CW00828531

Desky Kernowek

Other Cornish books from Evertype

Gwerryans an Planettys (H. G. Wells, tr. Nicholas Williams 2013)

Ky Teylu Baskerville (Arthur Conan Doyle, tr. Nicholas Williams 2012)

Flehes an Hens Horn (Edith Nesbit, tr. Nicholas Williams 2012)

Phyllis in Piskie-land (J. Henry Harris 2012)

An Beybel Sans: The Holy Bible in Cornish (tr. Nicholas Williams 2011)

Whedhlow ha Drollys a Gernow Goth (Nigel Roberts, tr. Nicholas Williams 2011)

The Beast of Bodmin Moor: Best Goon Brèn (Alan Kent, tr. Neil Kennedy 2011)

Enys Tresour (Robert Louis Stevenson, tr. Nicholas Williams 2010)

Whedhlow Kernowek: Stories in Cornish (A.S.D. Smith, ed. Nicholas Williams 2010)

Henry Jenner's Handbook of the Cornish Language (ed. Michael Everson 2010)

The Cult of Relics: Devocyon dhe Greryow (Alan Kent, tr. Nicholas Williams, 2010)

Jowal Lethesow: Whedhel a'm West a Gernow
(Craig Weatherhill, tr. Nicholas Williams, 2009)

Skeul an Tavas: A coursebook in Standard Cornish (Ray Chubb, 2009)

Kensa Lyver Redya
(Harriette Treadwell & Margaret Free, tr. Eddie Foirbeis Climo, 2009)

Adro dhe'n Bÿs in Peswar Ugans Dëdh
(Jules Verne, abridged and tr. Kaspar Hocking, 2009)

A Concise Dictionary of Cornish Place-Names (Craig Weatherhill, 2009)

Alys in Pow an Anethow (Lewis Carroll, tr. Nicholas Williams, 2009)

Form and Content in Revived Cornish
(Everson, Weatherhill, Chubb, Deacon, Williams, 2006)

Towards Authentic Cornish (Nicholas Williams, 2006)

Writings on Revived Cornish (Nicholas Williams, 2006)

Cornish Today (Nicholas Williams, 2006)

Desky Kernowek

A complete guide to Cornish

Nicholas Williams

evertype

2012

Published by Evertype, Cnoc na Sceiche, Leac an Anfa, Cathair na Mart, Co. Mhaigh Eo, Éire. *www.evertype.com*.

Editor: Michael Everson.

First edition 2012. Reprinted with corrections June 2012, March 2013, June 2013.

Evertype acknowledges that the publication of this book was made possible in part by the generous support of Agan Tavas, in recognition of the importance of this work in advancing the understanding of traditional Cornish. *www.agantavas.com*

Evertype acknowledges that the publication of this book was made possible in part by the generous support of Cussel an Tavaz Kernûak, who welcome it as a major contribution to learning and reviving Cornish. *www.cusselantavaz.com*

A catalogue record for this book is available from the British Library.

ISBN-10 1-904808-95-6 (paperback)
ISBN-13 978-1-904808-95-4 (paperback)

ISBN-10 1-904808-99-9 (hardcover)
ISBN-13 978-1-904808-99-2 (hardcover)

Typeset in Baskerville by Michael Everson.

Cover design by Michael Everson.
Photo by David Martyn Hughes, dreamstime.com/davidmartyn_info

Printed and bound by LightningSource.

TABLE OF CONTENTS

RAGLAVAR
FOREWORD

Desky Kernowek is intended to be a complete guide to revived Cornish both for the beginner and for the more advanced student. This book teaches the orthography known as Standard Cornish or *Kernowek Standard* (KS).

In 2008 a compromise orthography for Cornish was officially agreed and is now in public use. The agreed orthography is not completely satisfactory, however. KS seeks to address some of the problems in the 2008 orthography in the following ways:

1 KS spells according to pronunciation, rather than according to etymology. The learner does not need to learn differences in spelling when there is no difference in pronunciation; thus KS writes **lyver** 'book' and **nyver** 'number' (not *niver*). Similarly, this orthography writes **gwelyn** 'we see' and **melyn** 'mill' (not *melin*) because the two rhyme perfectly.

2 KS orthography employs a simple and consistent system for the distribution of the letters *i* and *y*.

3 KS prescribes diacritical marks over certain vowels in order to make clear distinctions in pronunciation that cannot be shown without such symbols. In this way KS can distinguish, for example, the long vowel in **cost** 'coast' from the short one in **còst** 'cost' and the differing quality of the two vowels in **cùssul** 'advice' and **dùstuny** 'witness'.

4 KS distributes the alternations **v/f** and **dh/th** in final position and in an authentic and coherent way.

5 KS uses the graphs **ai** and **au** for a class of loanwords with [eː] and [ɒː] respectively in both monosyllables and polysyllables.

6 KS uses the graphs **wh** and **qw**, rather than the less authentic *hw* and *kw*, and in this way (and in others) is closer to the orthography of the traditional language.

7 KS offers spelling options based on linguistic register only. The compromise orthography, on the other hand, treats "Revived Middle Cornish" and "Revived Late Cornish" as different forms of the language, and also allows two sets of graphs ostensibly on aesthetic grounds, although giving precedence to the less traditional of the two.

Perhaps some of these seven points may be helpful for any revision of the compromise orthography.

A full account of the pronunciation and spelling of Standard Cornish will be found at pages xxiii–xl. It was prepared by Michael Everson.

As well as explaining the various features of Cornish grammar and setting exercises for practice, in each lesson *Desky Kernowek* cites, in the original spelling and with English translation, phrases and sentences from the Middle and Late Cornish texts. These are intended to exemplify relevant points of inflection, syntax, and vocabulary. Since Cornish lacks native speakers, we are almost entirely dependent upon the remains of traditional Cornish for our knowledge of the language. It is important that learners should at every stage understand that what they are being taught is grounded in authentic Cornish, and is not a modern construct devised according to modern preferences and thus only partially related to the traditional language.

Because the different traditions of Revived Cornish focus on different periods for their reconstructions, it is desirable to centre on a variety of Traditional Cornish to which all can relate. The "foundation text" for the orthography used in the present book is William Jordan's *Creation of the World* of 1611, while looking forward to John Keigwin, William Rowe, and Nicholas Boson, on the one hand, and back to John Tregear, *Sacrament an Alter*, *Bewnans Ke*, and *Beunans Meriasek*, on the other. The whole corpus of Traditional Cornish has been used below in order to enlarge the vocabulary and to complete the paradigms. Such has been a necessary principle of Revived Cornish since its beginnings.

Some aspects of Standard Cornish spelling may be unfamiliar at first. The orthography is by its very nature a compromise, but the devisors have sought to do the following things:

a) to give due weight to the Cornish scribal tradition of the medieval period, which began its decline at the closure of Glasney in 1548
b) to offer a form of the language that is in its grammar and syntax close enough to later Cornish to be recognizably the same language

c) to suggest a variety of Cornish that is sufficiently close to the Celtic toponymy of present-day Cornwall as to appear to be part of the same linguistic tradition

d) to present a language that looks as though it could be learnt, written, and spoken without undue difficulty

e) to provide a robust orthography that equips the Revival with spellings which are as unambiguous as possible in their representation of the sounds of Cornish, and which at the same time remain faithful to the forms found the traditional Cornish texts—since these are our chief source for the language.

Throughout this book, words which are written in **bold type** are in the Standard Cornish which is to be learnt. Words which are written in ***bold italic type*** are written in the spellings of the traditional corpus (including the phonetic alphabet of Edward Lhuyd). Words which are from other languages like Welsh or Breton, and words written in other orthographies of Cornish (including Unified Cornish and Unified Cornish Revised) are written in *italic type*. In the paradigms in Appendix C, **bold type** indicates an attested form, ***bold italic type*** indicates a reconstructed form, and citations from the traditional corpus are written in bracketed ‹***bold italic type***›.

At lesson 40 a whole series of sentences from the texts is cited under various headings in the original spelling, in normalized orthography and with an English translation. The purpose of this section is to provide an authentic phrase-book for learners and more advanced speakers.

Since it is likely that *Desky Kernowek* will be used not only in classes but also by those learning by themselves, the key to the first 18 exercises is given at the end of the book.

My earlier grammar, *Clappya Kernowek* (Agan Tavas, 1997) was popular among learners of Cornish. I hope that this larger and more comprehensive book, in a more coherent orthography, will be equally popular.

In a work of this kind misprints and other errors are bound to occur. If any reader notices typographical or similar errors, the publisher will be very pleased to hear of them. Errata submitted will be made available online at *http://evertype.com/books/dk-errata.html* before their incorporation into subsequent editions of the dictionary.

Finally, I should like to thank Neil Kennedy most sincerely for reading the whole book in proof and for making many helpful comments.

Nicholas Williams
Dublin 2012

LEVERYANS HA SPELLYANS
PRONUNCIATION AND SPELLING

0.1 ORTHOGRAPHY

The pronunciation and spelling used in this book are those of Standard Cornish or **Kernowek Standard** (KS). KS is based on two principles: first, that the spelling of Revived Cornish must be based on attested traditional forms; and second, that the relationship between spelling and sounds seeks to be unambiguous.

Although Kernowek Standard takes as its starting point William Jordan's *Creation of the World* of 1611, it looks forward to later writers, e.g. Nicholas Boson, William Rowe, and John Keigwin, and back to John Tregear, *Sacrament an Alter*, *Bewnans Ke*, *Beunans Meriasek*, and the *Ordinalia*, etc. This use of all periods of Cornish is in accord with the principle of *tota Cornicitas*.

In the discussion below we have given both plain-text descriptions of the sounds as well as transcription in the International Phonetic Alphabet. For a summary explanation of the symbols see pages 445–447 at the end of the book.

0.1.1 WORD STRESS

Stress is marked in this book and in dictionaries with a middle dot (·) following the stressed vowel; in phonetic notation, a raised vertical line (ˈ) is written before the stressed syllable: **Ke·rnow** [ˈkɛɹnoʊ].

In most Cornish words the stress falls upon the penultimate syllable: **a·val** [ˈævəl] 'apple', **ava·low** [əˈvæloʊ] 'apples'; **myte·rnes** [mɪˈtɛɹnəs] 'queen', **myterne·sow** [mɪtɛɹˈnɛzoʊ] 'queens'. In some words, however, the word stress is anomalous, e.g. **myte·rn** [mɪˈtɛɹn] 'king'; **inwe·dh** [ɪnˈweːð] 'also'; **adro·** [əˈdɹoː] 'around'; **a·mary** [ˈæməɾi] 'cupboard'.

0.1.2 VOWEL LENGTH

Vowels in Cornish are typically described as being either long or short, but the quality of unstressed short vowels deserves special attention as well.

0.1.3 UNSTRESSED VOWELS

In general the unstressed vowel can be described as *schwa* [ə], but in practice *i*-colouring and *u*-colouring of reduced vowels is often found; Henry Jenner described this in §2.1.1 of his *Handbook*. The colouring can be described as a three-way distinction between *schwi* [ɨ], *schwa* [ə], and *schwu* [ʉ]; compare **gwelys** [ˈɡwɛlɨs] 'seen' and **gwelas** [ˈɡwɛləs] 'saw'. In some dialects of English similar distinctions are made: compare *Rose's* [ˈɹəʊzɨz] and *Rosa's* [ˈɹəʊzəz]. Note also that **arlùth** 'lord' could be written [ˈɑɹlʉθ], [ˈɑɹlʉθ], or [ˈɑɹləθ] depending how narrow the transcription is intended to be.

0.1.4 SHORT VOWELS

Stressed vowels in disyllables and polysyllables are short: **scrifa** [ˈskɹɪfə] 'to write'; **dhyso** [ˈðɪsə] 'to you (emphatic)'; **tasow** [ˈtæzoʊ] 'fathers'; **delyow** [ˈdɛljoʊ] 'leaves'; **myternesow** [mɨtɛɹˈnɛzoʊ] 'queens'; **caradow** [kəˈrædoʊ] 'beloved'. Stressed vowels in word-final position are usually long, in **tre** [tɹeː] 'home'; **tro** [tɹoː] 'turn' and **ky** [kiː]~[kəɪ] 'dog', for example. Weakly stressed words like **ha** [ha] 'and' and **pò** [pɔ] 'if', however, have short vowels. (The word **ha** is not written **hà** because of its frequency and because there is no alternation with any word [hæː].)

0.1.5 LONG VOWELS

A vowel in a stressed monosyllable is long before a single written voiced consonant, e.g. **mab** [mæːb] 'son'; **uj** [iːdʒ]~[yːdʒ] 'screech'; **hel** [heːl] 'hall'; **clem** [kleːm] 'claim'; **den** [deːn] 'man'; **cav** [kæːv] 'gets, will get'; **gov** [ɡoːv] 'smith'; **ros** [ɹoːz] 'rose'; **bedh** [beːð] 'grave', and **gor** [ɡoːɹ] 'knows'. A vowel in a stressed monosyllable is also long before **th**, **gh**, **sk**, and **st**: **whath** [ʍæːθ] 'still, yet'; **flogh** [floːx] 'child'; **Pask** [pæːsk] 'Easter'; and **cost** [koːst] 'coast'.

If a word is anomalously stressed on the final syllable, that syllable behaves like a stressed monosyllable. Thus **adro·** [əˈdɹoː] 'about' has long second syllable, just as **tro** [tɹoː] 'turn' has a long vowel. **Inwe·dh** [ɪnˈweːð] 'also' has a long vowel in the stressed syllable, exactly as **bedh** [beːð] 'grave' has a long vowel.

A vowel is short in stressed monosyllables before a voiceless consonant, e.g. **top** [tɔp] 'top'; **fyt** [fɪt] 'bout', and before a consonant written double, whether voiced or unvoiced, e.g. **coll** [kɔl] 'loss'; **garr** [ɡɑɹ] 'leg'; **coss** [kɔs] 'itch'. A vowel is also short before all consonant clusters other than **st** and **sk**: **horn** [hɔɹn] 'iron'; **part** [pɑɹt] 'part'; **fors** [fɔɹs] 'force'; **box** [bɔks] 'box tree'.

A vowel in a stressed monosyllable is short before pre-occluded consonants: **pedn** [pɛᵈn] (**penn** [pɛn]) 'head'; **gwadn** [gwæᵈn] (**gwann** [gwæn]) 'weak'; **cabm** [kæᵇm] (**camm** [kæm]) 'bent' and **tobm** [tɔᵇm] (**tomm** [tɔm]) 'hot'. (For pre-occlusion see 0.3.14 below.)

In stressed monosyllables **i** is always long: e.g. **tir** [tiːɹ] 'land'; **gwir** [gwiːɹ] 'right'; **scrif** [skɹiːf] 'writes'. In disyllables and polysyllables, however, **i** is pronounced short: **tiryow** ['tɪɾjoʊ] 'lands'; **gwiryon** ['gwɪɾjən] 'innocent'; **scrifa** ['skɹɪfə] 'to write'. If **i** is to be pronounced long in a disyllable or polysyllable, the length is shown by a circumflex, e.g. **sîra** ['siːɾə] 'father'; **mîsyow** ['miːzjoʊ] 'months'.

In stressed monosyllables **y** is pronounced short: **myn** [mɪn] 'kid'; **jyn** [dʒɪn] 'engine, device'; **bys** [bɪz] 'until'.

In stressed monosyllables **ë** and **ÿ** are pronounced long: **bës**, **bÿs** [beːz]~[biːz] 'world'. (See 0.2.8 below.)

When a vowel in a stressed monosyllable before a voiceless consonant is long, the anomalous length is shown by a circumflex: **câss** [kæːs] 'case'; **shâp** [ʃæːp] 'shape'; **hôk** [hoːk] 'hawk'; **Grêk** [gɹeːk] 'Greek'.

When a vowel in a stressed monosyllable is short before a voiced consonant or other lengthening consonant (**th**, **gh**, **sk**, **st**) the anomalous length is shown by a grave: **pàn** [pæn] 'when' (and **abà·n** [ə'bæn] 'since'); **còst** [kɔst] 'cost'. Note that the diacritic in the word **còst** [kɔst] 'cost' distinguishes the short vowel from the long vowel in **cost** [koːst] 'coast'.

0.2 CORNISH SPELLING: VOWELS

0.2.1 SHORT AND LONG *A*

Cornish **a**, when short, is pronounced like the *a* in Standard English 'man' [mæn], for example in **mabm** [mæᵇm] (**mamm** [mæm]) 'mother'; **lack** [læk] 'lack'. When long, Cornish **a** is pronounced like a lengthened equivalent of the short **a** [æː] (and can even be raised to [ɛː]), e.g. in **gwlas** [glæːz]~[gʷlæːz] 'kingdom, land'; **glas** [glæːz] 'blue, green'; **sav!** [sæːv] 'stand!'; **ladh!** [læːð] 'kill!' Both short and long **a** have an allophonic variant [ɑ] before final **-r**, as in **carr** [kɑɹ] 'car', **wàr** [wɑɹ] 'on', **war** [wɑːɹ] 'aware'.

In some words long **a** may be pronounced [ɒː], that is, with a vowel like a lengthened variety of the *o* in Standard English 'hot' [hɒt]. Such a pronunciation is shown by writing the vowel with a circumflex accent (ˆ): **tâl** [tɒːl]~[tæːl] 'forehead'; **clâv** [klɒːv]~[klæːv] 'sick'; **gwâv** [gwɒːv]~[gwæːv] 'winter'; **cân** [kɒːn]~[kæːn] 'song'.

â is also written in **dâ** [dæː] 'good', in order to distinguish it from **da** [də], the dialectal variant of **dha** [ðə] 'thy, your'. It is also written in **â** [æː] 'goes' to distinguish it from the verbal particle **a** [ə], and in **nâ!** [næː] 'no!' to distinguish it from the verbal particle **na** [nə] 'not'.

à is written in **pàn** [pæn] 'when' and **in bàn** [ɪn 'bæn] 'up, upwards', to show that the vowel is short; and in **wàr** [waɹ] 'upon' to show that the vowel is short and thus to differentiate the word from **war** [waːɹ] 'aware'.

0.2.2 SHORT AND LONG *E*

Cornish **e** when short is similar to the *e* in Standard English 'pen' [pɛn], for example in **settya** ['sɛtjə] 'to set'; **pedn** [pɛᵈn] (**penn** [pɛn]) 'head'; **pell** [pɛl] 'far'.

When **e** is short in a position where a long vowel is expected, for example, in **mès** [mɛz] 'but' and **ès** [ɛz] 'than', the vowel is written with a grave accent (ˋ) to indicate the anomalously short vowel. In this way **mès** [mɛz] 'but' is distinguished from the second element in **in mes** [ɪn 'meːz] 'out', and **ès** [ɛz] is distinguished from **es** [eːz] 'you were'.

When long, **e** is not unlike the vowel of Standard English 'rain' but without the *y* sound at the end ([eː], not [eɪ]). It occurs, for example, in **den** [deːn] 'man'; **wheg** [ʍeːg] 'sweet'; **teg** [teːg] 'beautiful'. As mentioned above, the anomalously long vowel in **Grêk** [gɹeːk] 'Greek' is shown by the circumflex accent.

A circumflex is sometimes written over **e**, when long by nature, in order to distinguish it from a word that is identical in pronunciation. Thus **êth** [eːθ] 'went' is spelt differently from **eth** [eːθ] 'eight', and **kê!** [keː] 'go!' is different in spelling from **ke** [keː] 'hedge'. In the words **yêth** 'tongue', **Yêdhow** 'Jew', and **yêhes** 'health', the circumflex indicates that these words may be pronounced as though written **eth**, **Edhow**, or **ehes**: [jeːθ]~[eːθ], ['jeðoʊ]~['eðoʊ], ['jɛhəs]~['ɛhəs].

0.2.3 SHORT AND LONG *O*

Cornish **o**, when short, is similar to the *o* in English 'pot' [pɔt], e.g. in **top** [tɔp] 'top'; **cot** [kɔt] 'short'; **brodn** [bɹɔᵈn] (**bronn** [bɹɔn]) 'breast'.

When long, Cornish **o** is similar to the *o* in German '*Ohm*' [oːm], e.g. in **ros** [ɹoːz] 'gave'; **con** [koːn] 'supper'; **noth** [noːθ] 'naked'.

When **o** is unexpectedly long, the length is shown by a circumflex, e.g. **hôk** [hoːk] 'hawk'; **côk** [koːk] 'fishing boat'.

0.2.4 *Ù* AND *Ú*

Short [ʊ] and long [uː] in Cornish are most frequently written **ù** and **û** respectively. The diacritics are necessary to distinguish these two vowels from short [ʏ] and long [yː], which are both written **u** (see 0.2.5 below).

Short **ù** is similar to the *u* in English 'full', e.g. **pùb** [pʊb] 'every'; **lùck** [lʊk] 'enough'; **cùsca** [ˈkʊskə] 'to sleep'; **tùchya** [ˈtʊtʃə] 'to touch'. Short **ù** can also appear in unstressed syllables, e.g. **arlùth** [ˈɑɹlʊθ] 'lord'.

Long **û** is similar to the *oo* of English 'food' and 'moon', e.g. **frût** [fɹuːt] 'fruit'; **gûn** [guːn] 'gown'.

Lhuyd writes **yu** [iʊ] in loanwords based on the root **ûs-** 'use', i.e., **yuzia** 'to use', **yuzhanz** 'usage'. Some speakers of Cornish may wish to pronounce the words **ûs** 'use' (noun), **ûsya** 'to use'; **ûsys** 'used, customary'; **ûsadow** 'custom' with initial [iʊ]—[iʊz], [ˈiʊzjə], [ˈiʊzɨs], [iʊˈzædoʊ]. In practice, however, the first syllable is probably best pronounced [juː] as in English 'use' and 'usual': **ûs** [juːz], **ûsya** [ˈjuːzjə], **ûsys** [ˈjuːzɨs], **ûsadow** [jʊˈzædoʊ] (this last having shortened its long vowel).

The sound of **û** is also represented by the spellings **oo** and **ou**; see 0.2.12 below.

0.2.5 SHORT AND LONG *U*

Cornish **u** when short is similar to the *i* in Standard English 'pin' [pɪn] for many speakers of Cornish; for other speakers it is similar to the short *ü* in German '*hübsch*' [hʏpʃ]. Examples are **uskys** [ˈɪskɨs]~[ˈʏskɨs] 'quick'; **budhy** [ˈbɪði]~[ˈbʏði] 'to drown'; **uthyk** [ˈɪθɨk]~[ˈʏθɨk] 'terrible'

When long, **u** is not unlike the *ee* of Standard English 'cheese' [tʃiːz] for many speakers of Cornish; for other speakers it has the rounded sound of the long *ü* in German '*grün*' [ɡʀyːn] or French '*lune*' [lyːn]. The long equivalent occurs, for example, in **tus** [tiːz]~[tyːz] 'men' and **fur** [fiːɹ]~[fyːɹ] 'wise'.

The preterite of **gwil** [ɡwiːl] 'to do' is **gwrug** and this can be pronounced with a long vowel as [ɡɹiːɡ] or [ɡɹyːɡ]. When it is used as an auxiliary, however, it is most often pronounced with a short vowel, i.e. as [ɹɪɡ], for example in **ny wrug ev dos** [ni ˈɹɪɡ ɛːv ˈdoːz] 'he did not come'.

In absolute final position **u** is pronounced [iʊ], e.g. in **du** [diʊ] 'black'; **tu** [tiʊ] 'side'; **gu** [ɡiʊ] 'woe'; and in **Jesu** [ˈdʒɛziʊ] 'Jesus'.

0.2.6 *I* AND *Y*

In stressed monosyllables **i** is pronounced long [iː], like the vowel in English 'green' or 'queen', e.g. **gwin** [ɡwiːn] 'wine'; **gwir** [ɡwiːɹ] 'true'; **sqwith** [skwiːθ] 'tired'; **tir** [tiːɹ] 'land'.

In disyllables and polysyllables derived from such words, orthographic **i** is pronounced like **y**, that is to say, as [ɪ]; e.g. **gwiryow** [ˈɡwɪɾjoʊ] 'rights'; **tiryow** [ˈtɪɾjoʊ] 'lands'; **sqwithus** [ˈskwɪθɨs] 'tiresome'. As has been noted, if **i** is pronounced long in disyllables and polysyllables it is written **î**: **mîsyow** [ˈmiːzjoʊ] 'months'; **sîra** [ˈsiːɾə] 'sire, father'.

When short [ɪ] occurs at the beginning of a word, it is written **i**, e.g. **inhy** ['ɪnhi] 'in her'; **ino** ['ɪnɔ] 'in him'; **igam ogam** ['ɪgəm 'ɔgəm] 'zig-zag'.

As has been mentioned above, the vowel written **y** is pronounced short as [ɪ] in stressed monosyllables, e.g. in **myn** [mɪn] 'kid goat'; **fyt** [fɪt] 'match, bout'; **mydn** [mɪᵈn] (**mynn** [mɪn]) 'will'; **dhybm** [ðɪᵇm] (**dhymm** [ðɪm]) 'to me'. The same short [ɪ] also occurs in stressed position in disyllables and polysyllables, e.g. **lyver** ['lɪvɔɹ] 'book'; **lyther** ['lɪθɔɹ] 'letter'; **nyver** ['nɪvɔɹ] 'number'; **venymys** [vɛ'nɪmɪs] 'poisoned'. In Middle and Late Cornish this stressed open [ɪ] in polysyllables seems to have alternated with [ɛ].

The same short vowel [ɪ] also appears in unstressed syllables, though it usually has a higher realization as [i] in final position, e.g. **dysqwedhys** [dɪs'kwɛðɪs] 'shown'; **dystrêwy** [dɪs'tɹɛʋi] (**dystrôwy** [dɪs'tɹoʋi]) 'to destroy'; **kelly** ['kɛli] 'to lose'.

In absolute final position the long vowel is written **y** rather than **i** in stressed monosyllables, e.g. in such words as **ky** [kiː] 'dog'; **chy** [tʃiː] 'house'; **pry** [pɹiː] 'clay'. This **y** may also be pronounced as a diphthong similar to **ey** [ɔɪ] (see 0.2.11 below); thus **chy** 'house' may be pronounced as though it were written **chey** [tʃɔɪ] and **ky** as though it were written **key** [kɔɪ].

0.2.7 THE DISTRIBUTION OF *I* AND *Y*

In stressed monosyllables, as we have seen, **y** represents a short vowel and **i** a long one, e.g. **myn** [mɪn] 'kid' but **min** [miːn] 'mouth, edge'. **î** is written when long in polysyllables, e.g. **desîrya** [dɛ'ziːɾjə] 'desire', **sacryfîs** ['sækɹɔ̣fiːs] 'sacrifice'.

In most disyllabic and polysyllabic words, however, there is no difference in pronunciation between **y** and **i**, since both are pronounced short [ɪ]. The distribution of **y** and **i** in such cases is for the most part a question of derivation. The short vowel is usually written **y**, but **i** is used in derivatives of monosyllables which contain **i**: e.g. **gwir** [gwiːɹ] 'true' and **gwiryon** ['gwɪɾjən] 'innocent'; **tir** [tiːɹ] 'land' and **tira** ['tɪɾə] 'to land'; **sqwith** [skwiːθ] 'tired' and **sqwithus** ['skwɪθɪs] 'tiring'.

Since in most disyllables and polysyllables **i** represents a short vowel, a long vowel in such cases is written with a circumflex **î**, e.g. **cîder** ['siːdɔɹ] 'cider', **sîra** ['siːɾə] 'father', **mîsyow** ['miːzjoʊ] 'months', and **decylîter** ['dɛsɪ'liːtɔɹ] 'decilitre'.

In this orthography, however, at the beginning of a word **i** is written rather than **y**, e.g. **inwedh** [ɪn'weːð] 'also'; **indella** [ɪn'dɛlə] 'thus'; **incens** ['ɪnsɛns] 'incense'; **isel** ['ɪzəl] 'low'; **inhy** ['ɪnhi] 'in her'.

There are a few exceptions to this rule: the verbal particle **y(th)** [ə(θ)] is written with a **y**, as are **yma** [ə'maː] 'there is' and **ymowns** [ə'moʊns] 'there are'. The adverbial particle appears as **yn**. This means that the adverbial particle **yn** [ən] is distinguished from the preposition **in** [ɪn] 'in'. We thus write **in gwir** [ɪn ˈɡwiːɹ] 'in truth, truly' and **in mes** [ɪn ˈmeːz] 'out' but **yn tâ** [ən ˈtæː] 'well'; **yn leun** [ən ˈløːn]~[ən ˈleːn] 'fully'.

> NOTE: In summary, the rules are easy to remember:
> i) use **i-** at the beginning of a word, and **-y** at the end of a word
> ii) use **i** for [iː] in monosyllables and for [ɪ] in words derived from them
> iii) use **y** for [ɪ] in monosyllables and polysyllables
> iv) use **î** for [iː] in polysyllables

0.2.8 *Ë* AND *Ÿ*

There is a large class of words in Cornish which can be pronounced either with a long [eː] or a long [iː] depending on whether the speaker prefers a "later" or "Western" pronunciation or an "earlier" or "Eastern" one. In order to show that either pronunciation is permissible, these are written with either **ë** or **ÿ**. Thus **bëdh** 'be!' can be pronounced [biːð] or [beːð], and **bÿs** 'world' can be pronounced either [beːz] or [biːz]. Any word with **ë** may be written with **ÿ**. So **bëdh** and **bÿdh**; **prëv** and **prÿv** 'reptile'; **ëst** and **ÿst** 'east', etc. are equally acceptable. In this book the **ë** variants have generally been preferred, apart from the words **ÿst** [iːst] 'east' (**ëst** [eːst]) and **ÿs** [iːz] 'grain' (**ës** [eːz]), which are distinguished from **Est** [eːst] 'August' and **es** [eːz] 'ease'.

> NOTE: It is very important to distinguish **y** from **ÿ**, as the first is short and the second long. The word **prÿv** has a long vowel [priːv] (as though it were English *preeve*) and should never be pronounced with a short vowel [pɹɪv] (as though it were English *privv*). Similarly **dÿdh** 'day' should rhyme with English *seethe*, rather than sound like the first syllable of **dither**.

0.2.9 SCHWA

Schwa is the mid-high unrounded neutral vowel (the unstressed vowel for example in English *local*, *lessen*, and *mason*). It is common in unstressed syllables and can be variously written as **a**, **e**, or **o**. It appears as **a** in **culyak** [ˈkɪljək]~[ˈkʏljək] 'cock, rooster'; **marhak** [ˈmɑɾək] 'rider'; **savas** [ˈsævəs] 'he stood'; as **e** in **gweles** [ˈɡwɛləs] 'to see'; **gwedhen** [ˈɡwɛðən] 'tree'; **Kernowek** [kɛɹˈnoʊək]~[kɛɹˈnuək] 'Cornish'; and as **o** in **gortos** [ˈɡɔɹtəs] 'to wait'; **colon** [ˈkɔlən] 'heart'; [ˈpɹɪzən] **pryson** 'prison'.

0.2.10 DIPHTHONGS AND DIGRAPHS WITH *A*

ay. This is phonetically /æ/ + /i/, but the first element may lower to bring the diphthong to [aɪ], rhyming with standard English 'my', 'thigh'. It is seen, for example, in **bay** [baɪ] 'kiss'; **fay** [faɪ] 'faith', and **may** [maɪ] 'so that'.

aw. This is pronounced [aʊ], and thus sounds similar to the diphthong in Standard English 'house'. It occurs in the Cornish words **maw** [maʊ] 'boy'; **naw** [naʊ] 'nine'; **paw** [paʊ] 'paw', and **saw** [saʊ] 'but, except'.

　　ai. This is not a diphthong, but rather another way of writing long **e** [eː]. It is written in borrowings like **train** [tɹeːn] 'train', in the plural **trainow** ['tɹeːnow]; in **paint** [peːnt] 'paint' and **paintya** ['peːntjə] 'to paint'; and in **trailya** ['tɹeːljə] 'to turn, to translate'.

　　au. This is not a diphthong, but rather a way of writing long [ɒː], for example, in **dauns** [dɒːns] 'dance'; **dauncya** ['dɒːnsjə] 'to dance'; **cauns** [kɒːns] 'pavement'. Sometimes the vowel shortens in polysyllables as in **auctoryta** [ɒk'tɔɾitə] 'authority', **Australya** [ɒs'tɹæljə] 'Australia', but it retains its quality and does not become short [ɔ].

0.2.11 DIPHTHONGS AND DIGRAPHS WITH *E* AND *Y*

　　ey. This is phonetically /e/ + /i/, but the first element is usually rather lower, so [əɪ] is more typical than [eɪ]. This diphthong appears as **ey** in both monosyllables, e.g. **teyr** [təɪɹ] 'three' (fem.); **seyth** [səɪθ] 'seven' and disyllables, e.g. **seythen** ['səɪθən] 'week'; **seytegves** [səɪ'tɛgvəs] 'seventeenth'.

　　ew. This is pronounced like a short **e** followed by short **ù** [ɛʊ], e.g. in **tew** [tɛʊ] 'fat'; **rew** [ɹɛʊ] 'frost' and **bew** [bɛʊ] 'alive'. It also occurs in dissyllables, e.g. **tewder** ['tɛʊdəɹ] 'fatness', though in hiatus with another vowel it may consonantalize: **bewa** ['bɛʊə]~['bɛwə] 'to live'; **rewys** ['ɹɛʊɨs]~['ɹɛwɨs] 'frozen'.

　　êw. This diphthong is also pronounced [ɛʊ], but it occurs only in words that also have a variant in **ôw** [oʊ]; e.g. **bêwnans** ['bɛʊnəns] 'life' (which has a variant **bôwnans** ['boʊnəns]) and **dystrêwy** [dɪs'tɹɛʊi] 'to destroy' (which has a variant **dystrôwy** [dɪs'tɹoʊi]). In any word, therefore, **êw** may be pronounced [oʊ] as well as [ɛʊ].

　　eu. This is not a diphthong but a way of writing a front-rounded vowel similar to the vowel in German *schön* 'beautiful' or French *jeune* 'young' [øː]. Speakers of revived Late Cornish pronounce **eu** as though it were **e**. It occurs, for example, in **leun** [løːn]~[leːn] 'full'; **beu** [bøː]~[beː] 'was'; **deu** [døː]~[deː] 'comes'; **eus** [øːs]~[eːs] 'is'. A short variety [œ]~[ɛ], also written **eu**, is found, for example, in **deuthowgh** ['dœθoʊx]~['dɛθoʊx] 'you came'; **deuva** ['dœvə]~['dɛvə] 'has come'; **deuta** ['dœtə]~['dɛtə] 'you come, will come'; **leuhy** ['lœhi]~['lɛhi] 'calves'.

　　yw. This diphthong is pronounced [iʊ] and occurs, for example, in **pyw** [piʊ] 'who'; **gwyw** [ɡwiʊ] 'worthy' and **lyw** [liʊ] 'colour'. In a handful of words, this diphthong is written **uw**, e.g. **Duw** [diʊ] 'God'; **buwgh** [biʊx] 'cow'; **duwhan** ['dɪʊʌ ʌən] 'misery', **pluw** [plɪʊ] 'parish', and **guw** [ɡɪʊ] 'spear'.

0.2.12 DIPHTHONGS AND DIGRAPHS WITH *O* AND *U*

ow. This is pronounced like a short **o** followed by short **ù** [oʊ] and occurs in both stressed and unstressed syllables, for example, in **pow** [poʊ] 'land, country'; **gow** [ɡoʊ] 'lie'; **tasow** ['tæzoʊ] 'fathers'; **geryow** ['ɡɛrjoʊ] 'words'. Before a vowel it is sometimes [u]: **Jowan** ['dʒoʊən]~['dʒuən].

ôw. This is also pronounced [oʊ] but is written only in words that have a variant pronunciation in **ew** [ɛʊ], e.g. **clôwes** ['kloʊəs] 'to hear', which can also be pronounced as though it were **clêwes** ['klɛʊəs]; and **côwsys** ['koʊzɪs] which can also be pronounced as though it were **kêwsys** ['kɛʊzɪs]. Any **ôw**, therefore, may also be pronounced as though it were **êw**.

oy. This is pronounced rather like the **oy** in English 'boy' or 'oil' [ɔɪ]; it occurs in native words and borrowings, for example, **moy** [mɔɪ] 'more'; **oy** [ɔɪ] 'egg'; **boya** ['bɔɪə] 'boy, page'; **rejoycya** [ɹɔˈdʒɔɪsjə] 'to rejoice'. See **ùy** below.

oo. This digraph may be pronounced like *oo* in English 'food' and 'school' [uː], or like long **o** [oː]. Where **oo** occurs in Cornish it is a reflex of an earlier *oy* or *uy*, e.g. **coos** [kuːz]~[koːz] 'wood'; **goodh** [ɡuːð]~[ɡoːð] 'goose'; **goos** [ɡuːz]~[ɡoːz] 'blood'; **scoodh** [skuːð]~[skoːð] 'shoulder'.

ou. This is also pronounced like the *oo* in English 'food' and 'school' [uː]; it occurs chiefly in English borrowings, e.g. **cloud** [kluːd] 'cloud'; **flour** [fluːɹ] 'flower'; **tour** [tuːɹ] 'tower'. In unstressed syllables ou shortens to [ʊ] or weakens still further: **doctours** ['dɔktʊɹz]~['dɔktʉɹz] 'doctors', **plesour** ['plɛzʊɹ]~['plɛzʉɹ] 'pleasure'.

ùy. This is pronounced [uɪ] and is very rare. Perhaps the only examples are **mùy** [muɪ], a variant of **moy** 'more' and **ùy** [uɪ], a variant of **oy** 'egg'.

0.2.13 *IA*, *IE*, AND *IO*

ia is not a diphthong, since in verse it is treated as two syllables. It is pronounced like the *ee* in English 'see' followed by the short unstressed vowel *schwa* ['iːə]. It occurs, for example, in **bian** ['biːən] 'small'; **bia** ['biːə] 'would be'; and **Maria** [məˈriːə] 'Mary'.

ie is pronounced like **ia** ['iːə]. It is found in a few words, e.g. **bien** ['biːən] 'I would be'; **biens** ['biːənz] 'they would be'; **destries** [dɛsˈtɹiːəs] 'destroyed' (the verbal adjective of **destria** [dɛsˈtɹiːə] 'to destroy').

io is written in some words. It occurs, for example, in **lion** ['liːən] 'lion'. In **tiogow** 'farmers', where the stress falls upon **-og-**, it represents two separate syllables: [tiˈɔɡoʊ].

0.3 CORNISH SPELLING: CONSONANTS

0.3.1 *B* AND *P*

b is pronounced as in English, e.g. **bian** ['biːən] 'small'; **brâs** [bɹɒːz]~[bɹæːz] 'great'; **bëdh!** [beːð] (**bÿdh!** [biːð]) 'be!'

p and **pp** are pronounced similarly to English *p*, *pp* [p]: e.g. **pell** [pɛl] 'far'; **cappa** ['kæpə] 'cap'.

0.3.2 *C, K, QW,* AND *CH*

c is pronounced [k] like English *k* before **r** and **l**, e.g. **crev** [kɹeːv] 'strong'; **cledh** [kleːð] 'left side'. It is also pronounced like English *k* before **a**, **o** or **u** (with or without diacritic), e.g. **cav** [kæːv] 'gets'; **coos** [kuːz]~[koːz] 'wood'; **cuv** [kiːv]~[kyːv] 'dear'; **cùsca** ['kʊskə] 'to sleep'.

c is pronounced [s] like **s** before **e**, **i** (with or without diacritic) and **y**, e.g. **certan** ['sɛɹtən] 'certain'; **cîder** ['siːdəɹ] 'cider'; **dauncya** ['dɒːnsjə] 'to dance'.

k is pronounced [k] as in English, but it is written only before **e, i, y**, and **n**: e.g. **kelly** ['kɛli] 'to lose'; **kig** [kiːg] 'flesh'; **kyn** [kɪn] 'although'. Before **n** it is pronounced, e.g. **knoukya** ['knuːkjə] 'to knock' and **knyvyas** ['knɪvjəs] 'to shear'.

qw is pronounced [kw] like the English *qu* in 'queen' and 'quick', e.g. **qweth** [kweːθ] 'garment'; **qwestyon** [kwɛsˈtjən] 'question'. Cornish **qw** is sometimes the result of the mutation of **gw**, e.g. **gwertha** ['gwɛɹθə] 'to sell' > **ow qwertha** [ə 'kwɛɹθə] 'selling'; **gwra** [gɹæː] 'he does' > **mara qwra** ['mɑɹə 'kɹæː] 'if he does'.

ch is pronounced like *ch* [tʃ] in English 'church': **chy** [tʃiː]~[tʃəɪ] 'house'; **chapel** ['tʃæpəl] 'chapel'; **chaunjya** ['tʃɒːndʒjə] 'to change'.

> NOTE: **Ch** is not written for Greek χ in modern borrowings: **catekîs** ['kætəˌkiːs] 'catechism'; **teknologieth** [ˌtɛknɔləˈgiːəθ] 'technology'.

0.3.3 *G* AND *GW*

g is pronounced like *g* in English 'got', 'gimmick', e.g. **gow** [goʊ] 'lie'; **glân** [glɒːn]~[glæːn] 'clean'; **wheg** [ʍeːg] 'sweet'.

gw is pronounced **g** + **w** before vowels, e.g. **gwana** ['gwænə] 'to wound'; **gwâv** [gwɒːv]~[gwæːv] 'winter'; **gwydn** [gwɪᵈn] (**gwynn** [gwɪn]) 'white'. Before **l** and **r**, however the **w** may or may not be pronounced, e.g. **gwrav** [gɹæːv]~[gʷɹæːv] 'I do'; **gwlas** [glæːz]~[gʷlæːz] 'country, kingdom'. For historic reasons the **w** is always written.

0.3.4 *GH* AND *H*

gh is like the *ch* [x] of Scottish 'loch', e.g. in **flogh** [floːx] 'child'; **whegh** [ʍeːx] 'six'.

h is like English *h* in English 'hat', e.g. in **hir** [hiːɹ] 'long'; **hun** [hiːn]~[hyːn] 'sleep'; **hordh** [hɔɹð] 'ram'. It should be noted that **gh** and **h** alternate with each other in inflected forms; **gh** is written at the end of a syllable, whereas **h** is written at the beginning of a syllable, for example, **flogh** [floːx] 'child' but **flehes** ['flɛhəz] 'children'; **kergh** ['kɛɹx] 'fetch!' but **kerhes** ['kɛɹhəz] 'to fetch.

In Late Cornish **h** between vowels was often lost, as in **bohosak**, **bohojak** 'poor' ([bʉ'hɔzək]~[bʉ'hɔdʒək] > [bo'ædʒək]), while final **gh** was either lost completely, e.g. **flogh** 'child' ([floːx] > [floː]) or was replaced by **th**, e.g. **sëgh**, **zëgh** 'dry' ([seːx]~[zeːx] > [zeːθ]). Neither development is written in this orthography.

0.3.5 *D*, *T*, *DH*, AND *TH*

d is pronounced [d] as in English, e.g. **dov** [doːv] 'tame'; **dâ** [dæː] 'good'; **peder** ['pɛdəɹ] 'four' (feminine). The cluster **dy** in **dyowl** [djoʊl] 'devil' becomes **j** [dʒ] after the definite article: **an jowl** [ən 'dʒoʊl].

t is pronounced [t] as in English. Before **e** and **y** it has a tendency to become **ch**. For this reason **te** [teː] (**ty** [tiː]) 'you' (singular) are **che** [tʃeː] (**chy** [tʃiː]) in Late Cornish pronunciation.

dh is pronounced [ð] like the **th** in English 'this' and 'that' [ð]. Final **dh** after **r** is often lost, e.g. **hordh** [hɔɹð] 'ram', for example becoming **hor'** [hɔɹ]. **Fordh** [fɔɹð] 'way, road' is often **for'** [fɔɹ]. In Standard Cornish the full forms **hordh** and **fordh** are always written, however.

th is pronounced [θ] like the *th* in English 'thick' [θɪk], 'thin' [θɪn]. Final **th** after **r** is sometimes lost. When it is, it also devoices the preceding **r**, for example in **porth** 'harbour', which is pronounced either [pɔɹθ] or [pɔɹ̥]. In Standard Cornish the full form **porth** is always written, however.

In certain cases, however, **th** in traditional Cornish really represents **t** + **h** in different syllables and are pronounced [t] + [h]. In such cases to avoid ambiguity, the cluster should be written **t'h**, e.g. **cot'he** ['kɔt'heː] 'to shorten'; **lent'he** ['lɛnt'heː] 'to decelerate'.

For the distribution of **dh** and **th** in final position see the note to 0.3.10.2.

0.3.6 *L*, *LL*, AND *R*

l is pronounced as in English [l], e.g. in **leun** [løːn]~[leːn] 'full'; **gweles** ['gwɛləs] 'to see'; **pel** [pɛl] 'ball'. The double form **ll** is similarly pronounced, e.g. **kelly** ['kɛli] 'to lose'. There are places, however, where **ll** derives from earlier **l** + **h** and may be pronounced thus, or as a geminate

or long consonant; for example, **pella** ['pɛlə] 'further' may be written
pelha and pronounced ['pɛlhə] or ['pɛlːə].

r is usually the alveolar approximant [ɹ] found in the traditional dialects
of the southwest of Britain, as well as in the English of Ireland and America.
This sound is found at the beginning and at the end of words, as well as
before and after other consonants: **ros** [ɹoːz] 'rose', **dor** [doːɹ] 'earth,
ground', **crejy** ['kɹɛdʒi] 'to believe'. The final *r* is never dropped as in RP
and similar dialects of British English. As noted at 0.3.5 there is a voiceless
r [ɹ̥], which can be used in **porth** [pɔɹθ]~[pɔɹ̥] 'harbour'; **gwerth** [gwɛɹθ]~
[gwɛɹ̥] 'sell!'; **warbarth** [waɹˈbɑɹθ]~[waɹˈbɑɹ̥] 'together'.

Between two vowels, **r** is a single tongue tap [ɾ], like *tt* in American
English *butter* or like the *r* in Spanish *pero*: **cara** ['kæɾə] 'to love', **bara**
['bæɾə] 'bread', **egery** [ɛˈgɛɾi] 'to open'.

0.3.7 THE ALTERNATION *LL ~ L* AND *DN (NN) ~ N*

When double **ll** is written after a stressed vowel, single **l** is written in
derived forms where it comes before a stressed syllable, for example, **tyller**
['tɪlɔɹ] 'place' but **tyleryow** [tɪˈlɛɾjoʊ] 'places'; **kelly** ['kɛli] 'grove' but
keliow [kɛˈlioʊ] 'groves'. A similar alternation is seen in with **dn** (**nn**):
cadnas ['kædnəs] (**cannas** ['kænəs]) 'messenger', **canasow** [kəˈnæzou]
'messengers'; **colodnek** [kəlˈɔdnək] (**colonnek** [kəlˈɔnək]) 'brave, stout-
hearted', but **colonecter** [kɔlʉˈnɛktɔɹ] 'bravery'.

0.3.8 *W* AND *WH*

w is pronounced [w] as in English. Before **l** and **r**, however, the **w** may
be silent, e.g. **gwlas** [glæːz]~[gʷlæːz] 'land, kingdom', **an wlas** [ən ˈlæːz]~
[ən ˈʷlæːz] 'the kingdom'; **gwra** [gɹæː]~[gʷɹæː] 'do!', **ev a wra** [eːv ə ɹæː]
'he will do'.

wh is pronounced [ʍ] like the *wh* of Scottish and Irish English, i.e. with
the devoicing clearly audible, e.g. in **wheg** [ʍeːg] 'sweet'; **whath** [ʍæːθ]
'still'; **dewheles** [dɛˈʍɛləs] 'to return' and **whilas** ['ʍɪləs] 'to seek'. In some
cases **wh** is the result of initial mutation, e.g. **maga whydn** ['mægə ʍɪᵈn]
'as white' < **gwydn** [gwɪᵈn] 'white'. In several traditional texts, historic **wh**
is sometimes written **w** which suggests that **w** and **wh** were falling together
as **w** in some forms of Cornish (as indeed they did in southern and western
dialects of English).

> NOTE: Spellings like ***hweg** 'sweet', ***hwath** 'yet', ***dehweles**
> 'return' are without warrant in traditional Cornish, and have never
> been used by native speakers of Cornish at any time in the history
> of the language.

0.3.9 *F* AND *V*

f is pronounced [f] as in English 'far' or the **ff** in 'off', e.g. in **fin** [fiːn] 'fine'; **flour** [fluːɹ] 'flour'; **fa** [fæː] 'beans'.

v is pronounced [v] as in English 'veal', 'vole', or 'love', e.g. in **sav!** [sæːv] 'stand!'; **lev** [leːv] 'voice'; **viaj** [ˈviːədʒ] 'journey', and **eva** [ˈeːvə] 'to drink'.

In initial position in some words, initial **f** is sometimes voiced to **v** in speech. The words in which **v** for earlier **f** occurs are relatively few in number. Such words may be written with **v**, providing that **v** is used consistently. If one writes **fenten** 'spring' and **folen** 'page' one should also write **fordh** 'road'; **forgh** 'fork'; **fow** 'cave' and **Frynkek** 'French'. If one writes **venten** and **volen**, however, one should also write **vordh**; **vorgh**; **vow** and **Vrynkek** 'French'.

0.3.10 ALTERNATION OF FINAL CONSONANTS

0.3.10.1 ALTERNATION OF FINAL *G/K* AND *B/P*

In Standard Cornish, inherited **g/k** and **b/p** alternate acccording to position, that is to say, the voiced consonant occurs after a stressed vowel and the voiceless consonant after an unstressed one. Thus we write **rag** 'for', **teg** 'beautiful', and **kig** 'flesh', but **marhak** 'rider', **carrek** 'rock', and **uthyk** 'dreadful'. Similarly in this orthography we write **mab** 'son', **glëb** 'wet', and **me a dÿb** 'I consider', but **methêwnep** 'drunkenness', **morrep** 'seashore', and **modryp** 'aunt'. This distribution corresponds both to the practice of our foundation texts (see page xxi above) and to the evidence of place-names.

The alternation **g/k** and **b/p** can be explained phonetically as follows: at the end of a syllable the highly-voiced quality of the preceding stressed vowel voiced the inherited lenis consonant after it, and this consonant was written *g* or *b*. In unstressed syllables there was no highly sonorous vowel, and in consequence the final lenis remained unvoiced and appears either as *k* or *p*.

0.3.10.2 ALTERNATION OF FINAL *DH/TH* AND *V/F*

The evidence for **dh/th** and **v/f** is more ambiguous than that for **g/k** and **b/p**, since much of it comes from Lhuyd, who seems in this matter to have to be have been influenced by his native Welsh, rather than by what he actually heard in Cornwall. If Lhuyd heard voiced **dh** in final unstressed position, as in his native Welsh, he would surely have written *dh* or *ð* on every occasion. Sometimes, however, he writes *th* or *ꞇ* rather than *dh* or *ð*. It might be argued that Lhuyd did indeed hear **dh** in final unstressed syllables rather than **th**, but that the practice of the medieval scribes, with which he was familiar, induced him to write **th** for **dh**. This suggestion lacks credibility, however, in the light of the totality of Lhuyd's transcription. Moreover forms like **genaffa** < **genef** + **va** CW 271 and **sewenaffa** < **sewenaf** + **vy** CW 1285 suggest that the simplex in **genaf** and **sewenaf** originally ended in a voiceless consonant.

In any case, Standard Cornish employs a distribution for inherited **dh/th** and **v/f** similar to that for **g/k** and **b/p**. We thus write **sedh!** 'sit!', **bëdh!** 'be!', **scoodh** 'shoulder', and **rudh** 'red', but **gorseth** 'gorsedd', **meneth** 'mountain', **nowyth** 'new', and **arlùth** 'lord'; similarly we write **gwrav** 'I make, I do', **nev** 'heaven', **gov** 'smith', and **cuv** 'beloved' but **manaf** 'I will', **genef** 'with me', and **orthyf** 'at me'.

It should be noted here that forms containing an unstressed vowel followed by -v, e.g. **a hanav** 'from me', **a yuhav** 'above me', **dredhev** 'by me', **genev/ṣenev** 'with me', **orthiv** 'to me', **ragov** 'for me', **ṵarnav** 'on me', **olav** 'I weep', are attested in Lhuyd's writing, but nowhere in native Cornish.

There is, incidentally, no evidence to suggest that the variations **g/k**, **b/p**, **dh/th**, and **v/f** in final position are determined by the initial segment of the following word.

0.3.10.3 ALTERNATION OF FINAL S/Z

There can be little doubt that in early Middle Cornish **s** behaved exactly like **g/k**, **b/p**, **dh/th**, and **v/f** in final position as described in 0.3.10.2 above. After a stressed vowel of whatever origin **s** was pronounced [z], e.g. **bos** [boːz] 'to be'; **tas** [tæːz] 'father'; **in mes** [ɪn ˈmeːz] 'out'. After an unstressed syllable, however, **s** was pronounced [s], e.g. **gwelys** [ˈgwɛlɪs] 'seen'; **gweles** [ˈgwɛləs] 'to see'; **myternes** [mɪˈtɛɹnəs] 'queen.' It is this system which is heard in the speech of many revivalists, so that, for example, Cornish **bos** 'to be' rhymes approximately with dialectal English *rose*, while **gwelys** 'seen' rhymes with English *trellis*.

The regular system of [z] after a stressed vowel and [s] after an unstressed one, appears to have been contaminated in the traditional language when a large number of English nouns with plurals ending in [z] and [ɪz] were borrowed into Cornish. When, for example, **carpentors** [kɑɹˈpɛntəɹz] 'carpenters'; **prysners** [ˈpɹɪznəɹz] 'prisoners'; **branchys** [ˈbɹæntʃɪz] 'branches'; **chainys** [ˈtʃeːnɪz] 'chains' were borrowed into Cornish, [z] and [ɪz] now to be found at the end of unstressed syllables. It should be remembered here just how common were plurals in -**s** and -**ys** in the language. They were so prevalent in fact, that in Tudor and Late Cornish they sometimes took the place of the original Celtic plurals, for example in

Tregear's *aweylers*, *aweylors* 'evangelists' (for expected *awayloryon), or Rowe's *poscaders* 'fishermen' (for expected *puscadoryon).

As a result of the influx of so many English plurals into Cornish, native words like **spyrys** ['spɪrɪs] 'spirit', **gweles** ['gwɛləs] 'to see', **lagas** ['lægəs] 'eye', **tavas** ['tævəs] 'tongue', etc. could now be pronounced with final [z], a pronunciation that is reflected in the Late Cornish texts in spellings like *spiriz*, *gwellaz*, *lagaz*, *tavaz*. Cornish learners have the choice of pronouncing such words with either final [s] or [z].

0.3.11 *S, SS, Ẓ*, AND *SC*

s in Cornish can represent two different sounds. It either resembles the *s* in English 'sing' [sɪŋ] or the *z* in English 'zing' [zɪŋ]. Initially **s** is usually pronounced [s], e.g. **sëgh** 'dry' [se:x]; **seyth** [səɪθ] 'seven'; **sav** [sæ:v] 'stand!' Between vowels **s** is pronounced [z], e.g. in **côwsys** 'spoken' ['kouzɪs]; **posa** ['pɔzə] 'to weigh'; **rosons** ['rɔzəns] 'they gave'.

In final position, after a long stressed vowel, **s** is pronounced [z], e.g. in **tas** [tæ:z] 'father'; **ros** [ro:z] 'he gave'; **coos** [ku:z]~[ko:z] 'wood'. If after a long stressed vowel the sound is [s], it is written **ss**, e.g. **grâss** 'grace' [gra:s], **Grêss** [gre:s] 'Greece' where the vowel is long but the final segment is voiceless.

Before **a**, **o**, and **u** (with or without diacritic) the group **sc** is pronounced as though it were **sk**, e.g. **scav** [skæ:v] 'light'; **scol** [sko:l] 'school' and **scubya** ['skɪbjə]~['skʏbjə] 'to sweep'. Before **e**, **i**, and **y**, however, **sc** is pronounced as though it were **s**, e.g. **ascendya** [ə'sɛndjə] 'to ascend'; **sciens** ['si:əns] 'science' and **dyscypel** [dɪ'sɪpəl] 'disciple'.

Final **s** representing the borrowed English plural is normally voiced as in English, e.g. **profettys** [prə'fɛtɪz] 'prophets'; **doctours** ['dɔktʉɪz] 'doctors, learned men'.

Final **ls** is pronounced as though it were **lz**, e.g. **âls** [ɒlz]~[ælz] 'shore, cliff'; **fâls** [fɒlz]~[fælz] 'false'; **gwels** [gwɛlz] 'grass'; **gwyls** [gwɪlz] 'wild'.

After a stressed vowel final **ns** is usually pronounced as though it were **nz**, e.g. **dans** [dænz] 'tooth'; **gwyns** [gwɪnz] 'wind'; **kyns** [kɪnz] 'before'; **gwrêns** [gre:nz]~[gʷre:nz] 'let him/them do'. After an unstressed vowel, however, final **ns** is pronounced as [ns], not [nz], e.g. **bedhens** ['bɛðəns] 'let him/them be'; **ugans** ['ɪgəns]~['ʏgəns] 'twenty'; **arhans** ['ærəns]~ ['æɾhəns] 'silver'; **revrons** ['rɛvrəns] 'reverence'; **sùbstans** ['sʊbstəns] 'substance'. Where **ns** occurs in the plural of an borrowed English singular in **-nt**, it is unvoiced, e.g. **marchons** ['maɹtʃəns] 'merchants'; **serpons** ['sɛɹpəns] 'snakes'.

English monosyllables ending in *-nce*, when borrowed into Cornish are written with final **-ns**, and are pronounced with final [ns], e.g. **pryns** [pɹɪns] 'prince'; **dauns** [dɒːns] 'dance'; **chauns** [tʃɒːns] 'chance'. **Sens** 'sense' is similarly pronounced with final [ns].

In the later Cornish sources there is hesitation between initial **s** and **z**. In many words initial **s** was clearly pronounced [z] in the later language. In Standard Cornish orthography such words may be written with **z** provided it is done consistently. If one writes **sëgh** 'dry'; **seythen** 'week' one should also write **Sadorn** 'Saturday', **Sul** 'Sunday' and **Sowsnek** 'English'. If one writes **zëgh** 'dry' and **zeythen** 'week', one should also write **Zadorn**, **Zul** and **Zowsnek**. In toponyms it is permissible to write **z** at all times, e.g. **Eglos Zenar** 'Zennor' and **Zawan Orgel** 'Zawn Organ'. The Cornish name for 'Penzance' (without pre-occlusion on the first element) should be written **Penzans** [pɛnˈzæns], where **z** represents [z] and **s** its voiceless equivalent [s].

0.3.12 *SH* AND *J*

sh is pronounced as *sh* in English 'shop'; e.g. **shoppa** [ˈʃɔpə] 'workshop, shop'; **shara** [ˈʃærə] 'share'. In certain cases, however, **sh** in traditional Cornish really represents **s** + **h** in different syllables and are pronounced [s] + [h]. In such cases to avoid ambiguity, the cluster should be written **s'h**, e.g. **lies'he** [ˈliːəsˈheː] 'to multiply'; **cales'he** [ˈkæləsˈheː] 'to harden'; **les'hanow** [lɛsˈhænou] 'nickname'.

When **ss** is followed by **y**, the cluster is pronunced [ʃ], e.g. **passyon** [ˈpæʃən] 'passion'; **processyon** [pɹəˈsɛʃən] 'procession'.

j is pronounced [dʒ] as in English 'jug', e.g. **jowal** [ˈdʒouəl] 'jewel'; **jentyl** [ˈdʒɛntɪl] 'gentle'; **Jowan** [ˈdʒouən] 'John'. **j** alternates with **s** in a number of words, for example, **usy/ujy** [ˈyzi, ˈydʒi] 'is'; **nyns/nynj** [nɪnz, nɪndʒ] not'; **wosa/woja** [ˈwɔzə, ˈwɔdʒə] 'after'; **kerensa/kerenja** [kəˈrɛnzə, kəˈrɛndʒə] 'love'.

0.3.13 *Y* AS A CONSONANT

When it is a consonant **y** as a consonant is pronounced like the *y* in English 'yoyo', e.g. **yagh** [jæːx] 'healthy', **de Yow** [də ˈjou] 'Thursday'; **yew** [jɛu] 'yoke'. Initial **ye** is often reduced to **e**: **yêhes** 'health', and **yêth** 'language' therefore, may be pronounced as though they were **ehes** and **eth** respectively. The **y** is always written, however, and the possibility of reduction is marked with a circumflex **yê**. See 0.2.2 above.

0.3.14 *M*, *N*, AND PRE-OCCLUSION

The consonants **m** and **n** are pronounced as in English, e.g. **mos** [moːz] 'to go'; **oma** [ˈɔmə] 'I am'; **nos** [noːz] 'night'; **ena** [ˈɛnə] 'there'. In some stressed short syllables, however, **m** is pronounced with an intrusive but unexploded **b** before it, e.g. **tabm** [tæᵇm] 'bit' and **obma** [ˈɔᵇmə] 'here'. Similarly after some short stressed syllables **n** is pronounced with an intrusive but unexploded **d** before it, e.g. **gwydn** [gwɪᵈn] 'white'; **pedn** [pɛᵈn] 'head'.

In Standard Cornish such pre-occluded pronunciations may be written **bm** and **dn**. If one does not wish to write pre-occlusion, however, one may write **mm** and **nn** respectively. Thus KS allows both **tabm** and **tamm**, and both **obma** and **omma**. The doubled consonants in **mm** and **nn**, however, are indications that a pre-occluded pronunciation is allowed. In this book pre-occlusion is written, except in quotations from texts without it.

If one does not wish to pre-occlude in a word at all, one *must* write single **m** and single **n**. It is for this reason that KS has **ino** [ˈmɔ] 'in him' (UC and UCR *ynno*) and **inia** [ɪˈniːə] 'to urge' (UC and UCR *ynnya*)—because the forms ***idno** and ***idnia** are not attested.

0.4.1 THE APOSTROPHE

The *apostrophe* is an important part of Cornish orthography. It often indicates the elision of a vowel, as in **dh'agas** (< **dhe agas**), **pandr'yw** (< **pandra yw**), or **dhodh'ev** (< **dhodha ev**). In order to ensure good typography, it is best not to leave a space before or after an apostrophe. If after, as in ***dhodh' ev**, the trailing apostrophe may be confused with a final single quotaton mark; if before, as in ***dhodh 'ev**, the burden is on the writer to ensure that the apostrophe goes the right direction (that is, that it looks like a *9 '* rather than a *6 '*). Much "helpful" word-processing software will turn an apostrophe after a space into a left single "smart quote", as in ***dhodh 'ev**, and this is an unsightly error. The rule "don't use a space on either side of an apostrophe" will help ensure better typography in Cornish. (In poetry and similar contexts the apostrophe may be written conventionally, however.)

In this orthography, the apostrophe is used conventionally *after* the verbal particle **th** in the colloquial register, e.g. **th'erof vy** (**yth esof** in the literary register). This is an orthographic convention, not an error; **'th erof vy** is not "more correct", and the leading apostrophe leads to the ***'th erof vy** trouble just described.

> NOTE: Forms like Lhuyd's *cera vi* and Tonkin's *thera vi* show that the form was analysed as a unit. For this reason **th'erof vy** is recommended over **th erof vy** without the apostrophe.

For **t'h** and **s'h** see §0.3.5 and §0.3.12 above respectively.

The leniting particle **a²** is not written after **pandra** 'what?' (< **py an dra**); thus **te a wrug hedna** 'you did that', but **pandra wrusta?** 'what did you do?' Since the leniting particle is not used before vowels in parts of the verbs **bos** 'to be' and **mos** 'to go' beginning with a vowel, **pandra** is elided to **pandr'** before such forms, e.g. **pandr'yw hedna?** 'what is that?', **pandr'esta ow qwil?** 'what are you doing?', **pandr'êth an fordh wàr nans mynysen alebma?** 'what went down the road a minute ago?' **Pandra** is not elided before forms of **bos** 'to be' which begin with a consonant: **pandra veu hedna?** 'what was that?', **pandra vëdh gwrës?** 'what will be done?'

A similar rule applies to the use of **fatla** 'how?' Thus **fatla wrusta hedna?** 'how did you do that?'; **fatla wrewgh why dewheles?** 'how will you (*pl.*) return?'; **fatl'yw dha vabm?** 'how is your mother?', but **fatla via hedna ragowgh?** 'how would that be for you (*pl.*)?'

0.4.2 QUOTATION MARKS

Because the apostrophe is frequently used in Cornish, "*double quotation marks*" are recommended for quoted speech, and '*single quotation marks*' for citations within quoted speech. This is advantageous in terms of legibility, because double quotation marks are more easily distinguished from the apostrophe. Of course, the choice remains with the writer.

0.4.3 THE HYPHEN

Standard Cornish does not write a hyphen in compounds like **lyther nowodhow** 'newsletter' (not *****lyther-nowodhow**), **jyn tedna** 'tractor' (not *****jyn-tedna**) and **sîra wydn** 'grandfather' (not *****sîra-wydn**).

The hyphen is, however, employed after prefixed adjectives and adverbs: **drog-labm** 'accident', **fâls-dùstuny** 'false witness', **tebel-wolies** 'grievously wounded'.

The hyphen is always written before the demonstrative suffixes **-ma** 'this' and **-na** 'that'; e.g. **an lyver-ma** 'this book', **an vuwgh-na** 'that cow', **an re-ma** 'these' and **an re-na** 'those'.

COT'HEANSOW
ABBREVIATIONS

AB = Edward Lhuyd, *Archæologia Britannica* (London 1707 [reprinted Shannon 1971])

Bilbao MS = Henry Jenner 'The Cornish Manuscript in the provincial library at Bilbao, Spain', *Journal of the Royal Institution of Cornwall* 21 (1924-25): 421-37

BK = Graham Thomas & Nicholas Williams (editors), *Bewnans Ke : The Life of St Kea* (Exeter 2007)

BM = Whitley Stokes (editor), *Beunans Meriasek: the life of St Meriasek, Bishop and confessor, a Cornish drama* (London: Trübner and Co. 1872)

Bodewryd MS = Andrew Hawke, 'A Rediscovered Cornish-English Vocabulary', *Cornish Studies: Nine* (2001): 83-104.

Borde = Andrew Borde, cited from J. Loth, 'Cornique moderne', *Archiv für Celtische Lexicographie* 1 (1900): 224-28

Borlase = William Borlase, *Antiquities of the County of Cornwall* (London 1754)

Carew = F.E. Halliday (editor), *Richard Carew of Antony, the survey of Cornwall* (London 1953)

CF = *The Charter Fragment*, text from E. Campanile, 'Un frammento scenico medio-cornico', *Studi e saggi linguistici* 60-80, supplement to *L'Italia Dialettale 26*

Chygwyn = The song 'Delkyow Sevy', quoted by William Pryce F f 4 v

CW = Whitley Stokes, *Gwreans an Bys: The Creation of the World* (London 1864 [reprinted 2003 by Kessinger Publishing, Montana, USA]

Exeter Consistory Court = Deposition of the Bishop's Consistory Court at Exeter (1572). Quoted from Martyn F. Wakelin, *Language and history in Cornwall* (Leicester University Press 1975): 89

JBoson = Cornish writings of John Boson in O.J. Padel, *The Cornish Writings of the Boson Family* (Redruth 1975)

JCH = *John of Chyanhor*, in O.J. Padel, *The Cornish Writings of the Boson Family* (Redruth 1975)

NBoson = Nicholas Boson, 'Nebbaz Gerriau dro tho Carnoack', in O.J. Padel, *The Cornish Writings of the Boson Family* (Redruth 1975)

JJenkins = two poems by James Jenkins, quoted in Pryce (1790)

JKeigwin = 1. John Keigwin's translation of the letter of Charles I in Tremenheere MSS, Morrab Library, Penzance, typescript edition by P.A.S. Pool (1995); 2. His translation of *Genesis* 1, from Gwavas collection, British Library Add MS 28554

JTonkin = two poems by John Tonkin (c. 1693 & c. 1695) in LAM: 224-228

LAM = Alan Kent and Tim Saunders (editors), *Looking at the Mermaid: A Reader in Cornish Literature 900-1900* (London 2000)

OCV = Eugene V. Graves, *The Old Cornish Vocabulary* (PhD thesis, Columbia University 1962)

Oliver Oldwanton = Michael Flachman (editor), 'The First English Epistolary Novel: "The Image of Idleness (1555)"', *Studies in Philology* 87, No. 1 (Winter 1990). University of North Carolina Press

OM = 'Origo Mundi' in Edwin Norris, *The Ancient Cornish Drama* (London 1859 [reprinted New York & London 1968]: i 1-219

OPender = letter by Oliver Pender (August 1711) in LAM: 239

PA = Harry Woodhouse (editor), *The Cornish Passion Poem in facsimile* (Penryn 2002)

PC = 'Passio Christi' in Edwin Norris, *The Ancient Cornish Drama* (London 1859 [reprinted New York & London 1968]: i 221-479

Pryce = William Pryce, *Archaeologia Cornu-Britannica* (Sherborne 1790 [reprinted Menston, Yorkshire 1972])

RD = 'Resurrexio Domini' in Edwin Norris, *The Ancient Cornish Drama* (London 1859 [reprinted New York & London 1968]: ii 1-199

Richard Symonds = Charles Edward Long (editor), *Diary of the Marches of the Royal Army during the Great Civil War; kept by Richard Symonds* (Camden Society 1859)

Rowe = J. Loth (editor), 'Textes inédits en cornique moderne', *Revue Celtique* 23, 173-200.

SA = *Sacrament an Alter,* text quoted from an unpublished edition by D.H. Frost (St David's College 2003)

Scawen MSS = proverbs and rhymes from Mr. Scawen's Manuscripts in W.C. Borlase, 'A Collection of hitherto unpublished Proverbs and rhymes, in the Ancient Cornish Language; from the Manuscripts of Dr Borlase', *Journal of the Royal Institution of Cornwall* 1886: 9-10

JBoson = Cornish writings of Thomas Boson in O.J. Padel, *The Cornish Writings of the Boson Family* (Redruth 1975)

TH = John Tregear, *Homelyes xiii in Cornyshe* (British Library Additional MS 46, 397) [text from a cyclostyled text published by Christopher Bice (s.l. [1969])

Ustick MSS = proverbs and rhymes from Ustick's Manuscripts in W.C. Borlase, 'A Collection of hitherto unpublished Proverbs and rhymes, in the Ancient Cornish Language; from the Manuscripts of Dr Borlase', *Journal of the Royal Institution of Cornwall* 1886: 11-12

WBodinar = P.A.S. Pool & O.J. Padel, 'William Bodinar's Letter, 1776', *Journal of the Royal Institution of Cornwall*, New Series, vol. 7 (1975-76), 231-36

WGwavas = writings by William Gwavas in Pryce and LAM.

KENSA DYSCANS
FIRST LESSON

1A.1 NOUNS AND GENDER

All nouns in Cornish are either masculine or feminine. There is no neuter, so everything is either 'he' or 'she', rather than 'it'. Words for males, e.g. **den** 'man', **maw** 'boy', **myte·rn** 'king', **tarow** 'bull,' etc. are masculine. Words for females, e.g. **benyn** 'woman', **myrgh** 'daughter', **myternes** 'queen', **buwgh** 'cow', etc. are feminine. The gender of other words has to be learnt, though this is not always as difficult as it might seem. The gender of nouns is given below.

1A.2 PLURALS

There are many different ways of forming the plural in Cornish, though any given word will have only one plural form:

1A.2.1 one can add an ending, e.g. **-ow** (**tas** *m.* 'father', **tasow** 'fathers'; **myternes** *f.* 'queen', **myternesow** 'queens'), **-yow** (**ger** *m.* 'word', **geryow** 'words'; **gwel** *m.* 'field', **gwelyow** 'fields'), **-on** (**Sows** *m.* 'Englishman', **Sowson** 'Englishmen'), **-yon** (**Kelt** *m.* 'Celt', **Keltyon** 'Celts'), **-as** (**cath** *f.* 'cat', **cathas** 'cats'; **yewgen** *f.* 'ferret', **yewgenas** 'ferrets'; **golvan** *m.* 'sparrow', **golvanas** 'sparrows' (nouns referring to animals or birds often form their plurals in **-as**), **-eth** (**mytern** *m.* 'king', **myterneth** 'kings'). Words ending in a final **-y** in the singular take **-iow** in the plural (**gwely** *m.* 'bed', **gweliow** 'beds'; **goly** *m.* 'wound', **goliow** 'wounds'). This enables us to distinguish in writing **gweliow** 'beds' from **gwelyow** 'fields'

Nouns or nominalized adjectives ending in **-ak** form their plurals in **-ogyon**, e.g. **marhak** 'horseman', **marhogyon** 'horsemen'; **bohosak** 'poor man', **bohosogyon** 'poor people'. They thus contrast with words in **-ek**, which form their plurals in **-ygyon**, e.g. **medhek** 'doctor, physician', **medhygyon** 'doctors'; **gowek** 'liar', **gowygyon** 'liars'.

Nouns ending in **-or** or **-yor** form their plurals in **-oryon** or **-yoryon**, e.g. **helhor** 'huntsman', **helhoryon** 'huntsmen'; **redyor** 'reader',

1

redyoryon 'readers'; **robbyor** 'robber', **robbyoryon** 'robbers'. Such words contrast with nouns in **-er**, which form their plurals in **-ers** ([ǝɹ], [ǝɹz]), e.g. **lêder** 'leader', **lêders** 'leaders', **marner** 'mariner, sailor', **marners** 'mariners.' They also contrast with nouns in -**our**, which form their plurals in **-ours** ([ʊɹ]~[ɵɹ], [ʊɹz]~[ɵɹz]), e.g. **doctour** 'doctor, learned man', **doctours** 'learned men'; **scryptour** 'scripture', **scryptours** 'scriptures'; **brybour** 'vagabond', **brybours** 'vagabonds'.

1A.2.2 one can change the vowel, e.g. **men** *m.* 'stone', **meyn** 'stones'; **davas** *f.* 'sheep', **deves** 'sheep' (*pl.*); **alargh** *m.* 'swan' (arch.), **elergh** 'swans'; **managh** *m.* 'monk', **menegh** 'monks'; **gavar** *f.* 'goat', **gever** 'goats' (**gyfras** also occurs). In two-syllable words where the vowel in the plural raises from **a** to **e**, the vowel in the unstressed final syllable often follows the same pattern (['dævǝs], ['dɛvǝs]; ['gævǝɹ], ['gɛvǝɹ]).

1A.2.3 one can change the vowel and add an ending, e.g. **mab** *m.* 'son', **mebyon** 'sons'; **car** *m.* 'relative', **kerens** 'relatives, parents'; **carr** *m.* 'car', **kerry** 'cars'

1A.2.4 one can change **t** to **s** or add **-s** or **-ys** in the case of borrowings from English: **marchont** *m.* 'merchant', **marchons** 'merchants'; **cothman** *m.* 'friend', **cothmans** 'friends'; **rom** *m.* 'room', **rômys** 'rooms'

1A.2.5 one can drop the feminine singulative ending to give a collective plural: **gwedhen** *f.* 'tree', **gwëdh** 'trees'; **hasen** *f.* 'single seed', **has** (collective) 'seed'

1A.2.6 parts of the body that come in pairs have a dual in **dew** *m.* or **dyw** f.: **scoodh** *f.* 'shoulder', **dywscoth** 'shoulders', **troos** 'foot', **dewdros** 'feet'. The plural **treys** is the form mostly used, however, for a person's two feet.

1A.2.7 some words have a different root in their plural: **chy** *m.* 'house', **treven** 'houses'; **maw** 'boy', **mebyon** or **coscar** 'boys', **tra** *f.* 'thing', **taclow** or **taclenow** 'things'; **dorn** *m.* 'hand' uses **dewla**, the dual of **leuv** *f.* 'hand', as a plural.

1A.3 THE INDEFINITE AND DEFINITE ARTICLES

'A, an' (the indefinite article) is not usually expressed in Cornish: **chy** 'a house', **oy** 'an egg', **flogh** 'a child', though there are instances of the word **udn** 'one' being used as an indefinite article in some texts.

The definite article 'the' is **an** for both genders, singular and plural. **An** contracts as follows: **in** 'in' + **an** becomes **i'n**; **dhe** 'to' + **an** becomes **dhe'n**; **ha** 'and' + **an** becomes **ha'n**, and **a** 'of' + **an** becomes **a'n**. Elsewhere **ha** becomes **hag** before vowels: **Adam hag Eva** 'Adam and Eve'.

NOTE: Tudor and Late Cornish often write **ha an** for **ha'n** and **ha in** for **hag in**.

1A.4 LENITION, SOFT MUTATION, OR THE "SECOND STATE"

Like all the other Celtic languages Cornish changes (mutates) the initial consonants of words in certain circumstances. The commonest initial mutation is *lenition* or *softening*. This mutation is often referred to as the *second state*, and is shown in grammars by a superscript [2] after the word that causes it. The soft mutation changes **b** to **v**; **m** to **v**; **d** to **dh**; **g** to ZERO (that is, disappears completely); **go** to **wo**; **p** to **b**; **t** to **d**; **c**, **k** to **g**; and **qw** to **gw**. The soft mutation operates after the definite article in two contexts:

1A.4.1 if the following noun is feminine singular: **benyn** *f.* 'woman', **an venyn** 'the woman'; **mowes** *f.* 'girl', **an vowes** 'the girl', **gwreg** *f.* 'wife', **an wreg** 'the wife'. Similarly **delen** *f.* 'leaf', **an dhelen** 'the leaf'; **garr** *f.* 'leg', **an arr** 'the leg'; **gwedren** *f.* 'glass, tumbler', **an wedren** 'the tumbler'; **pellen** *f.* 'ball', **an bellen** 'the ball'; **tesen** *f.* 'cake', **an desen** 'the cake'; **cath** *f.* 'cat', **an gath** 'the cat'.

1A.4.2 if the following noun is masculine plural and refers to persons: **mab** 'boy, son', **an vebyon** 'the sons'; **mytern** 'king', **an vyterneth** 'the kings', **clâv** 'invalid', **an glevyon** 'the invalids, the patients', **bohosak** 'poor person', **an vohosogyon** 'the poor'. **Tas** 'father', **an tasow** 'the fathers' is an exception.

1A.4.3 English loanwords (with English plurals) are not usually mutated in the plural: **an brybours** 'the vagabonds' (from Middle English *bribours* 'beggars, vagrants'), **an Grêkys** 'the Greeks', **an profettys** 'the prophets' (but **profus** 'prophet', **an brofusyon** 'the prophets, because **profus** is not an English borrowing.) **Marchont** 'merchant', **an varchons** 'the merchants' is an exception.

1A.5 MORE ON INITIAL MUTATION

Notice also the following: **dëdh** 'day', **an jëdh**; **dyowl** 'devil', **an jowl** 'the devil', *pl.* **dewolow** 'devils', **an dhewolow** 'the devils'; **margh** 'horse', **an vergh** 'the horses'; **men** 'stone', **an veyn** 'the stones', **den** 'man', **tus** 'men, people', **an dus** 'the men'; **dor** 'earth, ground', **an dor** 'the ground', **an nor** 'the earth, the world'.

1B EXAMPLES FROM THE TEXTS

1B.2 *ov geryov gruegh attendya* 'pay attention to my words' BM1632; *war oll an puscas in dowre* 'over all the fishes in the water' TH 2; *rage collenwall an romes* 'to fill the rooms' CW 241; *Gwra... maga ow deves* 'Feed my sheep' TH 44; *gans prevas a bub sortowe* 'with creeping things of every kind'

CW 111; *myterneth gwlasow* 'kings of countries' TH 6a; *chy, trevyn po tyrryow* 'house, houses or lands' TH 21a.

1B.4 *han venyn* 'and the woman' TH 2a; *An wethan a wothfes an da han drog* 'The tree of knowledge of good and evil' TH 2a; *rag an vyghternes real* 'for the royal queen' BK 2047; *tety valy bram an gathe* 'pooh, pooh, the cat's fart!' CW 1305; *Lowena ha ryelder the flowren an vyghterneth!* 'Joy and majesty to the flower of kings!' BK 1930-31; *ef a sawye an glevyon* 'he used to heal the sick' PA 25a; *han vohosogyen pub vr* 'and the poor always' BM 4261

1B.5 *pup deth vmma ware an nore vys* 'every day here on the earth SA 60; *bys may teffa an jeth hag egery* 'until the day happen to dawn' TH 18; *inter an gyth ha'n noos* 'between the day and the night' CW 85; *an veyn ma gura bara ʒis* 'make of these stones bread for yourself' PA 11c; *an dus prowd, an dus fure, an dus dyskys, an dus perfect* 'the proud people, the wise people, the learned people, the perfect people' TH 9; *in mes an nore* 'out of the earth TH 2; *an ore a thros in rag bestes peswartrosek* 'the earth brought forth four-footed animals' TH 2; *war oll an bestas in nore* 'over all the animals in the earth' TH 2; *ow tenna then dore* 'drawing down to the ground' TH 6; *mes an dore* 'out of the ground' CW 2083; *an jawl re'th ewno* 'the devil mend you!' OM 2527; *kyn fes tregys gans an Jowl!* 'thou thou dwell with the Devil' BK 45; *oll an thewollow* 'all the devils' CW 481.

1C.1 VOCABULARY

bara *m.* bread
benyn *f.*, **benenes** woman
bord *m.*, **bordys** table
buwgh *f.* **buhas** cow
carow *m.*, **kyrwas** stag
coos *m.*, **cosow** wood, forest
davas *f.*, **deves** sheep
dëdh *m.*, **dedhyow** day
delen *f.*, **delyow** (*pl.*) and **del** (coll.) leaf
escar *m.*, **eskerens** enemy
flogh *m.*, **flehes** child
gwedhen *f.*, **gwëdh** tree
gwel *m.*, **gwelyow** field
gwels *m.* grass
gwin *m.* wine
in dadn² under

Kernow *m.*, **Kernowyon** Cornishman
Kernow *f.* Cornwall
ky *m.*, **keun** dog
mab *m.*, **mebyon** boy, son
marchont *m.*, **marchons** merchant
medhek *m.*, **medhygyon** doctor
meneth *m.*, **menydhyow** mountain
mona *m.* money
mowes *f.*, **mowysy** girl
nos *f.*, **nosow** night
Pow an Sowson *m.* England
Sows *m.*, **Sowson** Englishman
tarow *m.*, **terewy** bull
tas *m.*, **tasow** father
wàr² upon

1C.2 TRANSLATE INTO ENGLISH:

1 An desen wàr an bord.
2 An gwin i'n wedren.
3 An gath ha'n ky.
4 An cathas ha'n keun.
5 An mytern ha'n vyternes.
6 An vyterneth ha'n myternesow.
7 An jëdh ha'n nos.
8 An vebyon ha'n mowysy.
9 An vedhygyon ha'n glevyon.
10 An varchons ha'n mona.
11 An cothmans ha'n eskerens.
12 An gerens ha'n flehes.
13 Dywscoth ha treys.
14 An delyow in dadn an wedhen.
15 An vuwgh ha'n tarow i'n gwel.
16 An kyrwas i'n cosow.
17 An deves wàr an meneth.
18 An buhas wàr an gwels.
19 An rômys i'n treven.
20 An Sowson in Pow an Sowson ha'n Gernowyon in Kernow.

1C.3 TRANSLATE INTO CORNISH:

1 The men and the women.
2 The children in the fields.
3 The sheep and the cows.
4 The grass on the mountains.
5 The trees in the woods.
6 The girls and boys under the tree.
7 The cats and the dogs.
8 The leaves on the tree and the leaves on the ground.
9 Friends and relatives.
10 The table in the room in the house.
11 The boys, the girls and the fathers.
12 The girl and the cat.
13 The boys and the bulls.
14 The king, the queen and the devil.
15 The devils and the women.
16 The fields and the mountains.
17 The Englishman, the devil and the cat.
18 The cows on the grass.
19 The doctor and the children.
20 The merchant and the money.

SECÙND DYSCANS
SECOND LESSON

2A.1 SOME COMMON ADJECTIVES

meur great
brâs large, big
bian small
coth old
yonk young
nowyth new
pell far, long
hir long
ogas near; **ogas dhe²** near to
cot short
drog bad
dâ good
uhel (pronounced [ˈju(h)əl]) high
isel low
ker dear, expensive, blessed
teg pretty, beautiful
wheg sweet, dear (in letter writing)
wherow bitter
du (pronounced [diʊ]) black
gwydn white
gwer green
glas blue (also **blou**)
melen yellow
rudh red
gell (light) brown
loos grey, old
tewl dark
spladn bright, apparent
cler clear

munys tiny
parys ready
terrys broken
trogh cut, blemished
peryllys dangerous
saw safe, sound
yagh healthy
clâv sick, unwell
yeyn cold
tobm hot
smoth smooth
garow rough, harsh
cortes polite
dyscortes rude
uskys quick
scav quick, light (of weight)
lent slow
poos heavy, serious, fetid
cosel quiet
medhel soft
cales hard
tanow thin, few
tew fat, thick
crev strong
gwadn weak
skentyl intelligent
fur wise
gocky foolish
dydhan entertaining, amusing

diek lazy
dywysyk industrious, hardworking
down deep
bas shallow
coynt odd, wily
stranj strange
clor mild
gwyls wild
dov tame
glân clean

plos dirty
bohosak poor
rych rich
rônd round
scant scarce
sëgh dry, thirsty
glëb wet
gwag empty, hungry
leun full

2A.2 MUTATION OF ADJECTIVES

Adjectives normally follow their noun: **den coth** 'old man'; **chy brâs** 'large house'; **flogh bian** 'little child'. The initial consonant of an adjective undergoes lenition after a feminine singular noun: **benyn goth** 'old woman', **buwgh wydn** 'white cow', **gwedhen wer** 'green tree'. The initial consonant of an adjective will also be lenited after a masculine plural noun referring to persons, **mebyon vian** 'little sons'. If the noun ends in **s**, or **th**, however, following **t**, **d** and **p** are usually left unmutated: **eglos** *f.* **teg** 'a beautiful church'; **nos** *f.* **dâ** 'good night'; **cath** *f.* **plos** 'dirty cat'.

The adjective is not mutated if either a verb comes between it and the noun: **buwgh wydn** 'a white cow' but **an vuwgh yw gwydn** 'the cow is white', **an venyn goth** 'the old woman', but **an venyn o coth** 'the woman was old'. Note also the different constructions **benyn vian goth** 'a small old woman' and **benyn vian ha coth** 'a small old woman'.

The word **mas** 'good' has a permanently mutated form **vas**, which means 'of use, of worth, acceptable': **nyns yw an margh vas** 'the horse is no good'.

2A.3 PREFIXED ADJECTIVES

Some adjectives are prefixed to their noun. In this case the whole is treated as one word and the initial consonant is lenited after the the prefix: **coth** 'old' + **gwas** 'fellow' (plural **gwesyon**), gives **cothwas** 'old fellow', **cothwesyon**. Other prefixed adjectives are usually written with a hyphen: **tebel** 'evil', **drog** 'bad, evil', **fâls** 'false' **hager** 'ugly, evil', and **leun** 'full': **tebel-venyn** *f.* 'evil woman', **an debel-venyn** 'the evil woman'; **drog-dhewas** 'an evil drink' (**dewas, dewosow** 'drink'); **drog-dhyweth** 'an evil end' (**dyweth** *m.* 'end, finish'); **fâls-duwow** (*pl.*) 'false gods' (**duw** *m.* 'god', **duwow** 'gods'; notice that the **d** here is not lenited after **s**); **hager-vernans** 'a nasty death' (**mernans** *m.* 'death'), **hager-oberow** 'evil

7

deeds' (**ober** *m.*, **oberow** 'deed, work'); **a leun-golon** 'with a full heart, willingly' (**colon** *f.*, **colonow** 'heart')

2A.4 PLURAL ADJECTIVES AS NOUNS

As suggested in 1A.4, some adjectives can receive the plural ending **-yon** to be made into plural nouns. We have seen **clâv** 'sick' > **clevyon** 'patients, ill people', **bohosak** 'poor' > **bohosogyon**. Here also can be included: **othomak** 'needy' > **othomogyon** 'needy people', **brâs** 'great' > **brâsyon** 'important people'; **gowek** 'mendacious' > **gowygygyon** 'liars'; **dyscryjyk** 'unbelieving' > **dyscryjygyon** 'unbelievers'; **muscok** 'insane' > **muscogyon** 'madmen'.

Plural adjectives are never used with plural nouns: **flourys brâs** 'large flowers', not **flourys *brâsyon**. The only exception is **aral** 'other', which has a special plural form **erel**: **den aral** 'another man', **tus erel** 'other men'. **Eskelly grehen** 'bat' (the flying mammal) can be mentioned here. The first element, **eskelly**, is the plural of **askel** *f.* 'wing' and **grehen** is the plural of **crohen** *f.* 'skin' with initial lenition.

Ken 'another' precedes its noun without mutation: **ken maner** 'another manner', **ken mytern** 'another king'; **Ken** is also used as a pronoun meaning 'something else' and as an adverb with the sense 'otherwise'.

2A.5 THE GENITIVE OF JUXTAPOSITION

When one noun follows another it becomes possessive in sense: **hot** *m.* 'hat' + **benyn** 'woman' gives **hot benyn** 'a woman's hat'; **jyn** *m.* 'machine' + **gortheby** 'answering' gives **jyn gortheby** 'answering machine'.

Notice that when the possessive noun is a proper noun or is preceded by the definite article, the first noun itself becomes definite, i.e. it behaves as though it had the definite article in front of it. **Tus** 'men' + **Kembra** *f.* 'Wales' gives **tus Kembra** 'the men of Wales', **ascorn** *m.* 'bone' (*pl.* **eskern**) + **an ky** 'the dog' gives **ascorn an ky** 'the bone of the dog, the dog's bone'.

Expressions like ***an yêth** *f.* **Kernow** for 'the language of Cornwall', ***an Orseth Kernow** for 'the Gorsedd of Cornwall' are incorrect. **Yêth Kernow** means 'the language of Cornwall', **Gorseth Kernow** means 'the Gorsedd of Cornwall', since **Kernow** is a proper name and thus definite.

If the article is used with the first noun, **a²** is used with the second: **an flehes a'n scol** 'the children of the school', **an dus a'n pow** 'the people of the country'. In the Cornish tale *Jowan Chy an Hordh* the expression **an** *ôst an tshei* 'the landlord' occurs four times. This is not an instance of the incorrect use of the article, since in modern spelling the phrase would be written **an ost a'n chy**.

NOTE: the wrong use of the definite article is a mistake frequently made by revivalists, most likely due to influence from English. Even R. Morton Nance himself wrote a book called **Lyver *an Pymp Marthus Seleven**, which first appeared in 1939. The title is not perfect, since **Seleven** 'St Levan' is a proper name and thus definite. It would have been wiser to have called the book **Lyver Pymp Marthus Seleven** 'the Book of St Levan's Five Miracles'.

2A.6 FEMININE NOUNS WITH FOLLOWING GENITIVE

The initial consonant of a noun used possessively immediately after a feminine noun is often lenited. This is because the second noun is effectively an adjective. Examples are common in place-names, e.g. **Carrek** *f.* **Veryasek** 'St Meriasek's rock'; **Tre Garasek** 'Tregassick' (from **tre** *f.* 'town, settlement' and the personal name, **Carasek** 'Caratacus, Caradog'). Where the collocation is not a set phrase the second noun is sometimes lenited, and sometimes not. One thus finds in traditional Cornish both **bednath Varia** and **bednath Maria** 'Our Lady's blessing'.

2B EXAMPLES FROM THE TEXTS

2B.1 **Brvz yu an venen-na** 'That women is large' AB: 243c; **nyns o mas bean** 'it was only small' TH 5; **ha in tyrmyn an testament nowith** 'and in the time of the new testament' TH 27a; **ogas o nyng esa pell** 'it was near, it wasn't far' PA 140b; **an lesson cut ma** 'this short lessorn' TH 26; **beautifull tege ha wheg** 'beautifully fair and sweet' TH 2; **Arluth ker, the arhadow a vith gwreys** 'Dear lord, your command will be done' BK 2034-35; **me ath ra parlet vhel** 'I will make you a high prelate' BM 1468; **rag own bos drys re esall** 'for fear of being brought too low' BK 1006; **nyng o dyag the wul obereth da** 'he was not lazy to do good works' TH 2a; **thy'm rosons bystyl wherow** 'they gave me bitter gall' RD 2601; **du yw y lyw** 'black is his colour' RD 2101; **deaw gopyl a gelemmy, dof gans pluf gwyn** 'two pairs of doves, tame with white plumage' BK 2044-45; **colom whek glas hy lagas** 'a sweet dove, blue her eye' OM 1135; **barve looz** 'grey beard' Bodewryd MS; **agan tavas ew ruth gans e gos** 'our tongue is red with his blood' SA 60; **Y'n howl yma rowndenab ha golow splan** 'In the sun there is roundness and brilliant light' BK 283-84; **caradowha ys an houl cler** 'more beloved than the clear sun' BK 1751-52; **Yma oma kuen munys** 'Here there are tiny dogs' BM 3223; **ha paris the verwall** 'and ready to die' SA 59; **ow holan yth ew terrys** 'my heart it is broken' CW 1263; **ow holan ew ogas troghe** 'my heart is almost broken' CW

1228; *te ru'm grug saw* 'you have made me well' BK 813; *the oll an re na a vo claff, not then re ew yagh* 'to all those who are sick, not to those who are healthy' TH 8a; *yma ow gwyll ow holan clave* 'it makes my heart sick' CW 1199; *Yein kuer, tarednow ha golowas* 'Cold weather, thunder and lightning' Pryce; *in wethan pur smoth heb mycke* 'in the tree very smoothly without a sound' CW 536; *yscar ha canfas garow* 'sackcloth and rough canvas' TH 60a; *aban osa mar gortes* 'since you are so courteous' RD 675; *Ens mes a'm golag uskys* 'Let him leave my sight quickly' BK 3188; *hemma yth ew gorryb skave* 'that is a frivolous answer' CW 1198; *Cowethe na vethen lent* 'Comrades, let's not be slow' BM 3245; *very grevaws ha poos* 'very grievous and serious' TH 4; *a mennen vy purguir sevel in cosel* 'if I wished to stand quietly' BM 2425-26; *rag y vos kyc methel gurys* 'because he has been created soft flesh' OM 928; *rag y bos an vnderstonding an gyrryow ma calys* 'because the understanding of these words is hard' TH 53; *ow howetha ew tanow* 'my companions are few' CW 121; *may hallo cane ellas nefre yn tewolgow tew* 'that he may for ever sing alas in thick darkness' OM 515-16; *Mal nagwunnen moaz gwadn trea* 'So that no one may go weak home' WGwavas; *Kyn nag off den skentyll pur* 'Though I am not a very intelligent man' PA 8a; *pe rêg e gwellaz fatal o geaze gwreaze anotha gen an teze feere* 'when he saw that he had been made fun of by the wise men' Rowe; *sow yth ota gy gockye* 'but you are foolish' CW 2324; *pys gans colon dywysyk* 'pray with an assiduous heart' RD 1370; *in pytt downe ow leskye* 'burning in a deep pit' CW 2034; *syght coynt y welys certen* 'I saw an odd sight indeed' BM 1786; *strange yth ew eve tha welas* 'strange it is to be seen' CW 1549; *my a'n gwra clor* 'I will render him meek' BK 2781; *ha kyrwas gwyls pur prety aragtha in le ohan* 'and wild stags before them very prettily instead of oxen' BK 960-61; *del vynnas Du whar ha dof* 'as God wished, mild and tame' BK 848; *pew a yll gull glan, neb ew conceyvys in mostethes* 'who can make clean him who was conceived in impurity?' TH 7; *me re'th clowas ow ty the Jovyn plos* 'I heard you swearing to dirty Jove' BK 115-16; *Mars on bohosak ha gwan* 'If we are poor and weak' BK 773; *rych os ha fuer* 'rich you are and wise' BK 1697; *mêz a kein gûn an manah pîs pŷrround* 'out of the back of the monk's gown a completely round piece' JCH §27; *mars es dor segh war an beys* 'if there is dry land on the earth' OM 1100; *Gwag ove, rave gawas haunsell?* 'I am hungry; can I have breakfast?' Pryce; *Du leun a ras, re'gas guytho* 'May God full of grace preserve you!' BK 2889-90; *Ha an huêl a kỳòaz skent* 'and work became scarce' JCH §2.

2B.2 *In kepar maner neb a rella don colan tha* 'Similarly whoever bears a good heart' TH 23a; *does ny vydnas an vrane vras* 'the great raven did not wish to return' CW 2464; *in Bretayn Ver curunys* 'crowned in Great Britain' BK 3136; *mytern yn bryten vyan* 'king in Little Britain' BM 169; *now in toppe an wethan deake* 'now in the top of the beautiful tree' CW 1907; *Dzhûan a ʒuiʌaz an vòr ʒôʌ* 'and Jowan kept to the old road' JCH §16; *ugge an teez goth tho merwal akar* 'after the old people die out' NBoson; *barve velin... barve widne* 'a yellow beard... a white beard' Bodewryd MS; *Mez ol krêv en karensa vâz* 'But all strong in excellent love' WGwavas.

2B.3 *theworth neb drog then* 'from some evil person' TH 32a; *ha'n throg-venyn a'm geysys!* 'and the evil woman who ridiculed me' BK 3144; *a lamec drog was yth os* 'Lamec, you are an evil fellow' CW 1655; *han tebel el hager bref* 'and the evil angel, vile serpent' PA 122c; *Out warnas, tebal-venyn!* 'Fie upon thee, evil woman!' BK 1210; *Te falge horsen nam brag vy* 'You false whoreson, don't threaten me' BM 3491; *ha nagh Astrot ha Jovyn ha'th fals duwaw in pub tu* 'and deny Astrot and Jove and your false gods on every side' BK 222-23.

2B.4 *a bur fals dyscryggygyon* 'O you utter false unbelievers' OM 1855; *nyns ough lemmyn gowygyon* 'you are nothing but liars' RD1510; *the vohosogyan guet ry in cheryte part ath peth* 'be sure to give in charity some of your wealth to the poor' BM 472-73; *kefrys brosyen ha kemyn* 'both the important people and the common man' BM 3215; *parys certen ath guereys the socra othomogyon* 'ready indeed by your help to succour people in need' BM 2552-53; *ha angy droaze thotha oll an glevyan* 'and they brought him all the sick people' Rowe.

2B.5 *myghtern israel arluth cref* 'the king of Israel, a mighty lord' PC 276; *Duk kernov hag oll y dus* 'the Duke of Cornwall and all his men' BM 2397; *envy intre te ha haes an venyn* 'hatred between you and the seed of the woman' TH 13; *Welcom, sokers, drys tus an bes owhy heb mar!* 'Welcome are you, helpers, beyond the people of the world!' BK 1732-34; *in toppe an wethan deake* 'in the top of the beautiful tree' CW 1907; *par dell ough rewlar an wlas* 'as you are ruler of the kingdom' BK 3069; *duk an Saxens, Chellery* 'the duke of the Saxons, Childerich' BK 3230; *gorfan an bees* 'the end of the world' Bodewryd MS; *Materen Frink, thera vi a menia* 'the King of France, I mean' JTonkin; *gennez en collan an pow* 'born in the heart of the country' NBoson.

2B.6 *Ov map benneth varya dys* 'My son, Mary's blessing to you' BM 63-4; *carrek veryasek holma gelwys vyth wose helma* 'this will be called St Meriasek's Rock hereafter' BM 1072-23; *honna a vythe ow skavall droose* 'that will be my footstool' CW 20.

2C.1 VOCABULARY

âls *f.*, **âlsyow** cliff, shore	**ena** there
best *m.*, **bestas** animal	**fresk** fresh
cloud *m.*, **cloudys** cloud	**gwels** *coll.* grass
coos *m.*, **cosow** wood	**Kernow** *m.*, **Kernowyon** Cornishman
dowr *m.*, **dowrow** water, river	**Kernowes** *f.*, **Kernowesow** Cornishwoman
dres across	
ebron *f.* sky	**Loundres** *f.* London
eglos *f.*, **eglosyow** church	

lowarth *m.* garden
lowr enough. **lowr a²** enough of, a number of
meur a² many
obma here
pons *m.,* **ponsow** bridge
pow *m.,* **powyow** country
ryb beside, near
saw but

tavern *m.,* **tavernyow** tavern, pub
warba·rth together
yma 'is' or 'are' (with plural nouns). It is used when describing position; it also means 'there is'
yw is (of characteristic)

2C.2 TRANSLATE INTO ENGLISH:

1 Yma lowr a Geltyon in Kembra.
2 An Gernowyon yw crev ha dywysyk.
3 Yma meur a dheves gwydn in menydhyow gwer an pow.
4 Yma lowr a flourys teg i'n lowarth hag yma meur a wëdh gwer i'n coos.
5 Yma lowr a vergh scav i'n gwel brâs.
6 An flehes i'n scol yw cortes ha skentyl.
7 An debel-venyn yw gocky.
8 An bestas i'n coos brâs yw gwyls, saw an keun obma yw dov.
9 An bara yw fresk ha gwydn saw an gwin yw coth ha rudh.
10 Yma lowr a dus warbarth i'n dre.
11 Yma pons nowyth dres an dowr.
12 Yma lowr a rômys in chy an Gernowes rych.
13 An dowr obma yw down, saw an dowr ogas dhe'n dor yw bas.
14 An othomogyon yw gwag, saw an dus rych i'n tavern yw lowen.
15 An flehes yw saw obma, saw an fordh vrâs yw peryllys.
16 An buhas tew yw gell ha'n vergh yw gwydn ha du.
17 Yma an benenes coth warbarth i'n eglos hag yma an gothwesyon warbarth i'n tavern.
18 Yma lowr a gloudys gwydn i'n ebron las.
19 An mytern ha'n vyternes yw rych, saw yma meur a vohosogyon i'n pow.
20 An vebyon wocky yw dewolow vian.

2C.3 TRANSLATE INTO CORNISH:

1 There are lots of poor people in Wales.
2 The Cornishmen are polite and industrious.
3 The water under the bridge is deep and dangerous.
4 There are many fat cows in the field and there are many thin sheep on the mountain.
5 The old fellow is amusing but the old woman is quiet.

6 There are many clever children in the school.

7 The cliffs are dangerous, but the children are safe here together.

8 The red wine is old but good.

9 The white bread is on the table.

10 There are many black horses under the trees.

11 The day is bright and the sky is blue.

12 The good king and the good queen are together in the church.

13 The old fellows are together under the large tree near the bridge.

14 The girls are industrious, but many of the boys in the school are lazy.

15 There are many mountains in Wales.

16 There are many young Cornishmen and young Cornishwomen in London.

17 The dogs and the cats are tame, but there are many wild animals in the dark wood.

18 The grass is dry and brown, but the leaves on the trees are soft and green.

19 The cake is ready and the children are hungry.

20 The cat is black and the dog is brown and white.

21 The doctor is here but the merchants are in the pub.

TRESSA DYSCANS
THIRD LESSON

3A.1 *YTH ESOF*, ETC.

We have already met **yma·** which means 'is, are' (of position) and 'there is, there are'. Here is the full paradigm of the this verb:

yth esof vy, yth esoma	I am
yth esos, yth esta	you are
yma· va, yma· ev	he is
yma· hy	she is
yma· an den	the man is
yma· Jowan	John is
yma· an flehes	the children are
yth eson, yth eson ny	we are
yth esowgh, yth esowgh why	you are
ymow·ns , ymow·ns y	they are.

The first person has a common variant **yth esoma** < **yth esof + ma**, where **ma** is a suffixed emphatic personal pronoun. The basic form of the second person singular is **esos**, but **yth esta** < **yth esos + ta**, with a suffixed second person pronoun is common. As well as **yma· va** one can use the ordinary person pronoun and say **yma· ev** 'he is'. Similarly with all three persons in the plural the emphatic pronouns **ny**, **why**, and **y** respectively may be used after the inflected form of the verb. The particle **yth** is weakly pronounced and sometimes reduced to **th**. In this orthography, reduced **yth esa** is written **th'esa**, rather than **'th esa**. The third person singular **yma** and plural **ymowns** are sometimes reduced to **ma** and **mowns** respectively; these should be written *without* an apostrophe (not **'ma** and **'mowns**). We have already seen that a plural noun, e.g. **an dus** 'the men', **an benenes** 'the women', **an flehes** 'the children', takes the singular form of the verb: **yma an benenes ena** 'the women are there', **yma an flehes obma** 'the children are here'.

14

Notice also that in later Cornish the **-s-** in this tense changes to **-r-** after **e**, so that one finds **th'eroma** 'I am', **th'eron** 'we are', **th'erowgh** 'you are', etc. The later paradigm is:

th'erof vy, **th'eroma**	I am
th'eros, **th'esta**	you are
ma va, **ma ev**	he is
ma hy	she is
ma an den	the man is
ma Jowan	John is
ma an flehes	the children are
th'eron, **th'eron ny**	we are
th'erowgh, **th'erowgh why**	you are
mowns , **mowns y**	they are.

3A.2 *YTH ESOF* WITH THE PRESENT PARTICIPLE

Yth esof, etc. form part of the verb **bos** (or **bones**) 'to be', and are known as the *long present*. As well as referring to position and meaning 'there is, there are', this tense has another important function: it is used with the Cornish equivalent of the present participle to make the present of other verbs, e.g. **cana** 'to sing', **ow cana** 'singing'. We can thus say **yma an flogh ow cana** 'the child sings (*or* is singing)'; **yma an benenes ow pobas** 'the women bake (*or* are baking)'; **yth esof ow mos** 'I go (*or* am going)'; **yma an cothwas ow tùchya pib** 'the old fellow smokes (*or* is smoking)'; **yma an cothmans owth eva warbarth i'n tavern** 'the friends drink (*or* are drinking) together in the pub'; **yma an profettys ow cria i'n gwylfos** 'the prophets cry (*or* are crying) in the wilderness'.

Here are some further verbs with their present participles:

kerdhes (pron. ['kɛrəz]) to walk	**ow kerdhes** walking
gwil to do, make	**ow qwil** doing, making
debry to eat	**ow tebry** eating
dos to come	**ow tos** coming
gweles to see	**ow qweles** seeing
redya to read	**ow redya** reading
scrifa (**screfa**) to write	**ow scrifa** writing
wherthyn to laugh	**ow wherthyn** laughing
ola to cry, to weep	**owth ola** weeping
sedha (**esedha**) to sit	**ow sedha** sitting
bewa to live	**ow pewa** living

triga (**trega**) to dwell	**ow triga** dwelling
gelwel to call	**ow kelwel** calling
gwana to pierce, to stab	**ow qwana** stabbing
tôwlel to throw	**ow tôwlel** throwing
perthy to bear	**ow perthy** bearing
kemeres to take	**ow kemeres** taking
cafos to get	**ow cafos** getting
desîrya to desire, to want	**ow tesîrya** desiring
omlath to fight	**owth omlath** fighting
agria to agree	**owth agria** agreeing
argya to argue	**owth argya** arguing
declarya to declare	**ow teclarya** declaring
sùffra to suffer	**ow sùffra** suffering
godra to milk (a cow)	**ow codra** milking
codha to fall	**ow codha** falling
crambla to climb	**ow crambla** climbing
cramyas to crawl	**ow cramyas** crawling
desky to learn, to teach	**ow tesky** learning, teaching
prena (**perna**) to buy	**ow perna** buying
gwertha to sell	**ow qwertha** selling
don to carry	**ow ton** carrying
cùsca to sleep	**ow cùsca** sleeping
fysky to rush	**ow fysky** rushing

Two things will be noticed from the above list. In the first place, if a verb begins with a vowel, **ow** becomes **owth** before it. In the second place, initial **b**, **d**, **g** and **gw** become **p**, **t**, **c** or **k** and **qw** respectively after **ow** of the participle. This is another Cornish mutation. Its technical name is *provection*, but it is more frequently known as the *hard mutation* or *fourth state*. In dictionaries words that cause provection are often shown with a superscript **4** after them. Actually provection is hardly known in Cornish apart from its use with **ow⁴** of the present participle, and after **mar⁴**, **mara⁴** 'if'. See Stagell A (Appendix A).

3A.3 NOUN OBJECT OF THE PRESENT PARTICIPLE

A noun object may come after **ow** + verb: **yma an wreg ow pobas bara i'n gegyn hag yma an gour ow codra an buhas i'n bowjy** 'the wife is baking bread in the kitchen, and the husband is milking the cows in the cowshed'.

3B EXAMPLES FROM THE TEXTS

3B.2–3 *ef a thueth a galyle lays nowyth ov tesky* 'he came from Galilee teaching new laws' PA 107cd; *ov corthya crist* 'worshipping Christ' BM 3449; *yma ynweth S paull ow scriffa the timothe* 'St Paul also writes to Timothy' TH 18a; *ha lymmyn yma Anastasius ena ow setha* 'and now Anastasius sits there' TH 48; *yma ow tybbry ha owh eva y damnation y honyn* 'he eats and drinks his own damnation' TH 51a; *an pith vsans ow quelas gans aga lagasow kyge* 'what they see with their bodily eyes' TH 56; *ema ef ow trega innaff ve* 'he dwells in me' SA 61; *ha me avel mordarow owth ola hag owth owtya* 'and I like a bull seal weeping and yelling' BK 23-4; *avell tane ow collowye* 'shining like fire' CW 125; *yn defyth in myske bestas yma ef prest ow pewa* 'in the desert among animals he is living always' CW 1481-82; *ow crowntya thymmo sylwans* 'granting me salvation' CW 1944; *than purpose na mowns ow toos* 'for that purpose they are coming' CW 2161.

3C.1 VOCABULARY

a·mary cupboard	**keus** cheese
boos *m.* food	**kyttryn** *m.*, **kyttrynow** bus
bys in to, into	**lebmyn** now
carr *m.*, **kerry** car	**lewyas** to steer, to drive
chair *m.*, **chairys** chair	**lyver** *m.*, **lyvrow** book
clappya to talk	**ogas dhe** near
côwsel to speak (takes **orth**);	**orth** at, to (with certain verbs)
daras *m.*, **darasow** door	**practys** *m.* practice, exercise
dres across	**shoppa** *m.*, **shoppys** shop
gans with	**stenor** *m.*, **stenoryon** tin miner
gorra put	**tan** *m.* fire
govyn to ask (takes **orth**);	**tro ha** towards
gwely *m.*, **gweliow** bed	**whath** still, yet
hedhyw today	**yn lent** slowly
kerdhes in mes gans to go out with, to date	**yn scav** quickly
	yn tâ (LC **yttâ·**) well
Kernowek Cornish language	**yn uskys** quickly

NOTE: **Kernowek** properly means 'Cornish language'. To express the idea of 'Cornish', e.g. 'Cornish cream' or 'Cornish wrestlers', it is probably better to use **Kernow** *f.* 'Cornwall'; **dehen a Gernow** 'cream of Cornwall', **omdowloryon Kernow** 'the wrestlers of Cornwall' (definite), **omdowloryon a Gernow** 'Cornish wrestlers' (indefinite). 'I am Cornish' is best translated **Kernow ov vy** 'I am a Cornishman' or **Kernowes ov vy** 'I am a Cornishwoman'.

3C.2 TRANSLATE INTO ENGLISH:

1 Yma lowr a Gernowyon ow côwsel Kernowek hedhyw.

2 Yma an benenes ow pobas hag yma an mowysy ow codra an buhas.

3 Yth esof ow scrifa an practys Kernowek i'n lyver.

4 Ymowns y ow kerdhes warbarth in dadn an gwëdh hag ow tôwlel an bellen wàr an gwels.

5 Yma an flehes ow cùsca in gweliow bian i'n rom brâs hag yma an dus coth ow wherthyn hag owth eva warbarth ryb an tan.

6 Yma lowr a gloudys gwydn ow fysky yn uskys dres an ebron.

7 Yth esta ow tesky Kernowek lebmyn hag yth esta ow redya an lyver teg.

8 Yma an vebyon ow crambla wàr an âlsyow uhel peryllys.

9 Yma an vebyon ow codha; ymowns y owth ola.

10 Yth eson ny ow ton an bara ha'n gwin dhe'n stenoryon in dadn an dor.

11 Yth esowgh owth omlath hedhyw saw yma an mowysy cosel ow redya hag ow scrifa Kernowek.

12 Yma an cothwas clâv hag yma ev ow sùffra.

13 Yth eson ny ow sedha wàr an chair medhel ryb an daras.

14 An mowysy yw gwag hag ymowns y owth ola.

15 Yma an buhas ow sedha wàr an gwels i'n gwel.

16 Yth eson ny ow qwary ryb an scol.

17 Yma an venyn yonk ow qwil tesen hedhyw.

18 Yma Jowan ow tesîrya pellen nowyth hag yma ev ow kerdhes troha'n shoppa i'n dre.

19 Yma an gwedrednow i'n amary ogas dhe'n daras hag yma an gwin wàr an bord.

20 Yth esta ow qwary hag ow wherthyn.

21 Yma Jenefer ha Jowan ow kerdhes in mes warbarth.

3C.3 TRANSLATE INTO CORNISH:

1 There are many cars in Cornwall.

2 Many people speak Cornish now.

3 You speak Cornish well, but I am still learning.

4 You (*pl.*) read Cornish in the new book.

5 I read and write Cornish but I speak English to Cornishmen.

6 I am carrying the glasses and the wine to the table under the tree.

7 We are playing with a ball near the church.

8 The girls are playing but the boys are arguing and fighting.

9 The children are hungry; they are crying.

10 The young people are coming across the bridge.

11 We buy food in the big shop.

12 We take the bus to the town.

13 I am going to Wales in the car today.

14 The merchant sells horses and cows in Cornwall.

15 The man is old and sick; he suffers and he walks slowly.

16 The boys are fighting beside the school.

17 The child is ill in bed and the doctor is hurrying to the house.

18 The Cornishwoman is walking in the mountains of Wales.

19 She is young and healthy. She is going out with a handsome young man.

20 The old woman is old but she is still healthy.

21 The old fellows are drinking together in the pub.

22 The merchants sell much wine to the foolish young people; the young people drink together—and they argue and fight.

PESWORA DYSCANS
FOURTH LESSON

4A.1 NEGATIVE OF THE LONG PRESENT OF *BOS*

Sentences with **esof** are rendered negative by use of the negative particle **nyns** or **nynj**. Either form is acceptable, but for brevity's sake we shall confine ourselves to **nyns**.

nyns esof, nyns esof vy, **nyns esoma**	I am not
nyns esos, nyns esta	you are not
nyns usy va, nyns ujy ev	he is not
nyns usy hy, nyns ujy hy	she is not
nyns usy an den, nynj ujy an den	the man is not
nyns usy Jowan, nynj ujy Jowan	John is not
nyns eus den (**vëth**)	no man is
nyns eus benyn (**vëth**)	no woman is
nyns eson, nyns eson ny	we are not
nyns esowgh, nyns esowgh why	you are not
nyns usons, nyns usons y	they are not.

4A.2 *USY* VERSUS *EUS*

Notice that **usy** (or **ujy**) is used with definite subjects, 'the man', 'John', 'the woman', 'the children', 'he', 'she', whereas **eus** is used with indefinite subjects, 'no man', 'no woman', 'no child'. It takes time to get used to this distinction, so practise constructing sentences of the following kinds:

Nyns eus den vëth obma No one is here, There's nobody here
Nyns eus flogh vëth i'n lowarth There is no child in the garden
Nyns usy an flogh i'n lowarth The child is not in the garden
Nyns usy Jowan i'n rom John is not in the room.

4A.3 NEGATIVES WITH THE PERIPHRASTIC PRESENT

You can also make sentences like the following:

Nyns esoma ow mos dhe'n dre de Yow I do not go to town on Thursday

Nyns usy hy ow wherthyn lebmyn; yma hy owth ola She's not laughing now; she's crying

Nyns eson ny ow prenassa i'n shoppa bian na fella We no longer do the shopping in the little shop

Nyns usy hy wàr an kyttryn; ow kerdhes yma hy She is not on the bus; she is walking

Nyns esoma ow côwsel Kernowek yn tâ; yth esoma whath ow tesky I don't speak Cornish well; I'm still learning.

Notice that in order to emphasize the participle, **yma va owth ola** can become **owth ola yma va**. Emphasizing a word by putting it at the beginning of its clause is a common feature of Cornish, and indeed of all the Celtic languages.

4A.4 INTERROGATIVE FORM OF *ESOF*, ETC.

To make questions with **esof** one omits the **nyns** from the negative:

esoma?, **esof vy?**	am I?
esta?	are you?
usy va?, **usy ev?**	is he?
usy hy?	is she?
usy an den?	is the man?
eus den vëth?	is anybody?
eus flogh?	is a child? is there a child?
eus benyn?	is a woman? is there a woman?
eus tra vëth?	is there anything?
eus keus?	is there cheese?
eus cres?	is there peace?
usy Jowan?	is John?
usy an dus?	are the people?
eson ny?	are we?
esowgh why?	are you (pl.)?
usons y?	are they?

As with negatives, so with questions. You must distinguish **eus?** 'is there any?' from **usy?** 'is?' (definite):

Eus den vëth obma? Is there anyone here?
Eus boos i'n gegyn? Is there food in the kitchen?
Eus buwgh vëth i'n gwel? Is there any cow in the field?
Usy Jowan i'n rom? Is John in the room
Usy an leth i'n gegyn? Is the milk in the kitchen?
Usy an mowysy ow codra an buhas? Are the girls milking the cows?
Usy an gothwesyon whath owth eva an gwin? Are the old fellows
  still drinking the wine?

Again, this takes a little getting used to, but it becomes easier with practice. The difference between an indefinite subject, e.g. anybody, a woman, a child, a cow, a dog, cheese, etc., and a definite subject, e.g. the people, the women, the children, the cows, the dogs, the cheese, etc., is the difference between speaking about *what* is there, and about *who or which one* is there.

4A.5 REPLIES
Cornish, like most of the other Celtic languages, usually manages without a separate word for 'yes' and 'no'. Instead the verb of the question is repeated. If the answer is 'no', **nyns** becomes **nag**:

Esta ow mos dhe'n dre? Nag esof. Are you going to the town? No.
Usy va ow kerdhes dhe'n scol? Nag usy. Does he walk to school?
  No.
Eus den vëth i'n gegyn? Nag eus. Is there anybody in the kitchen?
  No.
Esowgh why ow qwary gwëdhboll? Nag eson. Do you (*pl.*) play
  chess? No.

If the answer is 'yes', then the verb by itself is repeated:

Esta ow convedhes? Esof. Do you understand? Yes.
Usy hy ow pobas hedhyw? Usy. Is she baking today? Yes.
Eus boos i'n gegyn? Eus. Is there food in the kitchen. Yes.
Eus cres? Eus. Is there peace? Yes.

When the statement is repeated in full, remember that the verbal particles are **nyns** (**nynj**) negative and **yth** (**th'**) positive:

Usy Jory i'n rom? Nag usy, nyns usy ev i'n rom. Is Jory in the room? No, he is not in the room.

Esta owth eva gwin? Esof, yth esof owth eva gwin dâ. Do you drink wine? Yes, I drink good wine.

4A.6 NEGATIVE QUESTIONS

Negative questions are formed by placing the interrogative particle **a²** in front of the negative verb:

A nyns usy ev ow cortos? Isn't he waiting?

A nyns esowgh why ow côwsel Kernowek? Don't you (*pl.*) speak Cornish?

A nyns esoma ow scrifa lebmyn? Am I not writing now?

A nyns uson y whath i'n tyller? Are they not still in the place?

The interrogative particle **a²** is not always pronounced. The interrogative particle **a²** is used with most verbs. Forms of **bos** 'to be' and **mos** 'to go' (16A.4) that begin with a vowel are the exception and do not take the particle:

> NOTE: In later Cornish **ny(ns)** and **ny(nj)** are largely replaced by **na(g)** everywhere. It is probably wiser for beginners to maintain the destinction between **ny(ns)** and **na(g)**, however.

4A.7 'YES' AND 'NO'

If one must use the words for 'yes' and 'no', then the Cornish forms are **ea** (pronounced ['eə] and **nâ** (pronounced [næ:]) respectively: **nyns usy ev ow leverel ea na nâ** 'he says neither yes or no', **an gorthyp yw ea bò nâ** 'the answer is yes or no'.

> NOTE: Some speakers of Cornish used the word **gwir** 'true' to mean 'yes'. There is nothing wrong with this usage, but it is without parallel in the traditional language.

4A.8 'WHERE?' AND 'WHEN?'

'Where?' in Cornish is **ple**, which is added to the affirmative form in 3A.1 and **ple yth** contracts to **pleth**; **ple yma** and **ple ymowns** become **ple ma** and **ple mowns** respectively:

Pleth esof vy? Where am I? (but **Ple th'erof vy?**)

Pleth esta? Where are you?

Ple ma Jowan? Where is John?

Pleth esowgh why ow mos? Where are you going? (but **Ple th'erowgh why ow mos?**)

'When?' in Cornish is **py eur**, **peur** (literally 'which hour'), which is attached to the question form in 4A.4. **Peur** before consonants causes mixed mutation (7A.3)

Peur usy an dus ow tos obma? When do the people come here? or When are the people coming here?

Peur esta ow mos dhe'n gwely When do you go to bed?

Another ways of saying 'when?' is with the expression **pana dermyn** (literally 'which time?'). This is also attached to the question forms given in 4A.4:

Pana dermyn usons y ow mos tre? When do they go home?

Pana dermyn esta ow cùsca? When do you sleep?

4B EXAMPLES FROM THE TEXTS

4B.1 ***Teuthar, nyng egas in fas war the forth hyr*** 'Teuthar, you are not well upon your long road' BK 168-69; ***nyng vgy ow mesternges yn bys ma*** 'my kingdom is not in this world' PA 102a; ***in cambron an lagasek nyns usy eff malbe dam*** 'the sharp-eyed man isn't in any damned place in Camborne' BM 1018-19; ***Nyns es thyn naneyll feith… na tra vith arell ew da*** 'We have neither faith… nor any other good thing' TH 9; ***nenna nyns egow why in dan an la*** 'then you are not under the law' TH 16a.

4B.2 ***nynses onyn a ra da, nag es vn onyn*** 'there is not one who does good, there is not one' TH 7a; ***Nyng es Du saw onyn lel*** 'indeed there is only one God' BK 136; ***Hostes, eus boues de why?*** 'Hostess, have you any food?' Borde; ***Ez kêz? Ez po neg ez*** 'Is there cheese? There is or there isn't' Pryce; ***Nyng es tra vith dale talues en beez*** 'There is nothing that should be esteemed in the world' NBoson.

4B.3 ***Nyns esos ov attendya an laha*** 'you do not consider the law' BM 848-49; ***ny gesas ow dysky the honyn*** 'you do not teach yourself' TH 14a; ***Rag nyng esan ny ow cara*** 'For we do not love God' Du TH 9a; ***ken nyns ugens y ow regardya du*** 'although they do not regard God' TH 25; ***rag neg eran cregy nanyle regardia gerryow Dew*** 'for we do not believe nor regard the words of God' SA 59.

4B.4, 6 *esta ge ow jugia mett the veras war onyn an parna* 'do you judge me worthy to look upon one like this?' TH 7; *esta ge worth ow cara ve moy ys an re ma* 'do you love me more than these?' TH 43; *pa vaner a sort esta o qvelas agen saviour Christ* 'in what way do you see our Saviour Christ?' SA 60a; *nyns ugy crist ow leverall inweth* 'doesn't Christ also say?' TH 34; *Pelea era why moaz, moz* 'Where are you going, going?' Chygwyn.

4B.7 *the kuntel an flehyggyov ea numbyr a tremmyl* 'to gather the babies, yes, the number of three thousand' BM 1515-16; *Ea, ha the forsakya pub tra oll in bys rag kerensa du* 'Yes, and to forsake everything in the world for God's sake' TH 21a; *Ea, tristyough thyn* 'Yes, trust us' BK 2607; *Ya, ou golag ew garow* 'Yes, my appearance is savage' BK 1407; *Na na ny vythe in della* 'No, no, it won't be so' CW 264; *na na ny wreth in della* 'no, no, you won't do thus' CW 2014; *na með e vêster rei ðem* '"No", said his master, "give it to me."' JCH §10.

4B.8 *Caym lauar ple ma abel the vroder ov servont lel* 'Cain, tell me where is Abel, your brother, my loyal servant?' OM 571-72; *A! out! pleth af the guthy?* 'Ah! Alas! Where can I go to hide?' BK 118; *py vr fuf vy y wythes* 'When was I his guardian?' OM 576; *e a vednyaz thoranze seer puna termin reeg an steare disquethaz* 'he asked them assiduously when did the star appear' Rowe.

4C.1 VOCABULARY

amanyn *m.* butter
canker *m.*, **kencras** crab
degol *m.*, **degolyow** holiday
dhywar[2] from off
drehedhes to reach
glaw *m.* rain; **yma ow qwil glaw** it's raining
gorsaf *m.*, **gorsavow** station
gorvarhas *f.*, **gorvarhasow** supermarket
gwyns *m.*, **gwynsow** wind
in mes out, out of the house
kefrës also, as well
Kembrek *m.* Welsh language

keus *m.* cheese
lyverjy *m.*, **lyverjiow** library
marhas *f.*, **marhasow** market
miras (**meras**) to watch
mor *m.*, **morow** sea
nebes a little, some
nessa next
pellwolok *f.* television
prenassa to go shopping
soweth alas, unfortunately
strêt *m.*, **strêtys** street
train *m.*, **trainow** train
yn lowen happily

4C.2 TRANSLATE INTO ENGLISH:

1 Esowgh why ow mos dhe'n dre hedhyw? Nag eson, yth eson ny ow mos dhe'n mor wàr an train.

2 Pana dermyn usy an train ow trehedhes an gorsaf?

3 Ple ma Jowan ha Jenefer? Ymowns y ow sedha in dadn an wedhen vrâs i'n lowarth.

4 Eus keus i'n gegyn? Nag eus.

5 Eus leth pò bara i'n amary? Yma nebes leth, saw nyns eus bara vëth.

6 Usons y ow qwary yn lowen warbarth? Nag usons, soweth. Yma an vebyon owth omlath hag yma an mowysy owth ola.

7 Usy Jory obma? Usy, yma va i'n rom nessa ow miras orth an bellwolok.

8 Yma meur a dus ow kerdhes i'n strêt. Ymowns y ow mos dhe'n varhas.

9 Yth eson ny ow prenassa i'n worvarhas hedhyw.

10 A nyns esowgh why ow tos kefrës? Nag eson, yth eson ny ow cortos obma.

11 Esta ow côwsel Kernowek? Esof, yth esof ow côwsel Kernowek ha Kembrek kefrës.

12 Eus pons dres an ryver i'n dre? Eus, yma pons nowyth ha pons coth kefrës.

13 Ple ma an flehes? Ymowns y i'n lowarth ow crambla wàr an gwëdh hag ow miras orth an flourys.

14 A nyns usons y i'n scol? Nag usons, nyns usons y i'n scol hedhyw? Hedhyw yw degol.

15 Ple ma an medhek? Yma va i'n nessa rom ow miras orth Jory. Yma Jory clâv i'n gwely.

16 Yth eson ny ow tebry meur a vara, saw nyns eson ny owth eva gwin.

17 Usy an cothwas whath obma? Nag usy, yma va owth eva i'n tavern gans an gothwesyon erel.

18 Yma ow qwil glaw, soweth. Yma meur a gloudys loos i'n ebron.

19 Nyns eson ny ow mos in mes hedhyw.

20 Crev yw an gwyns hedhyw hag yma an delyow ow codha dhywar an gwëdh i'n lowarth.

4C.3 TRANSLATE INTO CORNISH:

1 Are the children crying? No, they are laughing together.

2 Where are the sheep? They are eating grass on the mountain.

3 Are you (*pl.*) going to the supermarket? No, we are going to the church. Today is a holiday.

4 Where is the doctor? Jory is sick in bed.

5 We are going to the town today. Are you going on the train? No, we are going on the bus.

6 The wind is strong and the yellow leaves are falling.

7 It is raining and the horses are under the trees in the field.

8 Where are the cows? They are sitting on the wet grass.

9 Isn't the old woman baking in the kitchen? No, she is here watching the television.

10 Aren't the children learning in the school today? No, they are reading in the library.

11 The boys are playing happily with the dog. The girls are talking together.

12 Where is Jennifer? She is on the train going to London.

13 Are there many young Cornishwomen in London? Yes, and young Cornishmen also.

14 Are the crabs still under the stone? No, they are in the sea now.

15 Where are the sheep? They are on the high mountains in Wales.

16 Is the man walking slowly? Yes, the old man is walking slowly. He is old and ill.

17 Where are you? I am sitting beside the fire watching the television.

18 Is it raining? No, but the day is cold.

19 Where is the old woman's house? It is in the dark wood.

20 Are the boys reading? No, they are still playing.

PYMPES DYSCANS
FIFTH LESSON

5A.1 IMPERFECT OF *ESOF*

So far we have dealt only with the verb in the present. If one wants to talk about where one was or what one was doing, the imperfect is used. Here are the various forms:

yth esen vy	I was
yth eses ta	you were
yth esa va, yth esa ev	he was
yth esa hy	she was
yth esa an den	the man was
yth esa Jowan	John was
yth esen, yth esen ny	we were
yth esewgh, yth esewgh why	you (plural) were
yth esens y	they were.

> NOTE: in later Cornish the **-s-** of this tense frequently appears as **-r-**, which in this orthography may be written by Late Cornish speakers. Moreover forms with **-j-** for **-s-** are also attested.

5A.2 NEGATIVES

To render these forms negative **yth** is replaced by **nyns** (or **nynj**) throughout:

Nyns esen vy ow mos I was not going
Nyns esa an dus ow wherthyn The people were not laughing.

5A.3 INTERROGATIVES

As with the present questions are asked by using the simple form without any verbal particle:

Esa Jowan wàr an kyttryn? Was John on the bus?
Esa flehes ena inwedh? Were there children there as well?
Esens y ow pobas hedhyw? Were they baking today?
Esewgh why ow kerdhes i'n dre? Were you (*pl.*) walking in the town?

If the reply is 'yes', the verb by itself is repeated:

Esesta ow carma? Esen Were you calling? Yes.
Esens y ow wherthyn? Esens Were they laughing? Yes.

If the reply is 'no', the verb is preceded by **nag** rather than **nyns**:

Esa ev obma? Nag esa Was he here? No.
**Esewgh why owth eva i'n tavern? Nag esen, nyns esen ny owth
  eva ena**. Were you drinking in the pub? No, we weren't drinking
  there.

Notice also:

Pleth esa Jory owth eva newher? A nyns esa va i'n tavern?
Where was Jory drinking last night? Wasn't he in the pub?

5A.4 DISJUNCTIVE PERSONAL PRONOUNS
When personal pronouns stand by themselves, they take the following
forms:

1 *sg.* **me** or **my** 'I, me'	1 *pl.* **ny** 'we'
2 *sg.* **te** or **ty** 'you'	2 *pl.* **why** 'you'
3 *sg.* **ev** 'he'; **hy** 'she'	3 *pl.* **y** 'they'

In later Cornish **me**, **my** is sometimes **vy**; in later Cornish also **te**, **ty** is
not infrequently pronounced **che**, **chy** and may be so written. In traditional
Cornish **why** 'you' (plural) is often used for the singular, particularly in
formal contexts, or when addressing a superior (compare the difference in
French between *tu*, *toi*, and *vous*). In the revived language the distinction is
not always observed. Note also that in the seventeenth-century tale *Jowan
Chy an Hordh* the use of **te** and **why** is rather inconsistent.

In later Cornish **y** 'they' is usually replaced by an emphatic form **anjy·**,
based on the third person plural ending of verbs.

The disjunctive personal pronouns are used in such expressions as **te ha me** 'you and me'. They can also be used with **ha** 'and' to render the sense 'while, as': **yth esa ev ow cana hag ev ow kerdhes an fordh ahës** 'he was singing as he walked along the road'.

5A.5 PREPOSITIONAL PRONOUNS

We have met the prepositions **dhe²** 'to', **gans** 'with', **orth** 'at, to', **dhyworth** 'from' and **a²** 'from, of'. These prepositions are among those that combine with the personal pronouns to form a single word. They conjugate as follows:

dhe² 'to'
1 *sg.* **dhybm** (**dhymm**), **dhèm** 'to me'
2 *sg.* **dhis** 'to you'
3 *sg.* **dhodho** 'to him'; **dhedhy** 'to her'
1 *pl.* **dhyn** 'to us';
2 *pl.* **dhywgh** 'to you'
3 *pl.* **dhedhans**, **dhodhans** 'to them'

Emphatic forms are also attested:
1 *sg.* **dhybmo** (**dhymmo**)
2 *sg.* **dhyso**

> NOTE: Later Cornish reduces **dhybmo vy**, **dhyso jy**, and **dhywgh why** to **dhe vy**, **dhe jy**, and **dhe why** respectively.

gans 'with' (**gen** in later Cornish)
1 *sg.* **genef**, **ge·nama** 'with me'
2 *sg.* **genes** 'with you'
3 *sg.* **ganso** 'with him'; **gensy** 'with her'
1 *pl.* **genen** 'with us'
2 *pl.* **genowgh** 'with you'
3 *pl.* **gansans** 'with them'

orth 'at, against, to' (also **worth**)
1 *sg.* **orthyf** 'at me'
2 *sg.* **orthys** 'at you'
3 *sg.* **orto** 'at him'; **orty** 'at her'
1 *pl.* **orthyn** 'at us'
2 *pl.* **orthowgh** 'at you'
3 *pl.* **ortans** 'at them'

dhywo·rth 'from' (**dhort** in later Cornish)
1 *sg.* **dhyworthyf, dhywortama** 'from me'
2 *sg.* **dhyworthys** 'from you'
3 *sg.* **dhyworto** 'from him'; **dhyworty** 'from her'
1 *pl.* **dhyworthyn** 'from us'
2 *pl.* **dhyworthowgh** 'from you'
3 *pl.* **dhywortans** 'from them'

a² 'of, from'
1 *sg.* **ahanaf** 'of me';
2 *sg.* **ahanas** 'of you';
3 *sg.* **anodho** 'of him'; **anedhy** 'of her'
1 *pl.* **ahanan** 'of us'
2 *pl.* **ahanowgh** 'of you'
3 *pl.* **anodhans** 'of them'

Ahanan 'of us, from us' can also mean 'from here, hence'.

The third person plural ending **-ans** of the prepositional pronouns is not attested in Cornish until the middle of the sixteenth century. Before that date the forms were **dhedha** 'to them', **gansa** 'with them', **orta** 'at them', **dhyworta** 'from them' and **anedha** 'of them'. Such forms are, of course, permissible in the revived language.

In the above paradigms the English meaning of each form has been given. From now on prepositional pronouns will be referred to only by person and number, without citing the meaning of each form.

5B EXAMPLES FROM THE TEXTS
5B.1 ***Dre henna yth esa ow meynya pub ordyr da*** 'By that he meant every good order' TH 40a; ***ena yth esa flowrys*** 'there were flowers there' CW 1050; ***yth esen dre pur hyreth war the lergh ovth ymwethe*** 'we were pining away for sheer longing for you' RD 1169-70; ***mayth egan owth umgelly ol clamderak*** 'so that we were fainting all in a swoon' BK 2332-33.
5B.2–3 ***ha mars ega thetha lell corfow po nag essa*** 'and whether they had real bodies or not' TH 55; ***ev a dhelledzhas an termen mal ða va prêv erra e urêg ʒuiʦa kŷmpez et i ʒever: erra po nag erra*** 'he spun out the time so that he could prove was his wife staying faithful to him: was she or wasn't she?' JCH § 39; ***ogas o nyn gesa pell*** 'it was near, it wasn't far' PA 140b; ***ha whath ena nyns esa materiall trumpet vith*** 'and still there was no material trumpet' TH 56a; ***whath ena nyns esa na marth, charet, na army*** 'still there wasn't there either horse, chariot or army' TH 56a; ***buz nag erra termen***

31

dem de screffa du straft arta 'but I did not have time to write back to you immediately' OPender.

5B.4: *may fe ellas aga han kepar ha my* 'so that like me their song should be alas' OM 309-10; *Te a ra cara theth kyscristyan kepar ha te the honyn* 'you shall love your fellow Christian like yourself' TH 20a; *flogh byen nowyth gynys hag ef yn quethow maylys* 'a new born baby and he wrapped in cloths' OM 806-07; *thy wore in doyr pur guir del grese kelmys ogh suyr ha ny kefrys* 'to bury him indeed, as I believe, you surely are bound and we as well' BM 4371-73.

5B.5.1 DHE: *nynges omma dean in wlase a greys thybm* 'there isn't in the country here a man who believes me' CW 2327-28; *Me a dryst this nos ha dyth* 'I trust you day and night' BK 3207; *esylly glan erell a vo ow ionya nessa thotho* 'other clean limbs joining next to it' TH 25a; *hag a leveris thethy hy* 'and said to her' TH 3; *Th'agan palas gwel ew thyn revertya gans cannow tek* 'It is better for us to return to our palace with sweet songs' BK 2061-62; *Theugh e tof ve glu ha lym* 'To you I swear bitter and sharp' BK 3204; *Jhesus a leverys thethans y* 'Jesus said to them' TH 43a.

5B.5.2 GANS: *te a vyth yn keth golow yn paradis genama* 'on this same day you will be in paradise with me' PA 139d; *Kynth ogh geneff dysplesijs* 'Though you are displeased with me' BM 492; *Ow unadow, a garadow, ew mos genas* 'my desire, beloved, is to go with you' BK 2947-49; *ganso eff ny ew kylmys in catholik vnite* 'with him we are bound in catholic unity' TH 48; *na rellan tuchia na myllia gynsy* 'that we should not touch or meddle with it' TH 3; *crist the vos conversant omma genan ny* 'that Christ is here conversant with us' TH 55a; *ow thowl ew monas genowgh* 'my plan is to go with you' BK 1358; *in aga mysk y ha gansans y* 'among them and with them' TH 49a.

5B.5.3 ORTH, DHYWORTH: *neb a rella golsowes worthow why, y ma ow golsowas wartha ve* 'who listens to you (pl.), listens to me' TH 35a; *worthaf ve sertan ny dale bos mellyes* 'certainly it is not worth meddling with me' CW 1219-20; *peth ave mos theworthas?* 'where will I go departing from you?' SA 63; *an place sure lowre ʒawarta me a wyth* 'I will keep the place from him indeed' CW 265-66; *mar teberthyth eredy meryasek theorthen* 'if you depart from us , Meriasek' BM 4264-65; *ny rug eff omdenna y favore thewortans y* 'he did not withdraw his favour from them' TH 23.

5B.5.4 A: *predery ahanaff gura* 'think of me' PA 193b; *ahanas tenaf asen* 'from you I draw a rib' CW 385; *Anotho te re gowsys* 'You have spoken of him' BK 213; *ha kemerogh exampyl anethy* 'and take an example from her' TH 49a; *in pub part kepar hag onyn ahanan ny* 'in every way like one of us' TH 15; *Gans gweras ahanowgh why ow eskar a vith lethis* 'With help from you my enemy will be killed' BK 3246-47; *the kaws da anothans then bys* 'to speak well of them to the world' JKeigwin.

5C.1 VOCABULARY

bohes venowgh seldom
cana to sing
de yesterday
dege·nsete the day before
 yesterday
dre² (**der**) through.
edhen *m.*, **ÿdhyn** (and **edhnow**)
 bird
goslowes listen (takes **orth**)
gwary·va *f.*, **gwaryvaow** theatre
gweres *m.* help, assistance
howl *m.* sun
in kerdh away
mabm *f.*, **mabmow** mother
mona *m.* money
namoy· *adv.* any more
nowodhow *pl.* news

ôn *m.*, **ên** lamb
pel *f.* **droos** football
ponya to run
pùpprës always
ry to give
ryver *m.*, **ryvers** river
terry to break
todn *f.*, **todnow** wave
treth *m.*, **trethow** beach
treveglos *f.*, **trevow eglos** village
ùnderstondya to understand
whetha to blow
warleny last year
yma va trigys he lives (dwells), he
 is living (dwelling)
yn crev strongly
yn fenowgh often

5C.2 TRANSLATE INTO ENGLISH:

1 Esewgh why ryb an mor de? Nag esen, yth esen ow kerdhes i'n dre.

2 Yth esen vy ow prenassa i'n worvarhas nowyth.

3 Nyns usy hy ow cafos mona dhywortans y namoy.

4 Ymowns ow ry lowr a weres dhedhans pùpprës.

5 Esewgh why obma yn fenowgh warleny? Esen.

6 Esa an flehes ow qwary gansans yn lowen? Esens, yth esa an vebyon ow qwary pel droos warbarth.

7 Yth esen ny ow miras orth an todnow ow terry wàr an treth.

8 Te ha me, yth esen ow kerdhes der an dreveglos ow coslowes orth an dus ow côwsel Kembrek.

9 Yma meur anodhans ow côwsel Kembrek yn tâ.

10 Eus lowr ahanowgh why owth ùnderstondya Kernowek? Nag eus, nyns eus den vëth ahanan ow tesky Kernowek, soweth.

11 Esa Jory ha Jenefer genowgh newher? Nag esens, yth esens warbarth i'n waryva.

12 Pleth esewgh why degensete? Yth esen ow crambla i'n menydhyow. Yma meur anodhans uhel ha peryllys.

13 Esowgh why ow cafos meur a nowodhow dhyworty lebmyn? Nag eson, nyns eson ny ow cafos nowodhow vëth. Nyns usy hy ow scrifa dhyn yn fenowgh.

14 Yth esoma ow qweles an medhek bohes venowgh. Yma va trigys in ken tyller lebmyn.
15 Esowgh why ow scrifa dhodho? Nag esof.
16 Esa ev ow côwsel orthys de? Nag esa, yth esa ow côwsel orth Jory degensete.
17 Esa ow qwil glaw de? Esa, hag yth esa an gwyns ow whetha yn crev.
18 Nyns esa Jowan genama. Yth esa ev gans an cothwas i'n tavern. Yth esa ev owth eva hag ow wherthyn ganso.
19 Esa buhas i'n gwel? Esa, hag yth esa tarow gansans. Ymowns y i'n gwel hedhyw whath.
20 Esa Jowan gans Jenefer i'n lyverjy? Nag esa, yth esa Jory gensy.

5C.3 TRANSLATE INTO CORNISH:

1 Are you coming with us? No, I am going with her and with him.
2 Were you beside the sea yesterday? Yes, I was walking on the beach with the dog.
3 Did you hear much news from her? No, she seldom writes to me.
4 Where were the old man and the old woman last night? They were sitting in the house watching the television.
5 Were they shopping in the supermarket the day before yesterday? Yes.
6 Do you always speak to her? No, I seldom speak to her.
7 I often speak to them in the town. They understand Cornish well.
8 There is a mountain near the village. We were climbing there.
9 The doctor lives by the bridge across the river.
10 The birds were singing in the trees, the lambs were running in the fields and the sun was in the blue sky.
11 Where were you? I was ill in bed.
12 Where was the doctor? I was talking to him.
13 The beautiful woman was singing, and I was listening to her and looking at her.
14 The wine was on the table and the glasses were on the table with it.
15 We were giving her (i.e. to her) much help.
16 We were walking with them in the wood. The birds were singing there.
17 There were many wild animals in the wood also. I was looking at them.
18 The children were running away from them.
19 Where was the mother? She was in the house baking.

WHEFFES DYSCANS
SIXTH LESSON

6A.1 THE SHORT PRESENT OF *BOS*

The forms of **bos** dealt with so far are used when talking about where someone or something is, or what someone or something is, or was, doing. If one wants to say what somebody or something is, e.g. 'he is a man', 'she is a woman', 'the dog is an animal', 'I am tired', 'we are Cornishmen', etc. one has to use a different form of the verb as follows:

me yw	I am
te yw	you are
ev yw	he is
hy yw	she is
ny yw	we are
why yw	you (plural) are
y yw	they are
an den yw	the man is
Jowan yw	John is
an venyn yw	the woman is
Jene·fer yw	Jennifer is
an dus yw	the men are
an daras yw	the door is.

When the pronoun or noun subject precedes it, the form **yw** is invariable, e.g. **me yw sqwith** 'I am tired'; **te yw diek** 'you are lazy'; **an maw yw gwag** 'the boy is hungry'; **an vowes yw skentyl** 'the girl is intelligent'; **an dus yw holergh** 'the people are late'; **an flogh yw abrë·s** 'the child is early'; **an daras yw melen** 'the door is yellow'; **y yw dywysyk** 'they are industrious'.

Remember that one says **yma hy ow wherthyn lebmyn** 'she is laughing now' and **yma hy obma** 'she is here', but **hy yw benyn** 'she is a woman' and **hy yw skentyl mès diek** 'she is clever but lazy'. In the third person singular and plural **yma** and **ymowns** may be used with an adjective complement, if the complement follows the verb: **yma ev clâv** 'he is sick', **ymowns y pòr deg** 'they are very beautiful'.

6A.2 NEGATIVE SHORT PRESENT OF *BOS*

If one wants to turn **me yw**, etc. into the negative, one uses **nyns** (or **nynj**), but each person must have its own special form as follows:

nyns ov vy, nyns oma	I am not
nyns os, nyns osta	you are not
nyns ywa, nyns yw ev	he is not
nyns yw hy	she is not
nyns on ny	we are not
nyns owgh why	you (plural) are not
nyns yns y	they are not
nyns yw an den	the man is not
nyns yw an venyn	the woman is not
nyns yw an flogh	the child is not
nyns yw an dus	the men are not
nyns yw an benenes	the women are not
nyns yw an flehes	the children are not.

Instead of **nyns os, nyns osta** one cans say **nyns os jy, nyns osa**, and **nyns ota**.

6A.3 INTERROGATIVE SHORT PRESENT OF *BOS*

To ask a question with these forms one removes the negative particle **nyns** or **nynj** to get sentences like:

Ywa brâs?	Is he big?
Osta parys wàr an dyweth?	Are you finally ready?
Yw an tavernyow egerys?	Are the pubs open?
Yw an carrjy degës?	Is the garage closed?
Oma Kernow?	Am I a Cornishman?
Yns y diek?	Are they lazy.

As before, if the answer is 'yes', one uses the verb by itself: **Yw hy teg? Yw** 'Is she pretty? Yes.' But if the answer is 'no', then the verb is preceded by nag: **Osta parys? Nag ov, nyns oma parys whath** 'Are you ready?

No, I'm not ready yet.' Similarly negative questions are introduced by **a +
nyns**: **A nyns osta parys whath?** 'Aren't you ready yet?'

6A.4 THE VERBAL PARTICLE *YTH*

We have seen that the long forms of **bos** are often preceded by the
particle **y(th)**: **yth esof, yth esos, yma**, etc. One can also use **yth** with
the short forms of **bos**: **yth ov, yth os, yth yw, yth on, yth owgh, yth
yns**. These forms are somewhat emphatic. **Yth ov vy sqwith** is more
forceful than **me yw sqwith**, for example.

6A.5 INVERSION

Here is a curious feature of Cornish grammar. If one puts the predicate,
i.e. the descriptive word (**sqwith, teg, diek, gwag, flogh, benyn**, etc.)
before the verb, the verb is identical in form with the question form. As
when it is preceded by **yth**, it has to show the right person, but it has no
particle before it: **diek osta** 'you're lazy'; **benyn yw hy** 'she is a woman';
flehes yns y whath 'they are still children'; **benegys osta jy inter
benenes** 'blessed art thou among women'. Sentences of this kind
emphasize the part which occurs first. **Sqwith ov vy** means 'I am *tired*',
with the emphasis on the tired.

When one says **me yw sqwith** 'I am tired', one is really saying 'it is I
who is tired'. It is clear from comparison with the other Celtic languages,
that there is an invisible part of the verb 'to be' at the beginning of such
sentences. **Me yw sqwith** 'I am tired' emphasizes **me**; **sqwith ov vy** 'I
am tired' emphasizes **sqwith**. One can also say **sqwith yth ov**, which
emphasizes **sqwith** even more .

6A.6 'WHAT?' AND 'WHICH?'

There are two words for 'what?' in Cornish. The first is **pandra·?** This
is a contraction of **py an dra** 'what the thing?' and it contracts to **pandr'**
before the vowel of **esof** and **ov**: **Pandr'esta ow qwil?** 'what are you
doing?' **Pandr'ywa** 'What is he? What is it?' (remember there is no neuter
in Cornish). The second word is **pëth** (**pÿth**). This is a contraction of **py
pëth** 'what thing?' It precedes the verb immediately: **Pëth esta ow pobas**
'What are you baking?' **Pëth ywa?** 'What is he? What is it?'

'Which?' can be translated **py**, e.g. **Py lyw yw an daras** 'What colour
is the door?' Another expression is **pana²?**, a contraction of **py ehen a²**
'what kind of?'. **Pana** causes lenition or the second state (see 1A.4 above).

6B EXAMPLES FROM THE TEXTS

6B.1 *owt aylas me yw marowe* 'Oh, alas, I am dead!' CW1570; *te ew Pedyr,*
ha war an garrak ma me a vyn buldya ow egglos 'you are Peter and upon
this rock I will build my church' TH 45a; *ny ew gwyth crabbys, na thora*
frut da vith 'we are crab-apple trees, that bring forth no good fruit' TH 9; *Ha*
why ew abo pagan! 'And you are a pagan hulk!' BK 951; *rag y yv calcoryan*
vrays 'for they are great calculators' BM 1375; *oges yma ov envy* 'my enemy
is near' BM 1013; *y nessevyn sur ymons serris dretho in certyn* 'his
relatives are surely angry because of him indeed' BM 1953–54; *Yma e pyr havel*
dhys 'He is very like you' AB: 242b; **Ma goz screfa compaz** 'Your writing is
correct' BF: 46.

6B.2 *th'e begy ken nyns of guyw* 'though I am not worthy to beseech him' BK
1493; *Tewdar, nyns os skyental* 'Tewdar, you are not wise' BK 322; *ha*
gortas da nyng ew hyer 'and a good wait is not long' BK 2766; *Ow galarow*
nyng yns lowes 'My pains, they are not slight' BK 181.

6B.4 *mabe Jared yth ov heb gowe* 'I am the son of Jared indeed' CW 2096; *Eth*
os floran drys peb i'n noer 'You are a flower beyond all people on the earth'
BK1765-66; *dotho oll yth on sensys* 'we are all beholden to him' BM 4177;
Eth ough ow nerth ha'm socckers 'You are my strength and my helpers'
BK 2733.

6B.5 *lemyn deffryth ove ha gwag* 'now I am weak and hungry' CW 1173; *Ha*
indella kylmis one ny the performya 'and thus we are bound to perform'
TH 27a; *ha buldyys owgh war an fondacion a'n abosteleth* 'and you are
built upon the foundation of the apostles' TH 33; *Welcom ough genaf in suer*
'You are surely welcome with me' BK 1619; *Try personne eternal yns hag*
un gwyer Thew byttygyns 'They are three eternal persons and one true God
nonetheless' BK 253-54.

6B.6 *praga pandrew an matter* 'why, what's the matter?' CW 2329; *agis negis*
pyth ywe 'your business, what is it?' PA 69b; *pyth ew cusyl orth an wrusyl?*
'what is the remedy against the insubordination?' BK 968-69; *Pandr'ota te*
indar fol, pan i'n preysyth araga'? 'What are you if not mad, since you
praise him in front of me?' BK 2245b-46b; *Gosoweth pandr'uge S. Ambros*
ow leverall 'Listen to what St Ambros says' SA 62a.

6C.1 VOCABULARY

arta again
aval *m.*, **avallow** apple
carrjy *m.*, **carrjiow** garage
clâvjy *m.*, **clâvjiow** hospital
coref (LC **cor**) *m.* beer, ale. **coref**
 clor *m.* mild ale
dyllas *coll.* clothes
fe·nester *f.*, **fenestry** (LC
 beyster, **beystry**) window

golhy to wash
gromercy dhis thank you (*sg.*);
 gromercy dhywgh thank you
 (*pl. or polite sg.*)
in gwir truly, really
jentyl kind
kig *m.* meat, flesh. **kig bowyn**
 beef. **kig porhel** pork
kigor *m.*, **kigoryon** butcher

lavurya to toil, to work
mar pleg if you please, please
mès but
paintya to paint
pandr'yw an mater? what is the matter?

plegya (takes **dhe²**) to please
pòr² very
porhel *m.*, **porhelly** pig
solabrë·s already
wàr an dyweth in the end, finally

6C.2 TRANSLATE INTO ENGLISH:

1 Osta parys wàr an dyweth? Nag ov, soweth. Yth esoma ow fysky, saw me yw pòr sqwith.

2 Pandr'ywa? Ev yw medhek. I'n clâvjy brâs yma va ow lavurya.

3 Yth esen ow paintya darasow an chy hedhyw. In gwir? Py lyw yns y lebmyn?

4 Gwer yw daras an strêt, saw daras an lowarth yw rudh ha gwydn.

5 Eses jy ow paintya an fenestry kefrës? Nag esen.

6 Yma maw nowyth ow lavurya i'n shoppa. Ywa dywysyk? Ev yw pòr dhywysyk ha cortes, saw nyns ywa skentyl, soweth.

7 Esowgh why ow tebry lowr a gig lebmyn? Nag eson, saw yma kig porhel ow plegya dhyn.

8 Yw kig porhel an kigor vas? Yw in gwir.

9 Nyns osta lowen hedhyw. Pandr'yw an mater? Me yw pòr drist. An flehes yw clâv.

10 Yth yw an dowr pòr dhown, a nyns ywa? Yw, ha pòr beryllys.

11 Yth esoma ow tos genes. Gromercy dhis, te yw pòr wheg dhybm.

12 Ple ma an carr? I'n carrjy yma va, saw nyns usy ev ow ponya yn tâ. Pandr'yw an mater?

13 Pana garr ywa? Carr coth yw.

14 Yth esen ow colhy dyllas hedhyw. Yns y sëgh? Nag yns whath. Yma ow qwil glaw.

15 Esta ow mos dhe'n dre hedhyw? Esof, yma gorvarhas nowyth egerys ena.

16 Yw hy brâs? Yw, ha pòr dcg yw hy kefrës.

17 Hager ha garow yw an bestas gwyls, saw nyns yns y peryllys.

18 Spladn yw an howl i'n ebron, saw nyns owgh why lowen.

19 Yth yw an gwyns pòr grev hedhyw ha'n todnow yw uhel.

20 Yw in gwir, hag yma meur a dhelyow melen war an dor.

21 Coth ha dâ yw an gwin rudh, saw wherow ywa dhybm.

6C.3 TRANSLATE INTO CORNISH:

1 What is the matter? I am sad today. The children are in the hospital.

2 What kind of house is it? It is a big dark house and it is on the cliff.

3 Do you eat much beef now? No, I eat a lot of pork.

4 Is the old man coming? No, he is old and slow.

5 Are the boys intelligent. Yes, they are intelligent, but unfortunately they are not always polite.

6 The cows are brown but the bull is white. Is it?

7 The sheep are white. They are on the mountain.

8 Is she pretty? She is very pretty, but she is not very sweet. She is rude.

9 I was painting the house the day before yesterday.

10 Really? What colour are the doors and windows? They are blue.

11 Is he a good doctor? No, but there are many good doctors in London.

12 What kind of cake is it? It is a sweet cake.

13 Where are Jennifer and John? They are together in the theatre. They like it (= It pleases them).

14 I am giving you (to you) the money. Thank you, you are very kind.

15 Are the mountains of Wales high? Many of them are very high indeed.

16 There is a new boy in the school. What sort of boy is he? He plays a lot of football.

17 The bridge over the river is not safe.

18 What are you doing? I am taking the ball from him.

19 Is it raining? No, but the clouds are dark and the wind is very strong.

20 Are you cold? No, we are not cold. We are sitting near the fire.

21 The apples are tiny. Yes, and they are very bitter as well.

SEYTHVES DYSCANS
SEVENTH LESSON

7A.1 POSSESSIVE ADJECTIVES

We have learnt how to say **an chy**, **an ky**, **an flehes**. When saying 'my house', 'her dog' or 'their children', one uses the possessive adjectives as follows:

ow³ 'my'	**agan** 'our'
dha² 'your'	**agas** 'your'
y² 'his'; **hy³** 'her'	**aga³** 'their.

Neither **agan** 'our' nor **agas** 'your' is followed by any mutation. Thus one says **tas** 'father' and **agan tas** 'our father', **bara** 'bread' and **agas bara** 'your (plural) bread'. **Dha²** 'your' and **y²** 'his', both cause lenition (or the second state). One says, therefore, **dha das** 'your father', **dha gath** 'your cat', **dha bedn** 'your head', **dha vabm** 'your mother', **dha arr** 'your leg' (**garr** 'leg', and **dha woos** (**goos** 'blood'), etc., and similarly **y das** 'his father', **y gath** 'his cat', etc.

7A.2 SPIRANTIZATION OR THE "THIRD STATE"

Ow³ 'my', **hy³** 'her' and **aga³** 'their' are followed by the mutation properly known as *spirantization*, but which is more commonly known as the third state. It affects three sounds only: **c** or **k** become **h**; **p** becomes **f**; and **t** becomes **th**; **cath** 'cat', gives **ow hath** 'my cat', **hy hath** 'her cat' and **aga hath** 'their cat'; **pedn** 'head' gives **ow fedn** 'my head', **hy fedn** 'her head', and **aga fedn** 'their head'. Notice also that **cl**, **cr** are not mutated: **ow cledha** 'my sword' (**cledha** *m.*, **cledhydhyow** 'sword'), **aga creft** 'their craft' (**creft** *f.*, **creftow** 'art, craft'). Spirantization is not uncommon in other contexts. See Stagell A (Appendix A).

7A.3 MIXED MUTATION

After certain prepositions **ow** 'my' becomes **'m**, e.g. **dhe'm** 'to my'; **a'm** 'of my'; **i'm** 'in my' and also after **ha** 'and', **ha'm** 'and my'. The reduced **'m** in these cases does not cause any mutation. **Ha'w³** 'and my' is also attested.

In similar circumstances **dha** 'thy' becomes **'th**: **dhe'th**, **a'th**, **i'th** and **ha'th**. This **'th⁵** causes a mutation know as mixed mutation, or the fifth state. The mixed mutation affects **b**, **m**, **d**, **g** and **gw** only. After **'th⁵**, **b** and **m** become **v**; **d** becomes **t**; **g** becomes **h**, and **gw** becomes **w**. Initially **go-**, **gu-** behave as though they were **gwo-** and **gwu-** respectively:

> **brâster** 'majesty': **dha vrâster** 'your majesty' > **dhe'th vrâster** 'to your majesty'
> **mab** 'son: **dha vab** 'your son' > **dhe'th vab** 'to your son'
> **dorn** 'hand': **dha dhorn** 'your hand' > **i'th torn** 'in your hand'
> **gavel** 'grasp': **dha avel** 'your grasp' > **i'th havel** 'in your grasp'
> **gwreg** 'wife'; **dha wreg** 'your wife' > **a'th wreg** 'of your wife'.

7A.4 PRONOUN OBJECTS OF THE VERBAL NOUN

The personal possessive adjectives are useful in another way. When one says **yma an venyn ow trehy an bara** 'the woman cuts the bread', literally one is saying 'the woman is at the cutting of the bread'. If, then, one wants to say 'the woman cuts it', in Cornish one must say **yma an venyn worth y drehy**. Note first, that **ow** of the participle becomes **orth** or **worth** before the possessive adjective. Note second, that **bara** is masculine, and therefore one uses the masculine possessive adjective. **Yma an venyn worth y drehy** means literally 'the woman is at his cutting'. The word **tesen** 'cake' is feminine; if one wanted to say 'the woman is taking the cake and is cutting it', one would say **yma an venyn ow kemeres an desen hag yma hy worth hy threhy**. This is at first sight a curious syntax, though it is universal in the Celtic languages. It has arisen because Celtic has no participle, and instead has to use the verbal noun preceded by a preposition. The verbal noun is a noun, not a verb. English says 'seeing him', whereas Cornish says **worth y weles**, literally 'at his seeing, at the seeing of him'.

7A.5 IDIOMATIC USE OF THE POSSESSIVE ADJECTIVE

In English compound adjectives like 'white-haired', 'quick-witted' are not uncommon. Similar expressions are found in Cornish, e.g. **peswartrosek** 'four-footed' and **udnlagajek** 'one-eyed'. More usually, however, such expressions are rendered in Cornish by the use of a phrase containing the possessive adjective, so that 'a white-haired old man' can be rendered **den coth, gwydn y vlew** 'an old man, white his hair', and 'a sharp-witted girl' would be **mowes, lybm hy skians.**

7A.6 *WARBYDN*, EARLIER *ERBYNN*

Er is a rather uncommon preposition which means 'by' in such phrases as **er an leuv** 'by the hand'. In Middle Cornish it is common, however, in the expression **erbynn** 'against'. The second element here is **bynn** < **pynn**, the old dative case of **penn, pedn** 'head'. **Erbynn** therefore means 'at the head of > against'. In the course of the sixteenth century **erbynn** was reshaped as though the first element were **wàr** 'upon' to give **warbynn, warbydn**. In order to use **warbydn** with a pronominal complement one has to use the possessive adjective:

wàr ow fydn	against me
wàr dha bydn	against you
wàr y bydn	against him
wàr hy fydn	against her
wàr agan pydn	against us
wàr agas pydn	against you *(pl.)*
wàr aga fydn	against them.

7B EXAMPLES FROM THE TEXTS

7B.1–2 *kepar dell rug ow thas ow dynvyn ve* 'just as my Father sent me' TH 35a; *honna o drog preyf heb nam a dullas eva tha vabm* 'that was an evil serpent indeed who deceived your mother, Eve' CW 1919-20; *Neb a garra y das po y vam, y vab po y virth... moy agesa ve* 'whoever loves his father or his mother, his son or his daughter... more than me' TH 21a; *agen tase ha mamm eva* 'our father and our mother, Eve' CW 1346; *fatell yllans gwetias favowre a thewleff aga thas a neff* 'how can they expect favour from the hands of their Father of heaven?' TH 55a.

7B.3 *a wrug kyns theth vam ha tas debbry an avall a ankan* 'who first made your mother and father eat the apple of misery' CW 1812-13; *po sure inter te hath wreage an garenga quyt a fyll* 'or indeed between you and your wife the love will fail completely' CW 834-35; *Lemen y3 torn my as re* 'Now into your hand I give her' CF 17.

7B.4 *neb a rella agys despisia why, y ma worth ow despisia ve* 'whoever despises you, he despises me' TH 41a; *Dar, nu'm clowyth orth the begy?* 'What, do you not hear me beseeching you?' BK 1242-43; *fatell vsy eff worth agan cara ny* 'that he loves us' TH 26; *pesough rag an re na esy worth agys vexia* 'pray for those who vex you' TH 22; *yma eff worth aga gwarnya the gemeras with* 'he warns them to take care' TH 32.

7B.5 *an golom glas hy lagas* 'the blue-eyed dove' OM 1109; *colom whek glas hy lagas* 'a sweet blue-eyed dove' OM 1135; *dev tek a bren rag styllyow ha compos y denwennow bras ha crom y ben goles* 'God, what a fine timber for planks and straight its sides and curved its lower end' OM 2441-43: *an harlot foul y berhen* 'the rascal, foolish his master' PC 2112; *a peue den drok y gnas* 'were he a man of evil nature' PC 2969.

7B.6 *Ha nebyn Mânah a trailiaz e ʒein uar bidn an tù[l]* 'And a certain monk turned his back against the hole' JCH § 34; *rag errya sure war ow fyn me ath wiske harlot jawdyn* 'for sinning indeed against me I'll strike you, you villainous scoundrel' CW 1112-13; *Mar te the brother ha gull trespas war the byn* 'If your brother happen to trespass against you' TH 31a; *han yeattys a yffarne ny ra prevaylya war y byn* 'and the gates of hell will not prevail against it' TH 44; *yma an turant heb mar er agis pyn drehevys* 'the tyrant has risen against you of course' BM 3239-40.

7C.1 VOCABULARY

adro dhe² around, about

ania to annoy, to tire

cân *f.*, **canow** song

cantol *f.*, **cantolyow** candle

coges *f.*, **cogesow** (female) cook

colon *f.*, **colonow** heart

côta *m.*, **côtys** coat

demedhys married

dorn *m.*, **dewla** (the dual of **leuv** *f.* hand') hand

edhen *m.*, **ÿdhyn** bird

êwna to mend

glanhe· to clean

gwreg *f.*, **gwrageth** wife

hirwarrow *m.* cranefly, daddy-long-legs

hùrtya to hurt

kerensa *f.* love

lagas *m.*, **lagasow** eye

lavrak *m.*, **lavrogow** pair of trousers

metya meet

mos warby·dn meet

myrgh *f.*, **myrhas** daughter

nessa next

neyja to fly, to swim

pocket *m.*, **pockettys** pocket

pora·n exactly

prias *m.*, **priosow** spouse

pùb jorna every day

pùptra everything

re a² too much

re² too

semlant *m.*, **semlans** appearance

sera *m.*, **serys** sir

serrys angry

spladna to shine

sqwerdys torn

tiak *m.*, **tiogow** farmer

troos *m.*, **treys** foot

whor *f.*, **whereth** sister

7C.2 TRANSLATE INTO ENGLISH:

1 Yma an ky ow ponya i'n gwel, saw yma an tarow orth y ania.

2 Yma an bara wàr an bord, hag yma gwreg an tiak orth y drehy.

3 Ple ma an flehes? I'n scol ymowns y hag yma an dhescadores orth aga desky.

4 Ow threys yw clâv. Yth esen ow qwary pel droos de.

5 A nyns osta sqwith whath? Nag ov, saw yth yw ow dyllas pòr blos solabrës.

6 Te yw ow herensa. Yth esof worth dha gara i'm colon.

7 Ow thas ha'm mabm yw serrys genef.

8 Ple ma dha vona? I'm pocket.

9 Plos yw dha dhewla. Pandr'eses ow qwil hedhyw? Yth esen owth êwna an carr. Coth ywa ha nyns esa ow ponya yn tâ.

10 Yma an hirwarrow ow neyja adro dhe'n gantol. Yma an gath ow miras orto.

11 Sqwerdys yw ow lavrak ha'm côta. Eus lavrak aral i'n amary? Eus.

12 Yma an gân ow plegya dhybm. Yth esof worth hy hana pùb jorna.

13 Pòr gortes yw an vowes nowyth, saw nyns usy hy worth ow ùnderstondya yn tâ.

14 Owgh why whath war y bydn? Nag on, saw nyns usy ev ow plegya dhybm.

15 Yma edhen brâs ha glas ow neyja i'n ebron. Esta worth y weles? Nag esof, yma an howl ow spladna i'm lagasow.

16 Yth esen ow côwsel orth dha gothmans de. Pòr wheg yns y, saw nyns usons y ow côwsel Kembrek.

17 Esta ow côwsel Kernowek? Esof, saw nyns esof ow convedhes pùptra.

18 Yw dha whereth demedhys? Yma onen anodhans demedhys hag in Loundres yma hy trigys.

19 Pandr'yw hy frias? Ev yw medhek ha'ga chy yw brâs ha pòr deg.

20 Yw prias dha whor Kernow? Nag yw, saw yma va ow cara Kernow hag yma va obma yn fenowgh.

7C.3 TRANSLATE INTO CORNISH:

1 Where are your children? They are in the school learning Cornish.

2 You were driving your car too fast.

3 My wife is a very good cook. She is baking bread today.

4 We eat her bread every day. We are eating it now.

5 There is too much butter on my bread.

6 Your cat was singing through the night. His voice is not sweet.

7 Where is John? He is in the garage underneath the car. Is he repairing it? Not exactly (**Nag usy**, **nyns usy poran**). He is looking at it.

8 My wife and my sons are going on the train to London today. Are you going with them? No, I am seeing the doctor today. I am not well. My foot is hurting.

9 She lives in a big house on the cliff, but her daughter lives in a tiny house in the next street. She is poor and her mother does not give her much money.

10 Your hands are dirty. What were you doing? I was playing football with my friends.

11 The book is on the chair. I am not reading it.

12 Where are your shoes? I am cleaning them.

13 He was speaking against learning Cornish and he was annoying me. Are you still against him? No, but I do not like him.

14 Do your sisters live in Cornwall? No, they live in London, but my daughter lives here.

15 Is your father coming? No, he is old and ill. He is in the hospital.

16 Are you painting the door? No, I am mending it and cleaning it.

17 What are you doing with the pork? I am cutting it.

18 My eyes are tired. I read too much every day.

19 The candle is not bright, but the cranefly is flying around it.

20 Your daughter is married, isn't she? No, she works in a school teaching tiny children. She loves them.

ÊTHVES DYSCANS
Eighth Lesson

8A.1 THE FUTURE OF *BOS*

If one wants to convert a sentence with **yw** into the future, all one has to do is change **yw** to **vëdh** (**vÿdh**):

me a vëdh (or **vÿdh**)	I shall be
te a vëdh (or **vÿdh**)	you will be
ev a vëdh (or **vÿdh**)	he will be
hy a vëdh (or **vÿdh**)	she will be
ny a vëdh (or **vÿdh**)	we will be
why a vëdh (or **vÿdh**)	you (plural) will be
y a vëdh (or **vÿdh**)	they will be
an den a vëdh (or **vÿdh**)	the man will be
an venyn a vëdh (or **vÿdh**)	the woman will be
an dus a vëdh (or **vÿdh**)	the people will be
an flehes a vëdh (or **vÿdh**)	the children will be.

> NOTE: From now on verbs will no longer be set out in tabular form. Tabular paradigms are found in Stagell C (Appendix C) below from page 348.

From the grammatical point of view **me a vëdh** and **me yw** are similar. The only real difference is the absence of the relative particle **a²** in **me yw**. As we have already noted, **a²** is not used with parts of **bos** 'to be' and **mos** 'to go' that start with a vowel.

We saw at 6A.5, when the predicate precedes **ov**, **os**, **yw**, etc., no verbal particle is required. Thus one says **lowen ov vy** 'I am happy', **gwag yw hy** 'she is hungry', etc. The verbal particle is also omitted before forms of **bos** beginning with a consonant: **lowen vëdh hy** 'she will be happy'.

Notice also that the future of **bos** can also have present habitual sense: **ev a vëdh obma pùpprës** 'he is always here'.

8A.2 THE USES OF THE FUTURE

After a pronoun or noun subject **a vëdh** can be used to express position. It can also be used with the participle, **ow cana** 'singing' or **ow qwil** 'doing', for example:

Hy a vëdh sqwith avorow She will be tired tomorrow

An flehes a vëdh obma yn scon The children will be here soon

Y a vëdh ow cana i'n tavern haneth They will be singing in the pub tonight

An mer a vëdh ow trehy an ryban rag an worvarhas nowyth obma avorow The mayor will be cutting the ribbon for the new supermarket here tomorrow.

8A.3 THE FUTURE NEGATIVE

If one wants to convert **a vëdh** into a negative, one must use a special form for each person. Because the verb **vëdh** (from **bëdh**) begins with a consonant, not a vowel, the negative particle is **ny**, not **nyns**:

1 *sg.* **ny vedhaf vy, ny vedhama**
2 *sg.* **ny vedhys jy, ny vedhyth jy**
3 *sg.* **ny vëdh** (or **vÿdh**) **ev**; 3 *sg. f.* **ny vëdh** (or **vÿdh**) **hy**
1 *pl.* **ny vedhyn ny**
2 *pl.* **ny vedhowgh why**
3 *pl.* **ny vedhons y**

The suffixed pronouns **vy, jy, ev, hy**, etc., are not always necessary, but it is best to use them to start with.

Ny vedhaf vy ow tos haneth wosa pùptra I shan't be coming tonight after all

Ny vëdh ev obma bys hanter dëdh He won't be here till midday

Ny vedhyn ny orth an Gùntelles Keltek hevleny We won't be at the Celtic Congress this year.

8A.4 THE INTERROGATIVE FUTURE

To convert negative sentences into questions **ny** is replaced by **a**:

A vedhys obma haneth? Will you be here tonight?

A vëdh Jowan ow tos genes? Will John be coming with you?

If the answer is 'yes', it is expressed by the verb itself without initial mutation: **A vedhys obma? Bedhaf.** If the answer is 'no', **na²** replaces **ny²**: **A vedhys obma haneth? Na vedhaf** 'Will you be here tonight? No'.

A negative question is expressed by **a + ny²** before the verb: **A ny vedhons y ow tos genowgh?** 'Won't they be coming with you?'. And the answer is **Bedhons** 'Yes' or **Na vedhons** 'No'.

8A.5 *BEDHAF*, ETC. WITH THE PARTICLE *Y(TH)*

Just as one can say **yth ov vy** 'I am', as well as **me yw** 'I am', so one can use the particle **yth** with **bedhaf, bedhys, bëdh,** etc. **Yth** before consonants is **y** and causes mixed mutation or the fifth state (see 7A.3). Unlike **'th**, the reduced form of **dha** 'your', **y⁵** changes **b** and **m** to **f** (rather than **v**): **y fedhaf, y fedhys, y fëdh (fÿdh),** etc. We thus say: **Ev a vëdh obma heb let** 'He will be here directly' or **Y fëdh ev obma heb let**.

8A.6 'WHO?'

'Who' in Cornish is expressed by the word **pyw?** which is followed immediately by **a** (except with parts of **mos** and **bos** beginning with a vowel): **Pyw a vëdh ow cana?** 'Who will be singing?' but **Pyw osta jy** 'Who are you?', **Pyw usy ow tos lebmyn?** 'Who is coming now?'

The expression **pywa** (< **pyw ywa**) 'who is it?' is used when responding incredulously: **Jowan a vëdh pronter yn scon. Pywa?** 'John will be a priest soon. What?'

8A.7 THE DAYS OF THE WEEK

The days of the week in Cornish are as follows:

> **de Sul** (or **de Zul**) Sunday
> **de Lun** Monday
> **de Merth** Tuesday
> **de Merher** Wednesday
> **de Yow** Thursday
> **de Gwener** Friday
> **de Sadorn** (or **de Zadorn**) Saturday

These are all adverbs: **me a vëdh obma de Yow** 'I'll be here on Thursday'; **y fëdh ow mab ow qwary de Sadorn** 'my son will be playing on Saturday'. The **de** is omitted when using the definite artice or when the name of the day is preceded by an adjective: **an secùnd Sul**

wosa Pask 'the second Sunday after Easter'. One sometimes finds **wàr** + the article + the name of the day, e.g. **wàr an Zul** 'on Sunday'. This is probably an Anglicism, and is best avoided.

Note also the expressions **dhe weyth na dhe Sul** 'neither on a weekday or a Sunday' and **gool ha gweyth** 'holiday and working day'.

8A.8 SOME TEMPORAL ADVERBS

hedhyw today
agensow recently
adhewedhes lately
avorow tomorrow
de yesterday
trenja the day after tomorrow
godreva in three days time
an jorna-ma wàr seythen today week (**seythen** *f.*, **seythednow** week)
i'n kensowha in the early part of the day
ternos on the next day
ternos vyttyn the next morning (**myttyn** *m.* morning)

bo·ragweyth one morning
Sulgweyth one Sunday
dohajë·dh afternoon, in the afternoon
gordhuwher evening, in the evening
myttyn *m.* morning, in the morning
newher last night
haneth tonight
bythqweth ever (in the past)
nefra ever (in the future)
traweythyow sometimes
nessa bledhen, an vledhen usy ow tos next year

8A.9 ADVERBIAL USE OF THE NAMES FEAST DAYS

de Halan an Vledhen 'on New Year's Day'; **de Yow Hablys** 'on Maundy Thursday'; **de Sul Blejyow** 'on Palm Sunday'; **de Pask myttyn** 'on Easter morning'; **de Fencost myttyn** 'on Whitsunday morning'; **de Halan Gwâv myttyn** 'on the morning of All Saints' Day'.

8B EXAMPLES FROM THE TEXTS

8B.1–2 *ha uelkom ti a vêð* 'and welcome you shall be' JCH §15; *why a vith kepar ha du hagys lagasow a vith clerys ha why a vith kepar ha duow* 'you (*pl.*) will be like God and your eyes will be cleared and you will be like gods' TH 3a; *ken sur ny a veth blamyes* 'otherwise we shall surely be blamed' BM 3249; *Arthur a vyth guarthevyas* 'Arthur shall be overlord' BK1488.

8B.3–5 *gon guyr y fethaf marow* 'I know truly I shall die' RD 2030; *gans ihesu y feth clowys hay petyconn colenwys* 'by Jesus he will be heard and his petition fulfilled' BM 4299-300; *them y fethow canhagowe* 'you will be messengers for me' CW 66; *Ny vef re goward bythquath na ny vethef hedre ven* 'I was never a coward, no will I be as long as I am alive' BK 931-32;

cayme na vethys in della 'Cain, you shall not be so' CW 1178; *yn mes y fethons gorrys* 'they shall be evicted' OM 342.

8B.6 *pew vs ahanow why a yll ow reprovia ve rag pegh* 'who is there of you who can reprove me for sin?' TH 3; *Mars o Christ Du mar rajak, pew o e das?* 'If Christ was so full of grace, who was his father?' BK 208-09; *pew ostashe es in wethan awartha gans troes ha cane* 'who are you who is in above in the tree with noise and song?' CW 548-49; *Pew vedna why gawas rag seera rag guz flo* 'Who will you get as father for your child?' Chygwyn; *pewa te ew cayne mab tha adam ny allaf cregye henna* 'What? You are Cain the son of Adam? I can't believe that' CW 1601-02.

8B.7 *kyns ys du merher the nos eff a deerbyn trestyns* 'before Wednesday evening he will encounter sorrow' BM 2254-55; *arta me a thue deth yov* 'I will come again on Thursday' BM 1472; *me a vyn mones de yow prest the helghya* 'I will go to hunt indeed on Thurday' BM 3159-60; *Du guener crist ihesu ker a ruk merwel ragon ny* 'on Friday beloved Jesus Christ died for us' BM 4316-17; *Kova tha gwitha benigas de Zil* 'Remember to keep Sunday holy' JBoson; *ma an mab leean ni e gana terwitheyaw war an Zeell* 'our parson sings it sometimes on Sunday' JBoson.

8B.8 *Gwra ouna guz furu hithow po avorou* 'mend your ways today or tomorrow' WGwavas; *agensow my a'n guelas* 'I saw him a while ago' RD 911; *ha dre henna ny a well nag ew an egglos tevys ha springis in ban athewethas* 'and thus we see that the church did not grow or spring up recently' TH 34a; *En eȝewon ny vynne bos an laddron ow cregy ternos* 'the Jews did not want the robbers to be hanging next day' PA 229ab; *rag gurthuhar ha myttyn nyng es thenny mar tha car* 'for in the evening and in the morning we have not got such a good friend' BK 827-28; *Me a'm byth drog neun hanath* 'I shall have a bad hunger tonight' BK 488; *ny vef yn scole rum levte bys yn newer gorȝewar* 'I was upon my word not in school until last night in the evening' BM 102-03; *rag bythqwath me nyn kerys* 'for I never loved him' CW 1289; *Neffra ny vyth ankevys* 'Never will it be forgotten' BK 1617; *An mam a gemar meth trewythyow rag boos mammeth* 'the mother is sometimes embarrassed to be breast-feeding' SA 59a.

8B.9 *Kyn fe mar freth du Halan an vlethan i'n kynsa deyth* 'Though he be so bold at the Kalends of the year on the first day' BK 1880-81; *Dewsull blegyow pan ese yn mysc y abestely* 'When he was among his disciples on Palm Sunday' PA 27a; *nyng egy cowse vith a deow habblys arrna theffa leverall an keth geyr ma* 'there is no talk of Maundy Thursday until he happens to say this same word' SA 66; *drefen na fynnyth crygy an arluth the thasserghy du pask vyttyn* 'because you will not believe that the Lord arose on Easter morning' RD 1106-07; *the gowse in aga hanow y oll then bobyll war du fencost myttyn* 'to speak in the name of them all to the people on the morning of Pentecost' TH 44a.

8C.1 VOCABULARY

aswon to recognize, to know
cessya to cease, to stop
dallath to begin
demedhy to marry (takes **gans**)
descadores *f.*, **descadoresow** (female) teacher
dewas *m.*, **dewosow** drink
dewheles to return
dres oll an jorna all day long
farwè·l dhis, **farwè·l dhywgh** goodbye
fol *m.*, **fôlys** fool
fordh *f.*, **fordhow** way, road
ger *m.*, **geryow** word
gonesyas *m.*, **gonesyjy** worker, workman
hanow *m.*, **henwyn** name
heb let without delay, immediately

i'n contrary part (or **dhe'n contrary**) on the contrary
kyns pedn within (of time)
màn at all (used with a negative verb)
martesen perhaps
mater *m.*, **maters** matter
mis *m.*, **mîsyow** month
offra to offer
nessa *adj.* next
popet *m.*, **popettys** doll
reqwîrya to require, to ask
selder *m.*, **selders** cellar
solabrë·s already
tê *m.* tea
yêhes (pronounced ['jɛhəz] or ['ɛhəz] *m.* health

8C.2 TRANSLATE INTO ENGLISH:

1 Me a vëdh obma arta an jorna-ma wàr seythen ha ny a vëdh ow wherthyn warbarth.

2 A vedhys obma avorow? Bedhaf, martesen.

3 Ow whor a vëdh ow mos gans ow mabm dhe'n eglos haneth ha'n chy a vëdh gwag.

4 Pandr'esta ow leverel? A nyns esta ow convedhes ow geryow?

5 Te yw fol ha drog ha nyns esoma orth dha gara, ha ny vedhaf vy ow temedhy genes an vledhen usy ow tos.

6 Ny vedhons y ow tos tre adermyn. Ny a vëdh warbarth oll an gordhuwher.

7 An flehes a vëdh owth ola yn scon. Y fëdh descadores nowyth ow tos dhe'n scol avorow.

8 Nyns yw dha vab dywysyk saw yma dha vyrgh pòr dhâ ow scrifa hag ow redya.

9 A vedhys ow tebry an desen? Na vedhaf, gromercy dhis. Hy yw re wheg dhybm.

10 Pëth yw dha hanow ha pyw osta? Me yw an maw nowyth hag yth esen ow côwsel solabrës orth dha wreg.

11 Pana dermyn a vedhys ow tallath lavurya obma? De Merher nessa, an jorna-ma wàr seythen.

12 Pywa, a ny vedhys ow tallath hedhyw?

13 Ow mabm yw clâv hag y fêdh hy ow mos dhe'n clâvjy de Sadorn.

14 Pandr'yw an mater gensy? Yma hy threys ow hùrtya, saw nyns usy an vedhygyon owth aswon an cleves.

15 Poos yw an mater. Hy a vëdh i'n clâvjy bys pedn mis.

16 Me a vëdh ow perna popet melen hy blew.

17 Ny a vëdh ow lavurya obma gool ha gweyth. Ny oll yw sqwith anodho.

18 A vedhowgh why ow cortos obma bys in dyweth an vledhen? Na vedhyn, y fedhyn ny ow tewheles dhe Gernow kyns pedn seythen.

19 Me a vëdh ow pobas tesednow dohajëdh hag y fëdh an flehes orth aga debry avorow.

20 Pyw yw an dhescadores nowyth? Benyn yonk, glas hy lagasow, yw hy, ha myrgh an dhescadores coth.

8C.3 TRANSLATE INTO CORNISH:

1 Who exactly and what exactly are you? I am the new boy, sir. My name is Jory and I will be starting here the day after tomorrow.

2 What, won't you be starting immediately?

3 I shall be starting on Tuesday, sir. I will not be working holidays and workdays together. My health is very good, I am very strong and I shall require a lot of good food and drink.

4 What? What are you saying? Will you be drinking beer, milk or water? I shall be drinking good wine, sir.

5 Good wine is very expensive and I am not rich. I shall not be offering you much wine.

6 You are not rich, sir, but you are not poor. There is much good wine in your cellar. I shall be drinking it every day.

7 On the contrary, my boy, you will not be drinking in my house at all. Goodbye.

8 The old fellow is foolish. He does not recognize a good worker.

9 The children will be coming home soon. I will meet them in the station.

10 Where will you be tomorrow? I shall be on the train on my way to London.

11 I shall be in bed. I am going to bed and I shall stay there for a week.

12 The girls will be going out and milking (**rag godra**) the cows.

13 I was working all day long (**oll an jëdh**) and soon I shall be sitting by the fire, drinking tea and watching the news on television.

14 Will your friends be coming again tonight? No, unfortunately. I am glad. What? I don't like them.

15 Is it still raining? Yes it is, but soon the rain will stop and the wind will be blowing the clouds away.

16 Goodbye, my dear children. I will not be here tomorrow. I will not be seeing you again.

17 Where will you be going? I shall be going back to my father's house and to my father's people (**pobel** *f.*).

18 The old men will be drinking in the pub tonight. They will be drinking too much. They always drink too much on Saturday evening.

19 They are not rich, but they drink a lot of beer, the silly old fools.

NAWVES DYSCANS
NINTH LESSON

9A.1 THE SHORT IMPERFECT OF *BOS*

We have already seen how to make the imperfect of **esof**. The imperfect of **ov** is similarly constructed:

1 *sg.* **en** (**vy**)	1 *pl.* **en** (**ny**)
2 *sg.* **es** (**jy**), **esta**	2 *pl.* **ewgh** (**why**)
3 *sg.* **o** (**va**, **ev**, or **hy**)	3 pl **êns** (**y**)

These forms describe what or who somebody or something was, rather than where he, she or it was. One can use the inflected from with **yth**: **yth en vy sqwith de** 'I was tired yesterday', or the third singular can be used with all persons, if the subject precedes: **me o sqwith de** 'I was tired yesterday'.

9A.2 SHORT IMPERFECT OF *BOS*:
NEGATIVE AND INTERROGATIVE

To make the negative and negative interrogative **nyns** (**nynj**) and **a nyns** (**a nynj**) are used: **Nyns o va medhek dâ** 'He was not a good doctor' and **A nyns o hy mowes skentyl?** 'Wasn't she a clever girl?'

The positive interrogative uses the verb without the prefixed particle: **Êns y dâ?** 'Were they good?' The answer is either **êns** 'yes' or **nag êns** 'no'.

9A.3 DEMONSTRATIVES

Cornish has a distinctive way of saying 'this', 'that', 'these' and 'those'. When 'this', 'these' are adjectives, they are rendered in Cornish with the article before the noun and **-ma** 'here' (< **obma**, **omma**) after it: **an den-ma** 'this man', **an venyn-ma** 'this woman', **an dus-ma** 'these men'. Similarly 'that', 'those' are expressed by combining the article with **-na** (< **ena** 'there'): **an den-na** 'that man', **an venyn-na** 'that woman', **an dus-**

na 'those men'. Note that **-ma** and **-na** are always joined to their noun by a hyphen.

'This', 'that', 'these' and 'those' in English are frequently pronouns, that is to say, they do not qualify any noun, but stand by themselves, e.g. 'what is this?' 'who is that?' 'what colour are those?' In such cases 'this (one)' is expressed in Cornish by **hebma** *m.* and **hobma** *f.* Similarly 'that (one)' is **hedna** *m.* and **hodna** *f.* Speaking of dogs, for example, one says: **teg yw hebma**, **saw nyns yw hedna teg** 'this one is nice, but that one is not'. If one were talking of cows, which are feminine, one would say **yma hobma ow pory, saw nyns usy hodna ow pory namoy** 'this one is grazing, but that one isn't grazing any more'. Besides **hebma** and **hobma** one also finds **helma** and **holma**.

Before vowels in **bos** the pronouns **hebma**, **hedna**, **hobma** and **hodna** are often reduced to **hèm**, **hèn**, **hòm**, **hòn**: **saw hèn yw uthyk!** 'but that is terrible! **hòm yw ow myrgh vian** 'this is my little daughter'.

For 'these' and 'those' as pronouns one uses **an re-ma** and **an re-na**, literally 'the ones here' and 'the ones there': **an re-ma yw terrys, mès saw yw an re-na** 'these are broken, but those are sound'.

9A.4 'EVERYBODY' AND 'MANY'

Cornish has several ways of saying 'everybody'. The simplest expression is **pob** 'everybody'. One can also use the adjective **pùb** 'every' with **onen** 'one' to give **pùbonen** 'everyone'. **Pùb** can also be used with the pronoun **huny** to give **pùb huny** 'everyone', or with the noun **den** 'man, person', to give **pùb den** 'everyone' or **pùb den oll** 'everybody' (literally 'everybody all'). **Oll** 'all' can be used to reinforce **pùb** with other nouns as well: **pùb dëdh oll** 'every day', **pùptra oll** (< **pùb tra oll**) 'everything'. Later Cornish also uses **kenyver** 'as many' with the sense 'each, every'. This combines with **onen** and **den** to give **kenyver onen, kenyver den** 'everybody, everyone'.

Huny is also used with **lies** 'many' to give **lies huny** 'many people, many a one'. Notice that both **pùb** 'every' and **lies** 'many' are always followed by the singular: **pùb dëdh** 'every day' and **lies tra** 'many things'.

> NOTE: **Huny** is incidentally restricted to use after **pùb**, **lies** and **kettep** 'each, every'. It is not to be used in any other context (see also 37A.1).

9A.5 'ANYTHING', 'NOTHING', 'ANYBODY', AND 'NOBODY'

'Anybody' can be expressed by **neb den**, **nebonen** or **neb**. 'Something', 'anything' is rendered by **neb tra** or **neppyth**. Since Cornish, like the other Celtic languages, lacks a word for 'nobody' and 'nothing', **den vëth** and **tra vëth** are used with a negative verb: **nyns esa tra vëth wàr an bord** 'there was nothing on the table'; **nyns usy den vëth obma** 'there is nobody here'. **Nagonen** is sometimes used with the negative instead of **den vëth**.

9A.6 IMPERSONAL 'ONE'

In the earliest texts the impersonal 'one' of English is sometimes rendered by the use of the autonomous forms of the verb (26A.1). On occasion **den** 'person' is used to render impersonal 'one'. Sometimes **onen** 'one' or **neb onen** 'someone' is so used: **hèn yw lowr rag movya den** (or **onen**) **dhe dhagrow** 'that is enough to move one to tears'.

9A.7 'ONLY'

The simplest way of rendering 'only' with verbs is to use the negative together with one of four words for 'but, except': **lemen**, **marnas** (**ma's**), **mès** or **saw**. One therefore says: **nyns yw hedna lemen** (**marnas, mès, saw**) **an gwyns i'n gwëdh** 'that is only the wind in the trees'. The negative should always be used with **lemen**, **marnas**, **mès** or **saw**. **Saw** by itself does not mean 'only'.

9A.8 EMPHATIC 'SELF'

'Self' used for emphasis is rendered in Cornish by the word **honen** preceded by the relevant possessive adjective: **ow honen**; **dha honen**; **y honen**; **hy honen**; **agan honen**; **agas honen**; **aga honen**. One therefore says: **yth esof ow mos dy ow honen** 'I am going there myself'; **ny agan honen a vëdh in Kernow kyns na pell** 'we ourselves will be in Cornwall before long'. **Honen** also has an idiomatic use: **yma va lebmyn y honen oll i'n chy** means 'he is now all by himself in the house'.

For the reflexive sense of 'self' in Cornish see 22A.7.

9A.9 'TO HAVE'

Cornish has a verb which means 'have' (see 23A.1–2 below). Most frequently, however, the notion of possession is expressed by the verb bos 'to be' and the prepositions **gans** 'with' or **dhe**[2] 'to'. There is a slight difference between the two prepositions when describing possession: **Yma mona genef** 'I have money (with me)' but **yma mona dhybm** 'I have money, I possess money'.

9A.10 IDIOMS WITH *GANS* AND *DHE*[2]

Note the following idiomatic phrases with gans: **dâ yw genef** 'I like, I am glad'; **drog yw genef** 'I am sorry, I do not like'; **câs yw genef** 'I hate'; **gwell yw genef** (**gwell** 'better') 'I prefer'; **meth yw genef** 'I am ashamed'; **edrek yw genef** 'I regret'; **marth yw genef** 'I am astonished'; **poos yw genef** 'I am reluctant'; **mal yw genef** 'I am eager'.

The following idioms contain **dhe[2]**: **yma own dhybm** 'I am afraid'; **yma nown dhybm** 'I am hungry'; **yma sehes dhybm** 'I am thirsty'; **yma whans dhybm** 'I desire'; **gwell yw dhybm** 'it is better for me, I had better'; **res yw dhybm** 'I must, I am compelled to'.

9B EXAMPLES FROM THE TEXTS

9B.1 *dall en ny welyn yn fas* 'I was blind; I did not see well' PA 220c; *in the pov yth esta gal* 'in your country you were a criminal' BM 2412; *indella yth o ov thays* 'thus was my father' BM 2206; *yth o tra eysy lowre the forberya* 'it was an easy enough thing to resist' TH 4.

9B.2 *na neill nyng o dyag the wull obereth da* 'he was not slow to do good works either' TH 2a; *inweth nyng o mabden abyll the weras y honyn* 'also man was not able to help himself' TH 12-12a; *Nyns o an rena dewov* 'Those were not gods' BM 1801; *byth nyng ens y coweʒe* 'never were they companions' PA 41b.

9B.3 *fatell yll an den ma ry thyny y gyk* 'how can this man give us his flesh?' TH 57; *Brvz yu an venen-na* 'That women is large' AB: 243c; *hebma yth ew sawer wheake* 'that is a sweet smell' CW 2493; *homma gans daggrow keffrys re's golhas yn surredy* 'this woman with tears as well has washed them' PC 519-20; *Pa'n dreu' hedna mêð Dzhûan* '"What is that?" said John' JCH §10; *ha honna ny ra agys desevia* 'and that will not deceive you' TH 34a.

9B.4 *pan a perfeccion a vewnans a gotha thotha bos in pub onyn ahanan ny* 'what perfection of life there should be in every one of us' TH 26a; *hag honor bras in pelder thu'm arluth drys pub huny!* 'and great honour forever for my lord above everyone!' BK 2668-69; *the canevar den gwyrrian a vo desyrius e gowis* 'to every righteous man who is desirous to obtain it' SA 60; *Ha kanifer bennen oggas e teen* 'And every woman with her behind near' JBoson; *kynifar uynnyn a ôr kouz Kernûak* 'everyone who can speak Cornish' AB: 223; *syndis ve dre govaytis yndella yw leas huny* 'he was destroyed by avarice; so are many people' PA 62d; *vn ladyr eff a yll robbya lyas den* 'one robber can rob many men' TH 25a.

9B.5 *ny amont tra vyth hemma* 'this does not count for anything' OM 439; *na havalder a'n tra vyth es en nef a wartha* 'nor the likeness of anything which is in heaven above' Pryce; *Te naras latha den vith* 'Thou shalt not kill anybody' TBoson; *Ha na ore den veeth durt peniel reeg an kol ma kensa dose* 'And no one knows from what this loss first came' NBoson; *ny ve nagonyn sawys bew* 'no one was saved alive' TH 39a.

9B.6 *y'n gylwyr Arthur Cornow* 'he is called Arthur the Cornishman' BK 1658; *tommans onan dour war tan* 'let water be heated upon the fire' PC 833; *mur a wokyneth yv mones the lesky peyth a yl den orto bewe* 'it is great folly to go to burn something that one could live on' OM 475-75; *pandra ill den vith leverell* 'what can one say?' TH 55a.

9B.7 *nynsyv eff lemen an lor pan vgy ov trehevel* 'it is only the moon when it is rising' BM 2102-03; *rag nyns yv mas tarosvan ha pur sempel the cara* 'for it is only an illusion and very easy to love' BM 2566-67; *nynses nagonyn da mas du* 'no one is good but God' TH 8a.

9B.8 *pan vynnogh agas honon why a gyl gul da thethe* 'when you yourselves wish you can do them good' PC 545-46; *me a vyn mos the vyras sur ow honan* 'I will go to look indeed myself' RD 1637-38; *ne ra an pronter vsya girreow e honyn, mas girreow Christ* 'the priest does not use his own words but the words of Christ' SA 62.

9B.9–10 *seghes sur thotho yma* 'surely he is thirsty' PC 2974; *Guel yv genen ny merwel es gorthya devle dyogel* 'we prefer to die rather than worship a devil indeed' BM 1234-35; *rak thythy yma thy'm whans* 'for I have a desire for it' RD 1938; *Ny res theugh bos duwenyk* 'you do not need to be sorrowful' BK 2659.

9C.1 VOCABULARY

acowntyas *m.*, **acowntysy** accountant

Alban *f.* Scotland (also **Scotlond** *m.*)

amowntyor *m.*, **amowntyoryon** computer

arhanty *m.*, **arhantiow** bank (for money);

broder *m.*, **breder** brother

badna at all (used with negative verbs; literally means 'drop').

bytegy·ns nonetheless

crytyca to criticize

dagrow *pl.* tears

doth discreet, well behaved

dres ena over there

dysqwedhes to show

eskys *f.*, **eskyjyow** shoe

fâss *m.*, **fâssow** face

gonys to cultivate, to work

goslowes listen to (takes **orth**)

gwyras *f.*, **gwyrosow** spirits, whisky

gwysca to wear

hag erel et cetera

medhow drunk, intoxicated

movya to move

pows *f.*, **powsyow** garment, dress

praisya to praise

qweth *f.*, **qwethow** garment

reknel *f.*, **reknellow** calculator

Spain *f.* Spain

uthyk dreadful, frightful

Wordhen *f.* Ireland

9C.2 TRANSLATE INTO ENGLISH:

1 Yth esa pùbonen ow miras orthyf ha meth brâs o genef.

2 Pyw usy obma whath? Nyns eus den vëth obma marnas dha whor dha honen ha'n medhek yonk. Mal o dhodho côwsel orty.

3 Yth esa lowr a vona gensy de. Pandr'esa hy ow qwertha i'n shoppa-na?

4 Pyw yw an re-na? Hèn yw an acowntyas ha'n venyn deg yw y wreg. Nyns usons y ow côwsel ger vëth a Gernowek, soweth.

5 Nyns yw hobma ow fows vy. Ow fows vy o rudh ha glân.

6 Yth esa lies buwgh ha lies margh ganso, ha meur a vona i'n arhanty, saw nyns o va lowen màn. Trist o ev. Y wreg o pòr glâv dres lies bledhen ha lebmyn marow yw hy.

7 Ple ma dha lavrak coth? Wàr an chair ryb an tan yma ev. Ev yw pòr blos. Yth esen ow lavurya i'n lowarth dres oll an jorna ha'n tyller o glëb.

8 Esta whath ow mos dhe Spain gans an re-na? Poos yw genef mos gansans. An den y honen yw pòr wocky ha'y wreg a cas genef.

9 Nyns eus ger vëth a Gernowek gensy, saw y fëdh hy owth argya gans pùbonen. Lowr yw hedna dhe vovya onen dhe dhagrow.

10 An vowes-na yw aga myrgh. Skentyl yw hy, mès dyscortes.

11 Aga mab yw an maw-na dres ena. Ev yw pòr wocky. Nyns usy ev ow côwsel orth den vëth. Gwell yw ganso gwary gans y amowntyor.

12 Eus dewas genowgh? Eus in gwir. Yma pùb sort a dhewas genen i'n tavern-ma, gwyras Alban, gwyras Wordhen, hag erel, saw gwell yw genef agan coref agan honen. Hèn yw pòr dhâ. Y fëdh kenyver onen worth y braisya.

13 Ev o dydhan ha jentyl, saw nyns esa va ow plegya dhybm.

14 Pywa? Esta whath ow crytyca ow broder? Nag esof, saw gwell yw dha whor genef.

15 Ple ma ow reknel nowyth? Yma an acowntyas ow tos haneth hag y fëdh res dhybm dysqwedhes an lyvrow dhodho.

16 Me o acowntyas ow honen i'n dedhyow-na, saw nyns esa an ober ow plegya dhybm màn.

17 Res yw dhybm leverel neppyth dhis. Pywa? Esta ow côwsel orthyf vy? Nag esof, yth esen ow côwsel orth an re-na, saw nyns usons y ow coslowes orthyf badna.

18 Cas yw genef an eskyjyow-na. Re gales yns ha'n lyw yw uthyk.

19 Res yw dhis aga gwysca bytegyns.

20 Yth en vy pòr wocky i'n termyn-na, saw lebmyn den fur ha doth ov, soweth.

9C.3 TRANSLATE INTO CORNISH:

1 I hate him. I prefer you.

2 I must listen to him, nonetheless.

3 He was very sweet to me yesterday, but I am reluctant to go with him on the train to London.

4 Who are those? They are my brothers and sisters. I prefer your father and mother.

5 Where are your old trousers? In the cupboard with the brown shoes.

6 Will you be wearing them (= it, him) today? Yes, I shall be working in the garden all day.

7 What is this? That is Irish whiskey. You silly fool. You drink too much.

8 I regret those words. You do not drink too much.

9 You work all day and you like a drink.

10 I prefer to sit with you by the fire watching the television.

11 I am ashamed. I drink much Irish whiskey and Scotch whisky. I was drunk yesterday and the day before yesterday.

12 Were you? Yes, I was. I was in the pub all day. My friends have too much money.

13 Who are those? That is the new doctor. That is his young wife. She is pretty, isn't she?

14 I am looking at the ugly dress (**an hager-bows**). She is also wearing dreadful shoes. She has very big feet.

15 You do not like her? I prefer the doctor himself. He is a young handsome (**teg**) man.

16 I do not like his big rough red hands and he has a silly face.

17 What is in your hand? This is my new calculator. It is very fast and very clever (**skentyl**).

18 I was talking to my accountant today. He was nice, but he was not happy with the books.

19 We haven't enough money and clothes are very expensive.

20 You buy too many clothes, you have too many garments and too many shoes. Soon we shall be very poor indeed.

DEGVES DYSCANS
TENTH LESSON

10A.1 THE PRETERITE (OR PAST) OF *BOS*

There is another past tense of **bos** which we have not yet examined, namely the preterite. This form is inflected as follows:

1 *sg.* **beuv, beuma**	1 *pl.* **beun**
2 *sg.* **beus, beusta**	2 *pl.* **bewgh**
3 sg **beu, beuva, beu hy**	3 *pl.* **bowns**

As with the other **b-** tenses of **bos** the preterite can be used after **y**^{5}: **y feuv, y feus, y feu**, etc., or it can be used in the impersonal way **me a veu, te a veu, ev/hy/an venyn a veu**, etc. **Ny** is used to render this tense negative: **ny veuv, ny veus, ny veu**. It is used by itself in positive answers: **A veus? Beuv**.

10A.2 THE USES OF THE PRETERITE OF *BOS*

The preterite expresses the idea of being at a certain point in the past, as distinct from the imperfect, which refers to being over a period. **Y feu ev** means 'he was and the matter is finished', whereas **yth o va** means 'he was for a while and something happened'. **Ev a veu den dâ** means 'He was a good man (and he is now no longer with us)', whereas **Ev o den dâ**, means 'He was a good man (and here are some of the good things he did)'. The preterite, because it implies a discernible change of state, can also be used to translate 'become', for example, **ev a veu medhek warleny** 'he became a doctor last year'.

Another important use of the preterite is in conjunction with the verbal adjective (past participle) to form the past passive. For example, if one wishes to say 'he was injured by a car', one says **ev a veu shyndys dre garr**.

Such sentences can be inverted by placing the verbal adjective before the verb, in which case **a**^{2} is normally omitted: **shyndys veu dre garr**. Notice that **dre²** 'by, through' is the preposition used in such constructions. If the agent is human, **gans** is used: **Abel a veu ledhys gans Caym y vroder** 'Abel was killed by Cain his brother'.

Notice the difference between **an chy a veu byldys** 'the house was built' and **an chy o byldys** 'the house had been built' (i.e. was in a state of having been built). Not all speakers of revived Cornish are careful to make this distinction.

The present and future passive can be made with the short present and the future of **bos** + the verbal adjective: **indella yth yw gwrës** 'thus it is made'; **indella y fëdh gwrës** 'thus it will be made'.

10A.3 THE VERBAL ADJECTIVE

The verbal adjective ends in **-ys**: **shyndya** 'to injure', **shyndys** 'injured'; **pôtya** 'to kick', **pôtys** 'kicked'; **gweles** 'to see', **gwelys** 'seen'; **derevel** 'to raise', **derevys** 'raised, built'; **leverel** 'to say', **leverys** 'said'; **côwsel** 'to speak', **côwsys** 'spoken'. Often an **a** in the stem become an **e** in the verbal adjective: **gasa** (**gara**) 'to leave', **gesys** (**gerys**) 'left'; **ladha** 'to kill', **ledhys** 'killed'; **cana** 'to sing', **kenys** 'sung'; **dampna** 'to condemn', **dempnys** 'condemned'.

Note also the following verbal adjectives: **gyllys** 'gone' (**mos** 'to go'); **devedhys** 'come' (**dos** 'to come'); **godhvedhys** 'known' (**godhvos** 'to know'); **gwrës** 'made, done' (**gwil** 'make, do'); **rës** 'given' (**ry** 'to give'); **drës** 'brought' (**dry** 'to bring'); **degys** 'carried' (**don** 'to carry'). **Gyllys** is used with the short present of the verb **bos** 'to be' with the sense 'have become, has become': **ow thas yw gyllys coth** 'my father has become old'; **me yw gyllys bodhar** 'I have grown deaf'.

10A.4 THE PERFECT WITH *RE*²

The preterite has a further use. If instead of **y⁵** or **a²** one puts **re²** before the preterite, the sense changes to that of the English perfect: **ev a veu** 'he was, he became', **y feu va** 'he was, he became', but **ev re beu** 'he has been'. **Re²** does not cause lenition with the initial **b-** of the preterite of the verb **bos** 'to be'. It does, however, lenite the initial consonant when used with other verbs. See Stagell A (Appendix A) below.

Me a veu means 'I was', but **me re beu** 'I have been'. One can also say **re beuv**, **re beuma** 'I have been', **re beus** 'you have been', etc., where **re²** stands instead of **y⁵**. If **ny** or **na** precede the preterite with perfect sense, the **re** is omitted. The sense may still be perfect: **ny veuv ena whath** 'I have not yet been there'.

10A.5 *PLE(TH)*? 'WHERE?' AND *KYN(TH)* 'ALTHOUGH'

We have already met the interrogative adverb **ple**[5] 'where' (4A.8). **Ple**[5] causes mixed mutation: **ple feusta?** 'where have you been?'

Kyn[5] 'although' is similar. It is **kynth** before vowels, **kynth usy va ow tos** 'although he is coming', but causes mixed mutation of initial **b-**: **kyn feu va shyndys, salow ywa arta** 'though he was injured, he has recovered'. **Kyn** is followed by **na(g)** when the sense is negative: **kyn nag osta plêsys genef** 'though you are not pleased with me'.

10A.6 THE CARDINAL NUMERALS 1–100

onen, **udn**	one	**udnek**	eleven
dew², **dyw²** *f.*	two	**dewdhek**	twelve
try³, **teyr³** *f.*	three	**tredhek**	thirteen
peswar, **peder** *f.*	four	**peswardhek**	fourteen
pymp	five	**pymthek**	fifteen
whegh	six	**whêtek**	sixteen
seyth	seven	**seytek**	seventeen
eth	eight	**êtek**	eighteen
naw	nine	**nawnjek**	nineteen
deg	ten	**ugans**	twenty

onen, **udn warn ugans**	twenty one
dew warn ugans	twenty two, etc.
deg warn ugans	thirty
dewgans	forty
onen, **udn ha dewgans**	forty one
dew ha dewgans	forty two, etc.
hanter-cans	fifty
try ugans	sixty
deg ha try ugans	seventy
peswar ugans	eighty
deg ha peswar ugans	ninety
cans	a hundred.

Onen is used when counting; **udn** comes before a noun and lenites a following feminine noun: **udn den** 'one man'; **udn venyn** 'one woman'. The numeral **udn** is sometimes used as an indefinite article.

When the definite article precedes **dew**, **dhyw** the initial **d** undergoes lenition: **an dhew flogh** 'the two children'. The distinction between **dew** 'two' before masculine nouns and **dyw** 'two' before feminines was lost early in Middle Cornish. The distinction is maintained here in spelling, though both forms are indifferently pronounced [dɪʊ]. **Teyr³** and **peder** are the forms of **try³** and **peswar** used with feminine nouns: **try³ hy** 'three dogs' but **teyr³ hath** 'three cats'. **Peder** is very rare. The masculine form **peswar** had a variant **pejwar**, which became **pajer** in later Cornish.

All numerals are followed by the singular form of the noun: **udn bluven** 'one pen'; **dew lyver** 'two books'; **teyr hath** 'three cats'; **peswar daras** 'four doors'; **pymp del** 'five leaves'; **whegh eskys** 'six shoes'; **seyth jorna** 'seven days'; **eth gwedhen** 'eight trees'; etc.

10A.7 *TRA* 'THING'

The word **tra** 'thing' is anomalous. It is preceded by masculine numerals: **try thra** 'three things', **peswar tra** 'four things', but it undergoes lenition after **udn** and **an**: **udn dra** 'one thing', **an dra** 'the thing', and it lenites the initial of a following adjective: **tra vian** 'a small thing'. It is always referred to by masculine pronouns. **Tra** has the plurals **taclow** or **taclenow**' compare **lies tra** 'many things' with **oll an taclow-ma** 'all these things'.

For the inauthentic plural *traow** see 38A.9, 38B.9.

10A.8 'LIKE', 'AS', AND 'SUCH'

The English preposition 'like' is rendered by **ave·ll** in Cornish: **yma hy ow cana avell edhen i'n ebron** 'she sings like a bird in the sky'. **Avell** conjugates as follows:

1 *sg.* **avellof**	1 *pl.* **avellon**
2 *sg.* **avellos**	2 *pl.* **avellowgh**
3 *sg. m.* **avello**; 3 *sg. f.* **avelly**	3 *pl.* **avellans** (or **avella**)

'Like' as a preposition can also be rendered **kepa·r ha(g)**: **yth esa Jowan owth ola kepa·r ha flogh** 'John was weeping like a child'. The conjunction 'as, like as' is rendered in Cornish by **dell²**: **nyns yw hedna ewn dell esof vy worth y ùnderstondya** 'that is not right as I understand it'. One can also use **kepa·r dell**: **yma hedna ow plegya dhybm kepa·r dell ywa** 'I like it as it is'. Note also the phrase **in mar veur dell** 'inasmuch as: **in mar veur dell veu Duw ollgalosek plêsys** 'inasmuch as it pleased Almighty God'.

10B EXAMPLES FROM THE TEXTS

10B.1 *Dal y fueff lues blythen* 'I was blind for many years' BM 4393; *ny fuf den thotho bythqueth* 'I have never been his servant' PC1238; *rak na fues kyns lymmyn fur* 'for you have not been sensible before now' PC 1194; *Bythquath ny ve thewhy parow* 'Never was there your equal' BK 1256-57.

10B.2-3 *acontis y fus flogh fur* 'you were accounted a sensible child' BM 338; *a thorn dew y festa gwryes* 'by the hand of God you were made' CW 309; *y fe danvenys omma the Englond an moyha notabill ha auncyent tus* 'the most notable and ancient men were sent here to England' TH 51; *gans y blew y fons syhys* 'they were dried with her hair' PC 521 *gans an Jowle y fowns tulles* 'they were deceived by the Devil' CW 1003.

10B.5 *Solabrys kynth of cryys, the'n turant ny vetha' mos* 'Already although I have been summoned, I dare not go to the tyrant' BK 445-46; *Kynth a ow ownter a bel, an nowothow a vith gwel* 'Though my uncle goes afar, the news will be better' BK 2764-65; *kyn fewgh mar hout, ewgh mes a'm veu hag omdennowgh* 'though you be never so haughty, get out of my sight and withdraw' BK 1953-55; *kyn fe an Joule war e scoyth, ny a'n dywoys avel goyth* 'though the Devil be upon his shoulder, we will bleed him like a goose' BK 2730-31.

10B.6 *yn vhelder my a vyn dek warn ugans y vos gures* 'in height I want it made thirty [cubits]' OM 959-60; *Deg uar niȝans* 'Thirty' AB: 166c; *yn weth dewthack warn ugans a virhas in pur thibblans* 'also thirty two daughters very clearly' CW 1984-85; *in oydge me ew in or ma try cans try vgans in prove ha whath pymp moy pan es thym coof in geth hythew* 'in age I am now three hundred and sixty in proof, and still five more when I think about it today' CW 2101-04; *Ma douthak meese en blethen, Quartar blethan ew tarthack sithen, Hanter blethan ew whe sithen warn igens, Oll an vlethan ew douthak sithen ha deugens* 'There are twelve months in a year; A quarter of the year is thirteen weeks, Half a year is twenty six weeks, The whole year is twelve weeks and forty' Bilbao MS

10B.7 *na the wetha taclenow wo vsyys in la moyses* 'nor to keep things that were usual in the law of Moses' TH 27a; *Mar crug an geir an tas a'n nef gonis in taglenno erall* 'If the word of the Father was at work in other things' SA 63; *Der taklow minniz ew brez teez gonvethes, avel an tacklow broaz; dreffen en tacklow broaz, ma angy mennow hetha go honnen; bus en tacklow minnis, ema angye suyah hâz go honnen* 'By little things people's minds are known, as much as in large things; because in great matters they often stretch themselves; but in little things, they follow their own nature' Pryce.

10B.8 *e yskar a vith maraw ha touchys kepar ha ky* 'his enemy will be dead and stricken like a dog' BK 2434-35; *Arlothas, guyn avel gurys, dun the'n chamber, me a'th pys* 'Lady, white as crystal, let us go to the bedroom, I beseech you' BK 2981-82; *now adam ma ow lordya avell duke in paradise* 'now Adam like a duke is lording it in paradise' CW 456-67; *kepar dell wruck S Thomas touchia corfe Christ* 'just as St Thomas touched the body of Christ' SA 60a; ***Kepar dell ough e soccor, why a the hag a'n confort*** 'As you are his assistance, you will come and comfort him' BK 2498-99.

10C.1 VOCABULARY

brathy bite, wound by biting
bysy busy, essential
clôwes to hear
cowethas *f.*, **cowethasow** company, society
creswas *m.*, **creswesyon** policeman
cresy to believe
dhe'n dor down, downwards
dystowgh immediately
esel *m.*, **esyly** member
frank free
gour *m.*, **gwer** husband
gwetyas to expect, to hope
hâtya to hate
i'n tor'-ma at the moment
kyffewy *m.*, **kyffewyow** party (convivial);
lel loyal, faithful

melo·dy *m.* melody, tune
menestrouthy instrumental music
tebel-was *m.*, **tebel-wesyon** evil fellow
paper nowodhow *m.*, **paperyow nowodhow** newspaper
predery to think, to consider
rom *m.*, **rômys** rooms
scubya to sweep
sevel to stand
wâstya to waste
whel *m.* work
whilas, whelas to seek, to look for
yma othem dhybm a^2 I need

10C.2 TRANSLATE INTO ENGLISH:

1 Yth esa dew vab gans Adam. Abel a veu ledhys gans y vroder Caym. Tebel-was o Caym.

2 Abel o tiak ha den dâ, lel y golon, saw tebel-was o an broder aral.

3 Yma deg warn ugans jorna in pùb mis ha me yw sqwith a'm bêwnans.

4 Ple feusta? Me re beu ow whilas whel dhe wil.

5 Y fêdh an gân kenys i'n eglos an jorna-ma wàr seythen, ha res yw dhybm hy desky dhe flehes an scol.

6 Deg warn ugans flogh bian ow cana an gân deg-na? Yma whans dhybm clôwes hedna!

7 Kyn nag ov vy den skentyl, yth esof ow cara menestrouthy ha melody.

8 Pandr'yw an taclow-na wàr an bord? An re-na yw an gwedrednow ha'n gwin rag an kyffewy haneth.

9 Drog yw genef saw nyns eus genef marnas teyr thesen wheg. An re-na ena a veu gesys gans an dus erel hag ymowns y gyllys tre.

10 Yma moy es hanter-cans esel i'n gowethas i'n tor'-ma, saw nyns usy marnas deg anodhans ow côwsel Kernowek yn tâ.

11 Y fëdh cans mowes ha hanter-cans maw ow coslowes orthys ow côwsel. Osta parys?

12 Yth esa meur a vona dhybm i'm pocket, saw y feu va kemerys dhyworthyf gans an greswesyon.

13 Yth ov vy bohosak lebmyn, ha res yw dhybm perna boos rag ow flehes. Yma try anodhans ow sevel obma. Yns y gwag? Yns, gyllys yns pòr wadn.

14 Pandr'yw pymp warn ugans ha pymp warn ugans? Hèn yw hanter-cans.

15 Osta plêsys gans an flehes? Kynth oma plêsys gansans, nyns ov vy plêsys genes jy.

16 Y fëdh ow whel gwrës dystowgh ha me a vëdh frank dhe vos genowgh why.

17 A vedhaf vy worth dha weles avorow? Na vedhys, ny vedhaf gwelys obma nefra arta.

18 Res yw dhybm dewheles dhe'm pow ow honen ha dhe bobel ow thas, ha hèn yw pell dhyworth an tyller-ma.

19 A veu va ledhys? Na veu, saw y dreys a veu terrys ha'y bedn shyndys.

20 Kynth ywa clâv i'n tor'-ma, ev a vëdh yagh yn scon.

10C.3 TRANSLATE INTO CORNISH:

1 You were seen yesterday near to my sister's house. What were you doing in the garden? We were killing two birds with one stone.

2 I was there yesterday. The wind was blowing and the sea was very rough.

3 This is a small thing, but it is very dear to me.

4 There were two cats on the road but they were both injured by your car.

5 Where are your brother and your sister? They have gone home. They don't like school.

6 There are seven days in every week and fifty two weeks in a year and yet there is never enough time.

7 You are always busy. Yes, twelve months a year without any holiday.

8 She has two cows, one bull, six sheep, four cats and a wild dog. What does her husband think? He has gone. He doesn't like animals.

9 He is like me. I don't like animals. I prefer flowers.

10 Do you hate animals? No, I don't hate them exactly. We have two cats and a tame bird. My son was bitten by a dog recently.

11 Has the food been brought yet? Yes, but only three children have come (**yw devedhys**).

12 Will you be marrying him soon? Yes, I hope to marry him today week.

13 What does your father think? My father does not think. He is always drunk. My brother likes him and my three sisters.

14 I love him though he is often not sensible (**fur**). He wastes money on me. He is sweet but foolish.

15 Two of them will be enough, I believe. We do not need sixty.

16 Where have you been? I have been looking for you all over the town.

17 I have been in the library reading the newspapers.

18 This house was built upon the beach. It will be falling down soon.

19 Your friends are known in this town. The people do not like them.

20 Has the work been done yet? No, we have been too busy sweeping the fifty-five rooms in this house.

UNEGVES DYSCANS
ELEVENTH LESSON

11A.1 THE CONDITIONAL OF *BOS*

The tenses in English containing 'would' or 'should', e.g. 'I would be happy to help', or 'if everything were all right, he would be here by now', are referred to as conditional. In Cornish such tenses have their own forms. The conditional of **bos** is as follows:

1 *sg.* **bien**	1 *pl.* **bien**
2 *sg.* **bies**	2 *pl.* **biowgh**
3 *sg.* **bia**	3 *pl.* **biens**

These forms are treated like **bedhaf** and **beuv**. One can either say **me a via lowen** 'I should be happy' or **y fien lowen** 'I should be happy'; **y fia hy parys dhe dylly** 'she would be prepared to pay.

One can also say **lowen vien dhe wil hedna** 'I should be happy to do that', with the predicate preceding the verb. Similarly **dâ via genef gwil gweres dhis** 'I should like to help you'.

11A.2 THE PLUPERFECT OF *BOS*

The conditional of **bos** has another function. If one puts the particle **re** before it (and remember that **re** does not cause any mutation before the **b-** of forms of **bos**), the sense is pluperfect: **re bien** then means 'I had been'. If one puts any other particle before the pluperfect, the **re** disappears: **re bia ev i'n cyta kyns hedna, saw ny via bythqweth i'n bedneglos** 'he had been in the city before then, but he had never been in the cathedral'.

> NOTE: The pluperfect use of **bien**, **bia** is confined in the traditional texts to the very earliest stratum of Middle Cornish. Such a use is unknown in the *Ordinalia, Beunans Meriasek, Bewnans Ke, Tregear* and the *Creation of the World*. The pluperfect of **bos** is,

however, well established in the revived language. See further the note on the pluperfect in other verbs at 14A.3 below.

11A.3 THE HABITUAL IMPERFECT OF *BOS*

We have already seen **esen** and **en**, the imperfect of the long and short forms of **bos** respectively. There is another imperfect of **bos** that is used when the sense is habitual, i.e. when speaking of something or somebody was continually or repeatedly. The tense conjugates as follows:

1 *sg.*	**bedhen**	1 *pl.*	**bedhen**
2 *sg.*	**bedhes**	2 *pl.*	**bedhewgh**
3 *sg.*	**bedha**	3 *pl.*	**bedhens**

Y fedha ev i'n gwely pùpprës 'he was always in bed'; **indella y a vedha gwrës** 'they used to be made like that'.

11A.4 ORDINAL NUMERALS

kensa first		**unegves** eleventh	
secùnd second		**dewdhegves** twelfth	
tressa, **tryja** third		**tredhegves** thirteenth	
pe·swora, **pe·swara** fourth		**peswardhegves** fourteenth	
pympes fifth		**pymthegves** fifteenth	
wheffes, **wheghves** sixth		**whêtegves** sixteenth	
seythves seventh		**seytegves** seventeenth	
êthves eighth		**êtegves** eighteenth	
nawves, **nawes** ninth		**nawnjegves** nineteenth	
degves tenth		**ugansves** twentieth	

kensa warn ugans	twenty-first
secùnd warn ugans	twenty-second
tressa warn ugans	twenty-third, etc.
degves warn ugans	thirtieth
unegves warn ugans	thirty-first, etc.
dewgansves	fortieth
kensa ha dewgans	forty-first
secùnd ha dewgans	forty-second
hanter-cansves	fiftieth
tryugansves	sixtieth
degves ha tryugans	seventieth

peswar ugansves	eightieth
degves ha peswar ugans	ninetieth
cansves	hundredth.

The initial consonant of ordinals does not undergo mutation.

> NOTE: Many revivalists used **nessa** for 'second'; **nessa** really means 'next' and is used for 'second' only in a series. The ordinary word for 'second' in the traditional language is **secùnd**.

11A.5 THE MONTHS OF THE YEAR

The names of the months of the year are as follows:

mis Genver January
mis Whevrel February
mis Merth March
mis Ebrel April
mis Me May
mis Metheven or **mis Efen** June
mis Gortheren or **mis Gorefen** July
mis Est August
mis Gwydngala, **mis Gwyngala** September
mis Hedra October
mis Du November
mis Kevardhu December

These names are also used without the preceding **mis** 'month'.

11A.6 THE DATE

There are two ways of rendering the date. One can write, for example, **an 12es (dewdhegves) a vis Gwydngala 2012** 'the twelfth of September 2012'; **an 28es (êthves warn ugans) a vis Ebrel 2120** 'the twenty-eighth of April 2120'. A simpler way is to write the bare number and the short name of the month: **23 Hedra 2001**; **8 Kevardhu 2117**. This shorter form of the date is to be recommended for letters and when dating cheques, etc. One can also abbreviate the names of the months themselves as follows: **Gen**; **Whe**; **Mer**; **Ebr**; **Me**; **Mvn**; **Gor**; **Est**; **Gwn**; **Hed**; **Du**; **Kev**. Thus one can also write, for example, **23 Hed 2001** and **8 Kev 2117**.

11A.7 'WHY?' AND 'HOW?'

'Why' in Cornish is rendered by the word **prag** (< **py rag** 'what for?'). The verb does not come immediately after **prag**, but is preceded by the particle **y⁵(th)**: **Prag yth esta ow leverel hedna?** 'Why do you say that?'; **Prag yth usy hy owth ola?** 'Why is she crying?' When the verb is negative, **y** is replaced by **na²(g)**: **Prag nag usons y obma whath?** 'Why aren't they here yet?'; **Prag nag usy an clogh ow seny?** 'Why doesn't the bell ring?'

'How?' can be expressed by **Fate·ll²**. Since **fatell** is actually a compound of **dell²**, it behaves in the same way: **Fatell esowgh why ow qwil taclow a'n par-na?** 'How do you do things like that?'; **Fatell vedhowgh why ow mos tre?** 'How will you be going home?' There is also another form of **fatell**, namely **fatla²**. This is often reduced to **fatl'** before vowels: **Fatl'usons y ow qwil hedna?** 'How do they do that?'

I'n vaner-ma is used in the texts for 'in this way, thus'. The interrogative derivative **in pana vaner** 'in which way' is occasionally used to ask 'how?'

11B EXAMPLES FROM THE TEXTS

11B.1–2 *lemen mar mynnyth dotya trueth vya ov map ker* 'now if you are going to be silly, it would be a pity, my dear son' BM 346-47; *Gwel vea the'n harlot dos in noeth der spethas ha spern* 'It would be better for the scoundrel to pass naked through thorns and brambles' BK 416-17; *henna vea hager dra* 'that would be a dreadful thing' CW 589; *Na vîa ragôh huei nei a vîa tîz oll dizurêyz* 'Had it not been for you, we should all be dead men' JCH §20.

11B.3 *an plos myngov neb a thuk peynis anwhek sur in grovs pren a vethe gelwys ihesu* 'the dirty liar who suffered bitter pains indeed on the cross, used to be called Jesus' BM 2379-82; *an pith a vetha gwrys syehar anotha* 'that which sacks used to be made of' TH 6a; *mas pub tra oll a rella pertaynya ha concernya an feithfull cristonnyan a vetha rulyys ha gouernys dre an abosteleth a crist* 'but everything which pertained to and concerned the faithful Christians who were ruled and governed by the apostles of Christ' TH 37a.

11B.4 *An kensa tra vgy ow tuchia an creacion a mab den* 'The first thing concerning the creation of man' TH 1; *yn secund dyth y fynna gruthyl ebron nef hynwys* 'on the second day I shall make a firmament called heaven' OM 17-8; *in y tressa chapter the Thimothe in second pistill* 'in his third chapter to Timothy in the second epistle' TH 18a; *bys an tresa han peswera denythyans* 'until the third and the fourth generation' JKeigwin; *in pympas dyth orth ow breis an puskas heb falladowe hag oll an ethyn keffrys me a gwra thom plegadow* 'on the fifth day according to my design without fail I will make the fishes and all the birds for my pleasure' CW 106-09; *hethyw yw an whefes dyth aban dalletheys gonys* 'today is the sixth day since I began to work' OM 49-50; *rag henna ef a benegas ann seythvas dyth* 'therefore he blessed the seventh day' JKeigwin.

11B.5 *An wehes deth in gortheren han gela veth mys est certen orth ov deser an viiives deth han tresse mys gvyngala dugol myhal yv henna in plu noala neffrea an keth feriov ma a veth* 'The sixth day in July, and the second will be in August indeed at my desire, the eighth day, and the third, that is Michaelmas, in the parish of Noala forever, these same fairs shall be' BM 2072-79; *in meys est an viiives deth an secund feer sur a veth sensys in pov benytha* 'in August on the eighth day the second fair will be held in the land forever' BM 2197-99; *yn dekvas dyth mys heddra in blethan myll whegh cans dewghans ha try* 'on the tenth day of the month of October in the year 1643' JKeigwin; *an Kensa journa a messe Heddra an centle, en plew Paule, in Cernow teage en blooth Creste an Arleuth whege meele sith cans ha hanter deege* 'the first day of the month of October was the assembly, in the parish of Paul, in fair Cornwall, in the year of Christ our sweet Lord, 1705' TBoson; *Durt Newlin in Bleau Pawle 22 East, 1711* 'From Newlyn, in the parish of Paul, 22 August 1711, WGwavas; *Flô vye gennes an mîz Merh, ni trehes e bigel en mîz East; E a roz towl dho proanter Powle, mîz Du ken Nadelik* 'A child was born in the month of March, we cut his navel in August; he gave a fall to the vicar of Paul in the month of November before Christmas' WGwavas; *Skrefis war an kenza dydh an miz Kevardhiu 1736* 'Written on the first day of December 1736' WGwavas; *Adheworth Newlyn, e'n Blew Paul, on 22ves mys Est, 1711* 'From Newlyn, in the Parish of Paul, the 22nd of August, 1711' OPender.

11B.6.1 *Mar tewhy demandea, praga a ruke an egglos dewys mar galys vnderstandyng* 'If you ask why did the church choose such a hard understanding' SA 64a; *Praga i'gas kerthow why e tef lynas in erbers* 'Why in your territories do nettles grow in the gardens?' BK 2295-96.

11B.6.2 *Ima lowarth onyn o bostia, fatla vgy faith an tasow coth a vam egglys in an sy* 'Many of them boast how the faith of the ancient fathers of the church is in them' SA 59a; *Why a welle an gallus a geir Christ fatla vgy ow conys* 'You see the power of Christ's word, how it works' SA 62a; *y praytha lavar fatla* 'I pray thee, tell me how' CW609.

11B.6.3 *hag a wor yn pa vaner ganso crous worth y baner wharre ef a thyspleytyas* 'and [I] know with a cross on his banner how shortly he displayed it' RD 526-28; *me a levar thys mar pleag yn pan vanar yn bema* 'I will tell you, if you please, how I came by it' CW 755-56.

11C.1 VOCABULARY

cansvledhen *f.*,
  cansvledhydnyow century
clogh *m.*, **clegh** bell
contentya to satisfy, to content
Degol *m.* **agan Arlodhes** the
  Annunciation' (25th March)

Degol *m.* **Myhal** Michaelmas' (29
  September)
Degol *m.* **Stefan** Boxing Day' (26
  December)
genys *adj.* born
gwâv *m.* winter

gwaynten *m.* spring
hâv *m.* summer
heb mar *adv. phrase.* of course
kynyaf *m.* autumn
loor *f.* moon
lowena dhis! *interj.* hello!
lytheredna to spell (also **spellya**)
mejy to reap
meyny *m.,* **meynys** household, family
Nadelyk *m.* Christmas

Pask *m.* Easter
pedn *m.* **bloodh** birthday, anniversary
powes to rest, to depend (+ **wàr**)
pronter *m.,* **prontyryon** priest, vicar
seny to ring, to sound
vysytya to visit
yn certan *adv. phrase.* certainly

11C.2 TRANSLATE INTO ENGLISH:

1 Lowena dhis. Fatl'osta hedhyw?

2 Dâ lowr, gromercy dhis. Fatl'osta dha honen? Prag yth esta ow leverel 'dâ lowr'?

3 Hedhyw yw an pympes dëdh a'n mis, mis Gwydngala.

4 Trenja a vëdh de Sul an wheffes. Hèn yw pedn bloodh ow gwreg. Res yw dhybm perna neppyth teg dhedhy.

5 A via dâ genes dos genen ny dhe'n mor avorow? Dâ via genef in gwir, saw res vëdh dhybm lavurya avorow, soweth.

6 Y fedhyn ny ow seny an clogh rag an ugansves prës. Prag?

7 A veu dha vroder plêsys gans an dhew lyver-na? Na veu yn tien. Nyns usy an kensa ow plegya dhodho, saw plêsys veu gans an secùnd anodhans.

8 Ev a veu demedhys yn fenowgh. Y beswora gwreg yw pòr deg saw nyns usy hy trigys obma na fella.

9 Prag? Ny vedha hy ow cara y flehes ev. Yma peswardhek anodhans trigys ganso in y jy brâs wàr an âls.

10 Ny via hy contentys gans dew flogh. Yma hy ow pewa i'n nawnjegves cansvledhen.

11 A veusta bythqweth obma kyns hedhyw? Na veuv, saw ow meyny re bia obma liesgweyth.

12 Y fedha tansys gwrës ha leskys an unegves nos warn ugans a vis Hedra.

13 Genver yw an kensa mis ha Whevrel yw an secùnd mis i'n vledhen. An tressa mis yw mis Merth.

14 Pandr'yw an kensa mis a'n hâv? Hèn yw mis Mê.

15 Nâ, mis Mê yw an gwaynten. Nag yw. Mis Ebrel yw dyweth an gwaynten.

16 Usy mis Est i'n hâv bò i'n kynyaf? I'n kynyaf yma va. An mis-na y fëdh an wonesyjy ow tallath mejy.

17 Pana dermyn a vëdh Degol agan Arlodhes? Hèn a vëdh an pympes dëdh warn ugans a vis Merth.

18 Pana dermyn a vëdh an Nadelyk? Yma hedna ow tos pùb bledhen an pympes dëdh warn ugans a vis Kevardhu.

19 Pana dermyn a vëdh de Sul Pask? Prag yth esta ow covyn?

20 Yma dëdh Pask determys der an vledhen ha der an loor.

11C.3 TRANSLATE INTO CORNISH:

1 Is this your first child? No, he is my fourth.

2 He was born on Boxing Day last year.

3 His birthday is the twenty-sixth of December.

4 Would you like to tell me his name? Certanly, he is called Stephen (**Stefan**).

5 When will you be leaving the hospital? The day after tomorrow, the seventeenth of April.

6 How do you go to school every morning? I come on the bus, but on Wednesday my father will be bringing me in the car.

7 Would you like to come with us on the train tomorrow? I certainly should, thank you.

8 How do you spell your name in Cornish? There are two ways.

9 He used to be happy to see me, but now he is too old to recognize me.

10 People used to speak the language here in the eighteenth century.

11 The sheep used to be on the mountain but now they stay near the house.

12 It will be the twentieth of November tomorrow. I shall be going to visit my second son and his third wife.

13 Where will you be next January? Why? I was only asking.

14 Would you be free at the moment? Yes, but I am going home immediately after work.

15 He was always laughing, but he was never really happy.

16 Were you ever in the cathedral? Of course, I used to sing there.

17 He is always drunk after five drinks. This is his sixth.

18 The vicar will be here before long. For the twentieth time, what will we be giving him to eat?

19 Last April was very cold and it was always raining. Next June will be hot.

20 Where do you learn such things? How do you hear them?

DEWDHEGVES DYSCANS
TWELFTH LESSON

12A.1 *GWIL* AS AN AUXILIARY

To date we have confined ourselves to one inflected verb, namely **bos** 'to be'. **Bos** is used in such sentences as **Yma hy ow cana** 'She sings, she is singing', **Me a vëdh ow tos avorow** 'I will be coming tomorrow' and **Y feu va shyndys** 'He was injured'. In each of those sentences **bos** forms a full verb with the present participle (**ow⁴** + verbal noun) or with the verbal adjective (in **-ys**). **Bos** is therefore said to be an auxiliary verb or auxiliary.

Bos is not the only auxiliary verb in Cornish, however. There are several others, of which the commonest is **gwil** (or **gul**) 'to do'. **Gwil** can be used for almost any tense in Cornish. Unlike **bos** which has separate present and future tenses, **gwil** has a present tense which also has to serve as a future (the present-future tense is a feature of most other verbs as well). The present/future tense of **gwil** is inflected as follows:

1 *sg.* **gwrav, gwrama**	1 *pl.* **gwren**
2 *sg.* **gwres** (or **gwreth**), **gwrêta**	2 *pl.* **gwrewgh**;
3 *sg.* **gwra**	3. *pl.* **gwrowns**

The older form **gwreth** of the 2 *sg.* is the origin of **gwrêta** < **gwreth** + **ta**.

12A.2 SYNTAX OF *GWRAV*, ETC.

One says **me a wra** 'I do, I will do'; **te a wra** 'you do, you will do'; **ev a wra** 'he does, he will do', etc. This is then used with the verbal noun of another verb to express the future: **me a wra dos** 'I shall come'; **te a wra scrifa lyther** 'you will write a letter'; **hy a wra metya hy mabm i'n cyta** 'she will meet her mother in the city'.

One uses the inflected form if one puts the verbal noun first: **gweles a wrav an tyller yn scon** 'I shall see the place soon'; **lavurya a wres yn holergh haneth** 'you will work late tonight'.

77

NOTE: One can also use **y⁵** with the inflected forms: **y whren mos alebma avorow** 'we will go from here tomorrow'. Traditional Cornish prose, however, tends to avoid introducing a verb with **y⁵** except in three cases:

   i) if it is part of **bos** 'to be': **y fëdh ev obma** 'he will be here';
   ii) if it is an auxiliary: **y codhvia dhis y wil** 'you should have done it'; **yth hevel dhybm bos gwir** 'it seems to me to be true';
   iii) if it is indirect speech: **ev a leverys y whre hedna** 'he said he would do that'. See §13A.5.

Speakers of the revived language would be well advised to confine themselves to these cases.

We must remember that **gwil** is a verb in its own right with the sense 'to make, to do':

Me a wra den a bry 'I make man from earth'
Gans crehyn an bestas-na me a wra dyllas dhybmo 'I shall make clothes for myself from the skins of those animals'.

12A.3 PRONOMINAL OBJECTS WITH *GWIL* + VERBAL NOUN

It is possible to use a pronominal object with verbs like **me a wra gweles** 'I shall see'. The verb **gweles** is a verbal noun, its logical object must be a possessive adjective (cf. **yma hy worth y weles** 'she sees him', etc. at 7A.4 above). We therefore say:

Me a wra y weles i'n dre I shall see him in town
Aga dystrêwy a wrav I shall destroy them
Hy a wra dha vetya trenja She will meet you the day after tomorrow.

12A.4 MORE PREPOSITIONAL PRONOUNS

Here are the forms of some more prepositional pronouns:

wàr² 'on, upon'
1 *sg.* **warnaf**
2 *sg.* **warnas**
3 *sg. m.* **warnodho**; 3 *sg. f.* **warnedhy**
1 *pl.* **warnan**
2 *pl.* **warnowgh**
3 *pl.* **warnodhans** (or **warnedha**)

rag 'for'; **dhyra·g** 'before, in front of' is inflected like **rag**
1 *sg.* **ragof**
2 *sg.* **ragos**
3 *sg. m.* **ragtho**; 3 *sg. f.* **rygthy**
1 *pl.* **ragon**
2 *pl.* **ragowgh**
3 *pl.* **ragthans** (or **ragtha**)

heb 'without'
1 *sg.* **hebof**
2 *sg.* **hebos**
3 *sg. m.* **heptho**; 3 *sg. f.* **hepthy**
1 *pl.* **hebon**
2 *pl.* **hebowgh**
3 *pl.* **hepthans** (or **heptha**)

ryb 'beside'
1 *sg.* **rybof** (also **ryboma**)
2 *sg.* **rybos**
3 *sg. m.* **ryptho**
3 *sg. f.* **rypthy**
1 *pl.* **rybon**
2 *pl.* **rybowgh**
3 *pl.* **rypthans** (or **ryptha**)

in 'in, into'
1 *sg.* **inof**
2 *sg.* **inos**
3 *sg. m.* **ino** (also **etna, etta**); 3 *sg. f.* **inhy**
1 *pl.* **inon**
2 *pl.* **inowgh**
3 *pl.* **inans, inhans** (also **ina** and **ettans**)

dre (LC **dreth**) 'through, by'
1 *sg.* **dredhof**
2 *sg.* **dredhos**
3 *sg. m.* **dredho**; 3 *sg. f.* **dredhy**;
1 *pl.* **dredhon**;
2 *pl.* **dredhowgh**
3 *pl.* **dredhans** (or **dredha**)

inter, **intra** (LC **ter**) 'between, among'
1 *sg.* **intredhof**
2 *sg.* **intredhos**
3 *sg. m.* **intredho**; 3 *sg. f.* **intredhy**
1 *pl.* **intredhon**
2 *pl.* **intredhowgh**
3 *pl.* **intredhans** (or **intredha**)

dres 'over, across'
1 *sg.* **drestof**
2 *sg.* **drestos**
3 *sg. m.* **dresto**; 3 *sg. f.* **dresty**
1 *pl.* **dreston**
2 *pl.* **drestowgh**
3 *pl.* **drestans** (or **dresta**)

a-ugh, **a-ught** 'above, over'
1 *sg.* **a-uhof**
2 *sg.* **a-uhos**
3 *sg. m.* **a-uho** (or **a-ughta**)
3 *sg.* **a-ughty**
1 *pl.* **a-uhon**
2 pl **a-uhowgh**
3 *pl.* **a-ughtans** (or **a-uha**).

12A.5 *INTER* AND *HEB*

Inter has some idiomatic uses: **inter dha dhewla** 'into your hands' and **terry inter dyw radn** 'to break into two parts'. **Inter**, **intra** is sometimes used with disjunctive pronouns: **inter me ha te** 'between me and you'.

Heb 'without' lenites the **g** in **gow** 'lie' in the expression **heb wow** 'without falsehood'. In early Middle Cornish **heb dhowt** 'without doubt' and **heb dhyweth** 'without end' are attested. Later, however, the unlenited variants **heb dowt** and **heb dyweth** become universal.

12B EXAMPLES FROM THE TEXTS

12B.1–3 ***lemmyn the besy del wraf*** 'now as I shall beg you' BK 783; ***Gwag ove, rave gawas haunsell?*** 'I am hungry; will I get breakfast?' Pryce; ***pan reta ow cusullya the gasa cres the'n harlot*** 'when you advise me to leave the scoundrel in peace' BK 988-89; ***Gorthya Jovyn te a ra*** 'You will worship Jove' BK 913; ***Mos the Arthor dyougal a ren, agen arluth ol*** 'We will go indeed to Arthur, the lord of us all' BK 1383-84; *No ny rewgh merwell* 'No, you will not die' TH 3a; *mar ny rowns ow gohelas hag omdenna* 'if they do not avoid me and withdraw' BK 1511-12.

12B.4.1 WÀR: *y varck warnaf y settyas* 'his mark upon me he set' CW1530; *A, owt warnas, te rybot* 'Oh, damnation upon you, you scoundrel' BK 987; *Warnotha, Du, tal dyel!* 'Upon him, O God, inflict vengeance!' BK 3283; *Hov dehesugh warnethy* 'Ho! Let fly upon her!' BM 3948; *mere warnan pub tenewhan omgwethen ny gans deel glase* 'look, let us put on us green leaves as clothes on every side' CW 857-58; *Joy warnowgh ha ryelder* 'Joy upon you and majesty' BK 2005; *warnothans kymar gallus* 'assume power upon them' CW 356.

12B.4.2 RAG: *in cheryta ragaf pys* 'in charity pray for me' BK 2828; *kin fe Soudan Babylon omma ragas ow pegy* 'though the Sultan of Babylon were praying for you here' BK 132-33; *Ne nahaf Du a vercy, ragtho kyn fena maraw* 'I will not deny the God of mercy, though I should die for it' BK 579-80; *Thum peiadov alema mones a vanna rygthy* 'I will go hence to my prayer for her sake' BM 4015-16; *Du re vynnas ragon ny guthyl marclus* 'God has desired to perform miracles for us' BK 861-62; *ple ma an Romans ow settya ragow' myrnans* 'where the Romans are plotting death for you' BK 2807-08; *eff a rug oll an da a ylly thethans y ha ragthans y* 'he did all the good he could to them and for them'TH 23.

12B.4.3 HEB: *ha lues heboff oma* 'and many apart from me here' BM 4546; *hebogh why sur na menogh ny a sped mater in pov ma* 'without you indeed not often do we succeed in any business in this country' BM 2692-93.

12B.4.4 RYB: *'Ma lever bean rebbam* 'I have a small book beside me' NBoson; *kenever a whelha ha vo o sevall rebta* 'whoever would see and would stand beside him' SA 60; *Fyntan dek ema ryban* 'There is a fair spring beside us' BK 799.

12B.4.5 IN: *ema ef ow trega innaff ve* 'he dwells in me' SA 61; *Inno ema ow fythya* 'In him he trusts' BK 889; *then wlas vgy y vab Jhesus crist inhy tregys* 'to the kingdom in which his son Jesus Christ dwells' TH 11a; *ha fowt disposicion da ynnan ny the receva* 'and lack of right disposition in us to receive' TH 13a; *ha ow gyrryow ve inno why* 'and my words in you' TH 39a; *an rena as tevas an spurissans innans* 'those who have the Holy Spirit in them' TH 38a; *an nef han oar han more ha myns es ythens y* 'the heavens and the earth and the sea and all that is in them' JKeigwin; *ha an prounterian da eze etangy* 'and the good clerics that are in them' JTonkin.

12B.4.6 DRE: *han segh gallas quyte drethaf* 'and the arrow has gone quite through me' CW 1573; *Drethos eth on lewenhys* 'By you we are delighted' BK 2039; *Me, Sertory, myghtern Lyby, a res dretho gans ow gu* 'I, Sertorius, king of Libya, will run him through with my spear' BK 2587-89; *rag innan agan honyn, na drethan agan honyn ny geffyn tra vith vas* 'for in us ourselves, nor through us ourselves we get nothing of good' TH 10; *in tradicions, delyuerys drethens y* 'in traditions delivered by them' TH 19.

12B.4.7 INTER: *yntretho ha'y gowethe* 'between him and his friends' PC 1288; *Pysell defferans a bewnans vs lymmyn intrethan ny* 'How great a difference of life is there now between us' TH 27; *lemmyn ol cres yntrethough* 'now peace among you all' RD 2433.

12B.4.8 DRES: *nynsus arluth dresto ef* 'there is no lord beyond him' RD 746.

12B.4.9 A-UGH: *saw un voys whek a belder a-ughaf in uhelder ow kowsal cler* BK 13-5; *mas an sorre a crist a dryg vghta* 'but the wrath of Christ remains over him' TH 40; *Arluth esos ahuhan, benegas re by pub prys* 'O Lord, who art above us, mayst thou be blessed always' BK 478-79; *than nef vghall a vghan* 'to the high heaven above us' CW 2077.

12B.5 *Inter dula du avan* 'Into the hands of God above' BM 5002; *ef a ve degys inter e thowla* 'it was delivered into his hands' SA 65; *haw fedn squatyes pur garow why an gweall ynter dew ran* 'and my head crushed very roughly (you can see it) into two parts' CW 1707-08.

12C.1 VOCABULARY

a les *adj. phrase.* of interest	**omsettya** to resist (takes **orth**)
a'y sav *adv. phrase.* standing	**pehas** *m.,* **pehosow** sin
assaultya to assault, to attack	**pols** a while
avowa admit	**repentya** to repent
chauns *m.* chance, opportunity	**resek** to run (chiefly of liquids)
cùssul *f.,* **cùssullyow** advice, counsel	**ryver** *m.,* **ryvers** river
derivas to tell, to inform	**scodhya wàr²** to rely upon
dyberth to separate, to depart	**settya** to set
fêkyl false, affected (*as prefixed adj.*)	**sogh** *m.,* **soghyow** ploughshare
gov *m.,* **govyon** smith	**styrya** to explain
gwetyas hope, expect	**sur** *adj.* sure, certain
haunsel *m.* breakfast	**trestya** to trust (takes **dhe**)
i'n gwetha prës *adv. phrase.* unfortunately	**war** *adj.* wary
	whedhel *m.,* **whedhlow** story
	ytho· *adv.* therefore

12C.2 TRANSLATE INTO ENGLISH:

1 Ny a wra debry an desen hag eva an gwin intredhon agan dew.

2 A wrêta goslwes orthyf pols? Na wrav. Ny wrama dha glôwes.

3 A ny wrewgh why avowa agas pehosow? Gwren, gwren ha ny a wra repentya anodhans.

4 Ny wrowns gasa an chy hebon, yth esof ow qwetyas.

5 Me a wra settya oll ow thaclow wàr an bord, ha sedha i'n chair brâs rybos.

6 Obma yma an paper nowodhow ragos. Eus tra vëth dâ ino? Nag eus.

7 Nyns esof ow redya paperyow nowodhow i'n tor'-ma. Ny vëdh whedhel vëth a les inhans i'n dedhyow-ma.

8 Yth esof ow miras orth an ebron a-uhon. Hy yw spladn ha glas.

9 An best gwyls a wra agan assaultya. Res yw dhyn bos war anodho.

10 Pòr dewl yw an coos. Cales vëdh cafos fordh vëth dredho hag in mes anodho.

11 Y fëdh gensy neppyth pòr deg ragos. Pywa? Hy a wra pobas tesen ragos jy ha ragof vy.

12 A wrav vy hy hafos yn scon? Te a wra hy hafos avorow wosa haunsel.

13 Nyns eus den vëth obma a wra ow gweres ow mos dres an ryver.

14 Osta parys dhe dhos genen wàr an dyweth? Nag ov, res yw dhywgh oll mos hebof.

15 Ny wren ny gwil hedna màn. Ny wren ny mos tyller vëth hebos. Yth eson ny ow scodhya warnas.

16 Fatla wrama gweres dhywgh ytho? Nyns ov marnas benyn wadn.

17 Res yw dhis côwsel orth dha wour ha leverel taclow kepar ha'n re-na dhodho.

18 Yth yw an den-na ryb an pons aswonys dhybm, saw pyw yw an venyn yonk a'y sav ryptho?

19 Hòn yw y vyrgh ev. Hy a wra agan vysytya haneth ha chauns a vëdh dhis dhe gôwsel orty.

20 Nyns esof vy ow trestya dhedhy. Fêkyl yw hy wharth, yth esof ow cresy.

12C.3 TRANSLATE INTO CORNISH:

1 I will not help you with things like that.

2 I was looking through my pockets. Was there any money in them?

3 I am relying on them to come in time. I was hoping to explain things to them.

4 When will you be giving them the cake? After breakfast perhaps.

5 Who is that woman standing by the large trees in the garden? She is the doctor's wife. She will be going home without him.

6 The smith is making a ploughshare. Will it be big enough for us?

7 Between the two of us, I do not believe she is his wife at all.

8 What? Who is she then? A foolish young woman.

9 We will go to the town by bus and meet the others near the bridge.

10 I will give my money into their hands. I certainly trust them.

11 The chair will break in two. You are too heavy for it.

12 This is the little house and that is the river running beside it. Isn't it pretty?

13 The river is very deep. I will not be swimming across it.

14 I have advice for them. What? They must come immediately to see me, or I will inform the police.

15 Here are the shoes. There is something in them. What? Small stones.

16 I am looking at the sky above us. Isn't is blue and bright?

17 The wood is very dark and it will be hard for us to go through it.

18 The animals are wild and they will attack us. We must beware of them.

19 The girl standing over there is my daughter. Who is the man standing beside her? That is her husband.

20 Will you and your family be coming with us? No, unfortunately, I have to work. You will be going without me and without them also.

TREDHEGVES DYSCANS
THIRTEENTH LESSON

13A.1 THE PRETERITE OF *GWIL*

One can render the past tense of any verb by using the preterite of **gwil** 'to do' together with the relevant verbal noun, for example: **me a wrug mos** 'I did go, I went'; **te a wrug gweles** 'you did see, you saw'; **ev a wrug convedhes an geryow yn tâ** 'he understood the words well'; **hy a wrug abma dhybm** 'she kissed me' (**abma** 'to kiss' is usually followed by **dhe²**).

If one wants to make the verb negative, however, the personal forms must be used. They are as follows;

1 *sg.* **gwrug, gwrug avy**
2 *sg.* **gwrussys, gwrusta**
3 *sg.* **gwrug, gwrug ev, gwrug hy**
1 *pl.* **gwrussyn**
2 *pl.* **gwrussowgh, gwrussowgh**
3 *pl.* **gwrussons, gwrussons y**

1 *sg.* **gwruga, gwrugaf** and 3 *sg. m.* **gwruga** (< **gwruge**) are also attested. In later Cornish, **gwrussowgh why**, **gwrussons y** are replaced by **gwrugowgh why** (pronounced as **gwrugo'why**) and **gwrug anjy** respectively.

One says:

A wrusta gweles an den a'y sav ena? Did you see the man standing there
A wrug ev dha elwel? Did he call you?
A wrussyn ny agas ania? Did we disturb you?
A wrussowgh why clôwes hedna? Did you (*pl.*) hear that?

Y whrug ev dos, **mos**, **gweles**, etc. 'he came, went, saw', etc. with the particle **y**[5] are sometimes used by Cornish speakers. As has been mentioned above (12A.2) such syntax is best avoided in prose.

When **gwrug** is used as an auxiliary to make the past tense of another verb, it is usually pronounced with a short vowel: **Ev a wrug gweles**, for example, is pronounced **Ev a rig gweles** with [ɹɪg]. When **gwrug** is a full verb, meaning, 'made, did', it tends to have a long vowel. In the sentence **Duw a wrug an bës ha pùptra ino** 'God made the world and everything in it', **wrug** may be pronounced [ɹiːg]. In Late Cornish 'made' is often **gwras** rather than **gwrug**.

13A.2 INDIRECT STATEMENT INTRODUCED BY *FATELL,* '*TELL*, AND *DELL*

Ev yw pòr skentyl 'He is very intelligent' is a direct statement. If one wants to report what someone believes, says or thinks, one uses indirect speech, e.g. 'The teacher thinks he is very intelligent'.

There are several ways of expressing indirect statement in Cornish. The simplest is to introduce the clause of reported speech with one of the two conjunctions **fate·ll**[2] 'how' or **dell**[2] 'as'. In later Cornish **fatell** is often reduced to **tell**, **ter**, **tr'** and **dell** to **der**, **dr'**. Notice that **fatell**, **dell**, when used to introduce indirect speech, must immediately precede their verb:

Yma an descador ow cresy fatell ywa pòr skentyl The teacher believes that he is very intelligent

An den yonk a leverys dell esa ow cortos y gowethes The young man said he was waiting for his girlfriend

Ny wrussons convedhes 'tell vedha res dhedhans chaunjya kenyver tra They did not understand that they would have have to change everything

Ev a leverys dell o va medhek He said he was a doctor.

NOTE: Indirect speech after **fatell** and **dell** is found in the earliest Middle Cornish and is probably related to the comparable construction in Middle Breton, e.g. *Chuy a lauar penos ez credit en Doue* 'You say how/that you believe in God' *Doctrin an Christenien* (1622). For a discussion of this and of indirect speech in Cornish in general see 'Indirect Statement in Cornish and Breton' in *Cornish Studies: Six* (1998), 172-82.

13A.3 INDIRECT STATEMENT WITH THE VERBAL NOUN

The verbal noun can also be employed to express indirect speech. This can be done in two ways. If the tense of the main verb is the same as that of the verb in indirect speech, one can use the verbal noun by itself: **yma hy ow leverel bos an medhek ow tos** 'she says the doctor is coming'. If, however, the two tenses do not agree, one has to put the subject of the reported verb first and introduce the verbal noun with **dhe²**: **yma hy ow leverel an medhek dhe dhos heb let** 'she says that the doctor will come without delay'; **yma hy ow cresy hy mab dhe bassya oll y apposyansow** 'she believes that her son passed all his exams'. **Dhe²** can also be used if the two tenses do not differ: **yma hy ow teclarya hy dhe gôwsel Frynkek** 'she claims she speaks French'.

If the subject of the verb in indirect speech is a pronoun, one says, for example, **yma hy ow leverel ev dhe dhos avorow** 'she says he will come tomorrow' or **yma hy ow leverel y vos obma solabrë·s** 'she says he is already here'.

13A.4 PERSONAL SUFFIXES ATTACHED TO THE VERBAL NOUN *BOS*

In traditional Cornish, the verbal noun **bos** is sometimes marked for person. If desired, this can be imitated in the revived language and we would then get indirect statements like: **esta ow tyby ow bosaf teg** 'do you think I am beautiful?'

In TH and CW in indirect speech the verbal noun **bos** is not introduced by a possessive adjective but by **y.** This **y** causes no mutation and person is indicated by an enclitic pronoun attached to the verbal noun (see 13B.4 for examples). The dummy **y** may derive in part from the use of **y(th)** in indirect speech (see 13A.5). Sentences such as the following are possible: **yth esof ow cresy y bosans y hy whereth hy** 'I believe they are her sisters' and **lavar dhedhans y bosama obma** 'tell them I am here'.

13A.5 INDIRECT STATEMENT WITH *Y*⁵(*TH*)

Indirect speech can also be introduced by the particle **y⁵(th)** and the inflected form of the verb, e.g. **yma hy ow cresy y fëdh tyller i'n carr ragon ny oll** 'she believes there will be space in the car for us all'; **me yw certan yth yw hy an ganores wella in Kernow** 'I am certan she is the best singer in Cornwall'.

When the indirect speech refers to future time the habitual imperfect of **bos** 'to be' must be used, and the imperfect of other verbs:

Ev a leverys y fedhen wolcùm He said I would be welcome
Jowan a bromysyas dhybm y whre va dos tre abrë·s John
promised me he would come home early.

13A.6 NEGATIVE INDIRECT STATEMENT

None of the above constructions can be used when the verb is negative.
In such cases the verb is identical with the answer form: **ev a wrug leverel
nag esa ow tos** 'he said he was not coming'; **yth esof ow cresy na wra
Peder cachya an train** 'I believe that Peter won't catch the train'; **yma
hy ow qwetyas na wra an descador govyn orty** 'she hopes the
teacher will not ask her'.

13B EXAMPLES FROM THE TEXTS

13B.1 *na ny wrugaf tha wellas nangew sure lyas blethan* 'nor did I see you
for many years now' CW 1662-63; *Ase rusta hager prat!* 'What an evil trick
you have played!' BK 84; *Gwra ge contynewa in pith a rusta dysky*
'Continue in that which you learnt' TH 18a; *pan rug an arluth Dew e
rebukya, whath na ruk Judas e vnderstandya* 'when the Lord God
rebuked him, still Judas did not understand him' SA 65a; *ha pan russyn ny
dre agan defout agan honyn cothe in stat a anken* 'and when we through
our own fault fell into a state of misery' TH 16; *ow negyssyow yth ew gwryes
par dell wrussowgh thym orna* 'my business has been completed as you
ordered me' CW 1883-84; *rag na rigga ve beska gwellaz skreef Bretten
coth veeth* 'for I never saw ancient British writing' NBoson; *No rig avee
biscath gwelles lever Cornoack* 'I never saw a Cornish book' WBodinar; *po
'ryȝo huei mvz ker* 'when you went away' JCH §44; *Pe rêg angye clowaz
an matern y eath caar* 'When they heard the king, they departed' Rowe.
13B.2 *ny a fyn leuerel ol yn pow sur the pub den ol fatel wrussyn ny
keusel orth an arluth ker ihesu* 'we will tell everyone in all the land that we
spoke to the dear lord Jesus' RD 1339-42; *Gothvethow fatell ew du agan
arluth ny* 'Know that God is our lord' TH 1; *yth ew recordys fatell rug
onyn sodenly apperya the Josue* 'it is recorded that one suddenly appeared
to Joshua' TH 55a; *pe reg Jesus clowaz tero Jowan towlaz tha bressen*
'when Jesus heard that John had been thrown into prison' Rowe; *pu reg laule
theese tell estah en noath?* 'who told you that you were naked?' Rowe; *Vn
venyn da a welas dell o Ihesus dystrippijs* 'a good woman saw that Jesus
had been stripped' PA 177a; *eue levarraz dr'o ua Gever Ul* 'he said that it
was "Goats All".' NBoson; *Pe reege a vennin gwellas tr'o an wethan da
rag booze, ha der o hi blonk tha'n lagagow* 'When the woman saw that
the tree was good for food and that it was pleasant to the eyes' Rowe.
13B.3 *ny gresaf awos an beys bos an hore whath marow* 'I do not believe
for the world that the whore is dead yet' OM 2752-53; *y vos byw my ny gresaf*
'I don't believe he is alive' RD 904; *Ny gresaf awos an bys bos maner*

thotho parkys a dyrath whath 'I do not believe for all the world that he has enclosed a manor of land for himself' BK 1189-91; *as yv ioy gynef gothfos an denses the thos the'n nef* 'what joy it is to me to know that the manhood has come to heaven' RD 2608-09; *Pan ew ow dewan mar drus, ef the vynnas bysmeras thym eth yw bern* 'When my anxiety is so perverse, it is a source of concern that he wished to disgrace me' BK 412-14.

13B.4 *ov sclandra mar mynnogh why ha leferel ov bosa omma cruel* 'if you wish to slander me and say that I am cruel here' BM 3747-49; *Me a wothya, parda! the vota ow recordya ow bosa den eredie* 'I knew by God! that you were making it clear that I was a man indeed' BK 351-53; *cresowh ow bosaf prince creif hag in weth thewhy cheften* 'believe that I am a powerful prince and your chieftain' CW 116-17; *fensan ow bosaf marowe soweth bythqwathe bos formys* 'I wish I were dead, alas, and never having been born' CW 1264-65; *So pew a leverough why y bosama* 'But who do you say I am?' TH 43a; *A te dore, remember y bosta, dore, dore* 'O you clay, remember that you are clay, clay' TH 7a; *crist ew gylwys bara, rag y bos eff food an ena* 'Christ is called bread, for he is food for the soul' TH 57a; *honna a rug pub vr desquethas y bossy an very spowse a crist* 'she who always showed that she was the very spouse of Christ' TH 34a; *a theth warnan ny dre reson y bosen gyllys in mes thean chy a thu* 'that have come upon us because we have gone away from the house of God' TH 40a; *Rag henna ow cothmans, dre reson y bosow gwarnys therag dorne, bethow ware* 'Therefore, my friends, because you have been warned in advance, beware' TH 18; *fatell rons y dos in crehyn devas, dre reson y bosans y ow pretendya an gyrryow a thu* 'that they come in sheeps skins, because they claim to have the words of God' TH 19a.

13B.5 *Rag an traytor a gewsys ha ʒe rag leas huny war lyrgh y vonas leʒys ʒen tressa dyth y seuy* 'For the traitor declared and to many that after he was killed he would rise on the third day' PA 240ab; *y leverys ef ynweth datherghy an tressa deth y wre* 'he said also he would rise on the third day' RD 4-6; *lemmyn me a grys yn ta y fynnaf vy mos pella esough haneth* RD 'now I believe full well that I will go further than you tonight' 1297-99; *hag a covsis donfon warlergh seluester hag y fethen heb awer a oll ov cleves sawys* 'and he told me to send for Silvester and that I should be without fear healed of all my disease' BM 1729-32.

13B.6 *Camen pylat pan welas na ylly crist delyffre* 'When Pilate saw that he could in no way save Jesus' PA 150a; *yth ewa poynt bras a error the supposya na rug crist kemeras y gyge mes a gyge an wyrhes maria y vam* 'it is a great point of error to suppose that Christ took his flesh only from the flesh of the Virgin Mary his mother' TH 12a; *Rys ew gwelas orth an wel nag ota ge mowas lows* 'It is necessary to see by the work that you are not a slack girl' BK 1115-16.

13C.1 VOCABULARY

ape·rt *adj. & adv.* open(ly), apparent
bys venary *adv.* for ever
cabm *adj.* bent, wrong
camgemerys *adj.* mistaken
cachya to catch
cudhys *adj.* hidden
drogober *m.*, **drogoberow** evil deed, crime
gorthyp *m.*, **gorthebow** answer
gwil ges to jest, to make fun of (takes **a²**)
gwiryon *adj.* innocent
gwiryoneth *m.*, **gwiryonethow** truth
haval *adj.* like, similar
i'n eur-na, **nena** *adv.* then

indelma *adv.* in this way
jùj *m.*, **jùjys** judge
kentrevak *m.*, **kentrevogyon** neighbour
kepa·r ha(g) *adj. & adv. phr.* like, as
kyns na pell *adv. phrase* before long
ladra to steal
pebys *adj.* baked
pryson *m.*, **prysons** prison
pysk *m.*, **pùscas** fish
spêna to spend
strayl *m.*, **straylyow** mat
tyby to consider, to think
yn few *adj. phrase* alive
yn tien *adj. phrase.* completely

13C.2 TRANSLATE INTO ENGLISH:

1 Yma va ow leverel na wrug ev gweles an dhew dhen a'ga sav in cres an fordh.

2 Cales yw cresy y vos ow terivas an gwiryoneth.

3 Yma pùbonen ow tyby fatell yns y whath yn few.

4 Me a wrug cafos an lyther-ma wàr an strayl myttyn hedhyw.

5 A wrusta cùsca yn tâ? Na wrug, yth esa an cathas ow cana dres an nos ha ny wrug avy cùsca màn.

6 Me a wrug leverel dhodho ow bos i'n tyller rag an coref hag ev a wrug cresy dhe'm geryow.

7 Yth esen ow qwetyas hy dhe dhewheles tre kyns na pell ha ny dhe vewa yn lowen warbarth bys venary.

8 Nyns esof vy ow cresy te dhe gachya an kyttryn lebmyn, saw heb mar y fëdh kyttryn aral ow tos yn scon.

9 Ev a wrug avowa fatell esa kerensa gudhys intredhans. Pyw? Intredho ev ha'm gwreg vy.

10 Y fedha bara pebys pùb jorna indella i'n chy-ma.

11 A nyns usy an Lyver Dâ ow leverel fatell yw res dhis cara dha gentrevak?

12 Ymowns y ow tyby an whedhel-na dhe vos gwir, saw apert yw dhe bùb huny y vos fàls yn tien.

13 Prag yth esta ow leverel y vos ev camgemerys i'n mater?

14 Hy a wrug gweles fatell o an flogh trist ha hy a wrug govyn orto prag.

15 Ny wrug hy cafos gorthyp vëth.

16 Nena me a wrug ùnderstondya rag an kensa près nag esa lowr a vona dhodho.

17 Nyns usy pùbonen i'n dreveglos ow cresy me dhe wil an drog-ober.

18 Kynth ov vy gwiryon, yma an jùj ow leverel y fëdh res dhybm spêna teyr bledhen in pryson.

19 Soweth ragos. Res yw dhybm derivas dhe'n paperyow nowodhow na wrussys ladra tra vëth.

20 Nyns esta ow cresy me dhe avowa tra kepar ha hedna.

13C.3 TRANSLATE INTO CORNISH:

1 She said she was happy to see me, but I did not believe her.

2 He believes that it was I who committed (= *did*) the crime.

3 You are mistaken. I did not do such a thing (**tra kepar ha hedna**).

4 He thought he would catch many fish, but he caught two only.

5 Why do you say that I do not love you?

6 Did you see the two girls standing by the river? No.

7 One of them is my sister, and she says you are wrong. The river is not deep.

8 What did she say? She said she understood the matter completely and that I was a fool.

9 Where did you buy that pretty dress? I told you already that I stole it from my sister.

10 I am only joking. I bought it in town the day before yesterday.

11 He says she is his sister, but I believe she is his girlfriend. She is not like him at all.

12 You must believe the words of the Good Book. It says: you shall love your neighbour as yourself.

13 Who is my neighbour? Not that dreadful man in the next house.

14 He said he had no money at all, and then I saw him in the pub laughing and drinking with his friends.

15 He said he was poor, but it is obvious that he was not telling the truth.

16 He admitted that he committed the crime, but the police do not believe him.

17 Who did it then? The people here think it was his brother.

18 I hope that you will return soon, and that you will bring your beautiful sister with you.

19 Why do you say that my sister is beautiful? Everybody says she wears dreadful clothes.

20 I said that I would not be pleased to come with you, but I must admit now I was only joking.

PESWARDHEGVES DYSCANS
FOURTEENTH LESSON

14A.1 THE IMPERFECT OF *GWIL*

The imperfect of **gwil** is conjugated as follows:

1 *sg.* **gwren**	1 *pl.* **gwren**
2 *sg.* **gwres**	2 *pl.* **gwrewgh**
3 *sg.* **gwre**	3 *pl.* **gwrêns**

This form is used when describing repeated or habitual action in the past: **agan tasow a wre pesy Duw yn freth in pùb caletter** 'our fathers prayed (used to pray) assiduously to God in all difficulties'. It also introduces verbs in indirect speech in the past, that would be future in direct speech: **ev a wrug leverel na wre va sùffra taclow a'n par-na** 'he said he would not endure such things' (his actual words were: **ny wrama sùffra taclow a'n par-na** 'I will not endure such things'.)

14A.2 IMPERFECT WITH *ÚSYA*

In English we often express repeated action in the past by means of the verb 'to use': 'My father used to say', 'we used to stay in Falmouth when we were young', etc. A similar idiom is attested in Cornish with **ûsya** 'to use, to be wont'. We can therefore say:

Me a wrug ûsya mos dhe'n scol wàr an kyttryn i'n dedhyow-na I used to go to school on the bus in those days

Te a wrug ûsya côwsel moy orthyf kyns ès ny dhe berna an bellwolok You used to talk to me more, before we bought the television.

14A.3 CONDITIONAL OF *GWIL*

We have seen that the conditional of **bos** is **bien**, **bies**, **bia**, etc. (11A.1). The equivalent tense of **gwil** is inflected as follows:

1 *sg.* **gwrussen**	1 *pl.* **gwrussen**
2 *sg.* **gwrusses**	2 *pl.* **gwrussewgh**
3 *sg.* **gwrussa**	3 *pl.* **gwrussens**

The conditional here, as with most other verbs, is formed by adding the endings **-sen**, **-ses**, **-sa**, etc. to the preterite stem. **Bos** and its compounds are exceptional in not using **-s-** in the conditional. The conditional of any verb can refer both to the future and to the past. **Bien** can therefore mean 'I would be' and 'I would have been'. **Gwrussen** is either 'I would do' or 'I would have done'.

> NOTE: the conditional of **bos**, when preceded by the particle **re** has pluperfect force, 'I had been'. As has been noted above, this use is confined to the very earliest stratum of Middle Cornish, i.e. in *Pascon agan Arluth* only. In revived Cornish the conditional of other verbs is sometimes used with pluperfect sense. Edwin Norris the editor of the Ordinalia expressly mentions that the conditional never has pluperfect sense in any of the three plays: 'The Fourth tense is named the Preterpluperfect in Welsh and Armoric… Its use in those languages is in accordance with its name, but it is more commonly employed as a subjunctive of conditional. In Cornish, so far as I have observed, it is used as a conditional only, and it is frequently confounded with the second tense' [i.e. the imperfect], *Ancient Cornish Drama* (1859) ii: 260-61. Since the conditional is never a pluperfect in our foundation texts, BM, TH, SA, BK and CW, it is not so used here. It cannot, of course, be considered incorrect.

14A.4 SUFFIXED PERSONAL PRONOUNS

In English when one wants to emphasize a possessive adjective, one merely pronounces it with greater vigour, for example: 'Somebody has been sitting in *my* chair!' or 'That's not *your* money!' Such a method of emphasis is unknown in any of the Celtic languages. In order to emphasize possession it is necessary to use a suffixed personal pronoun after the relevant noun: **Re beu nebonen ow sedha i'm chair vy!** and **Nyns yw hedna dha vona jy!**

The suffixed personal pronouns when used with nouns, prepositional pronouns and to emphasize infixed pronouns (18A.1) are as follows:

1 *sg.* **vy**	1 *pl.* **ny**
2 *sg.* **sy, jy**	2 *pl.* **why**
3 *sg. m.* **ev**; 3 *sg. f.* **hy, y**	3 *pl.* **y**

And when double emphasis is required, the following forms are used:

1 *sg.* **avy·**	1 *pl.* **nyny·**
2 *sg.* **dhejy·, tejy·**	2 *pl.* **whywhy·**
3 *sg. m.* **e·ev**; 3 *sg. f.* **hyhy·**	3 *pl.* **ynsy·**

The Celtic languages emphasize the subject of an inflected form by the use of enclitic pronouns similar to those listed above. In English one says '*I* didn't do it' or '*She* didn't lose them'. Cornish on the other hand has to say: **Ny wrug avy y wil** and **Ny wrug hyhy aga helly**. If the verb is positive, the impersonal syntax is emphatic enough: **Te a wrug y wainya** means '*You* won it', since the underlying sense of such a sentence is 'it is you that won it', where you is already emphasized by being at the head of its clause.

The suffixed nominative pronouns used with verbs in the plural are identical with those used with nouns; the singular suffixed subject pronouns used with verbs are different. They are as follows:

1 *sg.* **-ma, -a**
2 *sg.* **-ta**
3 *sg. m.* **va, ev**; 3 *sg. f.* **hy, y**

The doubly emphatic subject pronouns are **mavy·**; **tejy·**; **vae·v**; **hyhy·**. In the plural they are the same as those used with nouns.

14A.5 ADVERBS OF POSITION

The common adverbs of position are:

obma here	**dhe'n dor** down, downwards
ena there	**wàr nans** down, downwards
dy thither, to that place	**awoles** down, below
ade·r dro round about	**aba·rth awoles** down, below
in bàn (late **in màn, màn**) up, upwards	**in hans** over there
avà·n up, aloft	**alebma** from here, hence
awartha above	**alena** from there, thence
a-uhon above (in a text)	**dres ena** over there
dhe'n leur down, downwards	**ajy·** in, into
	aberveth in, into

in mes out, away
in kerdh away
dhe ves away
wàr ves outside
wàr jy inside
alê·s abroad, far and wide
ahë·s along
ogasty· nearly, almost
rybon nearby

obma in ogas nearby
in rag forward
adhelergh behind, in arrears
wàr dhelergh back, backwards
warlergh after, behind
tre homewards, home
in tre at home (i'n dre means 'in
  the town')
adre· from home

Note also **an pëth awartha dhe woles** 'upside down'.

14A.6 TEMPORAL AND FINAL CONJUNCTIONS

The commonest temporal conjunction is **pàn²** 'when', which immediately precedes its verb: **pàn wrug avy gweles hedna** 'when I saw that'. **Pàn²** is also the basis of **abà·n²** 'since', which has both temporal and consecutive sense. Like **pàn** it precedes the verb immediately, unless the verb is negative, in which case **na** follows both **pàn** and **abà·n**: **ny wrama mos tre, abà·n esta obma** 'I won't go home, since you're here'; **nyns ov vy certan adro dhe'n mater, abà·n na wrug avy redya an lytherow whath** 'I am not sure about the matter, since I have not yet read the letters'. 'Since' with a temporal sense can also be rendered by **dhia bàn²**: **ny wrug an medhek agan vysytya, dhia bàn veu va obma warleny** 'the doctor has not visited us since he was here last year'.

There are several ways of saying 'because' in Cornish. **Rag** can be used with a finite verb: **rag ev a wrug dos ava·rr** 'because he came early'. **Drefen** (stressed on the first syllable) 'because', **dre rêson** 'because' and **awos** 'because' are used with the verbal noun if the verb is positive: **me yw glëb drefen (dre rêson, awos) me dhe gerdhes der an glaw** 'I am wet because I walked through the rain'. **Na(g)** and a finite verb are used if the verb is negative: **ny wrug avy y weles, drefen (dre rêson) nag esa golow i'n tyller** 'I did not see him, because there was no light in the place'.

NOTE: The word **drefen** appears as *drefan* twice in BK and 14 times in CW. This suggests that the second syllable was unstressed in the traditional language, and that the word should not be pronounced *[dɹə'fɛn], but rather ['dɹɛfən].

14A.7 'BEFORE' AND 'AFTER'

The preposition **kyns** 'before' is used in such expressions as **kyns lebmyn, kyns ès lebmyn** 'before now', **kyns dyberth** 'before leaving', **kyns pedn seythen** 'within a week'. It is also an adverb: **ny wrug avy y weles kyns** 'I never saw him before'. 'Beforehand' is also sometimes rendered **ara·g dorn, dhyra·g dorn**. The expressions **kyns, kyns ès** function as conjunctions when used with the verbal noun. One can therefore say: **ev a wrug ow gelwel kyns dos**, or **kyns ès dos** 'he called me before coming'. One can also say **kyns ès ev dhe dhos, ev a wrug ow gelwel** 'before he came, he called me'.

'After' in a temporal sense is **wosa** (**awosa, woja**). As a conjunction **wosa** requires a verbal noun: **wosa redya an lyver, me a wrug y dhon arta dhe'n lyverjy** 'having read the book, I took it back to the library'. If one wishes to say 'after' as a temporal adverb one says **wosa hedna**: **me a wrug clôwes nebes painys termyn hir wosa hedna** 'I felt some pain for a long time after'.

Warlergh can also be used as a conjunction with the verbal noun: **warlergh spêna dew dhëdh ena, me o gesys heb mona** 'after spending two days there, I was left without money'. **Warlergh hedna** can be used to mean 'afterwards'.

14B EXAMPLES FROM THE TEXTS

14B.1 ***bost a wrens tyn ha deveth yn gweȝens worth y ehen*** 'they repeatedly boasted sharply and without shame that they would guard him in spite of all he might do' PA 242d; ***kyns ty a wre meystry thy'n*** 'before you used to lord it over us' PC 2982; ***ha y a re bostya hag a leuery, … yth esa ve ow syngy a paule, yth esa ve ow singy a Apollo*** 'and they used to boast and said,… I hold to Paul, I hold to Apollo' TH 33.

14B.2 ***fatell rug Judith, Hester, Job, Jheremye, gans mere moy tus benegas ha benenas in testament coth a rug vsia gwyska yscar ha canfas garow*** 'that Judith, Esther, Job, Jeremiah, and many more holy men and women in the Old Testament used to wear sackcloth and rough canvas' TH 6a; ***A ra tus vsya offra bois ha dewas the re, rag purpos vith arall… ?*** 'Are people accustomed to offer food and drink to other people for any other purpose…?' TH 52a.

14B.3 ***indelle ty gargesen drok thym ty a russa*** 'thus, you glutton, you would do me harm' BM 2423-24; ***Te a'm grussa fuer forsoyth ha'm whyppya gans guelan vloyth*** 'You indeed would sober me indeed and would whip me with a bare rod' BK 359-60; ***ne setsan warnas algat, na russan rag meth an bys*** 'I would not have attacked you at all, I would not for shame in the world' BK 607-08; ***Mar kressa an dean deskez feer na gwellaz hemma e a*** *venga kavaz fraga e ouna en skreefa-composter* 'If that learned and wise man were to see this, he would find cause to emend it in orthography' NBoson.

14B.4 *fystyn ov duf whek avy* 'hasten my dear son-in-law' PC 989; *po 'ryȝ avî dvz ðv'n dvrraz* 'when I came to the door' JCH §43; *bewe pel ny eltegy* 'you cannot live long' BM 2570; *the ij cheplen kemer y genes thegy eredy* 'your two chaplains, take them with you indeed' BM 4034-35; *ef a'n kyf na ve va vas* 'he will get it, so that he will not be better' BK 2737; *na byth moy ken mam neffre es hyhy te na whela* 'nor any mother apart from her never seek again' PA 198d; *lemyn saw ol on nyny* 'now we all are healed' OM 2024; *Ha lagagow angie ve gerres ha angie oyah tel er'angye en noath: ha angye a wrovas delkyow figgez warbarth, ha wraze tho angye aprodnieo* 'And their eyes were opened and they knew they were naked; and they wove fig leaves together, and made aprons for themselves' Rowe.

14B.5 *yn havall thymma obma ymadge dean gwregaf shapya* 'like myself here I created man' CW 2523-24; *thum wyles neb a thue dy* 'to seek me who will come thither' BM 4295; *peys I say golsowogh a der dro* 'Peace I say; listen all around' CW 1431; *Hayl, arluth gay, uhal in ban yn bona fay!* 'Hail, fair lord, high up in very deed!' BK 1760-62; *Omden, gas the folneb! Serf Du avan!* 'Withdraw, leave your folly. Serve God above' BK 281-82; *e thesa deow Helias: onyn awartha, ha Helias awolas* 'there were two Elijahs: one above and Elijah below' SA 60; *pana abbys a ve twolys thyn dore, pana colyges, pana chauntreys a ve towlys then dore?* 'what abbeys were cast down, what colleges, what chantries have been cast down?' TH 40a; *yn pytt ma y wreth trega genaf ve a barthe wollas* 'in the pit you will dwell with me down below' CW 1722-23; *mas pub tra in den o treylys an pith awartha the wolas* 'but everything in man was turned upside down' TH 4; *Ke aberveth, te harlot! i'n preson in mysk prevas* 'Go in, you scoundrel! into the prison among the worms' BK 418-19; *eff a clomder hag a in kerth kepar ha skesse* 'he withers and departs like a shadow' TH 7; *na rellan ny cristonnyan desquethes agan honyn da ha virtus, war ves in sight an bys only* 'that we Christians should not show ourselves good and virtuous externally in the sight of the world only' TH 26a; *ny a res thyn desquethas agan dader war gy in golan* 'we must show our goodness internally in the heart' TH 26a; *y a rug corruptia hag ogasty a stoppyas in ban an pure blonogath, an lyvely fyntan a vewnans* 'they corrupted and almost stopped up the pure will, the lively fountain of life' TH 22; *Fyntan dek ema ryban* 'There is a fine spring nearby' BK 799; *eth e adre me ny won* 'whether he has gone from home I do not know' BM 3254.

14B.6 *Drefan ef the wul drog thim, ough, tomhas ow galarow!* 'Because he has done me wrong, alas, my sorrows have become intense' BK 3201-02; *nynges owne thym ahanas drefan bose mar deake tha face* 'I am not afraid of you because your face is so fair' CW 562-63; *ny bydgyaf bones gwelys gans mabe den in bys ma bew drefan om boos omskemynes* 'I cannot tolerate being seen by any man alive in this world because I am accursed' CW 1509-11; *ha der reson ha drefan e vos mer goyth govynnys, ef a leverys efan, e fethowgh why dybynnys* 'and because and since it was demanded so insolently, he said publicly that you would be beheaded' BK 2268-72; *dre reson y the justyfia aga honyn dre aga contyrfett benegitter therag an presens an bobill* 'because they justified themselves by their counterfeit sanctity before the presence of the people' TH 9; *henew the leverell an vnyuersall egglos, dre reson nag ussy ow lurkya in cornettow* 'that is to say, the universal church, because it does not lurk in corners' TH 31a.

14B.7 *Te gwas, py stat e 'th esta kyns te the thos thu'm pow ma?* 'You, fellow, what state were you in before you came to this my country?' BK 590-91; *Ow arlothas, kyns ys nos ny a ra thewhy duur-ros* 'My lady, before nightfall we will make your rose water' BK 2990-91; *ha wosa y pregoth in pontus* 'and after he preached in Pontus' TH 47; *A wosa y bos mab den vnwith graffys in Crist ha gwrys kevrennak ay virnans* 'After mankind was grafted into Christ and made partakers in his death' TH 51a; *sav me warlergh drehevel a's dyerbyn dyougel yn galile* 'but I after rising will meet you indeed in Galilee' PC 896-98; *Mar pewas Christ, me a grys, warlergh mirwall, ow du Jovyn a'n dathorthas der e ras* 'If Christ lived, I believe, after he died, my god Jove raised him up by his grace' BK 316-19.

14C.1 VOCABULARY

arlùth *m.,* **arlydhy** lord
assentya to assent (also **bos assentys**) agree
assûrya to assure
awel *f.* wind, weather
chair howl *m.,* **chairys howl** deck chair
cùssulya to advise
dystowgh *adv.* immediately
êthgweyth *adv.* eight times
furneth *m.* wisdom
golow *m.,* **golowys** light
hevleny *adv.* this year
i'n tor'-ma (< **i'n torn-ma**) at this time
knofen *f.,* **know** *coll.* nut

lendya to lend (followed by **dhe²**)
managh *m.,* **menegh** monk
me a res I must
muscok *adj.* insane
nebes *adj. & pron.* a little (followed by a plural noun)
passya to pass
pendhescador *m.,* **pendhescadoryon** head teacher, principal
stair *m.,* **stairys** stair
strêt *m.,* **strêtys** street
tôwlel to throw
tybyans *m.,* **tybyansow** opinion

14C.2 TRANSLATE INTO ENGLISH:

1 An venegh a wrug ùsya gwysca dyllas du ha pesy êthgweyth pùb jorna.
2 Ny wrug hy bythqweth côwsel orthyf arta dhia bàn wrug hy clôwes an fàls-whedhel uthyk-na.
3 Ny a wre mos dhe'n mor pùb hâv ha spêna dyw seythen ena.
4 Nyns yw hobma dha vyrgh dhejy. Ow myrgh jy yw hy.

5 Ny veu to a-uhon dhia bàn wrug agan chy coth codha dhe'n dor in nos an gwyns brâs.

6 An Arlùth a wra kemeres in kerdh oll agan pehosow hag ev a wra agan golhy ha ny a vëdh glân yn tien.

7 Y feu pùptra tôwlys an pëth awartha dhe woles gans an pendhescador nowyth.

8 Why a res leverel dhybm kyns dyberth pandra wrewgh why gelwel an flogh.

9 Kynth yw ow amowntyor terrys, ny wrama perna onen nowyth dre rêson me dhe vos re vohosak i'n tor'-ma.

10 Ev a wrug agan assûrya na wre va gwil drog vëth wàr agan pydn.

11 Nyns esof vy orth y drestya. Ev a wrug ûsya leverel hedna dhe bùbonen.

12 Y a wrug ûsya mos adro in dyllas coynt dhyworth chy dhe jy ha govyn mona ha taclow wheg orth an gentrevogyon.

13 A wrewgh whywhy gwil indella i'n dedhyow-na? Na wren, ny a wre gortos i'n chy ha gwary warbarth ha debry avallow ha know.

14 Ny a res mos aberveth i'n chy dystowgh dre rêson bos glaw poos ow codha.

15 Kyns ès ny dhe wil indella, martesen ny a wra miras orth an pùscas ow neyja alebma hag alena i'n ryver bian.

16 Yw hedna dha whans tejy? Te yw muscok. Re yeyn yw an awel hag y fëdh nos kyns ès ny dhe dhewheles.

17 Ny wrama mos alebma genes tejy. Yma golow an jëdh ogasty gyllys.

18 Ow hothman wheg, ny res dhis bos serrys genef. Ny a wra dos wàr dhelergh yn scon ha nena ny a wra sedha warbarth ryb an tan ha miras orth an bellwolok hag eva coref.

19 Yth esof owth ùnderstondya lebmyn te dhe gôwsel an gwiryoneth. Te re wrug ow hùssulya kyns lebmyn ha pùpprës te a wre leverel an gwiryoneth gans furneth.

20 Ny a wra kerdhes wàr nans dhe'n chy bian ryb an pons ha miras orth an ebron hag orth an bobel ow passya i'n strêt ahës.

14C.3 TRANSLATE INTO CORNISH:

1 She used to bake bread every morning and on Sundays she baked a cake as well.

2 He said he was coming this evening but I do not believe him.

3 Would you steal the money? No, I would not.

4 Somebody has been sitting in my chair and broken it completely.

5 We will go down to the beach and sit on the deck-chairs and look at the sea.

6 She went out but she has not come in again.

7 Is that your horse standing under the tree? No, it is your horse.

8 When I left the house, everybody was asleep. When I returned, everybody was still asleep.

9 You must clean your room a little before you go to school.

10 I have not the time because I am late.

11 I will do it well after I come home this afternoon.

12 The vicar used to visit us a lot last year. He has not come down to the house once this year.

13 After reading that book, I am sure that he is completely mistaken.

14 I say that, because I now understand the truth of the mater.

15 That is only your opinion. I do not agree, and my opinion is not always wrong.

16 I fell down the stairs (**an stairys wàr nans**) last year and hurt my leg. I have been feeling pain ever since (*after*).

17 I will arise (**sevel**) and go to my father and will confess my sins to him.

18 I cannot (**nyns of abyl dhe**) do anything today because my computer is broken.

19 Why don't you buy a new one? I don't buy a new one because I am too poor.

20 I will lend you my machine. It is new and very good.

PYMTHEGVES DYSCANS
FIFTEENTH LESSON

15A.1 RELATIVE SENTENCES

In English relative (or adjectival) clauses can be introduced by a relative pronoun 'which', 'who(m)', 'that', or without any pronoun at all. One can therefore say: 'Show me the shoes that you will wear', 'Show me the shoes which you'll wear', or 'Show me the shoes you'll wear'. In Cornish such sentences require the relative particle **a²**. We have already met this particle in such expressions as **me a wrug** 'I did' (literally: it is I that did). Cornish therefore says:

> **Yw an re-na an eskyjyow a wrêta gwysca?** Are these the shoes that you will wear?
>
> **Hèm yw an lyther a wrug avy recêva hedhyw** This is the letter I received today
>
> **A ny wrusta gweles an dhescadores yonk a wre desky dha vyrgh warleny?** Did you not see the teacher who taught your daughter last year?

Negative relative clauses are introduced by **na(g)**: **Yw an re-ma an eskyjyow na wrêta gwysca?** 'Are these the shoes you will not wear'; **Hy yw an dhescadores na wrug desky ow myrgh** 'She is the teacher who did not teach my daughter'.

15A.2 RELATIVE CLAUSES WITH *BOS*

We have seen from expressions like **ev yw dha vroder** 'he is your brother' (but **ev a veu shyndys** 'he was injured') that the relative particle is not expressed with forms of **bos** 'to be' if they begin with a vowel. This is a general rule in Cornish (and is also true for parts of the verb **mos** 'to go', which we have not yet met; see 16A.4). One therefore says:

Yth esen ow côwsel orth an Vretones esa obma myttyn hedhyw
I was talking to the Breton woman who was here this morning
Pyw a wrug debry an desen o pebys gans Jenefer? Who ate the
cake which had been baked by Jennifer?

15A.3 INDIRECT RELATIVE SENTENCES

In the English sentence 'These are the shoes that you will wear
tomorrow', the phrase 'the shoes' is said to be the antecedent of the relative
verb 'you will wear'. So far our relative sentences in Cornish have been
confined to those in which the antecedent is either i) the logical subject of
the relative verb or ii) the logical object of the relative verb:

i) **Yth o an den uthyk-na a wrug assaya ladra ow sagh** It was that
   awful man who tried to steal my bag
ii) **Lavar dhybm oll an taclow a wrêta derivas dhe vowysy an
   class** Tell me all the things you will tell the girls of the class.

Quite frequently, however, the relationship between the antecedent and
the verb will be less direct, for example in the English sentences:

i) Is that the place where you saw him?
ii) This is the hook I left my coat on.
iii) Mary is the girl whose brother is in hospital.
iv) I have in my hand the hammer I mended the chair with.

These are known as indirect relative sentences. When the relative
pronoun is 'the place where', 'the shop where', 'the school where' or the
relative clause is simply introduced by 'in which', the relative particle used
in Cornish is **may**[5]:

i) **Yw hedna an tyller may whrussys y weles?** Is that where you
   saw him?

And similarly one would say **Hèm yw an shoppa may whrug avy y
berna** 'This is the shop where I bought it', **Yma va ow mos dhe'n scol
may feuma ow honen deskys** 'He goes to the school where I myself
was taught' and **Pòr dhrog yw an stât mayth eson ny** 'Very bad is the
state in which we are'.

The the case of sentences ii–iv listed above classical Middle Cornish uses
the particle **may**[5]**(th)** and an appropriate prepositional pronoun if
necessary:

ii) **Hèm yw an bagh may whrug vy gasa ow hôta warnodho** This is the hook I left my coat on.

iii) **Maria yw an vowes mayth usy hy broder i'n clâvjy** Mary is the girl whose brother is in hospital.

iv) **Yma i'm dorn genef an morthol may whrug avy êwna an chair ganso** I have in my hand the hammer I mended the chair with.

Often, however, **may⁵(th)** is replaced by **a²** in indirect relative sentences. Instead, therefore, of saying **Tristan yw an maw may whrug avy côwsel orto** 'Tristan is the boy I spoke to', one can say **Tristan yw an maw a wrug avy côwsel orto**. Notice that in indirect relative sentences of this kind, the particle **a²** is omitted before vowels in the verbs **bos** and **mos**, e.g. **an den usy ow tos tro ha'n scol** 'the man who is coming towards the school'.

15A.4 *NEB* AS A RELATIVE PRONOUN

Neb 'who' + **a²** can function as a relative pronoun. One can therefore construct direct relative sentences like the following:

Yth esa hy ow côwsel orth an vowes neb a wrug gwainya an pris She was talking to the girl who won the prize

Ev yw an pronter neb a wra agan demedhy He is the priest who will marry us.

Since **neb** can be preceded by a preposition, it may be used in indirect relative clauses:

Yw hyhy an venyn dhyworth neb a wrusta cafos an bows? Is she the woman you got the dress from?

An re-na yw an dus warbarth gans neb a wrussyn ny dos obma Those are the people together with whom we came here.

Or **neb may** 'to whom' can also be used: **an vowes neb may feu rës an pris** 'the girl to whom the prize was given'. The use of **neb** as a relative pronoun is probably based to some degree on English syntax, and is widely used in the revived language. It does, however, appear a little un-Celtic.

15A.5 'THE ONE … THE OTHER'

In Cornish 'the one … the other' is expressed by **an eyl … y gela**: **yth esa an eyl anodhans ow qweskel y gela** 'the one of them was hitting the other'. **Y gela** literally means 'his fellow, his companion', where the root form **kyla**, **kela** is related to Welsh *cilydd* 'companion' and Irish *céile* 'companion'. Middle Cornish had a form **hy ben**, that was used instead of **y gela**, if both terms were feminine.

15A.6 'AROUND, ABOUT'

'Around' as an adverb is translated in Cornish by **adro** or **ader dro**: **yma an whedhel-na ow mos adro** 'that story is going around'.

When a preposition, 'around, about' in Cornish is rendered **adro dhe**: **yma lies chy coth adro dhe'n eglos** 'there are many old houses around the church'; **yth esa oll hy flehes adro dhedhy** 'All her children were around her'.

In kerhyn also means 'around, about': **yth esa an hirwarrow ow neyja in kerhyn an gantol** 'the cranefly was flying around the candle'. When used with personal pronouns **in kerhyn** is inflected as follows:

1 *sg.* **i'm kerhyn**
2 *sg.* **i'th kerhyn**
3 *sg. m.* **in y gerhyn**; 3 *sg. f.* **in hy herhyn**
1 *pl.* **i'gan kerhyn**
2 *pl.* **i'gas kerhyn**
3 *pl.* **i'ga herhyn**.

Both **adro dhe²** and **in kerhyn** are used when talking about items of clothing: **an bows adro dhedhy** 'the dress she is/was wearing'; **an eskyjyow adro dhe'm treys** 'the shoes upon my feet'; **an dyllas i'gan kerhyn** 'the clothes we are/were wearing'.

15A.7 'ABOUT, CONCERNING'

When 'about' means 'concerning', it can be translated **adro dhe²**, cf. the title of Nicholas Boson's tract *Nebes Geryow adro dhe Gernowek* 'A Few Words about Cornish'.

Another way of saying 'about' is by using the preposition **a²**, for example, **me a glowas a'n drog-labm myttyn hedhyw** 'I heard about the accident this morning'.

The commonest way of rendering 'about, concerning' in Cornish of the sixteenth century is to use the English borrowing **ow tùchya** 'touching' and to say, for example, **nyns esof vy owth ùnderstondya tra vëth ow tùchya an mater** 'I do not understand anything about the matter'; **ny wrug ev clôwes ger vëth ow tùchya dh'y vroder** 'he has not heard a word about his brother'. It will be noticed from these examples that **ow tùchya** is sometimes followed by **dhe²**, and sometimes not.

15A.8 *IN KEVER*

Since the early days of the Cornish revival the expression **in kever** has been used to mean 'about, concerning' in such expressions as ***in kever an mater-ma** 'about this matter' and ***in kever hemma** 'about this'. Neither phrase can really be justified by the usage of traditional Cornish.

In the first place, **in kever** is very rare indeed in traditional Cornish. There are four examples in Middle Cornish and one in Late Cornish. In the second place, **in kever** never means 'about, concerning', but rather 'with respect to, regarding, towards'. In the third place **in kever** is never used with anything other than a possessive adjective. This is the crucial point, since there are other places in Cornish syntax where prepositions are used exclusively with possessive adjectives or where the prepositional governance of nouns and of personal pronouns differ (see the next section 15A.9).

Me re beu re asper in y gever 'I have been too harsh with him' can be justified from the texts; **me a vydn leverel dhis pùptra *in kever an lyver-ma** 'I will tell you everything about this book' is without warrant and is best rephrased.

At 15B.8 below I cite and translate all five instances of **in kever** from the Cornish texts.

15A.9 *BYS IN, BYS DHE; A'M GOVYS*

Bys means 'until' and it lenites in the expressions **bys vycken** 'for ever', **bys venary** 'for ever', **bys venytha** 'for ever' and also in **bys worfen bës** 'until the end of the world'. **Bys in** means 'to, up to' and is used before nouns and proper nouns: **bys in Pilat** 'to Pilate', **bys i'n meneth** 'to the mountain', **bys in Cambron** 'to Camborne', **bys i'n empydnyon** 'into the brain'. When governing a personal pronoun, however, **bys in** becomes **bys dhe**, i.e. **bys dhybmo, bys dhis, bys dhodho**, etc.

Such expressions as **bys *dhe Loundres** 'to London' are without warrant and are best replaced by **bys in Loundres** (see further 36A.1).

The expression **a'm govys** 'for my sake' is attested four times in traditional Cornish. There are no instances of the prepositional phrase with any other person, though if we had more Cornish we might possibly find ***a'y wovys** 'for his sake', for example. Like **in kever**, **a'm govys** seems to have been confined to use with possessive adjectives. The ordinary way of saying of 'for the sake of' in Cornish, both with nouns and pronouns, is

rag kerensa: **rag agan kerensa** 'for our sake' and **rag kerensa an tavas** 'for the sake of the language' are both admissible.

15B EXAMPLES FROM THE TEXTS

15B.1 *Pegh o an pith a rug then tas a neff humbrak mabden in mes a baradise. pegh o an pith a rug then kyge stryvya gans an spuris han spuris warbyn an kyge. pegh o an pith a thros mabden the suffra clevas, gwanegreth, deseyses ha infirmytes.* 'Sin was that which made the Father of heaven drive man out of paradise. Sin was what made the flesh strive against the spirit and the spirit against the flesh. Sin was what brought man kind to suffer illness, weakness, diseases and infirmities' TH 3.

15B.2 *An kensa tra vgy ow tuchia an creacion a mab den* 'the first thing which concerns the creation of mankind' TH 1; *yth ew havall the henna vsy agan Savyour ow leverall thyn* 'it is similar to that which our Saviour tells us' TH 19a; *po theworth an re na vsy ow swarvya theworth an Catholyk egglos* 'or from those who depart from the Catholic Church' TH 38; *an eal ega in wethan y cowses gyrryow efan* 'the angel who was in the tree spoke expansive words' CW 827-28.

15B.3.1 *ogh gouy rak ow map ker the weles yn keth vaner may whelaf lemmyn dyghtys* 'oh, woe is me, for my dear son to see you in the very way in which I see you now treated' PC 2945; *in mar ver dell ons y aga dew an wrethyan dretho mayth o res the lynyath mab den dos* 'inasmuch as they both are the root through which it was necessary for the lineage of mankind to come' TH 4a; *oll an drog pobill erell, inweth Jewys, turkys bo pobill discrysik ha bestas gwyls, a ra cara an re ew aga cothmans ha dretha mayth usans ow pewa* 'all the other evil people, Jews also and Turks and unbelievers and wild animals, love those who are their friends and through whom they live' TH 24.

15B.3.2 *Marow yv pup tra ese spyrys a vewnans ynno* 'dead is everything in which there was the spirit of life' OM 1089-90; *han re esa ow pewa in tyrmyn coth in dan an la han testament coith* 'and those who lived in ancient times under the law an the Old Testament' TH 27

15B.4 *Na thegough sor yn golon war neb a vyn ow sawye* 'Do not bear anger in your heart against her who will salve me' PA 37a; *neb may fe moghya geffys a gar moghye yn pup le* 'he to whom most was forgiven loves the most everywhere' PC 513; *Myschef re bo guelys cler war neb a'th tros in awher* 'May mischief be clearly seen upon him who brought you into grief' BK 3150-51; *eff a ve promysiis thethans y ha thega successors neb a ve, neb ew, ha neb a vith in egglos, neb yma an spurissans, hag a vith triges rag neffra* 'he was promised to them and to their successors, who were, who are and who will be in the church, in whom the Holy Spirit is and will dwell for ever' TH 36a.

15B.5 *mar posse an eyll tenewen rag y scoth hy a grevye* 'if he leant to the one side, it hurt him because of his shoulder' PA 205c; *yn fen kymmer an yl pen* 'take up one end strongly' OM 2787; *Du a vyn shamys ow bos ha'm gar syttys der hi ben* 'God wants me to be shamed with my leg crossed over the other' BK 3301-02; *An rema ew contrary an neyll thy gela* 'These things are contrary one to the other' TH 16a; *an neyll ew the lell cregy, han gela the vewa compys ha in lyndury* 'the one is to believe faithfully, and the other is to live right and in fidelity' TH 16a-17; *may teffa pub den ha benyn cara du drys pub tra, ha cara peb y gyla* 'if every man and woman were to love God above all things and if everyone loved each other' TH 22a; *ann eyl hennew owne, hay gela ew feith* 'one of these is fear and the other is faith' TH 51a.

15B.6 *cafus an bovs na hep gvry vs y'th kerghyn me a vyn* 'I will have that seemless robe that is about you' RD 1921-22; *dus oma ese yth cheer guyske the dylles yth kerhyn* 'come here, sit in your chair, put your garments on' BM 3001-02; *queth ruth certan purpur pal the wyske adro thotho* 'a crimson robe indeed, a purple mantle, for him to wear' PC 2128-29; *me a thuk curyn a spern nep try our adro thu'm pen* 'I bore a crown of thorns for about three hours around my head' RD 2554-55.

15B.7 *Tra an par na me a glowaz dro tho an karack Mean Omber* 'I heard something similar about the rock Mean Omber' NBoson; *Ma ko them cavaz tra a'n par ma en lever Arlyth an Menneth dro tho e deskanz Latten* 'I remember finding something of this kind in Montaigne's book about his Latin education' NBoson; *An rema ew an very gyrryow agan savyoure ow tochia an kerensa agan kyscristian* 'The following are the very words of our saviour about the love of our fellow Christian' TH 22; *why a wore lymmyn pandra ew an lell crygyans ow tochia thyn sacrament an aulter* 'you now know what is the correct belief concerning the sacrament of the altar' TH 58;

15B.8 *whet kerghough thy'mmo pilat yn y geuer del fuef badt* 'still fetch Pilate to me as I have been in error regarding him' RD 1885-86; *me a vyn pesy gevyans boys mar thyek yth keuer* 'I will beg forgiveness for being so lax towards you' BM 3359-60; *maria re buff re logh in the gever* 'Mary, I have been too disrespectful towards you' BM 3798-88; *hag amyndya ef a ra y'th kevar del vo reson* 'and he will be better towards you as would be reasonable' BK 916-17; *ev a dhelledzhas an termen mal ða va prêv erra e urêg ʒuiꞇa kýmpez et i ʒever: erra po nag erra* 'he stretched out the time so that he could prove whether his wife was keeping faithful towards him, was she or not' JCH §39.

15B.9 *reys yv thy's mones ytho bys yn egip the pharo* 'therefore you must go to Egypt to Pharaoh' OM 1420-21; *bys yn ierusalem ke the vyghtern dauid lauar* 'go to Jerusalem, say to King David' OM 1928-29; *me agis gyd rum ena pur uskis bys in cambron* 'upon my soul, I will guide you very quickly to Camborne' BM 981-82; *theworth Kewnans an Velyn bys in Tremustel Penpol* 'from Kewnans an Velyn to Tremustel by Penpol' BK 1197-98; *Ow canhas ker, ke thegy bys in Rom gans pen Lucy* 'My dear messenger, go to Rome with the head of Lucius' BK 2838-39; *saw gvraa vn dra a'm govys* 'but do one thing for my sake' OM 76; *venytha gorthyys re by del russys moy a'n govys* OM 107-08; *na gemerre denvyth greff na duwen am govys vy* 'let no one be grieved or sorrowful for my sake' BM 405-

06; *thywhywhy y fye cam boys lethys am govys vy* 'it would be a wrong for you to be killed for my sake' BM 1654-55; *ny fue ragtho y honan yn gothefys ef certan mas rak kerenge map den* 'it was not for himself he suffered it but for the sake of mankind' RD 3226-28; *kyn na rella agan yskar deservya the gafus gyvyans rag y gerensa y honyn, ny a gothyn gava thotha rag kerensa du* 'though our enemy should not deserve forgiveness for his own sake, we should forgive him for God's sake' TH 24; *mars esta worth y wull rag kerensa an dus* 'if you do it for the sake of the people' TH 48.

15C.1 VOCABULARY

bës *m.*, **bysow** world
Bretones *f.*, **Bretonesow** Breton woman
conyn *m.*, **conynas** rabbit
dauns *m.*, **daunycyow** dance
entra to enter, go in (takes **in**)
an eyl ... y gela the one ... the other; **an eyl ... hy ben** the one ... the other (with fem. nouns)
gorfen *m.*, end. **gorfen an bës** the end of the world
gorra own in to frighten

in gwir *adv.* in truth, indeed
lowarn *m.*, **lewern** fox
mab *m.* **den** mankind
namnygen *adv.* just now
palas to dig
prëv *m.*, **prevas** insect
sagh *m.*, **seghyer** bag
son *m.*, **sonyow** sound, noise
an termyn a dheu future
toll *m.*, **tell** hole
yn uthyk *adv.* terribly

15C.2 TRANSLATE INTO ENGLISH:

1 Pëth esta ow tyby adro dhe'n descador nowyth?
2 Nyns eus tybyans vëth genef ow tùchya dhodho.
3 A wrug hy dysqwedhes dhis an bows a wra hy gwysca haneth?
4 Hòn yw an venyn yw hy mab clâv.
5 Ea, yth esen ow côwsel orty namnygen. Yma myrgh dhedhy inwedh a wres gwary gensy warleny.
6 Res yw dhis miras orth an côta-ma i'm kerhyn. Usy va worth dha blêsya?
7 Yw hedna an toll may whrug an conyn entra? Nag yw, hèn yw an toll a wrussyn ny palas de.
8 Me a wrug degea an fenester may whrug an hirwarrow entra.
9 Usy prevas ow corra own inos? Nag usons, saw nyns esof vy ow cara an re-na a wra son brâs.
10 Pëth yw hanow an vowes vian a wrusta côwsel orty namnygen?
11 Esta owth ùnderstondya an taclow a wrug avy leverel dhis? Nebes anodhans.
12 Prag na vedhys ow tos dhe'n waryva genen ny? Ny vedhaf ow tos dre rêson nag esof ow cara an taclow a vedhowgh why ow leverel ow tùchya an gwary.

13 Yma lies tra i'n bës-ma nag eson ny owth ùnderstondya marnas radn vian anodhans.

14 Res yw dhis leverel dhybm pana shoppa may whrama cafos dyllas dâ.

15 An arlodhes esen vy ow côwsel orty, hy yw gwreg an pronter.

16 Pòr deg yw hy. Yma lies den yonk adro dhedhy.

17 Res yw dhis leverel dhybm pyw a wrusta clôwes an whedhel uthyk-na dhyworto.

18 Ny wrug avy clôwes an whedhel dhyworth den vëth. Y redya a wruga.

19 Hèm yw an chair a wrug hy gasa hy sagh warnodho.

20 Nyns usy va ena lebmyn. Res yw govyn orth an flehes adro dhodho.

15C.3 TRANSLATE INTO CORNISH:

1 Who was that lady who was talking to you just now? That was the principal's wife.

2 Is this the hole you dug yourself? No, it is the hole the rabbit went into.

3 You must show me the shoes you will be wearing at the dance tonight.

4 I will not show them to you, because I have not bought them yet.

5 This is the school I used to go to when I was a boy.

6 What is the name of the insect that is flying around the light? It is a daddy-long-legs.

7 I will tell you something else about it. When you catch it in your hands, it leaves a leg behind.

8 That is odd. Are there many insects that do such a thing?

9 Over there I see the businessman (**marchont**) you bought your car from.

10 Every day I pass the house he lives in.

11 I will tell you a little story about two foxes.

12 One said to the other, "We must go to the wood to get some food for our hungry children."

13 Is Mary the girl whose brother is in hospital?

14 Yes, her brother is the little boy who fell down the school stairs the day before yesterday.

15 You have got some odd opinions about many things. What kind of books do you get them from?

16 I read a book recently that frightened me terribly.

17 What was the book about? It was about the end of the world.

18 Do you believe everything that you read in books and newspapers?

19 I believe a few of them. I don't go around believing everything.

20 I was talking yesterday to a man who has written a long book about the future of mankind. I though he was very silly indeed.

WHÊTEGVES DYSCANS
SIXTEENTH LESSON

16A.1 THE PRESENT OF *DOS* 'TO COME'

The verb **dos** (also **dones**) 'to come' is important both as a full verb and as an auxiliary. Its present-future is conjugated as follows:

1 *sg.* **deuv, deuma, dov**	1 *pl.* **deun**
2 *sg.* **deuth, deuta**	2 *pl.* **dewgh**
3 *sg.* **deu**	3 *pl.* **dôns, downs**.

The **eu** in this verb is frequently unrounded and pronounced like **e**: **deu** [dø:]~[de:].

16A.2 THE PRETERITE OF *DOS*

This is conjugated as follows:

1 *sg.* **deuth**	1 *pl.* **deuthon**
2 *sg.* **deuthys**	2 *pl.* **deuthowgh**
3 *sg.* **deuth**	3 *pl.* **deuthons**

A perfect can be made from this tense and the perfective particle **re²**: **me re dheuth** 'I have come'.

16A.3 THE IMPERFECT AND CONDITIONAL OF *DOS*

The imperfect of **dos** is conjugated as follows:

1 *sg.* **deun**	1 *pl.* **deun**
2 *sg.* **deus**	2 *pl.* **dewgh**
3 *sg.* **do**	3 *pl.* **deuns**

The conditional of **dos** is conjugated as follows:

1 *sg.* **dothyen**	1 *pl.* **dothya**
2 *sg.* **dothyes**	2 *pl.* **dothyewgh**
3 *sg.* **dothya**	3 *pl.* **dothyens**

Notice that no example of the conditional of **dos** is found later than the fifteenth century.

16A.4 *MOS* 'TO GO'
This verb is similar in many ways to **dos**. It is inflected as follows:

Verbal noun
mos or **mones**

Present-future
1 *sg.* **av, ama**	1 *pl.* **en**
2 *sg.* **êth**	2 *pl.* **ewgh**
3 *sg.* **â**	3 *pl.* **ôns**

Imperfect
1 *sg.* **en**	1 *pl.* **en**
2 *sg.* **es**	2 *pl.* **ewgh**
3 *sg.* **ê**	3 *pl.* **êns**

Preterite
1 *sg.* **yth**	1 *pl.* **ethon**
2 *sg.* **ythys**	2 *pl.* **ethowgh**
3 *sg.* **êth** (LC **gêth** < **nag êth**)	3 *pl.* **ethons**

Conditional
1 *sg.* **gylsen**	1 *pl.* **gylsen**
2 *sg.* **gylses**	2 *pl.* **galsewgh**
3 *sg.* **galsa**	3 *pl.* **galsens**

Note that **ny** is **nyns** (or **nynj**) before vowels with this verb: **nyns av, nyns êth**, etc. The perfective particle used with the preterite is **res**, not **re**: **ev res êth** 'he has gone'. For another perfect of **dos** and **mos** see 25A.3 below. The idiom **mos ragtho**, literally 'to go for it', means 'to warrant, to guarantee'.

NOTE: First, that the conditional is not attested after the fifteenth century, and is very rare even in Cornish earlier than that. Second, that John Tregear uses **a²** with the preterite of **mos**: *eff a eth thy virnans* 'he went to his death' TH.

16A.5 REAL CONDITIONS

Real conditions are those in which the condition is, or was, a real possibility, rather than a supposition. 'You can have these, if you want', 'If he tries to escape, don't let him', 'It's odd their shoes weren't muddy, if they came over the fields', are all real conditions.

Real conditions are expressed in Cornish by means of the conjunctions **mar⁴**, **mara⁴** 'if'. **Mar** and **mara** become **mars** an **maras** respectively before vowels. If the main verb in the *if*-clause (or protasis) is future in sense, the future of the verb **bos** must be used:

Mars eus den vëth i'n rom, ple ma va kelys? If somebody is in the room, where is he hidden?
Mar pëdh mab genen, ny a wra y elwel Jowan If we have (i.e. will have) a son, we will call him John.

Negative real conditions can be made with **mar ny**: **mar ny vedhyn ny ena** 'if we are not there'. **Marnas**, **ma's** 'unless' can also be used:

Ny yllyn ny convedhes an eyl y gela ma's ny a gows an keth tavas 'We cannot understand each other unless we speak the same language'.

The present subjunctive is often used in such cases (see 19A.2 vii below).

16A.6 *DOS* IN CONDITIONAL SENTENCES

Conditions are frequently expressed in Cornish by using the verb **dos** as an auxiliary, with the main verb of the *if*-clause (or protasis) expressed by **ha** 'and' followed by the verbal noun:

Mar teu an mytern hag ôstya obma, ny a vëdh pòr lowen If the king lodges here, we will be very happy
Mar teun ny ha hâtya agan broder, pehadoryon on ny If we hate or brother, we are sinners

Mar tewgh ha'gan vysytya trenja, ny a wra pobas tesen vrâs ragowgh If you visit us the day after tomorrow, we will bake a big cake for you.

In such cases the verb need not be put into a special future tense, since **deuv**, **deuth**, **deu** is both present and future.

16B EXAMPLES FROM THE TEXTS

16B.1 *a thew ple tof na ple yth af* 'O God where will I come or where will I go?' RD 1665; *oll ny a thue the helma* 'we all will come to this' BM 4540; *A bele teta the'n tyr?* 'Whence do you come to the country?' BK 80; *y tuan war nans* 'we shall come down' BK 771.

16B.2–3 *ha ken ny thothye the'n nef* 'and otherwise he would not come to heaven' RD 2450; *ha fattel duthys yn ban* 'and how you came up' RD 2568; *rag henna e tuth thewhy* 'therefore we have come to you' BK 1597; *Me re deth thys gans an ger* 'I have come to you at the word' BK 2592; *Ny re dueth a lyas gwlas* 'we have come from many lands' BK 2611.

16B.4 *thage herhes mars ama* 'if I go to fetch them' BM 3288; *ny a yl boys morethek war the lergh ha herethek mars eth theorthen in suer* 'we can be mournful after you and full of sorrow if you indeed depart from us' BM 4313-15; *Nyns a ancof* 'Forgetting will not happen' (lit. 'go') BK 2065; *Mars eugh the Arthor por wyr* 'If in very truth you go to Arthur' BK 1357; *py le re seth* 'where he has gone' RD 789.

16B.5 *Nyns ew plagys ha punyshmentys, teball anetha aga honyn, mar pethans kemerys in forth tha* 'Plagues and punishments are not evil in themselves, if they are taken in good part' TH 24a; *Mar petha ve lyftys in ban theworth an nore, me a vyn tenna pub tra oll thymmo ve ow honyn* 'If I am lifted up from the earth, I will draw all things to myself' TH 53; *ha te a vith ef heb mar, mar pyth o'm gallus evy* 'and of course you shall have it, if it is in my power' BK 1077-78; *Freth y feth gweregys, mar peth rys dos the henna* 'And he will be aided vigorously, if it be necessary to come to that' BK 1846-47.

16B.6 *mar tema disquethas theugh certyn tacclow arall* 'if I show you certain other things' SA 60; *rag mar tema ha rowtya* 'for if I happen to domineer' BK 1639; *mar tene ny consyddra hag vnderstondia in ta* 'if we consider and understand well' TH 10; *Rag mar tewgh why ha cara an re vsy worth agys cara why* 'For if you love those who love you' TH 22; *mar tewgh why gylwall thegys remembrans* 'If you call to your remembrance' TH 36; *mar towns y ha suffra du the vos offendys* 'if they allow God to be offended' TH 25.

16C.1 VOCABULARY

abma to kiss
confessya to confess
denaha to deny
dyscans *m.* teaching
glanhe to clean
hager-awel *f.* bad weather
knoukya to knock, to strike
our *m.*, **ourys** hour
pardona to pardon, to forgive
　(takes direct object)

perthy cov to remember (takes **a²**)
pobel *f.*, **poblow** people
poynt *m.*, **poyntys** point; (after
　negative verb) at all
remembra to remember
reqwîrya to require
tewolgow *abs. pl.* darkness
wolcùbma to welcome

16C.2 TRANSLATE INTO ENGLISH:

1 An creswas a dheuth dhe'n chy hag ev a wrug knoukya wàr an daras.

2 A dheuta genef? Na dheuv, re vysy vedhaf.

3 Ev res êth solabrës. Pleth êth ev?

4 Pàn dheuthys aberth i'n sodhva, pyw esa obma? Nyns esov vy ow remembra.

5 Mar teu va ha terry an daras, pleth en ny?

6 Ny dhowns ajy. Res vêdh dhedhans mos tre adermyn kyns ès dos an nos.

7 Mar pëdh mab genen, pandra wren ny y elwel?

8 Mara teun ny ha denaha agan Arlùth, a wra va agan pardona?

9 Why re wrug clôwes pandra vedha leverys i'n dedhyow coth ha dyscans an termyn res êth.

10 Pandra wrêta mar teuma hag abma dhis?

11 Ev a dho obma pùb jorna, saw ny wre pobel an tyller y wolcùbma poynt.

12 Nyns ama tre wàr an kyttryn, dre rêson na vëdh kyttryn obma bys pedn try our.

13 Me â genes, mar teuta ha'y reqwîrya dhyworthyf.

14 Ev ê dy y honen oll.

15 Mars eus den vëth i'n nessa rom, prag nag usy va ow qwil son vëth?

16 Mar pëdh den vëth i'n rom, ny â dhe gen tyller rag côwsel an eyl orth y gela.

17 Mar tewgh why ha gwil neppyth kepar ha hedna, i'n eur-na an descador a vëdh pòr serrys genen.

18 Ny wra va dos obma arta, mar teun ny ha bos dyscortes dhodho.

19 Mar ny vedhys obma, res vëdh dhybm mos dy hebos.

20 Mar teun ny ha'y hâtya, ev a wra agan hâtya nyny.

16C.3 TRANSLATE INTO CORNISH:

1 Where shall we go after the house falls down?

2 If the house falls down, you mean.

3 I used to go to that school when I was young.

4 She says she will not come to visit us ever again, because she does not like the food we eat.

5 If we say we have no sin, the truth is not in us.

6 But if we confess our sins, he will pardon us and will not remember all our evil deeds.

7 If the bad weather comes soon, we will be ready for it.

8 If the sun does not shine tomorrow, we will not go to the beach.

9 Where will you go then? We'll go to town on the train.

10 When will you come home? Before the darkness falls.

11 If anyone does that again, the teacher will be very angry with him.

12 When she finally came home, the children were all asleep (**ow cùsca**) in bed.

13 They will not buy the house, if you do not clean the place up.

14 If I tell you the truth, will you believe me?

15 Where did you all go yesterday? We did not go anywhere. We stayed at home.

16 She went into the room and came out again immediately.

17 We went to the church in the village every Sunday.

18 If you look hard enough, you will see a face in the clouds.

19 Will you come home with me tonight and meet my mother and father?

20 Yes, I will, if you so desire.

SEYTEGVES DYSCANS
SEVENTEENTH LESSON

17A.1 THE INFLECTION OF THE REGULAR VERB

We have given a number of tenses of **bos**, **gwil**, **dos** and **mos**.

Any Cornish verb can have its own inflected forms, though such forms are relatively rare, given the tendency of the language to use auxiliaries. The verb most commonly used as a model for inflection is **cara** 'to love'. It conjugates as follows:

Verbal noun	Verbal adjective
cara	**kerys**

Present
1 *sg.* **caraf**
2 *sg.* **keryth, kerta**, **kerys**
3 *sg.* **car**

1 *pl.* **keryn**
2 *pl.* **kerowgh**
3 *pl.* **carons**

Imperfect
1 *sg.* **caren**
2 *sg.* **cares**
3 *sg.* **cara**

1 *pl.* **caren**
2 *pl.* **carewgh**
3 *pl.* **carens**

Preterite
1 *sg.* **kerys**
2 *sg.* **kersys**
3 *sg.* **caras**

1 *pl.* **kersyn**
2 *pl.* **kersowgh**
3 *pl.* **carsons**

Conditional
1 *sg.* **carsen**
2 *sg.* **carses**
3 *sg.* **carsa**

1 *pl.* **carsen**
2 *pl.* **carsewgh**
3 *pl.* **carsens**

The subjunctive and the imperative are discussed at 19A.1–4 and 22A.1–6 respectively.

17A.2 THE VERBAL NOUN

The commonest ending of the verbal noun is **-a** (**triga** 'to dwell', **scrifa** 'to write', **cana** 'to sing', **whetha** 'to blow'). There are, however, a number of other endings, for example **-es** (**gweles** 'to see', **clôwes** 'to hear', **kemeres** 'to take'); **-os** (**gallos** 'to be able', **cafos** 'to get', **gortos** 'to wait'), **-as** (**miras** 'to look', **knyvyas** 'to shear'); **-y** (**perthy** 'to bear', **kelly** 'to lose', **tylly** 'to pay'); **-ya**, which is usual in borrowings (e.g. **exaltya** 'to exalt', **offendya** 'to offend', **forsâkya** 'to forsake', **trailya** 'to turn'). The borrowing for 'to wait, to expect' has a stem **gwait-**, but its verbal noun is **gwetyas**.

> NOTE: **cawas** 'to get' is a variant of **cafos** and in later Cornish it seems to acquire a permanently lenited initial to give **gawas**. **Gwetyas** in the later language has a permanently provected initial and appears as **qwatyes, qwachas**.

The verbal noun, although it functions as an infinitive, is in fact a noun. As we have already seen, it takes possessive adjectives to express the direct object: **me a vydn hy gweles** 'I will see her', **res yw y wil** 'it must be done'. The verbal noun can also be the subject of a verb: **gwary wheg yw gwary teg** 'gentle play is good play'.

17A.3 THE PRESENT-FUTURE

One should remember that the present-future is much more frequently future than present in sense. **Me a wra** means 'I will do' rather than 'I do'. 'I do' is usually **yth esof ow qwil**.

A few verbs have a special future forms in the earlier texts. These include **gwelvyth, gwelyth** 'he will see'; **clôwyth** 'he will hear'; **carvyth** 'he will love', **prenvyth** 'he will pay for it' and **gyllvyth** 'he will be able'. Such forms are not common and are replaced in the later language by **a vydn gweles, a vydn clôwes**, etc.

The ending of the 2 *sg.* of the present-future was originally **-yth**, but by the sixteenth century this had been reshaped on the basis of **os** 'you are', to give **-ys**. Even so the earlier form is used with the suffixed pronoun to produce such forms as **gylta** (< **gyllyth + ta**) 'you can' ; **mynta** (**mynnyth + ta**) 'you wish and **gwelta** (< **gwelyth + ta**) 'you see'.

Many verbs have **a** in the stem in the first singular but **e** or **y** in the second and third person singular: **cafaf** 'I get', but 2 *sg.* and 3 *sg.* **kefyth**, **kyv**; **savaf** 'I stand' but 2 *sg.* **sevyth** and 3 *sg.* **sev**; **lavaraf** 'I say', but 2 *sg.* **leveryth**, and 3 *sg.* **lever**. From the sixteenth century onwards the 3 *sg.* increasingly is made to conform to the first person, and both **cav** 'gets, will get' and **laver** 'says, will say' are attested.

NOTE: For the transition from *lever* to *laver*, etc. in later Cornish see '*I*-Affection in Breton and Cornish' in *Cornish Studies: Fourteen* (2006), 24–43.

In the orthography used in this book there is no written difference in the vowel of **scrifa** 'to write', **miras** 'to look' and **triga** 'to dwell' on the one hand and **ev a scrif** 'he will write', **ev a vir** 'he will look' and **ev a drig** 'he will live' on the other. In the texts, however, a distinction is often noticeable, for we often find *screfa*, *meras*, *trega* but *a scryf*, *a vyr* and *a dryg*. A distinction will be found in this orthography, however, in **pesy** 'to pray' but **ev a bës** 'he will pray', and **cresy** 'to believe' but **ev a grës** 'he will believe'.

Unexpected forms in the present-future include the following forms: **gweres** 'will help' (**gweres** 'to help'); **gorta** 'will wait' (**gortos** 'to wait'); **re** 'will give' (**ry** 'to give'); **dora** 'will bring' (**dry** 'to bring'); and **deg** 'will carry' (**don** 'to carry'). Notice also 1 *sg.* **galwaf** 'I will call', **marwaf** 'I shall die' but 3 *sg.* **gelow** and **merow**.

In verse on occasion the inflected verb sometimes appears without any preverbal particle, e.g **gon gwir** 'I know the truth' BM 3704; **gwrav brâster** 'I make a firmament' CW 81; **uskys comondyaf hedna** 'swiftly I command that' CW 245.

17A.4 THE IMPERFECT

The imperfect usually ends in **-en, -es, -a, -en, -ewgh, -ens**. There are some verbs, however, which have **-yn, -ys, -y, -yn, -ewgh, -ens**, most notably **leveryn, leverys, levery**, the imperfect of **leverel** 'to say'. **Sevel** 'to stand', **gelwel** 'to call', and **gallos** 'to be able' also form their imperfects with **-yn, -ys, -y**, etc., as **gyllyn, gyllys, gylly**, etc. of **gallos** 'to be able'.

17A.5 THE PRETERITE

The commonest ending of the third person singular in this tense is **-as**. There are a number of verbs, however, which have **-ys** instead, e.g. **sevel** 'to stand' > **sevys** 'he stood'; **côwsel** 'to speak' > **kewsys** 'he spoke';

leverel 'to say' > **leverys** 'he said'; **debry** 'to eat' > **debrys** 'he ate'. Forms with **-as**, however, become increasingly common and we find **savas** 'he stood'; **debras** 'he ate'; **cowsas** 'he spoke' and **lavaras** 'he said'.

The stem not infrequently changes in the third person singular of the preterite before **-as**, for example, **serry** 'to be angry', preterite **sorras**; **kelly** 'to lose', preterite **collas**.

Notice also the irregular forms **ros** 'he gave' (from **ry** 'to give'), **dros** 'he brought' (from **dry** 'to bring'), and **dug** 'he bore, he carried (from **don** 'to carry'). For the rest of the paradigms see Stagell C (Appendix C).

17A.6 THE CONDITIONAL

The conditional in most verbs is based on the unaffected stem together with the endings **-sen**, **-ses**, **-sa**, **-sen**, **-sewgh**, **-sens**. Notice the irregular **rosen** 'I would give' < **ry** 'to give' and **drosen** 'I would bring' < **dry** 'to bring.

Increasingly in Cornish the inflected conditional was replaced by a periphrastic tense with either **mydnas** or **gwil**: **me a vynsa leverel** 'I should say' or **me a wrussa leverel** 'I should say'. **Me a garsa** 'I should like' and **me a via** 'I should be', however, are not replaced by periphrastic forms.

17A.7 CONSTRUCTION AFTER CERTAIN VERBS

A number of verbs are followed by the preposition **worth**, **orth**: **côwsel orth** 'to speak to' (though **côwsel dhe²** is also found); **miras orth** 'to look at' (or **miras wàr**); **govyn orth** 'to ask of'. Notice also **sevel orth** 'to refrain from'. One may either say **gwitha orth**, **gwitha dhyworth** or **gwitha rag** 'to preserve from'.

Gweres 'to help' takes either a direct object or the preposition **dhe²**. 'To help someone to do something' is **gweres ow qwil tra**. 'To help' can also be rendered by the phrase **gwil gweres dhe²**.

Gortheby 'to answer' is similarly followed by the direct object or by **dhe²**. **Cresy** 'to believe' takes a direct object of the thing believed but **dhe²** or **in** with the person believed. **Pesy** 'to pray' is followed either by the direct object or the preposition **dhe²**. 'To pray for somebody' is either **pesy gans nebonen** or **pesy rag nebonen.**

Dallath 'to begin' is usually followed directly by a verbal noun: **ev a dhalathas côwsel** 'he began to speak'; **dallath a²** and **dallath dhe²** are also attested.

17A.8 IDIOMS WITH *KEMERES* AND *PERTHY*

Perthy 'to bear' is used with **avy** 'hatred' to mean 'to envy, to bear malice towards'; with **awhe·r** 'distress' to mean 'to be anxious', and with **danjer** 'scruple, hesitation' to mean 'hesitate'. Further **perthy dowt** means 'to fear' and **perthy cov** 'to remember. 'To remember' by the sixteenth century is often **remembra**, however.

Kemeres 'to take' is also used to express emotional states: **kemeres own** means 'to become afraid'; **kemeres with** means 'to take care'; **kemeres pyteth** 'to take pity' and **kemeres mercy** 'to have mercy'. These last two are followed either by a^2 or **wàr²**. **Kemeres tregereth wàr** 'to have mercy upon' is also attested.

17A.9 INVERSION WITH THE DIRECT OBJECT

We saw above (6A.5 and 8A.1) that when the predicate precedes the verb **bos**, the verbal particle is a^2 or zero (that is, it is omitted). Something similar applies when a verb takes a direct object and the direct object comes before the verb. One says **an den a welys** 'I saw the man'. In verse one could also say **an den y'n gwelys** 'the man, I saw him' (for the infixed pronouns see 18A.1), but not *****an den y whelys.**

17B EXAMPLES FROM THE TEXTS

17B.2 *ow scryfa than philipians* 'writing to the Philippians' SA 66; *Na esyn ny miras wor an bara* 'Let us not look upon the bread' SA 65a; *ha genaf eth ew tecter i'n bys ma perthy anken* 'and it is a delight for me in this world to suffer anguish' BK 437-38; *rave gawas haunsell?* 'shall I have breakfast?' Pryce; *rag the servya pub termyn* 'to serve you always' BK 2037.

17B.3 *Ny thoutyaf an nowothow* 'I do not fear the news' BK 2429; *lavar pandra welta moy* 'say what more you see' CW 1824; *me a'n caruyth y'm colon* 'I will love him in my heart' PC 1703; *y an prenvyth by my sovle* 'they will pay for it, upon my soul' BM 2320; *Ef ew pen an vethogyan hag a ylwyth the sawya* 'He is the chief of doctors and will be able to heal you' BK 795-96; *why a clowith moy* 'you will hear more' TH 46; *ha enna ti an kâv* 'and there you will find him' JCH §22; *an sperys ny drige neffra* 'the spirit shall not live for ever' CW 2219.

17B.4 *ny gowsy mas honester* 'he used not to speak but seemliness' BM 2239; *ran in Germany a levery, omma yma crist, omma yma an egglos, ran in Bohem a lleuery, omma yma crist* 'some in Germany were saying, here is Christ, here is the church; some in Bohemia were saying, here is Christ' TH 32; *ha y a re bostya hag a leuery* 'and they used to boast and say' TH 33a; *kemmys dader prest a wre* 'he always did so much goodness' PC 3096.

17B.5 *rag the pyte a gemercys an flehys* 'because of your pity which you took upon the children' BM 1836-37; *then dishonor han disordyr a wylsyn ny* 'to the dishonour and disorder which we have seen' TH 39; *in pov ma eff re dyrhays del glovsugh* 'he has landed in this country as you have heard' BM 2244-45; *thy'm rosons bystyl wherow* 'they gave me bitter gall' RD 2601; *Ena pan sevys yn ban hy a gewsys del ylly* 'Then when she arose she spoke as she was able' PA 166a; *Ha e savaz am'àn amez e uili* 'And he got up out of his bed' JCH §26; *kemer tyyr sprus a'n aval a dybrys adam the das* 'take three pips from the apple which your father, Adam, ate' OM 823-24; *Judas a thebbras* 'Judas ate' SA 65a; *ha'n bara dzhei a dhabraz* 'and the bread they ate' JCH §46.

17B.6 *confort thum cervons dyson boys y carsen* 'Indeed I should like to be a comfort to my servants; BM 3651-52; *ny garsen orto metya* 'I should not like to meet him' BM 3207; *me a garsa gul both the vrys* 'I should like to do the will of your heart' BK 2851-52; *me an drossa tha baynes* 'I would bring him to torment' CW 468.

17B.7 *bys o'm arluth why a the gows orta in e dowr* 'you shall go to my lord to speak to him in his tower' BK 3036-37; *pandra gowsow thym lemyn* 'what will you say to me now?' CW 141; *ʒe veras worth crist y eth* 'they went to look upon Christ' PA 216b; *esta ge ow jugia mett the veras war onyn an par na* 'do you consider me worthy to look upon one like that?' TH 7; *hag eff a wovynnys worth y apostlis* 'and he asked his apostles' TH 43a; *da yv sevell worth vn pris* 'it is good to refrain from one meal' BM 121; *crist guyth ny orth tewolgow* 'Christ, keep us from darkness' BM 4073; *gwyth ve orth drog!* 'preserve me from evil!' BK 1249; *rag omwetha theworth peryll ha danger* 'to keep himself from peril and danger' TH 4; *buz gwitha ny dort droge* 'but keep us from evil' Pryce; *yn cheryte gueres thy'm* 'in charity help me' OM 1782; *Ef re thonvanas kyrwas in le ohan thu'm gweras* 'He has sent stags instead of oxen to help me' BK 832-33; *peys gena the crist a rays* 'Pray for me to Christ of grace' BM 3135; *hag e pegyn ragas the Thew caradow* 'and we will pray to dear God for you' BK 2777-78; *Me a vyn i'n gwelha prys i'n geren dallath entra* 'I will at the best of times start to get into the tub' BK 1148-49.

17B.8 *an vuscogyon orto a borʒas avy* 'the madmen bore him malice' PA 26c; *Na borth awher* 'Do not be anxious' BK 2848; *dybbry byth na borth danger* 'do not at all hesitate to eat' OM 168; *Nag a, na borth dout* 'No, he won't go, do not fear' BK 2482; *hag arta perthugh coff guel* 'and in the future remember better' BM 1064; *Pesugh mercy war ihesu ha remembrogh agis du* 'Pray Jesus for mercy and remember your God' BM 2160-61; *drefen kemeres pyta an flehys gruegh del rusta* 'because of taking pity on the innocent children as you did' BM 1704-05; *nena eff a gemeras owne a drega na fella in cost na* 'then he became afraid of remaining any longer in that district' TH 46a; *du galosek, neb ew y vercy vgh oll y oberow, a gemeras pyteth an anken essa mab den ynna* 'Almighty God, whose mercy is above all his works, took pity on the misery in which mankind was' TH 12a; *mar ten ha kemeras with inta* 'if we take good care' TH 18.

17B.9 *onan a welsons eno* 'one they saw there' PA 154c.

121

17C.1 VOCABULARY

an pëth *pron.* that which	**frût** *m.*, **frûtys** fruit
auctour *m.*, **auctours** author	**lev** *m.*, **levow** voice
cably to slander	**pain** *m.*, **painys** pain
cort *f.*, **cortys** court	**sconya** to refuse, to reject
cria to cry	**servont** *m.*, **servons**, **servysy**
Duw *m.*, **duwow** God, god	servant

17C.2 TRANSLATE INTO ENGLISH:

1 Me a grës te dhe vos camgemerys.

2 Hy a leverys hy dhe berthy own anodho.

3 Res yw dhis perthy cov ow bos obma rag gweres dhis.

4 Ny a welas namnygen an maw pàn dheuthon ny aberveth.

5 Mar tewgh why ha debry a frût an wedhen-na, why a verow.

6 Mès y a dhebras anodho, ha Duw a dowlas an den ha'n venyn in mes a'n lowarth.

7 Ev a glowvyth dhyworthyf mar teuma obma arta.

8 An vowes vian a gollas hy fopet i'n fordh.

9 Me a garsa gweles y fâss ev lebmyn.

10 An venyn a gemeras pyteth anodho ha hy a ros boos ha dewas dhodho, ha hy a dhros dyllas nowyth dhodho kefrës.

11 Ev a besys y wreg dhe ry ken chauns dhodho, saw hy a wrug y sconya.

12 Res yw dhyn sevel orth leverel tra vëth dhedhy ow tùchya hy gour hy.

13 An auctour brâs re scrifas lies lyver, saw ny redys vy onen vëth anodhans.

14 Pàn o va deg warn ugans bloodh, ev a forsâkyas chy y das hag ev êth bys i'n menydhyow.

15 A glôwsowgh why tra vëth? Na glôwsyn, saw yth eson ny whath ow qwetyas.

16 An servysy a dhros an vowes teg dhyrag an mytern hag ev a godhas dystowgh in kerensa gensy.

17 I'n eur-na an mytern a leverys an geryow-ma: Me a gar an vowes-ma, ha hy a drig genama i'm chy ha'm gwreg avy hy a vëdh, ha'gas myternes whywhy.

18 Saw yth esa tebel-venyn in cort an mytern a berthy avy orth an vyternes. Hy a gablas an vyternes dhyrag an mytern.

19 Hy a leverys indelma: Fâls yw an vyternes ha kynth usy hy ow leverel hy dhe gara ow arlùth an mytern, nyns usy hy ow leverel an gwiryoneth.

20 I'n eur-na an mytern a sorras hag ev a grias a lev uhel hag ev a dowlas an vyternes in mes a'y gort.

17C.3 TRANSLATE INTO CORNISH:

1 Were you afraid when he said that? Yes, I was very afraid indeed.

2 Did you see the cat standing in the middle of the road? Yes, but I thought it was a fox.

3 Then God said to them: If you eat of the fruit of the tree, you will surely die.

4 But if you do not eat of the fruit of the tree, you will live forever.

5 The servants of the king brought food and drink and they set everything before him.

6 The king said to his servants: You must bring me the beautiful girl who is sitting before my great house.

7 And they brought the woman to him, and she was very beautiful.

8 The king looked up and saw the woman, and immediately he fell in love with her.

9 Then the king cried in a loud voice: I will marry this woman and she shall be my wife and your queen.

10 And all the people of the king agreed and they said: As you say, O king, so shall the matter be.

11 We must take care, I am afraid, or we will surely die.

12 I do not remember whom I saw or what I said. I was very drunk.

13 Did you speak to him? No, I did not even (**unweyth**) see anybody.

14 He said he would bring us something to eat and something to drink, but he has not come yet.

15 Pilate (**Pilat**) said to the Jews (**Yêdhewon**): That which I have written, I have written.

16 When he stood up, everybody began to laugh.

17 I say this to you all: we must not lose heart.

18 I pray God to keep me from sin and to have mercy upon me.

19 I feel the pain but I do not understand why.

20 When she gave them the food, she also brought them some new clothes.

ÊTEGVES DYSCANS
EIGHTEENTH LESSON

18A.1 INFIXED PRONOUNS

When inflected forms of the verb are used, a pronominal object appears as an infixed pronoun between the verbal particle and the verb: **me a gar** 'I love', but **me a'n car** 'I love him', **me a's car** 'I love her'. The infixed pronouns are as follows:

'm	me
'th[5]	you
'n	him, it
's	her, it
'gan, 'n	us
'gas, 's	you (*pl.*)
's	them.

Notice that only one of these forms mutates the following consonant, **'th**, which causes mixed mutation: **me a'th venten** 'I will support you', **ev a'th teg** 'he will carry you', etc. Infixed pronouns may be reinforced by suffixed pronouns, e.g. **me a'th car jy** (14A.4).

18A.2 SUFFIXED OBJECT PRONOUNS

The use of infixed pronouns was clearly not always easy even for native speakers of Cornish, and there is a slight tendency in the texts to replace them with suffixed pronouns by themselves. Instead, therefore, of using the infixed forms cited above, one may postposit as object pronouns the forms listed at 14A.4 above. Instead of **ev a's gwelas** 'he saw them', one can say **ev a welas anjy**, and instead of **ny'th caraf poynt** 'I don't love you at all', one can say **ny garaf jy poynt** (see 18B.2 for some examples from the texts themselves). Since this simplified syntax is not common in the traditional language, an excessive use of it in the revived language might be considered inauthentic.

124

18A.3 *MYDNAS (MEDNAS)* 'TO WISH' AS A VERBAL AUXILIARY

Mydnas (or **mednas**) when a full verb originally meant 'to wish, to want'. **Mydnas** is conjugated as follows in the present-future:

1 *sg.* **ma(d)naf, mydnaf, mednaf** 1 *pl.* **mydnyn, mednyn**
2 *sg.* **mydnys, mynta, menta** 2 *pl.* **mydnowgh, mednowgh**
3 *sg.* **mydn, medn** 3 *pl.* **mydnons, mednons**

We saw at 12A.2 above that the future is often made with the present-future of **gwil**. **Mydnas** is also frequently used to express the future:

Me a vydn mos genes I will go with you
Prag na vynta ry an flourys dhedhy? Why will you not give her the flowers?

Overall the commonest way of expressing the future in traditional Cornish is with **mydnas**.

18A.4 THE IMPERFECT, PRETERITE AND CONDITIONAL OF *MYDNAS*

The imperfect of **mydnas** is inflected as follows:

1 *sg.* **mydnen, mednen** 1 *pl.* **mydnen, mednen**
2 *sg.* **mydnes, mednes** 2 *pl.* **mydnewgh, mednewgh**
3 *sg.* **mydna, medna** 3 *pl.* **mydnens, mednens**

This tense means 'wanted, would' as a continuing state in the past.
The preterite of **mydnas, mednas** refers to a single act of volition. It is conjugated as follows:

1 *sg.* **mydnys, mednys** 1 *pl.* **mynsyn, mensyn**
2 *sg.* **mynsys, mensys** 2 *pl.* **mynsowgh, mensowgh**
3 *sg.* **mydnas, mednas** 3 *pl.* **mynsons, mensons**

The conditional of **mydnas, mednas** means 'would, would want, would wish' and conjugates as follows:

1 *sg.* **mynsen, mensen** 1 *pl.* **mynsen, mensen**
2 *sg.* **mynses, menses** 2 *pl.* **mynsewgh, mensewgh**
3 *sg.* **mynsa, mensa** 3 *pl.* **mynsens, mensens**

In later Cornish forms with **-nj-** for **-ns-** in the conditional are very common: **menjen, menjes, menja**, etc.

Since the conditional **mynsen, mensen**, etc. means 'I would wish, I would', it is often used with the verbal noun as a way of expressing the conditional. Instead, therefore, of saying **me a via lowen** 'I should be happy', one can say **me a vynsa/vensa/venja bos lowen**. Similarly instead of **ev a wrussa gweres** 'he said he would help', one can say **ev a vynsa gweres**.

18A.5 *GALLOS* 'TO BE ABLE'
This is an important verb in Cornish and is conjugated as follows:

Verbal noun
gallos

Present-future
1 *sg.* **gallaf, gallama**	1 *pl.* **gyllyn**
2 *sg.* **gyllyth, gylta**	2 *pl.* **gyllowgh**
3 *sg.* **gyll, gylla** (< **gyll** + **ev**)	3 *pl.* **gyllons**

There is also a 3 *sg.* future form **gyllvyth**.

Imperfect
1 *sg.* **gyllyn**	1 *pl.* **gyllyn**
2 *sg.* **gyllys**	2 *pl.* **gyllowgh**
3 *sg.* **gylly**	3 *pl.* **gyllens**

Conditional
1 *sg.* **galsen**	1 *pl.* **galsen**
2 *sg.* **galses**	2 *pl.* **galsewgh**
3 *sg.* **galsa**	3 *pl.* **galsens**

The consonant group **-ls-** is often **-lj-** in later Cornish. Moreover in later Cornish also the conditional replaces the imperfect with the sense 'could, was able':
1 *sg.* **galjen**	1 *pl.* **galjen**
2 *sg.* **galjes**	2 *pl.* **galjewgh**
3 *sg.* **galja**	3 *pl.* **galjens**

18B EXAMPLES FROM THE TEXTS

18B.1 *ha henna neb nam carra ve ny vyn gwetha ow gyrryow* 'and he who does not love me, will not keep my words' TH 23a; *rag in sertan me a'th care* 'for assuredly I love you' BK 1080; *del i'n caraf in colan* 'as I love him in my heart' BK 3026; *neb agan cara ny pan en ny y yskerans* 'who loved us when we were his enemies' TH 24; *Me a'gys car dek mylblek moy ys ow mam* 'I love you tell thousand times more than my mother' BK 2925-26; *benithe me nys care* 'I shall never love them' BM 2044.

18B.2 *arluth prag y hysta vy* 'Lord, why have you forsaken me?' PA 201c; *ny a ra eff gowak* 'me make him mendacious' TH 8; *te a wore henna, fatell caraff ve ge* 'you know that, that I love you' TH 43; *me a wra ge dean a bry* 'I make you, O man, of clay' CW 345; *An hagar-breeve a thullas ve* 'The evil serpent tempted me' Rowe; *Ha Deu goras gi en ebron neve* 'And God set them in the firmament of heaven' JBoson.

18B.3 *ýbma na vadna vi ostia* 'here I will not lodge' JCH §24; *pan vidnaf ve comanndya* 'when I command' CW 36; *Meea na vidna cowza Sawzneck* 'I will speak no English' Carew; *pan fynnyth in the bassion ow bos keffrannak i'n bys* 'when you wish that I should share in your passion in the world' BK 480-81; *mara mynta y wothfas* 'if you wish to know it' CW 1635; *mar menta guellaz an ôst an tshei, kî ðv'n ʒeʒen* 'if you want to see the host of the house, go to the kitchen' JCH §22; *ny a vidn gwyll indella* 'we will do thus' CW 2527; *Pew vedna why gawas rag seera rag guz flo* 'Whom will you get as father for your child?' Chygwyn.

18B.4 *Gorthyans thu'm Arluth a nef a vynnas clowas ow lef* 'Glory to my Lord of heaven who was ready to hear my voice' BK 1-2; *Awos myl buns ny vynsen the welas, ru'n oferen!* 'For a thousand pouns I would not want to see you, by the mass!' BK 1211-12; *bo ken crist ny vensa leverell* 'otherwise Christ would not have said' TH 17a; *ny vensans y presumya war aga judgement aga honyn* 'they would not have presumed upon their own judgement' TH 36a; *Ni venja pea a munna seer* 'He would not have paid the money indeed' JTonkin; *ev a venga kavaz fraga e ouna en skreefa-composter* 'he would find reason to emend its orthography' NBoson

18B.5 *Ny allaf e amontya!* 'I cannot reckon it!' BK 2980; *Dar, ny ylta dyfuna?* 'Hey, can you not wake up?' BK 349; *splanna es an howle deverye why a yll warbarthe gwelas ow bosaf sertayn* 'you can altogether see that I am certainly brighter than the sun indeed' CW 131-33; *yth halsan rowlya pur gay* 'I could rule very merrily' CW 607; *en termyn a alga ny dry mar nebaz thagan sawder* 'at a time when we could bring so little for our safety' JKeigwin; *Why re dueth i'n uer gwelha may halsough dos* 'You have come at the best time you could have come' BK 1548-49.

18C.1 VOCABULARY

auctour *m.*, **auctours** author

caletter *m.*, **caletterow** hardness, difficulty

chaunjya to change

creatya to create

dauncya to dance

dewheles to return

dyscortes rude, impolite

Frynkek French (language)

heb mar without doubt, of course

kerhes to fetch

benow *f.* female

gorow *m.* male

pa·radîs *f.* paradise

poynt a skians *m.*, **poyntys a skians** good counsel, maxim

sewya to follow

tewel to be silent

Ùngarek *adj.* Hungarian

18C.2 TRANSLATE INTO ENGLISH:

1 Ple ma an auctour brâs? Me a vydn y weles. Me a'n gwelas solabrës.

2 A ylta jy leverel dhybm ple hallaf chaunjya mona Ùngarek?

3 Ev a ylly y wil kyns ès lebmyn, saw y wil ny vydnas. Praga? Dre rêson ev dhe vos diek.

4 Ev a'n dora, mar teu va obma avorow.

5 A vynta ry neppyth dhedhans, awos y dhe wil meur a whel ragon?

6 Saw mar mynta y ry dhybm arta, me a dhesk dhis poynt a skians.

7 Ny vanaf vy bos dyscortes dhis, saw res yw dhis tewel lebmyn ha gasa nebonen dhe gôwsel.

8 Ny vynsen leverel tra kepar ha hedna dhyrag an bobel-na.

9 Ny a alsa debry warbarth i'n tavern hag i'n eur-na te a alsa mos tre wàr an kyttryn.

10 Duw a greatyas mab den. Gorow ha benow ev a's gwrug.

11 Ev a leverys dhybm na vynsa ev y ry dhybm.

12 Mar mynta, me a'n re dhis.

13 A alsens y bos obma adermyn? Galsens.

14 Ny yllyn scrifa wosa ow dorn dhe vos hùrtys.

15 Te a lever na vynta dos genen. A ylta jy leverel praga? Na allaf.

16 A yllowgh why côwsel Kernowek? Gallama.

17 An den êth in mes a'n rom saw ny vydnas y wreg y sewya.

18 Fatl'alsa hedna bos gwir? Galsa, y halsa heb caletter vëth.

19 Me a vydn côwsel Kernowek orto, saw ny yllvyth ow gortheby.

20 Me ny vydnaf côwsel Sowsnek.

18C.3 TRANSLATE INTO CORNISH:

1 Can you please tell me the way to the beach?
2 Can you speak French? Yes, I can.
3 Will you come back tomorrow? No, I can't. I'll return the day after tomorrow.
4 Would she be able to help us? No.
5 She said she would not give him any money, but that she could give him food and clothes.
6 I saw him yesterday. Did you? I have not seen him yet
7 Who said that? I said it, did you not hear me?
8 What could we do to guard ourselves against him? Very little.
9 She will bring them tomorrow. But she brought them today.
10 What can he do? He can speak English and French and can sing and dance.
11 The vicar (**pronter**) said he would come this afternoon, but I cannot wait in the house for him.
12 Will you be going out? Yes, I have to fetch the children from school.
13 I will fetch them for you and I'll bring them here in the car.
14 Thank you, could you do that for me? Of course I could.
15 They have gone. How can you say that?
16 If he comes around here again, I won't see him
17 Did you receive my letter? Yes, I received it yesterday morning.
18 Did you read it? No, I have not read it yet. I shall read it now.
19 Can you hear me? I hear you well.
20 God was angry with them and he cast (**tôwlel**) them out of paradise.

NAWNJEGVES DYSCANS
NINETEENTH LESSON

19A.1 THE SUBJUNCTIVE

As well as the various indicative tenses which we have examined, Cornish has a subjunctive mood as well. The subjunctive of some important verbs is given below:

bos 'to be'

1 *sg.* **ben**	1 *pl.* **ben**
2 *sg.* **bes, besta**	2 *pl.* **bewgh**
3 *sg.* **be**	3 *pl.* **bêns**

gwil 'to do'

1 *sg.* **gwrellen**	1 *pl.* **gwrellen**
2 *sg.* **gwrelles**	2 *pl.* **gwrellowgh**
3 *sg.* **gwrella**	3 *pl.* **gwrellens**

dos 'to come'

1 *sg.* **deffen**	1 *pl.* **deffen**
2 *sg.* **deffes, de·ffesta**	2 *pl.* **deffewgh**
3 *sg.* **deffa**	3 *pl.* **deffens**

mos 'to go'

1 *sg.* **ellen**	1 *pl.* **ellen**
2 *sg.* **elles**	2 *pl.* **ellewgh**
3 *sg.* **ella**	3 *pl.* **ellens**

gallos 'to be able'

1 *sg.* **gallen**	1 *pl.* **gallen**
2 *sg.* **galles**	2 *pl.* **gallewgh**
3 *sg.* **galla**	3 *pl.* **gallens**

mydnas 'to wish'

1 *sg.* **mydnen**	1 *pl.* **mydnen**
2 *sg.* **mydnes**	2 *pl.* **mydnewgh**
3 *sg.* **mydna**	3 *pl.* **mydnens**

This tense is very similar to the imperfect of **mydnas**; see 18A.4.

cara 'to love'

1 *sg.* **carren**	1 *pl.* **carren**
2 *sg.* **carres**	2 *pl.* **carrewgh**
3 *sg.* **carra**	3 *pl.* **carrens**

The subjunctive of most other verbs can be made by taking the unaffected stem, devoicing (hardening) the final consonant, where possible, doubling it and adding the endings **-en**, **-es**, **-a**, etc., for example, **degaf** 'I carry' > **docken, dockes**, etc.; **debraf** 'I eat' > **deppren, deppres**, etc.; **lavaraf** 'I say' > **lavarren, lavarres**, etc.; **kemeraf** 'I take' > **kemerren, kemerres**, etc.; **gwelaf** 'I see' > **gwellen, gwelles**, etc.; **savaf** 'I stand' > **saffen, saffes**, etc. **Ry** 'to give' has a subjunctive **rollen, rolles**, etc., while **dry** 'to bring' has **drollen, drolles**, etc.

19A.2 THE SYNTAX OF THE SUBJUNCTIVE
The subjunctive has a number of uses:

i) it is used to express an indefinite future after **pàn²** 'when' (see 19A.6); **hadre·²** (LC **der²**) 'while'; **erna·²(g)** 'until'; **kyn⁵(th)** 'although'; **kettel²** 'as soon as'; **may⁵** 'in order that'; and **pyskytter may⁵** 'as soon as'

ii) the subjunctive is used in future relative clauses when the antecedent is indefinite

iii) it is also used with such words as **pyna·g oll** 'whoever, whatever'. 'Wherever' can be expressed by **ple pyna·g may⁵** or **pyna·g fordh may⁵**

iv) **may⁵** + the subjunctive of **gallos** is widely used to mean 'in order that, so that' (see 19A.5 below)

v) the subjunctive is used in the protasis of unreal conditions (see 20A.1–2).

19A.3 THE PRESENT SUBJUNCTIVE
The forms of the subjunctive cited above are in origin the past subjunctive. The texts also have instances of a present subjunctive. In the verb **gwil** 'to do', for example, the forms of the present subjunctive are

gwryllyf, gwrylly, gwrello, gwryllyn, gwryllowgh, gwrellons. Similarly the present subjunctive of **dos** 'to come' is **dyffyf, dyffy, deffo, dyffyn, deffowgh, deffons**.

As final **-o** and **-a** fell together in pronunciation in Middle Cornish, the third singulars **gwrello** and **gwrella** became indistinguishable from each other. Moreover other parts of the two paradigms were identical in pronunciation, i.e. **gwrellowgh** and **gwrellewgh**, **gwrellens** and **gwrellons**. Since in most verbs the two paradigms through phonetic development were largely indistinguishable, the present subjunctive began to be replaced by the past subjunctive. This phenomenon is already well established in the earliest Middle Cornish.

The present subjunctive in most verbs is confined to the first person and second person singular, e.g. **gwryllyf, gwrylly** and **dyffyf, dyffy**. These forms are used in particular when the subjunctive is used as a command. This so-called jussive use of the subjunctive also involves the particle **re²**: **re dhyffy arta yn scon** 'may you come again soon!' Negative jussive clauses are introduced by **bydner re²** where **bydner** = 'never': **bydner re wryllyf hedna dhis** 'may I never do that to you!' The present subjunctive is also retained in some fossilized phrases, e.g. **dell y'm kyrry** 'as you love me' i.e. 'if you please', and **mydny jy ken na vydny** 'whether you want to or not', for example.

The verb **ry** 'to give' has a special jussive form of the 3 sg., **roy**. This is used without **re²** and occurs in such phrases as **Duw roy dëdh dâ dhywgh why** > **Dùrda dhe why** 'God give you a good day, good day'.

19A.4 THE PRESENT SUBJUNCTIVE OF *BOS*

Unlike most other verbs, **bos** 'to be' is monosyllabic in the present subjunctive. In consequence the final syllable (being the only syllable) retained its distinctive vowel, and the present subjunctive of **bos** thus survived intact. In sixteenth century texts the present subjunctive of **bos** is attested as follows:

1 *sg.* **biv, byma, boma**	1 *pl.* **ben**
2 *sg.* **by, bos, bosta**	2 *pl.* **bewgh**
3 *sg.* **bo**	3 *pl.* **bôns, bowns**

19A.5 *MAY⁵* 'IN ORDER THAT'

'In order that', 'so that' are usually rendered in Cornish by **may⁵(th)**: **me a'n gwra may fo gwrës yn tâ** 'I will do it so it will be well done'. Frequently **may⁵** is used with the appropriate part of the subjunctive of **gallos** 'to be able' to express the same idea:

Me re wrug dry lyvrow genef, may hallen aga redya obma in cosoleth I have brought books with me, so that I may (in order to) read them here in peace
Yma an Gernowyon ow tasvewa aga thavas, may halla (LC **mal**) **pùbonen godhvos fatell yns y Keltyon** The Cornish are reviving their language, so that everyone may know that they are Celts.

19A.6 THE SUBJUNCTIVE AFTER *PÀN* 'WHEN'

When the verb after the conjunction **pàn** (LC **pa**) refers to future time, it must always appear in the subjunctive. 'He will tell us all about the matter when he comes' is thus rendered **Ev a vydn derivas dhyn adro dhe'n mater, pàn dheffa ev**; 'your father will be appalled when he hears about your behaviour' can be translated **dha das a vëdh diegrys pàn glôwa ev adro dhe'th omdhon**. 'I shall be very glad when the clothes are ready' in Cornish is **me a vëdh pòr lowen pàn vo parys an dyllas**. Forms like *pàn dheu, *pàn glôw/glôwvyth, *pàn vëdh are unattested in traditional Cornish.

19B EXAMPLES FROM THE TEXTS

19B.1–2 **bynar re'm bo lowena hedre ven bew** 'may I not have joy as long as I am alive' BK 2585-86; **ha sekretly bew hedre vy ow ro theso a vyth clere** 'and secretly as long as you live my gift to you will be apparent' BK 638-40; **Rag penagull a rella pregoth discans vith a vo contrary** 'For whoever may preach teaching that is contrary' TH 19a; **penagull a rella latha, a vith in danger a judgment** 'whoever kills, is in danger of judgement' TH 27.

19B.3 **penag a wryllyf amme** 'whomever I kiss' PC 1084; **pan deffy' ha dyryvyas a'm skyansow** 'when I come and tell of my knowledge' BK 1325-26; **Byner re gymmyrryf boys** 'May I never consume food' BK 1458; **mes a'n bys ma pan ylhy, te a'n kef war the forth hyr** 'but when you depart from this world, you will receive it in the long run' BK 583-84; **ha penagull a rylly lowsya** 'and whomever you release' TH 44; **mynny gy kyn na vynny ty a in kerth genen ny** 'whether you wish to or not, you will go away with us' BM 2967-68; **ffrut da byner re thokko** 'may it never bear good fruit' OM 583; **ha byner re thewellough** 'and may you never return' BK 745.

19B.4 **Arluth, re by confortys!** 'Lord, may you be comforted!' BK 1183; **Gorthys re bo Du a nef!** 'May God of heaven be glorified!' BK 1177; **Erna vony unwerhys, neffra ny veth da ow cher** 'I shall never be happy until we be of one mind' BK 1035-36; **erna vons e dyskevrys** 'until they are unmasked' BK 3160.

19B.5 **A wylta kyrwas enos del vynnas Du whar ha dof orth an ewyow devethys gansa may hallan gonys?** 'Do you see stags yonder as God willed gentle and tame come to the yokes, that I might plough with them?' BK 847-50; **dun the'n chamber, me a'th pys, may hyllyn omacountya** 'let us go to

133

the bedroom, I beseech the, that we may get to know each other' BK 2982-83; *may hallowgh bos curunys* 'that you may be crowned' BK 3014; *Lemen parusugh an beth in hanov crist del deleth may hallen y anclethyas* 'Now prepare the grave in the name of Christ as is right, that we may bury him' BM 4510-12.

19B.6 *arluth pan dyffy ӡet pow predery ahanaff gura* 'Lord, when you come to your country, think of me' PA 193b; *pan deffa an spuris na a wryoneth, eff a thiske theugh oll gwryoneth* 'when that Spirit of truth comes, he will teach you all truth' TH 17; *ha pan deffasta than plas ty a gyef in yet vdn eall* 'and when you come to the place, you will find an angel in the gate' CW 1752-53; *pan deffa an oyle a vercy te a vith kerrys then ioye* 'when the oil of mercy comes, you will be brought to joy' CW 2075-76; *tevder mes y skyans a pan glowe y vos scappys* 'Teudar will go out of his mind when he hears that he has escaped' BM 1029-30; *ow thase ken fova serrys pan glowa an nowethys* 'though my father will be angry when he hears the news' CW 1135-36; *pan vo gures my a thue thy's* 'when it is done I shall come to you' OM 988; *pan fo a'n beys tremenys yth a the'n nef* 'when he has passed from the world, he will go to heaven' RD 287-88; *pan vo an re ma marov wegennov ny a ra moy* 'when these are dead, we will produce further little darlings' BM 1564-65; *pan vo an dewetha gyrryow clowis* 'when the last words are heard' SA 59; *Pan vo mî ha'm g'rêg an moyha lûan warbàrh dho terri an dezan* 'When I and my wife are the happiest together to break the cake' JCH §45; *Po marh leòres* 'When a horse is stolen' AB: 232a.

19C.1 VOCABULARY

anoyntya to anoint
arghel *m.*, **argheleth** archangel
betraya to betray
causya to cause
consecrâtya to consecrate, to sanctify
corf *m.*, **corfow** body
crejyans *f.* belief
defendya to dispel; to defend
dysonora to dishonour
enef *m.*, **enevow** soul
Fôceùs *m. personal name* Phoceus
galosek mighty, powerful
golowy to illuminate
gwil mencyon to mention
gwrior *m.*, **gwrioryon** creator
gylty *adj.* guilty

Jesù Crist *m. personal name.* Jesus Christ
jùnya to join
keth *adj.* same (precedes its noun)
lowr gweyth *adv.* many times, frequently
maga to nourish
maga⁵ *conj.* how (before adjectives)
mostethus *adj.* dirty, defiled
norvës *m.* world
pa vaner ha sort *adv. phrase* in which way
pana hager *adj. phrase* how ugly
pensevyk *m.*, **pensevygyon** prince
percêvya to perceive
ras *m.* grace

sacryfia to sacrifice
savyour *m.*, **savyours** saviour
sawya to heal
scrifor *m.*, **scriforyon** writer
sêlya to seal

spîtfùl *adj.* spiteful, malicious
spyrys *m.* **spyryjyon** spirit, ghost.
   Spyrys Sans Holy Spirit
sùbstans *m.* substance, nature

19C.2 TEXT DHE REDYA
(*SACRAMENT AN ALTER*)

Red an devyn usy ow sewya ha scrif gorthebow dhe'n qwestyons (Read the following passage and write answers to the questions):

Indella yw corf agan Arlùth Duw in gwlas nev, yw settys lebmyn dhyragon i'n norvës. Nyns esof ow tysqwedhes dhywgh eleth naneyl argheleth, mès an very corf a'gan mêster ha pensevyk. Te a yll percêvya pa vaner ha sort esta ow qweles agan Savyour Crist. Pana hager yw agan sùbstans ny dhyrag Duw a'n nev! An enef a vab den, nyns yw nefra sawys marnas dre grejyans dhâ, hadre vo an enef in kig mab den. An kig yma ow causya an ena dhe vos jùnys dhe Dhuw a'n nev. Pàn vo an kig golhys, an enef a vêdh glanhës. An kig yw anoyntys, may halla an enef bos consecrâtys. An kig yw sêlys, may halla an enef bos defendys. An kig yw tùchys gans dewla, rag may halla an enef bos golowys gans an Spyrys Sans. Yma an kig ow tebry corf hag owth eva goos agan Arlùth Jesù Crist, rag may halla an enef bos megys worth Duw golosek ha'y vab ras, agan Savyour Jesù Crist.

Pàn wrug agan Savyour Crist leverel: ev yw gylty a'n corf ha'n goos a'gan Arlùth Crist, indelma yma ev ow tysqwedhes kepar dell wrug Jûdas betraya y Arlùth Duw. An Yêdhewon a veu spîtfùl warbydn agan Arlùth Crist. Indella ymowns y ow tysonora Crist pàn vownsy y worth y recêva ev ha'y gorf benegys ev gans dewla mostethus. Maga pell dell usy an keth den-ma, Fôceùs, lowr gweyth ow qwil mencyon a gorf hag a'n goos agan Arlùth Duw, yma ev ow tysqwethas nag o ev only den yw sacryfies, mès agan Arlùth Crist y honyn, an gwrior a bùptra oll.

1 Pandr'usy an scrifor (*writer*) ow tysqwedhes dh'y redyoryon (*readers*)?
2 Herwyth (*according to*) an scrifor, pëth yw hager dhyrag Duw?
3 Pyw a vêdh ow maga an enef?
4 Pyw o spîtfùl warbydn Crist?
5 Pandra wrug Jûdas?
6 An scrifor a lever tus dhe dhysonora Crist. Pana dermyn usons y ow qwil indella?

UGANSVES DYSCANS
TWENTIETH LESSON

20A.1 UNREAL CONDITIONS WITH *DOS*

'If you go any further, you will fall' is a real condition. 'If you were to go any further, you would fall' and 'If you had gone any further you would have fallen' are both unreal conditions. Real conditions have been discussed at 16A.5 above. In Cornish unreal conditions are most easily expressed by means of **mar⁴** + the subjunctive of **dos** + **ha** and the verb as verbal noun in the *if*-clause (protasis) and the conditional with **mydnas** + verbal noun in the other clause (apodosis):

> **Mar teffes ha mos pella** (see 24A.1) **in rag, te a vynsa codha** If you were to go further, you would fall
> **Mar teffa ev ha leverel hedna dh'y wreg, ny vynsa hy cresy dhodho** If he had told his wife that, she would not have believed him.

20A.2 UNREAL CONDITIONS WITHOUT *DOS*

There are other ways of expressing unreal conditions. The verb in the protasis can itself be in the subjunctive without using **dos**: **mara pe an mona dhodho, ev a vynsa y ry dhybm** 'If he had had the money, he would have given it to me'. Instead of the conditional of **mydnas** in the apodosis, the conditional of **gwil** can be used: **mara pe va ena moy avarr, ny a wrussa y dhry ev genen** 'if he had been there earlier, we would have brought him with us'. The verb in the apodosis can also be in the conditional without an auxiliary. In the earlier texts **mar(a)⁴** in unreal conditions is also replaced by **a⁴**: **me a'n gwrussa, a callen** 'I would do it if I could'.

20A.3 NEGATIVE UNREAL CONDITIONS

The simplest way of making negative unreal conditions is to use **na ve** 'had it not been for' + the subject + **dhe²** + verbal noun:

> **Na ve an venyn dhe scrija, an lader a wrussa scappya** Had the woman not screamed, the robber would have escaped

Ny vynsa ev bythqweth spêdya, na ve te dhe wil dhodho gweres
He would not have succeeded, if you had not helped him.

Alternatively **mar ny** + subjunctive can be used in the negative protasis, and the conditional in the apodosis: **me a via tebel-goweth, mar ny wrellen dha scodhya** 'I would be a poor friend, if I didn't not support you'.

20A.4 NECESSITY AND DUTY

One way of expression the idea of necessity is to use the idiom **res yw dhe** 'there is necessity to', e.g. **res yw dhybm gorfedna ow whel kyns ès mos tre** 'I must finish my work before I go home'. Later **res** was found in a mixed construction, in which **res** was used as a verb following a personal pronoun, but the prepositional pronoun was also used: **ny a res dhyn bos dâ** 'we must be good'. Later still **res** acquired the status of a full verb: **me a res gorfedna ow whel** 'I must finish my work'. When **res** is a verb, it has an imperfect **resa**: **ny a resa sevel ava·rr pùb myttyn i'n dedhyow-na** 'we had to get up early in those days'.

To express the idea of duty rather than absolute necessity in Cornish, one uses a number of verbs. One is the verb **codha** 'to fall', which is used impersonally in the present-future: **y coodh dhybm** 'I ought', the subjunctive **y cotha dhybm** 'I ought' or the conditional **y codhvia dhybm**. Or a mixed construction **me a goodh dhybm** can be used.

The verb **tylly** 'to pay' can also be used impersonally in the present-future to express duty: **me a dal gwil gweres dhodho** 'I ought to help him'. The conditional **dalvia** is also sometimes used: **me a dalvia y wil** 'I ought to do it'.

20A.5 VOLITION

In the revived language **me a vydn** is frequently used to mean 'I want to', yet in traditional Cornish the mean of the verb **mydnas** is less strong, and **me a vydn y wil**, for example, is a simple future 'I will do it', without any sense of volition. To translate 'I want to do it' or 'I wish to do it' it is probably better to say **mal yw genef y wil** 'I am eager to do it', **y carsen y wil** 'I should like to do it', **me a garsa y wil** 'I should like to do it', or **me yw whensys dh'y wil** 'I am desirous of doing it'. One can also, of course, say, **ervirys yw genef y wil** 'I am determined to do it' and **porposys ov y wil** 'I intend to do it'.

20B EXAMPLES FROM THE TEXTS

20B.1 *Rag mar teffa crist ha dos in dallath an bys whare whosa mab den the beha ha the vos kyllys, tus a russa supposia* 'For if Christ had come at the beginning of the world, soon after mankind had sinned and had been lost, people would have assumed' TH 13; *Mar teffa an epscobow han brontyryan in tyrmyn passis, in weth an dus leg, dysky ha practysya aga duty haga vocacyons, dre an exampill ma surly ny russa an egglos a crist dos then dishonor han disordyr a wylsyn ny* 'If the bishops and the priests in the past, and the laity also, had taught and practised their duty and vocations, through this example, surely the church of Christ would not have come to the dishonour and disorder we have seen' TH 39; *mar teffa an holl brodereth obeya according then commondmentys a thu, ny vynsa den vith styrrya na gwaya warbyn an colleges* 'if all the brotherhood had obeyed according to the commandments of God, no one would have stirred or moved against the colleges' TH 42a.

20B.2 *cous ganso me a garse y volungeth mara pe* 'I should like to speak to him, if it were his wish' RD 744-45; *saw yndella mara pe warbarth ol ny a vye marthys ates* 'but if it were so, we all together would be very pleased' RD 1022-24; *y terfensa myrgh emperour ʒy par kefis mara peya* 'he would deserve an emperor's daughter as his spouse if she were found' BM 185-86; *A trykkowgh bytte vlythan, gras e wothvean thewhy* 'Were you to remain for a year, I should be grateful to you' BK 1592-93; *A'm nygysyow a pen war, ru'm Arluth na'n gevas par! ny thothyan thys mar sotal* 'Had I been aware of my business, by my Lord who has no equal, I should not have come to you so speedily' BK 3117-19.

20B.3 *na ve bos fals an den ma nyn drossen ny bys deso* 'if this man were not false, we would not have brought him to you' PA 99b; *na ve y vose guir sans mar lues merkyl dyblans byth ny russe* 'if he were not a true saint, he would never have performed so many obvious miracles' BM 2051-53; *ha na ve agan savyowre crist intendys the ry the pedyr specyall auctorite a vgh aga hensa, pan a othom vea cowse hemma* 'and had our Saviour not intended to give to Peter special authority over their fellows, what need would there have been to utter this?' TH 44a; *An kyth office ma ny vynsa pedyr kemeras na ve crist the ry thotha an auctorite* 'Peter would not have accepted this same office, had Christ not given him the authority' TH 44a; *Me a thothya gans an ger, na ve ow maw thu'm lettya* 'I should have come at the word, had my servant not prevented me' BK 469-70.

20B.4 *reys yv dyberth otyweth* 'it is necessary to depart at last' BM 4255; *ha ris ew gul e thevys* 'and one must perform his ordinance' BK 2374; *Ny res theugh bos duwenyk awos lavarow drog-den* 'you ought not to be dispirited because of the words of an evil man' BK 2659-60; *ny a res pub vr casa aga oberow haga offencys* 'we must at all times hate their deeds and their offences' TH 26; *an pith a resa bos colynwys anotheff therag y pascion* 'that which had to be fulfilled concerning him before his passion' TH 15; *an pith a goth thyn gull* 'that which we ought to do' TH 20a; *ny a goth then consydra pandra vsy S paule ow cowse* 'we ought consider what St Paul says' TH 32a; *ha indella ny oll a goth thyn cresy* 'and thus we all ought to believe' TH 58; *ha gans charite y a gotha bos executys* 'and in charity they ought to be put to death' TH 24a; ***Bez e brederaz ter goʇa ðoðo bʋz aviziyz ðiueʇ ken guesgal enueʇ*** 'But he considered that he should think twice before striking once' JCH §40; ***Ha po'rŷʒ an [d]zhei ðʋz ðʋ'n tshei lebma gôʇfia an dzhei ostia*** 'And when they came to the house where they were to lodge' JCH §21; ***ny dallvea thotheff mar ver predery a throg thy kentrevak*** 'he ought not so much as think of evil towards his neighbour' TH 29; ***ny dalvea thetha bos refusyys gans particular person vith*** 'they ought not be rejected by any particular person' TH 38; ***Hag et eye ollaz hye dalveath gowas tane*** 'And on her hearth she should get fire' JJenkins; ***Why dalveya gowas an brossa mine*** 'You should get the largest stones' JJenkins.

20B.5 ***mal yv gynef y gaffos rak y worre th'y ancow*** 'I am eager to find him to put him to death' PC 2069-70; ***confort thum cervons dyson boys y carsen*** 'I should indeed like to be a comfort to my servants' BM 3651-52; ***gans golyas ha gans pynys me a garsa crist ʒe plesya*** 'with vigil and with fasting I should like to please Christ' BM 164-66; ***pronter boys me a garse*** 'I should like to be a priest' BM 522; ***Me a garsa thotha ef dusquethas unwyth pew of*** 'I should like to show him once who I am' BK 2067-68; ***Me a garsa in tefry cafas gorthyb in certan*** 'Indeed I should certainly like to receive an answer' BK 2100-01; ***me a garsa gul both the vrys ow arluth ker*** 'I should like to perform the wish of your heart, my dear lord' BK 2851-53; ***pana pask onn o Christ wensys tha thibbry gans e apostelath*** 'which paschal lamb Christ wished to eat with his apostles' SA 64a; ***rak satnas yv yrvyrys avel ys y' nothlennow th'agas kroddre*** 'for Satan is determined to sift you like grain in winnowing sheets' PC 880-82; ***Rag yth off purposyys dre weras a thu, the egery ha the thisquethas pena dra ew an kythsame egglos ma*** 'For I intend with God's help, to explain and to show what kind of thing this same church is' TH 31; ***Ith off ve dre weras a thu purposys the gowse an auctorite an egglos*** 'I intend with God's help to speak of the authority of the church' TH 35.

20C.1 VOCABULARY

an hackra flogh the ugliest child
baby *m.*, **babiow** baby
bëdh war! *v. phrase* beware!
camgemerys *adj.* mistaken
Cath *f.* **Ker** personal name Cheshire-Cat
consydra to consider
cuv *m.* **colon** darling
dagren *f.* **dagrow** tear
dewfrik *dual* nose
drehedhes to reach

dres ehen *adv. phrase* exremely, greatly
fienasow *pl.* anxiety
hanaja to sigh, to gasp
lath *f.* **lathow** yard (measure)
ledan *adj.* wide
mar calsa den if one could
mellya gans to bother with
pandr'o an mater what was the matter
pyneyl *pron. & adj.* which of two
renky (*pret.* **roncas**) to grunt

sewajya to assuage, to relieve
syght *m.*, **syghtys** sight
tron *m.* snout

ùnpossybyl *adj.* impossible
yn cosel *adv.* quietly
yn sevur *adv.* strictly

20C.2 TEXT DHE REDYA (*ALYS IN POW AN ANETHOW*)

Red an devyn usy ow sewya ha scrif gorthebow dhe'n qwestyonow:

An baby a roncas arta, hag Alys a viras orth y fâss gans meur a fienasow rag gweles pandr'o an mater ganso. Dewfrik an flogh o pòr rônd ha pòr ledan heb dowt vëth oll, ha moy haval o dhe dron porhel ès dhe dhewfrik baby bian; moy ès hedna yth esa y lagasow ow lehe dres ehen. Ow kemeres pùptra warbarth, ny blegyas an syght anodho dhe Alys. "Martesen nyns usy ev saw owth ola," yn medh hy dhedhy hy honen, ha hy a viras orth an lagasow arta may halla gweles esa dagrow inhans.

Nâ, nyns o dagren vëth dhe weles. "Mars esta ow trailya dhe borhel, a guv colon," yn medh Alys yn sevur, "ny vanaf vy namoy mellya genes. Bëdh war!" An dra via a wrug hanaja arta (poken renky arta—ùnpossybyl veu leverel pyneyl) hag y êth in rag pols.

Yth esa Alys ow tallath govyn worty hy honen pandr'alsa hy gwil gans an creatur pàn wrella hy drehedhes tre, pàn roncas ev unweyth aral mar grev, may whrug hy miras orth y fâss rag ewn own. Ny ylly hy bos camgemerys an termyn-ma. Nyns o va tra vëth ken ès porhel, ha hy a gonsydras y fia gocky dres ehen, mar teffa hy ha'y dhon na felha.

Rag hedna hy a settyas an best bian wàr an dor, hag y feu hy holon sewajys yn frâs pàn wrug hy y weles ow ponya yn cosel aberth i'n coos. "Mar teffa ha tevy in bàn," yn medh Alys dhedhy hy honen. "ev a via an hackra flogh bythqweth a veu; saw porhel teg lowr ywa, me a grës." Gans hedna hy a dhalathas predery a oll an flehes erel neb o aswonys dhedhy hy honen, hag yth esa hy ow leverel dhedhy hy honen, "mar calsa den unweyth cafos an fordh ewn rag aga chaunjya," pàn veu hy sowthenys gans Cath Ker hag ev esedhys wàr vranch a wedhen nebes lathow dhyworty.

1 Pandra wrug Alys pàn wrug an baby renky dywweyth?
2 Pana semlant esa wàr dhewfrik an baby?
3 Prag yth esa Alys ow cresy an baby dhe jaunjya dhe borhel?
4 Pàn wrug Alys convedhes an baby dhe vos porhel, pandra wrug hy ganso?
5 Prag y feu Alys nebes sewajys?
6 Pandr'esa in brës Alys pàn veu hy sowthenys gans Cath Ker?

KENSA DYSCANS WARN UGANS
TWENTY-FIRST LESSON

21A.1 *GODHVOS* 'TO KNOW'

Godhvos is important both as a full verb and as an auxiliary. Its basic sense is 'to know' of facts. As an auxiliary, however, it is used to mean 'to know how to, to have the capacity'. Its conjugation is as follows:

Verbal noun
godhvos

Verbal adjective
godhvedhys

Present
1 *sg.* **gòn, goraf, gorama**
2 *sg.* **godhes, go·dhesta**
3 *sg.* **gor**

1 *pl.* **godhyn, goryn**
2 *pl.* **godhowgh**
3 *pl.* **godhons**

Future
1 *sg.* **godhvedhaf**
2 *sg.* **godhvedhyth, godhvedhys**
3 *sg.* **godhvyth**

1 *pl.* **godhvedhyn**
2 *pl.* **godhvedhowgh**
3 *pl.* **godhvedhons**

Imperfect
1 *sg.* **godhyen**
2 *sg.* **godhyes**
3 *sg.* **godhya** (LC **goya**)

1 *pl.* **godhyen**
2 *pl.* **godhyewgh**
3 *pl.* **godhyens**

Conditional
1 *sg.* **godhvien**
2 *sg.* **godhvies**
3 *sg.* **godhvia**

1 *pl.* **godhvien**
2 *pl.* **godhviewgh**
3 *pl.* **godhviens**

Subjunctive

1 *sg.* **gothfen**	1 *pl.* **gothfen**
2 *sg.* **gothfes**	2 *pl.* **gothfewgh**
3 *sg.* **gothfa**	3 *pl.* **gothfens**

NOTE: The preterite of **godhvos** is nowhere attested in traditional Cornish. Although it could be reconstructed as ***godhvef** 'I realized', ***godhves** 'you realized', etc., in the interests of authenticity the tense is best avoided.

The imperfect refers to continuous knowledge: **me a wodhvia pùptra solabrë·s, pàn wrusta y leverel dhybm** 'I knew everything already, when you told me'.

21A.2 *ASWON, AJON* 'TO KNOW, TO RECOGNIZE'
When describing acquaintance with people or places one uses **aswon**, rather than **godhvos**: **yth esof owth aswon dha vroder yn tâ** 'I know your brother well'. **Aswon**, however, is also used to mean 'to acknowledge facts', e.g. **ny a yll gweles hag aswon an tavas Kernowek dhe vos tavas coth** 'we can see and acknowledge that the Cornish language is an ancient language' (John Boson).

21A.3 *MYNS, SEUL* AND THE RELATIVE PARTICLE *A*²
'All that', 'all who', etc. are usually translated in Cornish by **myns**, **kebmys** or **seul**. The subjunctive is used with all three when referring to an indefinite number of persons or things in the future:

Seul a vydna dos genen, res vëdh dhodho bos obma myttyn abrë·s avorow All those who want to come with us, must be here tomorrow morning early

Y fëdh henwys i'n lyvryk kebmys a rolla mona dhe'n eglos There will be named in the book all those who give money to the church.

Neb can also be used with this sense: **Neb a wrella y wil, ev a wra cafos an gober** 'Who ever does it, he will get the prize'. It is possible, however, to express the idea of 'all that', 'all who', etc. without using an antecedent at all, i.e. by allowing the relative particle to function as its own antecedent:

Me a wor a whelowgh why I know what you seek
Ev a wra kemeres a vydna He will take what he wants.

21A.4 ALTERNATIVE STATEMENTS

The ordinary word for 'or' in Cornish is **pò** or **bò**. This may be used twice in alternative statements: **bò kerdhes pò ponya tre me a wra** 'I will either walk or run home'. But note the use in: **may halla va prevy esa y wreg ow qwitha compes et y gever, esa pò nag esa** 'so that he might prove whether his wife was keeping faithful to him, was she or wasn't she' (see also 15B.8).

Alternative statements can also be rendered with **be va... pò: ev a vydn dos dhe'm gweles be va avorow pò trenja** 'he will come to see me whether it be tomorrow or the day after'.

21A.5 'EVEN, IF ONLY'

Kyn⁵(th) and the subjunctive is used in such sentences as **ny yll den vëth y ewna, kyn fe scoler pò den pòr skentyl** 'no man will be able to amend it, even though he be scholar or very wise man'. 'Even' in sentences of this kind can also be expressed by **unweyth** 'once', for example: **ny allaf ùnderstondya unweyth an radn sempel anodho** 'I don't even understand the easy part of it'. **Unweyth** (LC **eneth**) in conditions means 'only': **me a via pòr lowen, unweyth a callen y ùnderstondya** 'I should be very happy, if only I could understand it'.

21A.6 'SEEM, APPEAR'

In Cornish 'it seems' in 'it seems to me', for example, is rendered by the verb **yth hevel.** The imperfect is **yth hevelly** 'it seemed' and the conditional **yth havalsa** 'it would seem'. This last tense is also attested in the 3rd plural **yth havalsens** 'they would seem'. The verbal noun is **hevelly**, which is used to mean 'to liken, to appear'.

'To appear' in a more general sense is sometimes rendered by **omdhys-qwedhes**, literally 'to show oneself' or even **dysqwedhes** 'to show, to appear'. The English borrowing **apperya** 'to appear' is also well attested.

21B EXAMPLES FROM THE TEXTS

21B.1 *ny won eth e ahanan* 'I do not know whether he has gone hence' BK 12; *sera ny won convethas ages dewan in neb for* 'sir, I cannot understand your anxiety in any way' CW 1232-33; *Na ora vee dr'el an Kembreean gweel rag tho gwytha 'ge tavaz* 'I do not know what the Welsh can do to maintain their language' NBoson; *Ny wothys gwardya preson* 'You don't know how to guard a prison' BK 527; *mara custa lavar thym* 'if you can, tell

me' CW 2331; ***Ow negys ny wothvethys*** 'You will not know my business' BK
46; ***Te a wothvith the negys*** 'You will know your business' BK 1051; ***pan
worshyp, er agys fith, a wothya Arthor the ry*** 'what compensation, by your
faith, was Arthur able to give?' BK 2253-54; ***vn dra a won a'n gothfes a russe
the thythane*** 'one thing I know, which, if you knew it, it would amuse you' OM
151-52; ***Nyng es myghtern in neb gwlas na wothvean, rennothas!
dystogh lyha e vrusyl*** 'There is no king in any country, whose insubordination
I could not, by my father, immediately reduce' BK 1305-07; ***a cuffan y voʒa
gwyre me a sewsye tha thesyre*** 'if I knew it were true, I should follow your
desire' CW 672-73; ***an gwyr a ve derives a thorne the thorne, may halla
ynna bos gothvethis eysy*** 'the truth was related from hand to hand, so that it
could be easily known among them' TH 48.

21B.2 ***rak ganso yma hep fal mur a'y tus thotho haval na aswonyn an
profus*** 'for there are without fail many people like him, so that we will not
recognize the prophet' PC 988-70; ***kettel tersys an bara aswonys cryst a
gara*** 'as soon as you broke the bread, I recognized Christ whom I love' RD 1318-
19; ***bythqueth me nyn aswonys*** 'never have I known him' PA 84d; ***A
aswonsyn ve the stat, ne setsan warnas algat*** 'Had I know of your estate,
I should not have attacked you at all' BK 606-07; ***Ny yll henna gafus du thy
das, mas eff a aswonna an egglos the vos y vam*** 'That man cannot have
God as his father, unless he recognises that the church is his mother' TH 39a;
***an egglos a rome an brassa, an cotha egglos, han brassa assonys a oll
egglosyow*** 'the church of Rome, the largest, oldest church and the best known
of all churches' TH 47a; ***whath me ny won ʒe redya nag aswen ov leʒerow***
'I cannot yet read nor recognize my letters' BM 72-3; ***ha rag hedna ni el
guelas ha adzhan an tavaz Kernuak dha boz tavaz koth ha triuadh eu
dha boz kelles*** 'and therefore we can see and recognize that Cornish is an
ancient language and it is a pity that it should be lost' JBoson.

21B.3 ***Myns a vynhy ol a vyth gwrys*** 'All that you wish will be done' BK1676;
ha mer the breysya drys suel a welys heb mar 'and greatly to be praised
certainly beyond all those I have seen' BK 2243-44; ***in nergh korf kemmys a
vo in arvow rys ew thotha hastia thu'm arluth uhall*** 'as many in bodily
strength who are in arms must haste to my noble lord' BK 2369-71; ***Neb a rella
agys clowes why, eff am clow ve, ha neb a rella agys despisia why,
yma worth ow despisia ve, ha neb a rella ow despicia ve, yma ow
despicia henna a rug ow dynwyn ve*** 'He who hears you, he hears me, and
he who despises you, despises me, and he who despises me, despises him who
sent me' TH 41a.

21B.4 ***the prevy ha the thisprevy puptra scriffis, ewa scriptur, po nag ew***
'to prove and to disprove everything written, whether it is scripture or not' TH
36; ***ha mars ega thetha lell corfow po nag essa*** 'and whether they had real
bodies or not' TH 55; ***Ha mar crussons dibbry in dede po na russens,
ha fatell alsans apperia in corfow po na alsans*** 'And if they really ate or
not, and how they could or could not appear in bodily form' TH 55; ***be va dre
commondment du, bo dre neb one ny dre obediens kylmys the seruya***

'whether it be by the commandment of God, I by him whom we are by obedience bound to serve' TH 5; *be va foode an corfe po food an ena* 'whether it be food for the body or food for the soul' TH 57a.

21B.5 *Ne ren vry pew a's pewa, kyn fe va arluth mar vras* 'I did not care who owned it, even if he was so great a lord' BK 100-01; *Indella me a vynsa, kyn fe rys thym bos marow* 'Thus I would wish, even though I should have to die' BK433-34; *Kyn fe in cres menath horn, me a'n devyn a deu thorn in hast* 'Even if he were in the middle of an iron mountain, I will tear him quickly into two pieces' BK 3220-22; *vnwyth a caffen hansell me a russa amendie* 'if only I could have breakfast, I should improve' BM 110-11; *Ny sowrd clevas in mab pron na ra unwyth e lawsa* 'No sickness will arise in a man's body that it will not even remedy' BK 1124-25.

21B.6 *Ne hevelyth benegas* 'you do not seem blessed' BK 112; *orth fysmens age fays crustunyon yth havalsens* 'from the features of their faces they would seem to be Christians' BM 1205-06; *ymthysquethas ny vynna the plussyon auelough why* 'he did not wish to appear to dirty fellows like you' RD 1496-97; *e avednyaz thoranze seer puna termin reeg an steare disquethaz* 'he asked them certainly when the star appeared' Rowe; *ha grenz an teere zeeah disquethaz* 'and let the dry land appear' JKeigwin; *fatell rug agan Savyour, wosa y resurreccion, apperia in mor* 'that our Saviour appeared by the sea after his resurrection' TH 42a; *ny a rede fatell rug du apperya the Moyses in hevelep a flam a dan* 'we read that God appeared to Moses in the likeness of a flame of fire' TH 55a; *fatell ylly du po ell apperia in hevelep a den* 'that God or an angel can appear in the likeness of a man' TH 55a; *girryow an scripture a yll bos eaisy vnderstandis, kepare dell vgy apperia owrth an artickell ma* 'the words of the scripture can easily be understood, as appears from this article' SA 64.

21C.1 VOCABULARY

addya to add
aga thry *pron. phrase* the three of them
an Pednwyscor *m.* the Hatter
bohes confort little comfort
chair *m.* **brehek, chairys brehek** armchair
cornel *f.* **cornelly** corner
desmyk *m.*, **desmygow** guess, riddle
dhana *adv.* then, in that case
egery (*past* **egoras**) to open
elyn *m.*, **elydnow** elbow
galow *m.* invitation

herdhya to thrust, to push
hevelepter *m.* similarity
hunegan *m.*, **huneganas** dormouse
kebmer *imper.* take, have
kestalkya to talk together, to converse
me a dëb I consider
mênya to mean
miras stag orth to stare at
na vern that it doesn't matter
omdhydhana to amuse oneself
personek *adj.* personal
pluvak *f.*, **pluvogow** pillow

Scovarnak Merth *personal name*   **why a godhvia** you ought
the March Hare   **yn heglew** *adv.* audibly
spâss *m.* space, room   **yn town in cùsk** deeply asleep

21C.2 TEXT DHE REDYA (*ALYS IN POW AN ANETHOW*)
Red an devyn usy ow sewya hag ena gwra gortheby an qwestyonow:

Yth esa bord settys in mes in dadn wedhen dhyrag an chy hag yth esa Scovarnak Merth ha'n Pednwyscor ow kemeres tê orto; yth esa Hunegan esedhys intredhans yn town in cùsk; ha'n dhew aral orth y ûsya avell pluvak, aga elydnow ow powes warnodho hag y ow kestalkya dresto. "Bohes confort yw hedna rag an Hunegan," yn medh Alys dhedhy hy honen, "saw yma va in cùsk, hag ytho me a dëb na vern dhodho."

Brâs lowr o an bord, mès yth êns y oll aga thry herdhys warbarth orth udn gornel anodho. "Nyns eus spâss vëth! Nyns eus spâss vëth!" y a grias pàn wrussons y gweles Alys ow tos. "Yma lowr a spâss!" yn medh Alys nebes offendys ha hy a esedhas in chair brehek brâs orth udn pedn a'n bord.

"Kebmer nebes gwin," a leverys Scovarnak Merth, ow ry colon dhedhy.

Alys a viras orth an bord oll adro, saw nyns esa tra vëth marnas tê warnodho. "Ny welaf gwin vëth," yn medh Alys.

"Nyns eus," yn medh Scovarnak Merth.

"Ny veu cortes dhis dhana offra gwin dhybm," a leverys Alys yn serrys.

"Ny veu cortes dhis esedha obma heb cafos galow," yn medh Scovarnak Merth.

"Me ny wodhyen y vos agas bord why," yn medh Alys, "yma va settys rag lies moy ès try den."

"Y talvia dhis trehy dha vlew," yn medh an Pednwyscor. Ev re bia ow miras stark orth Alys, ha marth brâs dhodho dres nebes mynys, ha'n re-na a veu y kensa geryow.

"Why a godhvia sevel orth leverel taclow personek," yn medh Alys yn sherp, "pòr dhydhysk ywa."

Pàn glôwas an Pednwyscor hedna, ev a egoras y lagasow yn ledan, saw tra vëth ny leverys mès "Pandr'yw an hevelepter inter bran ha bord scrifa?"

"Dàr, ny a vydn omdhydhana lebmyn," a brederys Alys. "Pës dâ oma y dhe dhallath govyn desmygow—me a grës fatell allama gortheby hedna," hy a addyas yn heglew.

"Esta ow leverel te dhe bredery y hylta jy cafos an gorthyb dhodho?" yn medh Scovarnak Merth.

"Ea, poran," yn medh Alys.

"Te a dalvia leverel dhana an pëth esta ow mênya," a besyas Scovarnak Merth.

1 Pyw esa ow kemeres tê warbarth in dadn an wedhen?

2 Pleth esa esedhys an Pednwyscor, an Scovarnak ha'n Hunegan?

3 Pandra leverys an dhew pàn wrussons y gweles Alys?

4 Pandra wrug an Scovarnak offra dhe Alys ha prag na veu hy plêsys?

5 Pandra veu an dra dhyscortes a leverys an Pednwyscor dhe Alys.

6 Pëth a leverys Alys pàn glôwas hy desmyk an Pednwyscor?

SECÙND DYSCANS WARN UGANS
TWENTY-SECOND LESSON

22A.1 THE SECOND PERSON SINGULAR IMPERATIVE

The second person singular imperative is usually the root form of the verb: **kemeres** 'to take' > **kebmer** 'take!'; **gweles** 'to see' > **gwel** 'see!'; **perthy** 'to bear' > **porth** 'bear!'; **leverel** 'to say' > **lavar** 'say!'.

In some cases the the root ends in a vowel and this is apparent in the imperative: **gortos** 'to remain' > **gorta** 'remain!'; **whilas** 'to seek' > **whila** 'seek!' Note that **dysqwedhes** 'to show', has **dysqwa** 'show!' before a consonant and **dysqweth** before a vowel.

Where a dissyllabic verbal noun has **e** in the root, the second singular imperative can have **ë** or **ÿ**: **cresy** 'to believe' > **crës, crÿs** 'believe!'; **pesy** 'to pray' > **pës, pÿs** 'pray!' Some verbs have alternative forms in **e** in the verbal noun, e.g. **scrifa, screfa** 'to write', **triga, trega** 'to dwell', **miras, meras** 'to look', **piba, peba** 'to play the pipes'. In the second singular imperative the **i** only will appear: **scrif** 'write!'; **trig** 'dwell!', **mir** 'look!' and **pib** 'play the pipe!'

The following are irregular second singular imperatives: **bos** 'to be' > **bëdh** 'be!'; **godhvos** 'to know' > **godhvyth** 'know!' (though **gor** is also attested); **don** 'to carry' > **dog** 'carry!'; **mos** 'to go' > **ke** 'go!'; **dos** 'to come' > **deus** 'come!'; **gwil** 'to do' > **gwra** 'do!' This last can be used with any verbal noun, e.g. **gwra kerdhes in rag** 'keep walking!'

The verb **ry** 'to give' has an imperative **ro** or **roy** 'give!' **Ro** is not used before vowels. The imperative of **dry** 'to bring' is **dro**. A form **doroy** is sometimes used before vowels.

22A.2 THE SECOND PERSON PLURAL IMPERATIVE

Unlike the second person singular imperative, the second person plural imperative usually shows affection of the root: **perthowgh** 'bear!' (*pl.*); **leverowgh** 'say' (*pl.*) In verbs with alternating **e** ~ **ë/ÿ** the **e** will appear

148

in the second person plural imperative: **cresowgh** 'believe!' (*pl.*), **pesowgh** 'pray!' (*pl.*). If a verb has a variant stem in **e** and **i**, the **e** may appear in the second plural: **screfowgh** 'write!' (pl.); **tregowgh** 'dwell!' (*pl.*); **merowgh** 'look!' (*pl.*)

Irregular second person plurals include: **bedhowgh**! 'be!'; **godh-vedhowgh** 'know!'; **rewgh** 'give!', **drewgh** 'bring!'; **degowgh** 'carry!'; **kewgh** or **ewgh** 'go!' and **gwrewgh** 'do!' A variant form **gwrellowgh** 'do!' (*pl.*) is also attested. **Gwrewgh** may be used with the verbal noun of any verb to make a plural imperative: **gwrewgh sewya an den-na** 'follow (*pl.*) that man!'

22A.3 THE THIRD PERSON IMPERATIVE

To express the third person imperative, it is possible to use a jussive subjunctive, e.g. **re dheffo ev** 'let him come!'; **re bo an dra gwrës** 'let the thing be done!'

There does, however, exist a special form of the the third person imperative, which is identical for singular and plural: **deuns** is either 'let him/her come' or 'let them come'; **bedhens** means either 'let him/her be' or 'let them be'; **gwrêns** is either 'let him/her do' or 'let them do'. **Gwrêns** is particularly useful, since it can be used with the verbal noun of any verb to render the imperative: **gwrêns ev gortos ena** 'let him wait there', **gwrêns y cafos aga gober** 'let them get their wages'.

The third person imperative, both singular and plural, can be expressed by periphrasis with the verb **gasa** 'to allow, to let': **gas Jowan dhe vos gans an re erel** 'let John go with the others'; **gas an flehes dhe dhauncya lebmyn** 'let the children dance now'. **Gas Jowan dhe vos** is thus similar in sense to **êns Jowan** or **gwrêns Jowan mos**.

22A.4 THE OBJECT OF AN IMPERATIVE

The imperative proper can take a direct object: **roy an mona dhybm** 'give me the money'; **drewgh an flehes genowgh** 'bring the children with you (pl.)' If the object is a pronoun, it takes the form of the suffixed personal pronouns (see 14A.4) and is placed after the verb: **gwra y!** 'make them!', **dro y genes** 'bring them with you!'

As noted above, the second singular imperative of **dry** 'to bring' is **dro**. The subject pronoun **va** 'him, it' is sometimes suffixed to this form as a direct object: **dro va dhybmo** 'bring it to me'. It would seem that **dro** is the only attested verb to use **va** as an object after an imperative.

In the earlier texts a pronoun object sometimes appears as an infixed pronoun after the particle **a**: **a'n kemerens** 'let him take it'.

22A.5 THE NEGATIVE IMPERATIVE

Imperatives are rendered negative by the use of the particle **na²** (which does not become **nag** before vowels): **na wra** 'don't do'; **na wrewgh** 'don't do' (*pl.*); **na ankevowgh** 'don't forget' (*pl.*). The particle **na** may also be used with the third person imperative: **na wrêns ev côwsel** 'let him not speak'; **na dheuns y obma arta** 'let them not come here again'.

22A.6 THE FIRST PERSON PLURAL IMPERATIVE

Cornish possesses a separate form of the imperative for the first person plural in some verbs, e.g. **deun** 'let us come (or go)'; **bedhyn** 'let us be'; **gwren** 'let us do'. This last combines with the verbal noun of other verbs: **gwren pesy** 'let us pray'; **gwren perthy cov** 'let us remember'; **gwren y dhon alebma** 'let us take it hence'. These forms can all be rendered negative by the use of **na²**: **na vedhyn trist** 'let us not be sad'; **na dheun alebma** 'let us not go hence'; **na wren ankevy** 'let us not forget'.

By the later sixteenth century, however, such synthetic forms had largely given way to a periphrastic construction with gasa (see 22A.3 above). One can therefore say: **gesowgh ny dhe remembra** 'let us remember'; **gesowgh ny dhe bredery** 'let us consider'; **gesowgh ny dhe besy warbarth** 'let us pray together'. **Gesyn ny pesy** 'let us pray' and **gas ny dhe vos** 'let us go' are also attested. These constructions are rendered negative by the use of **na²**: **na esyn ny dhe gresy** 'let us not believe'. **Gas** can also be used with the first person singular imperative: **gas vy dh'y weles** 'let me see it'.

22A.7 THE REFLEXIVE

In the earliest Middle Cornish verbs are sometimes rendered reflexive by the use of the unstressed prefix **om²-** (or **ym²**): **golhy** 'to wash' > **omwolhy** 'wash (oneself)'; **gwitha** 'to keep' > **omwitha** 'keep oneself, avoid'; **dysqwedhes** 'show' > **omdhysqwedhes** 'show oneself, appear' (21A.6); **prevy** 'to prove' > **ombrevy** 'to prove oneself, show oneself'.

Notice the shift in sense in **tôwlel** 'to throw' but **omdôwlel** 'to wrestle'; **perthy** 'to bear' but **omberthy** 'to balance' (oneself); **ladha** 'to kill', **omladha** 'to kill oneself' but **o·mlath** 'to fight'; **omdho·n** 'to behave' but **o·mdhon** 'to conceive'; **kelly** 'to lose' > **omgelly** 'to faint'.

During the Middle Cornish period the prefix **om-** ceased to be productive and reflexives were made by use of the pronoun **honen** 'self'. If one imitates such reflexives in the revived language, one says, for example, **yth eson ny ow tecêvya agan honen** 'we deceive ourselves', **ev a wanas y honen dre wall** 'he stabbed himself by accident'.

Quite often in traditional Cornish both the prefix **om-** and the pronoun **honen** are used together in a mixed syntax. This can be imitated in the revived language to give such sentences as **y a allas omsawya aga honen** 'they were able to save themselves'.

22B EXAMPLES FROM THE TEXTS

22B.1 *dues gueres ny* 'come, help us' PC 308; *Meryasek beth lowen* 'Meriasek, be joyful' BM 4343; *doro thy'm a'n guyn guella* 'give me of the best wine' OM 1904; *Ke souyth ha north ha gura cry cref in pub cost* 'Go south and north and make a loud cry in every region' BK 2350-51; *Douoy an gòlou ðanna* 'Bring the light then' JCH §42; *Lavar thymmo, me a'th pys* 'Tell me, I beseech you' BK 938: *ɡyr tero an ðiz rag ha mana 'ryg an bad-ober* 'know that it was the ale-wife and a monk who committed the crime' JCH §31.

22B.2 *dewgh arag omma ʒa vee* 'come forth here to me' CW 62; *kewgh in kerth inweth gonʒa* 'co away with him also' CW 324; *Kemerogh, debbrogh, hem ew ow corff ve* 'Take, eat, this is my body' SA 62a; *bethough pur glor* 'be very gentle' BK 1278; *a'gys dyhowgh prederowgh* 'consider your right flank' BK 3260; *Eugh a'm golak in neb tol!* 'Go from my sight into some hole!' BK 2343; *Walkyow ha gwandrow warlyrth an spuris* 'Walk and wander according to the spirit' TH 16a.

22B.3 *Dens an re na pan vynnans* 'Let them come when they wish' BM 2467; *drens hy ov map dymo vy ha gruens ov servia deyly arta awose helma* 'let her bring me my son and let her serve me daily hereafter' BM 3696-98; *Lyvyryns theugh prag ema ow quarellya drys ow thyr* 'Let him tell why he is laying a claim against my country' BK 1836-37; *Gwrens e drubut ha'y sute* 'Let him perform his tribute and his suit' BK 1849; *bethans pur war!* 'Let them be on their guard!' BK 1262; *bethans gorrys in ye thywfridg* 'let them be put into his nostrils' CW 1854; *gas an haneth ma a virnans the vos thewortha ve* 'let this cup of death pass from me' TH 22a.

22B.4 *Te falge horsen nam brag vy* 'You false whoreson, do not threaten me' BM 3491; *Gwyth ve orth sham* 'keep me from shame' BK 1237; *ɡyr iustys lath e lath e* 'sir justice, kill him, kill him' PC 2356; *drova thymo desempys* 'bring it to me immediately' CW 844; *ke the gy kergh y yn mes* 'go you; fetch them out' PC 2290; *the ij cheplen kemer y genes thegy eredy* 'your two chaplains, take them with you indeed' BM 4034-35.

22B.5 *A'm dyrryvas na gemer marth* 'Of what I say be not astounded' BK 141-42; *na rens ef examnya den vith arell, mas y golan y honyn* 'let him not examine anyone else, but only his own heart' TH 23a; *Rag meth na vethens gegys a'y servys the omdenna* 'For shame, let him not be allowed to withdraw from his service' BK 1844-45; *Aragough na ren gwelas the servantes, tues vras ha coyth, bos wottywath drog telys* 'Before you let us not see your servants, great and wise people, being badly recompensed in the end' BK 754-756; *Cowethe na vethen lent* 'Comrades, let us not be slow' BM

3245; *na rewgh mas meras war an pow* 'only look at the country' TH 49a;
indella na rellow gull an pith a vynnow 'thus do not do what you want'
TH 16a; *nefra na wrewgh why dowtya* 'never fear' CW 1556.

22B.6 *gas ny the wull den* 'let us make man' TH 1; *Ha gwren ny consyddra
pan a royow a russyn recêva* 'And let us consider what gifts we have received'
TH 24a; *Gesow ny the consydra fatell essan ny ow deservia le gyvyans*
'Let us consider that we deserve less forgiveness' TH 24a; *gesowgh ny the
persuadya agan honyn* 'let us persuade ourselves' TH 54a; *gas ny tha vos
alemma* 'let us depart hence' CW 1332; *Na esyn vsya argumentys, mas
vsya exampels Christ* 'Let us not use arguments, but the very examples of
Christ' SA 61a; *Na esy'ny miras wor an bara ha'n dewas ew sittys
deragen* 'Let us not look upon the bread and the drink that is set before us' SA
65a.

22B.7 *saw whath rys ew mos thotha hag omthyvlamya orta* 'but still it is
necessary to go to him and apologize to him' BK 448-49; *guetyogh omprevy
manly* 'be sure to show yourselves manly' BM 1194; *Leud ema owth
umbrevy* 'She is showing herself to be lewd' BK 3001; *avel fals Judas
Scaryot a omgrogas orth scawan* 'like perfidious Judas Iscariot, who hanged
himself from an elder tree' BK 2536-37; *ny a gren agen barvov mar ny
omthegen the guel* 'we will shake our beards if we do not behave better' BM
3450-51; *Me vedn meare cressha tha dewhan ha tha humthan* 'I will
greatly increase your pain and your labour' Rowe; *mayth egan owth umgelly*
'so that we were fainting' BK 2332; *fetla wren omwetha bew* 'how shall we
keep ourselves alive?' CW 1047; *Gesow ny lymmyn the aswan agan honyn*
'Let us now recognize ourselves' TH 11a; *ny a gottha thyn omry agan honyn
the wetha ha the colynwall y commondment eff* 'we should devote
ourselves to keeping and to fulfilling his commandment' TH 21a; *lemmyn y
honan ny yl sur ymsawye* 'now indeed he cannot save himself' PC 2877-78;
rak hacre mernans certan eys emlathe y honan ny gaffe den my a grys
'for a nastier death than suicide no man could endure, I believe' RD 2072-74.

22C.1 VOCABULARY

a'y sav *adv. phrase* standing
boneyl ... bò either ... or
brâster *m.* majesty
bytegyns *adv.* all the same, however
cessya to cease
chauns *m.* chance, opportunity
cot hy anal *adj. phrase* 'short her
breath', out of breath
cowl *m.* **fug-grùban** mock turtle
soup
dêwys to choose

dùches *f.* duchess
dybarth to depart
dybedna to behead, to decapitate
dywvregh *dual* (two) arms
folya to follow
fug-grùban *m.* mock turtle
gwarek *f.*, **gwaregow** bow, arch
gwarior *m.*, **gwarioryon** player
gwarnyans *m.* warning
hager-awel *f.* storm
hanter-our *m.* half an hour

hedhy to stop. to cease
in dadn with *adv. phrase* in custody
park *m.* **crôkê** croquet pitch
plegys *adj.* folded
qwarellya to quarrel
qwit *adv.* quite, completely

sêsya to seize
skeus *m.* shade
stankya to stamp, to trample
strechya to delay
voys *m.* voice

22C.2 TEXT DHE REDYA (*ALYS IN POW AN ANETHOW*)

Red an devyn usy ow sewya ha scrif gorthebow dhe'n qwestyonow:

Alys a viras in bàn hag otta, yth esa an Vyternes a'y sav dhyrygthy, plegys hy dywvregh ha hy thâl màr dewl avell hager-awel.

"Dùrda dhywgh why, agas Brâster!" a dhalathas an Dhùches, isel, gwadn hy voys.

"Now, yth esoma ow ry gwarnyans teg dhis," yn medh an Vyternes, ow stankya wàr an dor gans an geryow, "boneyl te bò dha bedn a dal bos gyllys qwit, kyns ès pedn hanter mynysen! Gwra dêwys!"

An Dhùches a wrug dêwys ha gyllys o hy gans an ger.

"Gesowgh ny dhe bêsya gans an gwary," yn medh an Vyternes dhe Alys; hag Alys a gemeras re a own rag leverel tra vëth, mès hy a's folyas wàr dhelergh dhe'n park crôkê.

An warioryon erell a welas aga chauns pàn dhybarthas an Vyternes, hag yth esens y ow powes i'n skeus; bytegyns kettel wrussons y gweles an Vyternes, y oll a dhewhelys yn uskys dhe'n gwary; ny leverys an Vyternes mès udn ger: mar teffons ha strechya udn vynysen kyn fe, y fedhens gorrys dhe'n mernans.

Pàn esens y ow qwary, ny cessyas an Vyternes unweyth a gwarellya gans an warioryon erel ha cria "Gwrewgh y dhybedna!" bò "Gwrewgh hy dybedna!" Pàn vedha nebonen dampnys, an soudoryon a'n sêsyas ha res o dhedhans heb màr gasa aga ober avell gwaregow. Indella kyns pedn hanter-our nyns o gwarek vëth gesys, hag yth esa pùbonen, marnas an Mytern, an Vyternes hag Alys, in dadn with ha dampnys dhe'n mernans.

I'n eur-na an Vyternes a wrug hedhy, cot hy anal, ha leverel dhe Alys, "A wrusta gweles an Fug-Grùban whath?"

"Na wrug," yn medh Alys. "Ny woraf vy unweyth pandr'yw Fug-Grùban."

"Hèn yw an dra mayth usons y ow qwil Cowl Fug-Grùban anodho," yn medh an Vyternes.

"Ny wrug avy bythqweth naneyl gweles na clôwes a onen anodhans," yn medh Alys.

"Deus in rag ytho," yn medh an Vyternes, "hag ev a vydn derivas y story dhis."

1 Pleth esa an Vyternes a'y sav, pàn wrug Alys hy merkya?

2 Pëth o an dëwys a wrug an Vyternes ry dhe'n Dhùches?

3 Pàn dhybarthas an Vyternes, pandr'a wrug an warioryon erel?

4 Pëth esa an Vyternes ow qwil pùpprës ha hy ow qwary?

5 Prag nag o gesys marnas Alys, an Mytern ha'n Vyternes whath ow qwary?

6 Warlergh an Vyternes, pandra vynsa an Fug-Grùban gwil rag Alys?

TRESSA DYSCANS WARN UGANS
TWENTY-THIRD LESSON

23A.1 THE VERB *Y'M BEUS*

We have seen at 9A.9 that Cornish often expresses the idea of possession with the verb **bos** 'to be' and a preposition, for example: **yma mona dhybm** 'I have some money'. There is, however, a verb which means 'to have' by itself, namely **y'm beus**. This verb is itself a derivative of the verb **bos** 'to be', and it consists of the third person singular of the various tenses of **bos** preceded by a verbal particle and an infixed pronoun with dative sense ('to me', 'to you', 'to him', etc.). **Y'm beus mona**, therefore, literally means 'there is (**eus**) money to me (**'m**)', and is indentical in sense with the periphrastic **yma mona dhybm**.

Y'm beus has no verbal noun, verbal adjective or imperative. The third person singular, however, has separate forms for masculine and feminine. The various tenses may be conjugated as follows (although many of the following forms are actually unattested):

Present

1 *sg.* **y'm beus**	1 *pl.* **y'gan beus**
2 *sg.* **y'th eus**	2 *pl.* **y'gas beus**
3 *sg. m.* **y'n jeves**, *f.* **y's teves**	3 *pl.* **y's teves**

Future

1 *sg.* **y'm bëdh**	1 *pl.* **y'gan bëdh**
2 *sg.* **y'fëdh**	2 *pl.* **y'gas bëdh**
3 *sg. m.* **y'n jevyth**, *f.* **y's tevyth**	3 *pl.* **y's tevyth**

Imperfect

1 *sg.* **y'm bo**	1 *pl.* **y'gan bo**
2 *sg.* **y'fo**	2 *pl.* **y'gas bo**
3 *sg. m.* **y'n jeva**, *f.* **y's teva**	3 *pl.* **y's teva**

Imperfect Habitual

1 *sg.* **y'm bedha**	1 *pl.* **y'gan bedha**
2 *sg.* **y'fedha**	2 *pl.* **y'gas bedha**
3 *sg. m.* **y'n jevedha**, *f.* **y's tevedha**	3 *pl.* **y's tevedha**

Preterite

1 *sg.* **y'm be**	1 *pl.* **y'gan be**
2 *sg.* **y'fe**	2 *pl.* **y'gas be**
3 *sg. m.* **y'n jeva**, *f.* **y's teva**	3 *pl.* **y's teva**

Subjunctive

1 *sg.* **y'm bo**	1 *pl.* **y'gan bo**
2 *sg.* **y'fo**	2 *pl.* **y'gas bo**
3 *sg. m.* **y'n jeffa**, *f.* **y's teffa**	3 *pl.* **y's teffa**

Conditional

1 *sg.* **y'm bia**	1 *pl.* **y'gan bia**
2 *sg.* **y'fia**	2 *pl.* **y'gas bia**
3 *sg. m.* **y'n jevia**, *f.* **y's tevia**	3 *pl.* **y's tevia**

In the above paradigms the verbal particle throughout is **y**. If, however, the subject or object of the verb precedes the verb as a pronoun or a noun, **a** replaces **y**: **y'm beus govenek** 'I have hope', but **me a'm beus govenek** and **govenek a'm beus**. The particle **re** occurs with the jussive subjunctive: **bedneth an Tas re'gas bo** 'may you (*pl.*) have the blessing of the Father'; **re'th fo meth** 'may you be ashamed'; **bydner re'n jeffa lowena** 'may he never have joy'.

Because **y'n jeva** (< **y'n jevo**) of the imperfect and **y'n jeva** (< **y'n jeve** < *__y'n jeveu__) of the preterite have fallen together, the two tenses are not easily distinguished. It seems as though there was for the most part a single past tense, which could be either imperfect or preterite.

The verb **y'm beus** is on occasion used with the verbal adjective to create a perfect tense: **me a'm beus mab denethys** 'I have given birth to a son'.

23A.2 DEVELOPMENTS IN *Y'M BEUS*

The verb **y'm beus** was anomalous in Middle Cornish inasmuch as it was without personal endings. In consequence, it was liable to be reshaped in the texts. This reshaping can best be discussed under four separate headings:

i) the third singular masculine or femine is used with other persons. The masculine, for example, is used with feminine and plural subjects and with the first and second persons plural. One therefore finds such expressions, for example, as **an eglos** *f.* **a'n jevyth** 'the church will have' and **ny a'n jevyth** 'we will have'.

ii) the various persons are recharacterized with the relevant suffixed pronoun: **y'm bo** 'I had', for example, becomes **y'm boma**, and **y'fe** 'you had' becomes **y'festa**.

iii) the verb itself acquires personal endings, for example, **y'gas bëdh** 'we will have' becomes **y'gas bedhowgh** and **ma's teffa** 'that they may have' becomes **ma's teffons**

iv) second person singular forms beginning with **f < b** after **th⁵** are difficult to distinguish from parts of the verb 'to be' itself. **Te a'fëdh lowena** 'you will have joy' is so like **Te a vëdh lowena**, that the verb **bos** itself acquires possessive sense, and one finds such expressions as **me a veu own** 'I was afraid'.

None of the above developments can be considered incorrect, if used in the revived language. In the interests of simplicity, however, learners should perhaps confine themselves to the parts of **y'm beus** listed at 23A.1 above.

NOTE: Unified Cornish does not make use of any of the four developments in **y'm beus** mentioned above. Nance admitted that that ii) and iii) were common in Middle Cornish, but he considered such forms 'less correct'; see Nance's 1938 dictionary, page 203.

23A.3 *PEW* 'POSSESSES'

This is a defective verb with the sense 'to own, to possess'. In syntax it was originally similar to **y'm beus**, since **pew** derives from **py yw** 'to whom there is' > 'who owns'. **Pew** is found only in the third person singular in the present (**pew**) and the imperfect (**pewa**) and the second person singular present subjunctive (**pewfy**). Unlike **y'm beus** this verb can take an infixed pronoun as a direct object: **me a'n pew** 'I own it'. **Pew** has no imperative, no verbal noun and no verbal adjective.

NOTE: In his 1938 dictionary Nance reconstructed a full set of tenses and persons for this verb. Learners, and indeed all revivalists, would be well advised not to use any part of this verb that is not actually attested.

23B EXAMPLES FROM THE TEXTS

23B.1 *Mur varth am bus dyogel* 'Indeed I have great wonder' OM 371; *mar thues ovn bones knoukys* 'if you have fear of being beaten' PC 2245; *cryst guyr vn vap dev a nef yn bys ma nan geves par* 'Christ the only son of the God of heaven in this world, who has no peer' PC 1577-78; *Pylat eth yn mes ay hell yn vn lowarth an gevo* 'Pilate went from his hall into a garden he had' PA 140a; *ihesu agan mester da a'm danvonas the wovyn py le yn gevyth ef chy* 'Jesus, our good master, sent me to enquire where he will get a house' PC 668-70; *A traytors, re'gas bo spyt* 'O traitours, may you receive spite!' BK 2337; *A caffan neb a wothya y'n gevea gwereson* 'If I got someone who did know how, he would have a reward' BK 527-28; *flehys am bef denethys* 'I have engendered children' CW 1979.

23B.2.1 *an egglos an jevas an lell sens an scriptur* 'the church has the true sense of scripture' TH 36 fn.; *nynsevith eff bewnas, mas an sorre a crist a dryg vghta* 'he will not have life, but the wrath of Christ will dwell over him' TH 40; *ha ny an jevith agan reward gansans y* 'and we will have our reward with them' TH 22a; *ha ny an jeva promes a brassa royow* 'and we had a promise of greater gifts' TH 28; *why an jeva sufficient declaracion anotha* 'you had sufficient declaration thereof' TH 30a; *why as tevith sufficient instruccion* 'you will have sufficient instruction' TH 31a.

23B.2.2 *pesef agis bannothow maym beua the well grays* 'I pray your blessings that I may have better grace' BM 46-7; *dyworto ma'm boma gras* 'that I may have grace from him' OM 2077; *kyn nam boma lowena* 'though I may not have joy' CW 928; *thum corff am beua ȝehas y rosen hanter ov gluas* 'were I to have health for my body, I should give half of my kingdom' BM 1686-87; *Te a levar, tavas pan, na'th uesta Duw saw onyn* 'You say cloth-tongue, you have but one God' BK 260-61.

23B.2.3 *Benedicite pana syght am buevy haneth in noys* 'Blessed be God, such a sight I had in the night' BM 1725-26; *kemmys gyrryow teake am beff* 'I got so many fine words' CW 1017; *Pys the Vab ras, hethew ma'm byf an victory* 'Pray thy Son of grace, that today I may have the victory' BK 2814-15; *Ow negys ny wothvethys na worshyip te ny'fethyth* 'My business you shall not know nor will you have respect' BK 46-47; *a'fuys furneth th'e concyvya* 'did you but have wisdom to conceive it' BK 242-43; *gallos warnaf ny fyes na fe y vos grantys thy's* 'you would not have power over me, were it not granted to you' PC 2187-88; *Mar debal-los ny 'fyas, a pe vas the oberow* 'You would not have such ill repute, if your deeds were good' BK 1067-68; *rak na wrello dasserghy neffre nygen byen ny ioy hep thyweth* 'for were he not to rise again, we would not have eternal joy' RD 1028-30; *benytho arluth ath par pur thefry nygyn bethen* 'never in very truth will we have a lord like you' BM 4267-68; *peseff rag an keth re na mays tefons y luen ȝeheys* 'I pray for those same people that they may have full health' BM 4286-87; *byth nys tufons guel bugel* 'never would they have a better pastor' BM 2785.

23B.2.4 *me a levar thys mar pleag yn pan vanar yn bema* 'I will tell you, if you wish, how I came to have it' CW 755-56; *In meth Ihesus yn vr na mestry vyth te ny vea* 'Jesus said then, "you would have no authority"' PA 145a; *confortys yv ow colon pan clewys ow teryfas bones leghys the pascyon a fus tyn garow ha bras* 'comforted is my heart when I heard tell that the passion you had sharp, violent and great has been lessened' RD 503-06; *annethe kyn feste calge war na ra fethye inne* 'although you may have much of them, be careful that you do not trust in them' BM 2046-48; *ha pan deweth ha martirdom a veva in Rome* 'and what martyrdom and death he had in Rome' TH 47a; *me a vee owne, rag theram en noath* 'I was afraid, for I am naked' Rowe; *ha te a vyth mer a gras lemmyn rag gul ow negys* 'and you now will have much thanks for doing my business' BK 879-80; *Neb a'th cuthys in sertan a veth 'goef' er e ran!* 'He who afflicted you indeed will have "woe to him" as his share!' BK 2700-01; *ty a vyth mabe denethys* 'a son will be born to you' CW 1323; *pana rewarde a vethow why?* 'what reward will you have' TH 22; *mar pethama kibmiez tho gweel semblanz 'gun Aulsen coth brose* 'if I have permission to make comparison with great old Ausonius' NBoson; *promes a brassa royow dell vouns y* 'a promise of greater gifts than they had' TH 28.

23B.3 *te a'n pew heb falladow* 'you own it without fail' BK 1158; *Henna forsoth drys peb a bew an onor* 'That man indeed possesses honour above all men' BK 2002-2003; *Ne ren vry pew a's pewa* 'I did not care who owned it' BK 100; *war tu hay vam an pewo y ben a vynnas synsy* 'towards his mother to whom he belonged he wished to lean his head' PA 207c; *malegas nefra reby hag oll an tyer a bewfy* 'may you be cursed and all the land that you may own' CW 1158-59.

23C.1 VOCABULARY

arbednek *adj*. particular, specaill

Australya *f.* Australia

floren *f.* lock

gorra in dadn naw alwheth to lock up, to put under lock and key

i'n câss-na *adv. phrase* in that case

in udn hockya hesitatingly, reluctantly

injynor *m.*, **injynoryon** engineer

kebmys tra aral so many other things

marhogeth to ride

methek *adj*. ashamed, embarrassed

perhen *m.*, **perhednow** owner

posa to lean

rag ewn tristans *adv. phrase* in sheer sorrow

sodhva *f.*, **sodhvaow** office

tramor *adj*. overseas, foreign

troyllya to wind

ùncoth *adj*. unknown

yowynkneth *m.* youth, childhood

23C.2 TEXT DHE REDYA
(*WHEDHEL DHYWORTH AUSTRALYA*)

Red an devyn usy ow sewya ha scrif gorthebow dhe'n qwestyonow:

Me a'm beus lies cothman usy trigys in powyow tramor ha me a vydn derivas dhywgh whedhel adro dhe onen anodhans. An den arbednek-ma yw gelwys Jory hag yma va trigys in Australya le ma'n jeves ober dâ avell injynor. Ev ha'y wreg Anabel a's teves try flogh, dew vab hag udn vyrgh vian. Pàn esa Jory trigys in Kernow in dedhyow y yowynkneth, ny'n jevedha meur a vona rag y vabm o gwedhowes ha hy a's teva teylu brâs. Udn jëdh in Australya, pàn dheuth Jory tre dhyworth an sodhva mayth esa va ow lavurya, ev a welas maw ùncoth ow marhogeth wàr dhywros hag o pòr haval dhe dhywros mab cotha Jory, Davyth y hanow. Jory a wrug stoppya an carr, troyllya an fenester dhe'n dor ha govyn orth an maw pana vaner y'n jeva an dhywros. "Me a's beu rag Nadelyk warleny," yn medh an maw ha'm cothman a brederys ev dhe vos nebes methek. Rag hedna ev a leverys fatell o hy pòr haval dhe dhywros y vab y honen esa trigys i'n nessa strêt. "Wèl," yn medh an maw moy methek whath, "rag leverel an gwiryoneth me a gafas an dhywros posys warbydn wedhen adro dhe'n gornel. Saw nyns esa floren vëth warnedhy, hag yth hevelly dhybm hy dhe vos forsâkys gans hy ferhen." I'n eur-na Jory a wovydnas orth an maw dos ganso bys i'n tyller may cafas ev an dhywros. An maw a agrias in udn hockya ha wosa gorra y garr in dadn naw alwheth an den ha'n maw a gerdhas warbarth bys i'n nessa strêt. Ena y a gafas Davyth, mab Jory, ow whilas y dhywros hag ev owth ola ogasty rag ewn tristans. Jory a ros an dhywros ledrys dh'y vab arta, hag ena ev a drailyas dhe'n maw ùncoth. "Prag y whrusta ladra an dhywros?" yn medh ev. "Me ny'm beu dywros bythqweth," ev a worthebys. "Ow thas vy a verwys pàn en vy pòr vian, ha me ha'm mabm ha'm broder ha'm whor, ny'gan beus meur a vona." "I'n câss-na," yn medh Davyth, "an maw-ma a yll sensy an dhywros-na. Me a'm beus kebmys tra aral dhe wary gansans."

1 Ple ma Jory trigys ha ple veu va genys ha megys?
2 Pana sort a lavur a'n jeves ev ena?
3 Pàn welas ev an maw ùncoth wàr dhywros pandra wrug ev predery?
4 Pana dermyn a gafas an maw an dhywros herwyth y kensa geryow?
5 Esa an maw ow leverel an gwiryoneth pàn leverys ev hedna?
6 In pana vaner a'n jeva ev an dhywros in gwir?
7 Prag y whrug an maw ladra an dhywros?

PESWORA DYSCANS WARN UGANS

TWENTY-FOURTH LESSON

24A.1 COMPARATIVE AND SUPERLATIVE OF ADJECTIVES

For most adjectives in Cornish there is no difference in form between the comparative and the superlative. Both are made from the positive by doubling (where possible) and devoicing the final consonant and adding **-a**: **teg** 'fair' > **tecka** 'fairer, fairest'; **glëb** 'wet' > **gleppa** 'wetter, wettest'. Adjectives whose stems end in **l** may replace **-lla** in the comparative and superlative with **-lha**, e.g. **pell** 'far' > **pella**, **pelha** 'farther, farthest'.

There are a number of irregular comparatives and superlatives:

bian 'small';   **le** 'less';   **lyha** 'least';
  biadnha (**biatna**) 'smallest' is also attested.

meur 'much, great';   **moy** 'more';   **moyha** 'most'

ogas 'near';   **nes** 'nearer';   **nessa** 'nearest, next'

dâ 'good';   **gwell** 'better';   **gwella** (**gwelha**) 'best'

drog 'bad';   **gweth** 'worse;   **gwetha** 'worst';
  lacka 'worse, worst' is also attested.

Comparative and superlatives may both precede and follow their noun. If such an adjective follows a feminine singular noun, it will be lenited: **an gùssul wella** 'the best counsel'. With longer adjectives the comparative and superlative are more frequently rendered by means of **moy** 'more' and **moyha** 'most' respectively.

24A.2 *AGES, AVE·LL* 'THAN'

'Than' with comparatives is rendered by **ages** or **ès**. This conjugates pronominally as follows:

Present

1 *sg.* **(ag)esof**   1 *pl.* **(ag)eson**
2 *sg.* **(ag)esos**   2 *pl.* **(ag)esowgh**
3 *sg. m.* **(ag)esso**; *f.* **(ag)essy**   3 *pl.* **(ag)essa, (ag)essans**.

In later Cornish **ages**, **ès** are replaced by **ave·ll** (10A.8). A clause dependent upon a comparative is introduced by **ages dell** or **ès dell**: **yth o va gwell ès dell esen ow predery** 'he was better than I thought'.

24A.3 THE INCREMENTAL COMPARATIVE

To express the incremental comparative ('the more... the merrier', 'the bigger... the better', etc.) one has a choice of idioms. The commonest syntax is to **dhe²** with the comparative in both cases: **dhe vrâssa... dhe well** 'the bigger... the better'; **dhe yonca... dhe êsya** 'the younger... the easier'. One can also use **seul voy**: **seul voy y'n gwelaf, seul le usy ev orth ow flêsya** 'the more I see him, the less I like him'.

Dhe² is also used with the comparative to make the comparative adverb: **dhe voy** 'the more'; **dhe well** 'the better'; **dhe le** 'the less': **te a res lavurya dhe voy** 'you must work more'; **te a dalvia dhe le medhowy** 'you should get drunk less'.

Notice also **byttele·** (< **bÿth dhe le**) 'nonetheless'. **Bÿth well** 'any better' is used with negatives: **ny allama y wil bÿth well** 'I cannot do it any better'.

24A.4 THE EQUATIVE DEGREE

To express the idea of being 'as good as', 'as white as', 'as clever as', etc. one either used **maga⁵** or **mar²**: The noun or pronoun compared is introduced by **ave·ll**: **mar dhâ avellos jy dha honen** 'as good as you yourself'; **maga fery avell hôk** 'as merry as a hawk'; **maga whydn ave·ll an ergh** 'as white as the snow'.

When a verb is required in an equative construction, one can use the superlative. To render 'I shall do it as well as I can', for example, the superlative can be employed if it is followed by an unmutated (present) subjunctive or indicative: **me a vydn y wil gwella gyllyf** (or **gwella gallaf**) 'I will do it as well as I can'. One can also use **maga** or **mar**: **me a vydn y wil mar uskys dell allaf**.

Both Welsh and Breton have a special equative form of the adjective. The exclamatory use of the superlative may contain a trace of this (see the next note).

24A.5 THE EXCLAMATIVE ADJECTIVE

The superlative is used is used in an exclamative sense by combining it with a noun whose initial consonant undergoes lenition: **tecka wel!** 'what a beautiful sight!'; **drocka los** 'what a terrible pain!' (**glos** 'pain').

NOTE: It would seem that this construction has in the historic period been reinterpreted as adjective + **a²** + noun. It is likely, however, that the British equative is its ultimate origin. The exclamative use of the superlative is parallel with the similar use of the superlative and equative ('as good as', 'as fine as') in Breton, both modern and medieval: *O kaera bro* 'O fine country!'; *gwanat den* 'what a weak man!'; *gouazza sin eo an dra se* 'what a bad sign that is!'; *guelhet tra* 'what a good thing!' The equative is also used in exclamations in Middle Welsh: *uchet y kwynaf* 'how loudly I lament!'

If a verb is required with an exclamative adjective **assa²** (**ass** before vowels) is used: **assa via hedna teg!** 'how nice that would be!'; **ass oma sqwith** 'how tired I am!'

24B EXAMPLES FROM THE TEXTS

24B.1 *an gwelha corf a thug gu!* 'the noblest person who bore a spear' BK 1611; *pyth yy an gusyl wella* 'what is the best advice?' RD 1858; *war ow fay lacka mester* 'upon my faith a worse master' PC 2275; *ha me inweth mear lacka* 'and I also much worse' CW 1656; *malla ef signifia brossa mater ha eweth brassa conjunction intrethans* 'so that it may signify a greater matter and also a greater connection between them' SA 65; *Why dalveya gowas an brossa mine* 'you ought to obtain the biggest stones' JJenkins; *Ha che Bethalem en pow Judah, neg ooz an behathna amisk maternyow Judah* 'And you Bethlehem in Judah are not the smallest among the kings of Judah' Rowe; *eva neb o an gwanha in power han medalha vessell* 'Eve who was the weaker and the softer vessel' TH 4; *An uhelha Tas roy thewhy gul da!* 'May the highest Father grant to you to do well!' BK 2477-78.

24B.2 *my a'n musur lour yn ta… gans squyr compes ha scanntlyn na vo hyrre es am syn na vyth cotta war nep cor* 'I will measure it well enough, with accurate set-square and line, so that it be no longer than my mark nor any shorter at all' OM 2507-12; *guel yv vn den the verwel ages ol an bobyl lel* 'better is it for one man to die than all the loyal people' PC 446-47; *Pella agys oll an rema* 'Further than all these' TH 53a; *ny gavaf omma neb tew na susten moy es bestas* 'I do not find here any place or food more than animals' CW 1045-46; *Ny glowsyn cows a arloyth yn dan an howl ryelha agesowgh why* 'We have not heard of any lord under the sun more majestic than you' BK 2052-54; *Ma leiaz gwreage lacka vel zeage* 'There are many wives worse than brewer's grains' JJenkins.

24B.3 *The harhe a vo an rol the pelle why a wor ol hy a veth prest ov redya* 'The longer the roll, you all know, the longer it will be a-reading' BM 2842-44; *Rag an payn us thotha gwrys the voy eth ew lowenhys* 'For all the pain inflicted upon him, the more is he delighted' BK 716-17; *ny a wele an teez younk tho e clappia le ha le, ha lacka ha lacka* 'we see that the young people speak it less and less and worse and worse' NBoson; *y fowt ew the vrassa ha the voy* 'his fault is the greater and the more' TH 4; *the le inclynacion an geffa den the begh, the voy ha the vrassa ew y begh* 'the less inclination he may have to sin, the more and the great is his sin' TH 4a; *Sul voy ancov a rellogh the larchya preysys fethogh* 'The more deaths you cause, the more generously will you be praised' BM 2351-52.

24B.4 *maga whyn auel an leth* 'as white as milk' PC 3138; *mage fery avel hok* 'as merry as a hawk' BM 1901; *y thillas a ve gwris maga whyn avell an yrth* 'his clothes became as white as snow' TH 56a; *Me a's musyr a ver spys maga ledan avel hyer* 'I will measure it shortly as broad as long' BK 821-22; *Ha me a clov mar tha del reys* 'And I hear as well as is necessary' BM 2662-63; *Nyng es mar tha kenwesow in chy arluth i'n bys ma* 'There are not such good feasts in the house of any lord in this world' BK 1310-11; *me a'n herth guelha gyllyf* 'I will thrust it as best I can' PC 3012; *rag henna moes alemma my a vydn gwella gallaf* 'therefore I shall depart hence as well as best I can' CW 1709-10.

24B.5 *dev tek a wel yw homma* 'what a fair sight is that!' OM 753; *dev tek a bren rag styllyow* 'God, what a fine tree for planks!' OM 2441; *A thu asoma grefijs* 'God, how sorrowful I am!' BM 2522; *Ass yv helma mur a col in breten sur thynny oll* 'What a great loss is that for us all in Brittany' BM 4467-68; *du asson ny hyrethek ov queles corff meryasek ov mones in dor certen* 'God, how sad we are seeing the body of Meriasek laid in the earth indeed' BM 4526-28; *Assof engrys!* 'How angry I am!' BK 2156.

24C.1 VOCABULARY

abûsya to abuse

an côstys-ma this district, this region.

arlodhes *f.*, **arlodhesow** lady

cafos sawment to recover (from an ailment)

comendya to commend

consydra to consider

cowldevys *adj.* grown up, adult

dainty *adj.* choosy, fastidious

determys *adj.* determined

dermygy to imagine

dre lycklod *adv. phrase* in all probability

dre vrâs *adv. phrase* for the most part

fa·vera to favour
flattra gans nebonen to flatter someone
in kepa·r maner *adv. phrase* in such a way
kemerers preder a² to consider
maryach *m.*, **maryajys** marriage
nerv *m.*, **nervow** nerve
ny vanaf vy leverel ow bosaf tra vëth I will not say that I am anything
occasyon *m.*, **occasyons** occasion, reason

puns *m.*, **punsow** pound (currency)
promyssya to promise
revrons *m.* reverence, respect
sêmly *adj.* beautiful, handsome
sqwîthus *adj.* tiresome
Syr *m.* Sir
towl *m.*, **towlow** intention
trueth *m.* pity
truethek *adj.* wretched, pitiful
vexya to annoy

24C.2 TEXT DHE REDYA
(AN KENSA CHAPTRA A *GOTH HA GOWVREUS*)

Red an devyn usy ow sewya ha scrif gorthebow dhe'n qwestyonow:

"Mêster Benet wheg," y wreg a worthebys, "Fatl'yllowgh why bos màr sqwîthus! Why a dalvia godhvas tell esoma ow predery ev dhe dhemedhy onen anodhans."

"Yw hedna y dowl ev rag bos trigys omma?"

"Y dowl ef! Whedhlow! Fatl'yllowgh why côwsel indella! Saw martesen ev a vydn codha in kerensa gans onen anodhans. Rag hedna why a dal y vysytya pàn dheffa ev."

"Nyns esof vy ow qwelas occasyon rag hedna. Why ha'n mowysy a yll mos, boken why a alsa aga danvon aga honen oll bys dhodho, ha hedna martesen a via whath dhe well. Why yw màr sêmly avell den vëth a'n myrhas ha dre lycklod why a wra plêsya Mêster Bingley moy ages onen vëth anodhans."

"Ow frias wheg, th'esowgh why ow flattra genama. In gwir kyns obma me a veu ow radn vy a decter, saw na vanaf vy leverel ow bosaf tra vëth specyal lebmyn. Pan eus pymp myrgh cowldevys gans benyn, ny dalvia dhedhy predery a'y thecter hy honen."

"Yn fenowgh in câss a'n par-na ny vëdh meur a decter gans an venyn a alsa hy kemeras preder vëth anodho."

"Saw, a brias wheg, why a res porres mos ha vysytya Mêster Bingley pàn dheffa ev dhe'n tireth-ma."

"Hedna yw moy ès dell vanaf promyssya, trest dhybm."

"Saw, gwrewgh consydra agas myrhas. Ny yllowgh why desmygy pana sort a varyach a via hedna rag onen anodhans. Yma Syr William hag Arlodhes Lûcas determys dha vos dhodho rag an porpos-na yn udnyk, rag why a wor na wrowns y dre vrâs vysytya den vëth nowyth devedhys dhe'n tireth-ma. Why a res mos yn tefry, rag ny yllyn ny mos dh'y vysytya màr ny wrewgh why inwedh."

"Why yw re dhainty in gwir. Th'eroma ow cresy tell vydn Mêster Bingley bos pòr lowen dha'gas gweles why; ha me a vydn danvon dhodho der agas dorn why lyther cot ow ry dhodho cubmyas dha dhemedhy an vowes anodhans a vo va moyha plêsys gensy; saw res vëdh dhybm gorra aberveth ger dâ rag ow Lizzy vian wheg."

"Da via genama màr teffowgh why sevel orth gwil tra vëth kepar. Nyns yw Lizzy tabm vëth gwell ages an re erel, ha me a wor nag yw hy byth màr deg avell Jane na byth màr vedhel avell Lydya. Mès why a vëdh orth hy favera hy pùb termyn."

"Nyns eus tra vëth inhans, a vynsa comendya onen anodhans," a worthebys ev, "mowes wocky heb skians yw kenyver onen anodhans; saw yma in Lizzy moy a skians ages in hy whereth."

"Mêster Benet, fatl'yllowgh why abûsya agas flehes agas honen in kepar maner? Why a gav plesour brâs orth ow vexya vy. Nag eus trueth vëth oll genowgh a'm nervow truethek vy."

"Camgemerys owgh why ena, a brias wheg. Revrons brâs a'm beus rag agas nervow. Cothmans coth on ny an eyl dh'y gela. Me a'gas clôwas why dha wil mencyon anodhans gans meur a vry dres moy ages ugans bledhen."

"A! Ny wodhowgh why fatl'esoma ow sùffra!"

"Saw yma dhybm govenek why dha gafas sawment, ha bewa ha gweles lias den yonk ha pymp mil buns dhedhans i'n vledhen ow tos dhe'n côstys-ma."

1 Pes bledhen o Mêster ha Mêstres Benet demedhys pàn wharva an kescows-na?
2 Pes myrgh a's teva y warbarth?
3 Pyw o myrgh moyha kerys Mêster Benet ha praga?
4 Pandr'o an dra na vynsa Mêster Benet gwil rag y wreg ow tùchya Mêster Bingley?
5 Prag y whrug Mêster Benet demedhy y wreg i'n kensa le?
6 O va edrygys i'n mater?
7 Pàn wrug Mêstres Benet mencyon a'y nervow, prag na ros Mêster Benet dhedhy marnas gorthyp scav?

PYMPES DYSCANS WARN UGANS
TWENTY-FIFTH LESSON

25A.1 ADVERBS FROM ADJECTIVES

Some adjectives may be used adverbially. **Godhvos dâ** 'good knowledge' but **dâ me a wor** 'I know well'. Frequently, however, **yn⁵** is used to make an adverb of an adjective: **dâ** 'good' > **yn tâ** 'well'; **leun** 'full' > **yn leun** 'fully'; **men** 'vigorous' > **yn fen** 'vigorously'. Notice also that *__yn whir__ (< **gwir** 'true) is unattested, and that 'truly' is **in gwir**, where **gwir** is a noun and **in** (not **yn⁵**) is the preposition 'in'. Thus **in gwir** is literally 'in truth'.

The adverbial particle **yn⁵** has ceased to be productive by the sixteenth century. Instead, adverbs are sometimes made periphrastically with the words **maner** *f.* 'manner' and **fordh** *f.* 'way. Thus we find in sixteenth-century texts such expressions as **in kepar maner** 'similarly', **warlergh bad maner** 'badly', **in stranj fordh ha maner** 'strangely'.

In the earliest Middle Cornish the English suffix **-lych** is used to make adverbs of some borrowed adjectives, e.g. **falslych** 'falsely'; **hardlych** 'precisely'; **manerlych** 'fittingly'. By the sixteenth century, however, the usual way of turning a borrowed adjective into an adverb is to use the English suffix **-ly**: we thus find in texts of the period such adverbs as **ernestly, hastily, plainly, openly, surly, manly** 'courageously', **secretly, verily, impossybly**, etc. Of particular importance is **spessly** 'specially'.

25A.2 THE ADVERBIAL PRESENT PARTICIPLE IN *IN UDN*

The ordinary present participle is constructed with **ow⁴** (3A.2). There does exist a variant participle that is used in earlier Middle Cornish to describe an action that has already been mentioned. This participle replaced **ow** by **in udn²**. When, for example, one says 'he came towards the house running', the running describes the coming, which has already been mentioned. In Cornish the sentence could be rendered: **ev a dheuth tro ha'n chy in udn bonya**.

167

25A.3 *GALSOF* AND *DEUVEF*

Mos 'to go' in earlier Middle Cornish possesses a separate perfect tense, which is conjugated as follows:

1 *sg.* **galsof**	1 *pl.* **galson**
2 *sg.* **galsos**	2 *pl.* **galsowgh**;
3 *sg.* **gallas**	3 *pl.* **galsons**.

This tense is never preceded by any verbal particle and cannot be negative or relative. It clearly contains the same root as that seen in the verbal adjective **gyllys**.

The verb **dos** 'to come' has a separate perfect, which is conjugated as follows:

1 *sg.* **deuvef**	1 *pl.* **deuven**
2 *sg.* **deuves**	2 *pl.* **deuvowgh**
3 *sg.* **deuva**	3 *pl.* **deuvens**.

Unlike **galsof**, this tense is either used absolutely: **deuva an prës** 'the time has come', or it may be preceded by the perfective particle **re**: **re dheuva an dus** 'the people have arrived'. It is not, however, used in the negative nor in relative clauses.

25A.4 'TO BECOME' IN CORNISH

Cornish is without a single word for 'become' and one must use one of several ways to express the idea. One can, for example, simply use the verb **mos** 'to go' and thus say, for example, **mar teu va ha leverel tra a'n par-na, yth ama rudh** 'if he says something like that, I shall go red'.

In the past for 'became' with adjectives one can use **codha** 'to fall', e.g. **ha'n whel a godhas scant** 'and work become scarce'. If one wants to say that something or somebody has become + adjective, one can use the verbal adjective **gyllys** of **mos** 'to go' together with the present of **bos** 'to be' and the relevant adjective:

Y das yw gyllys pòr goth His father has become very old
Me yw gyllys sqwith I have become tired.

If on the other hand one wants to say 'they became friends', for example, or 'he became a doctor', the preterite of **bos** 'to be' affords the best translation:

Y a veu cothmans i'n tor'-na They became friends then
Ev a veu medhek hevleny He became a doctor last year
Hy a veu mabm an seythen dhewetha She become a mother last
week.

One can also use the preterite of **bos** 'to be' with the verbal adjective of
gwil 'to do, to make':

Hy a veu gwrës medhek hevleny She was made/became a doctor
last year
Ow mab a veu gwrës pedn-scoler agensow My son became head
boy recently.

In certain cases the verb **trailya** 'to turn' can be used to mean 'to
become', e.g. **trail dhe gig ha dhe woos** 'become flesh and blood.'

NOTE: For a long time now revivalists have been using either
*mos ha bos or ***dos ha bos** to translate 'become', e.g. ***hy êth
ha bos medhek** 'she became a doctor', ***ev a dheuth ha bos
clâv hag êth i'n clâvjy** 'he became sick and went to hospital'.
Both **mos ha bos** and **dos ha bos** are inventions of Nance's,
and neither has any warrant in the traditional language.

25A.5 *GOVY* AND *GWYDN OW BÊS*

The word **gu** 'woe, misery' combines with the person pronouns to mean
'woe is me, poor me', etc. The full paradigm is as follows:

1 *sg.* **govy**	1 *pl.* **gony**
2 *sg.* **gojy**	2 *pl.* **gowhy**
3 *sg. m.* **goe·v**; *f.* **gohy**	3 *pl.* **goy·**

Govy, **gojy**, **goev**, etc. not infrequently introduce a subordinate clause
or verbal phrase:

Govy pàn wrug avy dha serry! Alas that I angered you!
Goev codha mar bell Poor him that he fell so far!
Gohy rag leverel tra a'n par-na Poor her that she said such a thing!
Goev na yll gortheby Pity him who cannot answer.

'How lucky', 'how fortunate' is expressed in earlier Middle Cornish by **gwynvÿs** (literally 'white, fortunate world): **gwynvÿs a yll perna chy mar deg** 'fortunate is he who can buy such a nice house!' A possessive adjective can be placed between **gwydn** and **bës**: **gwydn dha vës pàn wrusta cafos an gober!** 'how luck you were to get the prize!'; **gwydn agan bës metya an eyl gans y gela** 'how lucky we were to meet each other!'

25A.6 'BEHOLD'

'Behold' in the sixteenth century is often rendered **lo!** 'lo!', **mir!** 'look!' or **mirowgh!**, **merowgh!** 'look! (pl.). There does, however, exist an earlier word for 'look! lo!': **otta** or **awotta** (**ot** or **awo·t** before vowels). Ot combines with personal pronouns as follows:

1 *sg.* **o·tta vy, o·ttama**	1 *pl.* **o·tta ny**
2 *sg.* **o·tta sy**	2 *pl.* **o·tta why**
3 *sg. m.* **o·tta va**; *f.* **o·tta hy**	3 *pl.* **ottensy**

Ot is also used with **obma** 'here', to give **ot obma** 'here is'.

25A.7 CAUSATIVE VERBS IN *-HE·*

There exists in Cornish a class of causative verbs derived from adjectives and nouns. The verbal noun ends in **-he·**, which bears the main stress. Such verbs include: **coselhe·** 'to pacify' (< **cosel** 'peaceful); **cot'he·** 'to shorten' (< **cot** 'short'); **crefhe·** 'to strengthen' (< **crev** 'strong'); **dallhe·** 'to blind' (< **dall** 'blind'); **duwhanhe·** 'to sadden' (< **duwhan** 'sorrow'); **glanhe·** 'to cleanse' (< **glân** 'clean); **lehe·** 'to lessen' (**le** 'less'); **lent'he·** 'decelerate' (< **lent** 'slow'); **lowenhe·** 'to cheer, to gladden' (< **lowen** 'joyful); **moghhe·** 'to increase' (< **moy** 'more'); **tekhe·** 'to beautify' (< **teg** 'beautiful'); **tirhe·** 'to land' (< **tir** 'land'); **uskys'he·** 'accelerate' (< **uskys** 'fast'); **yaghhe·** 'to heal' (< **yagh** 'healthy). Although the verbal adjective in **-hës** is the most frequently attested part of these verbs, other parts are also attested, most notably the verbal noun, the third person singular of the preterite in **-ha·s** and the third singular subjunctive in **-ha·ha**.

25A.8 'NEVER'

To render 'never' in Cornish one uses either **nefra** 'ever' or **bythqweth** 'ever' with a negative verb, e.g. **ny wrama hy gweles nefra arta** 'I will never see her again' (literally 'I will not ever see her again') and **ny wrug ev bythqweth abma dhybm kyn fe** 'he never even kissed me' (literally 'he did not ever even kiss me'). **Nefra** is used exclusively for the habitual present or the future; **bythqweth** (Later Cornish **byscath**) is used for the past. Although the word **nefra** derives from Old English *næfre* 'never', it may not be used for past reference. Expressions like **ny wrug avy *nefra y weles kyns lebmyn** 'I never saw him before' or **ny wrug hy *nefra demedhy** 'she never married' are quite wrong. One must rather say **ny wrug avy bythqweth y weles kyns lebmyn** and **ny wrug hy bythqweth demedhy**. The use of two different words for 'ever/never' in the future and in the past is a distinctive feature of all the Celtic languages.

25A.9 'WHILE'

'While' is often **hadre²**, but the conjunction **ha(g)** 'and' together with the present participle in **ow⁴** may also be used to mean 'while'. One can say, for example, **me a welas an drog-labm ha me ow kerdhes tre newher** 'I saw the accident while I was walking home last night', or **yth esa an flehes ow miras orth an bellwolok, ha'ga mabmow ow kestalkya i'n gegyn** 'the children were watching the television, while their mothers were chatting in the kitchen.' It is important to notice, however, that the clause introduced by **ha(g)** follows the main clause; it may not come first in the sentence.

25B EXAMPLES FROM THE TEXTS

25B.1 *me ny won in fays py ma an keth meneth na* 'I do not know well where that same mountain is' BM 1723-24; *Gor with in ta* 'Pay close attention' BK 193; *cref ew pan sorrhe en lun* 'he is strong when he becomes fully angry' BK 2202; *Me a garsa in tefry cafas gorthyb in certan* 'Indeed I should like certainly to receive an answer' BK 2100-01; *rag eff a recevyas corf Dew warlerth badd maner* 'for he received the body of God in a bad fashion' SA 65a; *trueth vye den yw gulan falslych y vones dyswrys* 'it would be a shame falsely to destroy an innocent man' PC 2437-38; *kepar dell esta se falsly ow reportia* 'as you falsely report' TH 48; *conceviis secretly in golan* 'conceived secretly in the heart' TH 28; *ha sekretly bew hedre vy* 'and secretly as long as you live' BK 638-39; *ha spesly lauer dethy* 'and especially tell her' BM 368; *ha specially the vos mynisters* 'and specially to be ministers' TH 52a; *ha thymmo ef a hyrhys spesly orthys aspya* 'and he specially ordered me to keep watch on you' BK 909-10; *Te a thu'm arluth hastely* 'You will go in hast to my lord' BK 554; *hay gommandement pur thefry a rose straytly* 'and he gave his commandment indeed very strictly' CW 632-33; *Veryly, verily, me a levar thewhy* 'Verily, verily, I tell you' TH 41a; *eth ew verely kyg ha verely gois agen arluth Jesus Christ* 'it is verily the flesh and verily the blood of our lord Jesus Christ' SA 61.

25B.2 *why a theth ʒym yn arvow dre dreyson yn un scolchye* 'you came to
me treacherously lurking in arms' PA 74ab; *y eth yn vn fystene* 'they went
hurring' PA 241d; *y fyys yn vn vramme* 'I fled breaking wind' RD 2094;
Tewough in un gyslyues! 'Be silent listening!' BK 1323; *deugh 'rag in un
thyena!* 'come forth panting!' BK 2349.

25B.3 *rak hyreth galsof pur claf* 'for longing I have become sick' RD 775;
galsof in claf 'I have become sick' BK 2944; *Owt, galsof gwan a'm
skyans!* 'Alas, I have become weak in my mind!' BK 3137; *galsos mur yn
dyscrygyans* 'you have descended greatly into disbelief' RD 1516. *Gallas
the'n fo* 'he has taken flight' BK 455; *Gallas garaw avel spern* 'He has
become as sharp as thorns' BK 2422; *ov envy in kerth galsons* 'my enemies
have gone away' BM 1069; *in kernov the ihesu gras theth desyr ty re dufa*
'to Cornwall, thanks be to Jesus, you have come as you desire' BM 622-24; *an
guyns thagen corse dufa* 'the wind has come to our course' BM 1086.

25B.4 *yth egh gvyn avel crystel* 'you will become as clear as crystal' BM 1521;
Ha an huêl a kỳðaz skent 'And work become scarce' JCH §2; *kynth os
gyllys feynt ha guan* 'though you have become faint and weak' BM 3672; *rag
yth ew ef cothe gyllys* 'for he has become old' CW 1791; *hagen saviour
Jesus Christ ew gwreis kigg ha gois* 'and our saviour Jesus Christ becomes
flesh and blood' SA 63; *yn vrna keskeweʒa y a ve ha specyall bras* 'then
they became companions and specially great ones' PA 110d.

25B.5 *Out govy harov harov* 'Oh, woe is me, alas, alas!' BM 1040; *govy na
vuma war kyns hager dyweth yv helma* 'woe is me that I was not wary
before now; this is a terrible death!' BM 4099-100; *O'm danger goef er bos!*
'Woe to him if he falls into my power!' BK 415; *A gony gony fyen ken marov
bras ha byen re corff mahum on oma* 'Woe to us, woe to us; let us flee!
Otherwise we will die, great and small her, by the body of Mahound' BM 3954-
56.

25B.6 *Myr, ow codres y'm sesya!* 'Look, he was seizing me with threats!' BK
2238; *meer an avall ma omma* 'look at this apple here' CW 849; *Mîr
Dzhûan með e vêster; ỳbma ða ṣûber* 'Look, John, said his master, here are
your wages' JCH §5; *merow lymmyn omma yma an apostyll* 'look now,
here is the apostle' TH 18; *Awot omma tra anath* 'Behold here a strange
thing' BK 486; *tomma gaya avall theys* 'here is a nice apple for you' CW
737; *Gans plenty a soudoryon awattave devethis!* 'Lo, I have come with
plenty of soldiers' BK 3243-44; *them shape ow honyn ytama why a weall
omma treylys* 'to my own shape behold me, you see here, transformed' CW
925; *Adam ottensy vmma* 'Adam, here they are' OM 102.

25B.7 *thyn ol yth yv coselheys* 'for us all is quietened' BM 2182; *uz na ellen
skant quatiez tho e wellaz crefhe arta* 'so that we can hardly expect to see
it strengthen again' NG; *ow dalhe lagasow an bobyll* 'blinding the eyes of
the people' TH 19a; *In ow holan tyn reg eth the vos kemmys duwhenhys*
'Pain has entered my heart that you are so grieved' BK 2556-57; *ann enaf a
veth glanhis* 'the soul will be cleansed' SA 60a; *may fo leheys mvr ay gallos*
'so that much of his power may he lessened' PC 44; *me ren moghheys eredy*

'I have made it great indeed' BM 2402; *hag awos own, me a dyrhas i'n forest a Rosewa* 'and because I was afraid, I landed in the forest of Rosewa' BK 97-99; *Ow holan ew lowenhys!* 'My heart is gladdened!' BK 2979; *an empour flour they golhy may fo tekkeys eredy* 'to wash the flower of emperors, that he may be beautified' BM 1600-01; *ny yllogh bones yaghheys* 'you cannot be cured' BM 1500.

25B.8.1 *gevyons me nvm byth neffre moy pegh o pan dyspresyas ys delo pan yn guerʒe* 'I shall never receive pardon; it was more of a sin when I despised him than when I betrayed him' PA 104cd; *ny's buth dour certan neffre* 'water indeed will never drown them' OM 1692; *an pyth a scrifys scrifis na ken ny scrifaf neffre* 'what I have written, I wrote; and I will never write differently' PC 28004-05; *hag ath peys vvel ha clour nefra na vena yn nor trelyes ʒe lust an bys me* 'and I beseech thee humble and mild that I may never in the world be turned to the lust of this world' BM 151-53; *ha honna ny ra agys desevia, na ny ra neffra fyllell* 'and this will not deceive you and never will it fail' TH 34a; *Neffra ny vyth ankevys* 'He will never be forgotten' BK 1617; *Ne vedn e nevra dvz vêz a ʒyndan* 'He will never get out of debt' AB: 230c.

25B.8.2 *pedyr te am nagh tergweth bythqueth arluth na vef ʒys* 'Peter you will deny me three times that I was never your lord' PA 49c; *bythqueth bay thy'm ny ryssys* 'never did you give me a kiss' PC 522; *Ellas emperour debyta mar mennyth oma latha flehys bythqueth na pehes* 'Alas, pitiless emperor, if you wish here to kill children that have never sinned' BM 1591-93; *hag in y ganow eff ny ve bythqueth kyffys deceypt vith na gyll* 'and in his mouth never was guile or deception found' TH 11; *Bythquath ny ve thewhy parow* 'Never was there your like' BK 1256-57; *a das kear ny won for thy na ny vef bythqwath ena* 'O dear father, I do not know the way thither and was I never there' CW 1738-39; *rag na rigga ve beska gwellaz skreef Bretten Coth veeth* 'for I never saw any Old British writing' NBoson; *No rig avee biscath gwelles lever cornoack* 'I never saw a Cornish book' WBodinar.

25B.9 *yʒ eth pesy may halle ʒy ʒas yn weth vgy a van hag ef rag own ow crenne* 'he also went to pray to his Father who is above, while he was trembling with fear' PA 53cd; *En eʒewon skyntyll keth resteffo mur vylyny ʒe veras worth crist y eth hag ef yn crous ow cregy* 'The crafty despicable Jews, may they get much shame, went to look at Christ, while he was hanging on the cross' PA 216ab.

25C.1 VOCABULARY

ave·s a² *prep. phrase* out of
composa to verify
dama *f.* mother
Ejyp *m.* Egypt
frankincens *m.* incense

hunros *m.*, **hunrosow** dream
lowender *m.* joy, happiness
myrr *m.* myrrh
owr *m.* gold
sa'bàn (< **sav in bàn**) get up!

steren *f., coll.* **ster** star   **Josef** *m.* Joseph
tresour *m.* treasure

25C.2 TEXT DHE REDYA
(WILLIAM ROWE: *MATHEW 2:8–15*)
Red an devyn usy ow sewya i'n eur-na derif an whedhel i'th eryow dha honen:

Hag ev a's danvonas dhe Bethalem hag a wrug leverel dhedhans: "Gwrewgh whilas sur rag an flogh yonk, ha pàn wrewgh why y gafos, drewgh ger dhybmo vy arta may hallen vy mos ha gordhya dhodho inwedh."

Pàn wrussons y clôwes an mytern, y êth in kerdh ha'n steren, a wrussons y gweles i'n ëst, êth dhyragthans erna wrug hy dos ha sevel dres an le mayth esa an flogh yonk. Pàn wrussons y gweles an steren, yth êns y lowen gans meur a lowender. Ha pàn êns y devedhys i'n chy, y a welas an flogh yonk gans Maria y dhama. Hag y a godhas dhe'n dor ha gordhya dhodho. Ha pàn wrussons y egery aga thresour, y a ros dhodho owr ha frankincens ha myrr. Hag y a veu gwarnys gans Duw hag y ow cùsca na wrellens y dos ogas dhe Herod. Hag y êth in kerdh dh'aga fow aga honen fordh aral.

Ha pàn êns y gyllys in kerdh, mirowgh, eleth nev a dhysqwedhas dhe Josef. Josef a'n jeva hunros indelma: "Sa'bàn ha kebmer an flogh yonk ha'y dhama ha ke dhe Ejyp ha bedhowgh ena erna wrellen dry dhis ger. Rag Herod a vydn whilas an flogh yonk rag y ladha."

Pàn wrug ev sevel, ev a gemeras an flogh yonk ha'y dhama i'n nos hag êth dhe Ejyp. Hag y feu ena erna veu marow Herod, may halja bos composys a veu côwsys gans Arlùth nev der an profet ow leverel: "Avês a Ejyp me a vydn cria ow mab."

WHEFFES DYSCANS WARN UGANS
TWENTY-SIXTH LESSON

26A.1 THE AUTONOMOUS FORM OF THE VERB

In Cornish, as we have seen, the passive is made with the verb **bos** 'to be' and the verbal adjective. This is not unlike English, where 'to be' and the participle express the passive. Thus Cornish **an lyther a vëdh scrifys avorow** is not unlike English 'the letter will be written tomorrow'. In the same way **an creswas a veu pystygys** 'the policeman was injured' and **pàn vo an whel gorfednys** 'when the work is finished' are similar to their English equivalents.

There does, however, exist in Cornish another way of expressing the passive. This involves the use of a passive (or better, autonomous) form of the verb. The autonomous verb is hardly attested at all in traditional Cornish outside the present-future tense, where it ends in **-er** or **-yr**. Using the autonomous form one can say **an mytern a elwyr Casvelyn** or **y helwyr an mytern Casvelyn** 'the king is called Casvelyn'; **an ober a wrer** or **y whrer an ober** 'the deed is being done'; **an soudoryon a ledhyr** or **y ledhyr an soudoryon** 'the soldiers are killed'. Notice incidentally that the ending of the autonomous present-future causes affection of **a** > **e** in the root syllable of the verb: **ladha** 'to kill' > **ledhyr** 'is killed'.

A pronominal object of the autonomous verb is expressed by an infixed pronoun after the appropriate verbal particle: **y'm gelwyr** 'I am called', but **prag na'n gwrer** 'why is it not done?"

NOTE: The autonomous form of the verb is obsolescent by the sixteenth century. It is noteworthy, for example, that *Origo Mundi* of the early fourteenth century begins: **An Tas a nev y'm gelwyr** 'I am called the Father of heaven' but *Beunans Meriasek* of the next century begins: **Me yw gelwys Dûk Breten** 'I am called the

Duke of Brittany'. In the earlier text the autonomous verb is used to express the passive sense, in the later **bos** + the verbal adjective. The autonomous verb cannot, of course, be proscribed for revivalists, but Cornish speakers can manage perfectly well without it.

26A.2 'TO' WITH VERBS

When the verbal noun is either the subject or object of a verb, 'to' is not expressed in Cornish: **ny via ewn y wil** 'it would not be right to do it'; **me a garsa y gafos** 'I should like to get it'; **ervirys yw genef mos gensy** 'I intend to go with her'; **me re ancovas y dhry genef** 'I forgot to bring it with me'; **ev a whilas ow lettya** 'he tried to prevent me'. In other cases, however, **dhe²** precedes the verbal noun, for example, **parys oma dhe gôwsel ortans** 'I am ready to speak to them'; **y feu an gowethas gesys dhe fyllel** 'the company was allowed to fail'; **ev a'm cùssulyas dh'y assaya** 'he advised me to try it'

After **pesy** 'to pray' 'to' is translated by **a²**: **ev a'm pesys a dhos ganso** 'he begged me to come with him'. With **erhy** 'to command' the person commanded is introduced by **dhe²**, and the second verb appears as a verbal noun; or a whole clause is introduced by **may⁵** + the subjunctive:

i) **Ev a erhys dhybm dos ganso** He ordered me to go with him
ii) **Ev a erhys may teffen ganso** He ordered me to go with him.

With the verb **comondya** 'to command' there are three possible constructions. One can use syntax similar to the syntax used with **erhy** in i) and ii) above. One can also treat the person commanded as the direct object and introduce the command with **may⁵** and the subjunctive; or the verb in the command may appear as the verbal noun preceded by **dhe²**. Thus 'God commanded Joseph to go down into Egypt' can be translated in four different ways:

i) **Duw a gomondyas dhe Joseph mos in nans dhe Ejyp**
ii) **Duw a gomondyas dhe Joseph mayth ella in nans dhe Ejyp**
iii) **Duw a gomondyas Joseph mayth ella in nans dhe Ejyp**
iv) **Duw a gomondyas Joseph dhe vos in nans dhe Ejyp**.

26A.3 'NOT TO' WITH VERBS

The Cornish equivalent of 'not to' is most often **na²**, or **ma na²** followed by the subjunctive: **hy a leverys dhybm na wrellen hy gelwel arta** 'she told me not to call her again'. One might also say **hy a leverys dhybm sevel orth hy gelwel arta** 'she told me to abstain from calling her again'.

After nouns and adjectives 'not to' can be rendered **bos heb**: **pòr dhrog yw genef bos heb scrifa dhis kyns lebmyn** 'I am very sorry not to have written to you before now'. One might also use **refrainya dhyworth, omwitha dhyworth**: **ow thowl yw omwitha (refrainya) dhyworth eva re alebma rag** 'my intention is not to drink too much from now on'.

Expressions like 'without my asking', 'without his knowing' are rendered in Cornish with the preposition **heb** 'without': **ev a'n gwrug ragof heb me dh'y wovyn** 'he did it without my asking'; **me a'n êwnas heb ev dhe wodhvos** 'I repaired it without his knowing'.

26A.4 CAUSATIVE USE OF *GWIL* 'TO DO, TO MAKE'

In English one can say 'my children made me do it', 'the dog made the cat run out into the street'. The commonest syntax in such cases is to use **dhe²** with the person or thing obliged to do the action and to introduce the action as a verbal noun: **ow flehes a wrug dhybm y wil**; **an ky a wrug dhe'n gath ponya in mes i'n strêt**.

A much less common syntax is to make the person or thing obliged the direct object and to introduce the verbal noun by **dhe²**: **gwrewgh ev dhe weles an lyver** 'make him see the book, show him the book'.

26A.5 EXCLAMATORY VERBAL NOUN

The verbal noun can be used in exclamations: **an jowl dhe'th lesky!** 'the devil burn you!'; **dhe'th cregy** 'may you be hanged!'; **dh'y lawa** 'praise him!'

26A.6 DEFECTIVE VERBS

Y coodh dhybm 'I should', **yma res dhybm** 'I must' and **y tal dhybm** 'I should' are all impersonal verbs rather than defective. A true defective verb is third singular **yn medh** '(he/she) says/said', third plural **yn medhans** 'they say/said'. In later Cornish **yn medh** is used in sentence initial, but it is probably preferable to confine one's use of it to after a direct quotation: **"Mydnaf," yn medh hy, "me a vydn dos genes yn lowen"** '"Yes", she said, "I will gladly come with you."'

Another defective verb is **deur**, which is found mostly in the expression **ny'm deur** 'I don't care'. Similar is the verb **bern**, which is found only after **ny** or **na**: **ny vern y salujy** 'there is no point in greeting him'. **Bern**, incidentally, is also a noun meaning 'concern', which is used with **bos** 'to be' to mean 'be of concern': **mars yw bern dhis an mater-ma** 'if this matter is of concern to you'.

Na fors has the appearance of a defective verb with the sense 'it doesn't matter': **Well, well, na fors** 'Well, well, it doesn't matter'. In fact **na fors** is a borrowing from Middle English *no force*. One can use **fors** in other constructions, i.e. **nyns eus fors** 'it doesn't matter' and **ny res dhyn fors** 'it doesn't matter for us'.

26A.7 'BOTH ... AND' AND 'NEITHER ... NOR'

English 'both... and' can be rendered in Cornish either as **ha ... ha ...** or **kefrës ... ha ...** . One can therefore say: **yth esa i'n tyller-na ha tus ha benenes** 'there were both men and women in that place' or **yth esa kefrës tus ha benenes i'n tyller-na**.

'Either ... or ... ' is rendered **pò ... pò ...** Thus 'I will see you either tomorrow or the next day can be rendered: **me a vydn dha weles pò avorow pò trenja**.

The word **ken** can mean 'otherwise'. **Poken** can be similarly used: **me a'n gwra, poken ny vëdh gwrës nefra** 'I will do it, otherwise it will never be done'.

'Neither ... nor ... ' is expressed by **naneyl ... ny ...** : **me ny wrug naneyl y weles na'y glôwes** 'I neither saw nor heard him'. The final position of **naneyl** in Late Cornish expressions like **dhe'n jorna-ma ow tegy na oryn pana lytherow naneyl** 'to this day bearing we do not know what letters neither' is based on English syntax.

26B EXAMPLES FROM THE TEXTS

26B.1 *Rag y hyller ervyre hay welas yn suredy* 'For it is possible to decide and to see quite clearly' PA 20a; *En tas a nef y'm gylwyr* 'I am called the Father of heaven' OM 1; *hag annethe crous y wrer* 'and from them a cross will be made' OM 1936; *menogh y rer y pesy* 'often people beseech him' BM 3440; *Avond, mar qurer y woodros* 'Forward, if he is threatened' BK 1426; *Ny gefyr agys paraw in dan howl in mor na tyer* 'Your like is not found on sea or land' BK 2406-07.

26B.2 *ol war barth I an naghas hag a yrghys y laȝe* 'all together they denied him and ordered him to be killed' PA 147d; *cayphas re hyrghys thywhy a thos the ierusalem the dysputye worth ihesu* 'Caiaphas has ordered you to come to Jerusalem to dispute with Jesus' PC 1648-50; *y a yrhys may whane yn corf Ihesus caradow* 'they ordered that it should pierce into the body of sweet Jesus' PA 218bc; *moyses me a commond thy's ha the aron kekyfrys mayth ylleugh yn mes a'm glas* 'Moses, I command you and Aaron also to depart from my kingdom' OM 1585-87; *hag vfel am comondyas thum mam the dre mayth ellen* 'and commanded me to go home humbly to my mother' BM 3774-75; *ha thynny a comondyas doys oll dotho the amma* 'and commanded us all to go to kiss him' BM 4429-30; *Du a commondyas an profet Ysay the wull proclamacion the oll an bys* 'God commanded the prophet Isaiah to make proclamation to all the world' TH 6a-7.

26B.3 *my a worhemmyn whare the'n glaw na moy na wrello* 'I shall command straightway the rain not to rain any more' OM 1091-92; *ov arlothes sur gyne dre thynnargh agas pygys na wrellough cammen lathe an profus a nazare* 'my lady indeed by a message through me has begged you that you should not execute the prophet of Nazareth' PC 2194-97; *hay gommandement pur thefry a rose straytly dres pub tra na wrellan mellya worty* 'and strictly he gave us indeed his commandment that above all things we should not meddle with it' CW 632-34; *Na vanna' heb the dolla, rag henna na gampolh a* 'I shall not without deceiving you, therefore do not mention it' BK 2143-44; *pana royow a russyn receva theworth du heb ny thega dyrfyn* 'what gifts we have received from God without our deserving them' TH 24a.

26B.4 *ef a rug ȝeȝe yn scon monas yn mes alene* 'he made them soon depart quickly thence' PA 30d; *ha me a ra ȝeugh spedye ow cafos crist yredy* 'and indeed I shall made you succeed in capturing Christ' PA 39b; *pegh o an pith a rug then kyge stryvya gans an spuris* 'sin was what made the flesh strive with the spirit' TH 3; *Pegh o an cawse a rug the oll an vssew a Adam ha Eva the vos genys in state a thampnacion* 'Sin was the cause that made all the offspring of Adam and Eve to be born in a state of damnation' TH 3; *Rag eff a ra then howle drehevell ha shynya kyffrys war an da han drog* 'For he makes the sun to rise and to shine on both the good and the evil' TH 22; *Gureuh vî dhv uelaz* 'Show me' AB: 250b.

26B.5 *avond tellek theth cregy* 'get hence, you ragamuffin, hang you!' BM 3492; *Taw, taw, harlot, the'th cregy!* 'Silence, silence, you scoundrel, hang you!' BK 472; *taw theth cregye* 'Silence, hang you!' CW 1003; *Ay tav an iovle theth lesky* 'Ho! Silence, the devil burn you!' BM 2098; *Gesugh creys vfel ha clovr in hanov du dy lawe* 'Give over humble and meek in the name of God, praised be he!' BM 1312-13.

26B.6 *Ny whelaff ve, y myth crist, ow blonogath ow honyn* 'I do not seek, said Christ, my own will' TH 22a; *In myth Arthur ema gwyer thotha ef in e ympyer* 'Arthur says that he has the right in his empire' BK 2425-26; *Mîr Dzhûan með e vêster; ẏbma ða ʒûber* 'Look, John, said his master, here are your wages' JCH §5; *Ha Dzhûan, ameð an dzhei, diou ʒennan nei* 'Hey, John, they said, Come with us' JCH §14; *A peth an beys num dur man* 'I do not care at all about worldly wealth' BM 2563; *wel wel na fors re appolyn ov du splan* 'well, well, no matter, by Apollo, my splendid god' BM 1058-59; *Nynsus fors awos henna* 'That does not matter' OM 2801.

26B.7 ***Adam otte an puskes ythyn a'n nef ha'n bestes kefrys yn tyr hag
yn mor*** 'Behold, Adam, both the fish, the birds of the heavens and the animals
on land and in the sea' OM 117-19; ***kefrys bresyon ha kemmyn*** 'both nobles
and commoners' BK 1275; ***bo clevas bo peth kescar po dre breson
presonys*** 'either sickness or dispersion of wealth or being imprisoned in prison'
PA 24c; ***Neb a garra y das po y vam, y vab po y virth, chy, trevyn po
tyrryow, moy agesa ve*** 'whoever loves his father or his mother, his son or his
daughter, house, houses or land, more than me' TH 21a; ***naneyll dre an
commine la a nature, na dre special gothfas an la a moyses*** 'neither by
the common law of nature nor by means of special knowledge of the law of Moses'
TH 14a; ***Nu'm let nanyl lanow na crug*** 'Neither high tide nor hill will stop
me' BK 2442.

26C.1 VOCABULARY

adhewedhes *adj. & adv.* recent,
recently

âls *m.*, **âlsyow** coast, cliff

an Garrek *f.* **Loos** St Michael's
Mount

clappyer *m.*, **clappyers** speaker

cov *m.*, **covyon** memory; **porth in
cov!** remember!

dhe vos scodhys wàr to be relied
upon

dhort *Late Cornish form of*
dhyworth from

dos adro to turn around

Falmeth *m.* Falmouth

gavar *f.*, **gever** goat

Geverangow *lit.* Hundreds (*a place
between Redruth, St Agnes and Truro,
where the four hundreds of Penwith,
Kerrier, Pyder and Powdar meet*)

govydnys *v. adj.* asked, required

gwadnhës *v. adj.* weakened,
attenuated

Hellës *f.* Helston

hag all *adv.* and all, also

idn *adj.* narrow, confined

le ha le, **ha lacka ha lacka** less
and less and worse and worse

An Lesard *m.* The Lizard

muskegys *adj.* confused

naneyl *adv.* neither

peca·r *Late Cornish form of* **kepar**
as, like

Pedn *m.* **an Wlas** Land's End

Porth *m.* **Ia** St Ives

Redrùth *m.* Redruth (*also* **Ewny
Redreth**)

scant *adv.* (*with negative*) hardly

stella *adv.* still, yet

tu ha(g) *prep.* towards

26C.2 TEXT DHE REDYA
(*NEBES GERYOW ADRO DHE GERNOWEK*)
Red an devyn usy ow sewya hag ena gwra gortheby an qwestyonow adro dhodho

Gàn tavas Kernowek yw mar bell wadnhës na yllyn ny scant gwetyas dh'y weles crefhe arta; rag pecar dell wrug an Sowson y dhanvon i'n pow idn-ma an kensa, indelna yma stella ow ton warnodho, heb gasa dhodho tyller vëth mès adro dhe'n âls ha'n mor. Oll ywa va clappys lebmyn ogasty yw dhort Pedn an Wlas dhe'n Garrek Loos ha tu ha Porth Ia ha Redrudh, hag arta dhort an Lesard tu ha Hellës ha Falmeth. I'n tyller idn-ma hag oll yma moy Sowsnek clappys dell eus Kernowek, rag radn a yll bos kevys na yll scant clappya na godhvos Kernowek, mès scant den vëth mès a wor godhvos ha clappya Sowsnek. Rag hedna, yth hevel dhyn, cales yw dhe wil dhodho gortos ha dos adro arta, rag wosa an dus dhe verwel in kerdh, ny a wel an dus yonk dh'y glappya le ha le, ha lacka ha lacka, hag indelna ev a vydn lehe dhort termyn dhe dermyn—rag an tavas Sowsnek yw clappys mar dhâ avell in tyller vëth; ha nyns yw an dus coth dhe vos scodhys wàr naneyl, pecar dell vydnowgh why gweles orth helma adro dhe'n Empyryk Angwyn, an brâssa ha'n cotha scoler in mesk oll an clappyers Kernowek adhewedhes. Rag govydnys dhe dhesmygy "Geverangow" ev a wrug predery wàr "gever", ha muskegys adro dhe "anco", ev a leverys dell o va "Gever oll" mès a ancovas dro dhe'n ger "cov" devedhys dhort "porth in cov."

1 Pandra na yllyn ny scant gwetyas, herwyth an scrifor?
2 Pleth esa Kernowek côwsys in y dhedhyow ev?
3 A ylly an clappyers a Gernowek côwsel Sowsnek inwedh?
4 Pëth o hanow an brâssa scoler Kernowek in dedhyow an scrifor?
5 Pana reson a'n jeva an scrifor rag predery nag esa Angwyn ow convedhes meur a'n tavas?

SEYTHVES DYSCANS WARN UGANS
TWENTY-SEVENTH LESSON

27A.1 THE HIGHER NUMERALS

These are **cans** 'a hundred', **dew cans** 'two hundred', **try cans**, **try hans** 'three hundred', **peswar cans** 'four hundred' and so on until **mil²** 'a thousand', **dyw vil²** 'two thousand', **tremmil²** or **teyr mil²** 'three thousand', **cans vil²** 'a hundred thousand'. 'A million' is either **mil vil²** or **mylyon**. The ordinals can be formed by the addition of **-ves** to each. **Cans** is masculine and has a plural **cansow**. **Mil** is feminine and has a plural **milyow**. Notice also **seyth ugans** 'a hundred and forty'. Like the lower numerals these are followed by the singular: **try cans den** 'three hundred men'. If **a²** is used after a numeral, however , the plural must follow: **tremmil ha peswar cans a bùscas** 'three thousand and four hundred fish'.

27A.2 YEARS

Years can be rendered as in English: **nawnjek hanter-cans ha naw** '1959'; **dyw vil, seyth warn ugans** or **ugans, seyth warn ugans** '2027'. To describe someone's age one uses the word **bloodh** *f.* 'years of age': **ow bloodh yw try ugans ha pymp** 'I am 65' or **an vowes vian yw teyr bloodh hedhyw** 'the little girl is three today'.

27A.3 'AGO'

There are two ways of saying 'ago' in Cornish. One can use the expression **nans yw** or **nanj yw** 'now it is', e.g. **y feu an lyver dyllys nans yw peder bledhen** 'the book was published four years ago', literally 'it is now four years. **Yth esof vy ow tesky Kernowek nans yw whegh mis** means 'I have been learning Cornish for six months now', but it can also be translated 'I started learning Cornish six months ago'.

The second way of saying 'ago' employs the word **alebma** 'hence', for example, **me a'n metyas nebes mîsyow alebma** 'I met him some months ago' (literally 'some months hence').

27A.4 MISCELLANEOUS EXPRESSIONS WITH THE NUMERALS

'We two', for example, is rendered **agan dew**, and 'the four of you' by **agas peswar**. 'Two by two' is **dew ha dew**. 'About a hundred and fifty' is **neb cans ha hanter-cans**, while 'nearly two hundred' is **ogas ha dew cans**. **Hanter** is 'half' and **qwartron** 'a quarter'. Other fractions can be expressed by the ordinal and the word **radn** *f.*, **radnow** 'share', e.g. **teyr degves radn** 'three tenths'; **an tressa radn a'n re-ma** 'a third of these'.

The time is expressed by using **our** *m.* 'hour', **mynysen** *f.* 'minute'. **Try our ha deg mynysen warn ugans** 'three hours and thirty minutes'. For times of the clock we can say: **ugans mynysen wosa seyth** 'twenty past seven'; **qwartron dhe naw** 'a quarter to nine', etc.

When reading out telephone numbers one uses **màn** for 'zero' and **dewblek** (or **dobyl**) for 'double': 2907665 is read **dew, naw, màn, seyth, whegh dewblek, pymp**.

27A.5 'HOW MUCH?' AND 'HOW MANY?'

'So many, as many', 'so much, as much' are usually rendered by **kebmys**: **kebmys a vo i'n chy** 'as many as are in the house'. There are a number of ways of translating 'how many?', 'how much?' The commonest way is **pygebmys**: **pygebmys eus genes?** 'how many have you?' **Pyseu·l** can also be used: **pyseul eus obma?** how many are here? One can also say **pyseul dhe voy a gotha dhyn bos lowen** 'by how much the more should we be happy'. **Pes** also means 'how many?', for example in **pes mildir?** 'how many miles?'

'How many?' can also be rendered by **py lies?** or **pana lies?**, for example **pana lies den a wrusta gweles ena?** 'how many people did you see there?' **Pesqweth** means both 'how often' and 'as often as'. **ny worama pesqweth a wrug hy ow thùlla** 'I do not know how often she deceived me' and **pesqweth a wrug hy ow thùlla, me a avas dhedhy** 'as often as she deceived me, I forgave her'.

'How often' can also be rendered **pana lowr torn** (literally) 'how many occasions': **a ylta jy remembra pana lowr torn a wrusta recêva mona dhyworto?** 'can you remember how often you received money from him?'

27A.6 LENGTH, WIDTH, HEIGHT, AND DEPTH

The measurements of length attested in the texts are **kevelyn** *m.* 'cubit'; **mesva** *f.* 'inch'; **tros'hës** *m.* 'foot'; **lath** *f.* 'yard' and **mildir** *f.* 'mile'.

When asking 'how long' one can say **pygebmys hës ywa?** 'how long is it?' 'How wide is it?' can be rendered **pygebmys les ywa?** For 'how high' and 'how deep' one can say **pygebmys uhelder** and **pygebmys downder**, though neither of these is attested. 'How far' is attested as **pana bellder?** One could therefore also say **pana uhelder usy ino?** 'what height is in it' and **pana dhownder usy ino** 'what depth is in it?'

For 'the canal is a hundred miles long, thirty feet wide and forty feet deep' in Cornish one would say **yma an dowrgledh cans mildir ahës, deg tros'hes alês ha dewgans tros'hes in downder**.

27A.7 'ONCE', 'TWICE', 'THREE TIMES', ETC.

'Once', 'twice', 'three times', etc. are expressed in Cornish by the word **gweyth** 'time', preceded by feminine forms of the numeral. Note that in **unweyth** 'once' the first element is never pre-occluded: **unweyth** 'once'; **dywweyth** 'twice'; **tergweyth** 'three times'; **pedergweyth** 'four times'; **pympgweyth**, etc. 'A hundred times' is **canqweyth** and 'a thousand times' **milweyth**.

'For the first time', 'on the first occasion', etc. can be rendered by means of the word **treveth**: **yth esof vy ow covyn rag an tressa treveth** 'I am asking for the third time'.

27A.8 ADDITION, SUBTRACTION, MULTIPLICATION, AND DIVISION

None of these is attested in the traditional language. In the revived language one expresses them as follows:

i) **dew ha dew a wra peswar** 'two and two make four'; **pymp ha hanter-cans ha try ugans a wra êtek ha try ugans** '55 and 23 make 78'

ii) **ugans marnas pymp yw pymthek** '20 minus five is 15'; **cans marnas deg warn ugans a wra deg ha try ugans** '100 minus 30 equals 70'

iii) **dew beswar yw êth** 'two fours are eight'; **udnek tergweyth yw tredhek warn ugans** '11 times three is 33'

iv) **cans rydnys inter deg yw deg** 'a 100 divided by 10 is 10'; **hanter-cans rydnys inter seyth yw seyth hag onen gesys** '50 divided by seven is seven and a remainder of one'. **Remnant** *m.* can also be used to mean 'remainder'.

The vigesimal system of counting in Cornish is distinctively Celtic, but it is also rather difficult to use. A simpler decimal system has been developed in Welsh and has been recommended for Cornish also. A decimal system of numeration would involve using no feminine forms from one to ten. From 11 to 99 one would count the units and the tens separately: **udn deg onen** 'eleven'; **dew dheg try** 'twenty-three'; **naw deg êth** 'ninety-eight'. With more complicated numbers; for example, 6972 one would deal with each part separately: **whegh mil**, **naw cans**, **seyth dek ha dew**. Ordinals would be replaced by cardinal numbers: **an dhavas udn cans, peswar deg ha try** 'the hundred and forty third sheep'.

27B EXAMPLES FROM THE TEXTS

27B.1 *moy ys cans vyl yn nomber* 'more than a hundred thousand in number' OM 1613-14; *try mylyon our* 'three million pieces of gold' RD 2258; *myl vyl dyaul a vye guan er y byn ef* 'a million devils would be of no avail against him' RD 132-33; *moy ages myl vyl enef yn bros pur dek* 'more than a million souls in a very nice broth' RD 141-42; *han re na a rug convertya ha trelya lyas myll a vyllyow then feith* 'and those converted and turned many thousand thousands to the faith' TH 51; *dens omma hage mammov tremmyl orth nyver heb wov* 'let them come here and their mothers, three thousand indeed' BM 1538-39; *pymp myll strekis del iove ha pedergwyth cans goly ha try vgons moy ganse ha pymʒek pur wyr ens y* 'five thousand weals, as I have heard, and four times a hundred wounds and sixty more as well and fifteen indeed they were' PA 227bc; *Tedna cans mil warbar* 'to catch a hundred thousand together' Pryce; *The'n cans myl deawl reg yllough* 'May you go to the hundred thousand demons' BK 744; *Merough ple ma an Romans ow settya ragow' myrnans, peswar cans meyl in un cor* 'See where the Romans are plotting your death, four hundred thousand in one contingent' BK 2808-10; *pan defa an termyn playne a pympe myell ha pymp cans vlethan an oyle a vercy in nena a vyth kevys* 'when the full time comes of five thousand and five hundred years, then the oil of mercy will be obtained' CW 1893-96; *try cans try vgans in prove* 'three hundred and sixty in fact' CW 2102; *tray hans myledere* 'three hundred miles' Borde.

27B.2 *An peth eu gwellez gena vee tho bose guthvethez ha dismiggiez eu lavar war cota dean brose en arghanz hunt tho canz bloath coth lebben* 'What was seen by me to be known and explained is the motto on the coat of arms of a great man in silver over a hundred years old now' NBoson; *pe nag oma buz dro tho wheeath bloah coth* 'when I was only about six years old' NBoson; *Bluth vee eue try egence a pemp* 'my age is sixty five' WBodinar; *poble coath pager egance blouth* 'the old people eighty years of age'

WBodinar; *Miz Ebral pempas dydh, sitack canz ha deg* 'The month of April, the fifth day, 1710' JBoson; *en blooth Creste an Arleuth whege meele sith cans ha hanter deege* 'in the year of Christ the dear Lord, 1705' TBoson.

27B.3 *Nans yw lemmyn tremenes nep dew cans a vlethynnow* 'Now have passed some two hundred years' OM 656-57; *gallas henna the ken tyr nans yv sythyn tremenys* 'that man went to another country a week ago' BM 2231-32; *na ny wrugaf tha wellas nangew sure lyas blethan* 'and I have not seen you indeed for many years past' CW 1602-03; *nang ew termyn tremenys a vlethydnyowe moy es cans* 'now the time has passed of many years' CW 1914-15; *skreefez rag an flehaz nab blethanniau alebma* 'written for the children some years ago' NBoson; *Me rig fanja guz lether zithan lebma* 'I received your letter a week ago' OPender.

27B.4 *deugh agas dew scon yn rak* 'come forward the two of you' PC 1867; *dew ha dew benaw ha gorrawe* 'two by two, male and female' CW2414.

27B.5 *ha gueles yn blethen hyr py gymmys hys may teffo* 'and to see in the long year how long it will grow' OM 2103-04; *ha pana peldar a ruga bewa ena* 'and how long he lived there' TH 47a; *Pysell defferans a bewnans vs lymmyn intrethan ny* 'How great is the difference of life now between us' TH 27; *Pan a lyas gwethfas a ve gesys heb confort? pan lyas flogh omthevas a ve gesys heb confort na succur? pan lyas testament ha blonogath an marow a ve tyrrys ha gesys heb colynwall gans intentys ha ordynans anethe?* 'How many widows have been left without support? How many orphan children have been left without support or assistance? How many wills and testaments of the dead have been disregarded and left unfulfilled with their intentions and instructions?' TH 40; *Pes myllder eus alemma de Londres?* 'How many miles is it from here to London?' Borde

27B.6 *ha tryhans keuelyn da an lester a vyth a hys* 'and three hundred good cubits the vessel will be in length' OM 955-56; *ha hanter cans keuelyn ynweth ty a wra y les* 'and fifty cubits also you shall make its width' OM 957-58; *yn vhelder my a vyn dek warn ugans y vos gures* 'I want it to be made thirty cubits in height' OM 959-60; *pan lowar turne a rug eff ernestly ha lamentably desyrya an mercy a thu* 'how many times he earnestly and lamentably desired the mercy of God' TH 8a.

27B.7 *Me a garsa thotha ef dusquethas unwyth pew of* 'I should like to show him once who I am' BK 2067-68; *guask gynsy dywyth an men* 'strike the rock with it twice' OM 1844; *Bedhez guesgyz dhiueth, ken gueskal enueth* 'be struck twice before striking once' JCH §10; *pedyr te am nagh tergweth* 'Peter, you will deny me three times' PA 49c; *ha pedergwyth cans goly* 'and four times a hundred wounds' PA 227b; *dek canquyth thy's lowene* 'ten hundred times joy to you' PC 574; *welcom mylwyth, ow sokors!* 'a thousand times welcome, my allies!' BK1548; *ke weth tresse treveth th'y* 'go again the third time thither' OM 799; *nena eff a gowsys thotha an tryssa trevath* 'then he spoke to him for the third time' TH 43.

27C.1 VOCABULARY

adâ·l *prep.* opposite, compared with
an bobel *f.* **chy** the household
Arlùth an Meneth *personal name.*
  Montaigne
awhe·r *m.* reason
Bryttas *pl.* Britons
coll *m.* loss
dien *adj.* complete
dyfedna to forbid
etna *late form of* **ino** in it

Frynk *f.* France
gwruga I did
Latyn *m.* Latin
Romans *pl.* Romans
scant *adv.* hardly (often with
  negative)
sians *m.* whim, desire
tra gwil *m.* wealth, wherewithal
yn meskys mixed, mingled

27C.2 TEXT DHE REDYA
(*NEBES GERYOW ADRO DHE GERNOWEK*, amendys)
   Red an devyn usy ow sewya ha scrif gorthebow dhe'n qwestyonow:

Rag me ow honen a veu genys in colon an pow-ma, le mayth yw an Kernowek an moyha côwsys, ha whath yma cov dhybm pàn nag en vy mès adro dhe whegh bloodh, na aljen y glappya na scant y wodhvos. An awher, yth esoma ow predery, yth o dhyworth sians ow dama, ow tyfedna orth an bobel chy ha'n gentrevogyon dhe glappya tra vëth dhybmo vy mès Sowsnek. Yma cov dhybm cafos tra a'n par-ma in lyver Arlùth an Meneth adro dh'y dhyscans Latyn.

Ena ow mos alês dhe scol ha woja hedna ow mos dhe Frynk, nyns eus cov dhybm dhe wodhvos meur i'n tavas Kernowek, erna wruga dos dhe gafos tra gwil i'n bës. Ha lebmyn yth esoma ow tôwlel dhe weles mar bell etna ogasty avell lies a'n gentrevogyon. Hag yma dhybm mar veur kerensa ragtho, mès ny allaf ry dhodho moy ès dell godhvia dhybm, rag yth ywa scant dien dhe vos gwelys in lies ger adâl bos gwrës in bàn dhyworth an Latyn bò an Sowsnek. Ha ny wor den vëth boneyl a wrug an coll-ma kensa dos dhyworth an Romans yn meskys gans an Bryttas, bò woja hedna dhyworth an Sowson, martesen dhyworth an dhew.

1 Ple feu an auctour genys?
2 Pyseul bloodh o va pan dhalathas ev desky an tavas Kernowek?
3 Prag na wrug ev y dhesky kyns hedna?
4 Pleth êth ev awosa?
5 Ev a lever bos fowt a eryow i'n tavas. Pyth yw an reson rag hedna in y dybyans ev?

ÊTHVES DYSCANS WARN UGANS
TWENTY-EIGHTH LESSON

28A.1 THE VOCATIVE

When addressing someone by his or her title, the vocative particle **a²** is frequently used: **a goweth** 'O friend'; **a vêster** 'O master'; **a venyn** 'O madam, O lady'. The particle is frequently omitted, however and the noun remains unmutated. The particle may be used with a proper name, but the initial is left unmutated: **a Myhal** 'O Michael'.

If the personal pronoun **te**, **ty** 'thou, you', precedes a noun used as a vocative, the initial consonant is lenited: **goslow orthyf, te dhen** 'listen to me, you man'.

28A.2 INTERJECTIONS

We have already noticed **ea** 'yes' and **nâ** 'nay, no'. Interjections expressing sorrow and regret include: **ella·s** 'alas'; **ala·ck** 'alack'; **ehan** 'alas'; **soweth** 'what a pity'; **tru** 'alas'; **ogh** 'oh' (in dismay); **owt** 'oh' (dislike); **harow** 'help, alas'. Other interjections include **ay** 'hey'; **a** 'oh'; **dar** 'eh, why' (astonishment); **pywa** 'what?' (astonishment); **tety valy** 'pshaw, pooh'; **how** 'hey, ho'; **fy** 'fie'; **agh** 'oh, fie'; **ho** 'hey'; **jowl** 'devil, hell'; **pyw an jowl** 'what the devil' and **a Dhuw** 'O God'.

Malbe² dàm, malbew² dàm is common in the texts and means 'devil the bit, damn all'. Similar are **malbe² vadna, malbew vadna** 'devil the drop, damn all' and **malbew onen** 'devil the one, nobody'.

Oaths are introduced by **re²**: **re Varia** 'by Our Lady' > **aria**; **re Vyhal** 'by St Michael'; **re'm leowta** 'upon my loyalty'; **ren ow thas** 'by my father'. **Wàr** is used in **wàr ow fêdh** 'upon my faith, upon my word'. **Tàn ow fêdh** 'upon my faith' is also found.

Further everyday expressions will be found in 40A, 40B, etc.

28A.3·THE POINTS OF THE COMPASS

The points of the compass are **north** 'north', **ÿst** or **êst** 'east'; **soth** 'south'; and **west** 'west'. The points between are **north ÿst** 'north east',

north west 'north west', **soth ÿst** 'south east' and **soth west** 'south west'. 'To the east' is **dhe'n ÿst** and 'to the east of' is **a ÿst dhe²**.

NOTE: Unified Cornish frequently uses the following purisms for the points of the compass: **cledh** 'north'; **howldrevel** 'east'; **dyhow** 'south' and **howlsedhas** 'west'. There is some evidence that in the very earliest Middle Cornish the points of the compass were **gogleth** 'north'; **dùryan** 'east'; **dyhow** 'south'; and **howlsedhas**; see *Cornish Studies: Fifteen* (2007), 17-21. These forms, seem to have been obsolete by the sixteenth century.

28A.4 PY(TH) 'WHERE?' AND 'WHITHER?'

Ple(th) is the commonest word for 'where?' Middle Cornish also had another adverb **py** 'where?' and 'whither?' It combines with **yma** to give **pyma**: **pyma va** 'where is he?'. It becomes **pyth** before vowels in **mos** 'to go' and **bos** 'to be': **pyth esta ow mos?** 'where are you going?'; **pyth av?** 'where shall I go?'

28A.5 LETTER WRITING

We have already seen the way in which the date is written in Cornish (11A.6). 'Dear' in letter writing is usually **wheg** (literally 'sweet') rather than **ker** 'dear'. 'Sir' is **syra**, **sera** (this is a different word from **sîra** 'sire, father'). Formal letters therefore begin: **Syra wheg** 'Dear Sir'. There are no attested examples of letters beginning 'Dear Madam', but **madama** 'madam' is attested elsewhere. One would therefore begin such a letter **Madama wheg** 'Dear Madam'.

We have a few examples from the Late Cornish period of signing off in letters. For yours faithfully one might say **Yth ov vy agas gwas** 'I am your servant' or possibly **yn lel dhywgh** 'faithfully to you', though there is no warrant in the texts for this latter expression. Perhaps the best way of saying 'yours sincerely' is to imitate John Boson with **gans oll ow holon vy** (literally 'with all my heart'). **Gans pùb bolùnjeth dâ** 'with every good wish' is also unobjectionable, though it is a modern invention.

Lowena dhis 'Joy to you' is sometimes used by revivalists to finish a letter. This should not be imitated, since in traditional Cornish **lowena dhis** is always used when meeting someone, not when taking one's leave.

28B EXAMPLES FROM THE TEXTS

28B.1 *lowene ȝys a vester* 'greetings to you, O master' PA 65b; *A vroder ov banneth thy's* 'O brother, my blessing to you' OM 1827; *reuerons thy'so a vam ker* 'reverence to you, O dear mother' RD 495; *Heyl dyso a venen tha*

'Hail to the, good lady' BM 3579; *A Thew, gohy ow holan* 'O God, pity my poor heart' BK 2277; *a das kere mere rase thewhy* 'O dear father, many thanks to you' CW 1953; *dvne ny warbarth a gowetha* 'let us go together, O friends' CW 2067; *taw pedyr te ny wozas* 'silence, Peter, you do not know' PA 46b; *moyses moyses saf ena* 'Moses, Moses, stand there' OM 1403; *ty myhall re stowte yth os* 'you, Michael, are too bold' CW 213; *A te then preder ath du* 'O you man, think of your God' BM 1908.

28B.2 *ogh govy ellas ellas* 'oh, woe is me, alas, alas' PC 2603; *ogh ellas gouy tru tru* 'oh, alas, alas, woe is me, alack, alack' PC 2627; *Ay tevdar ke war the gam* 'Hey, Teudar, steady on' BM 1048; *Ha sovdoryon lemmen ho* 'Hey, soldiers now, ho!' BM 2493; *Alak, tus vas, ha pell ew mer an bobill resys hethow in jeth theworth an kithsam rulle ma* 'Alack, good people and far have many of the people run these days from this same rule' TH 37; *Dar, ny ylta dyfuna?* 'What, can you not wake up?' BK 349; *Fy myllwyth the'n thew abo* 'A thousand times fie to the two hulks' BK 922; *Out, out, out, out, out! Owt, galsof gwan a'm skyans!* 'oh, oh, oh, oh, oh! Oh, I have become weak in the head!' BK 3136b-17; *tety valy bram an gathe* 'pshaw, the cat's farts' CW 2378.

28B.3 *nynsus guas a west the heyl an tollo guel* 'there is no fellow to the west of Hayle who would pierce it better' PC 2744-45; *North yst then chapel omma* 'north-east of the chapel here' BM 664; *nebes a weyst a carnebre* 'a little to the west of Carn Brea' BM 784; *agen tassens an barth north* 'our patron saint from the north' BM 3427; *Pan nowothou, pan guestlow us genowgh why a'n cost west?* 'What news, what pledges have you from the western region?' BK 2222-23; *Ke souyth ha north ha gura cry cref in pub cost* 'Go south and north and make a loud cry in every region' BK 2350-51; *ha pel ða êst ev a travaliaz* 'and far to the east he journeyed' JCH §3; *marrack en pedden west pow Densher* 'a knight in the west part of Devonshire' NBoson; *Wor duath gra gwenz noor east whetha pell* 'In the end the north-east wind will blow for long' JBoson; *Râg ma gwellez gen a ni e steran en est* 'For we have seen his star in the east' Rowe; *ha an stearan a reeg angye gwellhaz en east geeth deractanze* 'and the star they saw in the east went before them' Rowe.

28B.4 *pyma thym ov margh morel* 'where has my jet-black horse gone from me?' BM 2111; *pyma abell cowes henna* 'where is Abel; tell me that' CW 1191; *peth ave mos theworthas?* 'where will I go departing from you?' SA 63.

28B.5 *Mi a moaz tha'n venton, sarra wheag* 'I am going to the well, dear sir' Chygwyn; *cusal ha têg, sirra wheage, moas pell* 'soft and fair, dear sir, goes far' Pryce; *Sarah wheage onerez meth ewe da gene gasawaz than peath a eze laverez* 'Dear honoured sir, I am pleased to listen to what is said' TBoson; *Sara wheage, Me rig fanja guz lether zithan lebma* 'Dear sir, I received your letter a week ago' OPender; *heil a heil madama vras* 'hail, oh hail, great madam' PC 1935; *Agoz Obèruaz Hyvela* 'Your Humblest Servant' AB: 224; *Rag an termen ma [gwrenz] Deu boz genn'o* 'For the time being may God be with you' JBoson; ***Gen ol an kolan ve, ma ve goz guas*** 'With all my heart, I am your servant' JBoson.

28C.1 VOCABULARY

an hern *coll.* **gwâv** the winter pilchards

an hern *coll.* **hâv** the summer pilchards

breus *f.* judgement

cafos coler become angry

car vy *Late Cornish for* my kinsman

cries *v. adj.* called

Falmeth *m.* Falmouth

fanja to receive

gàs *Late Cornish for* **agas** your

gen oll ow holon vy yours sincerely (*lit.* with all my heart)

Gomer *m.* **mab Jafet mab Noy** Gomer son of Japhet son of Noah

grâss *m.* grace; *pl.* **grassow** thanks

holan *m.* **ker** expensive salt

hosket *m.*, **hoskettys** hogshead, barrel

in agan oos ny in our age

Lulyn *f.* Newlyn

mercy *m.* mercy, thanks

meur ras many thanks

ny alja *Late Cornish for* **ny ylly** he could not

Pluw *f.* **Pawl** the Parish of Paul

rag hedna *adv.* therefore

sconha *comp. adj.* sooner, earlier

scrifa *m.* **vas** good writing

seythen alebma *adv. phrase* a week ago

straft *adv.* straight away, immediately

Tour *m.* **Bâbel** the Tower of Babel

trueth yw y vos kellys it is a pity that it should be lost

tus *pl.* **Germogh** the people of Germoe

tus *pl.* **vuscok** madmen

28C.2 TEXTOW DHE REDYA.
(*LYTHEROW DHE WILLIAM GWAVAS*)

Red an dhew lyther-ma hag ena gwra gortheby an qwestyonow:

A. *Lyther dhyworth Jowan Boson dhe William Gwavas* (5 Ebrel 1710)

Mis Ebrel, an pympes dëdh, seytek cans ha deg

Car vy,

Me a wra ry mercy dhywgh rag gàs nowodhow orth an kensa den Kernowek. Ow sîra vy a wrug leverel dhybm yth o Gomer mab Jafet mab Noy an den a wrug clappya Kernowek i'n termyn may feu Tour Bâbel derevys, ha rag hedna ny a yll gweles hag aswon an tavas Kernowek dhe vos tavas coth ha trueth yw y vos kellys. Mès yma own dhybmo vy na vydn an tavas-ma nefra bos kevys arta in agan oos ny, na bêwnans heb dyweth.

Yma gàs scrifa compes, den fur owgh why,
ha skentyl lùk in tavas gàn pow ny.
Na wrewgh cafos coler rag scrifa vas:
Gen oll ow holon vy, me yw gàs gwas.

Jowan Boson.

Tus Germogh, cries stenoryon, yth yns tus vuscok, heb own Duw na'n bës. Ny allama leverel udn ger dâ wortans. Rag an termyn-ma, gwrêns Duw bos genowgh. JB.

B. *Lyther dhyworth Oliver Pender dhe William Gwavas* (22 Est 1711)

Dhyworth Lulyn in Plu Pawl
an 22es mis Est, 1711

Syra wheg,
Me a wrug fanja gàs lyther seythen alebma, mès nyns esa termyn dhybm dhe scrifa dhywgh straft arta, rag nyns eus mès lebmyn dyweth dhybm adro dhe'n holan ker. Meur ras dhe Dhuw, yth yw ogasty oll gwerthys. Yma own dhybmo vy, yma dyweth dhe nessa bledhen adro dhe'n hern. Nyns eus pris vëth eus ow mos whath ragthans y. An hern gwâv a vydn gwil drog dhe'n hern hâv, rag yma adro dhe dhyw vil hosket whath in Falmeth, gwerthys ha dhe vos gwerthys; hag ymowns ow scrifa ena wàr agan pydn ny.

Na wra gwitha hern re bell
kyns gwertha, rag pris dâ yw gwell.

[*ow tùchya Edward Lhuyd*]
Rag ny alja clappya na scrifa Kernowek kepar ha why. Yth o moy Kembrek an pëth a wrug ev gwil.

Oliver Pender

1 Pana davas esa Gomer mab Jafet ow côwsel, warlergh tybyans Jowan Boson?
2 Prag yma Jowan Boson ow cresy an tavas Kernowek dhe vos tavas coth?
3 Pandr'o an dhew dra nag o tus Germogh dowtys anodhans?
4 Prag na wrug Oliver Pender scrifa dhe William Gwavas sconha ès an lyther-ma?
5 Yma Pender ow ry grâssow dhe Dhuw dre rêson bos neppyth oll gwerthys ogasty. Pandra?
6 Pana vreus usy Pender ow ry adro dhe Gernowek Edward Lhuyd?

NAWVES DYSCANS WARN UGANS
TWENTY-NINTH LESSON

29A.1 THE VOCABULARY OF REVIVED CORNISH

Cornish contained many borrowings from French and English from the earliest Middle Cornish period, but Nance was often reluctant to admit them. Instead he preferred to use Celtic words which were attested only in Old Cornish, or which had been coined in Cornish on the basis of Breton and Welsh. Nance's linguistic purism was perhaps understandable; it may not have been wise. If we are attempting to resuscitate the ancestral language of Cornwall, we must surely do our best to revive it as it was spoken natively by the Cornish people. If we prefer the poorly attested or unattested word for the common one, we lay ourselves open to the charge that we are not reviving Cornish, but are constructing a language that is only tangentially related to historic Cornish.

29A.2 *WHARVOS* 'TO HAPPEN'

The verb **wharvos** is in some of its parts a compound of the verb **bos** 'to be'. The present **wher** is used in the expression **pandra wher dhis** 'what is the matter with you?' The future is **whyrvyth**. The subjunctive is **wharvo**, the preterite is **wharva**. The verbal adjective is either **wharvedhys** or **whyrvys**. **Happya** and **hapnya** 'to happen' are also attested.

29A.3 *TÀN!* 'TAKE!'

Tàn! 'take!' and the plural **tanowgh!** 'take!' are specialised imperatives of the verb **tedna** 'to draw, to extract'. They are colloquial in register.

29A.4 PREFIXES WITH VERBS

We saw at 2A.3 that some adjectives were prefixed to their nouns rather than put after them. One such adjectival prefix is **tebel** 'evil, bad'. **Tebel** can also be used adverbially, when prefixed to a verb: **tebel-wolia** 'to wound badly', **tebel-dhyghtya** 'to treat badly'. **Drog** 'bad' and **ewn** 'right' can also be prefixed to verbs: **drog-handla** 'to mistreat'; **ewn-gara** 'to love properly'. Another common verbal prefix is **cowl** 'fully', seen in **cowl-derevel** 'to build completely' and **cowl-wil** 'to complete'. The verb **cowllenwel**, **collenwel** 'to fulfil' is a compound of **cowl** 'fully' and **lenwel** 'to fill'.

Leun 'full' can also used with verbs, e.g. **leun-gresy** 'to believe fully'. The English borrowings **over** and **opyn** 'open' are used in the compounds **over-devy** 'to overgrow' and **opyn-weles** 'to see openly'.

29A.5 WORD ORDER AND EMPHASIS

We saw at 14A.4 that speakers of traditional Cornish did not use the tone of voice to emphasise, but rather employed suffixed pronouns and word order. If in Cornish one wishes to emphasize part of a sentence, one brings it to the head of its clause. In the English sentence 'I am the master here' one can stress either i) 'I' or ii) 'the master' or iii) 'here'. The Cornish equivalents have to be differently phrased:

i) **Me yw an mêster obma**
ii) **An mêster ov vy obma yth oma** or **An mêster ov vy obma**
iii) **Obma an mêster me yw**.

29B EXAMPLES FROM THE TEXTS

29B.1 *Ny alsa moy dyswryans wharvos neffra er ow fyn* 'No more destruction could happen against me' BK 3138-39; *saw lemmyn un marth a wher* 'but now a miracle is happening' BK 18; *rag y whyrvyth an tyrmyn* 'for the time will occur' OM 45; *yndella thy'n re wharfo* 'thus may it happen to us' OM 667; *ha tra na wharva bythquath* 'and a thing which never happened' BK 853; *Yn egip whyrfys yv cas* 'a matter has occurred in Egypt' OM 1415; *yma tra varth wharvethys* 'a remarkable thing has happened' OM 2082; *yt hapyas thy'm gul foly* 'it happened to me to work folly' PC 1438; *ha mar happyn thyn cotha dre gwannegreth* 'and if we happen to fall through weakness' TH 41.

29B.2 *Adam ystyn thy'm the thorn tan henna theworthef vy* 'Adam, stretch out your hand to me; take this from me' OM 205-06; *tannegh honthsel kyns sevel* 'take breakfast before getting out of bed' BM 960; *Tan at omma thys x puns* 'Take, here is ten pounds for you' BM 1464; *ha tan dis dewes ha boys* 'and take for yourself drink and food' BM 4243.

29B.3 *a ihesu gouy ragos mar tebeldyghtys the vos* 'O Jesus, woe is me for you, that you are so ill-treated' PC 2633-34; *mar calla y tebelfar* 'if I can, he will fare ill' BM 2281; *ha me tebelwolijs* 'and I badly wounded' BM 2490; *drokhandle del om kyry pan gyffy dalhen ynno* 'treat him roughly, as you love me, when you get hold of him' PC 991-92; *dre laha y coth dotho drokdywethe* 'by law he ought to come to an evil end' PC 1827-28; *iude mar a'm evn geryth* 'Jude, if you love me rightly' RD 1448; *arluth ytho pyw a wra couldreheuel ol the chy* 'Lord, who then will complete the building of your house?' OM 2339-40; *nanns yv an fossow coulwrys* 'now are the walls fully made' OM 2454; *y luen crygy me a wra* 'I will believe him fully' RD 482; *in ow thermyn me a'th luenworth* 'in my time I will I will worship you fully' BK 1225-26; *why am gweall over devys* 'you see me overgrown' CW 1507; *opyn guelys yv omma nag us du mas ihesu ker* 'it is openly seen here that there is no God but dear Jesus' BM 4152-53.

29C.1 VOCABULARY

assoylya to solve
camhenseth *m.* injustice
chastia to chastise
cheryta *m.* charity
compressa to oppress
coraj *m.* courage
cûr *m.* cure of souls
drog-pobel *f.* wicked people
epscop *m.*, **epscobow** bishop
execûtya to carry out, to execute
fâls-acûsacyon *m.* false accusation
fowt *m.*, **fowtys** fault
goheles to avoid
gormola *m.* praise
governans *m.*, **governansow** government
governour *m.*, **governours** governor
gwlascor *f.*, **gwlascorow** kingdom
hevelly to compare
inocent *m.*, **inocentys** innocent person
kerenjedhek *adj.* affectionate, loving
kessydhyans *m.* rebuke, punishment

lack *m.* lack
laha *m.*, **lahys** law
magata *adv.* as well, also
mes a fordh out of the way, wrong
meur-jersya to cherish greatly
offens *m.*, **offencys** offence
offys *m.*, **offycys** office, function
ordna to ordain, to order
pëth *m.* possessions, property
plag *m.*, **plâgys** plague, punishment
plain *adj.* plain, clear
prais *m.* praise
pregowthor *m.*, **pregowthoryon** preacher
prow *m.* advantage
pùnyshment *m.*, **pùnyshmentys** punishment
pùnyshya to punish
rebûkya to rebuke
regardya to regard, to consider
rewardya to reward, recompense
uhel-powers *pl.* powers that be
venjons *m.* vengeance

29C.2 TEXT DHE REDYA
(JOHN TREGEAR amendys)

Red an devyn usy ow sewya ha gwra gortheby an qwestyonow:

Obma me a vydn govyn udn qwestyon dhe vos assoylys: mar teu cheryta ha reqwîrya dhe bredery, dhe gows dâ ha dhe wil dâ dhe bùb den, dâ ha drog, fatell yll an rewlysy a'n wlas execûtya jùstys wàr dhrog-bobel gans cheryta? Fatell wrowns y tôwlel drog-pobel in pryson, kemeres in kerdh aga fëth ha traweythyow aga bêwnans warlergh laha an wlas, mar ny wrella cheryta sevel gansans ha'ga sùffra indella dhe wil? Dhe hebma yma gorthyp plain dhe vos rës. Nyns yw plâgys ha pùnyshmentys tebel anodhans aga honen, mar pedhons kemerys in fordh dhâ gans inocentys, ha dhe dhrog-pobel ymowns kefrës dâ hag a brow, hag y a yll bos execûtys warlergh cheryta, ha gans cheryta y a gotha bos execûtys. Rag an declaracyon a hebma, why a wra ùnderstondya fatell eus dhe jeryta dew offys, ha'n eyl yw contrary dh'y gela. Ha'n dhew a res bos gwrÿs ha bos ûsys wàr an re yw contrary in aga omdhon. An eyl offys a jeryta yw dhe veur-jersya an dus dhâ ha'n dus inocent, ma na vowns y compressys gans fâls-acûsacyon, mès dhe ry dhedhans coraj dhe wil dâ ha dhe dhurya in dader, ha'ga defendya dre gledha dhyworth aga eskerens. Ha'n offys a epscobow ha'n re a's teffa cûr a enevow yw dhe ry gormola ha prais dhe oll an dus dhâ rag oberow dâ, may hallens durya in dader; ea, ha dhe rebûkya ha dhe jastia der an ger a Dhuw offencys ha fowtys an dhrog-pobel. An offys aral yw dhe rebûkya ha dhe bùnyshya camhenseth heb favera den vÿth. Ha hebma yw dhe vos ûsys warbydn an dhrog-pobel magata dell ywa dhe rewardya ha defendya an re-na yw dâ hag inocent. Yma Sen Pawl indelma ow teclarya dhe'n Romans: An uhel-powers yw ordnys gans Duw ha nyns yns y dhe vos dowtys gans an re yw dâ, mès dhe bùnyshya an dhrog-pobel gans an cledha, ha dhe gemeres venjons wàr an dhrog-pobel. Indelma an dhew offys a vynsa bos execûtys yn tywysyk, rag goheles gwlascor an tebel-el, an pregowthor gans an ger, ha'n governour gans an cledha, ken nyns usons y ow regardya Duw na'n re usy in dadn aga governans, mar towns y ha sùffra Duw dhe vos offendys rag lack a gessydhyans, ha'n re usy in aga governans dhe vos dystrêwys kepar dell wra pùb tas kerenjedhek chastia y flogh y honen pàn dheffa ha gwil taclow mes a fordh, ken nyns ujy worth y gara.

1 An auctour a lever bos dew offys dhe jeryta. Pandr'yns y?

2 Yn arbednek pandr'yw offys an epscobow warlergh an auctour?

3 Pandr'usy an governour owth ûsya warbydn an re yw contrary in aga omdhon?

4 Mar ny wra an uhel-powers execûtya jùstys, pandra vydn wharvos, warlergh an auctour?

5 Yma an auctour owth hevelly an governour dhe das kerenjedhek. Prag?

6 Esta dha honen ow cresy bos ewn aga hevelly an eyl dh'y gela?

7 Esta dha honen ow cresy y vos warlergh cheryta gorra an dhrog-pobel dhe'n mernans?

DEGVES DYSCANS WARN UGANS
THIRTIETH LESSON

30A.1 'MONEY'

For 'money' in Cornish some people use the word **arhans**. This is not authentic, however, since **arhans** only ever means 'silver' in the texts, rather than 'money'. Moreover the internal consonant group (better **-rh-** than **-rgh-**) in the word for 'silver', is pronounced with a voiceless **r** and is sometimes written **rr**; it is not pronounced [rx]. The Middle and Late Cornish word for 'money', on the other hand, is **mona** *m*.

30A.2 'POUND'

In the Middle Cornish texts the word for 'pound' (money) is written **puns**. In Late Cornish 'pound' appears as **pens**. The form **pens** has led some commentators to believe that the Middle Cornish word **puns** represented **peuns*, and in Late Cornish this became **pens**, in the same way, for example, that **leun** 'full' became **len** and **eus** 'is' became **es**. This is a false conclusion, however. In the first place the expected Middle Cornish form is **puns**, not **peuns*; cf. Welsh *punt* 'pound'. In the second place **pyns** is also attested in Late Cornish alongside **pens**. It seems that once Middle Cornish [ʏ] was unrounded to [ɪ] in **puns**, the resulting **pyns** joined a group of words in which [ɪns] and [ɛns] were in free variation, e.g. **dyns ~ dens** 'teeth', **kyns ~ kens** 'before' and **syns ~ sens**. There is no evidence for **peuns*; the Cornish word for 'pound' is either **puns**, **punsow** or **pens**, **pensow**.

30A.3 THE WORDS *EUS* AND *USY*

The vowel in **eus** 'is' and **usy**, **ujy** 'is' (definite) were historically the same, but in the later language the first unrounds to **es** and the second to **ija**. This different development appears to be the result of vocalic harmony; and can be seen in various other pairs, e.g. **euth** 'terror' but **uthyk** 'terrible'; **feus** 'good fortune' but **fusyk** 'fortunate', **anfusyk**, **anfujyk** 'unfortunate'; **breus** *f.* 'judgement' but **brusy** 'to judge'; **beudh* 'drown!'

197

but **budhys** 'drowned'. In late forms like **bethys** 'drowned' and **eithick** 'terrible' the **e** may continue unrounded **eu**, but more probably is the result of the regular alternation of short **e** and **i** in open syllables (cf. **dewthack warnygans** CW 1981 but **ha deakwarnegans recknys** CW 1977). At all events the evidence suggests that it is better to write **uthyk, anfujyk, brusy** and **budhys**, with **u** rather than **eu**.

In some variaties of revived Cornish the words for 'already, just now' and 'already, formerly' are written ***seulabrys** and ***seuladhydh** respectively. There is no warrant for these spellings in the texts. The Cornish scribes always spell both items with **o** in the first syllable. In this book **solabrës**, **solabrÿs** and **soladhëdh**, **soladhÿdh** are the recommended spellings.

30A.4 'PUBLIC HOUSE'

A common word for 'public house, pub' in revived Cornish is ***dewotty**. This word is unattested, having been devised on the basis of Welsh *diotty* 'ale-house'. ***Dewotty** is unnecessary, in any case, because two words for 'ale-house, pub' are attested in the traditional language. The first of these is **tavern** *m*. or **chy tavern** which is attested in *Beunans Meriasek* and listed by Lhuyd. The second is **hostlery** *m*. cited by Pryce and Borlase. The plural of **tavern** was probably **taverns**, although **tavernyow** may have been an alternative plural. Although **hostlery**, *pl*. **hostlerys** is a borrowing from English 'hostelry' it was probably stressed on the second, rather than the first syllable. It is worth pointing out that Cornish **tavern** is the same word as Welsh *tafarn* 'tavern, ale-house' and Breton *tavarn* 'tavern, inn'. In the interests of authenticity, it would probably be wise to use **tavern** and **hostlery** in preference to ***dewotty**.

30A.5 'SHOP'

No word for 'shop' is attested in the Cornish texts. In consequence Nance devised the word ***gwerthjy** on the basis of the rare Welsh word *gwerthdy* 'shop'. The only attested Cornish word we have is **shoppa**, which can be seen in the place-names **Ponson Joppa** < **pons an shoppa** and **Parc Joppa** < **park an shoppa**. **Shoppa** is a borrowing from Middle English *shoppe* and means 'workshop' as much as 'shop for retail', but in the middle ages the distinction was much less clear than today. It is also noteworthy that the ordinary word for 'shop' in Welsh is *siop* < English 'shop'.

Given that the word **shoppa** occurs in Cornish toponymy, it seems sensible to prefer it to the wholly unattested word ***gwerthjy**.

30A.6 'HOUSES'

The Cornish word for 'house' is **chy** and variants **-jy** and **-ty** are found, for example, in **clâvjy** 'hospital' and **lêty** 'dairy'. These items are pluralized **clâvjiow** and **lêtiow** respectively. The simplex **chy**, however, has a suppletive plural **treven**. The form ***chiow** is not attested in traditional Cornish and cannot be recommended.

30B EXAMPLES FROM THE TEXTS

30B.1.1 *ha zozo y tysquethas owr hag arghans gwels ha gweth ha kymmys yn bys vs vas* 'and to him showed gold and silver, grass and trees, and all that is good in the world' PA 16bc; *fenten bryght avel arhans ha pedyr streyth vras defry ov resek adyworty* 'a spring as bright as silver and four streams running from it' OM 771-73; *me a'th cusyl dysempys byth na vy trest awos cost arhans nag our* 'I advise you not to be sad for the cost of silver or gold' RD 2229-31; *An pelle arrance ma ve resse, gen mere hurleyey, creve, ha brasse, do Wella Gwavas* 'This silver ball was given by many hurlers, strong and large, to William Gwavas' TBoson.

30B.1.2 *ha my a's pren thyworthy's otte an mone parys thy'so the pe* 'and I will buy it from you; here is the money ready to pay you' PC 1555-57; *ha me a vyn then benenes ry mona boys ha dewes the perna ha then flehys delles da* 'and I will give money to the women to buy food and drink and fine clothes for the children' BM 1671-74; *pronter ef a hevel suyr yma mona gans henna* 'he seems indeed to be a priest; that fellow has money' BM 1903-04; *Ith ew scryffys in viii-as chapter in actys an appostolis fatell rug Symon magus offra the ry mona the pedyr mar mynna pedyr ry power thotheff* 'It is written in the eighth chapter of the Acts of the Apostles that Simon offered Peter money if Peter would give him power' TH 46a; *Ha an mona an dzhei a gavaz; ha'n bara dzhei a dhabraz* 'And the money they found; and the bread they ate' JCH §46; *Dry dre an mona ha perna moy* 'Bring home the money and buy more' Pryce.

30B.2 *me a vynse a talfens myl pvns thotho a our da* 'I wish they would be worth a thousand pounds of fine gold for him' PC 211-12; *kyn teseryas punsov cans* 'even though you should desire of pounds a hundred' BM 1579; *eve a drayle thezo tha leas moy eas myllyow a bynsow* 'it will turn out to your advantage: more than thousands of pounds' CW 739-40; *deck pens en blethan* 'ten pounds a year' Pryce.

30B.3.1 *Mars ues den vith a vyn cows* 'If there is anybody who wishes to speak' BK 1496; *ihesu omma nyns ugy rak seuys yw* 'Jesus is not here, for he is risen' RD 782-83; *drefen nag es restorijs thymo gensy* 'because he has not been restored to me by her' BM 3786-67; *urth a hagar-awal igge va gweel do derevoll warren ny* 'because of the storms he makes to rise against us' NBoson; *Idzha'n lêauh dhv'n dên Ŷnk-na?* 'Has that young man the ague?' AB: 242a.

30B.3.2 *Mer ew the fues, the vannath ha'th ryelder* 'Great is your fortune, your blessing and your majesty' BK 1574-75; *me a yl bos cuthygyk ow bones mar anfugyk dres pup den ol vs yn beys* 'I can be very sorrowful because I am so unfortunate beyond all men in the world' PC1423-25.

30B.3.3 *may clamderha rag ewn ueth* 'so that he will faint for sheer terror' BK 2652; *vthyk yw clewas y lef* 'it is terrible to hear his voice' RD 2340; *Ithik, braz* 'huge, vast' AB: 68a; *Ithik tra* 'very much' AB: 122b; *Fatel ew reaz do chee eithick gwreage dah* 'That a necessity for you is a terribly good wife' JJenkins.

30B.3.4 *praga pandrew an matter a vyn dew buthy an beise* 'why, what is the matter; will God drown the world?' CW 2329-30; *Rhag oụn hui dho Kṿdha, po an reụ dhṿ dèrhi, a huei dhṿ vṿz bidhis* 'Least you fall, or the ice break and you be drowned' AB: 250a; *oll an beise a vyth bethys* 'all the world shall be drowned' CW 2315.

30B.3.5 *rag marow yv an voron gans ow whaffys sol a breys* 'for the wench has been dead by my blows for a long time now' OM 2746-47; *ow tybbry gynef yma a'm tallyovr yn keth bos-ma neb r'um guerthas sollabreys* 'eating with me from my plate of this same food is he who has already betrayed me' PC 744-46; *Benedycite pan wolov re bue oma sollabreys* 'Bless me, what light has been here just now' BM 1844-45; *Solabrys kynth of cryys, the'n turant ny vetha' mos* 'Although I have been called to the tyrant already, I dare not go' BK 445-46; *yrverys eu ru'm levte solathyth the avonsye* 'upon my word I have for a long time intended to promote you' OM 2611-12; *ny fue golhys sol a theth* 'it has not been washed for a long time' RD 1929; *a phelyp lous os y'th fyth ha ty gynef sollathyth* 'Philip, you are old in thy faith and thou with me for a long time' RD 2379-80; *omma avel bohosek solladeth ty re vewas* 'here like a poor man you have lived for a long time' BM 2939-40; *rag an trubut solathyth a stoppyas ef* 'for the tribute which he stopped a long time ago' BK 2255-56.

30B.4 *in tavern sur ov eva ymons pur ruth age myn* 'in the pub they're drinking indeed, with their mouths all red' BM 3308-09; *Tshy tavarn* 'A tavern' AB: 160b; *Hostleri* 'an inn, an alehouse' Pryce; *Hostleri* 'A tavern, alehouse' Borlase.

30B.6 *Neb a garra y das po y vam, y vab po y virth, chy, trevyn po tyrryow, moy agesa ve* 'whoever loves this father or his mother, his son or his daughter, a house, houses or lands more than me…' TH 21a; *Ny dale dieu gwile treven war an treath* 'You should not build houses on the sand' JJenkins; *Ko oagoaze tha e drevon ha bethow why looan* 'Approach his buildings and be joyful' TBoson; *Domus, Tshỳi [plur. Treven]* 'An house, a lodging, a dwelling' AB: 55c.

30C.1 VOCABULARY

bosty *m.*, **bostiow** restaurant
comondment *m.*, **comond-**
mentys commandment
Duw re dalla dhywgh may God
repay you
Duw re dhanvona God send
Duw re dharbarra nos dâ
dhywgh why God give you
good night
Duw re sowena dhywgh may
God prosper you

fara to fare
grassaf dhe Dhuw thank God
lowenek *adj.* merry, glad
maghteth *f.*, **meghtythyon** maid,
maiden
mâta *m.*, **mâtys** mate, fellow
ostel *f.*, **ostelyow** hôtel
oy *m.*, **oyow** egg
puns *m.*, *or* **pens**, **punsow** *or*
pensow pound (money)
qwart *m.*, **qwartys** quart

30C.2 TEXT DHE REDYA
(KESCOWS IN TAVERN, *ANDREW BORDE c.* 1547)

Pàn vo an kescows awoles redys genes, gwra desmygy dha honen in tavern pò in bosty pò in ostel ha scrif in mes kescows kepar intredhos hag ost pò ôstes.

Dùrda dhywgh why, mêster dâ
Duw re sowena dhywgh why, maghteth.
Wolcùm owgh why, gwreg dhâ.
Duw re dalla dhywgh why, syra.
Fatl'yw genowgh why?
Dâ, Duw re dalla dhywgh why, mêster dâ.
Ôstes, eus boos dâ dhywgh why?
Eus, syra, grâssaf dhe Dhuw.
Rewgh boos dâ dhe vy, ôstes dâ.
Maghteth, drewgh dhe vy bara ha dewas.
Gwreg dhâ, drewgh qwart gwin dhe vy.
Benyn, drewgh pùscas dhe vy.
Maghteth, drewgh oyow hag amanyn dhe vy.
Syra, bedhowgh why lowenek.
Ôstes, pandra wrav vy pe?
Syra, agas recken yw pymp dynar.
Pes mildir eus alebma dhe Loundres?
Syra, try hans mildir.
Bednath Duw genowgh why, ôstes.
Duw re dharbarra nos dâ dhywgh why.
Duw re dhanvona dhywgh fara yn tâ.

Duw genowgh why.

Me a'gas desîr why: comend vy dhe oll mâtas dâ.

Syra, me a vydn gwil agas comondment why.

Duw genowgh why.

UNEGVES DYSCANS WARN UGANS
THIRTY-FIRST LESSON

31A.1 THE DAYS OF THE WEEK

The days of the week in Cornish are as follows:

De Sul 'Sunday'
De Lun 'Monday'
De Merth 'Tuesday'
De Merher 'Wednesday'
De Yow 'Thursday'
De Gwener 'Friday'
De Sadorn 'Saturday'

The element **De** has adverbial force, so that **De Gwener**, for example, means 'on Friday' or 'on Fridays', rather than merely 'Friday'. The names of the week can also be used without **De**, e.g. **an kensa Gwener a'n mis usy ow tos** 'the first Friday of next month. In later Cornish **wàr an** sometimes replaces **De** to express adverbial sense, e.g. **wàr an Sul** instead of **De Sul** 'on Sunday(s)'. This is in imitation of English and is best avoided.

NOTE: In some forms of Cornish adverbial **De** before days of the week is written *Dy'* or *De'*, as though the **dh** of **dÿdh/dëdh** has been lost. This is mistaken. Historically forms like **De Sul**, **De Lun**, **De Merth** never contained the word **dÿdh/dëdh**. The initial element always ended in a vowel. This can be clearly seen from the Breton equivalents *disul, dilun, dimeurzh, dimerc'her, diriaou, digwener, disadorn*, and from Middle Welsh forms containing the related adverbial element *duw, dyw*, e.g. *duw/dyw Sul, duw/dyw Llun, duw/dyw Mawrth, duw/dyw Mercher*, etc. The adverbial **De** is never written *Dy* in traditional Cornish. Indeed the only attested spellings are **de**, **du**, and **dew**; with the last two compare the Welsh equivalents just cited. The adverbial **De** never has an apostrophe after it anywhere in traditional Cornish. Forms, therefore, like **Dy'Sul*, **Dy'Lun*, etc. are not authentic.

NOTE: The varieties of Cornish which write *dy'* before the names of days of the week, also tend to write 'Tuesday' as *Meurth* with *eu*, cf. Breton *(di)meurzh* and Welsh *Mawrth*. The word for 'Tuesday' is poorly attested in Cornish and appears only as **Merh**, that is with **e**. There is no evidence to indicate that in Middle Cornish the vowel was **eu**. Rather than rely on etymological spelling, it is perhaps wiser to remain close to the recorded forms and thus to write 'Tuesday' as **Merth**, **De Merth**.

31A.2 THE MONTHS OF THE YEAR

As we have seen at 11A.5 above, the months of the year in Cornish are as follows:

Genver, **mis Genver** 'January'
Whevrel, **mis Whevrel** 'February'
Merth, **mis Merth** 'March'
Ebrel, **mis Ebrel** 'April'
Me, **mis Me** 'May'
Metheven, **mis Metheven** 'June'
Gortheren, **mis Gortheren** 'July'
Est, **mis Est** 'August'
Gwydngala, **mis Gwydngala**, **Gwyngala**, **mis Gwyngala**,
   'September'
Hedra, **mis Hedra** 'October'
Du, **mis Du** 'November'
Kevardhu, **mis Kevardhu** 'December'.

Some of the months have variant names. **Whevrel** 'February' has a variant **Whervel**. **Metheven** 'June' is sometimes called **Efen**; **Gortheren** 'July' has a late form **Gorefen**.

NOTE: Because **Whevrel** derives from Latin *Februarius* and because the Welsh and Breton equivalents are *Chwefror* and *c'hwevrer* respectively, Nance used **Whevrer* for 'February'. Such a form is not attested, however, and there is no reason to adopt it.

Some forms of Cornish write the name for 'March' as *Meurth*. Since, however, the only attested form is Lhuyd's **Mîz Merh**, it is more authentic to spell the name **Merth**, **mis Merth**.

31A.3 WRITING THE DATE

Dates in Cornish may be written in both long and short forms. For example

De Gwener an pymthegves mis Hedra 2014
Friday the fifteenth of October 2014

Gwener 15 Hedra 2014
Monday, 15 October 2014

How to render dates such as 2014 has already been discussed at 27A.2.

31A.4 THE SEASONS AND MAJOR FESTIVALS OF THE YEAR

The names of the seasons are **gwaynten** *m.* 'spring', **hâv** *m.* 'summer', **kydnyaf** *m.* 'autumn' and **gwâv** *m.* 'winter'.

Some of the festivals during the year having been given at 8A.9 above. Here is a fuller list of festivals and saints' days:

De Halan an vledhen 'New Year's Day' (1 January)
Degol Stool 'Epiphany' (6 January)
Degol Maria Dallath an Gwaynten 'the Presentation' (2 February)
Degol Peran 'St Piran's Day' (5 March)
Degol Maria mis Merth 'the Annunciation' (25 March)
Cala'Me 'May Day' (1 May)
Golowan 'St John's Eve, Midsummer Eve' (23 June)
Calan Est 'Lammas' (1 August)
Degol Maria Hanter Est 'The Dormition of the Blessed Virgin, the Assumption' (15 August)
Gool Myhal, **Degol Myhal** 'Michaelmas' (29 September)
De Halan Gwâv 'All Saints' Day' (1 November)
Nos Nadelyk 'Christmas Eve' (24 December)
Nadelyk, **De Nadelyk** 'Christmas Day' (25 December)
Degol Stefan 'Boxing Day, St Stephen's Day' (26 December)

De Merth Enes 'Shrove Tuesday'
De Merher Lusow 'Ash Wednesday'

De Sul Blejyow 'Palm Sunday'
De Yow Hablys 'Maundy Thursday'
De Pask 'Easter Sunday'
De Fencost 'Whitsunday'
De Sul an Drynsys 'Trinity Sunday'

Corawys *m.* 'Lent'
Asvens *m.* 'Advent'

It must be admitted that not all the above are found in the texts. The attestations in traditional Cornish will be found at 31B.4.

31A.5 'GREAT' AND 'SMALL' IN CORNISH

There are two words in Cornish for 'great, large': **meur** and **brâs**. **Meur** as an adjective is much less used than **brâs** and tends to mean 'great, grand' rather than simply large in size. One speaks therefore of **Breten Veur** 'Great Britain', and **an Bardh Meur** 'the Grand Bard'. As we have seen, **meur** is also used as a pronoun in the expression **meur a²** 'much of, many of'. **Brâs**, on the other hand, is mostly used to mean 'large, big, of great size', e.g. **men brâs** 'a big stone', **chy brâs** 'a big house.' It is also used metaphorically, e.g. **pedn brâs** 'fathead, fool'. One can also use **brâs** with **arlùth** 'lord', **mêster** 'master' and similar words to denote a person whose authority is great. The plural **brâsyon**, as we have already seen, means 'important people, nobles'.

For 'small, little' in revived Cornish some speakers use the word *byghan*. It should be pointed out, however, that this form is not attested in the Cornish texts, though it does occur in place-names. Two examples of **beghan** in *Pascon agan Arluth* are the only examples in the texts of a medial **-gh-** in this word. There are a few examples of **byhan** and **behan**, with medial **-h-**. By far the commonest spellings for 'small' in early Middle Cornish, however, are **byan** or **byen**. TH and CW write this as **bean**, while Lhuyd writes **bîan** *passim*. This is an important point: it is apparent that the pronunciation of this word in Middle an Late Cornish was ['biːən] rather than *['brxən]. There is no need, therefore, to attempt in this word to pronounce **-gh-** [x] between vowels, a sound which is difficult for many speakers of English.

31B EXAMPLES FROM THE TEXTS

31B.1 ***Kova tha gwitha benigas De Zil*** 'Remember to keep holy the Sabbath day' JBoson; ***ma An mab leean ni E gana terwitheyaw war an zeell*** 'Our clergyman sometimes sings it on Sunday' TBoson; ***De lîn*** 'Monday' AB: 54c;

De merh 'Tuesday' AB: 54c; *kyns ys dumerher the nos eff a deerbyn trestyns* 'before Wednesday evening he will encounter sorrow' BM 2254-55; *me a vyn mones deyow prest the helghya* 'I will go indeed on Thursday to hunt' BM 3159-60; *Du guener crist ihesu ker a ruk merwel ragon ny* 'On Friday beloved Jesus died for us' BM 4316-17; *De Zadarn* 'Saturday; AB: 54c.

31B.2 *ʒenvar* 'the month of January' AB: 67a; *Huevral [cor. Huerval]* 'The month of february' AB: 59a; *Mîz merh* 'The month of March' AB: 86c; *Miz ebral* 'April' AB: 43b; *Dibre morgi en mîz Mea, rag dho geil maw* 'Eat a dog-fish in the month of May to make a boy' Pryce; *Ov gol a veth suer in mes metheven an kynsa guener* 'Indeed my festival shall be in the month of June, the first Friday' BM 4302-04; *Miz ephan* 'The month of June' AB: 74b; *vi deth in mys gortheren vn feer a veth in certen* 'the sixth day in the month of July there shall be a fair indeed' BM 2194-95; *Miz gorephan* 'The month July' AB: 74a; *in meys est an viijves deth an secund feer sur a veth sensys in pov benytha* 'in the month of August the eighth day the second fair shall be held for ever' BM 2197-99; *han gela veth mys est certen orth ov deser an viijth deth han tresse mys gvyngala* 'and the second will be in the month of August indeed as I wish, the eighth day, and the third will be be in the month of September' BM 2072-6; *Mîz guedn-gala* 'The month September' AB: 148c; *yn dekvas dyth mys heddra in blethan myll whegh cans dewghans ha try* 'in the tenth month, October in the year one thousand six hundred forty three' JKeigwin; *an Kensa journa a messe Heddra* 'the first day of the month of October' TBoson; *Mîz diu* 'November' AB: 100b; *mîz Du ken Nadelik* 'the month of November before Christmas' WGwavas; *Mis kevardhiu* 'The month of December' AB: 53c; *Skrefis war an kenza dydh an miz Kevardhiu* 'Written on the first day of the month of December 1736' WGwavas.

31B.4 *Kyn fe mar freth du Halan an vlethan i'n kynsa deyth* 'Though he be so bold on the Kalends of the year on the first day' BK 1880-81; *Degl stûl* 'epiphany or twelfth day' AB: 57a; *Enez* 'Shrove-tide' AB: 46b; *Dewsull blegyow pan ese yn mysc y abestely* 'On Palm Sunday, when he was among his apostles' PA 27a; *en gyth o deyow hablys may fenne ihesus sopye gans an re yn y seruys war an bys re ʒewesse* 'the day was Maundy Thursday when Jesus wished to sup with those in his service whom he had chosen in the world' PA 41cd; *nyng egy cowse vith a deow habblys arrna theffa leverall an keth geyr ma* 'there is no mention of Maundy Thurday until he happens to mention this same word' SA 66; *thomas ythos pur woky drefen na fynnyth crygy an arluth the thasserghy du pask vyttyn* 'Thomas, you are very foolish that you will not believe that the Lord rose again on Easter morning' RD 1105-08; *Ith ew scryffys fatell rug pedyr kemeras warnotha in presens a oll an appostlys the gowse in aga hanow y oll then bobyll war du fencost myttyn* 'It is written how Peter took it upon himself in the presence of all the apostles to speak in the name of them all to the people on the morning of Pentecost' TH 44a; *ix nobyl a cala'me a russe sokyr thynny* 'nine nobles on Mayday would be of help to us' BM 3338-89;

Guâve en Hâve terebah Goluan 'Winter in summer until St John's Eve' Ustick MSS; *dugol myhal yv henna* 'that is the feast of St Michael' BM 2077; *dugol myhall byth henna* 'that will be the feast of St Michael' BM 2201; *Ny gans Arthor in e sal, kyn tryken bys woyl Myhal, wylcum ny a vyth ena* 'We, though we stay with Arthur in his hall until Michaelmas, we will be welcome there' BK 1376-78; *Dew Whallan Gwa Metten* 'On the morning of Allsaints' Exeter Consistory Court; *E a roz towl dho proanter Powle, mîz Du ken Nadelik* 'He gave a throw to the Vicar of Paul in November before Christmas' WGwavas; *Nadelik; Deu nadelik* 'Natalis Christi' AB: 97a; *Ha Hâve en Guâve terebah Nedelack* 'And summer in winter until Christmas' Ustick MSS.

31B.5.1 *sevys gallas ʒe gen le den apert ha mur y breys* 'he has arisen and gone to another place, manifestly a man and great his worth' PA 255c; *my a pys dev mer y ras* 'I beseech God, great his grace' PC 117; *eff yv arluth mur y nel* 'he is a lord of great power' BM 3993; *erbyn Myghtern Bretyn Veor* 'against the king of Great Britain' BK1424; *Mer ew the fues, the vannath ha'th ryelder* 'Great is your fortune, your blessing and your majesty' BK 1574-75; *hag in yr ma gwraf assaya ʒa vos mur war an trone* 'and now I shall attempt to be great upon the throne' CW 200-01; *defalebys ove pur veare* 'I am very disfigured' CW 1665; *ha me ad wra arluth bras ow honore mar mynnyth* 'and I will make you a great lord if you will honour me' PA 16d; *ov tos yma syr pharo hag ost bras pur wyr ganso* 'Sir Pharaoh is coming and a great army with him indeed' OM 1651; *Yma eff in meneth bras* 'He is on the great mountain' BM 1956; *mar te den ha receva royow bras the worth y gothman po y soveran* 'if a man happen to receive great gifts from his friend or his sovereign' TH 4a; *I say Arthur is my nam, myghtern bras ha galosak* 'I say, Arthur is my name, a great and powerful king' BK 1399-400; *mar pethama kibmiez tho gweel Semblanz 'gun Aulsen Coth Brose* 'if I am permitted to make comparison with the Ancient Great Ausonius' NBoson; *Why dalveya gowas an brossa mine* 'You should get the largest stones' JJenkins

31B.5.2 *ʒeworte vn lam beghan yʒ eth pesy may halle* 'he went from them a little space that he might pray' PA 53c; *my ha'm gurek ha'm flogh byhan* 'me and my wife and my little child' OM 397; *longys reys yv thy's gyne vn pols byan lafurye* 'Longus, you must walk a little way with me' PC 3003-04; *mytern yn bryten vyan* 'king in Brittany' BM 169; *dugh genavy alemma benen gans the flogh byen* 'come away from here with me, woman, with your baby' BM 1549-50; *maria the vap byen gene dre yth a hythov* 'Mary, your little son will go home with me today' BM 3629-30; *kekyfrys byan ha bras* 'both small and great' OM 1673; *lemyn ol byan ha bras* 'now everybody, small and great' PC 2081; *brays ha byan* 'great and small' BM 257; *nyns o mas bean* 'it was only small' TH 5; *bean ha brase* 'small and great' CW 118; *den in mes bean ha brase* 'let us go out, small and great' CW 2481; *An lȳzûan bîan ʒen i'ar nedhez* 'the small plant with the twisted stalk' AB: 245a; *'Ma lever bean rebbam* 'I have beside me a little book' NBoson.

31C.1 VOCABULARY

bardhonek *m.*, **bardhonegow** poem
brag *m.* malt
bùs (< **mès**) but
campolla to mention
cùntell to collect, to gather
cunys *coll.* firewood, fuel
da jy, **da vy** to you (singular), to me
dendyl to earn
dreys *coll.* brambles
dywgh to you (*pl.*)
gen (= **gans**) with

gerys (< **gesys**) left
glow *coll.* coal
gwenenen *f.*, **gwenyn** *coll.* bee
gwlân *coll.* wool
lavuryans *m.* toil, labour
medra to aim, to emulate
olas *m.* hearth
padn *m.* **padnow** cloth
p'edery (< **predery**) to consider
sawgh (*pron.* **saw**) *m.* load; **worth**
  an sawgh by the load
seg, **zeg** *m.* brewer's grains, draff
tobma to warm, to heat

31C.2 TEXT DHE REDYA
BARDHONEGOW GANS JAMES JENKINS

Red an dhew vardhonek-ma ha scrif gorthebow dhe'n qwestyons:

(i)
Ma lies gwreg,
lacka 'vell zeg,
gwell gerys,
'vell kemerys;
ha ma lyes benyn
pecar ha'n gwenyn.
Y a vedn gweres da'ga thus
dendyl pëth a'n bÿs.
Flehes heb skians
a vedn gwil aga sians,
bùs mar qwrownjy p'edery
pandra dal aga gwary
ha medra yn tâ
pandra wrug sîra ha dama,
ny res dhedhans mos da'n coos
da gùntell aga boos,
bùs gen nebes lavuryans
y a venja dendyl gà boos ha dyllas.

209

(ii)

Côwsowgh da vy, che den mar fur,
da neb eus meur a pëth ha lies tir,
ha me a wrug clôwes an bobel ow campolla
fatl'yw res da jy uthyk gwreg dhâ.
Hy a wor gwil padn dâ gen hy gwlân,
hag et hy olas hy dalvyth gawas tan.
Ny dal dis perna cunys worth an sawgh,
na mos ow cùntell an dreys 'dro da'n keow
rag hedna a vedn bos côwsys 'dro da'n pow.
Gwell via perna nebes glow
ha hedna a vedn gàs tobma adhelergh ha arag;
ha why a ell eva cor' gwella mars eus dywgh brag.
Ny dal dywgh gwil treven wàr an treth,
bùs mar mednowgh derevel warbydn an pow yeyn
why a dalvia gawas an brâssa meyn,
Ha'n re-na a vedn durya wàr bydn mor ha gwyns.
Nag eus drog vyth gwrës lebmyn na kyns.

1. Pandr'usy an prydyth owth hevelly benenes dâ dhodho?
2. Pandra wrowns y gans aga thus?
3. Mar qwra flehes predery, pandra wrowns y gwil, warlergh an prydyth?
4. Pandr'yw res dhe'n den rych?
5. Fatl'usy hy ow tysqwedhes hy dhe vos dâ?
6. Prag y whrussa den cùntell dreys?
7. Ple whrussa den cùntell hedna?
8. Pandra na dal derevel wàr an treth?

DEWDHEGVES DYSCANS WARN UGANS
THIRTY-SECOND LESSON

32A.1 'FACE', 'NOSE', 'EARS', AND 'EYES'

In some forms of revived Cornish the customary word for 'face' is **enep**. This word occurs in the Old Cornish Vocabulary as **eneb** where it means 'page of a book'. Although **enep** is nowhere attested in Middle Cornish, it is used once by ?John Keigwin's translation of Genesis 1 in the expression **enapp an noare** 'the face of the earth'; moreover Lhuyd gives **enap** s.v. *Vultus* 'face' AB: 179a, without any indication that the word is Old Cornish; Lhuyd may therefore have heard the word when he was in Cornwall. The ordinary word for 'face' in Middle Cornish, however, is **fâss** (variously spelt *fas*, *face*, *fase*, *fays*, *fath*). This should perhaps be the default word for 'face' in revived Cornish also. In the plural **fâssow** can also mean 'pretence, hypocrisy' and 'minatory appearance'. The word **bejeth** 'face, visage' is attested in Late Cornish, which seems to be a reflex of an earlier **bysach* < Old French *visage*.

The default word for 'nose' in some forms of revived Cornish is **tron*, which is Nance's respelling of **trein** 'nasus [nose]' in the Old Cornish Vocabulary. **Tron* 'nose', however, is wholly unattested in either Middle or Late Cornish. Moreover its use is problematic, since it is identical in spelling and pronunciation with **tron** 'throne', a word that is well attested in the texts. The ordinary word for 'nose' in the texts is one of two forms of the word *friic* 'nostril' of the Old Cornish Vocabulary, namely either the dual **dewfrik** or the plural **frigow**. **Frigow** is probably the best word for 'nose' in the revived language.

The Cornish for 'eye' is **lagas** and the dual form **dewlagas** is found in the earliest Middle Cornish, i.e. in PA and in the Ordinalia. Neither singular nor plural occurs in BM. In TH, BK, CW and Late Cornish, however, the plural form is always **lagasow**, **lagajow** and **dewlagas** is unknown. Lhuyd gives *lagaz* 'eye', but he cites no plural. The scribe of the

Bodewryd glossary (first half of the seventeenth century) gives *lagas*, *lagasaw* 'eye, eyes'.

The word for 'ear' is **scovarn** *f.* and in the texts the plural is always **scovornow** (not the unattested *scovarnow). It should also noted that a dual ***dywscovarn** is unattested and there is no need to introduce it into the revived language.

32A.2 'HAND', 'HANDS', 'FEET', AND 'LEGS'

The Cornish word for 'hand' in the earliest texts is **leuv** *f.* (variously spelt *luf*, *luff*, *luef*, *lef*, *leff*). The plural appears to be unattested, being replaced by the dual **dewla** (variously spelt *dywle*, *dywla*, *dule*, *dula*, *dewle*, *dewla*, *dowla*). A variant with final [f], **dywlef**, **dewleff**, etc. is also found. As its vowel unrounded, the word **leuv** became indistinguishable from **lev** 'voice' and in the texts the singular **leuv** is increasingly replaced by **dorn** 'fist'. The plural was still **dewla**, however. It is for this reason that Lhuyd s.v. *Manus* 'hand' gives the Cornish equivalents as *Dorn*, *plur.* *Dula* (AB: 86a). The plural **dornow** continued to mean 'fists'. In the light of the evidence of the texts the revived language should perhaps for everyday use say **dorn** for 'hand' and **dewla** for 'hands'. Poetry, of course, is another matter.

The Cornish for 'foot' is **troos** m. A dual form **dewdros** is attested three times (once in PA and twice in PC). Much commoner, however, is the plural **treys** (also spelt *treis*, *tryes*, *tryys*) which is attested over 40 times. Thus the expression **treys ha dewla** is the ordinary way in Cornish of saying 'hands and feet', being attested at least nine times. This use together of the plural of the word for 'foot' and the dual of the word for 'hand' appears to be a common Celtic syntagm; cf. Welsh *traed a dwylo* 'feet and hands' and Irish *mo chosa agus mo dhá lámh* 'my feet and my hands'.

The Cornish for 'leg' is **garr** *f.* and the plural is **garrow**. Some speakers for 'legs' use a dual form ***dywarr**. This, however, is unattested and there is no need to introduce it into the revived language.

32A.3 'ANKLE' AND 'HEEL'

One of the Cornish words for 'ankle' is attested in OCV, where *talus* 'ankle-bone' is glossed *lifern*. This is almost certainly an error for **ufern**; cf. Breton *ufern*, *uferniòu* 'cheville' and Welsh *ucharnau* 'ankles'. Another word is **ʒybeddern** cited by Lhuyd under *Malleolus* 'a little hammer; the ankle or ankle bone' AB: 84b. **Goobiddar** 'ankels' [sic] in the Bodewryd glossary is a form of the same word. Given that **ʒybeddern** is singular and **goobiddar** plural, it looks as though the word is a feminine singulative

gobederen with a collective plural **gobeder**. **Gobederen** appears to be a compound of **go-** 'under, small' and ***pederen** 'bead', and probably referred originally to the use of sheep's ankle-bones as five-stones or dibs. This is speculation, however. 'Ankle' in Cornish is probably best rendered **ufern** *m.*, **ufernyow**.

The attested word for 'heel' in Cornish is **gwewen** *f.* The plural is unattested, but it was either collective ***gwew** or plural ***gwewednow/ *gwewennow**. Nance suggested ***sul** on the basis of Welsh **sawdl** and Breton **seul**. Some commentators respell this adventitious word ***seudhel**. There is no need to introduce ***sul**, ***seul** or ***seudhel** into Cornish. We have already the attested word **gwewen** *f.*, ***gwewednow** 'heel'.

32A.4 'ROOM'

The most widely used word in revived Cornish for 'room' in all senses is **stevel** *f.* This is a respelling of ***steuel*** in the OCV which glosses Latin *triclinium* 'a dining room'. Nance suggested using the plural *stevelyow*, presumably by analogy with Breton *gevel* 'tongs', plural *gevelioù*. The Breton singular corresponds to Cornish **gevel** 'pincers, tongs' from OC ***geuelhoern*** 'snuffers' (literally 'iron tongs'); so the plural is likely to have been similar in Breton and Cornish, i.e. Breton *gevelioù*, Cornish **gevelyow**. So Nance's **stevel**, **stevelyow** is probably correct. Some forms of Cornish, however, recommend a plural ******stevellow*, for which there is no evidence. **Stevelyow** is a more probable plural for the word.

The Cornish word for 'bedroom' is **chambour**, **chamber** which is well attested.

The Cornish word for 'bathroom' is sometimes given in dictionaries and wordlists as **stevel omwolhy**. Since **stevel** in OC means 'dining-room', it is perhaps not suitable to use it for a place where one both washes and relieves oneself. There is a further more important point, however. Apart from 'bedroom' the word for 'room' in traditional Cornish is **rom**, plural **rômys**. As with Middle English *roume*, Cornish **rom** can also mean an appointed place. In the interests of authenticity, **rom** should be the default word for 'room'.

32A.5 'TO GET'

Middle Breton has two forms of the verbal noun of the verb 'to get, to find', namely *caffout* and *kavout*. Similarly Cornish has two stems **cafos** and **cavos**. **Cavos** has a variant **cawas**, first attested as ***cawys*** in RD. Because **cafos/cavos/cawas** is so frequently used after **dhe**[2] 'to' and **y**[2] 'his, its', in later Cornish the word acquires permanent initial lenition. There are occasional instances of permanent lenition in TH also, for Tregear writes **gafus** on occasion, where **cafus** might have been expected.

There is no evidence that **cafos/cavos** means 'to get, to find' but **cawas** means 'to have'. **Cafos/cavos** itself frequently bears the sense 'to have'.

32B. EXAMPLES FROM THE TEXTS

32B.1.1 'FACE': *E ma reaze gennan thu keneffra lazoan toane haaz a eze wor enapp an Noare* 'I have given you every herb bearing seed that is upon the face of the earth' ?JKeigwin; *ma teth an goys ha dropye war y fas an caradow* 'so that the blood actually dripped upon his face, the beloved' PA 59b; *yn y fase y a drewys* 'in his face they spat' PA 95c; *the lef arluth a glewaf saw the face my ny welaf* 'thy voice, O Lord, I hear, but thy face I cannot see' OM 587-88; *gans queth me a vyn cuthe y fas hag onan a'n guysk* 'with a cloth I will cover his face and someone will strike him' PC 1370-71; *fas ihesu gynef yma yn hyuelep gurys a'y whys* 'I have the face of Jesus made in a likeness from his perspiration' RD 1704-05; *in ov fays cothys yma cleves vthyk num car den* 'A dreadful disease has come upon my face; no one loves me' BM 728-29; *eff a ve gylwys ell gans ran gyllwis mer therag an face a Du* 'he was called an angel by some called great before the face of God' TH 8; *Caradowder ema y'th fas ha golowder* 'There is amiability and brilliance in your face' BK 1755-57; *nyng es owne thym ahanas drefan bose mar deake tha face* 'I am not afraid of your because your face is so fair' CW 562-63; *ha spiriz Deu reeg guaya var budgeth an dour* 'and the spirit of God moved upon the face of the water' JBoson; *Pelea era why moaz, moz, fettow teag, Gen agaz bedgeth gwin ha agaz blew mellyn?* 'Where are you going, going, pretty maid, with your pale face and your yellow hair?' Chygwyn.

32B.1.2 'NOSE': *gor dotho nes the frygov* 'bring your nose near to it' BM 1454; *me an set ryb the frygov* 'I will set it next to your nose' BM 3399; *bethans gorrys in ye thywfridg* 'let them be put in his nose' CW 1854; *gorra sprusan yth ganow han thew arall pur thybblance in tha thewfreyge* 'to put a pip in your mouth and the other two very surely in your nose' CW 1931-33; *an dayer sprusan yw gorrys in y anow hay fregowe* CW 2087-88; *freegaw: freeg* 'nose; nostril' Bodewryd MS; *Naso... Frigaụ brâz* 'that hath a great nose' AB: 97a; *Nasus... Frigaụ* 'A nose' AB: 97a.

32B.1.3 'EYES': *y scornye hay voxscusy trewe yn y ʒewlagas* 'scorning him and cuffing him, spitting in his eyes' PA 83b; *me a tru sur vn clotte bras ware yn y theulagas* 'I will spit indeed a great gob smartly in his eyes' PC 1399-400; *roy thy'm gans ow dewlagas y weles wheth* 'may he grant to me to see him yet with my own two eyes' RD 791-92; *athyragon torth vara ef a torras arak agan lagasow* 'before us he broke a loaf of bread before our eyes' RD 1490-92; *why a vith kepar ha du hagys lagasow a vith clerys* 'you will be like God and your eyes will be made clear' TH 3a; *an venyn a welas y bos an frut da the thybbry ha teg the sight y lagasow* 'the woman saw that the fruit was good to eat and beautiful to the sight of her eyes' TH 3a; *an pith vsans ow quelas gans aga lagasow kyge* 'that which they see with their eyes of flesh' TH 56; *na ny'n gwelvith lagasaw i'n bys hagan* 'nor will eyes in the world see it yet' BK 1976-77; *E weflow ha'y lagasow ha'y goyntnans o mar fasow, mayth egan owth umgelly ol clamderak* 'His lips and his eyes and his countenance was so menacing that we were fainting all in a swoon' BK 2330-33; *gans tha lagasowe alees ty a weall pub tra omma* 'with your eyes wide open you see everything here' CW 694-95; *lagas, lagasaw* 'eye, eyes' Bodewryd MS; *n'ena agoz lagagow ra bos geres* 'then your eyes will be opened' Rowe; *Ha lagagow angie ve gerres* 'And their eyes were opened' Rowe.

32B.1.4 'EARS': *pur ankensy gans dornow thotho war an scovornow reugh boxsesow trewysy* 'very severely with fists upon his ears land painful blows' PC 1360-62; *ha ren thotho boxsusow gans dornow ha guelynny war an scovornow bysy* 'and let us land blows on his ears intently with fists and rods' PC 1389-91; *y a vynsa stoppya aga scovurnow* 'they would stop up their ears' TH 19; *gans agan lagasow ha scovornow, gans agan ganowow ha tavosow* 'with our eyes and ears, with our mouths and tongues' TH 21a; *Me a glowt e skovornow* 'I will box his ears' BK 1657; *skovarn, skovornow* 'eare, eares' Bodewryd MS.

32B.2.1 'HAND': *pandra synsyth y'th luef lemyn* 'what are you holding in your hand now?' OM 1442; *an luef a'm gruk me a wel* 'I see the hand that made me' RD 143; *Ny a vyn y carhara purguir na ala guaya na luff na troys* 'we will shackle him indeed so that he cannot move either hand or foot' BM 3573-75; *Adam ystyn thy'm the thorn* 'Adam, hold out your hand to me' OM 205; *otte ow fycher gyne yn ov dorn* 'See, here I have my pitcher in my hand' PC 656; *tan syns y'th dorn an giu ma* 'here, hold this spear in your hand' PC 3010; *an gwyr a ve derives a thorne the thorne* 'the truth was recounted from hand to hand' TH 48; *havall the den ha cletha noith in y dorne* 'like a man with a naked sword in his hand' TH 55a; *prag na bredersys a thorn dew y festa gwryes* 'why did you not consider that you had been made by the hand of God?' CW 308-09; *Ev a uaske e dvrn uar e ðaʒier ðv ðestrîa an dhêau* 'he strikes his hand on his dagger to kill them both' JCH §40

32B.2.2 'HANDS & FEET': *kenter scon dre the devtros my a's guysk* 'a nail quickly through your two feet, I will strike it' PC 2781-82; *an thyv yn mes a'y thywle hag a'y thew tros kekyffrys* 'I will draw the two out of his hands and from his feet also' PC 3153-54; *ha hager fest an dygtyas corf ha pen treys ha dewle* 'and treated him very cruelly, body and head, feet and hands' PA 130d; *me a vyn mos the vre ow arluth treys ha devle* 'I will go to anoint my Lord, feet and hands' PC 473-74; *ha'n kelmyns treys ha dule* 'and let them bind him hands and feet' PC 583; *ha kelmys treys ha dule ynny hy bethens taclyys* 'and bound hands and feet let him be nailed to it' PC 2163-64; *scorgis gans an ʒethewon kentrewys treys ha dula* 'scourged by the Jews, nailed hands and feet' BM 2602-03; *spykys bras a horne dre an treys ha dewleff* 'great spikes of iron through the feet and hands' TH 15a; *gans agan dewleff ha treys* 'with our hands and feet' TH 21a.

32B.2.3 'LEGS': *gans dour gorris yn bazon y wolhas aga garrow* 'with water put into a basin he washed their legs' PA 45c; *y arrow hay ʒeffregh whek* 'his legs and his sweet arms' PA 232a; *ov dywluef colm ha'm garrow* 'bind my hands and my legs' OM 1436; *pyw a thueth a'n beys yn ruth avel gos pen ha duscouth garrow ha treys* 'who has come from the world red as blood, head and shoulders, legs and hands?' RD 2499-501; *yagh yv ov corff ham garrov* 'healed are my body and my legs' BM 711; *me a pylse the pen blogh hag a russa dyso oma garrow pur trogh* 'I would strip your bald head and render very broken here your legs for you' BM 3828-31.

32B.3 'HEEL': *E ra browi tha pedn, ha chee ra browi e gwewan* 'He will bruise thy head, and thou shalt bruise his heel' Rowe.

32B.4 'ROOM' & 'BEDROOM': *Rag henna fystyn ke gura gorhel a blankos playnyys hag ynno lues trygva romes y a vyth gylwys* 'Therefore, hasten to make a vessel of planed timbers with many dwellings in her; they shall be called rooms' OM 949-52; *thega movya y the thewys onyn rag bos in rome esa Judas ynna* 'to urge them to choose someone to be in the appointed place that Judas had occupied' TH 44a; *tha golenwall an romys es yn nef der ow goth brase avoyd drethaf hawe mayny* 'to fill up the rooms in heaven vacated by me and my retinue through my great pride' CW 463-65; *rof thy's ov thour hel ha chammbour bethaf the wour* 'I will give you my tower, my hall and bedroom; I'll be your husband' OM 2110-11; *Arlothas, guyn avel gurys, dun the'n chamber, me a'th pys* 'Lady, white as crystal, let us go to the bedroom, I beseech you' BK 2981-82; *Cubiculum... Tshombar* 'A bedroom, a lodging-room' AB: 52c.

32B.5 CAFOS, CAVOS, CAWAS: *mal yv gynef y gaffos rak y worre th'y ancow* 'I should like to get him to put him to death' PC 2068-69; *me a vyn caffus an queth* 'I will get the cloth' RD 1875; *yn vr na ny reys thy'nny na den byth ol yn teffry caffus neffre na moy ovn* 'then we nor anybody at all indeed needs to have any more fear for ever' RD2170; *mar mynnyth cafus mowes my a'd wor scon bys thethy* 'if you want to have a girl, I will send you soon to her' OM 2071-72; *yma ow kul maystry bras rak mennas cafos enor* 'he is swaggering greatly because he wishes to have honour' PC 377-78; *y a veth purguir marov rag cafus sur age goys* 'they indeed will die to get their blood surely' BM 1598-99; *me a vyn cawys an povs* 'I shall get the garment' RD 1957; *y vab rag cawas dyskans sur danvenys ateva ʒyugh doctor wek* 'see here his son sent to you to get an education, sweet doctor' BM 85-87; *worthy rag cawas reuerens* 'worthy to be shown respect' BM 255; *the canevar den gwyrrian a vo desyrius e gowis* 'to every honest man who is desirous of having it' SA 60; *tha thew nyng eis otham vythe awoos cawas agen pythe* 'God has no need to have our possessions' CW 1133-34; *Rag me a venja cowas napeath* 'For I should get something' JTonkin; *dowt yth ow theis rag henna gawas meare y displeasure* 'you are afraid therefore greatly to have his disapproval' CW 204-05; *Gwag ove, rave gawas haunsell?* 'I am hungry; shall I have breakfast?' Pryce; ***Pew vedna why gawas rag seera rag guz flo*** 'Who will you get for a father for your child?' Chygwyn; ***Ny yll henna gafus du thy das*** 'That man cannot have God as his father' TH 39a; ***han speciall purposse o, crist the vynnas gafus aucthorite an parna in vn den*** 'and the special purpose was that Christ wished to have authority of that kind in one man' TH 46.

32C.1 VOCABULARY

ascor *m.* produce, offspring

bedhens *3sg imperative* let there be

bewens *3pl imperative* let them live

brÿs, brës *m.* mind

bys may fy loos until you be grey

dalethys *1st singular preterite of* **dallath** to begin

degens *3rd singular imperative of* **don** to bear

delen *f.,* **delyow** *pl.* leaf, *in pl.* foliage

dyllo to release, to publish

erber *m.,* **erberow** place of safety

encressyens *3pl imperative* let them increase

formya to create

formyor *m.,* **formyoryon** creator

frût *m.,* **frûtys** fruit

gorhemynna to command

gosteyth *adj.* obedient

grâss *m.* grace

gruthyl *variant vn. of* **gwil** to do, to make

kekemmys *pron.* as much as

losowen *f.,* **losow** *coll.,* **losowys** *pl.* plant, herb

may fedher that it will be

obery to work, to fashion

pàn y'n kylly when you lose it

perfeth *adj. & adv.* perfect, perfectly

prydydhieth *f.* poetry

rial royal, majestic

stergan *m.* starlight, stars

teffo *3rd singular subjunctive of* **tevy**

tevens *3rd singular imperative* let grow

tevy to grow

Trynyta *m.* Trinity

warnedha *variant of* **warnodhans** on them

whare· *adv.* presently

y'm gelwyr I am called

32C.2 TEXT DHE REDYA
(CREACYON AN BÿS MES A *ORIGO MUNDI*)

Red an devyn usy ow sewya awoles ha scrif gorthebow dhe'n qwestyonow:

> An Tas a nev y'm gelwyr,
> Formyor pùptra a vÿdh gwrÿs.
> Onen ha try on in gwir,
> an Tas ha'n Mab ha'n Spyrys;

ha hedhyw me a dhesîr
dre ow grâss dallath an bÿs.
Y lavaraf nev ha tir,
bedhens formys orth ow brÿs.

Lemmyn pàn yw nev dhyn gwrÿs
ha lenwys a eleth splann,
ny a vynn formya an bÿs,
par dell on try hag onen,
an Tas ha'n mab ha'n Spyrys.
Pòr rial yn sur certan
an re-ma yw oberys,
dell vynsyn agan honen.

I'n secùnd dÿdh y fynna'
gruthyl ebron 'nev' henwys;
rag yth hevel thymm bos dâ
i'n kensa dÿdh myns eus gwrÿs.
Bedhens ebron dres pùptra
rag cudha myns eus formys,
rag sensy glaw awartha
the'n norvÿs may fe dyllys.

I'n tressa dÿdh dybarth gwrav
intre an mor ha'n tiryow,
hag i'n tir gorhemynnaf
may teffo gwëdh ha losow.
Pùb gwedhen tevens a'y sav
ow ton hy frût ha'y delyow,
ha'n losowys erbynn hâv
degens has i'n erberow.

I'n peswora gwrÿs perfeth
the'n bës oll golowys glan;
ha'ga henwyn y a vëdh
an howl ha'n loor ha'n stergan.
Me a's set a-ugh an gwëdh
in cres an ebron avàn,
an loor i'n nos, howl i'n jëdh,
may rollons y golow splann.

I'n pympes dÿdh me a vynn
may fo formys dre ow nell
bestas, pùscas hag ëdhyn,
tir ha mor dhe gollenwel;
rag y whyrvyth an termyn
dredha may fedher dhe well.
Dhedha me a worhemmyn:
encressyens ha bewens pell.

Hedhyw yw an wheffes dëdh
abàn dhalethys gonys,
may whrug nev mor tir ha gwëdh
bestas, pùscas, golowys.
Gosteyth dhymmo y a vëdh,
kekemmys eus inha gwrÿs.
Mab den a bry yn perfeth
me a vynn y vos formys.

Dell on ny onen ha try
Tas ha Mab i'n Trynyta,
ny a'th wra, te dhen, a bry,
haval dh'agan fàss whare.
Ny a wheth in dhe vody
spyrys may hylly bewa,
ha'n bêwnans pan y'n kylly
dhe'n dor te a drail arta.

Adam sav in bàn yn clor
ha trail dhe gig ha dhe woos.
Preder me dhe'th whul a dhor
haval dhymm a'n penn dhe'n troos.
Myns eus i'n tir hag i'n mor
warnedha kemmer gallos;
i'n bÿs-ma rag dry ascor
te a vew bys may fy loos.

Adam, dell ov Duw a râss,
bos gwethyas a wrauntyaf dhis,
wàr paradîs me a'th as.

Saw gwra unn dra a'm govys:
wàr bùb frût, losow ha has
a vo inhy hy tevys
saw a'n frût ny'fŷdh cummyas,
yw prenn a skians henwys.

1 I'n devyn-ma pandra wrug Duw i'n kensa dëdh?
2 Pandra wrug Duw i'n secùnd dëdh?
3 Pandra wrug Duw i'n tressa dëdh?
4 Pana dhëdh a wrug Duw an creaturs bew?
5 Pandra wrug ev an jëdh-na?
6 Cubmyas a'n jeva Adam dhe dhebry a bùptra marnas onen. Pandr'o an dra-na?
7 Pandr'o hanow a'n dra a wrug Duw dyfedna?
8 A yllowgh why leverel tra vëth ow tùchya form an brydydhieth a-uhon?

TREDHEGVES DYSCANS WARN UGANS
THIRTY-THIRD LESSON

33A.1 'MAN', 'MEN', 'PERSON', AND 'PEOPLE'

The Cornish word **den** means 'man', i.e. 'adult male'. It is not usually employed to mean 'person, human being'. This, for example, is why the author of *Jowan Chy an Hordh* says **yth esa trigys in Seleven den ha benyn** 'there lived in St Levan a man and a woman', that is a man and his wife.

Just as **den** means 'adult male', so **tus** means 'adult males, men'. This can clearly be seen in Middle Cornish from the expression **tus, benenes ha flehes** 'men, women and children' which occurs three times in *Origo Mundi*. It is also clear from the expression **tus ervys** 'armed men' at PC 939 and RD 351. That **tus** means 'men, adult males' also in Late Cornish is clear from the way that Pryce translates **tus** as 'men':

Gorra tus in an skyber dhe dhrùshya Put men in the barn to thrash
Whelas tus dhe drehy kesow Look men to cut turf
Danvon rag tus dhe trehy gora Send for men to cut the hay (Pryce).

The three activities require physical strength and were usually to be done by men. On the other hand the lighter work of cutting furze could be done by women and Pryce says:

Whelas pobel dhe trehy eythyn 'Look people to cut furze' (Pryce).

That **tus** means 'adult males, menfolk' can also be seen from the poem by John Jenkins who says of good wives **Y a vedn gweres d'aga thus dendyl pëth a'n bÿs** 'They will help their menfolk earn their living'.

If one wants to say 'person' in Cornish without specifying the gender, one can say **den pò benyn** 'man or woman', or one can use the word

person, *pl.* **persons**. John Tregear, speaking of the eight people who survived the flood in the Ark says **êth person êns in oll myns a veu sawys** 'eight persons were they all told who were saved' TH 7. On occasion the expression **mab den** 'mankind' can be used for 'human being'.

As already noted, the default word for 'people' irrespective of gender is **pobel** *f.*

In some forms of revived Cornish a plural **denyon* has been suggested to mean 'men, adult males' as distinct from **tus** 'people'. Such a plural is unattested and cannot be recommended. If, for example, one wishes to write MEN and WOMEN on the door of public lavatories, one could write either **GWESYON** and **BENENES** or **MEBYON** and **MYRHAS**. There is no need for **denyon*.

33A.2 'HUSBAND' AND 'WIFE'

'Husband' in Cornish is **gour** and the plural is **gwer**. On occasion, however, the term **gour ty** is used, where **ty** is the unassibilated form of **chy** 'house'. Similarly the word **gwreg** *f.* 'wife', plural **gwrageth**, is sometimes reinforced by the addition of **ty** to give **gwreg ty** or **gwre'ty**. **Gwadn-wre'ty** (Lhuyd's *guadn-ʒyrti*) is attested twice and means 'bad wife, adulteress'.

The forms **gour ty** and **gwre'ty** are similar to expressions in the other Celtic languages; cf. Irish *fear an tí* 'man of the house, husband' and *bean an tí* 'woman of the house, wife'.

33A.3 'BABY'

The word **baban** occurs at BM 3405 where it means 'doll'. The word for 'baby' occurs once as a plural **babiow** at BM 1577 (***merugh an babyov wek*** 'look at the sweet babies'). **Baby** is, of course, a borrowing from English. Like the other Celtic languages Cornish prefers to use the word **flogh** 'child' for 'baby'. See the examples at 33B.3 below.

33A.4 'VIRGIN'

The word **gwerhes** *f.*, **gwerhesow** 'virgin' is never used except when speaking either of the Blessed Virgin Mary or in the plural when referring to virgin saints. There are two words in the texts for a young unmarried woman, a virgin, namely **maghteth** and **vyrjyn**. See the examples below 33B.4 below, where it is clear that both refer on occasion to the Blessed Virgin also.

The word **maghteth** is possibly what lies behind the curious form *fettow* in the song 'Delkyow Sevy'. **Maghteth** or **maghtath** was probably pronounced ['maɪtəθ] or ['maɪtə]. With initial lenition ['maɪtəθ] would be ['vaɪtəθ]. Because of the variation of initial [v] and [f], *['vaɪtəθ] was reshaped as *['faɪtəθ] and this appears as *fettow* in the song.

33A.5 'NATION' AND 'TRIBE'

The default word for 'nation' in revived Cornish has always been **kenedhel** (**kenethel**). This is a respelling of the word *kinethel* in OCV which glosses *generatio* 'generation'. The reflex of Old Cornish *kinethel* is unknown in Middle Cornish, where the ordinary word for 'nation' is **nacyon**, *pl.* **nacyons** (variously spelt *nacion*, *nascon*, *nasconn*, *nascyon*, *nassyoyn*, *nation*). This seems a more authentic word for 'nation' in the revived language.

For 'tribe' Nance (1938) suggest **lŷth**, a respelling of *leid* 'progenies vel tribus' [offspring or tribe] in OCV. Some have decided to emend *leid* to *loid* and to connect the word with the second element in *hebrenchiat luir* 'dux' [leader of an army] in OCV, which has been itself emended to *hebrenchiat luid*. It is unfortunately the case that there is no agreement about the correct shape for Old Cornish *leid* 'progenies vel tribus' in Middle Cornish. Moreover no such word is attested in the Middle Cornish texts. The only attested word for 'tribe' in Middle Cornish is John Tregear's **trib** (*tryb*).

33B EXAMPLES FROM THE TEXTS

33B.1.1 *A ty then myghtern pharo dev a'm danfonas thyso* 'O you man, king Pharaoh, God has sent me to you' OM 1479-80; *A then yonk fetel esta mur yv the lavyr oma heb y dyndyl* 'O young man, how are you? Great is your labour here without your deserving it' BM 3659-61; *ha remembra agan mortall genesegeth a russyn kemeras theworth Adam an kynsa den a ve gwrys* 'and to remember our mortal nature that we received from Adam, the first man that was created' TH 6a; *me a wor inta, why the bredery tha vos maga benegas agis an dean gwyrryan Elia*s 'I know well that you think you are as holy as the righteous man, Elijah' SA 60; *del o ef an kensa dean a ve gans an tas formyes* 'as he was the first man who was created by the Father' CW 2089-90; *Na ra chee gorwetha gen gwreg a'n dean arall* 'Thou shalt not lie with the wife of another man' Pryce.

33B.1.2 *tus benenes ha fleghys omma ny vethons gesys* 'men, women and children, they shall not be left here' OM 1588-89; *tus benenes ha fleghys ymons omma dyuythys ha'ga pyth degys ganse* 'men, women and children have come here and their possessions brought with them' OM 1611-13; *dun alemma the'n mor ruyth tus benenes ha flehys the'n tyreth a*

thythwadow 'let us go hence to the Red Sea, men, women and children to the Land of Promise' OM 1622-24; ***gans mere moy tus benegas ha benenas in testament coth a rug vsia gwyska yscar ha canfas garow*** '…with many more holy men and women in the Old Testament who used to wear sackcloth and rough canvas' TH 6a; ***Leben poue Jesus gennez en Bethalem a Judeah en deethyow Herod an matern, a reeg doaze teeze veer thor an Est tha Jerusalem*** 'Now when Jesus was born in Bethlehem of Judea in the days of Herod the King wise men came from the East to Jerusalem' Rowe; ***Ha ma leiaz bennen pokare an guenen; eye vedn gwerraz dege teez dendle peath a'n beaze*** 'And there are many women like the bees; they will help their men to earn their living' JJenkins.

33B.1.3 ***du a ve provokys warbyn an bys, may ruga cuthy ha dystrya gans lew Noye oll an bys, mas naye y honyn, y wreg, y iii mab haga iii gwreg, viii person ens in holl myns a ve sawys*** 'God was provoked against the world, so that he was grieved and destroyed by Noah's flood all the world except Noah himself, his wife, his three sons and their three wives; eight persons in all they were who were saved' TH 7; ***fatell rug Symon magus offra the ry mona the pedyr mar mynna pedyr ry power thotheff, penagull person a rella eff ha gora y thewleff warnotha may teffans ha receva an spuris sans*** 'that Simon Magus offered money to Peter if Peter would give him power, that whichever person upon whom he would lay his hands, that they should receive the Holy Spirit' TH 46a.

33B.1.4 ***Mab den heb ken ys bara nyn geuas ol y vewnans*** 'A person does not live by bread alone' PA 12a; ***ow spyrys ny dryc nefre yn corf map den vyth yn beys*** 'my spirit shall not dwell in the body of any person in the world' OM 925-26; ***rag me a grys fest yn ta lyes map den yn bys-ma rak y gorf an geuyth ovn*** 'for I believe very firmly that many are the persons in this word who will be afraid of his body' RD2078-80

33B.1.5 ***reys yv thy's gorre moyses aron a'th wlascor yn meys ha'ga pobel ol ganse*** 'you must send Moses, Aaron out of your kingdom and their people with them' OM 1572-74; ***ef yv arluth a allos hag a prynnas gans y wos pobel an beys*** 'he is a lord of power and with his blood he redeemed the people of the world' RD 1183-85; ***sawyah oll sorto clevas, ha oll pesticks mesk an boble*** 'healing all kinds of disease and all injuries among the people' Rowe; ***nag u an pobel coth tho bose skoothez war noniel*** 'the old people are not to be relied upon either' NBoson

33B.1.6 ***arvow lour thy'nny yma ha guesyon stout yn tor-ma a'n chache vskys*** 'we have enough arms and stout men now who will catch him quickly' PC 615-17; ***sav certan nyns o torn da danvon guesyon an par-ma gans arvow thu'm kemeres*** 'but indeed it was not a good deed to send men like this with weapons to arrest me' PC 1298-300.

33B.2 ***ha brassa ys profet han brassa bethqueth a sevys intre gore ha gwreg*** 'and greater than a prophet that ever arose between man and woman' TH 8; ***In weth S poull a commondias an gwer the cara aga gwregath kepar dell ra crist cara y egglos*** 'St Paul also commands the husbands to love their wives as Christ loves his church' TH 31; *Neb a'm gruk vy ha'm gorty ef a ruk agan dyfen aual na wrellen dybbry na mos oges the'n wethen* 'He who made me and my husband, he forbade us to eat an apple or to go near the tree' OM 181-83; *nefre gustyth th'y gorty me a orden bos benen* 'always obedient to her husband I ordain that woman shall be' OM 295-96; *nefra gostyth thy gorty me a ordayne bos benyn* 'always obedient to her husband I ordain that woman shall be' CW 894-95; *hy a vyჳ gwreg ty da* 'she will be a good wife' CF 13; *Adam yn dyweth an beys my a wronnt oel mercy theys ha the eua the wreghty* 'Adam at the end of the world, I shall grant you and your wife Eve, the oil of mercy' OM 328-30; *hag argh thotho growethe dre ov gorhemmynnadow wheth gans eva y wreghty* 'and order him by my commandment again to lie with Eve his wife' OM 635-37; *tha hena yma gwreghty benyn yw henwys eva* 'that man has a wife, a woman called Eve' CW 449-50; *adam kyns es dewath an bys me a wront oyle mercye theis ha tha eva theth wrethtye* 'Adam, before the end of the world I shall grant the oil of mercy to you and to Eve your wife' CW 940-42; *an guadnṣyrti ჳenz e follat a ᴅestrîaz an dên kôc en guili* 'the adulteress with her lover killed the old man in the bed' JCH §26; *Ha nessa metten an guadnṣyrti, hei a ᴅalasvaz ᴅv 'ụîl krei* 'And the next morning the adulteress, she began to make a hullaballoo' JCH §28.

33B.3 *eff a dall deneren nov rag baban a welogh why* 'it is worth nine pence as a doll, which you see' BM 3404-05; *parys thage dewosa me a veth ov arluth da merugh an babyov wek* 'ready to bleed them I shall be, my good lord; look at the sweet babies' BM 1575-77; *yma flogh genaf genys dre voth a'n tas dev in weth* 'I have given birth to a baby also through the will of God the Father' OM 672-73; *hag yn creys hy varennow vn flogh maylys gans lysten* 'and in the middle of its branches a baby wrapped in swaddling clothes' OM 837-40; *erbyn reson yv in beys heb hays gorryth thymo creys bones flogh vyth concevijs in breys benen heb awer* 'believe me, it is against reason in the world that any baby could be conceived rightly in the womb of a woman without male seed' BM 844-47; *Nansus thym vj vgons flogh dywans then empour trussogh may hallons boys dewogys* 'Now I have 120 babies; pack them off immediately to the emperor so that they can be bled' BM 1554-56; *na heb mear lavyer defry benytha nystevyth floghe* 'nor without great labour never shall she have a baby' CW 899-900; *yth esa vn virgyn wheake hay floghe pur semely maylyes vny defran wondrys whans* 'there was a sweet virgin and her baby beautifully wrapped in her bosom—wondrous longing' CW 1908-10; *Ha potho angye devethez en choy y a wellaz an Flô yonk gen Mareea e thama* 'And when they had come into the house, they saw the infant with Mary his mother' Rowe; *Flô vye gennes an mîz Merh, ni trehes e bigel en mîz East* 'A baby born in the month of March, we cut his navel in the month of August' WGwavas; *Pew vedna why gawas rag seera rag guz flo* 'Who will you get as father to your baby?' Chygwyn.

33B.4.1 *ha venytha me a grys the vos a werghes genys* 'and always will I believe that you were born of a Virgin' PC 402-03; *bynyges re bo an prys may fe a venen genys an wyrhes ker maria* 'blessed be the time when he was born of woman, of the Blessed Virgin Mary' RD 153-55; *y fue gynys a wyrhes ker maria* 'he was born of the Blessed Virgin Mary' RD 1199-200 *han werhes flour maria* 'and Mary the choicest Virgin' BM 631; *han wyrhes maria splan* 'and the bright Virgin Mary' BM 756; *maria mam ha guerhes* 'Mary mother and Virgin' BM 2973; *the supposya na rug crist kemeras y gyge mes a gyge an wyrhes maria y vam* 'to suppose that Christ took only his flesh from the flesh of the Virgin Mary his mother' TH 12a; *Jhesu Crist in substans, a ve genys an wyrhes maria* 'Christ in substance was born of the Virgin Mary' TH 54a; *Christ a gemeras kigg ha ve genys worth an worthias maria* 'Christ took flesh and was born of the Virgin Mary' SA 61; *Me a vyn, re'n gwerhesow! mos thu'm sofran alenha* 'I will by the Virgins! go thence to my sovereign' BK 1308-09; *Re'n gwerhesow! te 'bew an bys the'th unadow* 'By the Virgins! You possess the world to your desire' BK 1717-19.

33B.4.2 *maria mam ha maghteth* 'Mary mother and virgin' BM 634; *Gorthyans the crist map maghteth* 'Glory to Christ, son of a virgin' BM 1146; *hag a Varya genys, kekeffrys mayghtath ha mam* 'and born of Mary, both virgin and mother' BK 174-75; *ow voice oll yta changis avel mayteth in tevery* 'look, my voice is all changed, like a maiden indeed' CW 530-31; *me a weall vn mayteth wheake* 'I see a sweet maiden' CW 1835 *Mathtath, ro de vy barow ha dewas* 'Mayde, give me bread and drinke' Borde; *Mathtath drewgh eyo hag amanyn de vi* 'Mayde, brynge me egges and butter' Borde; *te, na de mabe, na de merth, de guas, na de maiteth, de chattol, na an vncouth es guy de yettes* 'thou, nor thy son, nor thy daughter, thy servant nor thy maid, thy cattle, nor the stranger that is within thy gates' TBoson; *Pelea era why moaz, moz, fettow teag* 'Where are you going, going, fair maid?' Chygwyn.

33B.4.3 *ha trewethow the dege virgin* 'and sometimes to a fair virgin' TH 31; *tha virgin deke pur havall* 'very like a fair virgin' CW 500; *now in toppe an wethan deake yth esa vn virgyn wheake* 'now in the top of the beautiful tree there was a sweet virgin' CW 1907-08.

33B.5.1 *hag in meske ol the nasconn henwys oys pronter grassijs* 'and in oll your nation you are called a gracious priest' BM 2549-50; *densa dy conuersasconn sur in mesk ol y nascon* 'a good man in his conduct sure in all his nation' BM 2917-18; *Du a wrappyas pub nacion in discregyans* 'God wrapped every nation in unbelief' TH 7a; *In the haes thege oll an nacions an bys a veth benegys* 'In thy seed all nations of the earth shall be blessed' TH 13; *Nebas e won ow nacion i'n bys ma* 'little I know my nation in this world' BK 35-6; *in dyspyt the'th nassyoyn, the vaw the honen a'th crog* 'despite your nation, your own servant will hang you' BK 465-66; *Lowena arag nation theso drys an re erall!* 'Hail before the nation to you above the others!' BK 1988-89.

33B.5.2 ***Ken rug oll an x tryb a Israell departia atheworth Roboam mab Salamon*** 'Though all the ten tribes of Israel departed from Rehoboam the son of Solomon' TH 50a.

33C.1 VOCABULARY

delkyow *late variant of* **delyow** *pl.* leaves

dhe'n dor *adv.* to the ground, down

galow *m.* calling

ledn *f.,* **lednow** blanket, cloth

venten *f., variant of* **fenten** *f.* spring, well

sevien *f.,* **sevy** *coll.* strawberry

trehor *m.,* **trehoryon** tailor

why a wra bos you will be

33C.2 TEXT DHE REDYA (*AN GÂN "DELKYOW SEVY"*)
Red an gân-ma ha scrif gorthebow dhe'n qwestyons:

Pyle a erowgh why ow mos, mos, a vaghteth teg,
gen agas bejeth gwynn, ha'gas blew melen?
Th'eroma ow mos dhe'n venten, sera wheg,
rag delkyow sevy a wra mowysy teg.

A wrav vy mos genowgh ow mowes, a vaghteth teg,
gen agas bejeth gwynn, ha'gas blew melen?
Gwrewgh, mar mennowgh why, sera wheg,
rag delkyow sevy a wra mowysy teg.

Fatla wrav vy agas gorra why dhe'n dor,
gen agas bejeth gwynn, ha'gas blew melen?
Me a vedn sevel arta, sera wheg,
rag delkyow sevy a wra mowysy teg.

Fatla wrav vy agas dry why gen flogh,
gen agas bejeth gwynn ha'gas blew melen?
Me a vedn y dhon, sera wheg,
rag delkyow sevy a wra mowysy teg.

Pyw vednowgh why gawas rag sîra rag gàs flogh,
gen agas bejeth gwynn ha'gas blew melen?
Why a wra bos y sîra, a sera wheg,
rag delkyow sevy a wra mowysy teg.

Pandra vednowgh why gwil rag lednow rag gàs flogh,
gen agas pedn du ha'gas blew melen?
Y sîra a vëdh trehor, sera wheg,
rag delkyow sevy a wra mowysy teg.

1 Pandr'yw porposys gans an den usy ow côwsel orth an vaghteth teg?
2 Pandra whyrvyth mar teu va ha cafos y whans?
3 Mar pëdh an vaghteth gans flogh, pandra vydn hy gwil?
4 Pyw a vëdh sîra pò tas an flogh?
5 Pëth yw y alow ev?
6 Usy an gân-ma ow qwil dhywgh perthy cov a gân in Sowsnek?

PESWARDHEGVES DYSCANS WARN UGANS
THIRTY-FOURTH LESSON

34A.1 'TO BURY', 'DITCH', AND 'TO MELT'

The Cornish for 'to bury' is variously spelt in the texts: *enclethyas*, *enclethyes*, *anclethyas*. where the **th** of the texts represents **dh** rather than **th**. In some forms of revived Cornish the verbal noun is on etymological grounds spelt **ynkleudhyas*. There is a little evidence in later texts to support initial **yn**; there is none at all for the medial **eu**. 'To bury' in Cornish is best spelt **encledhyas**.

The root of the word 'to bury' is also seen in the *Klêdh* 'A ditch or trench' AB: 61b and as *kledh* 'ditch' at AB: 244c. There is no evidence from the Cornish texts of a rounded vowel in this word, which should be written **cledh** in the revived language.

A verb with similar vocalism to **cledh** is **tedha** 'to melt, to thaw'. This is cited as *Dho tedha* s.v. *Deliqueo* [to melt, to dissolve] by Lhuyd at AB: 54a. There is no evidence to support a rounded vowel eu in this word either. It should be written **tedha** in revived Cornish.

34A.2 *YMA/YMOWNS, YW, EUS, USY/USONS*, AND *BËDH*

The different forms of the verb **bos** 'to be' are a source of difficulty for learners of Cornish. Here is a brief summary of the various forms of **bos** in the present and future.

> NOTE: In the Cornish texts **marow** 'dead' follows other parts of the verb **bos** 'to be' with the sense 'to die'.

34A.2.1 *YMA, YMOWNS*: these forms may be used only in main clauses. Four separate functions can be distinguished:

34A.2.1.1 to express the idea of being in a place or condition: **yma an medhek in drog-stât** 'the doctor is in a bad way', **yma hy wre'ty**

229

ganso 'his wife is with him'; **ymowns y i'n chambour warbarth** 'they are together in the room'

34A.2.1.2 **yma** may be used to express the idea 'there is, there are': **yma lies benyn obma** 'there are many women here'; **yma nebes gwin i'n votel whath** 'there is still a little wine in the bottle'

34A.2.1.3 with **ow** + verbal noun to express the simple present: **yma Jowan ow tos tro ha'n chy** 'John is coming towards the house'; **yma an flehes ow qwary i'n lowarth** 'the children are playing in the garden'; **ymowns y ow wherthyn** 'they are laughing'

34A.2.1.4 instead of **yw** in predicative sentences: **yma Jenefer kerys gans kenyver onen** 'Jennifer is loved by everybody'; **yma hy crohen pòr wydn** 'her skin is very pale'; **ymowns y shyndys genes!** 'they have been ruined by you! you have ruined them!'

If **yma**, **ymowns** are used in a subordinate clause after **may** 'where, in which' and **ple** 'where', they will appear as **ma**, **mowns**:

I'n gwetha prës ny worama ple ma hy 'Unfortunately I don't know where she is'; **certan oma hedna dhe vos an tyller may ma va** 'I am certan that't the place where he is'; **ple mowns y lebmyn?** 'where are they now?'

34A.2.2 *YW*: this is the commonest form of the third person singular present of the verb **bos** 'to be'. It has several uses:

34A.2.2.1 It can be used after the particle **yth** to introduce a predicative statement: **yth yw Jowan ow brâssa escar** 'John is my greatest enemy'; **yth yw an Arlùth ow golow** 'the Lord is my light'; it is also used with **yth** after **prag** 'why?': **prag yth yw mostys dha fâss?** 'why is your face dirty?'

34A.2.2.2 It can be used predicatively without any particle if the predicate precedes it: **ow hothman kerra yw Jowan lebmyn** 'John is now my dearest friend'; **sanses yw hy saw ny allama hy ferthy** 'she is a saint, but I can't stand her'

34A.2.2.3 **Yw** is used without particle immediately following its subject: **Jowan yw ow hothman** 'John is my friend'; **an venyn deg-na yw y wreg yonk** 'that beautiful woman is his young wife'

34A.2.2.4 **Yw** is used with the verbal adjective to make the passive: **pastys dâ yw gwerthys ena** 'good pasties are sold there'; **yth yw drog-oberow gwrës kenyver jorna** 'crimes are committed every day'

34A.2.2.5 **Yw** is used in negative main clauses after **nyns**: **nyns yw teg dha eryow** 'your words aren't fair' and in subordinate clauses after **nag**: **me a lever dhis nag yw teg dha eryow** 'I tell you, your words aren't fair'

34A.2.2.6 **Yw** can also be used without any preceding particle in questions: **yw Jory aswonys dhis** 'do you know Jory?'; **yw Tamsyn dha gares** 'is Tamsin your girlfriend?'

34A.2.2.7 **Yw** can also be used at the head of a relative clause: **me a gôwsas orth oll an dus yw parys dhe weres** 'I spoke to all the people who are willing to help'; **dysqwa dhybm an mowysy yw dâ rag cana** 'show me the girls who are good at singing'. Sometimes to avoid ambiguity **yw** should be preceded by **neb** 'who': **me a recêvas lyther dhyworth benyn hedhyw neb yw whensys dhe vetya genes** 'I received a letter today from a woman who is anxious to meet you'.

All parts of the short form of **bos** (**ov, oma**; **os, osta**; **yw**; **on**; **owgh**; **yns**) can be used in 1–7 above.

34A.2.3 *EUS*: **eus** is the indefinite member of the long form of **bos**. Its functions are similar to some of those of **yma** but only in in negative, interrogative or relative clauses where the subject is indefinite. **Eus** is therefore used:

34A.2.3.1 to mean 'there is not any': **nyns eus amanyn vëth i'n yeynor** 'there is no butter in the refrigerator'; **nyns eus den vëth obma** 'there is nobody here'; **nyns eus onen vëth ahanan ow wherthyn lebmyn** 'none of us is laughing now'

34A.2.3.2 to ask whether there is anything or anybody: **eus den vëth obma?** 'is there anybody here?'; **eus keus wàr an bord?** 'is there cheese on the table?'; **eus maw vëth ow mos in mes i'n glaw?** 'is any boy going out into the rain?'

34A.2.3.3 to introduce relative clauses where the antecedent is indefinite: **yth esoma owth examnya kenyver tra eus obma** 'I am examining everything that is here'; **pynag oll dra eus obma a vëdh tôwlys in mes** 'anything that is here, will be thrown out'.

34A.2.4 *USY* AND *USONS* are the definite members of the long form of **bos**. They can be used only when their subject is definite:

34A.2.4.1 in simple negative clauses: **nyns usy ow mabm i'n chy** 'my mother isn't in the house'; **nyns usy ev ow tendyl hedna** 'he doesn't deserve that'; **nyns usons y ow qweres** 'they don't help'

34A.2.4.2 in interrogative clauses: **a nyns usy ev obma?** 'isn't he here?'; **a nyns usy ev ow tos haneth?** 'isn't he coming tonight?'

34A.2.4.3 in subordinate clauses with a definite subject: **hèn yw an son a wra va, pàn usy ev ow sevel in mes a'y wely** 'that's the noise he makes when he gets up out of bed'; **lebmyn pàn usons y i'n lowarth, ny a yll côwsel** 'now that they are in the garden, we can talk'

34A.2.4.4 in relative clauses with a definite antecedent: **te a wor yn tâ nag yw hedna an pëth usy ev ow mênya** 'you know well that is not what he means'; **esta ow qweles an strôll usons y ow qwil?** 'do you see the mess that they are making?'

34A.2.4.5 For the other persons of the long form of **bos** there is no distinction between definite and indefinite forms. Such forms may be used in 1) positive, 2) negative, 3) interrogative, 4) relative and 5) other subordinate clauses. Here are some examples:

34A.2.4.5.1 **yth esoma obma** 'I am here'; **yth eson ny ow tos genowgh** 'we are coming with you'; **yth esta ow qweles pùptra** 'you see everything'

34A.2.4.5.2 **nyns esta ow convedhes** 'you don't understand'; **nyns eson ny ow whelas tra vëth a'n par-na** 'we are not looking for anything like that'

34A.2.4.5.3 **esoma i'gas fordh why?** 'am I in your way?'; **a nyns esowgh why ow lavurya i'n tor-ma?** 'aren't you working at the moment?'; **eson ny ow tybarth warbarth?** 'are we leaving together?'

34A.2.4.5.4 **ny vanaf vy clôwes an pëth esta ow comendya** 'I don't want to hear what you recommend'; **flows yw kenyver tra esowgh why ow leverel** 'everything that you say is nonsense'

34A.2.4.5.5 **me a wor pùpprës pàn esta ow leverel gow** 'I always know when you're lying'; **esedhowgh ena ha kemerowgh hanaf a dê abàn esowgh why obma wàr an dyweth** 'sit there and take a cup of tea, since you are here at last.'

34A.2.5 *BËDH (BÏDH)* is the third singular of **bedhaf, bedhys**, etc. 'will be', i.e. the future of **bos**. In the earlier Middle Cornish it sometimes has habitual force: **an eyl torn y fÿdh re hir, tres aral re got in gwir** 'at one time it is too long, another time too short indeed'; **bëdh dorn**

re verr, bëdh tavas re hir 'a hand is wont to be too short, a tongue is wont to be too long' This usage can be imitated in revived Cornish, provided there is no possibility of ambiguity.

It should also be remembered that in real conditions in future time containing the verb **bos** in the *if*-clause, **mar pëdhaf, mar pedhys, mar pëdh**, etc. are used. In Cornish therefore one says: **me a vydn côwsel orto, mar pëdh ev ena** 'I will speak to him, if he is there' and **mar pedhowgh why abrë·s avorow, ny â dhe'n vilva warbarth** 'if you are early tomorrow, we will go to the zoo together.'

With **pàn** 'when', however, the future of **bos** is not used, but rather the present subjunctive; see 19A.6.

34A.3 'WAS' (*O, BEU, ESA, BEDHA*)

As with the present of the verb **bos** 'to be', so with the past tenses, there are various forms in Cornish. Since English has but one form of 'to be' in the 3rd singular, i.e. 'was', the differing forms **o, beu, esa** and **bedha** are a source of difficulty for speakers of English. Let us look at these four forms in turn:

34A.3.1 *O*

O is the imperfect of the short form of **bos** 'to be'. **O** therefore is the imperfect corresponding to **yw**. **Yth o va dên skentyl**, for example means 'he was an intelligent man' and implies that more is going to be said about the intelligent things he did or said. If **o** is used with the verbal adjective the sense is pluperfect: **yth o an chy derevys solabrë·s pàn dheuth an corwyns** 'the house had already been built when the whirlwind came'; **yth o hy thas marow pàn wrug hy demedhy** 'her father was dead/had already died, when she married'.

34A.3.2 *BEU*

Beu is the third singular of **beuv, beuma, beus**, etc., the preterite of **bos**. It means 'was' at one particular moment; or it refers to something that happened and is now past. Thus Tregear can speak of Adam as **an kynsa den bythqweth a veu** 'the first man who ever was'.

Because **beu** describes a complete change of state, it is used with the verbal adjective to express the past passive: **ev a veu genys** 'he was born'; **oll an soudoryon a veu ledhys** 'all the soldiers were killed'; **an lyver-ma a veu dyllys in vledhen dyw vil ha deg** 'this book was published in the year 2010'.

As we have already seen, **beu** can be used to render 'became' in Cornish. For 'we became great friends after that' one could say **ny a veu cothmans brâs wosa hedna**. For 'he became a doctor last year' one could either say **ev a veu gwrës medhek warleny** or **ev a veu medhek warleny**. Consider the difference between **ev a veu pronter deg bledhen alebma** 'he became a priest ten years ago' and **ev o pronter bys i'n vledhen warleny** 'he was a priest until last year (but he has now been laicized)'.

If **beu** is used with the word **marow** 'dead', the sense is 'died': **y feu hy mabm marow an seythen eus passys** 'her mother died last week'. This way of using **beu marow** to mean 'died' is similar to *bu farw* 'he/she died' in Welsh and *ba marb* 'he/she died' in Middle Irish.

34A.3.3 *ESA (ERA)*

Esa is the 3rd person of **eses, eses, esa**, etc. the imperfect equivalent of **eus** and **usy**. It is used when describing how something or somebody was in a place or state for period, e.g. **pàn esen agensow in Loundres, me a vetyas gans dha vroder** 'when I was in London recently, I met your brother'; **nyns esen ny i'n côstys-na pàn wharva an drog-labm** 'we weren't in that area, when the accident occurred'.

Esa can be used with **ow** + verbal noun it is necessary to use a continuous form of another verb: **yth esen ow lavurya in Arwednek i'n termyn-na** 'at that time I worked in Falmouth'; **yth esa va ow screfa in fenowgh rag paper nowodhow an gowethas** 'he often wrote for the company newspaper'.

34A.3.4 *BEDHA*

Bedha is not so much imperfect as past habitual and refers to something that happened repeatedly. This is particularly apparent with the verbal adjective: **y fedha leth delyvrys dhe'n treven i'n dedhyow-na** 'milk used to be delivered to the houses in those days'; **y fedha tansys brâs anowys nos Golowan** 'a great bonfire used to be lit on Midsummer night'.

Another important use of this tense is with indirect speech. In English we say, for example, 'I told him I would be happy to help him'. In Cornish, if one uses a finite verb in the subordinate clause, it is not put into the conditional i.e. **y fien, y fies, y fia** 'would be', but into the past habitual, for example, **me a leverys dhodho y fedhen lowen dh'y** weres'; **hy a gresy y fedha ev ledhys gansans** 'she believed he would be killed by them'; see also 34A.5.

34A.4 IMPERFECT VERSUS PRETERITE IN OTHER VERBS

The verb **bos** 'to be' is unique in Cornish in having four tenses in the past, namely **en**, **es**, **o**, etc.; **esen**, **eses**, **esa**, etc.; **beuv**, **beus**, **beu**, etc., and **bedhen**, **bedhes**, **bedha**, etc. Other verbs have only imperfect and preterite, e.g. imperfect **leveryn**, **leverys**, **levery**, etc. versus preterite **leverys**, **leversys**, **leverys** (Late **lavaras**). The distinction in Cornish is an important one, but is not always respected by learners. Here, for example, is a published sentence in Cornish where the writer has failed to understand that the imperfect was necessary:

Yth esa tyller uhel a-ugh an waryva, may *whrug sedha Duw ow meras orth an dus 'There was a high place above the stage, where God sat, watching the people.'

This is a description of the practice in York and in Chester in the mystery plays and it describes the customary layout of the theatre, something that remained unchanged for years, if not for centuries. The preterite **may *whrug** is inadmissable here. It would have been correct to have written: **Yth esa tyller uhel a-ugh an waryva, may whre sedha Duw**... or better still **Yth esa tyller uhel a-ugh an waryva, may fedha Duw esedhys**.

Here is a similar example, describing in Cornish how the Israelites cooked manna in the wilderness every day:

Mès i'n gwylfos y *tybrys flehes Israel glûth an nev, a *bopsons yn tesednow pùb dëdh 'But in the wilderness the children of Israel ate the dew of heaven, which they baked into cakes every day'

The Israelites collected manna daily and cooked it daily. In both clauses here the imperfect must be used. The author ought to have written:

Mès i'n gwylfos flehes Israel a dhybry glûth an nev, a wrêns y pobas yn tesednow pùb dëdh.

34A.5 IMPERFECT VERSUS CONDITIONAL

We saw at 34A.3.4 above that with finite verbs in indirect speech the past habitual (**bedha**) is used rather than the conditional (**bia**). With other verbs the imperfect must be used in such cases: **ev a bromyssyas y whre va dos** 'he promised he would come'; **nyns esen ny ow qwetyas y clôwyn tra vëth dhyworto** 'we did not expect that we would hear anything from him'.

Some handbooks of Cornish teach that the conditional tense may be used as a pluperfect as well. This is very misleading. The use of **bien**, **dothyen**, **gwrussen**, etc. as pluperfect is confined to the earliest continuous text in Middle Cornish, *Pascon Agan Arluth* (PA). PA dates from the fourteenth century if not earlier and has many archaic features, for example, the *t*-preterite **pan gemert** 'when he took' (for later **pan gemeras**). Edwin Norris realized as early as 1859 that the pluperfect no longer functioned as a pluperfect in the Ordinalia (OM, PC, RD), but only as a conditional. Moroever in the later texts the conditional itself is increasingly rendered periphrastically. One does not, therefore, say **ev a gemersa** 'he would take' but **ev a vynsa kemeres** or **ev a wrussa kemeres**.

Pluperfect sense itself, in texts later than PA is usually rendered with the preterite. Alternatively in some cases the pluperfect can be made by periphrasis: **An carr o ledrys solabrë·s, pàn wrug avy drehedhes an strêt** 'The carr had already been stolen, when I reached the street'.

34B EXAMPLES FROM THE TEXTS

34B.1.1 *y anclethyas mar uskys* 'to bury him so quickly' OM 869; *the anclethyas crystenyon* 'to bury Christians' PC 1564; *y enclethyes vye da* 'it would be good to bury him' PC 3103; *may hallo bos anclethys* 'so that he can be buried' RD 3115; *ef a vyth sur anclethys* 'he will indeed be buried' PC 3134; *an corf ker the anclethyas* 'to bury the beloved body' PC 3140; *cummyas grantyys thy'm yma th'y anclethyas yn lowen* 'I have been granted permission to bury him joyfully' PC 3146-47; *parys rag y enclethyes* 'ready to bury him' PC 3161; *ihesu a fue anclethyys* 'Jesus was buried' RD 1; *me a wruk y anclethyes* 'I buried him' RD 439; *tus yn beth a'n anclethyas* 'people buried him in the grave' RD 1269; *the anclethias an dus vays* 'to bury the good people' BM 1323; *hag anclethys in beth men* 'and buried in the tomb' BM 4050; *a fue marov anclethyys* 'who was dead, buried' BM 4082; *thy anclethyes in certyn* 'to bury him indeed' BM 4471; *may hallen y anclethyas* 'that we may bury him' BM 4512; *marow ha inclithis* 'dead an buried' SA 61a; *hag in doer tha vos anclythys* 'and to be buried in the earth' CW 1851; *me a vyn y anclythyas* 'I will bury him' CW 2079; *marrow, hag ynclythys* 'dead and buried' Pryce; *crowses, maro ha inclythys* 'crucified, dead and buried' Pryce.

34B.1.2 *Dv e doula en kledh* 'To cast him into a ditch' AB: 244c.

34B.2.1 YMA, YMOWNS: *ow tybbry genen yma* 'he is eating with us' PA 43a; *hag yma yn hy myyn branch olyf glas* 'and in her beak is a branch of green olive' OM 1121-22; *yma gynef flowrys tek* 'I have with me beautiful flowers' PC 258; *yma daggrow ow klybye the dreys* 'tears are moistening your feet' PC 482-83; *Ima guel forth es honna* 'There is a better way than that' BM 900; *yma an turant heb mar er agis pyn drehevys* 'of course the tyrant has risen up against you' BM 3239-40; *yma parys tus arvov* 'armed men are ready' BM 3531; *Ima an profet Dauit in peswar vgans ha nownsag psalme ow exortya oll an bobyll* 'The prophet David in Psalm 99 exhorts all the people' TH 1; *gere Christ, ema gwiell an keth Sacrament ma* 'the word of Christ, it makes this sacrament' SA 62; *Ena ema y gastall* 'There is his castle' BK 56; *Ema Arthur devethys* 'Arthur has come' 2794; *'Ma 'ʒen ehaz nyi dhen* 'We have our health' AB: 242a; *Emâ a kîl err* 'It is snowing' AB: 250b; *Ema a kîl kezzar* 'It is hailing' AB: 250b-c; *Ma an gog en lûar wartha* 'The cuckow is in the higher garden' Ustick MSS; *Caym lauar ple ma abel the vroder* 'Cain, tell me, where is Abel your brother?' OM 571-72; *the nessevyn in ponfes ymons ragos in bysma* 'your relatives are in anxiety about you in this world' BM 1984-85; *so y mowngy oll ow casa henna thynny* 'but they all leave that to us' TH 53; *than purpose na mowns ow toos* 'they are coming for this purpose' CW 2161; *ha mouns screffa inna warbedden ni* 'and they write there against us' OPender; *me a wor ple mons parys* 'I know where they are ready' PC 2579

34B.2.2 YW: *curtes yw ha deboner* 'he is courteous and debonair' CF; *gweff yw ʒe vones leʒys* 'he is worthy to be killed' PA 95b; *lucyfer kelmys yv whath pur fast yn y golmennow* 'Lucifer is still bound very tightly in his bonds' PA 212c; *dyuythys ev ov deweyth* 'my end has come' OM 856; *lemyn sur yth yv evnhys* 'now indeed it has been corrected' OM 2525; *prag yth yw ruth the thyllas* 'why are your clothes red?' RD 2529; *Meryasek yth yv gelwys* 'He is called Meriasek' BM 970; *Guel yv genen ny merwel es gorthya devle dyogel* 'It is better for us to die than to worship a devil certainly' BM 1234-35; *The then fol yth ew haval* 'He is like a madman' BK 356; *An lavor gôth ewe lavar gwîr* 'The old saying is a true saying' Pryce; *mabe Jared yth ov heb gowe* 'I am the son of Jared without a lie' CW 2096; *benegas osta ge, Symon bariona* 'blessed are you, Simon bar Jona' TH 44; *ellas govy buthys on ny* 'alas, woe is me; we are drowned' OM 1705; *oma yth on devethys* 'we have come here' BM 1529; *a pup plos yth ough glanhys* 'you are cleansed of all filth' PC 865; *pur welcum ough genan ny* 'you are very welcome with us' BK 1633; *pobyl rome orth ij vernans delyfrys yth yns oma* 'the people of Rome, they have been delivered here from two deaths' BM 4168-69; *try fersons yns pur worthy* 'they are three persons much to be revered' CW 1960.

34B.2.3 EUS: *myns vs omma cuntullys* 'as many as are gathered here' PA 92b; *rag yth evel thy'm bos da yn kynsa dyth myns vs grvrys* 'for everything that has been made on the first day seems good to me' OM 19-20; *Peys warbarth myns us omma* 'Peace together, all who are here' BM 2499; *may fo va leall recordys a vyns tra es ynna gwryes* 'that it may be recorded about everything that has been made in them' CW 2173-74; *Mars ues den vith a vyn cows* 'If there is anyone who wishes to speak' BK 1496; *Hostes, eus boues dâ dewhy?* Hostess, have you any good food?' Borde; *Pes myllder eus alemma de Londres?* 'How many miles is London from here?' Borde; *mors eez du brage* 'if you have malt' JJenkins; *Eth egas ow kowsal da* 'you speak well' BK 626; *yth esan ny ow kafas oll pub dadder the worth du* 'we get all goodness from God' TH 11; *Neg eranny ow kemeras hemma rag common bara ha dewas* 'we do not take this for common bread and drink' SA 63a

34B.2.4 USY: *ȝy ȝas ynweth vgy avan* 'to his Father also who is above' PA 53d; *Eugh tynneugh an gasadow vsy ov cul fals dewow* 'Go, pull the hateful woman, who makes false gods' OM 2691-92; *in cambron an lagasek nyns usy eff* 'in Camborne the sharp-eyed one is not' BM 1018-19; *An kensa tra vgy ow tuchia an creacion a mab den* 'the first thing which concerns the creation of mankind' TH 1; *vrt an hagar auall igge va gweell do derevoll warneny* 'because of the storm that he causes to rise up against us' NBoson

34B.2.5 BÊDH: *lader cleves thym yma a veth gelwys an seson* 'I have a chronic disease which is called the ague' BM 679-80; *cayne me a vyth henwys* 'I am called Cain' CW 1500.

34B.2.6 MAR PÊDH: *yn certan mara pyth gurys sur warlergh an keth dev ma ny fyth ef neffre dyswrys* 'certainly if it is done, according to these two, he will never be destroyed' PC 2451-53; *mar qura gothvethys mar pyth yn scon dyswreys ef a vyth* 'if he does it, if it is known, soon he shall be killed' OM 1520-21; *mara pethaf bev blethen my a'n taluyth thyugh* 'if I live for a year, I shall repay you' OM 2386-87; *mar peth prevys dyogel in geth na fovt in bugel goeff doys then keth chargna* 'if a fault is found on that day in the pastor, woe to him to come to the position' BM 2839-41; *ha te a vith ef heb mar, mar pyth o'm gallus evy* 'and you will have it of course, if it is in my power' BK 1077-78; *mar pyth y frute hy tastys te a vyth dampnys ractha* 'if its fruit is tasted, you will be condemned for it' CW 377-78; *mar peth travith gwrez tho gwetha Curnooack, eue a dale bose gen rina eu ginnez ubba* 'if anything is done to preserve Cornish, it must be done by those who were born here' NBoson.

34B.3.1 O: *y bous ef o mar dek guris* 'his garment had been made so beautifully' PA 190c; *rag ef o tebel ethen neb a glewsys ov cane* 'for he was an evil bird that you heard singing' OM 223-24; *yth o ow fous ha'm brustplat purpur garow thu'm strothe* 'my shirt and my breastplate were rough purple cloth to constrict me' RD 2591-92; *nos tevle yth o namnygen* 'it was dark night a little while ago' BM 3680; *Eff o purguir den worthy ay genesygeth defry* 'He was a worthy man by birth indeed' BM 4386-87; *eff o lel servont ihesu* 'he was the loyal servant of Jesus' BM 4379; *I o chyf ow marogyon* 'They were the leaders of my knights' BK 3286.

34B.3.2 BEU: *ha kemmys a theseryas ʒoʒo eff a ve grontis* 'and as much as he desired was granted to him' PA 9d; *ny fuf den thotho bythqueth* 'I was never a man of his' PC 1238; *helhys vue in kerth heb fael* 'he was chased away without fail' BM 2249; *ʒiso y fue servont lel* 'to thee he was a loyal servant' BM 4339; *megys vue gans boys eleth* 'he was fed with the food of angels' BM 4464; *Dew a cowsas an ger ha ny a ve gwris* 'God spoke the word and we were made' SA 61a; *maga sow besca ve pesk* 'as sound as ever was a fish' JTonkin'; *gans luas y fons gwelys* 'by many they were seen' PA 210c; *der henna y fuff sawys* 'by him I was healed' BM 2154; *Dal y fueff lues blythen* 'I was blind for many years' BM 2393; *gans an Jowle y fowns tulles* 'by the Devil they were deceived' CW 1003; *out govy na vuff marov* 'Oh, alas that I did not die' BM 795; *ihesu crist map maria ha genys a lel werheys a fue marov in grovs pren hag anclethys in beth men* 'Jesus Christ son of Mary, and born of a true virgin, died on the cross and was buried in the tomb' BM 4048-50.

34B.3.3 ESA: *war ben dewlyn pan ese an nef y fe danuenys el ʒoʒo ʒy gomfortye* 'when he was on his knees from heaven was sent an angel to him to comfort him' PA 59ab; *fatell esa the crist mer a garensa worthan ny* 'that Christ had great love for us' TH 15a; *ha mars ega thetha lell corfow po nag essa* 'and whether they had real bodies or not' TH 55; *mal ða va prêv erra e urêg guica kympez et i ʒever: erra po nag erra* 'so that he could prove whether his wife was staying faithful to him, was she or not' JCH §39.

34B.3.4 BEDHA: *taw an el a bregewthy a'n wethen hag a'y vertv a'y frut a wrello dybry y fethe kepar ha dev* 'silence, the angel declared that whoever ate of the tree and of the power of its fruit would become like God' OM 229-32; *mar derre hy leuerys kepar ha dev y fethe* 'if he broke it, she said, he would be like God' OM 289-90; *nebes esen ov teby y fethe hy in for ma* 'little did I think it would be like this' BM 3250-51; *fatell vetha an kithsam kyge na a vetha rys rag an bewnans a oll an bys* 'that that same flesh would be that given for the life of all the world' TH 52; *fattell rug crist, dre y tempill, menya y corfe, an pith a vetha dre an Jewes gorys then mernans* 'that Christ, by his temple, meant his body, that which would be put to death by the Jews' TH 53; *hag y promysyas tha vee y fethan tha well nefra* 'and promised me that I should be for ever the better' CW 889-90; *der henna me a thowtyas gans peb a fethan lethys* 'because of that I feared I should be killed by everybody' CW 1636-37; *yn agan ethom pup tra pup vr parys thy'n vethe* 'in our need everything was always ready for us' PC 917-18; *mar corthyyth an plos myngov neb a thuk peynis anwhek sur in grovs pren a vethe gelwys ihesu* 'if you worship the dirty liar who suffered grim pains indeed on the cross, who was called Jesus' BM 2379-82; *an pith a vetha gwrys syehar anotha* 'the material from which sacks used to be made' TH 7.

34B.4.1 *Ihesu crist yn pow a dro pub er oll pregoth a wre* 'Jesus Christ in the country around always used to preach' PA 23a; *Hag y ee ʒe ben dewlyn ha hager mowys a wre* 'And they went down on bended knee and pulled ugly faces' PA 196a; *Rag gwan spyrn hag ef yn ten caman na ylly gwyʒe war nans na bosse y ben rag an arlont a vsye mar posse an eyll tenewen rag y scoth hy a grevye Ha whath gweth a wre an pren war ȝellargh mar an gorre* 'Because of dreadful thorns he could not in any way stop bending his head down, because of the crown which he was wearing and it tightly on him; if he leant forward to one side, it hurt his shoulder; and worse did the cross hurt if he leant his head backwards' PA 205a-d; *dal o ny wely banna* 'he was blind; he saw nothing' PA 217b; *govy y vones lethys kemmys dader prest a wre* 'alas that he is dead; so much good used he do' PC 3095-96; *by ny geusy ken ys wyr* 'never did he speak other than the truth' RD 1195; *ny gowsy mas honester* 'he used not speak anything but honesty' BM 2239; *may ruk y ij lyn hothfy mar vras scantlor y hylly trewythyov kerthes ay saeff* 'so that his knees swelled so greatly, scarcely could he sometimes walk upright' BM 4458-60; *ran in Germany a levery, omma yma crist* 'some in Germany were saying: here is Christ' TH 32.

34B.4.2 *moygha ȝoȝo drok a wre henna veȝa an guella gwas* 'whoever did him the greatest harm, he would be the best fellow' PA 112d; *me an glewas dyougel lyes guyth ov leuerel an temple y wre terry* 'I heard indeed many times saying that he would destroy the temple' PC 1307-09; *y leverys ef yn weth datherghy an tressa deth y wre pur wyr hep fyllel* 'he said also that he would rise again on the third indeed without fail' RD 4-6

34B.5.1 *pup den yn bys ma a wor den vythol na'n drehafse yn try dythwyth war nep cor* 'everybody in this world knows nobody could build it at all in three days' PC 386-88; *ol mens trespas a wruge thotho ef me a' n gafse* 'all the sins he has committed, I would forgive him' PC 1814-15; *A pesta den eredy, te a thoksa kehar claf* 'if you were a man, you would suffer painful sinews' BK 608-09

34B.5.2 *the pesy me a vynsa* 'I would ask you' BM 2556; *mar teffa du aga suffra the vsya aga naturall powers y a vynsa optaynya salvacion* 'if God had allowed them to use their natural powers, they would have obtained salvation' TH 13a; *bo ken crist ny vensa leverell, kepar dell ew scriffys in v. chapter a mathew* 'otherwise Christ would not have said, as is written in the fifth chapter of Matthew' TH 17a; *Lebmen Dzhûan e na vendzha servia na velha, bez e vendzha mvz teua ða e urêg* 'Now John, he would not serve any longer, but he would go home to his wife' JCH §11; *Eye venjah dendle go booz ha dillaz* 'They would earn their food and clothing' JJenkins

34B.5.3 *vnwyth a caffen hansell me a russa amendie* 'if only I were to have breakfast, I should improve' BM 110-11; *nena ny russa den vith resak in heresy* 'then no one would have run into heresy' TH 19a; *mernans ny wressans tastya mes in pleasure venarye y a wressa prest bewa* 'they would not taste death, but they would have lived indeed for ever in pleasure' CW 995-97; *Mar kressa an dean deskez feer na gwellaz hemma ev a venga kavaz fraga e ouna en skreefa-composter* 'If that wise and learned man had seen this, he would find reason to correct it in orthography' NBoson.

34C.1 VOCABULARY

a dhevîs *adv.* every inch, from head to toe

ancombra to confound, to hinder

archer *m.*, **archers** archer

astronymer *m.*, **astronymers** astronomer

cav *m.*, **cavyow** cave

crocer *m.* crozier-bearer

croffal *m.* complaint

dehesy to let fly, to shoot

den *m.*, **arvow**, **tus arvow** armed man, man of arms

den *m.*, **ervys**, **tus ervys** armed man

dedhewy to promise

devar *m.* duty

dragon *f.*, **dragonas** dragon

dûk *m.*, **dûkys** duke

dyblans *adj. & adv.* clear, clearly

dyswrës destroyed, ruined (< *dyswil* to destroy)

flàm *m.*, **flabmow** flame

gony *interj.* alas for us!

gonsy *variant of* **gensy** with her

gwann-rewl *f.* bad rule, poor arrangement

hail *interj.* hail

heb parow without equal

how *interj.* ho!

in hans dhe[2] *compound prep.* beyond

iredy *adv.* indeed

kyns ès dybarth before departing

livya to lunch

Mahom *m. personal name* Mahound

mollath Duw *interj.* God's curse

ôta *early variant of* **osta** thou art

pengasen *f.* paunch end, stomach

plâss *m.*, **plassow** place, palace

pras *m.*, **prasow** meadow

pryns *m.*, **pryncys** prince

scùmbla to defecate (*of animals*)

sportya to sport, to hunt

sqwerdya, **sqwardya** to tear

tirnans *m.* low-lying country

34C.2

TEXT DHE REDYA (*BEUNANS MERIASEK* 3896-3967)

Red an dyvyn-ma ha scrif gorthebow dhe'n qwestyonow:

First Magician

Me yw arlùth heb parow,
dûk inwedh astronymer.
Dhe helghya heb faladow,
dhe bryns par dell yw devar,
mos me a vynn
ha genef cowetha dâ.
An epscop pòr wir a dheu
dhe certan plâss er ow fynn.

Second Magician
Bysy yw dhyn bones war:
yma dragon vrâs heb mar
i'n cav omma rybon ny.
Mara teun ny er hy fynn,
marow on brâs ha bian.
Dâ yw bos fur, iredy.

Hunstman
Yma omma tus arvow
hag archers gans gwaregow
abyl pòr wir d'y ladha.
Ny dhowtya' gans ow heun
marnas y a vo re leun,
kyns ès dybarth hy squerdya.

Bishop of Poly
Me yw epscop a dhevîs
ha parlet, meur ow rassow.
Y tedhewys nans yw mis
mones in hans dhe'n prasow
erbynn Dûk Magùs a brîs,
den fur in y worthebow.
Ow crocer ôta parys
lemmyn dhe'm gormynadow?

Crozier-bearer
Me yw parys, arlùth dâ,
saw gwann-rewl yma omma
na yllyn livya kyn mos.
Gwag yw dhymm an pengasen.
A, mollath Duw i'n gegyn,
scant yw an dewas ha'n boos!

Bishop of Poly
Hail dhywgh, Dûk nobyl Magùs!
Me ha'm crocer Presagùs
re dheuth dhywgh why dhe sportya.
Na wethyn re dhe'n tirnans
rag yma dragon dyblans
hag onen vrâs sur omma.

First Magician
Now wolcùm Fader Bishyp.
Ny dheu dragon, me a dÿb
ogas dhyn ny.
Mar teu in syght, me a'n gor,
yma omma pobel lowr
rag hy ladha iredy.

Secund Magician
Na drestyen ny dhe henna.
Arlydhy deun alemma!
Otta hy sur devedhys!
Owt dredhy bedhyn marow
gans flàm tan mes a'y ganow.
Ny's gorta mil dhen ervys!

First Magician
How! dehesowgh warnedhy!
Nans eus rann lenkys gonsy!
Pyth yw an jowl a wren ny?
Mahom re'gas ancombra,
in agan mesk ow scùmbla
avell oy! Mark, otta hy!

A gony gony! Fien,
ken marow brâs ha bian,
re corf Mahom on omma!
Deun dhe'n Emprour Costentyn
ha dodho ev leveryn:
y wrians ev yw helma.
(*to Constantine*)
Hail, Syr Emprour Costentyn,
ha warnas ny a gry 'Owt!'
Dyswrës yw an pow lemmyn
ha der the wrians heb dowt
lies marow.

An dhragon vrâs eus i'n cav
unn den dhe gerdhes a'y sav
ny as na'n latha heb wow.

1 Pyw esa ow mos dhe helghya?
2 Pandr'o croffal an crocer?
3 Pana hanow a ros an epscop dhe'n astronymer?
4 Prag y whrug an epscop comendya na wrellens gwetha dhe'n tireth isel?
5 Pleth esa an dhragon trigys?
6 Pandra wrug an dhragon pàn veu hy gwelys gansans?
7 Yth esa an astronymer ow trestya dh'y dus ervys. O hedna fur?
8 I'n brës an astronymer pyw o dhe vlâmya rag an dhragon?

PYMTHEGVES DYSCANS WARN UGANS

THIRTY-FIFTH LESSON

35A.1 'PLACE'

The word **le** 'place' in Cornish is used for the most part in set phrases, i.e. **pùb le** 'everywhere'; **dhe gen le** 'to another place, elsewhere'; **in lowr le** 'in several places'; **neb le** 'somewhere'; **lies le** 'many places', **in le** 'instead of'; **in le may ma** 'where he is'; **in y le** 'in its (rightful) place'. Nance suggested the plural ***leow**, but no such form is attested.

The ordinary word for 'place', other than in set phrases, is **tyller**, plural **tyleryow**. **Tyller** can also be used with **pùb**, **lies**, **dhe gen**, etc. Notice also that the expression in **tyller clos** means 'in a secluded place'.

The word **plâss** (spelt *plas*, *plath*, *place*) is also used to mean 'place'. It can have the sense 'mansion, large house' as well.

35A.2 'TO UNDERSTAND'

The word used most frequently in revived Cornish for 'to understand' is **convedhes**. This item, however, is confined to Late Cornish sources, being attested only in CW and Pryce. Moreover **convedhes** does not exactly correspond to English 'to understand', but rather means 'to perceive, to grasp'. **Convedhes** itself is in origin the same verb as ***canfos**, ***canvos** 'to perceive' (cf. Welsh *canfod* 'to perceive, to behold'), a verb which occurs twice in BK. Lhuyd for 'To perceive or understand' gives ***adzhan** AB: 72a. This is the Middle Cornish verb **aswon** 'to know'.

The commonest and least unambiguous word in Cornish for 'to understand' is the English borrowing **ùnderstondya**, **ùnderstandya**, which is attested 32 times in TH and SA. The noun **ùnderstondyng**, **ùnderstondyng** occurs 23 times in TH and SA.

The word **comprehendya** is attested once, i.e. in CW, where it means 'to comprehend' in the sense 'embrace, encompass.'

35A.3 'TO TASTE'

The default word for 'to taste' in revived Cornish has always been
*blasa. This word is wholly unattested, however, having been devised by
Nance on the basis of Welsh *blasu* 'to taste' and Breton *blazañ* 'to taste'. The
noun **blas** occurs in the phrase ***ow flerye gans blas*** 'stinking with a tang'
PC 2160. The same root is seen in the adjective ***dyflas*** 'shameful' PC 2604,
and in the verb **dyvlasa** (*dyflase*) 'to disgust' PC 901.

The ordinary word for 'to taste' in traditional Cornish is **tâstya**, which
attested no fewer than 15 times. A speaker desiring to be authentic, will
naturally prefer the attested word **tâstya** to the unattested ***blasa**.

35A.4 'TO FEEL' AND 'TO SMELL'

The ordinary word for 'to feel' something is **clôwes**, for example, in **me
a glôwas an tan ow nessa dhybm** 'I felt the fire coming closer to me'.
Clôwes can also mean 'to smell' a smell, e.g. **me a glôwas sawour poos
i'n rannjy** 'I smelt a fetid odour in the flat'.

If one wants to talk about feeling something, for example, with the hands,
the verb **tava** (3rd singular present-future **tava**) can be used, e.g. **me a
davas an fos gans ow dewla erna gefys an sqwychel** 'I felt the wall
with my hands until I found the switch'.

When 'feel' refers to the feeling experienced by someone, the verb is
omglôwes, e.g. **fatell omglôwowgh lebmyn?** 'how are you feeling
now?'

35A.5 'SENSE' AND 'MEANING'

When the word 'sense' is used as a synonym for 'meaning', Tregear uses
the English borrowing **mênyng** 'meaning'. Another word is ***styr**, plural
*styryow, which though not actually attested, can be extracted from the
attested verb **styrya** 'to mean'. For the noun 'sense' Tregear also uses the
word **sens**. This has no attested plural, but ***sencys** can be assumed.

It is also possible to recast 'sense' as a verbal phrase; for example, instead
of 'I do not understand the sense of that statement', one could translate **Ny
worama convedhes pandr'usy an lavar-na ow styrya** 'I can't
understand what that remark means'. The verb **mênya** 'to mean' is also
found, for exeample in TH and John Tonkin. Another verb used both by
Tregear and SA is **sygnyfia** 'to signify, to mean'.

The word 'sense' is often used for one of the five senses, sight, hearing,
touch, taste and smell. It appears that there are no examples of this meaning
of 'sense' in traditional Cornish. Nance recommended **skians gweles**,

skians clôwes, etc. It might be just as well to say an **sens a weles**, **an sens a glôwes**, **an sens a dâstya**, etc.

35A.6 'REJOICE' AND 'TO ENJOY'

The word **lowenhe** in Cornish means both 'to gladden' and 'to be glad'. One can thus say **ny a lowenhas pàn wrussyn ny clôwes hedna** 'we rejoiced when we heard that' and **an nowodhow dâ-na a'gan lowenhas** 'that good news made us happy'. There is no attested verb ***omlowenhe**, which seems to have been devised by Nance. The word **rejoycya** is also well attested in the texts.

For 'to enjoy oneself' Nance recommended ***omlowenhe** 'to be joyful, to rejoice'. Since the word is not attested, it is best avoided. If one wants to say, for example, 'I am really enjoying the music', one could say **Meur a blesour dhybm yw an mûsyk** or **Yma an mûsyk worth ow flêsya yn frâs**. For 'I enjoyed myself last night' one might say **Ass o plêsont an nos newher** or **Me a gafas meur a blêsour i'n nos newher**. It would also be possible to use the verb **enjoya**, which is well attested in the texts.

35A.7 'STATE'

The earliest word for 'state, condition' in the texts is **studh**, which is found twice: The word **plît** 'plight, condition' also occurs in Middle Cornish from an early date. **Plît** and **stât** 'state, condition' later replace **studh** completely'. **Stât** also refers to a political state and an inherited estate. The verb **stâtya** means 'to convey land/real estate'. Since **plît** and **stât** are commoner than **studh**, there is no reason not to use them.

35B EXAMPLES FROM THE TEXTS

35B.1.1 *yn le mayth en yn trevow yn splan me as derevas* 'where I was in the towns I declared them openly' PA 9c; *scrifys yw yn leas le* 'it is written in many places' PA 22b; *En be3ow yn lower le apert a ve egerys* 'The graves in many placees were opened' PA 210a; *sevys gallas 3e gen le* 'he has arisen; he has gone to another place' PA 255c; *Arluth the voth my a wra del degoth thy'm yn pup le* 'Lord, thy will I will do, as is fitting for me everywhere' OM 640-41; *hy re gafes dyhogel dor dyseghys yn nep le* 'she indeed has found dry land somewhere' OM 1143-44; *worth an post yn le may ma y gelmy fast why a wra* 'you shall tie him fast to the post where he is' PC 2058-59; *ef a vyth sur anclethys yn le na fue den bythqueth* 'he will be buried surely in a place where no one has ever been' PC 3134-35; *Ef re thonvanas kyrwas in le ohan thu'm gweras* 'He has send stags instead of oxen to assist me' BK 832-33; *Hader vo bys in e le, in dan an houl ny 'fyth par* 'While the earth is in its place, you will have no peer under the sun' BK 1528-29

35B.1.2 *An ioul a trylyas sperys hag eth ȝy tyller tythy* 'The Devil changed
his intention and went to his native place' PA 18; *Pan doȝyans bys yn tyller*
mayȝ ese crist ow pesy lowene ȝys a vester yn meth Iudas an brathky
'When they had come to the place where Christ was praying, "Joy to thee, O
master," said Judas, the cur' PA 65ab; *saw pedyr crist a holyas abell avel*
vn ownek ȝe dyller an prins annas 'But Peter followed Crist at a distance
like one afraid to the dwelling place of prince Annas' PA 77bc; *ke war pynakyl*
a'n temple hagh ena gura ysethe nynsyw thy's tyller pur es 'Go up on
the pinnacle of the temple and there sit; it is not a very comfortable place for you'
PA 83-85; *kyns yn vn teller yn beys dev kendoner yth ege* 'once in a place
in the world there were two debtors' PC 501-02; *ihesu arluth cuff colyn the*
teller da rum gedya 'may Jesus, beloved Lord, guide me to a good spot' BM
628-29; *chapel guthel me a vyn rag gorthya maria wyn kynth yv teller*
guyls ha yne 'I will build a chapel to honour Mary the Virgin though the place
is bleak and narrow' BM 1143-45; *Rag ny ren ny redya in teller vith in*
scripture 'For we do not read in any other place in scripture' TH 2; *markyow*
pan dresy S austin in kythsam tellar ma ow scriffa 'Notice what St
Augustine writes in the very same place' TH 32a; *yth ew scriffys fatell rug*
agan Savyour, wosa y resurreccion, apperia in mor in tyllar gylwys
Tiberias 'it is written that our Saviour, after his resurrection, appeared in the
sea in a place called Tiberias' TH 42a; *ema tillar arall e mes Cucell a Nice*
'there is another passage from the Council of Nicea' SA 65a; *te a yl ou dogluthy*
ha the gavow dyskuthy, pan vynhy, in tellar clos 'you can sit me down
and disclose your sorrows to me in a private spot whenever you want' BK 2975-
77; *rag meth dean ny alemma tha gutha in tellar close* 'for shame let us
go hence to hide in a secluded place' CW 865-66; *En termen ez passiez ɤera*
triȝaz en St. Levan dên ha bennen en tellar kreiez Tshei an hɤr 'Once
upon a time there lived in St Levan a man and a woman in a place called the
House of the Ram' JCH §1; *ema stella teggo warnotha hep garra thotha*
telhar veeth 'it is still pressing against it without allowing it any place at all'
NBoson; *clappies mar da vel en telhar weth* 'spoken as well as in any place'
NBoson; *Gwrens an dour dadn an neue bos kontles var bar do idn tellar*
'Let the water under the heaven be gathered into one place' JBoson; *yn lyffrow*
del yw scrifys ȝen neȝyn gwyls rag nyeȝy tellyryow esa paris 'as is
written in the scriputres there were places ready for the wild birds to make their
nests' PA 206bc; *dre an kythsam tellyrryow ma an scriptur* 'by the very
same places in scripture' TH 33; *an egglos, not in telythyow erell* 'the
church, not in other places' TH 36a.

35B.1.3 *gvlan ef re gollas an plas a'm lef thyghyow* 'he has quite lost the
place on my right hand' OM 420-21; *ro thy'mmo grath a thos the'th plath*
gans the eleth 'give me grace to come to your place' PC 291-92; *Omma me*
re fundyas plas ryb maria a cambron 'Here I have founded a place beside
St Mary of Camborne' BM 990-01; *nyns ugy ow kemeras place (vel effect)*
in oll an bys 'it is not taking place (or effect) in all the world' TH 16a; *The Jesu*
gorthyans ha gras, eth esaf ynhe tho'm plas ys del desefsan ow bos

'To Jesus be glory and grace, I am closer to my place than I would have thought I was' BK 28-30; *ha pan deffasta than plas ty a gyef in yet vdn eall a ro gorthib theis in case* 'and when you come to the place, you will find at the gate an angel who will give you an answer in the matter' CW 1752.

35B.2.1 *me ne vethaf confethes om bos ynaff fallsurye* 'I shall not be found out, that there is falsehood in me' CW 532-33; *sera ny won convethas ages dewan in neb for* 'sir, I cannot understand your grief in any way' CW 1232-33; *me ny allaf convethas y bosta ge ow hendas* 'I cannot understand that you are my grandfather' CW 1609-10; *gans dean pen vo convethys worthaf ve sertan ny dale bos mellyes a vs neb tra* 'when it is understood by somebody that I should not be meddled with above anything' CW 1618-20; *henna yth ew convethys der an discans es thymma reis* 'that is understood by the teaching which has been imparted to me' CW 2153-54; *an howle han loor kekeffrys oll warbarth ew confethys* 'the sun and the moon also altogether have been understood' CW 2159-60; *Der taklow minniz ew brez teez gonvethes* 'Through small things is the mind of people understood' Pryce.

35B.2.2 *Ema Arthur devethys ha ny gansa canfethys* 'Arthur has come and we have been perceived by him' BK 2794-95; *Rag kueth, pan i'n canfethis, me re jangyas ow holor* 'For grief, when I heard it, I changed my colour' BK 3129-30.

35B.2.3 *why ara vnderstondia fatell vs the charite ii office, han neill ew contrary thy gela* 'you will understand that charity has two functions, and the one is contrary to the other' TH 24a; *pan rug an arluth Dew e rebukya, whath na ruk Judas e vnderstandya* 'when the Lord God rebuked him, still Judas did not understand him' SA 65a.

35B.2.4 *Rag lymmyn athewethas pub den sempill heb understonding na skyans a re supposia fatell yllens y bos iudges in maters a contrauercite* 'For now recently every simple person without understanding or knowledge supposed that they could be judges in matters of dispute' TH 37; *Mar tewhy demandea, praga a ruke an egglos dewys mar galys vnderstandyng an keth artickell ma* 'If you ask why did the church chose such a difficult understanding of this article' SA 64.

35B.2.5 *try yth on in vn substance comprehendys in vdn dew* 'we are three in one substance comprehended in one God' CW 10-1.

35B.3 *honna yw ol the vlamye a dorras an avel tek hag a'n dug thy'm the dastye* 'that woman is entirely to blame, who picked the fair apple and brought it to me to taste' OM 266-68; *pan russys thotho dybry ha tastye frut a'n wethen* 'when you gave him to eat and caused him to taste the fruit of the tree' OM 283-85; *ow tastya, ow gwellas, ow predery, gans oll an circumstans anetha fatell ruga pell contynewa ynna* 'tasting, seeing, considering with all the circumstance of them, how long he continued in them' TH 8a; *Judas a ruk tastia corf an arluth* 'Judas tasted the body of the Lord' SA 65a; *ef a tastyas kigg an arluth Dew* 'he tasted the flesh of the Lord God' SA 65a; *mar pyth y frute hy tastys te a vyth dampnys ractha* 'if its fruit be tasted you will be condemned for it' CW 377-78; *me a levar thys eva mar gwreth tastya an frute ma* 'I tell you, Eve, if you taste this fruit' CW 618-19; *dew a ornas contrary na thefan tastya henna* 'God ordained on the other hand that we should not taste that' CW 630-31; *genas a pe va tastys maga fure te a vea yn pub poynt sure avella* 'were you to taste it you would be as wise indeed in every particular as He' CW 641-42; *ny allaf ra pell perthy pan vo reys tastya anothy* 'I cannot forbear too long, since it is necessary to taste of it' CW 690-91; *ha by god nynges ʒym dowte tha dastya an keth avall* 'and by God, I have no fear to taste that same apple' CW 705-06; *mar gwreth tastya anotha eve a drayle theʒo tha leas* 'if you do taste of it, it will turn to your advantage' CW 739-40; *mar gwrean tastya an frut na avell dew ny a vea* 'if we tasted of that fruit, we would be like God' CW 781-82; *tast gy part an avallow po ow harenga ty a gyll* 'do you taste part of the apples or you will lose my love' CW 831-32; *hy a dorras an avall teake hag an dros thym tha dastya* 'she picked a fair apple and brought it to me to taste' CW 879-880; *mernans ny wressans tastya mes in pleasure venarye y a wressa prest bewa* 'they would taste death but would live forever in pleasure' CW 995-97; *a vs kyek an bestas na na a veast na lodn in beyse ny wressan bythqwath tastya* 'beyond flesh of those animals or of any bullock in the word we have never tasted' CW 1470-42; *lymbo ew ornys thotha da ragtha ef ha[y] gowetha ny dastyans an payne bras* 'Limbo has been ordained for him ; good for him and his companions—they will not taste the great torment' CW 2061-63.

35B.4.1 *pan clewfyf vy an tan tyn parhap y wrussen fye* 'when I feel the fire, perhaps I should flee' OM 1351-52; *rag ny glewsyug yn nep plas sawor an par ma bythqueth* 'for you have not smelt in any place ever a fragrance of this kind OM 1990-91; *rag ru'm fay rak ewen anwous ny glewaf yender thu'm trovs* 'for upon my word for sheer chill I cannot feel coldness in my foot' PC 1222-23.

35B.4.2 *kynth usons ovth omwul creff me a dava age grueff* 'though they are pretending to be strong, I shall touch their faces' BM 2366-67; *gorta gas vy the dava drefan gwelas mar nebas* 'wait, let me feel you, because I see so little' CW 1591-92

35B.4.3 *sevugh inban a tus vays fetel omglowugh omma* 'arise, good people; how do you feel here?' BM 708-09.

35B.5.1 *kynsa the wothfes fatell res thyn scripture bos vnderstondyys warlerth an generall menyng a egglos crist* 'first to know how we must understand scripture according to the general meaning of the church of Christ' TH 18; *Ran an aweylors, onyn po arell, a rug y egery plenly an very menyng anotha* 'One of the evangelists, one or another, explained it very clearly, the very meaning of it' TH 53; *An menyng an gyrryow ma ew kemerys in lyas forth* 'The meaning of these words are taken in many ways' TH 53

35B.5.2 *Dre reson y bos an egglos an cyta vgy agan savyour ena ow menya* 'Because the church is the city that our Saviour means there' TH 17a;

Dre henna yth esa ow meynya pub ordyr da keffrys yn egglos ha yn commonwelth 'By that I mean all good order both in the church and in the commonwealth' TH 40a; *Materen Frink, thera vi a menia* 'The king of France, I mean' JTonkin.

35B.5.3 *hemma ew the styrrya, I wysce ath face te a thebbyr the vara* 'this means: in the sweat of your brow you shall eat your bread' TH 6; *hemma ew the styrrya, neb a rug benega, han rena neb ew benegys, yth ens oll onyn* 'that means: he who blessed an those who are blessed, they are all one' TH 13.

35B.5.4 *fatell ma gwryoneth ha justice in kysam text ma ow signifia pub kynde oll a virtu ha daddar* 'that truth and justice in this same text means all manner of virtue and goodness' TH 26a; *eff a rug signifya pan kynde a virnans a re eff suffra* 'he signified what kind of death he should suffer' TH 53a; *rag malla ef signifia brossa mater* 'so that he might mean a greater matter' SA 65.

35B.5.5 *hag yth esans ow pewa warlerth an letterall sens a la moyses* 'and they lived according to the literal sense of the law of Moses' TH 26a; *du a ros power hag auctorite then catholik egglos the gafas an lell sens han vnderstonding an scriptur* 'God gave power and authority to the Catholic Church to obtain the true sense and understanding of scripture' TH 36; *an egglos an jevas an lell sens an scriptur* 'the church has the true sense of scripture' TH 36 (margin).

35B.6.1 *a arluth yth of lowen ty the vynnes dos gynen omma th'agan lowenhe* 'Lord, I am joyful that you wished to come among us here to gladdedn us' RD 1165-67; *lauar thy'm mara kyllyth yn nep poynt ov lowenhe* 'tell me whether you can in any point gladden me' RD 1689-90; *Innan agan honyn, ny yllyn ny lowenhe, rag ahanan agan honyn nyg on mas peghadorryan* 'In ourselves we cannot rejoice, for of ourselves we are only sinners' TH 10a; *Ny lowenhaf in ow dythyow neffra lam* 'Never in my days will I rejoice at all' BK 2930-31.

35B.6.2 *ha gans perfect colonow the reiosya in sight agan creator ha redemar* 'and with perfect hearts to rejoice in the sight of our Creator and Redeemer' TH 1; *te neb vgy ow reiosya in la, dre transgression an la yth esas ow dyhonora du* 'you who rejoice in the law, by disobeying the law, you dishonour God' TH 14a; *yma ow reiossya in mer y Epistlis, warbyn y yskerens ha yskerens a onyn vith an epscobow* 'he rejoices in many of his epistles against his enemies and the enemies of any of the bishops' TH 50a; *rag henna woʒa hemma nefra ny wren rejoycya* 'therefore henceforth we will never rejoice' CW 1271-72; *ny gemeras yddrag vyth mes y regoyssyas pur vear* 'he was not contrite, but he rejoiced greatly' CW 2048-49.

35B.6.3 *myns a vynna inioya an meritys ay pascion* 'as many as wish to enjoy the merits of his passion' TH 12a; *ny rowng enioya gwlas neff* 'they shall not enjoy the kingdom of heaven' TH 16a; *rag enioya an myrnans han pascion a crist, an kythsam ii poynt ma ew the vos requyrys in agan*

251

part ny 'to get the benefit of the death and passion of Christ these very same two points are required' TH 16a.

35B.6.4 *me yv myghtern re wruk cas ol rag dry adam ha'y has a tebel stuth* 'I am a king who battled entirely to bring Adam and his seed from an evil predicament' RD 2516-18; *ha fattel duthys yn ban dre the gallos the honan ha war the corf mar drok stuth* 'and how did you come up by your own power and your body in such an evil state' RD 2568-70.

35B.6.5 *kyns ol pan pleyt y me fe* 'first of all in what condition is he?' RD 2053; *pahan pleyt yma pilat yn le may ma* 'what condition is Pilate in where he finds himself' RD 2058-59; *ellas claf yv ow colon the vos yn plyt a par-na* 'alas, my heart is sick that you should be in a condition of that kind' RD 2637-38; *tru gony doys then pletma* 'woe that we have come to this state' BM 610

35B.6.6 *Der y peth grueys den ryel ha gorys then stat vhel* 'By his riches made a nobleman and brought to the high estate' BM 436-37; *So in mer ver dell ew an stat na kyllys, ha mabden dre an koll a henna cothes in extreme miseri* 'But inasmuch as that state has been lost, and manking by the loss of it fallen into extreme misery' TH 3; *I a gollas an originall innocency stat a vongy in aga creasion* 'They lost the original innocence, a state they possessed at their creation' TH 4; *han gothfas a vab du, then stat a den perfect, warlyrth an measure an lene oys a crist* 'and the knowledge of the Son of God, to the condition of a perfect man, according to the measure of the complete age of Christ' TH 42; *Ow stat o del vynnas Christ* 'My condition was as Christ wished' BK 593; *Eugh, myr py stat ema Ke* 'Gos, see in what condition Ke is' BK 886; *ny vannaf orth eale na moy dos thom stat ma menas me* 'I don't want any angel to come to my condition other than me' CW 134-35; *yth oma pur dewhanhees ortha welas in state ma* 'I am very grieved to see you in this state' CW 1225-26.

35B.6.7 *Mar peth stat the den arel grueys annotho dyogel ov liche wek me yv plesijs* 'If it is made the estate of some other man indeed, my dear liege, I am pleased' BM 422-24; *rag an trubut a wovyn na goyth nahen war nebas ous the'n stat a Rome, mars e ben ef dybynnys* 'for the tribute he demands, nothing else is owing to the state of Rome apart from his severed head' BK 2113-17; *the days ha me ny a yl statya an tyr dyogeyl mar mynen the den areyl* 'your father and I, we can bequeathe the land indeed if we wish to someone else' BM 412-415.

35C.1 VOCABULARY

anfusyk *m.*, **anfusygyon**
unfortunate person

aqwytya to repay, to settle, to pay
for

banknôta *m.*, **banknôtys**
banknote

bosty *m.*, **bostiow** cafe, restaurant

costya to cost

câss lytherow *m.*, pocket-book,
wallet

dalhen *m.* grip, grasp; **settya**
dalhen in to seize

dhesempys *adv.* immediately
drog-oberor *m.*, **drog-oberoryon** criminal
dyscudha to discover, to find out
gorlenwel to fill up, to fill to overflowing
gwesty *m.*, **gwestion** guest (in restaurant or hotel)
gwrydnyans *m.* squeezing, extortion
gyvyans *m.* pardon, forgiveness
hel *adj.* generous
kyttryn *m.*, **kyttrynow** bus
labm *m.* jump, leap; **wàr udn labm** all at once

molethy to curse
omvetya to meet, to converge
perhednak *m.*, **perhenogyon** owner, proprietor
qwarel *m.*, **qwarels** pane of glass
rûth *f.*, **rûthow** crowd
scobmyn *m.*, **scobmow** fragment
servont *m.*, **servysy** servant
shakya to shake
sols *m.* shilling
sorn *m.*, **sornow** corner, cranny
tabm *m.*, **tybmyn** piece, bit
totta *adv.* quickly
whare *adv.* directly, immediately

35C.2 TEXT DHE REDYA
('AN BANKNOTA' IN MES A *NEBES WHEDHLOW BERR*)

Red an devyn usy ow sewya ha scrif gorthebow dhe'n qwestyons

De Sadorn dohajëdh. An strêtys o gorlenwys a dus; hag in cres an dre, le may whre omvetya an kyttrynow, mar vrâs o an rûth na ylly den scant kerdhes. Desempys y feu clôwys son gweder terrys dhe scobmow. I'n rûth, nebonen re bia herdhys warbydn fenester an bosty ha'n qwarel a veu scattys dhe dybmyn. Wàr udn labm y teuth servysy in udn bonya in mes a'n bosty, ha totta y a wrug settya dalhen i'n drog-oberor.

"An qwarel a gòst sur hanter-cans sols," yn medh perhednak an chy. An den a worthebys, cortes ha vaner: "Agas gyvyans a besaf, syra, bytegyns nyns oma vy dhe vlâmya, na ny'm beus kebmys mona warnaf."

"Pob a yll leverel indella: whelowgh in y bockettys ev," veu cùssul onen a'n rûth.

Sevel ortans ny ylly an anfusyk, ha res veu plegya. An servysy a wrug scon tedna y gâss lytherow in mes a'y bocket, hag ot! ino nyns esa tra vëth saw carten, warnedhy y hanow ha'y drigva.

"Rewgh an câss dhybmo vy," a grias perhednak an bosty, "Yth esoma ow convedhes taclow a'n par-na: pùbonen a'n jeves y sorn cudhys." Hag in gwir, ev a dednas a'n sorn whare udn banknôta hanter-cans puns. Gwir yw y vos nebes ûsys, mès nyns o dhe weth awos hedna.

An den a besys na wrellens y kemeres an nôta dhyworto, hag ev orth y dhon mar bell. Mès perhednak an bosty o bodhar dhe bùb pejadow, hag ev a ros dhodho pymp puns ha dew ugans, ow qwitha ragtho y honen an nôta hanter-cans puns.

"Pymp puns rag qwarel a'n par-na?" a grias an den, dhodho sorr brâs. "Hanter-cans sols a alsa y aqwytya yn tâ. Hebma nyns yw mès gwrydnyans pur!" hag yth esa an westion erel a'n keth tybyans-na.

Mès sconya a wrug an perhednak, ow leverel gweder dhe vos hedhyw fèst yn ker, hag inwedh y cotha tylly nebes dhodho ev rag oll an ancombrynsy a wodhevys. Bytegyns, rag omwil den hel, ev a worras deg sols aral dhe'n pymp puns ha dew ugans; ha'n den êth dhe ves in udn volethy.

Udn den coth, neb o esedhys i'n bosty, a besys cubmyas a weles an banknôta hanter-cans puns.

Ev a wrug y whythra a bùb tenewen, orth y sensy warbydn an golow, hag ena yn medh ev, ow shakya y bedn: "An nôta-ma yw fâls."

Pùbonen a wharthas yn lowen saw unsel perhednak an bosty, hag y ow tyby heb mar ev dhe gafos an pëth a dhendylas.

1 Fatla veu an gweder terrys?
2 Pandra wharva i'n tor-na?
3 Pygebmys o valew an fenester warlergh an perhednak?
4 Pandra veu kefys in pocket an anfusyk?
5 Prag y feu an "drog-oberor" mar serrys?
6 Pandra veu dyscudhys pàn êth an "drog-oberor" in kerdh?
7 Pandr'o tybyans an rûth adro dhe hedna?

WHÊTEGVES DYSCANS WARN UGANS
THIRTY-SIXTH LESSON

36A.1 'TOWARDS', 'UNTIL', AND 'TO'

'Towards' in Cornish is rendered by **wor' tu ha**(g), e.g. **me a gerdhas wor' tu ha'n gorsaf** 'I walked towards the station'. **Wor' tu ha**(g) also appears as **tro ha**(g), e.g. **ev a veras tro ha'n daras** 'he looked towards the door'.

When 'until' is a conjunction, it is translated into Cornish by **erna²**(g) followed by the subjunctive or by **bys may⁵**(th) followed by the subjunctive. Thus one says **me a vydn gortos erna dheffa hy** 'I shall wait until she comes' or **me a vydn gortos bys may teffa hy**.

When 'until' is a preposition, it is translated by **bys**, which lenites the initial of the following word, e.g. **bys an present dëdh-ma** 'until this present day', **bys venary** 'forever' (literally 'until always'), **bys vycken** 'forever' (literally 'until always').

The default word for 'to' is of course **dhe²**, but when the sense implies motion towards, **bys in, bys dhe²** are often used. It is important, however, to notice the strict difference in usage between the two. **Bys in** is used with nouns and proper names, e.g. **ny êth bys i'n penvêster** 'we went to the headmaster', **yma an train-ma ow mos bys in Penzans** 'this train goes to Penzance'. **Bys dhe²** on the other hand is used exclusively with personal pronouns: **an flogh a bonyas bys dhyn** 'the child ran to us', **pàn dheuth an venyn bys dhodho** 'when the woman came to him'. It is quite wrong to say **ny oll êth bys *dhe Drûrû** 'we all went to Truro.' In 1966 a memorial was erected in St Keverne by Mebyon Kernow to Michael Joseph and Thomas Flamank, the leaders of the 1497 uprising. The Cornish inscription reads: *Dhe gof Myghal Josep An Gof ha Thomas Flamank Hembrynkysy an Lu Kernewek a geskerdhas bys *dhe Loundres ha godhevel ena dyalans…* 'To the memory of Michael Joseph, the Smith, and Thomas Flamank, leaders of the Cornish army, which marched to London, and who there suffered punishment…' The phrase *bys *dhe Loundres* should have been *bys yn Loundres*.

36A.2 'AT'

Revivalists have long been taught that 'at' in such expression 'at Bodmin', 'at Rome', etc. should be rendered in Cornish by **dhe²**. It is difficult to see where this notion originated, since in traditional Cornish **dhe²** is never used with geographical names with this sense. 'At Rome', 'at London', etc. are always expressed by use of the preposition **in**, not **dhe²**, i.e. **in Rom**, **in Loundres**, etc. If one wants to say, for example, 'the Gorseth this year was held at Liskeard' and when the ceremony did not take place in the town but just outside, one would say **y feu an Orseth hevleny sensys ryb Lÿs Kerwys**, i.e. 'the Gorseth was held this year beside Liskeard'.

36A.3 'TO LIVE' AND 'TO DWELL'

'To live' in Cornish, when it means, 'to be alive' is **bewa**. When the sense is 'to live somewhere, to dwell', the expression used is **bos tregys**. So 'I live in Bodmin but I work in St Austell' in Cornish would be **Yth oma tregys in Bosvena, saw yth esoma ow lavurya in Austol**.

Revivalists, however, have long been taught that 'I live in Bodmin', for example, is **Me a drig in Bosvena**. This is an error as can be seen from numerous examples in traditional Cornish. **Me a drig** does not mean 'I live, I dwell', but 'I shall stay, I shall remain'.

36A.4 'WELCOME'

It is quite common outside Cornish towns to see a notice saying **X a'gas dyn(n)argh**, 'X greets you' where X stands for the name of the town in question. This translates the English 'Welcome to X'.

There are a number of points to be noticed here. In the first place the verb **dynerhy** is not used of greeting someone to one's own place, but greeting him in his own. In the second place the third singular present-future is not attested in Late Cornish and is thus never found with pre-occlusion. The corresponding noun 'greeting, salutation' is now found twice in BK with *e* in the second syllable, rather than *a*. It might therefore be sensible to spell the word **dynergh** 'greets' with a single **n**, in order to avoid unwarranted pre-occlusion. The verb **dynerhy** is attested six times altogether and the noun **dynergh** twice.

The verb **wolcùmma, wolcùbma** 'to welcome' is attested four times but the adjective **wolcùm** (*wolcum, wolcom, welcom, welcum*) 'welcome' is attested 70 times. The traditional Cornish for 'Welcome to X' would be **Wolcùm owgh why in X**. If revivalists believe that such an expression is insufficiently Cornish, **X a'gas dynergh** is the alternation.

36A.5 'RIVER' AND 'VALLEY'

Nance in his English-Cornish dictionary for 'river' gives **avon** *f.*, **avenow**. **Avon** (*auon*) is found only in OCV where it glosses the Latin *flumen* 'river', and *fluvius* 'river'. Lhuyd gives *auan* for 'river' on several occasions and **Awen-Tregare** is attested in the seventeenth century as the name of Tregare Water. Otherwise the word is unknown. In geographical names 'River' is usually rendered by **Dowr**. In the Middle Cornish texts, moreover, the word for 'river' is **ryver**, plural **ryvers**.

The word **nans** 'valley', plural **nansow**, is well attested in place-names. It occurs only once in the Cornish texts, however, in the plural form *nanssow*. Other words or 'valley' that are as well or better attested in the literature include **tnow**, plural **tenwyn**, and the English borrowing **valy**.

36A.6 'COUNTRY' AND 'KINGDOM'

The Welsh national anthem *Hen Wlad fy Nhadau* has been translated into Cornish as **Bro Goth agan Tasow**. **Bro** for 'country' is very rare indeed, being attested only once and in the earliest long text, namely PA. The default word for 'country' in Cornish is **pow**, plural **powyow**. Another common word is **gwlas** *f.*, **gwlasow**, which tends to mean 'country' in the sense of 'area ruled, jurisdiction'.

To translate 'United Kingdom' some revivalists use the expression **Ruwvaneth Unys**. It should be pointed out, however, that the word **ruwvaneth is unattested as such, being a respelling of Old Cornish *ruifanaid* 'regnum, kingdom', seen also in OCV in *guailen ruifanaid* 'sceptrum, rod of kingship, sceptre.' The ordinary word for 'kingdom' in Middle and Late Cornish is **gwlascor** *f.*, *plural* **gwlascorow**. 'United Kingdom' in Cornish is best translated **Gwlascor Unys**.

36A.7 'ENGLAND' AND 'WALES'

In his English-Cornish dictionary (1952) under 'England' Nance suggests **Pow Saws, Pow an Sawson* and **Bro Saws*. *Saws* and *Sawson* are spelt **Sows** and **Sowson** respectively in the orthography used in this book. Neither **Pow Sows* nor **Bro Sows* is found anywhere in traditional Cornish. Of Nance's three suggestions only **Pow an Sowson** is actually attested.

The best attested word for 'England' is not perhaps likely to find favour with revivalists: John Tregear refers to 'England' as **Inglond** three times.

In his 1952 dictionary under 'Wales' Nance gives *Kembry f.*, presumably by analogy with Welsh *Cymru*. Nance was certainly aware that Lhuyd used **Kembra**, **Kimbra**, with a final **a** rather than **y**, though he preferred to write ***Kembry***, presumably on the grounds that ***Kembry*** was the original Middle Cornish form. **Kembra** has now appeared independently twice in BK and was clearly in use in the Middle Cornish period. Revivalists would be well to replace Nance's *Kembry* with the only attested form **Kembra**.

36A.8 'SCOTLAND' AND 'IRELAND'

Since the beginning of the revival the word for 'Scotland' has been **Alban**. This is not attested in the traditional writers, though Lhuyd uses **Alban** once. Lhuyd also, however, uses the expression **Skot-Vrethonek** for 'Scottish British, Scottish Gaelic' once. It is now apparent, however, that in traditional Cornish the ordinary word for 'Scotland' was **Scotland**, **Scotlond** which has now come to light three times in BK. **Scotlond** should perhaps replace **Alban** for general use.

Nance in his 1938 dictionary gives **Ywerdhon* for 'Ireland', which in the orthography used in this book would appear as ***Iwerdhon***. With ***Iwerdhon*** compare Welsh *Iwerddon* and Breton *Iwerzon*. It should, however, be pointed out that ***Iwerdhon*** is not attested. The Cornish name for Ireland is attested twice (see the examples at 36B.8) and in both cases the initial syllable is lost. Moreover the stressed vowel is written **o** rather than **e**. The revived Cornish for 'Ireland' should perhaps be **Wordhen** *f.* rather than ***Iwerdhon***.

36A.9 'FRANCE' AND 'GERMANY'

For 'France' Nance gives **Frynk**. One sometimes, however, sees the unattested ***Pow Frynk*** used as well. The attested forms are *Frynk*, *Frenk*, *Vrink*, and it is this form which should perhaps always be used in the revived language.

Germany is called *Almayn* once in RD. Thereafter the common name for the country is **Jermany** (spelt *Germany*), which may well have been stressed on the second syllable. Revivalists can therefore use either **Almayn** or **Jermany** in their speech and writing.

36A.10 'ROMANS' AND 'SAXONS'

In his 1951 dictionary for 'Roman' Nance gives *Roman*, and he suggests that the plural should be **Romanas*. In fact the plural is attested in three separate texts and it is always **Romans**. **Romans** should therefore be the default plural in the revived language.

Similarly the word Saxon has an attested plural **Saxons** (*Saxens*) in two texts. This should be the plural in the revived language also.

In *Testament Noweth* of 2002 plurals like **Corynthyanas*, **Efesyanas*, **Galacyanas* were used. In the light of **Romans**, **Saxons** and further forms in TH, such forms should perhaps be replaced by names ending in **-ans**.

36B EXAMPLES FROM THE TEXTS

36B.1.1 *war tu hay vam a'n pewo y ben a vynnas synsy* 'towards his mother to whom he belonged he wished to hold his head' PA 207c; *War tua Frynk fystynnyn* 'Let us hasten to France' BK 2735; *Stop an wethen trogha'n dor* 'Bend the tree towards the ground' OM 201; *Cherubyn kemmer clethe fystyn trogha parathys* 'Cherub, take a sword, make haste to paradise' OM 331-32; *Adam ke yn mes a'n wlas troha ken pow the vewe* 'Adam depart from the land towards another country to live' OM 343-44; *kumyas pesa rag moys lema troha ham pov* 'I beg permission to go hence towards my country' BM 2778-80; *fystenowgh tro han daras rag omma ny wrewgh trega* 'hasten to the door, for here you shall not stay' CW 980-81.

36B.1.2 *na nefre ny debre boys erna govsen orth y ganov* 'nor shall I ever eat food until I speak to him face to face' BM 3984-85 *The'n myrnans ernag elha, e yskar ny the thu'm chy* 'Until he dies, his enemy will not come to my house' BK 2402-03; *Canhas, guarn an anprevion na vyth hueth war ow holan erna vons e dyskevrys* 'Messenger, warn the miscreants that there will be no joy in my heart until they are unmasked' BK 3158-60.

36B.1.3 *yn bys ma rak dry ascor ty a vew bys may fy loys* 'in this word to produce offspring you shall live until you are old' OM 71-72; *ty a wra y worre scon a thesempys yn pryson an casadow bys may hallo bos iuggys* 'you shall put him immediately in prison forthwith, the wretch, until he can be judged' RD 1977-80; *the wull an obereth a mynystra rag edyfya an corfe a crist, bys may teffan ny oll ha dos warbarth in vn vnyte a crisgians ha feith* 'to do the works of ministering to build up the body of Christ until we all come together in a unity of belief and faith' TH 42.

36B.1.4 *reys yv thy's mones ytho bys yn egip the pharo* 'you must go therefore to Egypt to Pharaoh; OM 1421-22; *gabryel fystyn whare bys yn ierusalem ke* OM 1927-28; *scon alemma why a spetd bys yn meneth olyuetd* 'soon hence you will hasten to the Mount of Olives' RD 2397-98; *me agis gyd rum ena pur uskis bys in cambron* 'I will guide you upon my soul quickly to Camborne' BM 981-82; *Ow canhas ker, ke thegy bys in Rom gans pen Lucy* 'My dear messenger, go you to Rome with the head of Lucius' BK 2838-39.

36B.1.5 *na ve bos fals an denma nyn drossen ny bys deso* 'had this man not been false, we shouldn't have brought him to you' PA 99b; *mar mynnyth cafus mowes my a'd wor scon bys thethy* 'if you want to get a girl, I will bring you soon to her' OM 2071-72; *dun bys thotho hep lettye* 'let us go to him without delay' PC 1455; *bys thy's vmma yn vn lam ef a vyth kyrhys* 'to you here all at once he will be fetched' RD 885-86; *Bys dotho me agys led* 'To him I will lead you' BM 2530.

36B.2 *my a wyth an gueel a ras yn ierusalem nefre* 'I will keep the rods of grace at Jerusalem ever' OM 2059-60; *syre me a leuer thy's pur wyr ef a fue genys pur evn y bethlem iudi* 'sir, I will tell you indeed that he was born very truly at Bethlehem in Judea' PC 1605-07; *yma tregys in cambron den ov cul merclys dyson* 'there dwells at Camborne a man working miracles' BM 687-78.

36B.3.1 *War lyrgh mab den ʒe begha reson prag y fe prynnys yw ihesus crist ʒe ordna yn neff y vonas tregys* 'After man had sinned the reason that he was redeemed is that Jesus Christ ordained that he should dwell in heaven' PA 7ab; *py tyller yma moyses ha py cost yma trygys* 'where is Moses and in what region does he dwell' OM 1551-52; *guyn y vys a vo trigys yn the seruys* 'happy is the man who dwells in thy service' RD 122-23; *pan a confort ha commodite ew hemma ragan ny an cristonnyan, the gafus crist tregys innan ny!* 'what a comfort and advantage is this to us Christians to find that Christ dwells in us!' TH 39a; *Yma tregys in Kembra in Urbe Legionum* 'He lives in Wales in the City of Legions' BK 1292-93; *En termen ez passiez ʒera triʒaz en St. Levan; dên ha bennen en tellar kreiez Tshei an hʋr* 'Once upon a time there lived in St Levan a man and a woman in a place called Chy an Hordh' JCH §1.

36B.3.2 *ha nena ny a dryg in du ha gans du, ha du a dryg innan ny* 'then we shall dwell in God, and God will dwell in us' TH 30; *rag henna bys venary eve a dryg ena deffry in paynes bras avel ky* 'therefore forever he will remain there indeed in great torment like a dog' CW 2052-53.

36B.4.1 *Then ioul mur neb o tus keth ʒe belat a leueris lowenna gwelha ʒe feth herodes reth tenyrghys* 'Those who were servants of the great devil said to Pilate, "Rejoice, cheer up! Herod has sent you greeting' PA 115ab; *syre pilat lowene thy's genef ythos dynerghys gans cesar an emperour* 'sir Pilate, joy to thee; you are greeted by Caesar the emperor through me' RD 1627-29; *Syr Teuthar a'th tenyrhys* 'Sir Teudar has sent you greetings' BK 908.

36B.4.2 *wolcum fest ough yn chymma* 'you are very welcome in this house' PC 1207; *wolcum ogh omma deffry wy hag ol agis pobell* 'you are welcome here, you and all your people' BM 241-42; *Welcom ogh agan soueran yn keth plassma pur certan* 'Welcome are you, our sovereign, in this same place very surely' BM 246-47; *Welcum o'm gwlas, agys messag mars ew vas* 'Welcome to my kingdom, if your message is good' BK 2010-11.

36B.5.1 *Torneuan an auan* 'a bank of a river' AB: 141a.

36B.5.2 *teuleugh ef yn trok a horn yn dour tyber yn nep corn may fo buthys* 'throw him in a box of iron into the River Tiber in some corner so he may drown' RD 2162-64; *yn dour tyber ef a fue yn geler horn gorrys dovn* 'he was put deep into the River Tiber in a coffin of iron' RD 2319-20; *An duk a'n gevith pur wyer rag e laver ol an tyr a Thowr Hombyr the Scotland*

'The duke will have for his labour all the land from the River Humber to Scotland' BK 3235-37.

36B.5.3 *hag orth an ryuer surly a josselyne chapel guthel me a vyn* 'and by the river indeed of Josselin I shall build a chapel' BM 1141-43; *Neb a crisse ynna ve kepar dell levar an scribis, ryvars a thowre a ra resek in mes anetha y* 'Whoever believe in me, as the scribes say, rivers of water will pour from them' TH 53.

36B.5.4 *In erna ȝen menyȝyow why a ergh warnough coȝe yn ketella an nanssow wy a bys ragas cuthe* 'Then you will command the mountains to fall upon you; similarly you will pray the valleys to hide you' PA 170ab.

36B.5.5 *Me a gergh erba rasaw drys keel, drys gwel, drys prasaw, drys tnow, drys gun, drys mene'* 'I will fetch herb of grace over bower, over field, over meadows, over valley, over moor, over mountain' BK 1159-61; *byth ny falla' ve an fals orth y houlya drys tenuyn ha menythyow* 'never will I fail to follow him, the renegade, across valleys and mountains' BK 2312-14; *An vyghternath par govyn a nug thygo drys tenuyn* 'the kings by request will fly to thee across valleys' BK 2527-28.

36B.5.6 *me a vyn heb falladowe vn dean formya in valy ebron devery* 'I shall without fail form a man in the Valley of Ebron indeed' CW 338-40.

36B.6.1 *Rag henna pylat a ros ȝen vorogyon aga ro may lavarsans hadolos yn pub tyller dris an vro ȝe vos tus yrvys yn nos warneȝe kymmys a dro nag ens y hardh ȝe wortos* 'Therefore Pilate gave the soldiers their pay, that they should say falsely that everywhere throughout the land there were so many armed men about against them that they did not dare remain' PA 250a-d.

36B.6.2 *lemyn ke aspy in ta mars us tyr segh in neb gulas* 'now go, search well if there is dry land in any country' OM 1119-20; *rag ny evaf bys deth fyn genough annotho na moy bys may thyllyf yn ow gulas* 'for I shall not drink of it with you until doomsday until I come into my kingdom' PC 724-36; *an pith ew only vniversall in pub gwlas dyskys ha cresys* 'the thing only that is universally taught and believed in every country' TH 34a; *Ow bannath genas, cosyn! In gulas nef re omgyffyn* 'My blessing to you, cousin! May we find ourselves in the kingdom of heaven' BK 3048-49.

36B.6.3 *ov colon yv claf marthys bos drog an par-ma cothys yn ov glascor yn tor-ma* 'my heart is wondrous sick that evil of this kind should have befallen my kingdom at this moment' OM 1568-70; *yma ov treyle deffry ol an wlascor a iudi* 'he is indeed converting all the kingdom of Judea' PC 1593-94; *ha war an gwlascur cheften nessa ȝen myterne vhell* 'and chieftain over the kingom nearest to the honoured king' BM 3-4; *rag avoydya gwlaskur an teball el* 'to avoid the kingdom of the devil' TH 25; *moy agys Du, me a grys, in e dron in gwlaskor nef* 'more than God, I believe, on his throne in the kingdom of heaven' BK 1650-51; *râg ma Gulasketh Neue tha dorn* 'for the kingdom of heaven is at hand' Rowe; *gwrênz doz thy gulasker* 'thy kingdom come' Pryce.

36B.7.1 *Anglia... Poụ an Zoụzn* 'England' AB: 42c; *lymmyn the drelya the gen pow ny a ynglonde* 'now to turn to our own country of England' TH 50a-51; *in cristoneth nyns es onyn an gevas mar ver cawse the favera an sea han stall a rom dell gevas englond* 'in Christendom there is not a country that has such great cause to favour the see and stall of Rome as England' TH 51; *ha y fe danvenys omma the Englond* 'and was sent here to England' TH 51

36B.7.2 *emesk nei Tîz Kimbra* 'among us, the people of Wales' AB: 222; *ken yụ hedda rêol por ụîr en Kembra* 'though that is regular very truly in Wales' AB: 224; *a Dowl an Jowl in Kembra* 'from the Devil's Drop in Wales' BK 1164; *Yma tregys in Kembra in Urbe Legionum* 'He lives in Wales in the City of the Legions' BK 1292-93.

36B.8.1 *en Ehual-dir an Alban* 'in the Highlands of Scotland' AB: 222.

36B.8.2 *Augel, myghtern in Scotland* 'Augel, king of Scotland' BK 1280; *a Thowr Hombyr the Scotland* 'from the River Humber to Scotland' BK 3237; *Now, myghtern Scotland, Augel* 'Now, Augel, king of Scotland' BK 3284.

36B.8.3 *Ha e tha Worthen eath e whonnen* 'And he went to Ireland himself' JTonkin; *hag en G'laskor Uordhyn* 'and in the kingdom of Ireland' AB: 222.

36B.9.1 *War tua Frynk fystynnyn* 'Let us hasten to France' BK 2735; *ha ugge hedda mose tho Frenk* 'and after that going to France' NBoson; *Nenna e eath car rag Frink* 'Then he went away to France' JTonkin; *Materen Frink, thera vi a menia* 'The king of France, I mean' JTonkin; *Brethonek Pou Lezou en Vrink* 'the British of Brittany in France' AB: 222.

36B.9.2 *yth egen yn cres almayn orth vn prys ly* 'I was in the middle of Germany eating lunch' RD 2147-48; *ran in Germany a levery, omma yma crist* 'some in Germany were saying, "Here is Christ"' TH 32; *Merowgh inweth war germany* 'Look also at Germany' TH 49a; *the whelas myns a geffa a bagans in Germany* 'to seek as many as he can find of pagans in Germany' BK 3231-32.

36B.10.1 *yma S pawle in kynsa chapter thyn romans, ow affirmya playn* 'St Paul in the first chapter to the Romans affirms clearly' TH 14; *Yma S poule indelma ow declaria thyn romans* 'St Paul thus declares to the Romans' TH 25; *An Romans a vyth wystyys* 'The Romans will be ravaged' BK 2136; *Merough ple ma an Romans* 'See where the Romans are' BK 2808; *durt an Romans meskez gen a Brittez* 'from the Romans mixed with the Britons' NBoson.

36B.10.2 *ha vi c. blethan wosa crist an Saxons a ve spredys drys oll an wlas* 'and 600 years after Christ the Saxons were spread through all the land' TH 51; *Me re thanvanas deffry duk an Saxens, Chellery* 'I have sent indeed the duke of the Saxons, Childerich' BK 3229-30.

36B.10.3 *in xi chapter in kynsa pistill then Corinthians* 'in the ninth chapter of the first epistle to the Corinthians' TH 51a; *in iiii-a chapter thyn Ephesians* 'in the third chapter to the Ephesians' TH 41a; *ha S pawle a gylwys an galathians fooles* 'and St Paul called the Galatians fools' TH 9a;

ema Chrisostom ow scryfa than philipians 'St John Chrysostom writes to the Philippians' SA 66.

36C.1 VOCABULARY

badh *m.*, **badhas** boar

bryntyn y gnas of noble nature

cola *(followed by* **orth**) to listen to, to harken to

coscar *coll.* retinue, companions

cowel *m.*, **cowellow** basket, cradle

cùhudhans *m.* accusation

dhe dybmyn to pieces, to bits

empres *f.*, **empresow** empress

emprour *m.*, **emprours** emperor

fèst *adv.* very

fos *f.*, **fosow** wall

gorowra to gild, to cover with gold

gosys *adj.* bloody, covered in blood

guw *m.*, **guyow** spear, lance

gwres *f.* ardour, heat

iniadow *m.* urging, insistence

in ketelma *adv.* in this very way, just like this

joust *m.*, **joustys** joust

jouster *m.*, **jousters** jouster, competitor in a joust

knighyas *m.* whinnying (of horses)

kyny to keen, to lament

lÿs *f.*, **lesyow** court

meppyk *m.*, **meppygow** baby boy

milgy *m.* **milgeun** hound

ogas; **in y ogas** near him

omdowl *m.* wrestling

omwheles to upset, to overturn

perswâdya to persuade

rygol *m.*, **rygolyow** groove

sarf *f.*, **syrf** serpent, snake

scoos *m.*, **scojow** shield, escutcheon

tenewen *m.*, **tenwednow** side

tournay *m.* tourney, medieval tournament

wàr ow fay *interj.* upon my faith, upon my word.

36C.2 TEXT DHE REDYA
'AN KY' IN MES A *WHEDHLOW AN SEYTH DEN FUR A ROM*
Red an dyvyn-ma ha scrif gorthebow dhe'n qwestyons

Yma an Empres ow wheles perswâdya an Emprour dhe worra mab an Emprour dhe'n mernans

"Yth esa kyns in Rom udn marhak, ha'y lÿs orth tenewen fos an cyta. Hag udn jÿdh y feu tournay ha joustys inter an varhogyon. Hag yth êth an arlodhes ha'y hoscar in bàn wàr an fos rag miras an joustys, heb gasa den vëth i'n lÿs saw unsel udn vab an marhak ow cùsca in y gowel, ha'y vilgy a'y wroweth in y ogas.

Hag awos knighyas an vergh, ha gwres an jousters, ha son an guyow owth omweskel warbydn an scosow, gorowrys aga rygolyow, y tyfunas sarf in fos an castel ha mos bys in lÿs an marhak, ha gweles an mab in y gowel, ha slynkya snell bys dhodho. Mès kyns ès hy dhe settya dalhen ino, an milgy scav a labmas warnedhy. Ha gans an omlath ha'n omdowl intredhans, an cowel a veu omwhelys ha'y bedn awoles ha'n meppyk ino. Ha'n ky scav ha lybm, bryntyn y gnas, a ladhas an sarf ha'y gasa sqwerdys dhe dybmyn ryb an cowel.

Ha pàn dheuth an arlodhes ajy hag aspia an ky ha'n cowel gosys, dos warbydn an marhak hy a wrug, in udn arma ha scrija, ow kyny an ky dhe ladha hy udn vab. Ha'n marhak rag ewn sorr a ladhas an ky. Hag awos plegya dh'y wreg, ev a dheuth dhe viras orth an meppyk. Ha pàn dheuth, yth o an meppyk fèst yn tâ in dadn an cowel, ha'n sarf in darnow munys in y ogas.

Ass o drog gans an marhak ladha ky mar dhâ avell hedna, awos lavar hag iniadow y wreg! In ketelma yw wharvos dhyso jy, mar teuta ha ladha dha vab awos cùhudhans hag iniadow dha wreg."

Hag ena an Emprour a dos dos na vedha an mab ledhys an jydh-na.

Ha wosa gorfedna aga cùssulyow ha'ga debâtya, y teuthons dhe'n hel. Ha pàn wodhya an Empres bos gwell gans an Emprour cows ages debry, dallath an cows hy a wrug dre wovyn orto mar peu ledhys an mab.

"Nag yw, wàr ow fay!" yn medh ev.

"Me a wor," yn medh hy, "yth yw tus fur Rom, neb re wrug hedna. Bytegyns y whyrvyth dhyso, mar teuta ha cola ortans, poran kepar dell wharva kyns dhe'n badh gwyls awos an bugel."

"Pandra veu hedna?" yn medh an Emprour.

"Wàr ow fay! ny'n lavaraf marnas te a rollo dha er y fydh ledhys an mab avorow."

"Ledhys ev a vydh, re'm ena!" yn medh ev.

1 Pleth esa trigys an marhak?

2 Prag yth êth an vyternes in bàn war an fos?

3 Pandra wharva pàn nag esa an vyternes i'n chambour?

4 Pàn dheuth hy dhe'n dor arta, pëth a welas hy?

5 Pandra a gresys an vyternes dhe vos wharvedhys?

6 Pàn welas an marhak y honen an deray i'n chambour, pandra wrug ev?

7 Pana stât esa an meppyk bian ino in gwiryoneth?

8 O an marhak fur pàn wrug ev gweskel unweyth heb predery dywweyth?

SEYTEGVES DYSCANS WARN UGANS
THIRTY-SEVENTH LESSON

37A.1 'THIS ONE', 'THE OTHER ONE', 'THE ONLY ONE', AND 'YOUR ONE'

For 'this one' Cornish says **hebma** *m*. or **hobma** *f*. For 'that one' Cornish says **hedna** or **hodna**. To render 'it is a good one' Cornish says **onen dâ yw**. **Onen** in such cases will take the gender of the thing referred to, for example: **an gath-ma yw onen dew** 'this cat is a fat one', not **onen tew**, because **cath** 'cat' is feminine.

It is not possible, however, to use this pronominal **onen** with any of the possessive adjectives. One cannot use the definite article with pronominal **onen** either. Such expressions as **an udn onen* 'the only one' or **an onen blou* are impossible in Cornish. Because of this apparent gap in the Cornish lexicon, some revivalists have recourse to the word **huny**. **Huny** in traditional Cornish, however, is used only after **pùb**, **lies**, and **kettep**, i.e. in **pùb huny** 'everyone', **lies huny** 'many people' and **kettep huny** 'everyone'. **Huny** may not be used like Breton *hini*, and thus expressions like **an huny blou* 'the blue one' or **an huny-ma* 'this one' are inadmissable.

In order to translate the pronominal 'one' of English into Cornish, it is often necessary to repeat the relevant noun: 'Which dress did you buy? I bought the blue one' is to be translated **Pana bows a wrusta perna? Me a bernas an bows vlou**. 'This one' and 'that one' are most naturally translated into Cornish as **hebma/hobma** and **hedna/hodna**, e.g. **Me a bew hebma** 'This one is mine'; **Dhe byw usy hodna?** 'Whose is that one?'

Huny cannot be not be used either to mean 'the one who, he who', e.g. **an huny usy ow lavurya* 'the one/person who works'. Authentic Cornish in such cases employs **hedna/hodna**: **hedna usy ow lavurya** 'the one/he who works', **hodna usy ow côwsel** 'the one/she who speaks'.

265

Alternatively a noun antecedent may be used: **an den usy ow lavurya** 'the one/he who works', **an venyn usy ow côwsel** 'the one/she who speaks'.

37A.2 'ONLY'

Essentially there are three ways of saying 'only' in Cornish. The most traditional way is to use **saw** (**unsel**), **mès**, **marnas** or **lemen** (all meaning 'except, but') after a negative; here the negative is absolutely necessary. Thus **ny vanaf vy perna tra vëth saw hedna** 'I will buy that only', **ny vëdh den vëth saw unsel ow broder ena** 'only my brother will be there', **ny vydn ev ry mès nebes mona dhyn** 'he will give us only a little money', **ny vanaf debry marnas bara hag amanyn** 'I will eat only bread and butter', **ny wrug ev lemen nebes ober** 'he did only a little work'.

A second way of rendering 'only' is to use the phrase **yn udnyk** 'only', e.g. **me a vydn côwsel Kernowek orthys yn udnyk** 'I will speak only Cornish to you', **me a'm beus mona lowr yn udnyk rag an viaj tre** 'I have only enough more for the journey home'. The expression **yn udnyk** (spelt *en ydnek*), however, is attested only in Lhuyd's Cornish, and we cannot be sure that it is an authentic phrase rather than one devised by Lhuyd on the basis of Welsh *yn unig* 'only'.

The third way of saying 'only' in Cornish is perhaps the least likely to commend itself to revivalists, namely the use of the English borrowing *only*. It should be pointed out, however, that **only** is attested nearly 40 times in traditional Cornish and occurs in four different texts, BM, TH, SA and CW. It is quite clear therefore than **only** 'only' had been an essential feature of the the Cornish lexicon from the early sixteenth century at the latest.

37A.3 'TO SERVE', 'SERVICE', AND 'SERVANT'

The default word for 'to serve' in Unified Cornish has always been **gonys**. Unfortunately, however, this usage not based on traditional Cornish, where **gonys** as a verb means 'to work, to create' and 'to cultivate (land)'. The ordinary word for 'to serve' in traditional Cornish is **servya**, both in the sense 'to serve somebody' and 'to serve, to be sufficient'.

'Service' in English has two main senses. The first is that of the act of serving someobody, e.g. 'he was conscientious in his service to the college'. The second is that of a church service. Unified Cornish has always used the noun **gonys** for both. Again this usage is not based on the traditional language, where 'service' in the first sense was usually **servys**. The second sense is an extension of the first, where God is served. We have no reference in the texts to a church service, but Cornish service to God is referred to as **servys**. In revived Cornish 'service' in such expressions as 'translation service', 'police service' should be rendered by **servys**. Similarly a church service should be called **servys eglos**.

The default word for 'servant' in Cornish is **servont** and the plural **servons** is also attested. Most frequently, however, 'servants' is rendered **servysy**, **servyjy**. It appears that in the traditional language the word **servont** has **servysy** rather than **servons** as its default plural. This should be the position in the revived language as well.

37A.4 'FREE' AND 'FREEDOM'

Nance believed that the element **reeth**, **reath** in place-names like **Goon Reeth** and **Wheal Reath** meant 'unrestricted, free' and was comparable with Welsh *rhydd* 'free'. He therefore used *ryth* to mean 'free' in Unified Cornish. **Reeth, reath** in such toponyms, however, is more likely to be for Middle Cornish **ruth** (our **rudh**) 'red' than **rydh* 'free'.

The word **frank** 'free' occurs in the Godolphin motto: **Frank ha leal etto ge** [**Frank ha lel ôta jy**] 'Free and loyal art thou'. Otherwise the only attested word for 'free' in Cornish is the English borrowing, **fre**.

There is no attested word for 'freedom' in Cornish. In the light of **frank** 'free', ***franchys** *m.* is probably the best word to use.

37A.5 'SHORT'

The word **berr** (UC *ber*) is attested only in set phrases, e.g. **a verr spis** 'in a short time', **wàr verr lavarow** 'in a few words, in a word' and in the second line of the englyn: **Bedh dorn rêver, dhon tavaz rê hîr** 'The hand is too short for the too long tongue'. This englyn belongs to the very earliest period of Middle Cornish and is perhaps not typical of the later language. Nance and Caradar both used **berr** as their default word for 'short', particularly in the light of Welsh *byr* 'short' and Breton *berr* 'short'. Cornish **berr** 'short' was not a wise choice, however. In the texts **berr** 'short' has most often a lenited initial, i.e. *a ver spys*, *war ver lavarow*; but *ver* is also a common way of spelling **veur** < **meur** 'great; much', and there was risk in Middle Cornish of confusion. This may have contributed to the fairly early demise of **berr**, which was replaced by **cot** 'short' (see examples at 37B.5). **Cot** should be the ordinary word for 'short' in the revived language.

37A.6 'WARRIOR' AND 'WAR'

For 'warrior' Nance respelt **cadwur** in OCV as Middle Cornish *casor*. The updated form is not correct, however, since the **r** in the following syllable of **cadùr/cador** would have prevented assibilation of the intervocalic -**d**-; cf. **peder** 'three' *f.*, **pehador** 'sinner', and **pùscador** 'fisherman'. The word for 'warrior' is now attested from BK where it appears as **gwerryor, gwerrour** with the plural **gwerrours**. **Gwerryor** is clearly related to the verb **gwerrya** 'to wage war' seen at BM 3454.

For 'war' Nance used **bresel** *f.*, **breselyow**, presumably on the basis of Breton *brezel* 'war'. Unfortunately **bresel** in Cornish does not mean 'war', so much as 'disagreement' or 'insubordination'. On grounds of authenticity it seems better to use **gwerryans** 'waging of war, war.'

37A.7 'TO CONQUER' AND 'VICTORY'

For 'to conquer' Nance suggested **fetha, tryhy** and **conqwerrya**. **Fetha** is well attested in the Ordinalia, BM and BK. *****Tryhy** on the other hand is wholly unattested. **Conqwerrya** is attested in the Ordinalia and in BK. The related word **conqwerrour** 'conqueror' is found in BM and BK. Notice that the consonant group **-nqw-** in these two words is to be pronounced [nkw] rather than [nk]. The English borrowing **overcùmya** is found in BM and TH eight times altogether.

For 'victory' Nance suggested **trygh, budhygoleth** and **vyctory**. *****Trygh** and *****budhygoleth** are both unattested. **Vyctory**, on the other hand (variously spelt *vyctory, victory, victuri*) is found in RD, BM, TH and BK, six times altogether. In the interests of authenticity, **vyctory** ought to be the default word for 'victory' in the revived language.

37A.8 'ANIMAL' AND 'LION'

In his English-Cornish dictionary (1951) under 'animal' Nance gives *myl*, *eneval* and *lon* respectively. *Myl* is Nance's respelling of *mil* 'animal' in the Old Cornish Vocabulary. *Eneval* is attested once only—in the plural form **enevalles** at PC 205. Nance's *lon*, our **lodn**, is attested once in CW and twice by Lhuyd, who says it means 'bullock, steer'. Lhuyd also gives *lodon davaz* as 'Vervex, wether sheep'.

Curiously Nance does not cite the commonest word in the texts for 'animal': **best** (*best, beast*), plural **bestas** (*bestas, bestes, beastas*) which is attested almost fifty times. Nance and other revivalists have probably been reluctant to use **best, bestas** on the grounds that it is a borrowing from English. But this is by no means certain. **Best** is more likely to be a borrowing from Latin *bestia*.

In his English-Cornish dictionary of 1952 s.v. 'lion' Nance gives first the word *lew*, plural *lewas*. This word is not attested in Middle Cornish, being a respelling of *leu* 'leo [lion]' in OCV. It is quite apparent, however, that the ordinary word for 'lion' in the Middle Cornish texts was **lion** (*lyon*, *luon*) and no other word for 'lion' is attested in them. **Lion**, plural **lions** should be the ordinary word for 'lion' in the revived language.

37B EXAMPLES FROM THE TEXTS

37B.1.1 *ffesont onan fat ha da the'n tas dev a'n nef guella my a offryn hep lettye* 'a pheasant, a fat and good one I shall offer without delay to the Father, God of the best heaven' OM 1192-94; *Awot omma onan da ragon ordenys parys* 'Behold here a good one ordained, ready for us' OM 1719-20; *rag yma dragon dyblans hag onen vras sur omma* 'for indeed certainly there is a dragon here and a big one' BM 3934-35.

37B.1.2 *syndis ve dre govaytis yn della yw leas huny* 'he was ruined by covetousness; so are many' PA 62b; *map then vyternes helen neb yv pen ol y ehen del glowas lues huny* 'a son to queen Helena, who is the head of all his kindred as many people have heard' BM 1158-60; *ol y pobel ymons y orth y sywe pup huny* 'all his people, they are following him, everybody' OM 1687-88; *Hayl, arluth heel drys pub huny!* 'Hail, my lord, generous above everybody' BK 1700-01; *ha Du re thanvanna ras warnough in katap huny!* 'and may God send you grace every one!' BK 2571-72.

37B.2.1 *nyns us den orth ov seruye len ha guyryon me a greys yn ol an beys sav noe ha'y wrek ha'y flehes kefrys* 'there is no one serving me loyally an truly, I believe, in all the world except Noah only, his wife and his children also' OM 929-32; *pyth ev an ethom dy'nny cafus lafur an par-na aban vynnyth pup huny lathe ol an nor vys-ma sav vnsel ov tus hammy* 'what need is there for us to have to labour so, since thou wishest to kill everyone, all this world apart only from my family and me?' OM 968-71; *nyns a den vyth bynytha a'n keth re-na the'n tyr sans marnas calef ha iosue* 'no one with ever go to the Holy Land apart only for Caleb and Joshua' OM 1878-80; *nyng es dean vytholl in byes tha wythell an kethe murder mes te haw mabe cotha cayne* 'there is no one in the world who could have done the same murder but only you and your elder son Cain' CW 1250-52; *an golovder me a wor nynsyv eff lemen an lor pan vgy ov trehevel* 'the brilliance I know, it is only the moon as it rises' BM 2100-02.

37B.2.2 *mez hedda a kodha en ydnek heruedh skrefyanz an Zoṷznak* 'but that occurred only according to English orthography' AB: 223; *ma nebaz Esperans dhebm, niz en ydnek, trẏ vedn neb Pednzhivikio 'ṣoz honan, kemerez huîth* 'I have some hope, not only that some gentlemen themselves will take care...' AB: 224.

37B.2.3 *ha thymmo na regh grasse mas only the crist avan* 'and do not thank me but only Christ above' BM 31551-2; *Ny rug crist cara y cothmans only, mas inweth y yskerens* 'Christ did not love only his friends, but also his enemies' TH 22a; *not der faith only, mas eweth in very deed* 'not by faith only, but also in very deed' SA 59a; *y praytha thymma lavar a wrug dew cowsall tha gye only heb dean arall vyth omma* 'prithee, tell me, did God speak only to you without any other person here?' CW 2348-50.

37B.3.1 *hethyw yw an whefes dyth aban dalletheys gonys* 'today is the sixth day since I began to work' OM 49-50; *me a commonnd scon dotho th'y teller kyns ens arte noe gonys may hallo* 'I command it quick to return to its place so that Noah may be able to till' OM 1094-96; *paseil moy gallus, the gonys, ha changya an pith nag o derag dorne* 'how much the more power to work and to change that which was not before' SA 62a; *Me a vyn dallath gonys, rag mas ew ar thyaha* 'I shall begin to plough, for good is peaceful cultivation' BK 868-69; *in erbers i'n pow adro an lynes in tyawgal prag e tevons heb den vith th'aga gonys?* 'why do the nettles grow indeed, 'in the gardens in the land all around without anybody's cultivating them?' BK 2131-34.

37B.3.2 *an tas a'n nef caradow roy thotho grath th'y seruye* 'may the beloved Father of heaven give him grace to serve him' OM 679-80; *en keth guas ma yth ese gans ihesu worth y seruye* 'this same man was with Jesus serving him' PC 1405-06; *pronter boys me a garse corff iheus thy venystra mar myn ov descans servya* 'I should like to be a priest to administer the body of Christ, if my education serves' BM 522-24; *meryasek in ov bevnans me a vyn prest the servya* 'Meriasek, in my life I shall continually serve you' BM 3850-51; *Ima an profet Dauit in peswar vgans ha nownsag psalme ow exortya oll an bobyll the ry prayse hag honor the du ha thy servya in lowendar* 'The prophet David in Psalm 119 exhorts all the people to give praise and honour to God and to serve him in joy' TH 1; *Nyng ew ow thowl servya an Jowl* 'It is not my intention to serve the devil' BK 2937-38; *Che ra gorthy tha Arleth Deew, hag eu e honnen che ra servya* 'Thou shalt worship thy Lord God and him alone shalt thou serve' Rowe.

37B.3.3 *guyn y vys pan ve gynys a allo gul thy's servys* 'happy the man in his birth that can do thee service' OM 1476-77; *Ov flehys wek eugh why dre ov banneth genogh neffre na letyogh vy am servys* 'My dear children, go home; my blessing with you always; do not keep me from my service [to God] BM 2676-78; *Rag meth na vethens gegys a'y servys the omdenna* 'For shame let him not be allowed to evade his service' BK 1844-45; *nyng es tra in bys ma gwryes mes thewhy a wra service* 'there is nothing in this world but that does you service' CW 2515-16.

37B.3.4 *map dev os ha den ynweyth saw ol the len servygy* 'thou art son of God and man also; save all thy faithful servants' PC 278-79.

37B.4.1 *Frank ha leal etto ge* 'Free and loyal art thou' Pryce.

37B.4.2 *na ny vea vices ha drokoleth mar fre vsyys* 'nor would vices and evil be so freely practised' TH 39; *Sau ol theso me a'n gaf rag the vos gyntel ha fre* 'But I will forgive you everything because you are noble and liberal' BK 1097-98; *Hayl, arluth fre!* 'Hail, liberal lord' BK 1680.

37B.5 *yn scon dyswreys ef a vyth ha the'n mernans cot gorrys* 'soon he will be destroyed and shortly put to death' OM 1521-22; *cot yv the thythyow the gy nahen na grys* 'short are your days; do not believe otherwise' RD 2037-38; *ren arluth then beys am ros me a ra pur cot y guyns* 'by the Lord who set me in the world, I shall make his wind very short' BM 2252-53; *ny ra bewa omma mas termyn cut* 'he lives here only a short while' TH 7; *rag henna degow in kerth in agis colonow an lesson cut ma* 'therefore take away in your hearts this short lesson' TH 26; *ha wosa an tyrmyn cut a vethyn ny omma in present ha mortall bewnans ma* 'and after the short while that we shall be here in this present and mortal life' TH 26; *an moar brase yn cutt termyn adro thom tyre a vyth dreys* 'the great sea in a short while will be brought around my land' CW 88-89; *in cutt termyn ages negys cowsow y praya* 'in a short while speak your business, I pray' CW 592-93.

37B.6.1 *bresell cref a ve sordijs en grows pu elle ȝy don* 'a strong dispute arose about the cross, who should carry it' PA 160c; *Ternoys y sordyas bresel gans an eȝewon goky* 'The next day a dispute arose among the foolish Jews' PA 238a; *Aron whek pyth a cusyl a reth thy'm orth am vresyl a son a'n debel bobel* 'Dear Aaron, what advice would you give me about the dispute and clamour of the evil people?' OM 1813-15; *rak ef a gergh thyworthy'n kemmys na worthyo iouyn hag a wra thy'n drok bresul* 'for he will take from us as many as do not worship Jove and will give us an evil contest' PC 1916-18; *A consler cam, pyth ew cusyl orth an wrusyl* 'you crooked adviser, what is to be done about the insubordination?' BK 967-69; *Nyng es myghtern in neb gwlas na wothvean, rennothas! dystogh lyha e vrusyl* 'There is no king in any country whose insubordination, I swear by my sire, that I could not immediately lessen' BK 1305-07.

37B.6.2 *Lowena this, myghtern freth, gwerror fers ha galosak!* 'Hail to thee, impetuous king, a fierce warrior and a powerful one!' BK 1996-97; *Me, Excerces, ew guerror fers ha myghtern in Itury* 'I, Excerces, am a fierce warrior and king of Ituria' BK 2597-99; *duk Bitini, Pollitetes, gwerryor stowt* 'the duke of Bithynia, Pollites, a brave warrior' BK 2705-06; *Lemmyn, ow gwerrors gwelha, dun ahanan in un rowt* 'Now, my choicest warriors, let us depart in a host' BK 2787-88; *an turant yv ongrassyas menogh y car ewyas ha guerrya purthyogel* 'the tyrant is graceless; he loves often to ride out and make war' BM 3452-54

37B.7.1 *y fyth agan enefow dre leuarow dev mygys ha fethys an dywolow* 'our souls will be nurtured by the word of God and the devils overcome' PC 75-77; *yth orden agan lathe rak na yl agan fethe dre lauarow* 'he will order us to be slain for he cannot conquer us by words' RD 253-55; *gwyn ow bys bos thym fethys lavyr ha dewhan an beyse* 'happy I am that I have overcome the labour and the sorrow of the world' CW 2004-05.

37B.7.2 *an harlot bras adam plos a thesefse warnan conquerrye neffre* 'the dirty scoundrel Adam would have presumed to conquer us forever' OM 907-09; *settys of rag the gerya, ha dyswul ha conquerya the yskerans der gras Christ* 'I am determined to assist you, and to destroy and conquer your enemies by the grace of Christ' BK 1483-85.

37B.7.3 *Me yv empour ha governour conquerrour tyr arluth worthy* 'I am emperor and governor, a conqueror of territory, a worthy lord' BM 930-33; *myghtern bras ha galosak ha conquerror* 'a great and powerful king and conqueror' BK 1400-01.

37B.7.4 *mar qureth y ouercummya the crist ny a vyn treyla* 'if you overcome it, we will turn to Christ' BM 4012-13; *Eff a promysyas fatell vetha onyn genys mes an stok han has a Eva, a re overcommya agan eskar ny an teball ell* 'He promised that one would be born of the stock and seed of Eve, who would overcome our enemy, the devil' TH 13; *whath hemma a vea sufficient lowre the ouercummya an re a vynna gull resystens* 'still that would be adequately sufficient to overcome those who would resist' TH 50a.

37B.8.1 *mil* 'animal' OCV; *moruil* 'whale' OCV.

37B.8.2 *yn pympes dyth me a vyn may fo formyys dre ov nel bestes puskes hag ethyn* 'on the fourth day I will that by my power be created animals, fish and birds' OM 41-3; *neffre yn dour hedre vo ny thue dresto na varwo gour gruek na best* 'never why he is in the river no one will pass over it without dying, man, woman nor animal' RD 2225-27; *noth off avel best oma war lur ov pedrevanas* 'I am naked as a beast here crawling on the ground' BM 4217-18; *Eff an grug Souereign rewler ha pen war oll an pusces in dowre, war an ethen in eyer, ha war oll an bestas in nore* 'He made him sovereign ruler and head over all the fishes in the water, over the birds of the air and over the animals of the land' TH 2; *yn defyth in myske bestas yma ef prest ow pewa* 'in the wilderness among the animals he lives always' CW 1481-82; *ken es beast nagew henna* 'that is nothing other than an animal' CW 1558; *Lebben an hagar-breeve o moy foulze avell onen veth ell an bestaz an gweale a reege an Arleth Deew geele* 'Now the serpent was more treacherous than anyone of the animals of the field that the Lord had made' Rowe.

37B.8.3 *leu* 'lion' OCV; *folle yn ta y whela ys del wra lyon y pray drey den yn peyn a calla* 'very much more madly he seeks to bring man to pain than a lion seeks his prey' PA 21cd; *yma agys yskar an teball ell kepar ha lyon ow huga ow mos adro ow whelas rag agys devowrya* 'your enemy the devil is like a roaring lion going about seeking to devour you' TH 3a-4; *Whath luon goyth in y ugo thys a ynclyn* 'Moreover a wild lion in his lair bows down to you' BK 1777-79.

37C.1 VOCABULARY

a leun-golon *adv.* phrase with a full heart, very willingly

ascra *f.* bosom, fold in garment

besydhya to baptize; **besydhys** baptized

bylen *adj.* villainous, ugly

conscians *m.* conscience

daffar mûsyk *coll.* musical instruments

darn *m.*, **darnow** piece, coin

dybreder *adj.* thoughtless, heedless

dynya to lure, to entice

gyttern *m.*, **gytterns** guitar, zither
harp *m.*, **harpys** harp
iffarn *m.* hell
kervya to carve; **kervys** carved
lawethan *m.*, leviathan, huge
monster
lùst *m.*, **lùstys** lust, desire
sans *m.*, **sens** saint
sin *m.* **an grows** the sign of the
cross

stag ena *adv. phrase* on that very
spot
stap *m.*, **stappys** step
tolgh *m.*, **tolhow** hillock
traitury *m.* treachery
valy *m.*, **valys** valley
whedhlor *m.*, **whedhloryon**
narrator.

37C.2 TEXT DHE REDYA
"VALY AN RE MAROW" IN MES A *WHEDHLOW KERNOWEK*

Red an devyn-ma usy ow sewya ha scrif gorthebow dhe'n qwestyons:

Inwedh me a welas tra uthyk ena. Pàn esen ow kerdhes in udn nans bian ogas dhe Ryver an Lùstys, me a welas lies corf marow. Hag i'n nans-na me a glôwas sonyow a ilow wheg lies ehen gytterns ha harpys, hag euth brâs a'm kemeras.

Hës an valy o seyth mildir dhe'n lyha, martesen eth; ha pynag oll den a wrello entra ino yn tybreder, ev a via marow kyns kerdhes hanter an valy. Rag hedna, ny vydna tus an pow dos ogas dhodho.

Whans a'm beu entra dhe'n nans-na, hag a leun-golon me a besys Duw, hag omsona, ha wosa hedna me êth dy. Hag ena me a welas kebmys corfow marow, ma na wrussa den vëth y gresy, marnas ev a'n gwelas. I'n valy-na a'n eyl tenewen dhybmo, yth esa carrek vrâs, ha warnedhy yth esa kervys bejeth bylen den, leun a draitury, ow meras orthyf. Me a gemeras own me dhe verwel stag ena: mès an geryow-ma a dheuth dhe'm brës: "An ger a veu gwrës kig hag a dregas intredhon ny," ha mc a wrug sin an grows. Ena me êth mar ogas dhodho ma nag esa seyth pò eth stap intredho ev ha me.

Alena me a wrug omdedna bys i'n hanter aral a'n valy, ha crambla wàr bedn tolgh growynek ha meras a bùb tu dhybm, mès tra vëth ny welys; saw me a glôwas an harpys ow cana, heb den vëth orth aga seny. Ha pàn wrug avy dos dhe bedn an tolgh, me a welas lies darn a arhans ow spladna wàr an dor. Me a gùntellas meur anodhans ha'ga sensy i'm ascra, ow predery aga don genef ha'ga dysqwedhas avell marthùs. Hag ena ow honscians a wrug dhybm aga thôwlel dhyworthyf, heb don onen vëth anodhans. Hag indella dre râss Duw me a dheuth in mes a'n nans yn saw.

Pàn gonvedhas tus an pow me dhe dhos alebma yn few, marth brâs a's teva ahanaf, ow leverel ow bos sans besydhys. Y a leverys an corfow-na dhe vos corfow tus, ha bos lawethan a iffarn ow qwary an harpys rag dynya tus dhe dhos ena, may halla aga ladha.

1 Pandra welas an whedhlor i'n nans bian?
2 Pana dhaffar mûsyk a glôwas ev?
3 Pleth esa an bejeth bylen?
4 Prag y whrug an whedhlor tôwlel an arhans dhyworto?
5 Pandra a gresy tus an pow adro dhe'n whedhlor?
6 Pyw esa ow qwary an harpys ha praga?

ÊTEGVES DYSCANS WARN UGANS
THIRTY-EIGHTH LESSON

38A.1 'AGREE' AND 'AGREEMENT'

The verb **unverhe** 'to be of one mind, to be reconciled' is attested twice and **unver** 'unanimous' is found once. The noun **acord** 'agreement' is attested five times and **acordya** 'to agree' occurs twice (PA and BM). The word **agria** (*agrea*, *agrya*) 'to agree' is used several times in TH; and Lhuyd uses the word **agrians** 'agreement.' It would seem, then, that the ordinary words for 'to agree' in Cornish are **acordya** and **agria**.

38A.2 'TO BUILD'

Derevel, **drehevel** with the sense 'to build' is attested in the earliest Middle Cornish and it is also used in Late Cornish by John Boson. 'To build', however, is **byldya** (*buldya*, *buyldya*, *byldya*) in TH and CW. Moreover the verb **gwil** 'to do, to make' can also be used when speaking of building a temple or a church. The use of the verb 'to do, to make' to mean 'to build' is a feature of other Celtic languages.

38A.3 'CHAIR'

Nance recommended the word *cadar f.*, *caderyow* for 'chair'. **Cader**, however, is known only from OCV and from place-names. The word for 'chair' in Cornish is **chair**, plural **chairys**. See the examples given at 38B.3 below. **Chair** should perhaps replace **cader** as the everyday word.

38A.4 'CLOUD'

Nance's preferred word for 'cloud' is **comolen f.*, with the plural **comolow* and the collective **comol*. Neither singular, plural nor collective is attested anywhere in Cornish. The nearest we find is **comolek** (*komolek*) 'dark or close (of weather)' cited by Lhuyd for both Cornish and Breton. The only attested word for 'cloud' in Cornish is ***cloud**, **cloudys**. The singular is not attested, but the plural is found twice.

38A.5 'COURT'

The word **lÿs**, **lës** *f.* 'court' is known only from place-names. The word for 'court, court of law' in Cornish is **cort**, which is attested twice: see the examples at 38B.5 below.

38A.6 'FLOWER'

In UC the default term for 'flower' is either **blejan m.*; *blejyewen f., pl. blejyow*; or **blejen f., pl. blejennow*. **Blejan* is apparently based on **blodon** 'flos [flower]' in OCV and Lhuyd's **bledzhan** 'flower' (AB: 240c). *Blejyewen* seems to be Nance's UC respelling of Lhuyd's **bledzhîan** (AB: 10b). The collective *blejyow* derives from the single attestation **Dewsull blegyow** 'Palm Sunday' (literally 'Flower Sunday' PA 27a). In the Middle Cornish texts, however, neither **blejan*, **blejen* nor *blejyewen* is attested anywhere. In traditional Cornish the word for 'flower' is **flour** or **flouren**, and the plural is **flourys**, spelt *flour*, *flowre*; *flowren*; *floris*, *floures*, *flowres*, *flourys*, *flowrys*. **Flour**, **flouren** can also mean 'flower, choice one' e.g. *flour ol an bys* 'pick of the world' OM 2122; and is used adjectivally with the sence 'choice, chosen', e.g. in *epscop flour* 'splendid bishop' BM 1434. In revived Cornish **flour**, **flourys** should perhaps replace ***blejen**, **blejyow** as the default word for 'flower'.

38A.7 'MORTAL'

In his 1938 dictionary Nance gives **marwyl* 'mortal'. This word is his own coinage and is nowhere attested. The only word for 'mortal' in Cornish is **mortal** (**mortall**), which is attested five times in TH.

38A.8 'POISON', 'TO POISON'

The commonest words for 'poison' in revived Cornish are **gwenyn** and **venym**. **Gwenyn** is attested only in the Old Cornish compound **guenoinreiat** 'veneficus [poisoner]'. The word does not occur in Middle or Late Cornish. **Venym** (< Middle English *venym*, *venim* 'venom, poison') is attested twice in *Origo Mundi*. **Poyson** is also attested. In the interests of authenticity the default words for the noun 'poison' in revived Cornish should be **venym** and **poyson**.

There are two attested words for 'to poison': **posnya** and **venymya**.

38A.9 'THING'

The Cornish word for 'thing' is **tra**, and the plural ***traow** is used twice by Lhuyd; he can hardly have heard this in use, for it unattested anywhere in Old, Middle or Late Cornish. Lhuyd's ***traow** was probably suggested to him by Breton *traoù* 'things'. The traditional Cornish for 'things' is the suppletive **taclow** or **taclenow**. In the interests of authenticity Lhuyd's ***traow** is best avoided.

38B EXAMPLES FROM THE TEXTS

38B.1.1 *Vnferheys kepar del on berth in eglos sent sampson bethens eff consecratis* "As we are agreed let him be consecrated within the church of St Samson' BM 2982-84; *Erna vony vnwerhys, neffra ny veth da ow cher* 'Until we be reconciled, my mood will never improve' BK 1036-36; *y fons vnver yntreʒe* 'they were agreed among themselves' PA 39c.

38B.1.2 *Kyn na goff den skentyll pur par del won lauaraff ʒys yntre du ha pehadur acord del ve kemerys* 'Although I am not a very clever man, as I know I will tell you that an agreement was made between God and sinner' PA 8ab; *my ny dorraf bys vycken an acord vs lemyn gureys yntre my ha lynneth den* 'I shall not break ever the agreement made between me an the race of man' OM 1239-41; *gesow ny oll gans vn accorde the ry thotheff agan voyses gans ioy pub vr* 'let us all with one accord give him our voices with joy always' TH 11.

38B.1.3 *yn deweth ny acordye y golon gans y lauar* 'in the end his heart did not agree with what he said' PA 40d; *trest ambus boys acordys orth ihesu crist a vercy* 'I trust to be in agreement with Jesus Christ of mercy' BM 494-95.

38B.1.4 *ny a goth thyn dysky fatell ew an lell diskans han feith a crist hay egglos onyn, ha fatell vsans pub vr ow hagrya* 'we should learn that it is the true teaching and the faith of Christ and his church, and they they always agree' TH 34a; *ha y ma S Augustin ow hagrea the hemma in y 102 Epistill* 'and St Augustine agrees with this in his 102nd epistle' TH 48; *pan esans ow hagrea gans an sea ha stall a rome, yth esans, hag y a rug, florysshya in religion a crist ha in rychis an bys* 'when they agreed with the see and stall of Rome they were and they flourished in the religion of Christ and in wordly wealth' TH 49a; *ha pan uêl e Agreanz, po kessenyans* 'and when he sees the agreement or harmony...' AB: 223.

38B.2.1 *awotta omma neb yll tempell du dowst oll squardye ha ʒe voth y ʒrehevell* 'here is someone who can reduce all the temple to dust and at his will build it up' PA 195cd; *ha my a fystyn agy ov trehevel an fosow* 'and I shall hurry inside to build the walls' OM 2319-20; *kyn fe dyswrys an temple the'n dor quyt na safe man me a'n dreha sur arte* 'though the temple be destroyed entirely so that it is not standing, I surely will build it up again' PC 344-46; *en termen an Tur Babel vo derevalz* 'in the time when the Tour of Babel was built' JBoson.

38B.2.2 *Cyte a ve settys bo byldys war meneth* 'A city set or built upon a hill'
TH 17a; *ha war an garrak ma me a vyn byldya ow egglos* 'and upon this
rock I shall build my church' TH 44; *ha war an power ma eff a rug buldya
y egglos* 'and upon this power he built his church' TH 45a; *praga ew genas
she omma buyldya lester mar worthy in creys powe thaworthe an
moare* 'why must you build such a fine vessel here in the middle of the country
far from the sea?' CW 2296-98.

38B.2.3 *yn dewellens pecadow gul alter sur da vye* 'in repentance of sins it
would be good to build an altar' OM 1173-74; *orden bos gureys temple
golow* 'order a magnificent temple to be built' OM 2260; *yn enour dev my a
vyn yn dre-mme gruthyl temple* 'in God's honour in this town I will build a
temple' OM 2283-84; *Dauid ny wreth thy'mo chy yn certen bys venary*
'David, you will not ever indeed build me a house' OM 2233-34.

38B.3 *me a's ordyn though wharre cheyrys ha formys plente* 'I shall
arrange them for you shortly, chairs and plenty of chairs' PC 2228-29; *dus oma
ese yth cheer guyske the dylles yth kerhyn* 'come here, sit in your chair,
and put on your clothes' BM 3002-03; *cam an par na then stall po cheare
an scribys han phariseis* '...wrong of that kind to the stall or chair of the
Scribes and Pharisees' TH 48a; *Mar pith den vith ioynys the chear pedyr,
po sensy then stall a pedyr, yth ew ow servont ve* 'If anyone is joined to
the chair of Peter or hold to the stall of Peter, he is my servant' TH 49.

38B.4.1 *C[ornish] & Ar[moric] Teual, komolek* 'dark or close' AB: 162.

38B.4.2 *Ego sum Alpha et Omega heb dallath na dowethva pur wyre me
ew omma agy than clowdes war face an dower in sertan* 'I in very truth
am Alpha and Omega, without end or beginning here within the clouds upon
the face of the water certainly' CW 1-5; *hag a vyn diskynnya than noore in
dan an clowdys hag ow both gwethill ena* 'and will descend to the earth
beneath the clouds and do my will there' CW 75-77.

38B.5 *me a vyn mones heb bern lemen the corte an mytern* 'I shall go
willingly now to the King's court' BM 3176-77; *Ma tha vee treall en cort an
Vaternes* 'I have a trial in the Queen's court' Bilbao MS.

38B.6 *ny dyf guels na flour yn bys yn keth forth-na may kyrthys* 'no grass
or any flower at all grows in that same way I trod' OM 711-13; *rag pan deffa
an welsan ha dalleth seeha an flowre a ra clamdera ha cotha the ves*
'for when the grass begins to dry up the flower will wilt and fall away' TH 7a; *eff
a deffe in ban kepar ha flowren* 'he springs up like a flower' TH 7; *palm
ha floris kekyffris er y byn degis a ve* 'palms and flowers also were brought
to meet him' PA 29d; *A frut da ha floures tek menestrouthy ha can whek*
'...of goodly fruit and beautiful flowers, music and sweet songs' OM 769-70; *yma
gynef flowrys tek* 'I have with me beautiful flowers' PC 258; *ow benneth ol
ragas bo ow tos yn onor thy'mmo gans branchis flourys kefrys* 'may
you all have my blessing coming to me in honour with branches, flowers also'
PC 265-67; *ha fatell ew oll an glory an broghter han lowender a vabden
kepar ha flowres in prasow* '...and that all the glory and splendour and joy
of man are like flowers in the meadows' TH 7; *an tryssa dyth me a wra than*

gwyth sevall yn ban ha doen dellyow teke ha da ha flowres wheag in serten 'on the third day I will make the trees arise and bear beautiful goodly leaves and sweet flowers indeed' CW 92-5; *lower flowrys a bub ehan yn place ma yta tevys* 'many flowers of every kind, behold, have grown in this place' CW 363-64; *ena yth esa flowrys ha frutes teke aga lew* 'there were flowers and fruits of fine hue there' CW 1050-51.

38B.7 *ha remembra agan mortall genesegeth a russyn kemeras theworth Adam* '…and remember our mortal birth which we received from Adam' TH 6a; *dre agan mortall yskar an teball ell* 'through our mortal enemy, the Devil' TH 10; *eff a ve den mortall, hag yth o gwrys in pub part kepar hag onyn ahanan ny* 'he became a mortal man and he was made in every respect like one of us' TH 15; *wosa an tyrmyn cut a vethyn ny omma in present ha mortall bewnans ma* 'after the short time that we shall be here in this present and mortal life' TH 26.

38B.8.1 *shyndyys of gans cronek dv ha whethys gans y venym* 'I have been injured by a black toad and am swollen by its poison' OM 1778-79; *sawyys yv ov ysyly ol a'n venym ham cleves* 'all my limbs have been cured of the poison and of my disease' OM 1797-98.

38B.8.2 *an poyson a serpons yma indan aga tavosow* 'the poison of serpents is under their tongues' TH 7a; *Rag edyfya spiritually an holl corfee, in feith, ha rag lell defence then holl corffe, theworth an poyson a heresy* 'To build up spiritually all the body in faith, and as a true defence for all the body against the poison of heresy' TH 42.

38B.8.3 *an dour ha'n eys yv posnys mayth ens mur a tus dyswreys* 'the water and grain have been poisoned, so that many people have died' OM 1559-60; *gans nader yth of guanheys hag ol warbarth vynymmeys* 'I have been bitten by a viper and I am altogether poisoned' OM 1756-57.

38B.9.1 *ny vendzha e besgueth hanual an Trào kreiez en Ladin*, **Quercus, rhamnus, hædus…** 'he would never have called the things referred to in Latin as *Quercus, rhamnus, melis, lepus, haedus* AB: 223; *pôrletryz ha pôrskientek en traou erel* 'very educated and very wise in other matters' AB: 224.

38B.9.2 *ha dy'so my a leuer yntrethon taclow pryve* 'and to you I will tell private things between us' OM 935-36; *the wruthyl vn pols byhan takclow pryve* 'to do private things for a while' PC 91-2; *kepar ha commondementys ha taclenow forbyddys* 'like commandments and forbidden things' TH 15; *fatell rug du requiria innan ny certan taclennow the vos colynwys* '… that God required in that certain things should be fulfilled' TH 16; *certyn tacclow arall mere moy agis helma* 'certain other things much greater than this' SA 60; *Gear Christ ill changia takclennow the nappith na ve travith derag dorn* 'The word of Christ can change things to something that did not exist before' SA 61a; *Mar crug an geir an tas an nef gonis in taglenno erall* 'If the word of the Father worked in other things' SA 63; *mere a dacklow ram lowta* 'many things upon my word' CW 765; *I costyans showre a vona an keth tacklowe es omma* 'They cost a large sum of money, the same things that are here' CW 2445-46; *rag debre an tacklow ewe per trink* 'for to eat the things is very bitter' JTonkin; **Der taklow minniz ew brez teez gonvethes** 'Through small things are peoples mind perceived' Pryce; **ha an tacklow a vedn gwaynia klôs theez rag nevera** 'and the things that will gain glory for you forever' Pryce; **Gwrâ, O Materne, a tacklow ma** 'Do, O King, these things' Pryce.

38C.1 VOCABULARY

amowntya to count, to avail

an den moyha a gyrry the man you love the most

Arberth *m.* Arberth (place in SW Wales)

bommen, bobmen *f.*, **bomennow, bomednow** blow, whack

brew *m.*, **brewyon** wound, cut, injury

darbary to prepare, to provide

drehedhes to reach

dyber *m.*, **dybrow** saddle

fronn, frodn *f.*, **fronnow, frodnow** rein

gwastas *adj.* level, steady

hus *m.* magic

in despît dhe² *compound prep.* in spite of

inia to incite, to urge

jolyf *adj.* frisky, lively

kentryna to spur

lamm, labm *m.*, **lammow, labmow** leap, stride

leven *adj.* level, even

marhoges *f.*, **marhogesow** horsewoman

moren *f.*, **moronyon** maiden, young woman

paly *m.* velvet, brocade

Pwyll *m.* Pwyll (prince of Dyfed)

ren ow enef *interj.* upon my soul

terlemmel, terlebmel to frisk, to prance

toth *m.* speed

wàr gamm *adv.* moderately, steadily

wondrys *adj.* wonderful, remarkable

yn compes *adv.* straight, directly

yn hell *adv.* slowly

yn tefry *adv.* indeed.

38C2 TEXT DHE REDYA
PWYLL IN ARBERTH
(warlergh AN MABYNOGYON IN KERNOWEK gans CARADAR)
Red an devyn-ma ha scrif gorthebow dhe'n qwestyons:

Unn prÿs mayth esa Pwyll in Arberth, y gort, y feu gool darbarys dhodho, ha lu brâs a dus ganso. Ha wosa an kensa debry, sevel in bàn a wrug Pwyll, ha mos wàr benn gorseth a-ugh an gort, o gelwys Gorseth Arberth.

"A Arlùth," yn medh onen a'n gort, "an orseth-ma yw wondrys. Den bryntyn vëth, pynag oll a vo, a wrella esedha warnedhy, nyns â ev alena erna wrella onen a dhyw dra wharvos—ev a'n jevyth bomennow ha brewyon, poken ev a welvyth marthus."

"Own ny'm beus a gafos bomennow pò brewyon," yn medh Pwyll, "in mesk lu a'n par-ma. Saw marthus mar pÿdh, dâ via genef y weles; yth âv dhe'n orseth hag esedha."

Esedha a wrug wàr an orseth. Ha pàn o va esedhys ena, y a welas benyn wàr geyn margh pòr wynn, meur y vrâster, ha gwysk owr splann a baly in hy herhyn, ow tos in rag wàr an fordh vrâs ryb an orseth.

Yth esa an margh ow kerdhes hell ha compes, dell hevelly dhe'n re-na a's gwelas, hag ow tos adâl an orseth.

"A dus," yn medh Pwyll, "eus nebonen ahanowgh usy owth aswon an varhoges?"

"Nag eus, Arlùth," yn medhons y.

"Gwrêns nebonen mos wàr hy fynn rag godhvos pyw yw hy," yn medh ev.

Onen anodhans a savas in bàn ha pàn dheuth ev wàr hy fynn wàr an fordh, gyllys o hy dresto. Ev a bonyas wàr hy lergh scaffa gylly hag ev wàr droos.

Saw dhe voy yth o y doth, dhe bella yth esa hy dhyworto. Ha pàn welas na ylly ev hy sewya màn, ev a dhewhelys dhe Pwyll ha leverel, "Arlùth, ny dal dhe dhen vëth hy sewya wàr droos."

"Hèm yw gwir," yn medh Pwyll, "Kê dhe'n gort. Kebmer an kensa margh a welyth ha kê in rag wàr hy lergh.

Ev a gemeras an margh ha mos in rag. Hag ev a dheuth dhe woon o gwastas ha leven, ha kentryna y vargh. Ha seul voy yth inias y vargh, dhe bella yth o hy dhyworto. Bytegyns hy ny hevelly mos uskyssa ages kyns. Y vargh ev a dhalathas fyllel, ha pan wrug ev percêvya kerdh y vargh dhe wannhe, ev a dhewhelys dhe Pwyll.

"Arlùth," yn medh ev, "sewya an arlodhes ny dal màn. Me ny aswonaf i'n pow-ma margh moy uskys ès hemma, saw hy sewya ny amownt dhymm."

"Ren ow enef," yn medh Pwyll, "res yw bos neb hus omma. Gesowgh ny dhe vos tro ha'n gort."

Y a dheuth dhe'n gort ha spêna an jëdh-na. Ha ternos y a savas in bàn ha spêna an jëdh-na kefrÿs, bys pàn veu termyn debry. Ha wosa an kensa debry, yn medh Pwyll, "Ny a wra mos, an keth re may feun ny de, dhe benn an orseth. Ha te," yn medh e dhe onen a'y goscar, "dro genes an margh moyha uskys a wodhes i'n pras." Ha'n maw a wrug indella.

Y a dhrehedhas an orseth ha'n margh gansans. Ha pàn êns y esedhys, y a welas an venyn wàr geyn hy margh ha'n keth gwysk adro dhedhy, ow tos war an keth fordh.

"Ot omma an varhoges de," yn medh Pwyll: "Bÿdh parys, a vaw, dhe wodhvos pyw yw hy."

"Arlùth," yn medh ev, "henna me a wra yn lowen."

Gans henna an varhoges a dheuth adâl dhedhans. Indella an maw a lammas wàr y vargh, ha kyns ev dhe settya y honen in y dhyber, yth o hy gyllys dresto, hag yth esa spâss intredhans. Saw hy thoth nyns o moy ès dell o an jëdh kyns.

Ena ev a worras y vargh dhe gerdhes, ow tyby hy drehedhes yn scon ha henna in despît dhe doth clor y vargh y honen. Saw ny wrug ev spêdya màn; ev a ros ytho an fronnow dh'y vargh. Saw whath hy dheuth ev nes dhedhy ages dell o pàn esa ow mos wàr y gamm. Ha dhe voy y whre va inia y vargh, dhe bella yth esa hy dhyworto. Whath ny wrug hy marhogeth moy uskys ès kyns.

An maw a dhewhelys dhe Pwyll. Hag y êth dhe'n gort. An nessa jorna y êth arta dhe'n orseth hag esedha. Ha nyns esens y marnas termyn cot ena, erna wrussons y gweles an varhoges ow tos wàr an keth fordh, i'n keth maner ha'n keth toth.

"A was," yn medh Pwyll, "me a wel an varhoges. Ro dhymm ow margh."

Pwyll a ascendyas wàr y vargh ha kettel veu va ascendys, hy o gyllys dresto. Trailya wàr hy lergh a wrug ev ha gasa y vargh dhe derlemmel yn jolyf. Hag ev a dyby y whre va dos bys dhedhy wàr an nessa pò an tressa lamm. Saw ny dheuth ev moy ogas dhedhy ages kyns. Ev a inias y vargh ha gwil dhodho resek uskyssa gylly, bytegyns ev a welas nag esa ow spêdya dhe dhos nes dhedhy. Ena yn medh Pwyll:

"A voren, rag kerensa an den moyha a gyrry, gorta vy,"

"Gortaf yn lowen," yn medh hy, "hag yn tefry y fia dhe les an margh mar teffes ha govyn solabrÿs."

1 Pleth esa Pwyll pàn dhalathas an whedhel?
2 Pëth o arbednek ow tùchya Gorseth Arberth?
3 Pàn esa Pwyll ha'y dus esedhys wàr an orseth, pandra welsons?
4 Pëth o an dra goynt ow tùchya an varhoges?
5 Pandra wrug an maw rag gwil dh'y vargh mos moy uskys?
6 A wrug ev spêdya dhe gachya an arlodhes?
7 Prag na ylly an gwas dos nes dhe'n venyn wàr geyn margh?
8 An venyn a stoppyas rag Pwyll y honen. Fatla wharva hedna?

NAWNJEGVES DYSCANS WARN UGANS
THIRTY-NINTH LESSON

39A.1 'DOWN' AND 'DOWNWARDS'

When 'down' means 'downstairs, down below' it is rendered in Cornish by **awoles**, e.g. **a welta jy an chy bian-na i'n valy awoles** 'do you see the small house down in the valley?' If 'down' means 'downwards, to a lower place' Cornish says **wàr nans**, e.g. **ev a wrug lebmel wàr nans dhywar an fos ha terry y ufern** 'he jumped down from the wall and broke his ankle.' **In nans** can also be used. Furthermore the expression **dhe'n dor** is also commonly used in this sense, e.g. **an chy a veu tôwlys dhe'n dor** 'the house was pulled down' or **an wedhen a godhas dhe'n dor dres nos** 'the tree fell down during the night'.

Both **wàr nans** and **dhe'n dor** are adverbial phrases. Neither is a preposition. If one wants to say, for example, 'he ran down the road' one has to say **ev a bonyas an fordh wàr nans**. Similarly 'the car rolled down the hill' would be **an carr a rollyas an vre wàr nans**. Late Cornish speakers often pronounce **dhe'n dor** as **en dor** or simply **dor**.

'Upside down' is rendered in Cornish as **awartha dhe woles**, e.g. when she came she turned everything upside down **pàn dheuth hy, hy a dôwlas pùptra awartha dhe woles**.

39A.2 'LATER'

The word **dewetha** is the comparative degree of **dewedhes**, and is an adjective. It is possible, therefore, to say **ot obma dyllans dewetha a'n keth lyver** 'here is a later edition of the same book'. **Dewetha** cannot be used adverbally to mean 'later, in a while'. In Cornish 'I will speak to you later' can be translated **Me a vydn côwsel orthowgh wosa hebma**. 'She said she would meet me later' would be **Hy a leverys y whre hy metya genef wosa hedna**.

39A.3 'FOR THE SAKE OF'

The expression **a'm govys vy** 'for my sake, on my behalf' is attested four times in traditional Cornish. It is not possible to say whether the phrase was used with any other person, nor whether **a *wovys** could be used with nouns. Nor is it necessary to know, since the commonest expression for 'for the sake of' in traditional Cornish is **rag kerensa**. We have attested examples, for example, of **rag dha gerensa** 'for thy sake', **rag y gerensa** 'for his sake', **rag kerensa Crist** 'for Christ's sake', **rag kerensa Duw** 'for God's sake' and **rag kerensa an dus** 'for the sake of the men'. **Rag kerensa** can be used with both nouns and possessive adjectives and should therefore be the default rendering in the revived language.

39A.4 'JUDGE', 'TO JUDGE', AND 'JUDGEMENT'

For the noun 'judge' some revivalists use **brusyas*, a word devised by Nance, but unattested in traditional Cornish. George's *Gerlyver Meur* (2009) spells this word **breusyas* and gives as a source Lhuyd's **brudzhiaz** at AB: 81a. Lhuyd's **brudzhiaz**, however, is the Cornish equivalent of *Lixus* 'boiled' (KS **bryjys**), and George's citation is erroneous. Nance (1938, 1952) also gives **brusyth*, itself a Middle Cornish respelling of Old Cornish **brodit** 'iudex [judge]'. The form **brusyth* is probably mistaken, however. Old Cornish **pridit** 'poeta [poet]' appears in Middle Cornish as **prydyth** BK 2497. It is likely therefore that the Middle Cornish form of Old Cornish **brodit** would have been **brudyth*, not **brusyth*.

Borlase gives **barn** 'to judge' and **barner** 'a judge'. The only attested word for 'judge' in the Middle Cornish texts, however, is **jùj**, plural **jùjys**.

The verb **brusy** 'to judge' is well attested in the texts, being attested four times. Much commoner, however, is the verb **jùjya** (*iuggya, iuggye, iugge, iudgia, judgia, judgya, yugge, yvgge*) which is attested at least 27 times.

The word **breus** (*brus, brues, breus*) 'judgement' is attested 24 times, in many cases in the expression **dëdh breus** 'the day of judgement'. As the vowel in **breus** lost its rounding ([bɹøːz] > [bɹeːz]), it would have become identical in pronunciation with the words both for 'mind' and for 'womb'. This may explain why John Tregear frequently uses **jùjment** (*judgement, jugement, iugment, jugment*) 'judgement', but has no instances of **breus**.

39A.5 'TO LEND', 'TO BORROW', 'CREDITOR', AND 'DEBTOR'

There is no attested word in traditional Cornish for 'to lend'. Nance's notion that **cola** 'to pay attention to, to heed' could be used to mean 'to lend' is based on a misunderstanding and cannot be defended. In his English-Cornish dictionary (1952), however, Nance suggested the borrowings *prestya* and *lena* as ways of saying 'to lend'. **Lêna** is from Middle English *lene* 'to lend' (the *-d* in English *lend* is not original). Neither **prestya** nor **lêna** is attested in Cornish. In the absence of any attested word **lêna** (or perhaps **lendya**) and **prestya** are acceptable.

No word for 'to borrow' is attested in the texts, although Borlase gives **benthygya** (*benthygio*) 'to borrow', which looks as though it may be the Welsh word *benthygio* 'to borrow, to lend'. **Benthygya** derives from **benthyg** 'thing borrowed, loan', itself from Latin *beneficium*. Nance (1952) also suggests the unattested *chevysya* for 'to borrow.' Since **benthygya** is actually attested, whatever its origins, it would seem to be the word of choice.

The attested word **dettor** does not mean 'debtor' but 'creditor'. The Cornish for 'debt' is **kendon** and the word for 'debtor' is **kendonor**. 'To owe, to be in debt' in traditional Cornish is **bos in kendon.**

39A.6 'TEACHER'

For 'teacher' Nance (1952) gives *dyscajor*. This is from Lhuyd's coinage, **deskadzher**, which means 'professor' rather than 'teacher,' and is badly formed. The **r** in the final syllable prevents the assibilation of **-d-** in the ending **-ador** as can be seen from **pùscador** 'fisherman' and **pehador** 'sinner'. The correct form, therefore, would have been **descador**. Another word for 'schoolmaster' in Cornish is **mêster** or **scolvêster**.

The word **dyscor** (*dyskar*) 'teacher' in Cornish is used once by John Tregear. **Dyscor** now, however, is used to mean 'learner'. Another way of saying 'learner' is to use one of the two words for 'disciple, pupil', i.e. **dyskybyl** or **dyscypyl**.

39A.7 'COURSE'

Nance suggested *stus*, *stes* (KS **steus** *f.*) 'course (series)' on the basis of Breton *steud* and Welsh *ystod*. The ordinary word for 'course, route', however, in traditional Cornish is **cors**, and this word can be used for 'course' in all senses.

39A.8 'FRUIT', 'GRAPE', AND 'VINEYARD'

The word *fruit* 'fructus [fruit]' < Latin *fructus* occurs in the Old Cornish Vocabulary. This Nance respelt as *fruyth* and it appears in the 2008 compromise orthography as *frooth*. John Boson writes *ffrueth*, *frueth* and Borlase has *ffrwyth* 'effect, fruit'. These all are based on Welsh. The word for 'fruit' in Middle Cornish, however, is not this word but **frût, frûtys**, borrowed from Middle English. **Frût, frûtys** should be the default word in the revived language also.

In his Cornish-English dictionary (1938) for 'grape' Nance suggests *gwinreunen f., gwinreun coll.* on the basis of Welsh *gwinrawn coll.* Since the discovery of Tregear's Homilies, however, the traditional word for 'grape' is now attested in the form **gwedhen grappys** 'vine', literally 'grape tree'. ***Grappa, grappys**, as the only attested word in Cornish should perhaps be the default word for 'grape' in the revived language.

In his Cornish-English dictionary (1938) for 'vineyard' Nance suggested **gwinlan f.*, an unattested word formed on the basis of Welsh *gwinllan*. Since the discovery of Tregear's Homilies, we have an attested word for 'vineyard', namely **vynyard** (*vyne yarde*) which is found three times. **Vynyard** was clearly the ordinary Cornish word in the sixteenth century. It should perhaps be the ordinary word in the revived language also.

39B EXAMPLES FROM THE TEXTS

39B.1.1 *Yma eff in meneth bras del glowevy sur myl pas theworth an grond awoles* 'He is on a high mountain, as I hear indeed, a thousand paces from the ground below' BM 1956-58; *eth esa deow Helias: onyn awartha, ha Helias a wolas* 'there were two Elijahs; one above and Elijah down below' SA 60; *han noore inwethe awollas scon worthe compas a vyth gwryes* 'and the earth down below also soon will be completely made' CW 18-19; *an tryssa degree awolas me a wra try order moy* 'of the third degree down below I shall make three more orders' CW 59-60.

39B.1.2 *Rag gwan spyrn hag ef yn ten caman na ylly gwyʒe war nans na bosse y ben rag an arlont a vsye* 'For the evil thorns and it tight he could in no way prevent himself from leaning his head downwards, because of the garland he was wearing' PA 205ab; *Lemmyn nyng ew vas an towl mayth esave ow towtya, y tuan war nans* 'Now the matter is not good so that I fear that we shall decline' BK 769-71; *A'n nef my a theth yn nans eua wek gvella the cher* 'I came down from heaven; Eve, be of good cheer' OM 165-66.

39B.1.3 *mars os mab du a vur brys dijskyn ha ʒen dor ke* 'if thou art the son of God of great importance, descend and go down' PA 14d; *toul an welen ol yn tyen the'n dor vskys* 'throw all the rod entirely quickly down' OM 1447-48; *kyn fe dyswrys an temple the'n dor quyt na safe man me an dreha sur arte* 'though the temple be demolished down to the ground so that it did not stand at all, I will indeed build it again' PC 344-46; *deyskyn then dor mata ha the borse mes ath ascra me am beth hath margh uskis* 'get down, mate, and I shall have your purse from your pocket and your horse quickly' BM 1887-89; *My a vyn settya envy intre te ha haes an venyn hag eff a putt then dore theth pen in dan y dros* 'I will set enmity between you and the seed of the woman and he will put down your head under his foot' TH 13; *Na rase plegy en dore dothans* 'Thou shalt not bow down to them' TBoson.

39B.1.4 *mas pub tra in den o treylys an pith awartha the wolas* 'but everything in man was turned upside down' TH 4.

39B.2.1 *in dewetha sermon ha homelye I fe declarriis thewgh why pandra ew an egglos* 'it was explained to you in the last sermon and homily what the church is' TH 35a; *Evyn an dewetha nois a rug eff bos in company gans y aposteleth the rag y virnans* 'Namely the last night that he was in the company of his apostles before his death' TH 51a-52; *the signifia thynny fatell o an bois na defferis bys in dewetha deth a ve agan Sovyour conuersaunt gans y appostlis* 'to indicate to us that that food was deferred until the last day that our Saviour was conversant with his apostles' TH 52; *pan vo an dewetha gyrryow clowis a onen a vo in y gwely marnance* 'when the last words of someone on his deathbed are heard' SA 59; *me a vedn gweel duath an skreef ma durth an dewetha reem 'vez a'n Kensa Caon Horace* 'I will finish this essay from the last verse of the Horace's first ode' NBoson.

39B.2.2 *eff a vith awosa hemma desquethis thewgh dre weras a thu* 'it will be demonstrated to you later with the help of God' TH 16; *Rag henna, tus vas, gwregh awosa hemma avoydya pub kynd a pehosow* 'Therefore, my good people, avoid hereafter all every kind of sin' TH 16; *Eff a vith particularly disquethis ha settys in mes theugh wosa hemma* 'It will be particularly shown and set out for you later' TH 20; *lymmyn a wosa hemma eff a vith desquethis ha previs thewgh omma fatell ve* 'now later it will be shown and proved to you here how it was' TH 47a; *Ea, lowar c. blethan a wosa henna Eff a promysyas the viterne Dauid* 'Yes, many hundreds of years later he promised king David...' TH 13a; *Awosa henna ny a redd fatell rug lyas onyn an disciplis a crist a scryffas aweylys* 'Later we read that many of the disciples of Christ wrote gospels' TH 37a; *ha wosa henna in dede eff a ros henna according the promysse* 'and later he granted that according to the promise' TH 51a.

39B.3 *yn della ef a vynne may halle dre baynys bras merwel rag ze gerense* 'thus he wished that he might die through great torment for thy sake' PA 70cd; *Bersabe flour ol an bys certus rag the gerense syr vrry a fyth lethys* 'Bathsheba, flower of all the world, for your sake Sir Uriah shall be killed' OM 2121-23; *fatel fue cryst mertheryys rak kerenge tus an beys why a welas yn tyen* 'how Christ was martyred for the sake of the people of the world' PC 3220-22; *mur a peyn a wothefys rak kerenge tus a'n bys* 'much torment he suffered for the sake of the people of the world' RD 832-33; *lemen rag y gerense regh them queth rag ov huthe* 'now for his sake give me a garment to cover myself' BM 3040-41; *Lymmyn Sure one ny fatell rug an abosteleth a crist suffra myrnans rag kerensa crist* 'Now we are sure that the apostles of Christ suffered death for Christ's sake' TH 36a; *Ef a'm pernas gans e wos, gothaf torment mayth ew own ha galarow thymmo rag e gerensa* 'He redeemed me by his blood, so that it is right for me to suffer torment and affliction for his sake' BK 429-32; *Cushez yw an nore râg tha crengah; gen dewan chee ra debre notha oll dethyow tha vownyaz* 'Accursed is the ground for thy sake; in sorrow shalt thou eat of it all the days of thy life' Rowe.

39B.4.1 *thyrag iug ny fyth iuggys* 'he will not be tried before a judge' PC 2388; *an egglos an Jevas an lell sens an scriptur ha yth ew iudg a henna* 'the church has the true meaning of scripture and is the judge of that' TH 36n; *Rag lymmyn athewethas pub den sempill heb understonding na skyans a re supposia fatell yllens y bos iudges in maters a contrauercite* 'For recently now all simple men without understanding or wisdom believe that they can be judges in matters of dispute' TH 37; *Rag an tyrmyn an prontyr, ha rag an tyrmyn an Judge* 'For a time the priest, and for a time the judge' TH 42a; *ha rag an tyrmyn the vos ivdge in stede a crist* 'and for a time to be judge in place of Christ' TH 48a. *Ihesus a ve danvenys ha ʒeworth an prins annas gans tus ven aʒesempys bys an ebscop cayphas dreʒo crist may fe bresys* 'Jesus was dispatched and from Prince Annas by stalwart men immediately to Bishop Caiaphas, that Christ might be judged by him' PA 88a-c; *me ny gafa moys kyns reson gans gwyr ʒy vrvsy* 'I cannot find any more than before reason justly to judge him' PA 117d; *deth brus eff a thue certan thagen brusy kyk in kneys* 'on the day of judgement he will indeed come to judge us flesh in skin' BM 4053-54; *deth brus eff a thue purfeth the vrusi an drok han mays* 'on the day of judgement he shall come to judge the evil and the good' BM 4086-87.

39B.4.2 *Ha ʒeso y tanvonas y allus crist rag iudgye* 'And he has sent you his authority to judge Christ' PA 116a; *dre vur stryff y fe Iuggijs ys degy crist y honon* 'by great dispute it was adjudicated that Christ should carry it himself' PA 160d; *ytho why kemereugh e ha herwyth agas laha ha concyans guregh y iuggye* 'therefore you, take him and according to your law and conscience do you judge him' PC 1977-79; *lader of a fue iuggys ha ryp ihesu cryst gorrys* 'I am a robber who was judged and placed beside Christ' RD 265-66; *ef a whylas ihesu Cryst myghtern a nef ha falslych y'n iuggyas ef gans cam pur bras* 'he sought Jesus Christ, the king of heaven, and falsely with very great injustice he judged him' RD 2261-64; *ha ny vith eff deceyvys, mas eff a ra lell iugia ha descernya mars uga in perfect charite* 'and he will not be deceived, but he will truly judge and discern whether he is in perfect charity' TH 23a; *ha ef a vyn dos the Judgia oll an bobell* 'and he will come to judge all the people' TH 59.

39B.4.3 *dre guyr vrus sur y cothe dotho gothaf bos lethys* 'by true judgement surely he ought to endure to be killed' OM 2237-38; *ny dogoth thy'nny lathe den uyth ol yn nor bys-ma felon na lader kyn fe hep brus iustis uynytha* 'we ought not ever kill any man in all the world, though he be felon or robber, without the judgement of a magistrate' PC 1981-84; *geseugh vy the worthyby kyns ry brues the vos dyswrys* 'let me answer before giving judgement for us to be killed' PC 2493-94; *may fo crousys ow bres yv dismas iesmas ha ihesu* 'my judgement is that Dismas, Jesmas and Jesus be crucified' PC 2504-05; *eff re ros thyn deth hyr lour pan vo an vrus wy a wour* 'he has given us a long enough day; when Judgement comes you will know' BM 1930-31.

39B.4.4 *hag eff a thesyrryas na rella du entra the Jugment ganso eff* 'and he desired that God should not enter into judgement with him' TH 8a; *rag dre gyrryow an par na den a goth in daunger a Judgment* 'for by words of that kind a man falls into danger of judgement' TH 29a; *yma S Augustyn lyas tyrmyn ow submyttya oll y Judgment hay oberow then Catholik egglos a crist* 'St Augustine often submits all his judgement and his works to the Catholic church of Christ' TH 37a; *yma S. paul ow leverell fatell ra an vnworthy recevans an sacrament ma dry iudgement ha dampnacion* 'St Paul tells that the unworthy reception of this sacrament brings judgement and damnation' TH 53a; *theworth oll the preceptys hath commondementys hath iugementys* 'from all thy precepts and thy commandments and thy judgements' TH 10.

39B.5 *kyns y vn teller yn beys dev kendoner yth ege the vn dettor me a grys* 'once in a certain place in the world there were two debtors to one creditor, I believe' PC 500-02; *Dha bos en kyndan* 'To owe, to be indebted' AB: 53c; *Ne vedn e nevra dvz vêz a ʒyndan* 'He'll never get out of debt' AB: 230c.

39B.6.1 *ʒen an mêr-fyr ha'n mêr-skientek A'hro an Deskadzher Davies* 'by the very wise and very learned teacher, Professor Davies AB: 222; *Ma'n Deskadzher Davies... a hanᵤal ʒerlevran Kernûak Levarva Cotten, Liber Landavensis* 'Professor Davies...calls the Cornish vocabulary of the Cottonian Library *Liber Landavensis*' AB: 223; *ha yth esas ow tristya fatell ota gydyar then re ew dall ha golow then re vs in tewolgow, ha dyskar then re nag ew fure* 'and you trust that you are guide to the blind, and light to those in darkness, and teacher to those who are not wise' TH 14a.

39B.6.2 *thyvgh lauara ow dyskyblyon pyseygh toythda ol kescolon* 'to you I say, my disciples, pray immediately all of one accord' PC 1-2; *the thyskyblon yv serrys mur* 'thy disciples are greatly angered' RD 884.

39B.6.3 *ʒen meneth olyff y ʒeth hay ʒyscyplys an sewyas* 'he went to the Mount of Olives and his disciples followed him' PA 52ab; *ʒy ʒyscyplys y trylyas yscafas ol ow coske* 'he turned to his disciples; he found them all asleep' PA 55c; *me a'n guyth sur deth ha nos awos y dysciplys plos* 'I shall guard it indeed day and not because of his dirty disciples' RD 390-91; *nyns ew worthy the vos dissipill na seruant thym* 'he is not worthy to be a disciple or servant of mine' TH 21a; *An discipels nyng o abel thy gyrreow age arluth Christ* 'The disciples were not able for the words of their lord Christ' SA 62a; *ha e ruk e distributia the e discipels* 'and he distributed it to his disciples' SA 64a.

39B.6.4 *maister mebion* 'schoolmaster' OCV; *kegy gans ov mab kerra bys yn mester a grammer* 'go with my most beloved son to a grammar schoolmaster' BM 35-36; *Me yv mayster a gramer gvrys yn bonilapper vniveriste vyen* 'I am a grammar schoolmaster, educated in Bonilapper, a small univerity' BM 76-78; *ha meister then Sempill ha ignorant* 'and teacher to the simple and ignorant' TH 14a; *Ith ew marthussyan the welas fatell rug an rena esans y ow kemeras rag aga doctors bras, ha scoll meisters, y a rug aga abusia, seducia, ha ga mockya* 'It is wondrous to behold how those whom they took for their great doctors and teachers, they abused, seduced and mocked them' TH 49a

39B.7 *powesough lymmyn vn cors me agas pys* 'rest now for a course, I beg you' PC 2146-47; *an guyns thagen corse dufa* 'the wind has veered to our course' BM 1086; *Py du y syngough an cours?* 'In what direction do you hold course?' BK1380.

39B.8.1 *ha war an pren frut degis may fe sur ʒagan sawye may teth frut may fen kellys rag adam ʒe attamye* 'and that a fruit might be borne to save us on the tree whence we were lost since Adam first broached it' PA 153cd; *War bup frut losow ha has a vo ynny hy tevys* 'Upon every fruit, herb and seed that has grown in it' OM 77-78; *A frut da ha floures tek menestrouthy ha can whek* 'Of good fruit and beautiful flowers, music and sweet singing' OM 769-70; *an frut vs in paradys ny a thebyr, mas an frut an wethan vs in nes in cres paradis du agan defennas na rellan tuchia na myllia gynsy* 'of the fruit which is in paradise we shall eat, but of the furit of the tree which is near to the middle of paradise God forbade us to touch it or meddle with it' TH 3a; *me a heath ran an frutyes hag a thro parte anetha* 'I shall reach some of the fruits and will bring part of them' CW 1842-43; *ena yth esa plenty a bup kynde a frutys, beautyfull tege ha wheg the veras warnetha* 'there there were plenty of fruits of all kinds, beautifully fair and delicious to look upon' TH 2; *lower flowrys a bub ehan yn place ma yta tevys ha frutes war bub gwethan* 'many floweres of every kind in the place behold there grow and fruits upon every tree' CW 363-65.

39B.8.2 *Yma agan meister, redymer ha Sovyour Jhesu crist, in aweyll a S Jowan, ow comparya ha ow hevely y honyn the wethan grappys* 'Our master, redeemer and Saviour Jesus Christ compares himself to a vine' TH 39a.

39B.8.3 *pan rug du dre y profet Esay settya in mes thynny pycture ay egglos in dan an hanow a vyne yarde* 'when God through Isaiah his prophet set out for us a picture of his church under the name of a vineyard' TH 40; *y myth eff, me a vyn kemeras the veis an ke aw vyne yard* 'he says, I will take away the fence from my vineyard' TH 40; *hag eff a suffras an drog pobyll the denna thyn dore an paell han kee ay vyne yarde* 'and he allowed the evil people to pull down the palings and fence of his vineyard' TH 40a.

39C.1 VOCABULARY

â *interj.* ah, oh!

awos a allo inspite of all he can do

biscath *Late variant of* **bythqweth** ever (in the past)

bloodh vy *Late for* **ow bloodh vy** my age

bodh *m.* wish, will

câss o ganso he was concerned

chartour *m.*, **chartours** charter

cres *f.* creed; **wàr an gres** by the creed, upon my faith

côk *m.*, **cûkow** fishing boat

darwar *2nd sg. imperative of defective verb* be cautious, be careful

deboner *adj.* debonair

dieskyna *early form of* **skydnya** to go down, to descend

dregyn *m.* harm

erhy to order, to command; **mara'th ergh dhis** if he commands you

fêkyl-geryow *pl.* hypocritical words

freth *adj.* eager, assiduous; **yn freth** assiduously

hadre vywhy as long as you shall live

i'n dre ny *Late for* **i'gan tre ny** in our village

lavar dhesy *emphatic 2nd sg. imperative* say!

les *m.* interest, advantage

mara'n kefyth in danjer if you get him in your power

mêkya to pretend, to dare

nakevys *Late for* **ankevys** forgotten

ny venna' *variant of* **ny vanaf** I will not

pajer ugans *Late for* **peswar ugans** eighty

re'n oferen *interj.* by the mass

sensy chy to keep house; **sens e fast** hold him fast

soth *m.* sooth, truth; **ha gensy soth** and she is truthful

tebmyk *m.*, **temygow** fragment

termyn me veu when I was

ty to swear; **me a'n te** I swear it

39C.2 TEXTOW DHE REDYA

A.

"TEBMYK AN CHARTOUR"

Fêkyl-geryow nebonen usy ow whelas demedhy den yonk gans mowes yonk

Golsow, te coweth;
byth na borth meth.
Dieskyn ha powes
ha dhymmo deus nes

mar codhes dha les;
ha dhis y rof mowes
ha fest onen deg.
Genes mara pleg
â, tan hy

kemmer hy dhe'th wreg.
Sconya dhis ny vêk
ha ty a vŷdh hy.

Hy a vÿdh gwreg ty dâ
dhis dhe sensy chy.

Pòr wir a lavara'
ha govyn worty.
Lemmyn i'th torn me a's re
ha wàr an gres me a'n te
nag eus hy far

a'n barth-ma dhe bons Tamar.
Me a'th pës, worty bÿdh dâ
hag oll dha vodh hy a wra,
rag flogh yw ha gensy soth;
ha gas hy dhe gafos hy bodh.

Kyn ès mos, dhymmo
emmowgh.
eugh alemma ha festynowgh.

Dallath avarr; yn freth darwar
own ma portho.
Ev omsettya worthys sy
camm na vetho.
Mara'th ergh dhis gul neb tra
lavar dhesy "Byth ny venna'".
Lauar dhodho, "Gwra mar mennyth."
Awos a allo ny wra tra vÿth.

I'n eur-na y'th sens dhe vos mêstres
hadre vywhy hag arlodhes.

Câss o ganso re'n oferen.
Cortes yw ha deboner.
Dhis dregyn ny wra.

Mara'n kefyth in danjer,
sens e fast indella.

B.
LYTHER WILLIAM BODINAR

Bloodh vy yw try ugans ha pymp.

Th'erof vy den bohojak a'n pùscas.

Me a wrug desky Kernowek termyn me a veu maw.

Me veu da mor gen sîra vy ha pymp den moy in côk.

Me a wrug scantlowr clôwes udn ger Sowsnek côwsys i'n cok rag seythen warbarth.

Na wrug avy biscath gweles lyver Kernowek.

Me a wrug desky Kernowek ow mos da mor gen tus coth.

Nag eus moy avell pajer pò pymp i'n dre ny a yll clappya Kernowek lebmyn,

pobel coth pajer ugans bloodh.

Kernowek yw oll nakevys gen pobel yonk.

A. above is the so-called Charter Fragment, the oldest continuous text in traditional Cornish, dating from the middle of the fourteenth century.

B. was written in the year 1776 is the last continuous text of traditional Cornish.

Let us determine that Cornish may never again cease to be spoken in Cornwall.

293

DEWGANSVES DYSCANS
FORTIETH LESSON

In this final lesson you will find many phrases and expressions taken from the Traditional Cornish texts. It is well worth becoming familiar with these, because they reflect the living language. It will also be seen that the orthography used in this book is well-suited to represent Cornish of all periods.

40A GREETINGS

Myttyn dâ dhywgh why
Metten da tha why—Pryce
Good morning to you.

Serys, dhywgh why lowena
syrys thywhy lowene—PC 2154
Greetings, gentlemen.

Dùrda dhywgh why, sera
Dur da dewhy, serra—Borde
Good morrow to you, sir.

Dùrsona dhywgh, maghteth
Durzona dewh, mathtath—Borde
God speed you, girl.

Duw re'gas blessya
Dew ragges blessye—Richard Symonds
God bless you.

Vatl'yw genowgh why?
Vatel ew gena why—Borde
How are you?

294

Yth ov vy pòr lowen dh'agas gweles why an myttyn-ma
Etho ve por loan tha gwelles why a metten ma—Pryce
I am very glad to see you this morning.

Welcùm fest owgh i'n chy-ma
wolcum fest ough yn chymma—PC 1207
You are very welcome in this house.

Welcùm, tus vas, owgh why dhymmo
Wylcum, tus vas, owhy thymmo—BK 1806-07
Welcome, good people, are you to me.

Welcùm owgh obma defry, why hag oll agas pobel
wolcum ogh omma deffry wy hag ol agis pobell—BM 241-42
You are welcome here indeed, you and all your people.

Ewgh bò tregowgh, welcùm vedhowgh, kyn fewgh why
    seythen omma
eugh bo tregugh, wolcum vethugh kyn fewy sythen omma—
    BM 4566-68
Go or stay, you will be welcome even if you're a week here.

Welcùmma den benary nefra ny dheu in ow chy, kyn teffa ow
    thas a'm denys
welcumma den benary nefre ny ʒue yn ov chy, kyn teff' ov ʒas
    am denes—BM 249–51
A more welcome person will never come to my house, even if my
    father who reared me were to come.

Me a's desîr why, comend vy dhe oll mâtas dâ
Mee's desyer why comende ve the olde olle matas da—Borde
I pray you, commend me to all good fellows.

Sera, me a vydn gwil agas comondment why
Syrra, me a vyden gewel ages commaundement why—Borde
Sir, I will do your commandment.

40B EVENING AND BEDTIME

Me a vedn gàs gweles arta gordhuwher
Mi vedn ɡyz guelaz arta ɡ̇ydhihụar—AB: 244c
I'll see you again in the evening.

**Trig genen, a goweth ker, rag namnag yw gordhuwher ha
dewedhes**
*tryk gynen a gouwyth ker rak namnag yw gorthuer ha
dewethas—RD 1305*
Stay withu us, dear friend, for it is almost evening and late.

Obma ny vadnaf vy ôstya, mès i'n nessa chy
ẏbma na vadna vi ostia bez en nessa tshei—JCH §24
Here I will not lodge, but in the next house.

Duw re dhebarra nos dâ dhywgh why
Dew re bera nos da dewhy—Borde
God give you a good night.

Ow huvyon, lebmyn cùscowgh hag oll warbarth powesowgh
*ow cufyon leman coskeugh hag ol warbarth poweseugh—PC
1093–94*
My dear friends, sleep now and all rest together.

Res yw dhymm porres cùsca; posyjyon i'm penn yma
*rys yv thy'm porrys coske possygyon yn pen yma—OM 1905–
06*
I desperately need to sleep; there is drowsiness in my head.

A Dhuw ker, ass oma sqwith
A dev ker assoma squyth—OM 684
O dear God, how tired I am.

**Me re beu in mes dres nos, meur ow anwos ha'm ponvos,
pan vëdh lies ow cùsca**
*Me re bue in mes dres nos mur ov anwys ham ponfos pan
veth lues ov cosca—BM 4187–89*
I have been out at night, in bitter cold and misery, when many others
are asleep.

Ha gorwedhowgh i'n gwely cala-na
ha gurvedhu en guili kala na—Borlase
And lie in that straw bed.

Pan esen vy et ow gwely, me a welas golow ha me a savas in màn
po ᴄera vi itta 'o guili, mî a uelaz gulou, ha mi a savaz am'àn—JCH §33
When I was in my bed, I saw a light, and I got up.

40C MISCELLANEOUS EXPRESSIONS

Dùrdala dhywgh why, mêster dâ
durdala de why master da—Borde
Thank you, good master.

Senjys on ny dhywgh why
Sendzhyz ôn nei ᴆv huei—JCH §20
We are beholden to you.

Gwrës dâ, che gwas vas ha lel
Gwrêz dah, chee gwaz vâz ha leal—Pryce
Well done, thou good and faithful servant.

Gromercy dhywgh why warbarth
Gramercy ᴣywy warbarth—BM 258
Thanks to you together.

Tewdar jentyl, gromercy a'th veneson
Tewdar gyntel, gromercy a'th veneson—BK 641–42
Gentle Teudar, thank you for your blessing.

Gromercy dhyso, dremas!
Gramersy theso, dremas!—BK 823
Thank you, good sir!

Meur a ras dhywgh why, syra, ow ry cùssul dhymm
mear a rase thewhy sera ow ry cusyll ᴣym—CW 702–03
Many thanks, sir, for advising me.

A das ker, meur ras dhywgh why
a das kere mere rase thewhy—*CW 1953*
Dear father, many thanks to you.

Py hanow os, benyn vas?
py hanow os benen vas—*RD 1697*
What is your name, madam?

Lavar dhymmo dha hanow
lauar thy'mmo the hanow—*OM 233*
Tell me your name.

A ble teuta dhe'n tir?
A bele teta the'n tyr?—*BK 80*
From where did you come into the country?

Praga? Pandr'yw an mater?
praga pandrew an matter—*CW 2329*
Why? What's the matter?

Pan nowedhys eus genes?
pana nowethis es genas—*CW 1886*
What news have you?

Mars yw an nowodhow dâ, te a vÿdh rewardys
marsew an nowothow da te a vythe rewardyes—*CW 732–33*
If the news is good, you will be rewarded.

Nowodhow yma genaf na bleg dhywgh why, me a grÿs
Nawothow ema gena' na pleg thewhy, me a grys—*BK 934–35*
I have news that will not please you, I believe.

Te javal, yw hedna gwir?
Te javal, ew henna gwyr?—*BK 78*
You scoundrel, is that true?

Te a glôw ken nowodhow kyns ow gweles vy arta
ty a glow keen nawothow kyns ow gwellas ve arta—*CW 724–25*
You will hear different news before seeing me again.

Hebma yw yeyn nowodhow
hemma ew yeyne nawothowe—*CW 1262*
This is terrible news.

Gwell yw goslowes
gwel yw gyzywaz—*Borlase*
It is better to listen.

Me a vydn bos dielys
me vedn bos dyliez—*Borlase*
I shall get my revenge.

**Dhe'n cans mil dyowl rej yllowgh ha bydner re
dhewhellowgh, why na tebel-nowodhow!**
*The'n cans myl deawl reg yllough ha byner re thewellough,
why, na tebal nawothow!*—*BK 744–46*
May you go the hundred thousand devils and may you never return,
you nor the bad news!

40D FAMILY

Lowena dhis, a dasyk
Lowena this, a dasak—*BK 1972*
Joy to you, dear father.

Ujy gàs tas byw?
Ydzhi 'gỳz tâz bêu?—*AB: 246a*
Is your Father living?

Sîra, dama ha vy ow honen
Seerah dama ha vee honan—*Bilbao MS*
Father, mother and I myself.

Vy, ow gwreg ha flehes
Vee o gwrege ha flehes—*Bilbao MS*
I, my wife and children.

I'n myttyn pàn vowgh why ow sevel, why a res cows dh'agas tas ha gàs dama wàr agas pedn dêwlin: Bednath Duw, ha udn bednath warnaf vy, me a bÿs dhe Dhuw
En Metten pan a why sevel, why rez cawse tha guz taz, ha guz damma, wor aguz pedndowlin: Bednath Deew, ha an bedneth wara vee, me a pidge thu Deew—Pryce
In the morning when you rise, you must say to your father and mother upon your knees: the blessing of God and a blessing upon me, I pray God.

Yw an vowes-na gàs whor?
Yu an vvz-na ʒÿz hôr?—AB: 246a
Is that girl your sister?

Yw hodna gàs whor why?
Eu hodda ʒyz hôr huei?—AB: 244c
Is that your sister?

Yma ev pòr haval dhis
Yma e pyr havel dhys—AB: 242b
He is very like you.

Ow broder wheg, deun dhe dre
Ow broder whek dun the dre—OM 525
My dear brother, let's go home.

Ow mab, merk an geryow-ma
ow mabe merke an gyrryow ma—CW 1952
My son, mark these words.

40E MEN AND WOMEN

Groweth i'n gwely ahës may hyllyf genes cùsca
growet yn guely a hys may hyllyf genes coske—OM 2127–78
Lie at length in the bed so I can sleep with you.

Kemerowgh with a'gas cal
Komero 'vyth goz kal—JBoson
Take care of your cock.

Damsel, er dha jentylys dysqwa dhybm a'th kerensa, rag bythqweth me ny welys benyn dhybm a well blegya whath in neb le

Damsel er the gentylys dysque thy'm a'd kerense rag bytqueth my ny welys benen thy'm a wel plekye wheth yn nep le—OM 2105–09

Damsel, for kindness, grant me of your love, for never did I see a woman whom I liked more anywhere.

Arlodhes, gwynn avell gwrys, deun dhe'n chambour, me a'th pÿs, may hyllyn omacowntya

Arlothas, guyn avel gurys, dun the'n chamber, me a'th pys, may hyllyn omacountya—BK 2983–81

Lady, white as crystal, let us go to the bedroom, I beg you, so that we can get to know each other.

Me ny allaf dha naha, lemen pùptra oll grauntya dhyworthyf a wovynny

my ny allaf the nahe lemyn pup tra ol gronntye theworthyf a wovynny—OM 2129–31

I cannot deny you but grant you everything you ask of me.

Ma lies gwreg lacka avell zeg, gwell gerys avell kemerys

Ma leiaz gwreage lacka vel zeage, gwell gerres, vel kommeres—JJenkins

There are many wives worse than brewer's grains, better left than taken.

Ev a dhylâtyas an termyn m'alla va prevy era y wreg ow qwitha compes et y gever, era pò nag era

ev a dhelledzhaz an termen mal ða va prêv erra e urêg guiᴅa kÿmpez et i ʒever: erra po nag erra—JCH §39

He spun out the time so that he could prove whether his wife was keeping faithful to him, was she or not.

Lewd yma owth ombrevy

Leud ema owth umbrevy—BK 3001

She is proving lewd.

Mars eus dhis duwhan gwysca an corn, roya tre arta

Marsoyse thees duan Guisca an corne Rogha tre arta—Oliver Oldwanton

If you are grieved to wear the cuckold's horn, give it back again.

Lebmyn an ôstes a'n chy, hy a gonsylyas gen neb udn vanagh era i'n dre dhe dhestria an den coth i'n gwely in termyn an nos ha'n rest a'njy ow repôsya

Lebmen an hostez an tshei, hei a kẏnsiliaz ṣen nebyn vanah a erra en tre, a ȯv destrîa an dên kôc en guilli en termen an noz, [ha'n rest a andzhẏi rẏppozia]—*JCH §25*

Now the landlady, she plotted with a certain monk who was in the town to kill the old man in the bed at night, while the rest of them were reposing.

Ny wòn vëth ple hallaf mos. A, Duw a vydn shâmys ow bos ha'm garr settys der hy ben

Ny won vith ple hallaf mos A, Du a vyn shamys ow bos ha'm gar syttys der hi ben—*BK 3300–02*

I do not know where I can go. Oh, God wants me to be shamed with one leg crossed over the other.

40F MARRIAGE

Benyn vas ha dremas
Bennen vâz ha dre maz—*Pryce*
Bride and groom.

Demedhowgh Jowan an den dhe Agnes an venyn rag banys ynjy i'n eglos ny Zulyow try
Demytho Jowan an dean tha Agnez an bennen rag beneas angy en eglez ny Zelio tri—*Pryce*
Marry John the man to Agnes the woman for they have been banned in our church on three Sundays.

Ow frias, gwellha dha jer. Gas dha ola ha'th uja
ow fryas gwella tha geare gas tha ola hath ega—*CW 1308–09*
My spouse, cheer up. Leave off your weeping and lamenting.

Te a dhemeth, ow mab wheg, dhe neb arlodhes wordhy, ha ny a vëdh dhe greffa der an maryach benytha
ty a thommeth ov map wek the neb arlothes worthy ha ny a veth the creffa der an maryach benitha—*BM 329–32*
You will marry, my dear son, some worthy lady, and we will be the stronger through the marriage for ever.

Kemmer hy dhe'th wreg. Sconya dhis ny vêk ha te a vÿdh hy. Hy a vÿdh gwre'ty dhâ.
kymmerr y ȝoȝ wrek sconya ȝys ny vek ha ty a vyȝ hy hy a vyȝ gwreg ty da—CF
Take her as your spouse. She will not attempt to refuse you and you will have her. She will be a good wife.

Rag hedna wosa hebma yn chast gwren ny kesvewa, ha carnal joy i'n bys-ma ny a vydn warbarth naha
rag henna woȝa hemma in chast gwren ny kesvewa ha carnall ioye in bys ma ny a vyn warbarth naha—CW 1313–16
Therefore hereafter let us live chastely together, and we will together forgo sexual pleasure in this world.

40G BABIES AND CHILDREN

Pàn wrugowgh why mos in kerdh, th'eren vy gyllys try mis gen flogh, ha lebmyn ma dhe ny meppyk wheg i'n gwely
po 'ryȝo ḥuei mυz ker, thera vi ȝillyz trei mîz ȝen 'hlôh; ha lebmen ma όυ nei meppig huêg en guili—JCH §44
When you went away I was three months pregnant, and now we have a sweet little boy in the bed.

An vabm a gebmer meth traweythyow rag bos mabmeth
An mam a gemar meth trewythyow rag boos mammeth—SA 59a
The mother is sometimes embarrassed to be breast-feeding.

Flehes a'm buev denethys a Eva ow frias ker dewdhek warn ugans genys a vebyon
flehys am bef denethys a Eva ow freas kear dewthack warnygans genys a vibbyan—CW 1979–82
Children I have begotten of Eve, my dear spouse, thirty born sons.

Rachel owth ola rag hy flehes ha ny venja hy bos comfortys rag th'ownjy ledhys
Rachal wholo rag e Flehaz ha na venga hye boaze comfortyes, rag tho an gye lethez—Rowe
Rachel weeping for her children, and she would not be comforted for they are dead.

Pan lies flogh omdhevas a veu gesys heb confort na succour?
pan lyas flogh omthevas a ve gesys heb confort na succur—
   TH 40a
How many orphan children were left without comfort or succour?

Merowgh, an babiow wheg
merugh an babyov wek—BM 1577
Look, the sweet babies.

I'n lyfryow scrifys yma bos collenwys lowena a anow a'n
   flehys dâ ha'n re munys ow tena
yn lyfryow scryfys yma bos collenwys lowene a ganow an
   fleghys da ha'n re mvnys ow tene—PC 435–38
I'n the scriptures it is written that joy is fulfilled from the mouths of the
   children and nursing infants.

Ev â dre genef hedhyw. Deus, deus, a vaby
eff a dre gena hythyv dus dus a vaby—BM 3634–35
He will go home with me today. Come, come, baby.

Rag why yw tender in oos ha flehes yonk a gar boos
rag wy yv tender yn oys ha flehys yonk a gar boys—BM 115–16
For you are tender in age and young children love food.

40H HEALTH AND SICKNESS

Th'ov vy lowen gàs gweles in yêhes dâ
Tho ve loan guz gwellas en ehaz da—Pryce
I am glad to see you in good health.

Yma gàn yêhes ny dhyn
'Ma 'ʒen ehaz nyi dhen—AB: 242a
We have our health.

Me a'n pÿs a leun-golon yêhes dhymmo a dhanvon
me a'n pys a luen golon yeghes thy'mmo a thanfon—RD 1715–
16
I pray him with all my heart to send me health.

**Ev yw an fysycyen ha'n methek a wrug sawya oll agan
dysêsys**
*Eff ew an phisicion han metheg a rug sawya oll agan
deseyses*—TH 11
He is the physician and doctor who healed all our diseases.

Manaf gweles agas dowr
Mannaf gueles agys dour—BM 1440
I will inspect your urine.

Gwra vy saw hag y fëdh gwell benytha in dha vêwnans
grua vy sav hag y feth guel benithe in the vevneyns—BM
1466–67
Cure me and things will be better in your life for ever.

Lebmyn me a wor defry pandr'yw an clevejow
lemen me a wor defry pendra yv an clevegov—BM 1456–57
Now I know indeed what the ailments are.

**Ha benytha ken maner, dell gows dhyn ny an lyver, ny
yllowgh bones yaghhës**
*ha benitha ken maner del govs thynny an lefer ny yllogh
bones yaghheys*—BM 1498–1500
And never otherwise, as the book tells us, can you be cured.

Ny sord cleves in mab bronn na wra unweyth y lowsa
Ny sowrd clevas in mab pron na ra unwyth e lawsa—BK
1124–25
No sickness arises in anybody that it will not simply alleviate.

40I COOKING AND EATING

Gorrowgh an bara i'n forn
Gora an bara en foarn—*Pryce*
Put the bread in the oven.

Bara, bleus ha brudnyon
Bara blease ha brudnyan—*Bilbao MS*
Bread, flour and oatmeal.

Yw an bara pebys lùck?
Eu an bara pebes luck?—*Pryce*
Is the bread baked enough?

An bara-ma kemerowgh dhywgh lebmyn yn kettep penn hag anodho oll debrowgh
an bara-ma kymereugh theugh lemman yn kettep pen hag anotho ol dybreugh—*PC 761–63*
Take this bread for you all now and eat of it every one.

Ÿs i'n nor
Ise en noare—*Bilbao MS*
Corn in the ground

Kergh, barlys ha gwaneth
Kerth barlys ha gwaneth—*CW 1066*
Oats, barley and wheat.

Barlys, gwaneth ha kergh
Barles gwanath ha keer—*Bilbao MS*
Barley, wheat and oats

Mana yw gelwys bara, saw whath nyns yw gwrÿs a gynda vëth a ÿs
Manna ew gylwis bara, so whath nyns ew gwrys a kynde vyth a eys—*TH 57a*
Manna is called bread, but it is not made of any kind of grain.

Ma ow gwreg vy ow pobas myttyn, ha hy a wra gwil tesen ragos
ma gurêg vî a pobaz metten, ha hei 'ra guîl tezan ragez—JCH §11
My wife is baking this morning, and she will make a cake for you.

Sav in màn, kebmer dha ly ha kê dhe'n hal
Sâv aman, kebmer tha lî ha ker tha'n hâl—Pryce
Get up, take your breakfast and go to the moor.

Gwag ov vy; a wrav vy gawas haunsel?
Gwag ove, rave gawas haunsell?—Pryce
I am hungry, can I have breakfast?

Unweyth a caffen haunsel, me a wrussa amendya
vnwyth a caffen hansell me a russa amendie—BM 110–11
If I could only have breakfast, I should improve.

Dhe'm godhvos wosa livya me a dhysk moy, ow mêster
ʒum gothvas wosa lyfye me a ʒysk moy ov mester—BM 104–05
To my knowledge, I will learn more, master, after having breakfast.

Tanowgh haunsel kyns sevel
tannegh honthsel kyns sevel—BM 960
Have breakfast in bed.

Saw gwadn rewl yma obma, na yllyn livya kyns mos
sav guan revle yma oma na yllyn lefya kyn moys—BM 3924–25
But here is a poor arrangement, that we can't have breakfast before leaving.

Benyn, drewgh pùscas dhe vy
Benen, drewh pyscos de vi—Borde
Woman, bring me some fish.

Maghteth, drewgh oyow hag amanyn dhe vy
Mathtath drewgh eyo hag amanyn de vi—Borde
Girl, bring me eggs and butter.

Gwag yw dhybm an pengasen. A, mollath Duw i'n gegyn!
Scant yw an dewas ha'n boos.
gvak yv thym an pengasen a molleth du in gegen schant yv an
dewes han boys—BM 3927–29
My stomach is empty. God's curse on the kitchen! The drink and food
are scanty.

Wosa cows ha lavurya an vaner a via dâ kemeres croust hag
eva
Wose cous ha lafurye an vaner a vye da kemeres croust hag
eve—OM 1899–901
After talking and working it would be a good thing to have lunch and
to drink.

Mownjy ow rostya ha ow pryjyon
'ma 'n dzhÿi a rostia ha prÿdzhan—AB: 248a
They are roasting and boiling.

Gwaityowgh dyghtya boos lowr dh'agan soper ragon
gueyteugh dygtye bos lour th'agan soper ragon—PC 639–40
Make sure to prepare enough food for us for our supper.

Me re dhesîryas fest meur debry genowgh why haneth
my re thysyryas fest mer dybry genogh why haneth—PC 718–19
I have greatly wanted to eat with you tonight.

Evowgh gàs cowl
Evough agos kowl—AB: 231c
Eat up your soup.

Eus conys dhywgh?
Ez konnez dhiu'?—AB: 242a
Have you had supper?

Ot omma gaya aval dhis
tomma gaya avall theys—CW 737
Here is a nice apple for you.

Gwil crampes avallow
gil krampez l'avalou—Borlase
To make an apple pie.

Hag erbys an goverow a vëdh ow boos dhe'm prejyow
hag erbys an goverov a veth ov bos thum preggyov—BM 1972
And the herbs of the brooks will be my food for my meals.

40J DRINK

Na gwin ny ûsyen badna
na gwyne ny vsyan badna—CW 1474
Nor did we use any drop of wine.

Ha'n gwin esa wàr an voos, ev a radnas intredha
Han gwyn esa war en foys ef a rannas yn treza—PA 45a
And the wine which was on the table, he shared among them.

Ny evaf cîder na gwin na dewas marnas dowr pur
ny eve cydyr na gwyn na dewes marnes dour pur—BM 1969–70
I drink neither cider nor wine nor any drink but pure water.

Ha why a yll eva an cor gwella mars eus dhywgh brag
Ha why el evah cor gwella mors eez du brage—JJenkins
And you can drink the best ale if you have malt.

I'n pow-ma nyns eus gwell gwin, rag hebma yw pyment fin
yn pov-ma nyns us guel guyn rag hemma yv pyment fyn—OM 1914–15
In this land there is no better wine, for this is fine piment.

Na wrewgh eva re, mès evowgh rag gàs sehes, ha hedna moy pò le a vedn gwitha corf in yêhes
Na reugh eva re, mez eva rag guz zehas; ha hedna muy po le vedn gwitha corf en ehaz—Pryce
Don't drink too much, but drink for your thirst, and that more or less will keep body in health.

I'n tavern sur owth eva ymowns pòr rudh aga min
in taven sur ov eva ymons pur ruth age myn—BM 3308–09
They are surely drinking in the pub with their mouths all red.

Me a vydn abarth an Tas mos ahanan toth garow dhe le na dhyfyk penlas

Me a vyn abarth an Tas mos ahanan toyth garaw the le na thyfyk penlas—BK 1266–68

I will go hence in the name of the Father in great haste to a place where the finest liquor does not fail.

Ow! medhow yw an javal pò gockyhës, by my sowl!

Ow, methew ew an javal py gokyhes, by my sowl!—BK 354–55

Oh, the wretch is drunk or out of his mind, upon my soul!

A, pennow medhow! Owt in ow dedhyow criaf warnowgh, ladron dreus!

a pennov methov ot in ov dythyov creyaff warnogh ladron drues—BM 1045–47

Ah, you drunkards! In my day I cry out upon you, bold thieves!

Wèl, wèl, me a be an scot

Wel wel me a bee an scot—BM 3340

Well, well, I'll pay the bill.

40K CLOTHES

Kemmer dha gygel rag nedha dhyn ny dyllas.

kymmer the gygel rag nethe thy'nny dyllas—OM 366–67

Take your distaff to spin clothes for us.

Agan corfow noth gallas. Mir warnan pùb tenewen. Omgwethyn ny gans del glas

agen corfow nooth gallas mere warnan pub tenewhan omgwethen ny gans deel glase—CW 856–57

Our bodies are naked. Look on us from every side. Let us clothe ourselves in green leaves.

Inwedh me a vydn nedha rag gwil dyllas dhe'm cudha ha dhe'm flehes eus genys

ynweth me a vyn netha rag gule dillas thom cutha ha thom flehys es genys—CW 1037–39

Also I will spin to make clothes to cover myself and for my children who have been born.

Pandra vednowgh why gwil rag lednow rag gàs flogh?
Pendre vedda why geil rag lednow rag 'as flo—Chygwyn
What will you do for clothes for your baby?

Nyns yw crejy dhe beggars hag a vo aga dyllas clowtys gans dyvers pannow
nyns yv crygy the beggars hag a fo aga dyllas cloutys gans dyuers pannow—RD 1507–09
One cannot believe beggars whose clothes are patched with various cloths.

Yma gàs dyllas gwrÿs
Ema 'ȝÿz dillaz gurŷz—AB: 248b
Your clothes are made.

Me ny welys i'n wlas-ma bythqweth dyllas a'n sewt-na sur
my ny wylys yn wlas ma bythqueth dyllas a sevt na sur—RD 2549–51
I have never seen clothes of that colour indeed in this kingdom.

Ea, ha'n poor creatùrs a Grist gesys dhe fâmya rag fowt boos, dewas hag othem dyllas, ow cria owt
Ea, han pore creaturs a crist gesys the famya rag fowt bos, dewas, hag ethom dyllas, ow crya out—TH 40a
Yes, an Christ's poor creatures left to starve for lack of food, drink and need of clothes, crying out.

Kemerowgh with a'gas lavrak poos
Kymero 'wyth goz lavrak pouz—JBoson
Take care of your heavy trousers.

Hy a wor gwil padn dâ gen hy gwlân
Hye oare gwile padn da gen hye glân—JJenkins
She can make good cloth with her wool.

Gans crehyn an bestas-na me a wra dyllas dhybmo
gans krehen an bestas na me a ra dyllas thyma—CW 1477–78
With the skins of those beasts I shall make clothes for myself.

**Ha velvet ker yw dha aray, damask, baudkyn, inwedh
cendal, byss ha satyn, ea, pùrpur pal ha pannow gay.**
*ha velvet ker eu the aray, damask, boytkyn, inweth cendal,
bys ha satynn, ye, porpor pal ha pannow gay—BK 1722–28*
And expensive velvet is your apparel, damask, baudkin and also silk
cloth, rich linen and satin, yea, purple in mantles and brightly-
coloured cloths.

**In le ow dyllas owrlyn, pùrpur, pannow fin certan lebmyn
me a wysk qweth loos**
*in le ov delles ourlyn purpur pannov fyn certyn lemen me a
wesk queth los—BM 1965–67*
Instead of my silk clothes, purple, fine fabrics now I shall wear grey
cloth.

**Ny vÿdh dhe well ow aray awos dha ro, by this day! Ny a
wysk blou ha more**
*ny vith the wel ow aray awos the ro, by thys day! Ny a wysk
blow ha more—BK 3062–64*
My appearance will be no better in spite of your gift, by this day—we
shall wear blue and murrey.

Gwysk dha dhyllas i'th kerhyn
guyske the dylles yth kerhyn—BM 3003
Put on your clothes.

An hevys adro y geyn
An hevez adrô y ꝫein—AB: 250a
The shirt on his back.

**Kyn whysca padn teg avês, in y nessa hevys reun pùb dëdh y
whysca certan**
*kyn wyske pan tek aveys in y nesse hevys ruen pup deth y
weska certen—BM 4442–44*
Though he wore fine fabric on the outside, next to his skin he indeed
wore a hair shirt every day.

An lodrow adro'gàs garrow
An lydroṵ adrô 'z garro—AB: 250a
The stockings on your legs.

An vanek adro'gàs dorn
An manak adrô 'z dʋrn—*AB: 250a*
The glove on your hand.

Gwescowgh an genter-ma et eskys vy
Guisgo an ӡenter-ma ed eskaz vi—*AB: 230c*
Knock this nail into my shoe.

Disk dha skyjyow qwyk dhe ves
dysk the skyggyow quyk the ves—*OM 1406*
Quick, take your shoes off.

**Ev a wrug exaltya y vêster Crist, hag a leverys fatell o ev
ùnwordhy rag bocla y eskyjyow**
*eff a rug exaltia y mester crist hag a leverys fatell o eff
vnworthy rag bocla y skyggyow*—*TH 8*
He exalted Christ his master and said that he was unworthy to buckle
his shoes.

An eskyjyow dro'gàs treys
An esӡizoу a dro 'z treiz—*AB: 250a*
The shoes on your feet.

40L MONEY

Ena anjy a vargydnyas rag try funs an vledhen gober
Ena dzhei a varӡiniaz raӡ trei penz an vleðan ӡuber *JCH §4*
Then they agreed on three pounds a year as wages.

Ha why a yll dendyl gàs bêwnans obma
ha huei el dendal 'ӡӱz bounaz ӱbma—*JCH §2*
And you can earn your living here.

Dry dre an mona ha perna moy
Dry dre an mona ha perna muy—*Pryce*
To bring home the money and buy more.

Dü yw an mona re'm fay
due yv an mona rum fay—*BM 1873*
The money is all gone, upon my faith.

Ev a dal deneren naw
eff a dall deneren nov—*BM 3404*
It is worth nine pence.

Tàn, ot obma dhis deg puns
Tan at omma thys x puns—*BM 1464*
Take, here are ten pounds for you.

Ry dhe stenor deg puns i'n vledhen
Ry tha stêner deck pens en blethan—*Pryce*
To give a tinner ten pounds a year.

Ny vedn ev nefra dos avês a gendon
Ny vedn e nevra dvz vêz a ꝫyndan—*AB: 230c*
He'll never get out of debt.

Te vaw, prag na wrusta dre don agan wajys obma?
Ty vav prag na ruste dre don agen wagys ome—*BM 3334–35*
You, boy, why didn't you bring us our wages home here?

Awos mil buns ny vynsen dha weles, re'n oferen!
Awos myl buns ny vynsen the welas, ru'n oferen!—*BK 1211–*
12
For a thousand pounds I wouldn't want to see you, by the mass!

Ha mona lowr gans gàs gwreg
ha mona lour gans goz gureg—*JBoson*
And may your wife have enough money.

**Kyns in udn tyller i'n bÿs dew gendoner yth eja dhe udn
dettor, me a grÿs. An eyl dhodho a della pymp cans dyner
monies ha hanter-cans y gela**
*kyns yn vn teller yn beys dev kendoner yth ege the vn dettor
me a grys an nyl thotho a delle pymp cans dyner monyys
ha hanter cans y gyle*—*PC 501–06*
Once upon a time in a place in the world there were two debtors to
one creditor. The one owed him five hundred minted pence, and the
other fifty.

Ha me a's pern dhyworthys. Otta an mona parys dhyso dhe be
ha my a's pren thyworthy's otte an mone parys thy'so the
  pe—PC 1555-57
And I will buy it from you. Here is the money ready to pay you.

Ha'n mona anjy a gavas, ha'n bara anjy a dhebras
Ha an mona an dzhei a gavaz; ha 'n bara dzhei a dhabraz—
  JCH §46
And they found the money and ate the bread.

40M WORK

Mos dhe balas me a vydn rag sostena bêwnans dhyn—res yw
  porres lavurya
mos the balas my a vyn rag sustene beunans thyn rys yw
  porrys lafurrye—OM 681-83
I shall go to dig to provide us with food to live—it is very necessary to
work.

Pana whel a yllysta gwil, yn medh an tiak? Pùb whel oll, yn
  medh Jowan
Panna huêl allosti ʒuîl með an tîak: pỳb huêl 'ulla með
  Dzhûan—JCH §4
What kind of work can you do? asked the farmer. Every sort of work,
said John.

Gorra tus i'n skyber dhe dhrùshya
Gorah tees en an skeber tha drushen—Pryce
To send men into the barn to thresh.

Crev yw gwredhyow an spedhes, mayth yw ow dywvregh
  terrys worta menowgh ow qweytha
kref yv gvrythyow a'n spethes may thyv ov dyv-vregh terrys
  worte menough ov quethe—OM 687-89
Tough are the roots of the brambles, so my arms are broken by
working at them again and again.

Gorra an vowes dhe shakya an cala
Gorah an vose tha shakiah an kala—Pryce
To put the girl to shake the straw.

Bargydnya gen den dhe mos dhe whel sten
Bargidnia gen dean da mose da whele sten—Pryce
To bargain with a man to go to a tin work.

Carya an stùff stênus dhe'n stampys
Coria an stuff stênes tha an stampes—Pryce
To carry the tin stuff to the stamping-mill.

Whelas tus dhe drehy kesow
Whelas tus tha trehe kesow—Pryce
To seek men to cut turf.

Whelas pobel dhe drehy eythyn
Whelas poble tha trehe ithen—Pryce
To seek people to cut furze.

Aras an kensa an todn
Aras an kensa an todn—Pryce
First to plough up the grass.

Yth esa ev ha'y helhor, cresowgh, avell pàn dheuthon, owth aras scav ha bysy ha kyrwas gwyls ha prety aragtha in le ohen
eth esa ef ha'y hethlor cresough, avel pan dohan, owth aras scaf ha besy ha kyrwas gwyls pur prety aragtha in le ohan—BK 958–61
He and his huntsman were, believe, when we came ploughing quickly and busily with wild and very handsome stags before them instead of oxen.

Yma ev ow clojyas
ma e a klodzhas—Borlase
He is harrowing.

Gorra an sogh ha'n troher dhe'n gov
Gora an soch ha an troher tha an gove—Pryce
To send the ploughshare and the coulter to the smith.

Gorra an dens harrow dhe'n gov dhe lebma
Gora an dens harraw tha an gove tha lebma—Pryce
To send the harrow tines to the smith to be sharpened.

Danvon rag tus dhe drehy gora
Danen rag teese tha trehe gorra—*Pryce*
To send for men to cut hay.

Trehy grônd bêten rag gonys sùgal
Trehe ground beaten rag gones sogall—*Bilbao MS*
To cut beat ground to sow rye.

Whelas mejwesyon dhe vejy an ÿs
Whelas megouzion dhe medge an îsse—*Pryce*
To seek reapers to reap the corn.

Whelas colmoryon dhe gelmy an ÿs
Whelas colmurion dhe kelme an îsse—*Pryce*
To seek binders to bind the corn.

40N SEASONS, DAYS, AND MONTHS

Gwâv in hâv tre ba Golowan ha hâv in gwâv tre bo Nadelyk
Guâve en hâve terebah Goluan ha hâve en guâve terebah
  Nedelack—*Ustick MSS*
Winter in summer until Midsummer and Summer in Winter until
  Christmas

In hâv porth cov a gwâv
En hâv per kou gwâv—*Pryce*
In summer remember winter.

Howl soth, torr leun, paradhys an gwaynten
Houl sooth, Tor lean, paravy[s] an gwaynten—*Pryce*
The sun in the south, a full belly—the paradise of spring.

Ena tregens gwâv ha hâv
ena tregans gwave ha have—*CW 1700*
There let him dwell winter and summer.

Rag own why dhe godha, pò an rew dhe derry, ha why dhe
  vos budhys
Rhag oᴜn hui dho Kᴠdha, po an reᴜ dhᴠ dèrhi, a huei dhᴠ vᴠz
  bidhis—*AB: 250a*
Lest you fall or the ice break and you be drowned.

Rag dowt why dhe slyppya
Rag dout why dho sleppia—Borlase
Lest you slip.

Kyns pedn seythen
Kynz pedn zythin—AB: 250b
Within a week.

Kyns ès de Merher dhe nos
kyns ys dumerher the nos—BM 2254
Before Wednesday evening.

Arta me a dheu de Yow
arta me a thue deth yov—BM 1472
I will come again on Thursday.

Hedhyw sur yw de Gwener
hezyv sur yv dugwener—BM 120
Today indeed is Friday.

De Sul Blejyow pàn esa in mesk y abestely, y whrug dhe re anedha mos dhe'n dre ha dygelmy an asen
Dewsull blegyow pan ese yn mysc y abestely y wreg ʒe re aneʒe mos ʒen dre ha degylmy an asen—PA 27a–c
On Palm Sunday when he was among his apostles he got some of them go to the town and unbind the ass.

Maner o dhe'n Yêdhewon wàr dÿdh Pask worth an jùstys a'n pryson govyn onen
maner o ʒen eʒewon war dyth pasch worth an iustis an preson govyn onon—PA 124cd
It was a custom of the Jews on the day of the Passover to ask for one man from prison from the justice.

Degol Myhal bÿdh hedna
dugol myhall byth henna—BM 2201
That will be Michaelmas.

Tommas, yth os pòr wocky drefen na vynnyth crejy an Arlùth dhe dhasserhy de Pask vyttyn
thomas yth os pur woky drefen na fynnyth crygy an arluth the thasserghy du pask vyttyn—*RD 1105–08*
Thomas, you are very silly, since you will not believe that the Lord arose on Easter morning.

Yth yw scrifys fatell wrug Peder kemeres warnodho in presens a oll an apostlys dhe gows in aga hanow y oll dhe'n bobel wàr de Fencost myttyn
Ith ew scryffys fatell rug pedyr kemeras warnotha in presens a oll an appostlys the gowse in aga hanow y oll then bobyll war du fencost myttyn—*TH 44a*
It is written that St Peter took it upon himself in the presence of all the apostles to speak in the name of them all to the people on the morning of Pentecost.

De Halan Gwâv myttyn in Eglos de Lalant
Dew Whallan Gwa metten in Eglos De Lalant—*Exeter Consistory Court 1572*
On the morning of All Saints' day in Lelant Church.

Ev a ros towl dhe bronter Pawl mis Du kyn Nadelyk
E a roz towl dho proanter Powle mîz Du ken Nadelik—*WGwavas*
He gave a fall to the vicar of Paul in November before Christmas.

Naw nobyl a Gala'Me a wrussa soker dhyn ny
ix nobyl a calame a russe sokyr thynny—*BM 3338–39*
Nine nobles on the first of May would have been a help to us.

Ow gool a vëdh sur in mis Metheven an kensa Gwener
Ov gol a veth suer in mes metheven an kynsa guener—*BM 4303–04*
My feast will surely be on the first Friday in June.

An wheffes dëdh in Gortheren ha'n gela vëth mis Est certan
An wehes deth in gortheren han gela veth mys est certen—*BM 2070–03*
The sixth of July and the other will be in August indeed.

Ha'n tressa mis Gwyngala
han tresse mys gvyngala—BM 2076
And the third in September.

In Castel Sùdley i'n degves dÿdh mis Hedra i'n vledhen mil whegh cans dewgans ha try
yn Castel Sudley yn dekvas dyth mys heddra in blethan myll whegh cans dewghans ha try—JKeigwin
In Castle Sudley on the tenth day of October in the year 1643.

An kensa jorna a vis Hedra an cùntell in plu Pawl in Kernow teg
an kensa journa a messe Heddra an centle en plew Paule in Cernow teage—TBoson
The meeting on the first day of October in the parish of Paul in fair Cornwall.

Screfys wàr an kensa dÿdh a'n mis Kevardhu 1736
Skrefis war an kenza dydh an miz Kevardhiu 1736—WGwavas
Written on the 1st December 1736.

400 WEATHER

Fatl'usy ow colowy ha taredna!
Patl ÿzhi a kÿlÿui ha trenna—AB: 248a
How it thunders and lightens!

Hager-awel ha awel teg
Hagar awell ha auel teag—Pryce
Bad weather and fine weather.

Yma ow qwil ergh
Emâ a kîl err—AB: 250b
It's snowing.

Yma ow qwil keser
Ema a kîl kezzar—AB: 250b
It's hailing.

Yeyn kewer, tarednow ha golowys, ergh, rew, gwyns ha clehy ha keser
Yeyn kuer, tarednow ha golowas, er, reu, gwenz ha clehe ha kezer—Pryce
Cold weather, thunder and lightning, snow, frost, wind, ice and hail.

Dhe wil glaw
Dho ʒîl glâu—AB: 122b
To rain.

Cabmdhavas i'n myttyn, glaw a yll bos ettan
Cabmthavaz en mettyn, glaue el boz etten—Pryce
Rainbow in the morning, rain can be in it.

40P LETTERS

Lebmyn why â bys in Arthùr gans lyther clos
lemmyn, why a bys in Arthur gans letherclos—BK 1820
Now you will go to Arthur with a sealed letter.

Dodho degowgh lytherow
dotho degogh lytherov—BM 2796
Take letters to him.

Sera wheg, Me a wrug fanja gàs lyther zeythen alebma, mès nag esa termyn dhybm dha screfa dhywgh straft arta
Sarra Wheage, Me rig fanja guz lether zithan lebma, buz nagerra termen dem de screffa du straft arta—OPender
Dear Sir, I received your letter a week ago, but I did not have time to reply to you immediately.

Th'ov vy lowen dhe glôwes dhyworthowgh why
Tho ve loan tha clowas thort why—Pryce
I am glad to hear from you.

Ny woraf vy screfa namoy
N'ora vi skrefa na muî—AB: 250b
I cannot write any more.

40Q ANIMALS

Eus leth lùck gen an vuwgh?
Ese leath luck gen veu—Pryce
Has the cow enough milk?

Gorra an ohen i'n ardar
Gora an ohan en arder—Pryce
To put the oxen to the plough.

Buwgh, lejek ha leugh
Bew leoyock ha leaw—Bilbao MS
Cow, heifer, and calf.

Tarow, ojyon ha denewes
Tarrow odgan ha denowes—Bilbao MS
Bull, ox, and steer.

Hordh, davas hag ôn
Hor davas ha oane—Bilbao MS
Ram, sheep, and lamb.

Deves, ên, gever ha menas
Devas ean gever ha menas—Bilbao MS
Sheep, lambs, goats, and kids.

Rag nynj on ny kelmys dhe vos cyrcùmcîsys, na dhe offra in bàn dhe Dhuw leuhy, ohen, deves ha gyfras
Rag nyg one ny kylmys the vos circumcisis, na the offra in ban the thew ley, oghan, devas, ha gyffras—TH 27a
For we are not bound to be circumcized, nor to offer up to God calves, oxen sheep, and goats.

Ha margh yw best heb parow
ha margh yw best hep parow—OM 24
And a horse is a beast without equal.

Casek, margh hag ebol
Casek mar ha eball—Bilbao MS
Mare, horse, and colt.

Me a wel gwas wàr geyn margh
Me a weyl guas war geyn margh—BM 1884
I see a fellow on horseback.

Mos dhe'n gov dhe hernya an vergh
Moas tha an gove tha herniah an verh—Pryce
To go to the smith to shoe the horses.

Ena why a gev asen hag ebol in unn golmen
ena why a gyf asen hagh ebel yn vn golmen—PC 176–77
There you will find an ass and a foal tied up together.

**Mergh, gwarthek, mogh ha deves drewgh aberveth
desempys**
mergh guarthek mogh ha deves dreugh abervet desempys—
   OM 1065–66
Bring in immediately horses, cattle, pigs, and sheep.

Yma an ky ow grysla
man kei y grisla—Borlase
The dog is showing his teeth.

Ky ha cath ha logosen
ky ha cathe ha logosan—CW 407
Dog and cat and mouse.

Dhe'm duw Jovyn in y fàss me a offryn lawen cath
Thum du iovyn in y fath me a offren lawen cath—BM 3412–13
To my god Jove in his face I shall offer a tom cat.

**Yma obma keun munys. Pymp lonn bowyn dyvynys y a
dhepsa in dew dhëdh.**
*Yma oma kuen munys v lon bowyn dufunys y a depse in ij
   deth*—BM 3223–25
Here are tiny dogs. In two days they would eat five cut-up beeves.

Gavar, ewyges, carow
gaver yweges karow—OM 126
Goat, hind, and stag.

Seul a vynno bos selwys, golsowens ow lavarow, a Jesù dell veu helhys wàr an bÿs avell carow
Suel a vynno bos sylwys golsowens ow lauarow a ihesu del ve helheys war an bys avel carow—PA 2ab
Whoever would be saved, let him listen to my words, how Jesus was hunted in the world like a stag.

Whath lion gooth in y ogo dhis a inclyn
Whath luon goyth in y ugo thys a ynclyn—BK 1777–79
Yet the wild lion in his den will submit to you.

Yma agas escar an tebel-el kepar ha lion owth uja, ow mos adro ow whelas rag agas devorya
yma agys yskar an teball ell kepar ha lyon ow huga ow mos adro ow whelas rag agys devowrya—TH 3a–4
Your adversary the devil like a roaring lion goes about seeking to devour you.

Bleydh brâs i'n fordh-na defry pòr wir yma
blyth brays in for na defry pur guir yma—BM 1104–05
There is indeed very truly a big wolf that way.

Yma agan Savyour worth aga gelwel y bleydhas, rag y a wra devorya enevow an re-na kebmys ina a gryssa
yma agan Savyoure worth aga gylwall y blythes, rag y a ra devourya enevow an re na kymmys inna a crissa—TH 19a
Our Saviour calls them 'wolves', because they devour the souls of as many as believe in them.

40R BIRDS

Me a wrug gweles an carnow ujy an gùllys ha'n ÿdhyn mor aral ow qwil aga neithyow
Mi 'rig guelaz an Karnou idzha an gullez ha'n idhen môr aral kîl ÿ͝ſe neitho—AB: 245a
I saw the rocks where the gulls and other sea birds make their nests.

Colom wheg, glas hy lagas, ke, neyj a-ugh lies pow
colom whek glas hy lagas ke nyg a-vgh lues pow—OM 1135–36
Sweet dove, with blue eye, go, fly over many lands.

Lebmyn hanwaf goodh ha yar, a sensaf ëdhyn heb par dhe vegyans den wàr an bës
lemyn hanwaf goyth ha yar a sensaf ethyn hep par the vygyens den war an beys—OM 129–31
Now I name goose and hen, which I consider peerless birds to nurture man in the world.

Kyns ès bos culyak kenys tergweyth y whreth ow naha
kyns ys bos kullyek kenys ter guyth y wregh ov naghe—PC 903–04
Before the cock crow, three times you will deny me.

Hoos, payon, colom, grugyar, swàn, bargos, bryny ha'n er
hos payon colom grvgyer swan bargos bryny ha'n er—OM 132–33
Duck, peacock, dove, swan, buzzard, crows and the eagle.

An tellek Arthùr, re'n Tas, a vÿdh boos dhe'n bryny brâs
An tyllyk Arthur, re'n Tas! a vith boys the'n bryny bras—BK 2690–91
The ragamuffin Arthur, by God, will be food for the carrion crows

Ha gwren leverel, Dhe'n dor, lost pêcok, *vel* payon, prowt
ha gwren leverall, then dore, lost peacok, vel payon, prowt—TH 9
And let us say, Down, proud tail of peacock (or Pavo).

Dew gopyl a gelemy dov, gans pluv gwynn
deaw gopyl a gelemmy, dof gans pluf gwyn—BK 2045–46
Two pairs of tame doves, with white feathers.

Maga fery avell hôk
mage fery avel hok—BM 1901
As merry as a hawk.

Gwir dhymm te a dherivas, an varghvran na dhewhela; yma war garynyas brâs ow tebry fest dybyta
Guyr thy'm ty a tharyvas an vargh-vran na thywhele yma war garynnyas bras ov tybry fest dybyte—OM 1105-08
You told me the truth about the raven, that it would not return; it is feasting on great carrion without mercy.

Er, bargos, gelvinak, kevelek, golvan, gwradnen
Er, Bargez, Ṡ̈ylvinak, Kyvelak, Golvan, Gṵradnan—AB: 241b
An eagle, a buzzard, a curlew, a woodcock, a sparrow, a wren.

40S FISH

Y rov henwyn dhe'n pùscas: porpos, sowmens, syllies, oll dhymm gostyth y a vÿdh, lenesow ha barvusy
y rof hynwyn the'n puskes porpus sowmens syllyes ol thy'm gustyth y a vyth lenesow ha barfusy—OM 135–38
I will give names to the fishes: porpoise, salmon, eels, they will all be obedient to me, ling and cod.

Mos dhe'n mor dhe gachya pùscas
Mos tha an mor tha catchah pyzgaz—Pryce
To go to sea to catch fish.

Gorra an rosow i'n dowr rag hern
Gora an rosow en dour rag hearn—Bilbao MS
To set nets in the water for pilchards.

Tedna cans mil warbarth
Tedna cans mil warbar—Pryce
To draw a hundred thousand together.

An hern gwâv a vedn gwil drog dhe'n hern hâv
an hern gwave vedn geele droeg d'an hern have—OPender
The winter pilchards will do damage to the summer pilchards.

Ma canow vy wàr hern gen côk ha roos kemerys en sans Garrek glas i'n Coos
Ma canow vee wor hern gen cock ha rooz kameres en zans Garrack glase en Kooz—JBoson
My songs are about pilchards with boat and net taken in the holy green Rock in the Wood.

40T TREES, FLOWERS, AND FRUIT

Pùb gwedhen tevens a'y sav ow ton hy frût ha'y delyow, ha'n losowys erbynn hâv degens has in erberow
pup gvethen tefyns a'y saf ov ton hy frvt ha'y delyow ha'n losowys erbyn haf degyns has yn erberow—OM 29–32
Let every tree grow upright, bearing its fruit and its leaves, and the herbs by summer time let them bear fruit in sheltered places.

Lowr flourys a bùb ehen i'n plâss-ma otta tevys, ha frûtys wàr bùb gwedhen, gwâv ha hâv kefrÿs
lower flowrys a bub ehan yn place ma yta tevys ha frutes war bub gwethan y teyf gwaf ha have keffrys—CW 363–66
Many flowers of all kinds look grow in this place, and fruits grow on every tree both in winter and summer.

An losowen bian gen y arr nedhys eus ow tevy in a'n hallow ny yw cries pleth Maria
An lÿzûan bîan ʒen i'ar nedhez, ez a tivi en an halou nei, ez kreiez Plêth Maria—AB: 245a
The small plant with the twisted stalk, which grows on our hills, is called Lady's tresses

Kepar dell wra an gwels seha, an flour a glamder
kepar dell ra an gwels seha, an flowre a glomder—TH 7
Just as the grass withers, the flower fades.

Rag delkyow sevy a wra mowysy teg
Rag delkiow sevi gwra muzi teag—Chygwyn
For strawberry leaves will make girls beautiful.

Palm ha bayes, byxyn, erbys genef yma
palm ha bayys byxyn erbys gynef yma—PC 261
Palm and bays, branches of box, herbs have I.

Ny dÿv gwels na flour i'n bÿs i'n keth fordh-na may kerdhys
ny dyf guels na flour yn bys yn keth forth-na may kyrthys—OM 712–13
No grass or flower at all grows in that same way where I walked.

Ny yw gwŷdh crabbys na dhora frût dâ vëth. Ahanan agan honen ny dhryn in rag ma's dreys, spern, lynas ha spedhes
ny ew gwyth crabbys, na thora frut da vith, ahanan agan honyn ny thryn in rag mas dreys, sperne lynas ha spethas—TH 9

We are crab-apple trees, which yield no fruit. On our own we do not produce anything but briars, thorns, nettles and brambles.

Duw a gomondyas an profet Esay dhe wul proclamacyon dhe oll an bŷs fatell yw mab den gwels ha fatell yw oll an glory, an brâfter ha'n lowender a vab den kepar ha flourys i'n prasow, rag pàn dheffa an welsen ha dallath seha, an flowr a wra clamdera ha codha dhe ves.
Du a commondyas an profet Ysay the wull proclamacion the oll an bys fatell ew mab den gwels, ha fatell ew oll an glory an broghter han lowender a vab den kepar ha flowres in prasow, rag pan deffa an welsan ha dalleth seeha an flowre a ra clamdera ha cotha the ves—TH 6a–7

God commanded the prophet Isaiah to proclaim to all the world that mankind is grass, and that all the glory, the splendour and joy of mankind are like flowers in the meadows, for when the grass begins to wither, the flower fades and dies.

Gwell via dhe'n harlot dos yn noth der spedhes ha spern
Gwel vea the'n harlot dos in noeth der spethas ha spern—BK 416–17

It would be better for the scoundrel to pass naked through brambles and thorns.

Praga i'gas kerthow why y tev lynas in erbers heb gonys vëth?
Praga i'gas kerthow why e tef lynas in erbers heb gonys veth?—BK 2295–97

Why in your jurisdiction do nettles grow in uncultivated kitchen gardens?

Hag erbys an goverow a vëth ow boos dhe'm prejyow
hag erbys an goverov a veth ov bos thum preggyov—BM 1971–72

And herbs of the streams will be my food for my meals.

**Yma agan mëster, redêmer ha savyour Jesù Crist in awayl a
Sen Jowan ow comparya hag owth hevelly y honen dhe
wedhen grappys ha ny oll dhe'n barrow**
*Yma agan meister, redymer ha Sovyour Jhesu crist, in aweyll
a S Jowan, ow comparya ha ow hevely y honyn the wethan
grappys, ha ny oll thyn barrow*—TH 39a
Our master, redeemer and saviour Christ, in St John's gospel compares
and likens himself to a grape vine, and us all to the branches.

Ena yth esa flourys ha frûtys teg aga lyw dh'agan maga
ena yth esa flowrys ha frutes teke aga lew thagan maga—CW
1050–52
In that place there were flowers and beautifully coloured fruits to
nourish us.

40U HEAVENLY BODIES

**Ha'ga henwyn y a vÿdh an howl, ha'n loor ha'n stergan; me
a's set a-ugh an gwëdh in cres an ebron avàn**
*h'aga hynwyn y a vyth an houl ha'n lor ha'n stergan my a set
ahugh an gveyth yn creys an ebron avan*—OM 35–38
And their names will be the sun, and the moon and the stars; I will set
them above the trees in the middle of the sky above.

**I'n peswora dÿdh bÿdh gwrÿs an howl ha'n loor yn tefry,
ha'n ster inwedh kekefrÿs rag gwil golow benary**
*in peswera dyth bith gwryes an howle han loer in tevery han
steare inweth kekeffrys rag gwyle golow benary*—CW 100–
03
On the fourth day will be made the sun and the moon indeed, and the
stars also as well to give light for ever.

An loor i'n nos, howl i'n jëdh may rollons y golow spladn
An lor yn nos houl yn geyth may rollons y golow splan—OM
39–40
The moon in the night, sun in the day, that they may give brilliant
light.

An golowder me a wor, nyns yw ev lemen an loor, pan ujy ow trehevel
an golovder me a wor nyns yv eff lemen an lor pan vgy ov trehevel—BM 2101–03
The light I know, it is only the moon when it is rising.

Ha Duw a wras dew wolow brâs, an brâssa rag an jëdh ha'n biadnha rag an nos; ev a wras an steradnow inwedh.
Ha Deu gwras deau gullou brôz, an broza rag an deth ha an behatna rag an noz, e gwras an sterradnou aveth—JBoson
And God made two large lights, the bigger for the day, and the smaller for the night; he made the stars also.

Ny vÿdh skians vëth i'n bÿs mès y aswon ev a wra der an planettys mes ha chy
ny vyth skeans vyth in beys mes y aswon ev a wra der a planantis mes ha chy—CW 1407–09
There will be no knowledge in the world, except he know it through the planets inside and out.

Der howl ha ster awartha ev a wra decernya an pÿth a vëdh wosa hebma kekefrÿs a dhrog ha dâ
der howle ha steare awartha ef a ra oll desernya an pyth a vith woʒa hemma kekefrys a throg ha da—CW 1410–13
By sun and stars above he will decern that which will be after this both of evil and good.

An planettys eus awartha ha'n ster inwedh magata ow poyntya ymowns pòr efan
an planattis es awartha han steare inweth magata ow poyntya mowns pur efan—CW 2154–56
The planets on high and the stars also as well are pointing quite clearly.

An howl ha'n loor kekefrÿs oll warbarth yw convedhys; dhe'n porpos-na ymowns ow tos
an howle han loor kekeffrys oll warbarth ew confethys than purpose na mowns ow toos—CW 2159–61
The sun and the moon also, all together they are understood; to that purpose they are coming.

40V COUNTRIES

Sten Sen Agnes: an gwella sten in Kernow
Stean San Agnes an guella stean en Kernow—*Pryce*
St Agnes tin: the best tin in Cornwall.

Ny wòn gov in oll Kernow a whetho gans megynow certan bÿth well.
ny won gof yn ol kernow a whytho gans mygenow certan byth wel—*PC 2712–14*
I do not know of a smith in all Cornwall who blows any better indeed with bellows.

Lebmyn dhe drailya dh'agan pow ny a Inglond, hebma a yll bos lel côwsys, a oll an gwlasow in Cristoneth, nyns eus onen a'n jeves mar veur caus dhe favera an se ha'n stall a Rom dell y'n jeves Inglond.
lymmyn the drelya thegen pow ny a ynglonde, hemma a yll bos lell cowsys , a oll an gwlasow in cristoneth nyns es onyn an gevas mar ver cawse the favera an sea han stall a rom dell gevas englond—*TH 50a–51*
Now to turn to our own country of England, this can be truly spoken, of all the kingdoms in Christendom there is not one that has as great cause to favour the see and stall of Rome as has England.

Dres meyn, dres gryn, dres trosow, a Dowl an Jowl in Kembra
drys myn, drys gryn, drys trosow, a Dowl an Jowl in Kembra—*BK 1163–64*
Over stones, over gravel, over breakers, from the Devil's Drop in Wales.

An Arvorek, pò dell yw hy cries genen ny in Kembra, an Lesawek
an Arvorek, po del yụ i kreiez ʒen a nei en Kembra, an Lezauek—*AB: 222*
The Armorican, or as it is called by us in Wales, the Letavian.

An duk a'n jevyth pòr wir rag y lavur oll an tir a Dhowr Hombyr dhe Scotlond
An duk a'n gevith pur wyer rag e laver ol an tyr a Thowr Hombyr the Scotland—BK 3235–36
The duke will have for his labour all the country from the River Humber to Scotland.

Now, mytern Scotlond, Augel, ha Syr Gawen yw marow
Now, myghtern Scotland, Augel, ha Syr Gawen ew maraw—BK 3284–85
Now the king of Scotland, Augel, and Sir Gawain are dead.

Hag ev dhe Wordhen êth y honen rag cows gen y gar Trip Cùnen
Ha e tha Worthen eath e whonnen rag cowas gen e gare Trip-Cunnen—JTonkin
And he to Ireland went himself to talk to his friend Tyrconnel.

ha'n Kelezonek pò an Scot-Vrethonek eus leverys in Uheldir an Alban hag in gwlascor Wordhen
ha 'n Kelezonek po 'n Skot-Vrethonek ez laveryz en Ehual-dir an Alban hag en G'laskor Uordhyn—AB: 222
And the Caledonian or the Scoto-British which is spoken in the Highlands of Scotland and in the kingdom of Ireland.

Me a jest dhe'n uhelha arlùth eus a-ugh an loor, istyn qwarel na wrelha erbynn Mytern Breten Veur, Arthùr, gour mas
Me a gest the'n ughelha arluth us a-ugh an loer, ystyn quaral na relha erbyn Myghtern Bretyn Veor Arthor, gour mas—BK 1421–25
I declare to the highest lord, who is above the moon, that he should not urge a dispute against the King of Great Britain, Arthur, a goodly hero.

Wàr tu ha Frynk fystenyn
War tua Frynk fystynnyn—BK 2735
Let us hurry to France.

Nena ev êth in kerdh rag Frynk
Nenna e eath car rag Frink—JTonkin
Then he went away to France.

Mytern Frynk, th'esof vy ow mênya
Materen Frink, thera vi a menia—*JTonkin*
I mean the King of France.

Me yw gelwys Duk Breten ha sevys a woos rial
Me yw gylwys duk bryten ha seuys a goys ryel—BM 1–2
I am called Duke of Brittany and a scion of royal blood.

Nyns eus in Breten Vian ow farow pòr wir heb dowt
nyns us in breten vyen ov parov pur guir heb dovt—BM 517–
18
There is not my peer in Brittany indeed without doubt.

**Merowgh inwedh wàr Jermany ha kemerowgh exampel
anedhy**
*Merowgh inweth war germany, ha kemerogh example
anethy*—TH 49a
Look also at Germany, and take her as an example.

**Me re dhanvonas defry duk an Saxons, Chellery, dhe whelas
myns a geffa a bagans in Jermany**
*Me re thanvanas deffry duk an Saxens, Chellery, the whelas
myns a geffa a bagans in Germany*—BK 3229–32
I have indeed sent Childerich, the duke of the Saxons, to seek as many
as he could find of pagans in Germany.

**Ha whegh cans bledhen wosa Crist an Saxons a veu spredys
dres oll an wlas**
*ha vi c. blethan wosa crist an Saxons a ve spredys drys oll an
wlas*—TH 51
And 600 years after Christ the Saxons had spread through all the land.

**Radn in Jermany a levery, Obma yma Crist, obma yma an
eglos; radn in Bohem a levery, Obma yma Crist, obma
yma an eglos**
*ran in Germany a levery, omma yma crist, omma yma an
egglos, ran in Bohem a lleuery, omma yma crist, oma yma
an egglos*—TH 32
Some in Germany were saying, Here is Christ, here is the church;
some in Bohemia were saying, Here is Christ, here is the church.

Hag ena ny a vedn y asa in mesk an bobel eus worth y gara dhe weles an pëth eus gwrÿs in Pow an Flemen in mesk an dus

ha enna ni e ved'n e ara amesk an poble ez e gara moaz tha wellaz an peath ez gwreze en Poww an Flemmen amesk an tiz—JTonkin

And there we'll leave him among the people who love him to see what is going on in Flanders among the people.

Gans oll ow gwlas vy parys, me, mytern Norgagh inwedh, a dheu ganso dres an bÿs dh'y socra dyhow ha cledh, dres sÿgh ha lynn

Gans ol ow gwlas ve parys, me, Myghtern Norgagh inweth, a thy gansso drys an bys th'y socra dyhow ha cleth, drys sygh ha lyn—BK 1429–33

With all my kingdom ready, I, the king of Norway also, will come across the world to assist him right and left, over dry land and water.

Ewgh dhymmo dres oll an pow kefrÿs Rom ha Lùmbardy

Eugh thymo dres ol an pov kefrys rome ha lumbardy—BM 1533–34

Go for me through all the land, both Rome and Lombardy.

Arlùth, ow tevos a Spain yth ejen in cres Almayn orth unn prÿs ly yn pòr wir pàn veuv gelwys

arluth ow tevos a spayn yth egen yn cres almayn orth vn prys ly yn pur wyr pan fuf gylwys—RD 2147–50

Lord, coming from Spain I was in the middle of Germany at a meal indeed when I was summoned.

Welcùm, Mytern Spain defry!

Welcum, Mightern Spain deffry!—BK 2643

Welcome, King of Spain indeed!

Mytern Grêss ov i'm tour

Myghtern Grece ove o'm towr—BK 2417

I am the king of Greece in my tower.

Me, Evander, dûk Syry, a'n dielha

Me, Evander, duk Syry, a'n dyelha—BK 1693–94

I, Evander, duke of Syria, shall be avenged on him.

Yma ow trailya defry oll an wlascor a Jûdy ow tallath in Galyle
yma ov treyle deffry ol an wlascor a iudi ov talleth yn galile—
PC 1593–95
He is turning all the kingdom of Judea indeed starting in Galilee.

Pòr wir ev a veu genys pòr ewn in Bethlem Jûdy
pur wyr ef a fue genys pur evn yn bethlem iudi—PC 1606–07
Very truly he was born rightly in Bethlehem of Judea.

Kebmer an flogh yonk ha'y dhama ha kê dhe bow an Yêdhewon
kebar an flô yonk ha e thama, ha ke tha pow an Ethewan—
Rowe
Take the young child and his mother and go to the land of the Jews.

Welcùm os, Mytern Partys, ha Mytern Ejyp kefrÿs!
Welcum os, Myghtern Partys, ha Myghtern Egyp kefrys!—BK
2640–41
You are welcome, King of the Parthians, and the King of Egypt also!

Davyd dhe Araby kê, dhe veneth Tabor whare
David the araby ke the veneth tabor whare—OM 1943–44
David, go to Arabia, to Mount Tabor immediately.

Welcùm, Mytern Itùry hag inwedh Mytern Lyby
Welcum, Myghtern Itury hag inweth Myghtern Lyby—BK 2644
Welcome King of Ituria and also King of Libya.

Tommas, te â dhe Eynda
thomas ty a the eynda—RD 2457
Thomas, you will go to India.

Me, Mùstensar, an tebel-gour, ov mytern in Afrycans
me, Mustensar, an tebal-gower, of myghtern in Affrycans—
BK 2655–56
I, Mustenar, the evil man, am king in Africa.

Ha nyns êns y ma's parcel bian a Afryca
ha nys ens y mas parcell bean a aphrica—TH 32
And they were only a small part of Africa.

Why pobel why in pow Ameryca ùncoth dhe ny
Why poble hui, en pow America, uncuth dho nei—WGwavas
You people in the land of America, unknown to us.

40W LANGUAGES

Pàn ve leun ow dhos a win ny garaf cows mès Latyn
pan ve luen ov ʒos a wyn ny gara covs mes laten—BM 79–80
When my wine glass is full of wine I prefer to speak Latin only.

A yllowgh why clappya Kernowek?
Elo why clapier Kernuack?—Pryce
Can you speak Cornish?

Desky Kernowek. Desky Sowsnek.
Deske Cornoack. Deske Sowsenack—Borlase
To learn Cornish. To learn English.

**I'n tavas Greca, Latyn ha'n Hebrow, in Frynkek ha
  Kernowek deskys dâ**
*En tavaz Greka, Lathen ha'n Hebra, en Frenkock ha
  Carnoack deskes dha*—JBoson
In the Greek language, Latin and the Hebrew, well versed in French
  and Cornish.

Me ny vydnaf cowsa Sowsnek
Meea na vidna cowza Sawzneck—Carew
I will speak no English.

**Me a wrug scantlowr clôwes udn ger Sowsnek côwsys i'n côk
  rag seythen warbarth**
*Me rig scantlower clowes eden ger sowsnack cowzes en cock
  rag sythen warebar*—WBodinar
I scarcely heard a single word of English spoken in the boat for a week
  at a time.

**Rag ny alja ev clappya na screfa Kernowek pecar ha why.
  Th'esa moy a Gembrek an pëth a wrug ev gwil**
*Rag na algia ea clappia na screffa Curnoack pecarra why.
  Thera moy Gembrack peath rig ea gweele*—OPender
For he could not speak Cornish like you. What he did was more Welsh.

Th'esoma ow soposya indelna dhe'n lyha rag an Breten ha'n Kernowyon, bos an Frynkek fin parys dhe gemeres wàr an eyl ha'n Sowsnek nobla wàr y gela

therama suppoga andelna tho an liha rag an Bretten ha an Curnowean: voz an Frenkock feen parrez tho cummeraz wara niel, ha an Sousenack nobla war e gilla—*NBoson*

I suppose thus at least for the Bretons and the Cornish that the fine French is ready to displace the one and the nobler English the other.

An pÿth yw menowgh, ea, lemmyn ha pùb eur in agan yêth ny hag in agan comen talk gelwys charyta

An pith ew meno, ea lymmyn ha pub vr, in agan eyth ny, hag in agan comyn talke, gylwys charite—*TH 20a–21*

What is often, yes, now and always in our language and common parlance called charity.

Gàn tavas Kernowek yw mar bell gwadnhës, ùs na yllyn scant qwetyas dh'y weles crefhe arta

Gun tavaz Carnoack eu mar pel gwadnhez, uz na ellen skant quatiez tho e wellaz crefhe arta—*NBoson*

Our Cornish language is so far weakened, that we can hardly expect to see it strengthen again.

Rag radn a yll bos kevys na yll scant clappya na godhvos Kernowek, bùs scant den vëth bùs a wor godhvos ha clappya Sowsnek

rag radden el bose keevez na el skant clappia na guthvaz Curnooack, buz skant den veeth buz ore guthvaz ha clappia Sousenack—*NBoson*

For some can be found who can hardly speak or understand Cornish, but hardly anybody but can understand and speak English.

Rag hedna ny a yll gweles hag ajwon an tavas Kernowek dhe vos tavas coth ha trueth yw ev dhe vos kellys

rag hedna ni el guelas, ha adzhan an tavaz Kernuak dha boz tavaz koth ha triuadh eu dha boz kelles—*JBoson*

Thus we can see and recognize that the Cornish language is an ancient tongue and it is a pity it should be lost.

40X IMPRECATIONS

Mollath Crist ha'm trevyjy wàr gorf Arthùr, mab an pla!
Mollath Christ ha'm trefugy war gorf Arthur, map an pla—
BK 2303–04
The curse of Christ and my citizens upon the body of Arthur, the
devil's spawn!

Wheth war gamm, venjans i'th las!
whyth war gam vyngeans y'th glas—PC 2716
Careful with your blowing—vengeance in your guts!

What, venjans dhis, a benn pyst
What vyngeans thy's a pen pyst—OM 2641
What? Vengeance on you, you fool!

Venjans wàr dha bedn crehy!
vengens war tha ben krehy—CW 2326
Vengeance on your scurvy pate!

Mollath Duw in da las!
Molla Tu en da laaz—Carew
God's curse in your guts!

Mil venjans warnas jy!
Mille vengeance warna thy—Carew
A thousand vengeances upon you!

Taw, dhe'th cregy, gaja meur!
Taw, the'th cregy, gage mmer!—BK 176
Shut up, hang you, you braggart!

**Taw, taw, harlot, dhe'th cregy! A dhrog-dheweth re vyrwhy.
In mes a'm golok omden!**
*Taw, taw, harlot, the'th cregy! A throg thewath re wyrwhy. In
mes a'm golak omden!—BK 472–74*
Silence, silence, scoundrel, hang you! May you die an evil death. Get
out of my sight!

Hay, 'rag! Caugh an Jowl i'th vin!
Hay, 'rag! Caugh an Jowl y'th vyn! BK 346
Hey, get a move on! The Devil's shit in your mouth!

Te, glovarak, re'th foja caugh!
Te, glovorag, re 'foga caugh!—BK 1250–51
You leprous fellow, shit to you!

Caha i'n gwely
kaha En gwille—WGwavas
Shit-abed (scoundrel).

Te falj horsen, na'm brag vy. Avond tellek, dhe'th cregy!
Te falge horsen nam brag vy avond tellek theth cregy—BM
3491–92
You false bastard, don't threaten me. Get away, you tattered fellow,
hang you!

A, mollath dhe'n horsen cabm ha dhe jy inwedh ganso!
a molath then horsen kam ha thage in weth gansa—CW 804–
05
Oh, curse the crooked bastard, and you as well with him!

Me a wra dhe'n horsen cabm bos calessa prysonys
me a wra then horsen cam boos calassa presonys—CW 2037–
38
I will make the crooked bastard be more severely imprisoned.

40Y PROVERBS, RIDDLES, AND RHYMES

**Kemmer with na wrewgh gara an vordh goth rag an vordh
nowyth**
Kemer uîth na 'rey gara an vòr' gôth rag an vòr noueth.—
JCH §6
Take care not to leave the old road for the new road.

**Kebmer with na wrewgh why ôstya in chy le ma vo den coth
demedhys dhe benyn yonk**
*Kebmer uîth na ray ostia en tshei lebma vo dên kôth
demidhyz dhꝺ bennen iyꞯk*—JCH § 8
Take care not to lodge in a house where an old man is married to a
young woman.

Bedhens gweskys dywweyth kyns gweskel unweyth
Bedhez guesgyz dhiueth, ken gueskal enueth—JCH §10
One should think twice before acting.

Cowsa nebes ha cowsa dâ, mes côwsa nebes an gwella
Rowsa nebaz ha rowsa dâ, mèz rowsa nebaz an gwella—*Pryce*
To speak a little and to speak well, but to speak little is best.

Cows nebes, cows dâ, ha dâ vëdh côwsys arta
Cows nebas, cows da, ha da veth cowsas arta—*Scawen MSS*
Speak little, speak well, and well will be spoken again

An lavar coth yw lavar gwir:
Bëdh dorn re verr, bëdh tavas re hir,
Mès den heb davas a gollas y dir
An lavar kôth yu lavar guîr,
Bedh dvrn rê ver, dhvn tavaz rê hîr;
Mez dên heb davaz a gvllaz i dîr—*AB: 251c*
The old saying is a true saying:
The hand is wont to be too short, the tongue is wont to be too long,
But a man without a tongue, lost his chance.

Nynj eus goon heb lagas na ke heb scovarn
Nyng es goon heb lagas na kei heb scovarn—*Scawen MSS*
There is no down without eye nor hedge without ear.

Gwell yw gwetha avell gofyn
Guel yw gwetha vel goofen—*Scawen MSS*
It is better to keep than to ask.

Gwra dâ, rag dha honen dha honen te a'n gwra
Grua da, rag tha hannen te yn gura—*Scawen MSS*
Do good, for yourself you do it.

Flogh a veu genys in mis Merth;
** Ny a drehys y vegel in mis Est;**
Ev a ros towl dhe bronter Powl
** in mis Du kyns Nadelyk**
Flogh vye gennes en miz-Merh
* Ni trehes e bigel en miz-East;*
E a ros towl dho Proanter Powle
* Miz-Du ken Nadelik*—*Pryce*
A child was born in March;
  We cut his navel in August;
He gave a fall to the Parson of Paul
  in November before Christmas.

Kensa bledhen byrla ha bay
  Nessa bledhen lùll a lay
Tryja bledhen, kemerowgh ha dog e;
  Peswora bledhen, mollath Duw warnodho ev a wrug hy dry
  hy obma!
Kensa blethan, byrla a' baye,
  Nessa blethan, lull a' laye,
Tridgya blethan, comero ha dog a,
  Peswara blethan, mollath Dew war ef reeg dry hy uppa—
  Pryce.
The first year hugs and kisses,
  The next year lullaby,
The third year, take and bring,
  The fourth year: God's curse on him who brought her here!

Pobel abell a bew castylly
Pobyll abell bew castilly—Scawen MSS
People afar own castles.

Neb na gar y gy a'n gwra devyjor
Neb na gare y gy an gwra deveeder—Scawen MSS
He that loves not his dog, will make him a sheep-worrier.

An men eus ow rollya ny vydn nefra cùntel bèst
A mêan ez a rhyllio ne vedn nevra kuntl best—Lhuyd & Borlase
A rolling stone gathers no moss.

A varwo awos arveth, nynj yw gwyw dhe varogeth
A varwo awos arveth nyng ew guyw the vorogath—BK 928–29
He who would die from insults, isn't worthy to ride into battle.

Eus keus? Eus pò nag eus. Mars eus keus, dro keus. Mar nag
eus keus, dro an pëth eus.
Ez kêz? Ez po neg ez; mars êz kêz, dro kêz; po neg ez kêz, dro
  peth ez—Pryce
Is there cheese? There is or there isn't. If there's cheese, bring cheese. If
  there is no cheese, bring what there is.

STAGELL A
Appendix A

Summary of Initial Mutation

The initial mutations of Cornish can be tabulated as follows:

1	2	3	4	5
P	B	F	.	.
C, K	G	H	.	.
Qw	Gw	Wh	.	.
T	D	Th	.	.
Ch	J	.	.	.
B	V	.	P	F, V
M	V	.	.	F, V
D	Dh	.	T	T
G	–, W	.	C, K	H, Wh
Gw	W	.	Qw	Wh, W
Radical	**Soft**	**Spirant**	**Hard**	**Mixed**

A.1 LENITION

The second state, soft mutation is more correctly known as *lenition*. Lenition occurs after the definite article, when the noun is feminine singular, **an venyn** 'the woman', or masculine plural referring to people, e.g. **an dus** 'the men, the people', except where the noun is a late borrowing from English, e.g. **an doctours** 'the doctors'. **An vergh** 'the horses' and **an varchons** 'the merchants' are exceptional. **An** also lenites the word **tra** 'thing', **an dra** 'the thing'.

The adjective is lenited after a feminine noun in the singular or a masculine noun referring to people in the plural, e.g. **benyn dhâ** 'a good woman'; **tus vas** 'good people'.

342

Lenition occurs **unn**, **udn** 'one', when the following noun is feminine singular, e.g. **udn venyn** 'one woman'. **Udn** also lenites **tra** 'thing', **udn dra** 'one thing'. **Onen** 'one', used pronominally to refer to a feminine noun also lenites, e.g. **buwgh ha fest onen deg** 'a cow and a very fair one'. The vocative particle **a** lenites, e.g. **a venyn dhâ** 'O good woman', moreover the noun is lenited if used vocatively after **te**, **ty** 'thou, you', **te dhen** 'you man'.

Lenition occurs after **dew**, **dyw** 'two', e.g. **dew dhen** 'two men'; **dyw venyn** 'two women'. Notice also that the initial of **dew**, **dyw** is lenited by the definite article, e.g. **an dhew flogh** 'the two children'.

The verbal particle **a** lenites, e.g. **me a welas** 'I saw'. With inversion the particle is normally suppressed, but lenition occurs nonetheless, e.g. **gwelys veu** 'he was seen'. The negative particles **ny** and **na** both induce lenition, e.g. **ny dheuth** 'did not come'; **na dheuth** 'that did not come'. The perfective particle **re** causes lenition, except with **b-** in **bos** 'to be', e.g. **re dheuth** 'has come' but **re beu** 'has been'. **Dell** 'as'; **fate·ll** 'how'; and **kettel** 'as soon as' cause lenition, e.g. **dell wrug avy** 'as I did'; **fate·ll wrusta?** 'how did you?'; and **kettel wella ev** 'as soon as he sees'. Lenition also occurs after **erna·** 'until'; **hadre·** 'while, until'; **pàn** 'when'; **abàn** 'since'; and **dhia bàn** 'since'. **Mar** 'as, so' lenites a following adjective: **mar bell** 'so far'.

The possessive adjectives **dha** 'thy, your' and **y** 'his' cause lenition, e.g. **dha jy** 'your house'; and **y das** 'his father'.

The following prepositions are followed by lenition: **dhe** 'to'; **dhia** 'from'; **dre** 'through'; **a** 'from, out of'; **wàr** 'upon'; **in dadn** 'under'; **re** 'by' (in oaths), e.g. **re Varia** 'by our Lady'. **Heb** 'without' lenites only in certan set phrases, e.g. **gow** 'lie', but **heb wow** 'without a lie'.

The word **pòr** 'very' lenites a following adjective: **gwir** 'true' > **pòr wir** 'very true'. Lenition also affects the the first consonant of the second element after some prefixes: **prëv** 'serpent, snake' > **hager-brëv** 'evil serpent'; **benyn** 'woman' > **tebel-venyn** 'wicked woman'; **den** 'man' > **drog-dhen** 'bad man'; **tevys** 'grown' > **over-devys** 'overgrown'; **cubmyas** 'permission' > **leun-gubmyas** 'full permission'.

A.2 SPIRANTIZATION

The third state, breathed mutation, is properly known as *spirantization*. Spirantization occurs after **try**, **teyr** *f.* 'three', e.g. **try thiak** 'three farmers'; and **teyr hath** 'three cats'. It also occurs after the possessive adjectives **ow** 'my'; **hy** 'her'; and **aga** 'their': **ow thas** 'my father'; **hy fedn** 'her head'; and **aga herens** 'their parents'.

Na 'not any' spirantizes in the expressions **na hens** 'not before'; **na fella, na felha** 'no longer'; and **nahe•n** 'not otherwise'.

The unstressed **de, du** 'day' spirantizes **Calan** 'first day of the month' in the adverbial phrases **de Halan an vledhen** 'on New Year's Day', and **de Halan Gwâv** 'on All Saints' day'; and it spirantizes the initial of **Pencost** 'Pentecost' in **de Fencost** 'at Pentecost, at Whitsun'. **De Yow** 'Thursday' spirantizes **Cablys** in the adverbial phrase **de Yow Hablys** 'on Maundy Thursday'.

A.3 PROVECTION

The fourth state or *provection* (hardening) occurs after **mar, mara** 'if', e.g. **mar teu va** 'if he comes'; **mara qwelaf nebonen** 'if I see anybody'. It also occurs after **a** 'if', used in unreal conditions, e.g. **a pe va obma** 'if he had been here'.

The particle **ow** used with the verbal noun to form the present participle also provects, e.g. **gwandra** 'to wander' > **ow qwandra** 'wandering'; **bewa** 'to live' > **ow pewa** 'living'; **gortos** 'to wait' > **ow cortos** 'waiting'.

A.4 MIXED MUTATION

The mixed mutation most commonly occurs after the verbal particle **y** and its derivative **may** 'so that': **beu** > **y feu** 'was'; **bo** > **may fo** 'so that (he) may be'. Mixed mutation also occurs after **ple** 'where?'; **py** 'where?'; **peur** 'when?'; and **kyn** 'although': **ple feusta?** 'where have you been?'; **py fÿdh ev?** 'where will he be?'; **peur feu hedna?** 'when was that?'; **kyn fe** 'though it be'.

The adverbial particle **yn** causes mixed mutation: **dâ** > **yn tâ** 'well'; **bew** > **yn few** 'alive'. The form **yn whir** 'truly' is unattested in traditional Cornish; 'truly' in the texts is always **in gwir** 'in truth', where **in** [ın] is the preposition 'in', not the adverbial particle **yn** [ən].

Maga 'as, so' also causes mixed mutation: **maga fery avell hôk** 'as merry as a hawk'; **maga whydn avell ergh** 'as white as snow'. Notice also **magata** (< **maga** + **dâ**) 'as well, also'.

The second person singular infixed pronoun causes mixed mutation, e.g. **me a'th teg** 'I will carry you'. The reduced form **'th** of **dha** 'thy, your' also causes mixed mutation: **i'th torn** 'in your hand'. Notice however that **th** in both these cases mutates **b** and **m** to **v**, not **f**: **me a'th venten** 'I will support you'; **ev a'th venyk** 'he will bless you'; **th** in these cases also mutates and **gw** to **w**, not **wh**: **ro hebma dhe'th wreg** 'give this to your wife'; and **ev a'th welvyth** 'he will see you'.

A.5 NASALIZATION

Nasalization is not part of the system of initial mutations in Cornish. Nasalization does, however, occur with the word **dor** 'earth' after the definite article: **an nor** (< **dor**) means 'the earth, the world', whereas **an dor** means 'the earth, the ground'.

A.6 ANOMALOUS MUTATION

The word **dyowl** 'devil' after the definite article always appears as **jowl**: **an jowl**. Similarly **dëdh** (**dÿdh**) 'day' after the article is (**an jëdh**) (**an jÿdh**) 'the day'.

The Middle Cornish verbal noun of the verb 'to find, to get' is **cafos** or **cawas**. In Late Cornish the second of these forms is usual, but with permanent lenition of the initial consonant: **gawas**.

In Middle Cornish the verb 'to expect' is **gwetyas** in the verbal noun. This appears in Late Cornish with permanent provection as **qwetyas** (**qwachas**).

A.7 OMISSION OF MUTATIONS

The above brief description of initial mutations is rather schematic. In the Middle Cornish texts mutation is sometimes not shown. It is rare, for example, for the verbal noun to be written with spirantization after **ow** 'my'. John Tregear, for example, writes **worth ow cara ve** 'loving me' six times, but he has no example at all of *__worth ow hara ve__.

Mutation is frequently avoided in order not to render a word unrecognizable. We thus find, for example, *a vaghtyth glan* 'of a pure maid' (not **a vaghtyth *lan**) at PC 3027 and *the glanhe* 'to cleanse' (not **the *lanhe**) at TH 10a.

By the Late Cornish period the system of mutation seems to have been under some strain and it is noteworthy, for example, that Nicholas Boson writes *tha gubber* 'your wages' (**dha gober**); *komeraz e kibmias* 'take his leave' (**kemeres y cubmyas**); *tho gweel dotha* 'to make it to' (**dhe gwil dhodho**), rather than the expected **tha wubber*, **e gibmias* and **tho weel dotha*.

STAGELL B
Appendix B

Summary of Cornish Verbal Usage

He speaks: **Ev a gôws** or **yma va ow côwsel**.

He speaks every day: **Ev a vÿdh ow côwsel pùb dëdh**.

He speaks Cornish well: **Yma va ow côwsel Kernowek yn tâ**.

He was speaking when I can in: **Yth esa va ow côwsel pàn wrug avy dos ajy**.

He used to speak to us every day: **Ev a vedha ow côwsel orthyn pùb dëdh** or **Ev a wrug ûsya côwsel orthyn pùb dëdh** or **Côwsel orthyn a wre pùb dëdh**.

He will speak to us now: **Ev a vydn côwsel orthyn lebmyn** or **Ev a wra côwsel orthyn lebmyn** or **Côwsel a wra orthyn lebmyn**.

He said he would speak to us today: **Ev a leverys y whre va côwsel orthyn hedhyw** or **Ev a leverys fatell vydna côwsel orthyn hedhyw** or **Ev a leverys ev dhe gôwsel orthyn hedhyw**.

If he speaks, don't answer him: **Mar teu va ha côwsel, na wra y wortheby** or **Mar qwra va côwsel, na wra y wortheby**.

He spoke to me: **Ev a wrug côwsel orthyf** or **Ev a gowsas orthyf**.

He has spoken and we must listen to him: **Ev re wrug côwsel ha ny a res goslowes orto**.

346

Had he spoken, I should not have answered: **Mar teffa ev ha côwsel, ny vynsen y wortheby** or **A qwrella ev côwsel, ny wrussen y wortheby**.

Had he not spoken, I should have answered myself: **Na ve ev dhe gôwsel, me a vynsa gortheby ow honen.**

If he does not speak, I shall not speak to him: **Marnas ev a wra côwsel, ny vanaf vy côwsel orto ev**, or **Mar ny wra va côwsel, ny wrama côwsel orto ev**.

Let him speak: **Gwrêns ev côwsel** or **Gas ev dhe gôwsel** or **Gesowgh ev dhe gôwsel** or **Re wrello ev côwsel**.

May he never speak again: **Bydner re wrello côwsel nefra arta**.

Let us be silent so that he can speak: **Gesowgh ny dhe dewel may halla ev côwsel.**

We will be silent so that he may speak: **Ny a vydn tewel may halla ev côwsel.**

We were silent to let him speak: **Ny a wrug tewel may halla ev côwsel**.

Let us turn away from him, lest he speak to us: **Gesowgh ny dhe drailya dhyworto, rag dowt ev dhe gôwsel orthyn.**

He can no longer speak: **Ev ny'n jeves côwsel na fella.**

Ne cannot speak any longer: **Ny yll ev côwsel na fella.**

He will not be able to speak: **Ev ny'n jevyth côwsel**, or **Ev ny yllvyth côwsel**.

He cannot speak or understand Cornish: **Ny wor ev côwsel na convedhes Kernowek.**

STAGELL C
Appendix C

Verbal Paradigms

Traditional Cornish has a strong tendency to use verbal auxiliaries, **bos** 'to be'; **mydnas** 'to wish'; **gwil** 'to do'; **gasa** 'to let'; **gallos** 'to be able', **godhvos** 'to know, to be able' and **dos** 'to come'. The use of **gwil** 'to do' in particular is widespread at all periods of the language. TH very infrequently indeed uses verbal forms other than the impersonal 3rd singular present, imperfect and preterite of any verb, preferring to use one of the auxiliary verbs. Given that TH is our only prose text of any length, it should form our model for the syntax of everyday revived Cornish. Poetry is, of course, another matter.

Starting with Nance, the authors of various handbooks of revived Cornish have reconstructed complete paradigms for numerous verbs. In so doing the authors have given a false impression of the traditional language. A recent example is Ray Edwards, *Cornish Verbs* (3rd edition, Kesva an Taves Kernewek 2010; ISBN 9781902917900), which lists a huge number of inflected forms of verbs. The overwhelming majority of them are unattested. The absence of so many inflected forms in the Cornish texts is not fortuitous, but is intimately related to the way in which historic Cornish preferred periphrasis with auxiliaries to inflection of the verb itself. It will be apparent from the paradigms given below, that inflected forms of even the commonest verbs are sparsely attested.

In this Appendix, I give such inflected forms as do occur in BM, TH, SA, BK and CW in Standard Cornish spelling. I have also, on occasion added inflected forms from NBoson and JCH. These texts together I refer to as our foundation texts. I have also added forms for the same tenses in order to complete the paradigm and mention which inflected forms are actually attested, and which are conjectural.

The Roman numerals are to be interpreted as follows: I = verbal noun; II = the present future (IIa = future, where it exists); III = imperfect; IV =

preterite; V = subjunctive; VI = conditional; VII = imperative; VIII = verbal adjective.

In these lists I start with **bos** 'to be' and **y'm beus** 'I have'. It will be noticed in connection with **bos** 'to be' that the verb has more than one present/future and more than one imperfect tense. These are listed as II, IIa, IIb, IIc, IId, III, IIIa and IIIb respectively. **Dos** 'to come' and **mos** 'to go' also have separate perfects; these are listed under IVa.

The persons are indicated as follows 1 = 1 sg.; 2 = 2 sg.; 3 = 3 sg.; 4 = 1 pl.; 5 = 2 pl.; 6 = 3 *pl.* Where there are separate masculine and feminine forms in the 3 sg., these are indicated as 3 *m.* and 3 *f.* respectively.

C.1 'TO BE'

I   *Verbal Noun*
     bos, bones

II   *Present Future*
     1 **ov, oma**   4 **on**
     2 **os, osta**   5 **owgh**
     3 **yw, ywa**   6 **yns**

IIa *Future*
     1 **esof, eroma**   4 **eson, eron**
     2 **esos, esta**   5 **esowgh, erowgh**
     3 **eus**   6 **usons**

IIb *Present Future*
     3 **usy, ujy**

IIc *Present Future*
     3 **yma**   6 **ymowns, ymôns**

IId *Present Future*
     1 **bedhaf**   4 **bedhyn**
     2 **bedhyth, bedhys**   5 **bedhowgh**
     3 **bëdh, bÿdh**   6 **bedhons**

III *Imperfect*
     1 **en**   4 **en**
     2 **es**   5 **ewgh**
     3 **o**   6 **êns**

IIIa *Imperfect*
1 **esen**, *eren*   4 **esen**, *eren*
2 **eses**, *eres*   5 **esewgh**, *erewgh*
3 **esa**, **eja**, **era**   6 **esens**, *erens*

IV   *Preterite*
1 **beuv**, **beuma**   4 **beun**
2 **beus**, **beusta**   5 **bewgh**
3 **beu**   6 **bowns**

V   *Subjunctive*
1 **ben**   4 **ben**
2 **bes**, **besta**   5 **bewgh**
3 **be**   6 **bêns**

V has old present subjunctive forms:
1 **biv**, **byma**   4 **bon**
2 **by**, **bosta**   5 **bowgh**
3 **bo**   6 **bowns**
These are used in jussives: **gordhys re by**, **bydner re bo**, etc.

VI   *Conditional*
1 **bien**   4 **bien**
2 **bies**   5 **biewgh**
3 **bia**   6 **biens**

VII   *Imperative*
1 –   4 **bedhyn**
2 **bëdh**, **bÿdh**   5 **bedhowgh**
3 **bedhens**   6 **bedhens**

C.2 'TO HAVE'

I   *Verbal Noun*

—

II *Present Future*

1 y'm beus	4 y'gan beus
2 y'th eus	5 y'gas beus
3 *m.* y'n jeves	6 y's teves
3 *f.* y's teves	

IIa *Future*

1 y'm bÿdh	4 y'gan bÿdh
2 y'fÿdh	5 y'gas bÿdh
3 *m.* y'n jevyth	6 y's tevyth
3 *f.* y's tevyth	

III *Imperfect*

1 y'm bo	4 y'gan bo
2 y'th o	5 y'gas bo
3 *m.* y'n jeva	6 y's teva
3 *f.* y's teva	

IV *Preterite*

1 y'm beu, y'm beuv	4 y'gan beu
2 y'feu	5 y'gas beu
3 *m.* y'n jeva	6 y's teva
3 *f.* y's teva	

V   *Subjunctive*

1 y'm bo, y'm byv, y'm boma	4 y'gan bo, y'gan ben
2 y'th fe, y'th fo, y'th foja	5 y'gas bo
3 *m.* y'n jeffa	6 y's teffa, y's teffons
3 *f.* y's teffa	

VI *Conditional*

1 y'm bia	4 y'gan bia, y'gan bien
2 y'fia	5 y'gas bia
3 *m.* y'n jevia	6 y's tevia
3 *f.* tevia	

The verbal particle **y** has been used throughout in the above paradigms.

NOTE: This verb in the texts is much more varied and unstable than Nance's schematization of it in *Cornish for All* and elsewhere (see 23A.1–2 above).

OTHER VERBS

C.3   'TO GET, TO FIND'

I   *Verbal Noun*

cafos, cavos, cawas, gawas

II   *Present Future*

1 **cafaf**	4 **kefyn**
2 **kefyth**	5 **kefowgh**
3 **kev, cav**	6 **cafons**

1, 5 and 6 are not attested in our foundation texts, but they occur in early Middle Cornish. An autonomous form **kefyr** is found in BK.

III   *Imperfect*

1 *kefyn*	4 *kefyn*
2 *kefys*	5 *kefowgh*
3 *kefy*	6 *kefens*

This tense does not appear to be attested in traditional Cornish.

IV   *Preterite*

1 *kefys*	4 *kefsyn*
2 *kefsys*	5 *kefsowgh*
3 **cafas**	6 **cafsons**

On;y 3 and 6 are attested in our foundation texts. The other forms appear to be unknown anywhere in traditional Cornish.

V   *Subjunctive*

1 **caffen, kyffyf**	4 **caffen, kyffen**
2 *caffes*, **kyffy**	5 **caffowgh, kyffowgh**
3 **caffa**	6 **caffons**

1 **Caffen**, 2 **kyffy**, 4 **kyffen** and 5 **caffowgh, kyffowgh** are attested in our foundation texts. 1 **Kyffyf**, 3 **caffa**, 4 **caffen** and 6 are found in early Middle Cornish. **Caffes* is unattested.

VI   *Conditional*

1 **cafsen**	4 *cafsen*
2 *cafses*	5 *cafsowgh*
3 *cafsa*	6 *cafsens*

1 is attested in BM. The other persons seem to be unattested anywhere in traditional Cornish.

VII   The imperative of this verb seems to be unattested anywhere.

VIII   *Verbal Adjective*

kefys, kevys

In the above paradigm, outside the verbal noun and the present-future third person indicative, the root cited is **kef-**, **caf-**. The voiceless final segment seems guaranteed *inter alia* by ‹*kefys*›, ‹*keffys*›, ‹*kyffys*›, the only form of the verbal adjective until the seventeenth century. In Later Cornish ‹*kevys*›, ‹*kevez*› 'got, found' is the only attested form. **Caf-**, **kef-** was the original stem of this verb and **cav-**, **kev-** are later and analogical. Both stems occur in both Welsh and Breton: MW *caffaf* 'I get' but *keveis* 'I got'; MB *kaff* 'gets' and *kav* 'gets'.

C.4 'TO LOVE'
I   *Verbal Noun*
    cara
II *Present Future*

1 **caraf**		4 **keryn**	
2 **kerta**		5 **kerowgh**	
3 **car**		6 *carons*	

II 6 is a reconstruction.
III *Imperfect*

1 *caren*		4 *caren*	
2 *cares*		5 *carewgh*	
3 **cara**		6 *carens*	

Only III 3 seems to be attested in our foundation texts.
IV *Preterite*

1 *kerys*		4 *kersyn*	
2 *kersys*		5 *kersowgh*	
3 **caras**		6 *carsons*	

Only IV 3 seems to be attested in our foundation texts.
V   *Subjunctive*

1 *carren*		4 *carren*	
2 *carres*, **kerry**		5 *carrowgh*	
3 **carra**		6 *carrens*	

Only V 2 **kerry** and 3 **carra** appear to be attested in our foundation texts.
VI *Conditioal*

1 **carsen**		4 *carsen*	
2 *carses*		5 *carsowgh*	
3 **carsa**		6 *carsens*	

Only VI 1 and 3 are attested in our foundation texts.
VII *Imperative*
    The imperative is not attested in our foundation texts
VIII *Verbal Adjective*
    kerys

C.5 'TO HEAR'
I *Verbal Noun*
clôwes
II *Present Future*

1 **clôwaf**		4 *clôwyn*	
2 **clôwyth**		5 **clôwowgh**	
3 **clôw**		6 *clôwons*	

II 4 and 6 are reconstructions
IIa *Future*
3 **clôwyth**
An earlier form ‹*clewvyth*› is attested in the *Ordinalia*.
III *Imperfect*
The imperfect is not attested in our foundation texts.
IV *Preterite*

1 **clôwys**		4 **clôwsyn**	
2 **clôwsys**		5 **clôwsowgh**	
3 **clôwas**		6 **clôwsons**	

An autonomous form **clôwas** is attested in BK.
V *Subjunctive*

1 *clôwen*		4 *clôwen*	
2 *clôwes*		5 *clôwowgh*	
3 **clôwa**		6 *clôwens*	

Apart from V 3 all forms in V are reconstructions.
VI *Conditional*
The conditional of this verb is apparently not attested in Cornish;
note the periphrastic expressions **ev a venja clôwes** and **me a
venja clôwes** at JCH §§40, 43.
VII *Imperative*

1 –		4 *clôwyn*	
2 **clôw**		5 **clôwowgh**	
3 *clôwens*		6 *clôwens*	

VII 3, 4 and 6 are reconstructions.

C.6 'TO SPEAK'
I   *Verbal Noun*
     côwsel, **cows**
     A Late Cornish form **cowsa** is also attested.
II   *Present Future*

1 **cowsaf**	4 **côwsyn**
2 **côwsyth**	5 **côwsowgh**
3 **côws**	6 *côwsons*

     II 6 is a reconstruction.
III *Imperfect*

1 **côwsyn**	4 *côwsyn*
2 *côwsys*	5 *côwsewgh*
3 **côwsy**	6 *côwsens*

     Only III 3 is attested in our foundation texts. 1 **côwsyn** is attested
     in PA.
IV   *Preterite*

1 *côwsys*	4 *côwsyn*
2 *côwsys*	5 *côwsowgh*
3 **côwsys**, **cowsas**	6 *cowsons*

     Apart from IV 3 all forms are reconstructions
V   *Subjunctive*

1 *cowsen*	4 *cowsen*
2 *cowses*	5 *cowsowgh*
3 **cowsa**	6 *cowsens*

     Apart from V 3 all forms are reconstructions.
VI   *Conditional*
     The conditional of this verb is not attested in our foundation texts.
VII *Imperative*

1 –	4 *côwsyn*
2 **cows**	5 **côwsowgh**
3 **côwsens**	6 *côwsens*

     VII 2 and 5 are attested in our texts; 3 **côwsens** (‹*kevsyns*›) is
     attested in RD.
VIII *Verbal Adjective*
     côwsys, **côwjys**.

C.7   'TO BELIEVE'

I   *Verbal Noun*
    cresy, **crejy**

II   *Present Future*

1 **cresaf**		4 **cresyn**	
2 *cresyth*		5 *cresowgh*	
3 **crës**, **crÿs**		6 **cresons**	

Apart from 1 and 3 II is a reconstruction; **cresyn** and **cresons** are attested in earlier Middle Cornish.

III   *Imperfect*
    The imperfect of this verb is not attested

IV   *Preterite*
    The preterite of this verb is not attested

V   *Subjunctive*

VI   *Conditional*

1 *cressen*		4 *cressen*
2 *cresses*		5 *cressowgh*
3 **cressa**, **cryssa**		6 *cressens*

The conditional VI and the subjunctive V are indistinguishable from each other; only V/VI **cressa** is attested in our foundation texts. V 3 ‹*crysso*›, ‹*cresso*› occur in the Ordinalia.

VII   *Imperative*

1 –		4 *cresyn*
2 **crës**, **crÿs**		5 **cresowgh**
3 *cresens*		6 *cresens*

Apart from 2 and 5 these forms are reconstructions.

VIII   *Verbal Adjective*
    cresys, **crejys**.

C.8 'TO CARRY'
I   *Verbal Noun*
     don
II   *Present Future*
     1 *degaf*   4 *degyn*
     2 *degyth*   5 *degowgh*
     3 **deg**, **dog**   6 *degons*

Of II only 3 is attested in our foundation texts.

III   *Imperfect*

The imperfect of this verb is not attested.

IV   *Preterite*
     1 *dug*   4 *dugon*
     2 *duges*   5 *dugowgh*
     3 **dug**   6 *dugons*

Of IV only 3 is attested in our foundation texts.

V   *Subjunctive*
     1 *dogen*   4 *dogen*
     2 *doges*   5 *dogowgh*
     3 **doga**, **docka**   6 **dockons**

Only 3 and 6 are attested in our foundation texts. The rest of this tense is conjectural.

VI   *Conditional*
     1 *doksen*   4 *doksen*
     2 *dokses*   5 *doksowgh*
     3 **doksa**   6 *doksens*

Only 3 is attested in our foundation texts.

VII *Imperative*
     1 –   4 **degen**
     2 **dog**   5 **degowgh**
     3 **degens**   6 **degens**

All these forms are attested.

VIII *Verbal Adjective*
     degys.

C.9   'TO EAT'
I   *Verbal Noun*
debry
II   *Present Future*

1 **debraf**	4 *debryn*
2 **debryth**	5 *debrowgh*
3 **deber**	6 *debrons*

Only II 1, 2 and 3 are attested.

III   *Imperfect*
The imperfect is unattested in our foundation texts.

IV   *Preterite*

1 *debrys*	4 *depsyn*
2 *depsys*	5 *depsowgh*
3 **debras**	6 *depsons*

Only IV **debras** is attested. An earlier ‹*dybrys*› occurs in the Ordinalia

V   *Subjunctive*

1 *deppren*	4 *deppren*
2 *deppres*	5 **depprowgh**
3 **deppra**	6 *depprons*

Only 5 is attested in our foundation texts; 3 as ‹*deppro*› is attested in PA and the *Ordinalia*.

VI   *Conditional*

1 *depsen*	4 *depsen*
2 *depses*	5 *depsowgh*
3 **depsa**	6 *depsens*

Only 3 is attested in this tense. The other forms are conjectural.

VIII   *Verbal Adjective*

1 –	4 *debren*
2 **deber**	5 **debrowgh**
3 *debrens*	6 *debrens*

Only 2 and 5 are attested.

C.10 'TO COME' (this is also an auxiliary in conditional sentences)

I *Verbal Noun*
   dos, **dones**

II *Present Future*

1 **deuv, dov, deuma**	4 **deun**
2 **deth**; **deta**	5 **dewgh**
3 **deu, deuva**	6 **downs**

III *Imperfect*
     The imperfect of this verb does not appear to be attested in our foundation texts.

IV *Preterite*

1 **deuth**	4 **deuthen**
2 *deuthys*	5 *deuthowgh*
3 **deuth**	6 *deuthons*

Only 1, 3 and 4 of this tense are attested in our foundation texts.

IVa *Preterite*

1 *deuvef*	4 *deuvyn*
2 *deuves*	5 *deuvowgh*
3 **deuva**	6 *deuvons*

Apart from 3 this whole tense is reconstruction.

V *Subjunctive*

1 **deffen, dyffyf**	4 **deffen**
2 **deffes, dyffy**	5 *deffowgh*
3 **deffa, deffo**	6 **deffons**

Only 5 is a reconstruction.

VI *Conditional*

1 **dothyen**	4 *dothyen*
2 *dothyes*	5 *dothyowgh*
3 **dothya**	6 *dothyens*

Only 1 and 3 are attested in our foundation texts; 6 **dothyans** is attested three times as a pluperfect in PA.

VII *Imperative*

1 –	4 **deun**
2 **deus, des**	5 **dewgh**
3 **deuns**	6 **deuns**

VIII *Verbal Adjective*
      devedhys.

C.11 'TO SIT'
I   *Verbal Noun*
       sedha, **esedha**
II   *Present Future*
       1 *sedhaf*   4 *sedhyn*
       2 *sedhyth*   5 *sedhowgh*
       3 **eseth**, **esa**   6 *sedhons*
       Apart from 3 this tense is a reconstruction.
III   *Imperfect*
IV   *Preterite*
V   *Subjunctive*
VI   *Conditional*
       These are all unattested in our foundation texts.
VII   *Imperative*
       1 –   4 *sedhyn*
       2 **eseth**   5 **esedhowgh**, **sedhowgh**
       3 *sedhens*   6 *sedhens*
       Apart from 2 and 5 these forms are unattested in our texts.
VIII   *Verbal Adjective*
       esedhys, **sedhys**.

The verbal noun is **sedha** in our foundation texts, but **esedha**, spelt
‹*esethe*›, ‹*ysethe*› occurs in early Middle Cornish.

C.12 'TO BE ABLE'

I   *Verbal Noun*
     gallos

II   *Present Future*

1 **gallaf**	4 **gyllyn**
2 **gyllyth, gyllysta, gylta**	5 **gyllowgh**
3 **gyll**	6 **gyllons**

     An autonomous form **gyller** is attested in BK.

IIa   *Future*
     3 **gyllvyth**
     This appears as ⟨*ylwyth*⟩ in BK.

III   *Imperfect*

1 **gyllyn**	4 **gyllyn**
2 *gyllys*	5 **gyllewgh**
3 **gylly**	6 **gyllens**

     III 2 is conjecture; 4 and 5 are indistinguishable from II 4 and 5.

IV   *Preterite*
     No preterite of this verb is attested in our foundation texts.

V   *Subjunctive*

1 **gallen**	4 **gallon**
2 **galles, gylly**	5 **gallowgh**
3 **galla**	6 **gallons**

     A form *gyllyf* at V 1 is attested in the Ordinalia.

VI   *Conditional*

1 **galsen, galjen**	4 **galsen, galjen**
2 **galses, galjes**	5 **galsewgh, galjewgh**
3 **galsa, galja**	5 **galsens, galjens**

C.13 'TO KNOW' (this verb also has a sense 'to be able')

I   *Verbal Noun*

godhvos, gothfos

I *govos* at OM 2102 and Lhuyd's **godhaz** imply that the consonant cluster in the verbal noun was voiced. On the other hand the very common spelling ‹**gothfos**›, ‹**gothfes**›, ‹**gothfas**› as late as TH seems to indicate that there was a variant with a voiceless cluster.

II   *Present Future*

1 **gòn, goraf vy, gorama**	4 **godhyn, goryn**
2 **godhes, gosta**	5 **godhowgh**, *gorowgh*
3 **gor**	6 **godhons**

6 is not attested in our foundation texts, but <ny wothons> is atttested in the *Ordinalia*.

IIa   *Future*

1 –	4 –
2 **godhvedhys**	5 –
3 **godhvyth**	6 –

The two future forms are attested in BK as 2 **ny wothvethys** and 3 **a wothvith** respectively.

III   *Imperfect*

1 **godhyen**	4 *godhyen*
2 **godhyes**	5 *godhyowgh*
3 **godhya**	6 **godhyens**

     III 4 and 5 are conjectural.

IV   *Preterite*

The preterite of this verb is not attested anywhere in traditional Cornish.

V   *Subjunctive*

1 **gothfen**	4 *gothfen*
2 **gothfes**	5 *gothfowgh*
3 **gothfa**	6 *gothfens*

     Only V 1, 2 and 3 are attested in our foundation texts.

VI   *Conditional*

1 **gothvien**	4 *gothvien*
2 *gothvies*	5 *gothviowgh*
3 *gothvia*	6 **gothviens**

Nance made a distinction between the indicative pluperfect *gothvyen* and the subjunctive pluperfect *gothfyen* which is entirely without warrant. Only 1 and 6 are attested in our foundation texts.

VII   *Imperative*

1 –	4 **godhvedhen**
2 **godhvyth**, **gor**	5 **godhvedhowgh**
3 **godhvedhens**	6 **godhvedhens**.

The form **gor** seems to appear in JCH §31. Only 2 and 5 are attested in our foundation texts.

VIII   *Verbal Adjective*
godhvedhys.

C.14   'TO REPLY'

I   *Verbal Noun*
gortheby

II   *Present Future*

1 **gorthebaf**	4 *gorthebyn*
2 *gorthebyth*	5 *gorthebowgh*
3 **gorthyp**	6 *gorthebons*

Apart from 1 and 3 this tense is reconstruction

III   *Imperfect*
The imperfect is not attested in our foundation texts.

IV   *Preterite*

1 *gorthebys*	4 *gorthepsyn*
2 *gorthepsys*	5 *gorthebsowgh*
3 **gorthebys**, **gorthebas**	6 *gorthepsons*

IV 3 only is attested in our foundation texts. **Gorthebas** is based on ‹*gwerebaz*› in Rowe.

V   *Subjunctive*

VI   *Conditional*
These are unattested in our foundation texts.

VII   *Imperative*

1 –	4 *gortheben*
2 **gorthyp**	5 **gorthebowgh**
3 *gorthebens*	6 *gorthebens*

All persons in VII are conjectural apart from 2 and 5.

VIII   *Verbal Adjective*
gorthebys.

C.15 'TO SEE'

I   *Verbal Noun*
     gweles

II   *Present Future*

1 **gwelaf**	4 **gwelyn**
2 **gwelyth**, **gwelta**	5 **gwelowgh**
3 **gwel**	6 *gwelons*

     II 6 is a reconstruction.

IIa   *Future*
     This, the special future, is represented in our foundation texts only
     by 3 **gwelvyth**.

III   *Imperfect*

1 **gwelyn**	4 **gwelyn**
2 **gwelys**	5 **gwelewgh**
3 **gwely**	6 **gwelens**

     In III only 1 and 4 are attested in our foundation texts.

IV   *Preterite*

1 **gwelys**	4 **gwelsyn**
2 **gwelsys**, **gwelsta**	5 **gwelsowgh**
3 **gwelas**	6 **gwelsons**

     IV 6 is not attested in our foundation texts, but **gwelsons** is attested
     twice in PA.

V   *Subjunctive*

1 *gwellen*, **gwyllyf**	4 *gwellen*
2 *gwelles*, **gwylly**	5 *gwellowgh*
3 **gwella**, **gwelha**	6 *gwellons*, *gwelhons*

     Apart from 1 **gwyllyf**, 2 **gwylly**, 3 **gwella**, **gwelha** all forms in V
     are reconstructions.

VI   *Conditional*

VII   *Imperative*
     These are not attested in our foundation texts.

VIII   *Verbal Adjective*
     gwelys.

C.16 'TO MAKE, TO DO'
I *Verbal Noun*
gwil, **gul**
II *Present Future*
1 **gwrav, gwrama** 4 **gwren**
2 **gwres, gwreth, gwreta** 5 **gwrewgh**
3 **gwra** 6 **gwrowns**
2 appears in Late Cornish as **gwras**.
III *Imperfect*
1 **gwren** 4 **gwren**
2 **gwres** 5 **gwrewgh**
3 **gwre** 6 **gwrêns**
III 3, 4 and 5 are attested in our foundation texts. 1, 2 and 6 occur in earlier Middle Cornish.
IV *Preterite*
1 **gwrug, gwrugaf** 4 **gwrussyn**
2 **gwrussys, gwrusta** 5 **gwrussowgh, gwrugowgh why**
3 **gwrug, gwras** 6 **gwrussons, gwrug anjy**
V *Subjunctive*
1 **gwrellen, gwryllyf** 4 **gwrellen**
2 **gwrelles, gwrylly** 5 **gwrellowgh**
3 **gwrella** 6 **gwrellons**
VI *Conditional*
1 **gwrussen** 4 **gwrussen**
2 *gwrusses* 5 *gwrussewgh*
3 **gwrussa** 6 **gwrussens**
VI 2 and 5 do not appear to be attested in our foundation texts.
VII *Imperative*
1 – 4 **gwren**
2 **gwra** 5 **gwrewgh**
3 **gwrêns** 6 **gwrêns**
VIII *Verbal Adjective*
gwrës, gwrÿs
This is the most frequently used auxiliary in Cornish and as such it is remarkably well attested.

C.17 'TO TAKE'
I   *Verbal Noun*
        kemeres
II   *Present Future*
        1 *kemeraf*   4 *kemeryn*
        2 *kemeryth*, *kemerta*   5 *kemerowgh*
        3 **kebmer**   6 *kemerons*
        Apart from II 3 all the above forms are conjecture.
III   *Imperfect*
        The imperfect of this verb does not appear to be attested.
IV   *Preterite*
        1 **kemerys**   4 *kemersyn*
        2 **kemersys**   5 *kemersowgh*
        3 **kemeras**   6 *kemersons*
        Only the three persons 1, 2 and 3 of the singular are attested in our
        foundation texts.
V   *Subjunctive*
        1 *kemyrren*, **kemyrryf** 4 *kemerren*
        2 *kemerres*, *kemyrry*   5 *kemerrowgh*
        3 **kemerra**   6 *kemerrons*
        V 1 **kemyrryf** and 3 **kemerra** are the only forms attested in our
        foundation texts.
VI   *Conditional*
        1 *kemersen*   4 *kemersen*
        2 *kemerses*   5 *kemersowgh*
        3 **kemersa**   6 *kemersens*
        Of VI only 3 is attested anywhere in Cornish.
VII   *Imperative*
        1 –   4 *kemeryn*
        2 **kebmer**   5 **kemerowgh**
        3 **kemerens**   6 *kemerens*
        In VII 4 and 6 are reconstructions.
VIII   *Verbal Adjective*
        kemerys.

C.18 'TO SAY'

I   *Verbal Noun*
    leverel
    A form **lavaral**, **lawl** is attested in Late Cornish.

II   *Present Future*
    1 **lavaraf**   4 **leveryn**
    2 **leveryth**, **leverta**   5 **leverowgh**
    3 **lever**, **laver**   6 *leverons*
    II 2 **leverta** is attested in the *Ordinalia*, but not in our foundation
    texts. 6 is not attested.

III   *Imperfect*
    1 *leveryn*   4 *leveryn*
    2 *leverys*   5 *leverewgh*
    3 **levery**   6 *leverens*
    Of III only 3 is attested in our foundation texts.

IV   *Preterite*
    1 **leverys**   4 **leversyn**
    2 **leversys**   5 **leversowgh**
    3 **leverys**, **laveras**   6 **lavarsons**
    Leversys, **leversowgh**, and **lavarsons** are attested in PA and the
    Ordinalia, but not in our foundation texts.

V   *Subjunctive*
    1 *lavarren*   4 *lavarren*
    2 *lavarres*   5 *lavarrowgh*
    3 **lavarra**   6 *lavarrons*
    Apart from V 3 this tense is unattested.

VI   *Conditional*
    This is not attested in our foundation texts.

VII   *Imperative*
    1 –   4 **leveryn**
    2 **lavar**   5 **leverowgh**
    3 *leverens*   6 *leverens*
    VII 3 and 6 are reconstructions.

VIII   *Verbal Adjective*
    leverys.

C.19 'TO WISH'

I   *Verbal Noun*
mydnas, **mednas**

II   *Present Future*

1 **manaf, madnaf, mydnaf**	4 **mydnyn, mednyn**
2 **mydnys, mynta, menta**	5 **mydnowgh, mednowgh**
3 **mydn, medn**	6 **mydnons, mednons**

III   *Imperfect*

1 **mydnen, mednen**	4 *mydnen, mednen*
2 **mydnes, mednes**	5 *mydnewgh, mednewgh*
3 **mydna, medna**	6 *mydnens, mednens*

The plural forms of III are all reconstructions.

IV   *Preterite*

1 **mydnys**	4 *mynsyn*
2 **mynsys**	5 *mynsowgh, mensowgh*
3 **mydnas, mednas**	6 *mynsons, mensons*

All the plural forms in IV are reconstructions.

V   *Subjunctive*

1 **mednen, mydnyf**	4 *mednyn*
2 **mednes, mynhy**	5 **mednowgh**
3 **mydna, mynho**	6 **mednons**

All these persons are attested except 4.

VI   *Conditional*

1 **mensen, menjen**	4 **mensen, menjen**
2 **menses, menjes**	5 **mensewgh, menjewgh**
3 **mensa, menja**	6 **mensens, menjens**

C.20 'TO GO'

I   *Verbal Noun*
    mos, **mones**

II *Present Future*

1 **av**, **ama**	4 **en**
2 **êth**	5 **ewgh**
3 **â**	6 **ôns**

III *Imperfect*

1 **en**	4 *en*
2 **es**	5 **ewgh**
3 **ê**	6 **êns**

Only III 3 is attested in our foundation texts.

IV *Preterite*

1 **êth**	4 **ethyn**
2 **êthys**	5 **ethowgh**
3 **êth**	6 **ethons**

In IV only 1 and 3 are attested in our foundation texts.

IVa *Preterite*

1 **galsof**	4 *galson*
2 **galsos**	5 *galsowgh*
3 **gallas**	6 **galsons**

Only 1, 3 and 6 are attested in our foundation texts; 2 is attested in the *Ordinalia*.

V   *Subjunctive*

1 **ellen**, **yllyf**	4 **ellen**
2 **elles**, **ylly**	5 **ellowgh**
3 **ella**	6 **ellons**

VI *Conditional*
    The conditional of this verb is not attested in our foundation texts.

VII *Imperative*

1 –	4 **deun**
2 **kê**	5 **ewgh**, **kewgh**
3 **êns**	6 **êns**

VIII *Verbal Adjective*
     gyllys.

C.21 'TO GIVE'

I   *Verbal Noun*

ry

II   *Present Future*

1 **rov**	4 *ren*
2 **reth**	5 **rewgh**
3 **re**, **ro**	6 *rêns*

II 4 and 6 are not attested in our foundation texts.

III   *Imperfect*

The imperfect of this verb is not attested.

IV   *Preterite*

1 **rys**	4 *resen*
2 **ryssys**	5 *resowgh*
3 **ros**	6 **rosons**

IV 3 only is attested in our foundation texts; 1, 2 and 6 occur in the *Ordinalia*.

V   *Subjunctive*

1 **rollen**	4 **rollen**
2 *rolles*	5 *rollowgh*
3 **rolla**, **roy**	6 **rollons**

V 1, 3 (**roy**) and 4 only occur in our foundation texts; 6 is attested in the *Ordinalia*.

VI   *Conditional*

1 **rosen**	4 **rosen**
2 **roses**	5 **rosewgh**
3 **rosa**	6 **rosens**

Only 1 and 3 are attested in our foundation texts.

VII   *Imperative*

1 –	4 **ren**
2 **ro**, **roy**	5 **rewgh**
3 *rêns*	6 *rêns*

VII 2 and 5 only occur in our foundation texts; 4 occurs in the *Ordinalia*.

VIII   *Verbal Adjective*

rës, **rÿs**.

C.22 'TO BRING'
I *Verbal Noun*
   dry
II *Present Future*
   1 **drov**   4 **dryn**
   2 **dreth**   5 *drewgh*
   3 **dora**, **dro**, **dre**   6 *drêns*
   II 5 and 6 are conjectural.
III *Imperfect*
   The imperfect of this verb is not attested in our foundation texts.
IV *Preterite*
   1 *drys*   4 *dressyn*
   2 *dressys*   5 *dressowgh*
   3 **dros**   6 *drosons*
   Only IV 3 is attested; the rest are conjectural.
V *Subjunctive*
   1 *drollen*   4 *drollen*
   2 *drolles*   5 *drollowgh*
   3 **drolla**   6 *drollens*
   Only V 3 is attested.
VI *Conditional*
   1 *drossen*   4 **drossen**
   2 *drosses*   5 *drossewgh*
   3 **drossa**   6 *drossens*
   Only VI 3 is attested in our foundation texts; 4 is attested in PA.
VII *Imperative*
   1 –   4 *dren*
   2 **dro**, **doroy** 5 **drewgh**
   3 **drêns**   6 *drêns*
   VII 4 and 6 are reconstructions.
VIII *Verbal Adjective*
   drës, **drÿs**.

C.23 'TO STAND'
I   *Verbal Noun*
       sevel
II   *Present Future*
       1 *savaf*   4 *sevyn*
       2 *sevyth*   5 *sevowgh*
       3 **sev**   6 *sevons*
       II 3 only is attested in our foundation texts.
III   *Imperfect*
       The imperfect of this verb is not attested in our foundation texts; *y sevy* is attested in PA.
IV   *Preterite*
       1 *sevys*   4 *sefsyn*
       2 *sefsys*   5 *sefsowgh*
       3 **sevys, savas**   6 *safsons*
       Apart from IV 3 this tense is a reconstruction; the form **savas** occurs in JCH.
V   *Subjunctive*
VI   *Conditional*
       These are unattested in our foundation texts.
VII   *Imperative*
       1 –   4 *sevyn*
       2 **sav, sa'**   5 **sevowgh**
       3 *sevens*   6 *sevens*
       Only VII 2 and 5 are attested in our foundation texts.
VIII   *Verbal Adjective*
       sevys.

STAGELL D
Appendix D

Jowan Chy an Hordh
in Standard Cornish spelling

1 I'n termyn eus passys th'era trigys in Seleven den ha benyn in tyller cries Chy an Hordh.

2 Ha'n whel a godhas scant, hag yn medh an den dhe'n wreg, "Me a vedn mos dhe whelas whel dhe wil, ha why a yll dendyl agas bôwnans obma."

3 Cubmyas teg ev a gemeras, ha pell dhe'n ëst ev a dravalyas, ha wàr an dyweth ev a wrug dos dhe jy tiak hag a wrug whelas ena whel dhe wil.

4 "Pana whel a yllysta gwil?" yn medh an tiak. "Pùb whel oll," yn medh Jowan. Ena anjy a vargynyas rag try fens an vledhen gober.

5 Ha pàn yth era dyweth an vledhen, y vêster a dhysqwedhas dhodho an try fens. "Mir, Jowan," yn medh y vêster, "obma dha wober. Bùs mar menta y ry dhèm arta, me a vedn desky dhis poynt a skians."

6 "Pandr'yw hedna?" yn medh Jowan. "Nâ," yn medh y vêster, "ry dhèm, ha me a vedn leverel dhis." "Kemerowgh dhan," yn medh Jowan. Nena yn medh an mêster: "Kebmer with na wreth gara an vordh goth rag an vordh nowyth."

7 Nena anjy a vargynyas rag bledhen moy rag pecar gober. Ha pàn th'era dyweth an vledhen, y vêster a dhros an try fens. "Mir, Jowan," yn medh y vêster, "Obma dha wober, bùs mar menta y ry dhèm, me a dhesk dhis ken poynt a skians."

8 "Pandr'yw hedna?" yn medh Jowan. "Nâ," yn medh y vêster. "Ry dhèm, ha me a vedn leverel dhis." "Kemerowgh dhan," yn medh Jowan. Nena yn medh y vêster, "Kebmer with na wrewgh why ôstya in chy le'ma fo den coth demedhys dhe venyn yonk."

9 Ena anjy a vargynyas rag bledhen moy, ha pàn th'era dyweth an vledhen, y vêster a dhros an try fens. "Mir, Jowan," yn medh y vêster, "obma dha wober, bùs mar menta y ry dhèm arta, me a dhesk dhis an gwelha poynt a skians oll."

10 "Pandr'yw hedna?" yn medh Jowan. "Nâ," yn medh y vêster, "Ro dhèm, ha me a laver dhis." "Kemerowgh dhan," yn medh Jowan. Nena yn medh y vêster: "Bedhys gweskys dywweyth kyn gweskel unweyth, rag hedna yw an gwelha poynt a skians oll."

11 Lebmyn Jowan, ev ny venja servya na velha, bùs ev a venja mos tre dh'y wreg. "Nâ," yn medh y vêster, "gwrewgh mos chy, ha ma an wreg vy ow pobas myttyn, ha hy a wra gwil tesen ragos dha dhros tre dhe'th wreg."

12 Ha anjy a worras an naw pens i'n desen, ha pàn wrug Jowan kemeres y gubmyas, "Obma," yn medh y vêster, "ma tesen ragos dhe dhon tre dhe'th wreg. Ha pàn vo che ha'th wreg an moyha lowen warbarth, nena grewgh terry an desen ha nahens."

13 Cubmyas teg ev a gemeras ha tu ha tre ev a dravalyas, ha wàr an dyweth ev a wrug dos dhe Goon Sen Eler, hag ena ev a vetyas gen try marchant a Tre Ryn, tus pluw, ow tos dre mes a fer Keresk.

14 "Ha, Jowan," yn medh anjy, "dewgh genen ny. Lowen on ny dh'agas gweles why. Ple veu che mar bell?"

15 Yn medh Jowan, "Me a veu ow servya, ha lebmyn th'eroma ow mos tre dhe'm gwreg." "Hâ," yn medh anjy, "Ewgh abarth dhe ny, ha welcùm che a vêdh."

16 Anjy a gemeras an vordh nowyth ha Jowan a withas an vordh goth.

17 Ha mos ryb keow Chy Woon, ha nyns o an varchons gyllys pell dhort Jowan, bùs ladron a glenas ort anjy.

18 Ha anjy a dhalathas dhe wil cry. Ha gans an cry a wrug an varchons gwil, Jowan a grias inwedh, "Ladron, ladron!"

19 Ha gans an cry a wrug Jowan gwil, an ladron a forsâkyas an varchons. Ha pàn wrug anjy dos dhe Varhas Yow, ena anjy a vetyas arta.

20 "Ha Jowan," yn medh anjy, "senjys on ny dhe why. Na ve ragowgh why, ny a via tus oll dyswrës. Deus abarth dhe ny, ha welcùm te a vêdh.

21 Ha pàn wrug anjy dos dhe'n chy le'ma godhvia anjy ôstya, yn medh Jowan, "Me a dal gweles an ost a'n chy."

22 "An ost a'n chy?" yn medh anjy, "Pandr'a venta gwil gen an ost a'n chy? Obma yma gàn ôstes ny ha yonk yw hy. Mar menta gweles an ost a'n chy, kê dhe'n gegyn, ha ena te a'n cav."

23 Ha pàn wrug ev dos dhe'n gegyn, ena ev a welas an ost a'n chy, ha den coth o ev, ha gwadn, ow trailya an ber.

24 Ha yn medh Jowan, "Obma ny vadnaf vy ostya, bùs i'n nessa chy." "Na whath," yn medh anjy, "Gwra cona abarth dhyn ny, ha welcùm te a vêdh."

25 Lebmyn an ôstes a'n chy, hy a gùssulyas gen neb udn managh era i'n dre dhe dhestria an den coth i'n gwely in termyn an nos ha'n rest a'anjy ow repôsya, ha gorra an fowt wàr an varchons.

26 Ha pàn th'era Jowan i'n gwely, th'era toll in tâl an chy, ha ev a welas golow. Ha ev a savas in màn in mes a'y wely. Ha ev a woslowas ha ev a glôwas an managh ow leverel, ha trailys y geyn dhe'n toll, "Martesen," yn medh ev, "ma nebonen i'n nessa chy, a wrug gweles agan hager-oberow." Ha gans hedna an wadn-wre'ty gans hy follat a dhestrias an den coth i'n gwely.

27 Ha gans hedna Jowan gans y golhan a drohas der an toll mes a geyn gon an managh pîss pòr rônd.

28 Ha nessa myttyn an wadn-wre'ty, hy a dhalathas dhe wil cry ter veu hy dremas hy destries. Ha rag nag era den na flogh i'n chy bùs an varchons, anjy a dhal cregy ragtho.

29 Ena anjy a veu kemerys ha dhe'n clogh-prednyer anjy a veu ledys. Ha wàr an dyweth Jowan a dheuth wàr aga fydn.

30 "Ha Jowan," yn medh anjy, "ma cales lùck dhyn ny. Ma agan ost ny destries newher ha ny a dal cregy ragtho."

31 "Why oll? Merowgh why, anjùstys yw," yn medh Jowan. "Gor ter o an dhewas-wreg ha managh a wrug an bad-ober."

32 "Pywa?" yn medh anjy. "Pyw a wrug an bad-ober?" "Pyw a wrug an bad-ober?" yn medh Jowan. "Mar ny'm beus tra a dheffa prevy pyw a wrug an bad-ober, me a vedn cregy ragtho."

33 "Leverowgh dhana," yn medh anjy. "Newher," yn medh Jowan, "pàn th'era'vy et ow gwely, me a welas golow, ha me a savas in màn, ha th'era toll in tâl an chy.

34 Ha neb udn managh a drailyas y geyn wàrbydn an toll. "Martesen," yn medh ev, ma nebonen i'n nessa chy a yll gweles agan hager-oberow."

35 Ha gans hedna gen ow holhan me a drohas pîss der an toll mes a geyn gon an managh, pîss pòr rônd. Ha rag gwil an geryow-ma dhe vos prevys, obma an pîss et ow focket dhe vos gwelys."

36 Ha gans hedna an varchons a veu fries, ha'n venyn ha'n managh a veu kemerys ha cregys.

37 Nena anjy a dheuth warbarth in mes a Varhas Yow. Ha wàr an dyweth anjy a wrug dos dhe Goos Kernwhyly in Beryan.

38 Ena th'era vordh dhyberth ha'n varchons a venja arta dhe Jowan mos tre abarth anjy, bùs rag an termyn ev ny venja, mès ev a venja mos tre dh'y wreg.

39 Ha pàn th'o ev gyllys dhort an varchons ev a dhylâtyas an termyn m'alla va prevy era y wreg ow qwitha compes et y gever, era pò nag era.

40 Ha pàn wrug ev dos dhe'n daras, ev a venja clôwes den aral i'n gwely.
Ev a wescas y dhorn wàr y dhagyer dhe dhestria an dhew. Bès ev a
brederas ter godha dhodho bos avîsys dywweyth kyn gweskel unweyth.

41 Ha ev a dheuth in mes arta. Ha nena ev a gnoukyas. "Pyw eus ena
abarth Duw?" yn medh hy.

42 "Th'erof vy obma," yn medh Jowan. "Re Varia, pyw a glôwaf vy?" yn
medh hy. "Mars owgh why Jowan, dewgh chy." "Doroy an golow
dhana," yn medh Jowan. Nena hy a dhros an golow.

43 Ha pàn wrug Jowan dos chy, yn medh ev, "Pàn wrug avy dos dhe'n
daras, me a venja clôwes den aral i'n gwely."

44 "Ha Jowan," yn medh hy, "pàn wrugough why mos in kerdh, th'eren
vy gyllys try mis gen flogh, ha lebmyn yma dhe ny meppyk wheg i'n
gwely, dhe Dhuw re bos grassyans."

45 Yn medh Jowan, "Me a vedn leverel dhis. Ow mêster ha'm mêstres a
ros dhèm tesen hag a leverys dhybm, pàn vo me ha'm gwreg an moyha
lowen warbarth dhe derry an desen, ha nahens. Ha lebmyn ma câss dhe
ny rag bos lowen.

46 Nena y a dorras an desen, ha th'era naw pens i'n desen. Ha'n mona
anjy a gavas ha'n bara anjy a dhebras, ha ny veu udn froth na myken na
tra wàr an norvës. Ha indella ma dyweth ow drolla adro dhedhans.

STAGELL E
Appendix E

Answers to Exercises 1–18

E.1C.2 Translate into English:
1 The cake on the table.
2 The wine in the glass.
3 The cat and the dog.
4 The cats and the dogs.
5 The king and the queen.
6 The kings and the queens.
7 The day and the night.
8 The boys and the girls.
9 The doctors and the patients.
10 The merchants and the money.
11 The friends and the enemies.
12 The parents and the children.
13 Shoulders and feet.
14 The leaves under the tree.
15 The cow and the bull in the field.
16 The stag in the woods.
17 The sheep on the mountain.
18 The cows on the grass.
19 The rooms in the houses.
20 The Englishmen in England and the Cornishmen in Cornwall.

E.1C.3 Translate into Cornish:
1 An dus ha'n benenes
2 An flehes i'n gwelyow
3 An deves ha'n buhas.
4 An gwels wàr an menydhyow.
5 An gwëdh i'n cosow.
6 An mowysy ha'n vebyon in dadn an wedhen.
7 An cathas ha'n keun.
8 An delyow wàr an wedhen ha'n delyow wàr an dor.
9 Cothmans ha kerens.

10 An bord i'n rom i'n chy.

11 An vebyon, an mowysy ha'n tasow.

12 An vowes ha'n gath.

13 An vebyon ha'n terewy.

14 An mytern, an vyternes ha'n jowl.

15 An dhewolow ha'n benenes.

16 An gwelyow ha'n menydhyow.

17 An Sows, an jowl ha'n gath.

18 An buhas wàr an gwels.

19 An medhek ha'n flehes.

20 An marchont ha'n mona.

E.2C.2 Translate into English:

1 There are many Celts in Wales.

2 The Cornish are strong and industrious.

3 There are many white sheep in the green mountains of the land.

4 There are many beautiful flowers in the garden and there are many green trees in the wood.

5 There are many swift horses in the large field.

6 The children in the school are polite and intelligent.

7 The evil woman is foolish.

8 The animals in the great wood are wild, but the dogs here are tame.

9 The bread is fresh and white but the wine is old and red.

10 There are many people together in the town.

11 There is a new bridge over the water.

12 There are many rooms in the house of the rich Cornishwoman.

13 The water here is deep, but the water near the land is shallow.

14 The needy people are hungry, but the rich men in the tavern are happy.

15 The children are safe here, but the big road is dangerous.

16 The fat cows are brown and the horses are white and black.

17 The old women are together in the church and the old men are together in the pub.

18 There are many white clouds in the blue sky.

19 The king and the queen are rich, but there are many poor people in the country.

20 The foolish boys are little devils.

E.2C.3 Translate into Cornish:

1 Yma lowr a vohosogyon in Kembra.

2 Yma an Gernowyon cortes ha dywysyk.

3 Yma an dowr in dadn an pons down ha peryllys.

4 Yma lowr a vuhas tew i'n gwel hag yma lowr a dheves tanow wàr an meneth.

5 An cothwas yw dydhan saw an venyn goth yw cosel.

6 Yma lowr a flehes skentyl i'n scol.

7 An âlsyow yw peryllys, saw an flehes yw saw warbarth obma.

8 An gwin rudh yw coth saw dâ.

9 Yma an bara gwydn wàr an bord.

10 Yma lowr a vergh du in dadn an gwëdh.

11 An jëdh yw spladn ha'n ebron yw glas.

12 Yma an mytern dâ ha'n vyternes dâ warbarth i'n eglos.

13 Yma an gothwesyon warbarth in dadn an wedhen vrâs ogas dhe'n pons.

14 An mowysy yw dywysyk, saw lowr a'n vebyon i'n scol yw diek.

15 Yma lowr a venydhyow in Kembra.

16 Yma lowr a Gernowyon yonk hag a Gernowesow yonk in Loundres.

17 An keun ha'n cathas yw dov, saw yma lowr a vestas gwyls i'n coos tewl.

18 An gwels yw sëgh ha gell, saw an delyow wàr an gwëdh yw medhel ha gwer.

19 An desen yw parys ha'n flehes yw lowen.

20 An gath yw du ha'n ky yw gell ha gwydn.

21 Yma an medhek obma saw yma an varchons i'n tavern.

E.3C.2 Translate into English:

1 Many Cornishmen speak Cornish today.

2 The women are baking and the girls are milking the cows.

3 I am writing the Cornish exercise in the book.

4 They are walking together under the trees and throwing the ball on the grass.

5 The children are sleeping in little beds in the big room and the old people are laughing and drinking together beside the fire.

6 Many white clouds are hurrying across the sky.

7 You are learning Cornish now and you are reading the beautiful book.

8 The boys are climbing upon the high dangerous cliffs.

9 The boys are falling; they are crying.

10 We are carrying the bread and the wine to the tinners under the earth.

11 You are fighting today but the quiet girls are reading and writing Cornish.

12 The old man is old and he is suffering.

13 We are sitting on the soft chair beside the door.

14 The girls are hungry and they are crying.

15 The cows are sitting upon the grass in the field.

16 We are playing beside the school.

17 The young woman is making a cake today.

18 John wants a new ball and he is walking towards the shop in the town.

19 The tumblers are in the cupboard near to the door and the wine is on the table.

20 You are playing and laughing.

21 Jennifer and John are going out together.

E.3C.3 Translate into Cornish:

1 Yma lowr a gerry tan in Kernow.

2 Yma lowr a dus ow côwsel Kernowek lebmyn.

3 Yth esta ow côwsel Kernowek yn tâ, saw yth esof vy whath ow tesky.

4 Yth esowgh why ow redya Kernowek i'n lyver nowyth.

5 Yth esoma ow redya hag ow scrifa Kernowek saw yth esoma ow côwsel Sowsnek orth Kernowyon.

6 Yth esof vy ow ton an gwedrednow ha'n gwin dhe'n bord in dadn an wedhen.

7 Yth eson ny ow qwary gans pellen ogas dhe'n eglos.

8 Yma an mowysy ow qwary saw yma an vebyon owth argya hag owth omlath.

9 An flehes yw gwag; ymowns y owth ola.

10 Yma an dus yonk ow tos dres an pons.

11 Yth eson ny ow perna boos i'n shoppa brâs.

12 Yth eson ny ow kemeres an kyttryn dhe'n dre.

13 Yth esof vy ow mos dhe Gembra i'n carr hedhyw.

14 Yma an marchont ow qwertha mergh ha buhas in Kernow.

15 An den yw coth ha clâv; yma va ow sùffra hag ow kerdhes yn lent.

16 Yma an vebyon owth omlath ryb an scol.

17 Yma an flogh clâv i'n gwely hag yma an medhek ow fysky dhe'n chy.

18 Yma an Gernowes ow kerdhes i'n menydhyow in Kembra.

19 Hy yw yonk ha yagh. Yma hy ow kerdhes in mes gans den yonk teg.

20 An venyn goth yw coth saw hy yw yagh whath.

21 Yma an gothwesyon owth eva warbarth i'n tavern.

22 Yma an varchons ow qwertha lowr a win dhe'n dus yonk gocky; yma an dus yonk owth eva warbarth—ymowns y owth argya hag owth omlath.

E.4C.2 Translate into English:

1 Are you going to the town today? No, we are going to the sea on the train.

2 When does the train reach the station?

3 Where are John and Jennifer? They are sitting under the big tree in the garden.

4 Is there cheese in the kitchen? No.

5 Is there milk or bread in the cupboard? There is a little milk, but there is no bread.

6 Are they playing happily together? No, unfortunately. The boys are fighting and the girls are crying.

7 Is George here? Yes, he is in the next room watching the television.

8 Many people are walking in the street. They are going to the market.

9 We are shopping in the supermarket today.

10 Aren't you coming as well? No, we are staying here.

11 Do you speak Cornish? Yes, I speak Cornish and Welsh as well.

12 Is there a bridge over the river in the town? Yes, there is a new bridge and an old bridge also.

13 Where are the children? They are in the garden climbing the trees and looking at the flowers.

14 Aren't they at school? No, they are not at school today. Today is a holiday.

15 Where is the doctor? He is in the next room looking at George. George is sick in bed.

16 We eat a lot of bread, but we don't drink wine.

17 Is the old man still here? No, he is drinking in the pub with the other old men.

18 It is raining, alas. There are many grey clouds in the sky.

19 We are not going out today.

20 The wind is strong today and the leaves are falling off the trees in the garden.

E.4C.3 Translate into Cornish:

1 Usy an flehes owth ola? Nag usons, ymowns y ow wherthyn warbarth.

2 Ple ma an deves? Ymowns y ow tebry gwels wàr an meneth.

3 Esowgh why ow mos dhe'n worvarhas? Nag eson, yth eson ny ow mos dhe'n eglos. Hedhyw yw degol.

4 Ple ma an medhek? Yma Jory clâv i'n gwely.

5 Yth eson ny ow mos dhe'n dre hedhyw. Esowgh why ow mos wàr an train? Nag eson, yth eson ny ow mos wàr an kyttryn.

6 An gwyns yw crev hag yma an delyow melen ow codha.

7 Yma ow qwil glaw hag yma an vergh in dadn an gwëdh i'n gwel.

8 Ple ma an buhas? Ymowns ow sedha wàr an gwels glëb.

9 A nyns usy an venyn goth ow pobas i'n gegyn? Nag usy, yma hy obma ow miras orth an bellwolok.

10 A nyns usy an flehes ow tesky i'n scol hedhyw? Nag usons, ymowns ow redya i'n lyverjy.

11 Yma an vebyon ow qwary yn lowen gans an ky. Yma an mowysy ow côwsel warbarth.

12 Ple ma Jenefer? Yma hy wàr an train ow mos dhe Loundres.

13 Eus lowr a Gernowesow yonk in Loundres? Eus, ha Kernowyon yonk kefrës.

14 Usy an kencras in dadn an men whath? Nag usons, ymowns y i'n mor lebmyn.

15 Ple ma an deves? Ymowns y wàr an menydhyow uhel in Kembra.

16 Usy an den ow kerdhes yn lent? Usy, yma an cothwas ow kerdhes yn lent. Ev yw coth ha clâv.

17 Pleth esta? Yth esof vy ow sedha ryb an tan ow miras worth an bellwolok?

18 Usy ow qwil glaw? Nag usy, saw an jëdh yw yeyn.

19 Ple ma chy an venyn goth? Yma va i'n coos tewl.

20 Usy an vebyon ow redya? Nag usons, ymowns y ow qwary whath.

E.5C.2 Translate into English:

1 Were you beside the sea yesterday? No, we were walking in the town.

2 I was shopping in the new supermarket.

3 She doesn't get money from them any more.

4 They always give them lots of help.

5 Where you here often last year? Yes.

6 Did the children play happily with them? Yes, the boys played football together.

7 We were watching the waves breaking on the shore.

8 You and I, we were walking through the village listening to the people speaking Welsh.

9 Many of them speak Welsh well.

10 Do many of you understand Cornish? No, no one of us is learning Cornish, unfortunately.

11 Were George and Jennifer with you last night? No, they were together in the theatre.

12 Where were you the day before yesterday? We were climbing in the mountains. Many of them are high and dangerous.

13 Do you get much news from her now? No, we don't get any news at all. She does not write often to us.

14 I see the doctor seldom. He lives in a different place now.

15 Do you write to him? No.

16 Was he speaking to you yesterday? No, he was talking to George the day before yesterday.

17 Was it raining yesterday? Yes, and the wind was blowing strongly.

18 John was not with me. He was with the old man in the pub. He was drinking and laughing with him.

19 Were there cows in the field? Yes, and there was a bull with them. They are still in the field today.

20 Was John with Jennifer in the library? No, George was with her.

E.5C.3 Translate into Cornish:

1 Esta ow tos genen ny? Nag esof, yth esof ow mos gensy hy ha ganso ev.

2 Eses ryb an mor de? Esen, yth esen ow kerdhes wàr an treth gans an ky.

3 Eses ow clôwes lowr a nowodhow dhyworty? Nag esen, yma hy ow scrifa dhybm bohes venowgh.

4 Pleth esa an cothwas ha'n venyn goth newher? Yth esens ow sedha i'n chy ow miras orth an bellwolok.

5 Esens y ow prenassa i'n worvarhas degensete? Esens.

6 Esta ow côwsel orty pùpprës? Nag esof, yth esoma bohes venowgh ow côwsel orty.

7 Yth esof vy ow côwsel yn fenowgh ortans i'n dre. Ymowns y owth ùnderstondya Kernowek yn tâ.

8 Yma meneth ogas dhe'n dreveglos. Yth esen ny ow crambla ena.

9 Yma an medhek trigys ryb an pons dres an ryver.

10 Yth esa an ÿdhyn ow cana i'n gwëdh, yth esa an ên ow ponya i'n gwelyow hag yth esa an howl i'n ebron las.

11 Pleth eses jy? Yth esen i'n gwely clâv.

12 Pleth esa an medhek? Yth esen ow côwsel orto.

13 Yth esa an venyn deg ow cana, hag yth esen ow coslowes orty hag ow miras orty.

14 Yth esa an gwin wàr an bord hag yth esa an gwedrednow wàr an bord ganso.

15 Yth esen ny ow ry lowr a weres dhedhy.

16 Yth esen ny ow kerdhes gansans i'n coos. Yth esa an ÿdhyn ow cana ena.

17 Yth esa lowr a vestas gwyls i'n coos kefrës. Yth esen ow miras ortans.

18 Yth esa an flehes ow ponya dhywortans.

19 Pleth esa an vabm? Yth esa hy i'n chy ow pobas.

E.6C.2 Translate into English:

1 Are you ready at last? No, unfortunately. I am hurrying, but I am very tired.

2 What is he? He is a doctor. He works in the big hospital.

3 I was painting the doors of the house today. Really? What colour are they?

4 The front door is green, but the back door is red and white.

5 Were you painting the windows as well? No.

6 A new boy is working in the shop. Is he hardworking? He is very hardworking, but he is not intelligent unfortunately.

7 Do you eat enough meat now? No, but I like pork.

8 Is the butcher's pork any good? Yes indeed.

9 You are not happy today. What is the matter? I am very sad. The children are ill.

10 The water is very deep, isn't it? Yes and very dangerous.

11 I am coming with you. Thank you, you are very kind to me.

12 Where is the car? It is in the garage, but it isn't running very well. What is the matter?

13 What kind of car is it? It is an old car.

14 I was washing clothes today. Are they dry? Not yet. It is raining.

15 Are you going to the town today? Yes, a new supermarket has opened there.

16 Is it big? Yes, and it is very beautiful as well.

17 Ugly and violent are the wild animals, but they are not dangerous.

18 The sun is bright in the sky, but you are not happy.

19 The wind is very strong today and the waves are high.

20 Yes indeed, and there are lots of yellow leaves on the ground.

21 Old and good is the red wine, but I find it bitter.

E.6C.3 Translate into Cornish:

1 Pandr'yw an mater? Me yw trist hedhyw. Yma an flehes i'n clâvjy.

2 Pana jy ywa? Chy brâs tewl ywa hag yma va wàr an âls.

3 Esta ow tebry lowr a gig bowyn lebmyn? Nag esof, yth esof ow tebry lowr a gig porhel.

4 Usy an cothwas ow tos? Nag usy, coth ywa ha lent.

5 Yw an vebyon skentyl? Yns, y yw skentyl, saw nyns yns y cortes pùpprës, soweth.

6 An buhas yw gell, saw an tarow yw wydn, a nyns ywa?

7 An deves yw gwydn. Ymowns y wàr an meneth.

8 Yw hy teg? Hy yw pòr deg, saw nyns yw hy pòr jentyl. Pòr dhyscortes yw hy.

9 Yth esof ow paintya an chy degensete.

10 In gwir? Pana lyw yw an darasow ha'n fenestry? Y yw glas.

11 Ywa medhek dâ? Nag yw, saw yma lowr a vedhygyon dhâ in Loundres.

12 Pana desen yw hy? Tesen wheg yw.

13 Ple ma Jenefer ha Jowan? Ymowns y warbarth i'n waryva. Yma hy ow plegya dhcdhans.

14 Yth esof ow ry an mona dhywgh. Gromercy dhywgh. Why yw re wheg.

15 Yw uhel menydhyow Kembra? Lowr anodhans yw pòr uhel in gwir.

16 Yma maw nowyth i'n scol. Pana vaw ywa? Yma va ow qwary lowr a bel droos.

17 Nyns yw saw an pons dres an ryver.

18 Pleth esta ow qwil? Yth esof vy ow kemeres an bellen dhyworto.

19 Usy ow qwil glaw? Nag usy, saw tewl yw an cloudys ha'n gwyns yw pòr grev.

20 Owgh why yeyn? Nag en. Yth esen ny ow sedha ogas dhe'n tan.

21 Munys yw an avallow. Yns, hag y yw pòr wherow kefrës.

E.7C.2 Translate into Cornish:

1 The dog is running in the field, but the bull is disturbing him.
2 The bread is on the table, and the farmer's wife is cutting it.
3 Where are the children? They are in the school and the teacher is teaching them.
4 My feet are sore. I was playing football yesterday.
5 Aren't you tired still? No, but my clothes are very dirty already.
6 You are my love. I love you in my heart.
7 My father and my mother are angry with me.
8 Where is your money? In my pocket.
9 Your hands are dirty. What were you doing today? I was mending the car. It is old and it was not running well.
10 The cranefly is flying around the candle. The cat is looking at it.
11 My trousers and coat are torn. Is there another pair of trousers in the cupboard? Yes?
12 I like the song. I sing it every day.
13 The new girl is very polite, but she doesn't understand me well.
14 Are you still against him? No, but I don't like him.
15 A large and blue bird is flying in the sky. Do you see it? No, the sun is shining in my eyes.
16 I was talking to your friends yesterday. They are very sweet, but they don't speak Cornish.
17 Do you speak Cornish? Yes, but I don't understand everything.
18 Are your sisters married? One of them is married and she lives in London.
19 What is her husband? He is a doctor and their house if large and very beautiful.
20 Is your sister's husband a Cornishman? No, but he loves Cornwall and he is often here.

E.7C.3 Translate into Cornish:

1 Ple ma agas flehes? Ymowns y i'n scol ow tesky Kernowek.
2 Yth eses ow lewyas dha garr re uskys.
3 Ow gwreg vy yw coges dâ. Yma hy ow pobas bara hedhyw.
4 Yth eson ny ow tebry bara pùb dêdh. Yth eson ny worth y dhebry lebmyn.
5 Yma re a amanyn wàr ow bara vy.
6 Yth esa agas cath ow cana i'n nos. Nyns yw wheg y lev.
7 Ple ma Jowan? Yma va i'n carrjy in dadn an carr. Usy ev worth y êwna? Nag usy, nyns usy poran. Yma va ow miras orto.
8 Yma ow gwreg ha'm mebyon ow mos wàr an train dhe Loundres arta hedhyw. Esta jy ow mos gansans? Nag esof, yth esof vy ow qweles an medhek hedhyw. Me yw clâv. Yma ow throos ow hùrtya.
9 Yma hy trigys in chy brâs wàr an âls, saw yma hy myrgh trigys i'n chy munys-na i'n nessa strêt. Hy yw bohosak ha nyns usy hy mabm ow ry lowr a vona dhedhy.
10 Dha dhewla yw plos. Pëth eses ow qwil? Yth esen ow qwary pel droos gans ow hothmans.
11 Yma an lyver wàr an chair. Nyns esoma worth y redya.
12 Ple ma dha eskyjyow? Yth esoma worth aga glanhe.

13 Yth esa ev ow côwsel warbydn desky Kernowek hag yth esa ev worth ow ania. Osta whath wàr y bydn? Nag ov, saw nyns usy ev ow plegya dhybm.

14 Usy agas whereth trigys in Kernow? Nag usons, ymowns y trigys in Loundres, saw yma ow myrgh trigys obma.

15 Usy agas tas ow tos. Nag usy, ev yw coth ha clâv. Yma va i'n clâvjy.

16 Esowgh why ow paintya an daras? Nag esof, yth esof orth y êwna hag orth y lanhe.

17 Pandr'esta ow qwil gans an kig porhel? Yth esof vy worth y drehy.

18 Sqwith yw ow lagasow. Yth esof vy ow redya re pùb dëdh.

19 Nyns yw spladn an gantol, saw yma an hirwarrow ow neyjya adro dhedhy.

20 Agas myrgh yw demedhys, a nyns yw hy? Nag yw, yma hy ow lavurya in scol ow tesky flehes munys. Yma hy worth aga hara.

E.8C.2 Translate into English:

1 I shall be here again today week and we will be laughing together.

2 Will you be here tomorrow? Yes, perhaps.

3 My sister will be going with my mother to the church tonight and the house will be empty.

4 What are you saying? Don't you understand my words?

5 You are foolish and bad and I do not love you, and I will not be marrying you next year.

6 They will not be coming home early. We shall be together all the evening.

7 The children will be crying soon. A new teacher will be coming to the school tomorrow.

8 Your son is not industrious but your daughter is very good at writing and reading.

9 Will you be eating the cake? No, thank you. It is too sweet for me.

10 What is your name and who are you? I am the new boy and I was talking to your wife already.

11 When will you be beginning to work here? Next Wednesday, this day week.

12 What, won't yo be beginning today?

13 My mother is ill and she will be going to the hospital on Saturday.

14 What is the matter with her? Her feet hurt, but the doctors don't recognize the disease.

15 The matter is serious. She will be in the hospital for a month.

16 I shall be buying a doll with yellow hair.

17 We work here on holidays and week days. We are all tired of it.

18 Will you be staying here until the end of the year? No, we shall be returning to Cornwall within a week.

19 I shall be baking cakes in the afternoon and the children will be eating them tomorrow.

20 Who is the new teacher? She is a young woman with blue eyes, and the daughter of the old teacher.

E.8C.3 Translate into Cornish:

1 Pyw osta poran ha pandr'esta poran? Me yw an maw nowyth, a syra. Ow hanow yw Jory ha me a vëdh ow tallath obma trenja.

2 Pywa, a ny vedhys ow tallath obma heb let?

3 Me a vëdh ow tallath de Merth, a syra. Ny vedhaf ow lavurya gool ha gweyth warbarth. Ow yêhes yw pòr dhâ. Me yw pòr grev hag othem vëdh dhybm a lowr voos hag a dhewas dâ.

4 Pywa? Pandr'esta ow leverel? A vedhys owth eva coref, leth pò dowr? Me a vëdh owth eva gwin dâ, a syra.

5 Gwin dâ yw pòr ger ha nyns oma rych. Ny vedhaf owth offra lowr a win dhis.

6 Nyns owgh why rych, a syra, saw yma lowr a win dâ dhywgh i'gas selder. Me a vëdh worth y eva pùb dëdh.

7 I'n contrary part, ow maw vy, ny vedhys owth eva i'm chy vy màn. Farwèl dhis!

8 An cothwas yw gocky. Nyns usy ev owth aswon gonesyas dâ.

9 An flehes a vëdh ow tos tre yn scon. Me a vydn aga metya i'n gorsaf.

10 Ple fedhys avorow? Me a vëdh wàr an train wàr ow fordh dhe Loundres.

11 Me a vëdh i'n gwely. Yth esof ow mos dhe'm gwely ha me a vydn gortos ena bys pedn seythen.

12 An mowysy a vëdh ow mos in mes rag godra an buhas.

13 Yth esen ow lavurya oll an jëdh hag yn scon me a vëdh ow sedha ryb an tan, owth eva tê hag ow miras worth an nowodhow wàr an bellwolok.

14 A vëdh dha gothmans ow tos arta haneth? Na vedhons, soweth. Me yw lowen. Pywa? Nyns usons y ow plegya dhybm.

15 Usy ow qwil glaw whath? Usy, saw yn scon an glaw a wra cessya ha'n gwyns a vëdh ow whetha an cloudys in kerdh.

16 Farwèl, a flehes ker. Ny vedhaf vy obma avorow. Ny vedhaf vy worth agas gweles arta.

17 Ple fedhys ow mos? Me a vëdh ow mos arta dhe jy ow thas ha dhe bobel ow thas.

18 An gothwesyon a vëdh owth eva i'n tavern haneth. Y a vëdh owth eva re. Y fedhons y owth eva re pùpprës de Sadorn gordhuwher.

19 Nyns yns y rych, saw ymowns y owth eva lowr a goref, an fôlys gocky coth.

E.9C.2 Translate into English:

1 Everybody was looking at me and I was very ashamed.

2 Who is still here. There is nobody here except your own sister and the young doctor. He wanted to speak to her.

3 She had a lot of money yesterday. What was she selling in that shop?

4 Who are those? That is the accountant and the pretty woman is his wife. They don't speak a word of Cornish unfortunately.

5 This is not my dress. My dress was red and clean.

6 He had many cows and many horses, and a lot of money in the bank, but he wasn't happy at all. He was unhappy. His wife was very ill for many years and now she is dead.

7 Where are your old trousers? They are on the chair beside the fire. They are very dirty. I was working in the garden all day long and the place was wet.

8 Are you still going to Spain with those people? I am reluctant to go with them. The man himself is very silly and I hate his wife.

9 She doesn't speak a word of Cornish, but she is always arguing with everybody. That is enough to move someone to tears.

10 That girl is their daughter. She is intelligent, but rude.

11 Their son is that boy over there. He is very silly. He doesn't talk to anybody. He prefers to play with his computer.

12 Have you drink? Yes indeed. We have every kind of drink in this pub, Scotch whisky, Irish whiskey, etcetera, but I prefer our own beer. That is very good. Everybody praises it.

13 He was amusing and kind, but I did not like him.

14 What? Are you still criticizing my brother? No, but I prefer your sister.

15 Where is my new calculator? The accountant is coming today and I will have to show him the books.

16 I was an accountant myself in those days, but I didn't like the work at all.

17 I must say something to you. What? Are you talking to me? No, I was talking to those people, but they are not listening to me at all.

18 I hate those shoes. They are too hard and the colour is dreadful.

19 You will have to wear them all the same.

20 I was very silly at that time, but now I am a wise and sensible man, alas.

E.9C.3 Translate into Cornish:

1 Cas yw ev genef. Gwell osta jy genef.

2 Res yw dhybm goslowes orto bytegyns.

3 Ev o pòr wheg dhybm de, saw poos yw genef mos ganso wàr an train dhe Loundres.

4 Pyw yw an re-na? Y yw ow breder ha'm whereth. Gwell genef yw dha das ha'th vabm.

5 Ple ma dha lavrak coth? In amary gans an eskyjyow gell.

6 A vedhys worth y wysca hedhyw? Bedhaf, me a vëdh ow lavurya i'n lowarth oll an jëdh.

7 Pandr'yw hebma? Hèn yw gwyras Wordhen. Te fol gocky. Yth esta owth eva re.

8 Yma edrek dhybm a'n geryow-na. Nyns csta owth eva re.

9 Yth esta ow lavurya oll an jëdh hag yma dewas ow plegya dhis.

10 Gwell yw genef sedha ryb an tan genes ow miras orth an bellwolok.

11 Meth yw genef. Yth esof vy owth eva re a wyras Alban hag a wyras Wordhen. Me o medhow de ha degensete.

12 Es jy? En, me o medhow. Yth esen i'n tavern oll an jëdh. Yma re a vona dhe'm cothmans.

13 Pyw yw an re-na? Hèn yw an medhek nowyth. Hòn yw y wreg yonk. Hy yw teg, a nyns yw?

14 Yth esof ow miras orth an hager-bows. Yma hy ow qwysca eskyjyow uthyk kefrës. Yma dhedhy treys pòr vrâs.

15 A nyns usy hy ow plegya dhis? Gwell yw genef an medhek. Ev yw den yonk teg.

16 Nyns usy y dhewla brâs garow rudh ow plegya dhybm, hag yma fâss gocky dhodho.

17 Pandr'eus i'th torn? Hòm yw ow reknel nowyth. Hy yw pòr uskys ha pòr skentyl.

18 Yth esen ow côwsel orth ow acowntyas hedhyw. Ev o jentyl, saw nyns o va lowen gans an lyvrow.

19 Nyns eus lowr a vona genen ha dyllas yw pòr ger.

20 Yth esta ow perna re a dhyllas, yma dhis re a bowsyow ha re a eskyjyow. Yn scon ny a vêdh pòr vohosak in gwir.

E.10C.2 Translate into English:

1 Adam had two sons. Abel was killed by his brother Cain. Cain was a bad fellow.

2 Abel was a farmer and a good man and faithful, but the other brother was a bad fellow.

3 There are thirty days in each month and I am tired of my life.

4 Where have you been? I have been looking for work.

5 The song will be sung in the church this day week, and I must teach it to the school children.

6 Thirty little children singing that beautiful song? I want to hear that!

7 Though I am not a clever man, I love music and melody.

8 What are those things on the table? Those are the glasses and the wine for the party tonight.

9 I am sorry but I have only three sweet cakes. Those there were left by the other people and they have gone home.

10 There are more than fifty members in the society at the moment, but only ten of them speak Cornish well.

11 There will be a hundred girls and fifty boys listening to you speaking. Are you ready?

12 I had a lot of money in my pocket, but it was taken from me by the policemen.

13 I am poor now, and I have to buy food for my children. Three of them are standing there. Are they hungry? Yes, they have become weak.

14 What is twenty-five and twenty-five. That is fifty.

15 Are you pleased with the children? Although I am pleased with them, I am not pleased with you.

16 My work will be finished directly and I shall be free to go with you.

17 Shall I be seeing you tomorrow? No, I shall not be seen here ever again.

18 I must return to my own country and to my father's people, and that is far from this place.

19 Was he killed? No, but his legs were broken and his head injured.

20 Although he is sick at the moment, he will be well soon.

E.10C.3 Translate into Cornish:

1 Why a veu gwelys de ogas dhe jy ow whor. Pandr'esewgh why ow qwil i'n lowarth? Yth esen ny ow ladha dew edhen gans udn men.

2 Me a veu ena de. Yth esa an gwyns ow whetha ha'n mor o pòr arow.

3 Hèm yw tra vian, saw pòr ger ywa dhybm.

4 Yth esa dyw gath wàr an fordh saw y fowns y aga dyw shyndys dre dha garr.

5 Ple ma dha vroder ha'th whor? Y yw gyllys tre. Nyns usy an scol worth aga flêsya.

6 Yma seyth dëdh in pùb seythen ha dyw seythen ha hanter-cans in pùb bledhen, saw ny vëdh nefra lowr a dermyn.

7 Te yw bysy pùpprës. Ov, dewdhek mis i'n vledhen heb degol vëth.

8 Yma dhedhy dyw vuwgh, udn tarow, whegh davas, peder cath ha ky gwyls. Pandr'usy hy gour ow predery? Gyllys ywa. Nyns eus bestas worth y blêsya.

9 Ev yw kepar ha me. Nyns eus bestas ow plegya dhybm. Gwell yw flourys genef.

10 Yw bestas cas genes? Nag yns, nyns yns y cas genef poran. Yma dhyn dyw gath hag edhen dov. Ow mab a veu brathys gans ky agensow.

11 Yw an boos drës whath? Yw, saw nyns yw devedhys marnas try flogh.

12 A vedhys ow temedhy ganso yn scon? Bedhaf, yth esof ow qwetyas demedhy ganso an jorna-ma wàr seythen.

13 Pandr'usy dha das ow predery? Nyns usy ow thas vy ow predery màn. Ev yw medhow pùpprës. Yma va ow plegya dhe'm broder ha dhe'm teyr whor.

14 Yth esof orth y gara, kyn nag ywa fur pùpprës. Yma va ow wâstya mona warnaf. Ev yw wheg mès gocky.

15 Dew anodhans a vëdh lowr, yth esof ow cresy. Nyns eus othem dhyn a dheg ha hanter-cans.

16 Ple feusta? Me re beu worth dha whilas dres oll an dre.

17 Me re beu i'n lyverjy ow redya an paperyow nowodhow.

18 Y feu an chy-ma derevys wàr an treth. Y fëdh ow codha dhe'n dor yn scon.

19 Dha gothmans yw aswonys i'n dre-ma. Nyns usons y ow plêsya an bobel.

20 Yw an whel gwrës whath? Nag yw, ny re beu re vysy ow scubya an pymp rom ha hanter-cans i'n chy-ma.

E.11C.2 Translate into English:

1 Joy to you! How are you today!

2 Well enough, thank you. How are you yourself? Why do you say 'well enough'?

3 Today is the fifth day of the month, the month of September.

4 The day after tomorrow will be Sunday the sixth. That is my wife's birthday. I must buy her something nice.

5 Would you like to come with us to the seaside tomorrow? I should like to indeed, but I have to work tomorrow, unfortunately.

6 We will be sounding the bell for the twentieth times. Why?

7 Was your brother pleased with those two books? He wasn't entirely. He doesn't like the first one, but he liked the second one of them.

8 He was often married. His fourth wife is very pretty but she doesn't live here any more.

9 Why? She didn't like his children. Fourteen of them live with him in his big house on the cliff.

10 She wouldn't be satisfied with two children. She lives in the nineteenth century.

11 Were you ever here before today? No, but my family had often been here.

12 A bonfire used to be made and burnt on the thirty-first night of October.

13 January is the first month and February is the second month in the year. The third month is the month of March.

14 What is the first month of the summer? That is the month of May.

15 No, the month of May is the spring. No. April is the end of the spring.

16 Is the month of August in the summer or the autumn? It is in the autumn. In that month the labourers begin to reap.

17 When is the Annunciation? That is the twenty-fifth day of the month of March.

18 When is Christmas? That comes every year on the twenty-fifth day of the month of December.

19 When is Easter Sunday? Why do you ask?

20 The date of Easter is determined by the year and the moon.

E.11C.3 Translate into Cornish:

1 Yw hebma agas kensa flogh? Nag yw, ev yw ow fympes.

2 Y feu va genys Degol Stefan warleny.

3 Y bedn bloodh yw an wheffes dëdh warn ugans a vis Kevardhu.

4 A garsowgh why leverel dhybm pëth yw y hanow. Yn certan, ev yw gelwys Stefan.

5 Pana dermyn a vedhowgh why ow casa an clâvjy? Trenja, an seythves dëdh a vis Ebrel.

6 Fatl'esta ow mos dhe'n scol pùb myttyn? Yth esof ow tos wàr an kyttryn, saw de Merher y fëdh ow thas orth ow dry i'n carr.

7 A garses dos genen wàr an train avorow? Carsen yn certan, gromercy dhis.

8 Fatl'esta ow spellya dha hanow in Kernowek? Yma dyw fordh.

9 Y fedha ev lowen dhe'm gweles, saw lebmyn ev yw re goth dhe'm aswon.

10 Y fedha an bobel ow côwsel an tavas obma i'n êtegves cansvledhen.

11 Y fedha an deves wàr an meneth saw lebmyn ymowns y ow cortos ogas dhe'n chy.

12 Y fëdh an ugansves dëdh a vis Du avorow. Me a vëdh ow mos dhe vysytya ow secùnd mab ha'y tressa gwreg.

13 Ple fedhys nessa Genver? Prag? Nyns esen marnas ow covyn.

14 A vies frank i'n tor'-ma? Bien, saw yth esof ow mos tre dystowgh wosa whel.

15 Ev a vedha ow wherthyn pùpprës, saw ny veu va bythqweth lowen.

16 A veusta bythqweth i'n bedneglos? Heb mar, me a vëdha ow cana ena.

17 Ev a vëdh medhow pùpprës wosa pymp dewas. Hèm yw y wheffes.

18 An pronter a vëdh obma yn scon. Rag an ugansves prës, pandra vedhyn ny ow ry dhodho dhe dhebry?

19 Mis Ebrel dewetha o pòr yeyn hag y fedha ow qwil glaw pùpprës. Nessa Metheven a vëdh tobm.

20 Pleth esta ow tesky taclow a'n par-na? Pleth esta worth aga clôwes?

E.12C.2 Translate into English:

1 We will eat the cake and drink the wine between us two.

2 Will you listen to me for a moment? No. I will not hear you.

3 Will you not admit your sins? Yes, we will and we will repent of them.

4 They will not leave the house without us, I hope.

5 I will put all my things on the table, and sit in the big chair beside you.

6 Here are the newspapers for you. Is there anything good in them? No.

7 I do not read newspapers now. There is never any story of interest in them these days.

8 I am looking at the sky above. It is bright and blue.

9 The wild animal will attack us. You must be careful of it.

10 The wood is very dark. It will be hard to find any way through it and out of it.

11 She will have something very nice for you. What? She will bake a cake for you and for me.

12 Will I get it soon? You will get it tomorrow after breakfast.

13 There is nobody here who will help me to get across the river.

14 Are you ready to come with us finally? No, you will all have to go without me.

15 We will not do that at all. We will not go anywhere without you. We depend upon you.

16 How will I help you then? I am only a weak woman.

17 You must talk to your husband and tell him things like those.

18 The man by the bridge is known to me, but who is the young woman standing beside him?

19 That is his daughter. She will visit us tonight and you will have a chance to talk to her.

20 I don't trust her. Her laugh is insincere, I believe.

E.12C.3 Translate into Cornish:

1 Ny wrama dha weres gans taclow a'n par-na.

2 Yth esen ow miras der ow fockettys. Esa mona vëth inhans?

3 Yth esoma ow scodhya warnodhans dhe dhos abrës. Yth esen ow qwetyas styrya taclow dhedhans.

4 Pana dermyn a vedhys ow ry an desen dhedhans? Wosa haunsel martesen.

5 Pyw yw an venyn-na ow sevel ryb an gwëdh brâs i'n lowarth? Hy yw gwreg an medhek. Hy a vëdh ow mos tre ganso.

6 Yma an gov ow qwil sogh. A vëdh ev brâs lowr ragof?

7 Intredhon agan dew, nyns esof vy ow cresy hy dhe vos y wreg ev màn.

8 Pywa? Pyw yw hy ytho? Benyn wocky yonk.

9 Ny a vydn mos dhe'n dre wàr an kyttryn ha metya gans an re erel ogas dhe'n pons.

10 Me a vydn ry ow mona inter aga dewla. Yth esof vy ow trestya dhedhans in gwir.

11 An chair a vydn terry inter dyw radn. Te yw re boos rygthy.

12 Hèm yw an chy bian ha hèn yw an ryver ow resek ryptho. A nyns ywa teg?

13 An ryver yw pòr dhown. Ny vedhaf vy ow neyja dresto.

14 Yma genef cùssul ragthans. Pandra? Res yw dhedhans dos dhe'm gweles heb let, poken me a vydn y dherivas dhe'n greswesyon.

15 Ot obma an eskyjyow. Yma neppyth inhans. Pandra? Meyn vian.

16 Yth esof ow miras orth an ebron a-uhon. A nyns yw hy glas ha spladn?

17 An coos yw pòr dewl ha cales vëdh dhyn mos dredho.

18 An bestas yw gwyls hag y a wra agan assaultya. Res yw dhyn bos war anodhans.

19 An vyrgh a'y sav dres ena yw ow myrgh vy. Pyw yw an den a'y sav rypthy? Hèn yw hy gour.

20 A vedhys jy ha'th veyny ow tos genen? Na vedhaf, soweth, res yw dhybm lavurya. Why a vêdh ow mos hebof vy ha hepthans y kefrës.

E.13C.2 Translate into English:

1 He says he did not see the two men standing in the middle of the road.

2 It is difficult to believe that he is telling the truth.

3 Everybody believes that they are still alive.

4 I found this letter on the mat this morning.

5 Did you sleep well? No, the cats were crooning all night and I did not sleep at all.

6 I told him I was present for the beer and he believed my words.

7 I was expecting that she would return home soon and that we would live together happily for ever.

8 I don't believe that you will catch the bus now, but of course another bus will be coming soon.

9 He confessed that there was clandestine love between them. What? Between him and my wife.

10 So bread used to be baked in this house every day.

11 Doesn't the Good Book say that you must love your enemy?

12 They believe that that story is true, but it is apparent to everybody that it is wholly false.

13 Why do you say that he is mistaken in the matter?

14 She saw that the child was sad, and she asked him why.

15 She received no answer.

16 Then I understood for the first time that he didn't have enough money.

17 Not everybody in the village believes that I committed the crime.

18 Although I am innocent, the judge says that I will have to spend three years in prison.

19 Alas for you. I must inform the newspapers that you did not steal anything.

20 You don't believe that I would confess something like that.

E.13C.3 Translate into Cornish

1 Hy a wrug leverel hy fatell o hy lowen dhe'm gweles vy, saw ny wrug avy cresy dhedhy.

2 Yma va ow cresy fatell wrug avy an drog-ober.

3 Why yw camgemerys. Ny wrug avy tra kepar ha hedna.

4 Yth esa ev ow cresy ev dhe gachya lies pysk, saw ny wrug ev cachya marnas dew.

5 Prag yth esta ow leverel nag esoma worth dha gara?

6 A wrusta gweles an dhyw vowes a'ga sav ryb an ryver? Na wrug.

7 Onen anodhans yw ow whor vy, hag yma hy ow leverel te dhe vos camgemerys. Nyns yw down an ryver.

8 Pandra wrug hy leverel? Hy a wrug leverel hy dhe ùnderstondya an mater yn tien ha me dhe vos fol.

9 Ple whrusta perna an bows teg-na? Me a wrug leverel dhis solabrës me dh'y ladra dhyworth ow whor?

10 Nyns esoma marnas ow qwil ges. Me a wrug hy ferna i'n dre degensete.

11 Yma va ow leverel hy dhe vos y whor, saw yth esoma ow cresy hy dhe vos y gowethes. Nyns yw hy haval dhodho màn.

12 Res yw dhis cresy dhe eryow an Lyver Dâ. Yma va ow leverel fatell yw res dhis cara dha gentrevak kepar ha te dha honen.

13 Pyw yw ow hentrevak? Nyns ywa an den uthyk-na i'n nessa chy.

14 Ev a wrug leverel nag esa mona dhodho, hag ena me a wrug y weles i'n tavern ow wherthyn hag owth eva gans y gothmans.

15 Ev a wrug leverel y vos bohosak. Saw apert yw nag esa ev ow leverel an gwiryoneth.

16 Ev a wrug avowa ev dhe wil an drog-ober, saw nyns usy an greswesyon ow cresy dhodho.

17 Pyw a wrug y wil ytho? Yma an bobel obma ow cresy fatell veu y vroder.

18 Yth esoma ow qwetyas fatell wrêta dewheles yn scon ha fatell wrêta don genes dha whor deg.

19 Prag yth esta ow leverel ow whor dhe vos teg? Yma pùbonen ow leverel hy dhe wysca dyllas uthyk.

20 Me a wrug leverel na vedhen plêsys dhe dhos genes, saw res yw dhybm avowa lebmyn nag esen marnas ow qwil ges.

E.14C.2 Translate into English:

1 The monks used to wear black clothes and pray eight times a day.

2 She never spoke to me again after she heard that dreadful untrue story.

3 We used to go the the seaside every summer and spend a fortnight there.

4 That girl is not your daughter. She is *my* daughter.

5 We have not had a roof over our heads since our old house fell down in the night of the big wind.

6 The Lord will take away all our sins and he will wash us and we shall be wholly clean.

7 Everything was turned upside down by the new head teacher.

8 You must tell me before you depart what you will call the child.

9 Although my computer is broken, I will not buy a new one because I am too poor at the moment.

10 He assured us that he would not do us any harm.

11 I do not trust him. He used to say that to everybody.

12 They used to go about in funny clothes from house to house and ask for money and sweets from the neighbours.

13 Used you do thus in those days? No, we remained at home and played together and ate apples and nuts.

14 We must go into the house immediately because heavy rain is following.

15 Before we do thus, perhaps we will look at the fish swimming hither and yon in the little river.

16 Is that your wish? You are mad. The weather is too cold and it will be night before we return.

17 I will not go hence without you. The daylight has almost gone.

18 My dear friend, you do not need to be angry with me. We will return soon and then we will sit together beside the fire and watch the television and drink beer.

19 I understand now that you were speaking the truth. You advised me before now and you always told the truth with good sense.

20 We will walk down to the little house beside the bridge and look at the sky and at the people passing along the street.

E.14C.3 Translate into Cornish:

1 Hy a ûsyas pobas bara pùb myttyn ha de Sul hy a wre pobas tesen kefrës.

2 Ev a wrug leverel y whre va dos hedhyw gordhuwher, saw nyns esof vy worth y gresy.

3 A wrusses ladra an mona? Ny wrussen màn.

4 Nebonen re beu ow sedha i'm chair vy ha'y derry yn tien.

5 Ny a wra mos wàr nans dhe'n treth ha sedha wàr an chairys howl ha miras orth an mor.

6 Hy a wrug mos in mes saw ny wrug hy dos ajy whath.

7 Yw hedna dha vargh jy ow sevel in dadn an wedhen? Nag yw, dha vargh jy ywa.

8 Pàn wrug vy gasa an chy, yth esa pùbonen ow cùsca. Pàn wrug vy dewheles, yth esa pùbonen ow cùsca whath.

9 Res yw dhis glanhe dha jambour nebes, kyns ès te dhe vos dhe'n scol.

10 Nyns usy an termyn dhybm, dre rêson me dhe vos holergh.

11 Me a vydn y wil yn tâ, wosa me dhe dhos tre hedhyw dohajëdh.

12 An pronter a wre agan vysytya yn fenowgh warleny. Ny wrug ev dos wàr nans dhe'n chy unweyth hevleny.

13 Wosa redya an lyver, me yw certan ev dhe vos camgemerys yn tien.

14 Yth esoma ow leverel hedna lebmyn, dre rêson me dhe ùnderstondya an mater.

15 Nyns yw hedna marnas dha dybyans jy. Nyns ov vy acordys, ha ny vëdh ow thybyans vy camgemerys pùpprës.

16 Me a godhas an stairys wàr nans warleny hag a hùrtyas ow garr. Me re beu ow clôwes pain bythqweth wosa hedna.

17 Me a vydn sevel ha mos dhe'm tas hag avowa ow fehosow dhodho.

18 Nyns ov abyl dhe wil tra vëth hedhyw dre rêson bos terrys ow amowntyor.

19 Prag na wrêta perna onen nowyth? Ny wrama perna onen nowyth rag me yw re vohosak,

20 Me a vydn lendya ow jyn vy dhis. Nowyth ywa ha pòr dhâ.

E.15C.2 Translate in English:

1 What do you think about the new teacher?

2 I have no opinion about him.

3 Did she show you the dress she will be wearing tonight?

4 That is the woman whose son is sick.

5 Yes, I was talking to her just now. She has a daughter as well whom you used to play with last year.

6 You must look at this coat on me. Do you like it?

7 Is that the hole the rabbit entered? No, that is the hole we dug yesterday.

8 I closed the window the cranefly came in by.

9 Do insects frighten you? No, but I don't like those that make a loud noise.

10 What is the name of the little girl you spoke to a moment ago?

11 Do you understand the things I told you? Some of them.

12 Why won't you be coming to the theatre with us? I shan't be coming because I don't like the things that you will be saying about the play.

13 There are many things in this world of which we understand only a small part.

14 You must tell me in which shop I can get good clothes.

15 The lady I was talking to, she is the vicar's wife.

16 She is very pretty. There are many young men around her.

17 You must tell me from whom you heard that dreadful story.

18 I didn't hear it from anybody. I read it.

19 That is the chair that she left her bag on.

20 It isn't there now. We must ask the children about it.

E.15C.3 Translate into Cornish:

1 Pyw o an arlodhes esa ow côwsel orthys namnygen? Hòn o gwreg an pendescajor.

2 Yw hebma an toll a wrusta palas dha honen? Nag yw, an toll ywa a wrug an conyn entra ino.

3 Res yw dhis dysqwedhes dhybm an eskyjyow a vethys ow qwysca orth an dauns haneth.

4 Ny wrama aga dysqwedhes dhis, dre rêson na wrug avy aga ferna whath.

5 Hòm yw an scol mayth esen ow mos dhedhy pan veuma maw.

6 Pëth yw hanow an prëv-na usy ow neyja adro dhe'n golow? Hirwarrow ywa.

7 Me a vydn leverel dhis neppyth aral adro dhodho. Pàn esta worth y gachya i'th tewla, yma va ow casa garr wàr y lergh.

8 Hèn yw coynt. Eus lowr a brevas usy ow qwil tra a'n par-na?

9 Dres ena me a wel an marchont a wrusta perna dha garr dhyworto.

10 Pùb jorna yth esoma ow passya an chy usy va trigys ino.

11 Me a vydn derivas dhis whedhel bian adro dhe dhew lowarn.

12 An eyl a wrug leverel dh'y gela, "Res yw dhyn mos dhe'n coos dhe gafos nebes boos rag agan flehes gwag."

13 Yw Maria an vowes usy hy broder i'n clâvjy?

14 Yw, hy broder yw an maw bian neb a godhas stairys an scol wàr nans degensete.

15 Yma dhis tybyansow coynt adro dhe lowr a daclow. Pana sort a lyvrow esta worth aga hafos in mes anodhans?

16 Me a wrug redya lyver agensow a worras own uthyk inof.

17 Pëth o an lyver adro dhodho? Yth o va adro dhe worfen an bës.

18 Esta ow cresy pùptra esta ow redya i'n paperyow nowodhow?

19 Yth esoma ow cresy radn anodhans. Nyns esoma ow mos adro ow cresy kenyver tra.

20 Yth esen ow côwsel de orth den re wrug scrifa lyver hir adro dhe'n termyn a
dheu a vab den. Yth esen ow tyby ev dhe vos pòr wocky in gwir.

E.16C.2 Translate into English:
1 The policeman came to the house and he knocked on the door.
2 Will you come with me? No, I am too busy.
3 He has gone already. Where did he go?
4 When you came into the office, who was here? I don't remember.
5 If he breaks the door, where will we go?
6 They won't come in. They will have to go home in time before night comes.
7 If we have a son, what shall we call him?
8 If we deny our Lord, will he pardon us?
9 You have heard what used to be said in the old days and the teaching of times
past.
10 What will you do if I kiss you?
11 He came here every day, but the people of the place used not welcome him at
all.
12 I will not go home by bus, because no bus will be here for three hours.
13 I will go with you, if you ask me.
14 He used to go there by himself.
15 If there is somebody in the next room, why isn't he making any sound?
16 If there is somebody in the room, we will go to another place to talk to each
other.
17 If you do something like that, then the teacher will be very angry with us.
18 He will not come here again, if we are rude to him.
19 If you are not here, I shall have to go without you.
20 If we hate him, he will hate us.

E.16C.3 Translate into Cornish:
1 Pleth ên ny, wosa dhe'n chy codha dhe'n dor?
2 Mar teu an chy ha codha dhe'n dor, yth esta ow styrya.
3 Me a wre mos dhe'n scol-na pàn veuma yonk.
4 Yma hy ow leverel na wra hy dos dh'agan metya nefra arta, dre rêson nag usy hy
ow cara an boos eson ny ow tebry.
5 Mar teun ny ha leverel nag eus pehas dhyn, nyns usy an gwiryoneth inon.
6 Saw mar teun ny ha confessya agan pehosow, ev a wra agan pardona ha ny wra
va remembra agan drog-oberow.
7 Mar teu an hager-awel yn scon, ny a vêdh parys rygthy.
8 Mar ny wra an howl spladna avorow, nyns en dhe'n treth.
9 Ple whrewgh why mos nena? Ny â dhe'n dre wàr an train.
10 Pana dermyn a wrewgh why dos tre? Kyns ès an tewolgow dhe godha.
11 Mar teu nebonen ha gwil hedna arta, an descador a vêdh pòr serrys ganso.
12 Pàn dheuth hy tre wàr an dyweth, yth esa an flehes ow cùsca i'ga gwely.
13 Ny wrowns perna an chy, mar ny wrêta glanhe an tyller.
14 Mar teuma ha leverel an gwiryoneth dhis, a wrêta ow cresy?

15 Pleth êthowgh why oll de? Ny êthon ny dhe dyller vëth. Ny a wrug gortos tre.

16 Hy êth aberth i'n rom hag a dheuth in mes dystowgh arta.

17 Ny ê dhe'n eglos i'n dreveglos pùb Sul.

18 Mar teuta ha miras cales lowr, te a wra gweles fàss i'n cloudys.

19 A wrêta mos tre genef haneth ha metya gans ow mabm ha'm tas?

20 Gwrav, me a wra dos, mars esta ow tesîrya indella.

E.17C.2 Translate into English:

1 I believe you are mistaken.

2 She said she was afraid of him.

3 You must remember that I am here to help you.

4 We saw the boy just now when we came in.

5 If you eat of the fruit of that tree, you will die.

6 But they ate of it, and God threw the man and the woman out of the garden.

7 He will hear from me if I come here again.

8 The girl lost her doll on the road.

9 I should like to see his face now.

10 The woman took pity on him and she gave him food and drink and she brought him new clothes also.

11 He begged his wife to give him another chance, but she refused him.

12 We must not say anything to her about her husband.

13 The great author has written many books, but I have not read any of them.

14 When he was thirty years old, he forsook his father's house and he went into the mountains.

15 Have you heard anything? No, but we are still waiting.

16 The servants brought the beautiful girl before the king and he immediately fell in love with her.

17 Then the king said these words: I love this girl, and she will live with me in my house and my wife shall she be, and your queen.

18 But there was an evil woman in the king's court who was envious of the queen. She slandered the queen before the king.

19 He said thus: False is the queen and though she says she loves my lord the king, she is not speaking the truth.

20 Then the king became angry and he cried out with a loud voice and he threw the queen out of the court.

E.17C.3 Translate into Cornish:

1 A wrusta kemeres own pàn leverys ev hedna? Gwrug, me a gemeras own pòr vrâs.

2 A wrusta gweles an gath ow sevel in cres an fordh? Gwrug, saw me a gresys hy bos lowarn.

3 I'n eur-na Duw a leverys dhedhans: Mar tewgh why ha debry a frût an wedhen, yn certan why a verow.

4 Saw mar ny wrewgh why debry a frût an wedhen, why a wra bewa bys venary.

5 Servysy an mytern a dhros boos ha dewas hag a settyas pùptra dhyragtho.

6 An mytern a leverys dh'y servysy: Res yw dhywgh dry dhybm an vowes teg usy ow sedha dhyrag ow chy.

7 Hag y a dhros dhodho an venyn, ha hy o pòr deg.

8 An mytern a viras in bàn ha gweles an venyn, ha dystowgh ev a godhas in kerensa gensy.

9 I'n eur-na a grias in mes, uhel y lev: Me a vydn demedhy an venyn-ma ha hy a vëdh ow gwreg vy ha'gas myternes why.

10 Hag oll pobel an mytern a agrias hag y a leverys: Kepar dell esta ow leverel, a vytern, indella y fëdh an mater.

11 Res yw dhyn kemeres with, yma own dhybm, poken yn certan ny a verow.

12 Nyns esoma ow perthy cov pyw a welys vy na pëth a leverys vy. Me o pòr vedhow.

13 A wrusta côwsel orto? Na wrug, ny wrug avy unweyth gweles den vëth.

14 Ev a leverys y whre va dry neppyth dhyn dhe dhebry ha neppyth dhe eva, saw nyns ywa devedhys whath.

15 Pilat a leverys dhe'n Yêdhewon: An pëth a scrifys, a scrifys.

16 Pàn savas ev in bàn, pùbonen a dhalathas wherthyn.

17 Me a lever hebma dhywgh why oll: res yw dhyn sevel orth kelly colon.

18 Me a bës Duw dhe'm gwitha rag pegh ha dhe gemeras pyteth ahanaf.

19 Me a glôw an pain, saw ny worama prag.

20 Pàn ros hy an boos dhedhans, hy a dhros dhedhans nebes dyllas nowyth inwedh.

E.18C.2 Translate into English:

1 Where is the great author? I will see him. I have seen him already.

2 Can you tell me where I can change Hungarian money?

3 He was able to do it before now, but he didn't want to do it. Why? Because he is lazy.

4 He will bring it, if he comes here tomorrow.

5 Will you give them something, because they have done a lot for us?

6 But if you give it to me again, I will teach you a maxim.

7 I don't want to be rude to you, but you must be quiet now and let someone else speak.

8 I wouldn't have said anything like that in front of those people.

9 We could eat together in the pub and then you could go home on the bus.

10 God created mankind. Male and female he created them.

11 He told me he would not give it to me.

12 If you wish, I will give it to you.

13 Could they be here on time? Yes.

14 I couldn't write because my hand was hurt.

15 You say you won't come with us. Can you say why? No.

16 Can you speak Cornish? Yes.

17 The man left the room but his wife didn't wish to follow him.

18 How could that be true? It could, it could without any difficulty.

19 I will speak Cornish to him, but he won't be able to answer me.

20 I will not speak English.

E.18C.3 Translate into Cornish:

1 A yllowgh why leverel dhybm mar pleg an fordh bys i'n treth?

2 A yllowgh why côwsel Frynkek? Gallaf, me a yll.

3 A wrêta dewheles avorow? Na wrav, ny allama. Me a vydn dewheles trenja.

4 A alsa hy agan gweres? Na alsa.

5 Hy a leverys na wre hy ry mona vëth dhodho, saw hy dhe allos ry boos ha dyllas dhodho.

6 Me a'n gwelas de. A welsys? Ny'n gwelys whath.

7 Pyw a leverys hedna? Me a'n leverys, a ny wrusta ow clôwes?

8 Pandr'alsen ny gwil rag omwitha dhyworto? Pòr vohes.

9 Hy a wra aga dry avorow. Saw hy a's dros hedhyw.

10 Pandr'yll ev gwil? Ev a wor côwsel Sowsnek ha Frynkek hag a wor cana ha dauncya.

11 An pronter a leverys y whre va dos hedhyw dohajëdh, saw ny allama gortos i'n chy ragtho.

12 A vedhys ow mos in mes? Bedhaf, res yw dhybm kerhes an flehes dhyworth an scol.

13 Me a's kergh ragos hag a's dora obma i'n carr.

14 Gromercy dhis, a alses gwil hedna ragof? Galsen heb mar.

15 Gyllys yns. Fatla ylta leverel hedna?

16 Mar teu va ha dos adro obma arta, ny vanaf vy y weles.

17 A wrusta fanja ow lyther? Gwrug, me a'n fanjas myttyn de.

18 A wrusta y redya whath? Na wrug, ny wrug y redya whath. Me a vydn y redya lebmyn.

19 A ylta jy ow clôwes? Me a'th clôw yn tâ.

20 Duw a veu engrys gansans, hag ev a's towlas in mes a baradîs.

GERVA KERNOWEK-SOWSNEK
Cornish-English Glossary

This is not a complete wordlist, but rather a consolidated glossary containing the words in each Vocabulary in chapters 1–39.

a² *prep.* of, from; **a'm** of my; **a'th** of thy, of your

abàn *conj.* since

a·barth awoles *adv.* down below

aberveth *adv.* in, into

abma *v.* to kiss (followed by **dhe²**)

a·brës *adv.* early, on time

abyl *adj.* able

acord *m.* agreement, accord

acordya *v.* to agree

acowntyas *m.*, **acowntysy** accountant,

adâ·l *adv* opposite

Adam *m. personal name* Adam

addya *v.* to add

ader dro *adv.* round about

adermyn *adv.* in time, on time

adhelergh *adv.* behind, in arrears

adhewedhes *adv.* lately

adre· *adv.* rom home

adro· dhe² *prep.* about, concerning

aga³ *poss. adj.* their; **aga thry** the three of them

agan *poss. adj.* our

agas *poss. adj.* your

agensow *adv.* recently

ages, **ès** *conj.* than *in comparisons (see 24A.2)*

agh *interj.* oh, fie

agria *v.* to agree

â! *interj.* oh!, ah!

ahanaf, ahanas, anodho, anedhy, etc. *prep. pron. inflected forms of* **a²** of, from (*see 5A.5*)

ahanan *prep. pron.* of us, from us; *adv.* hence

ahës *adv.* along

a·jy *adv.* into

ala·ck *interj.* alack, alas

Alban *f.* Scotland (*found once in Lhuyd's Cornish*)

alebma *adv.* from here, hence; ago; **alebma rag** *adv. phrase* from now on

alena *adv.* from there, thence

alês *adv.* abroad, far and wide

Almayn *f. place-name* Germany (*see also* **Jermany**)

âls *f.* cliff, shore, **âlsyow**

alwheth *m.*, **alwhedhow** key,; **gorra in dadn naw alwheth** to put under lock and key

Alys *f. personal name* Alice

amanyn *m.* butter

amary *m.*, **amarys** cupboard

amowntya *v.* to count, to avail

amowntyor *m.*, **amowntyoryon** computer

an *def. art.* the

Anabel *f. personal name* Annabel

ancombra *v.* to bother, to hamper

ancombrynsy *m.* bother, embarrassment

anedha *prep. pron.* of them, *earlier form of* **anodhans** (*see 5A.5*)

anfusyk *adj.* unfortunate; *m.*, *pl.* **anfusygyon** unfortunate person

anger *m.* anger; **cafos anger** to become angry

ania *v.* to annoy, to tire

anjy *pron.* they, them (*late form of* **y** they, them)

anowy *v.* to light, to ignite

anoyntya *v.* to anoint

ape·rt *adj. & adv.* apparent, open(ly)'

apperya *v.* to appear

aqwytya *v.* to pay for, to settle, to reward

ara·g *adv.* in front

aral *adj.* other, *pl.* **erel**

arbednek *adj.* special

Arberth *m.* Arberth (*in SW Wales*)

archer *m.*, **archers**, archer
arghel *m.*, **argheleth** archangel
argya *v.* to argue
arhanty *m.*, **arhantiow** bank *(financial)*
arlodhes *f.*, **arlodhesow** lady
arlùth *m.*, **arlydhy** lord
arta *adv.* again
arv *f.*, **arrow** arm, weapon; **tus arvow**
   armed men
Arwednak *m. place-name* Falmouth
askel *f.* **eskelly** wing; **eskelly grehen** bat
   (mammal)
ascor *m.* produce
ascra *f.* bosom, fold in clothing
ass, assa² *v. part.* how, how greatly
assaultya *v.* assault, attack
assaya *v.* to try
assentya *v.* to assent, to agree; **bos**
   assentys to agree
assoylya *v.* to solve
astronymer *m.*, **astronymers** astronomer
Asvens *m.* Advent
assûrya *v.* to assure
aswon *v.* to recognize, to know
a-ugh *prep.* above, over; **a-uhof, a-uhos**,
   etc. inflected forms (see 12A.4); **a-uhon** above
   (in a text)
auctour *m.*, **auctours** author
Australya *f.* Australia
av, ama, êth, *etc. v. present-future of* **mos** *(see*
   16A.4)
aval *m.*, **avallow** apple
avàn *adv.* up, aloft
a·varr *adv.* early
avell *prep.* like, as *before nouns*; **avellof,**
   avellos, avello, *etc. (see 10A.8)*; **ave·ll**,
   'vell *used to mean* than *in Late Cornish*
   comparatives
avês a² *comp. prep.* out of
avorow *adv.* tomorrow
avy *m.* envy, malice; **perthy avy orth** to
   bear malice against
awan *f.* river
awel *f.* wind, weather
awosa *adv. variant of* **wosa** after *q.v.*
avowa *v.* to acknowledge, to confess
awartha *adv.* above; **an pëth awartha**
   dhe woles upside down
a·wher *m.* sorrow, distress; reason *(for*
   anxiety); **perthy awher** to be distressed
awoles *adv.* down, below
a·wos *conj.* because
ay *interj.* hey
baban *m.*, **babanas** doll
baby *m.* **babiow** baby
badh *m.* **badhas** boar
badna *m.* drop; *used with negatives to mean* not
   at all

bagh *m.*, **bahow** hook
banknôta *m.*, **banknôtys** banknote
bara *m.* bread
bardhonek *m.*, **bardhonegow** poem
bas *adj.* shallow
bëdh *v.* 2nd singular imperative *of* **bos**
bedhaf, bedhys, bëdh, *etc. v. future of* **bos**
   (see 8A.3); **bedher** *autonomous future*
bedhen, bedhes, bedha, *etc. v. past*
   habitual of **bos** *(see 11A.3)*
bedhens *v.* 3rd singular & plural imperative of
   bos
bedhyn *v.* 1st plural imperative *of* **bos**
bednath *f.*, **benothow** blessing
bejeth *m.* face, countenance
ben, bes, be, *etc. v. subjunctive of* **bos** *(see*
   19A.1)
benegys *adj.* blessed
benow *f.* female
benyn *f.*, **benenes** woman
bern *m.* concern; *defective v.*; **ny vern** there
   is no point in
berr *adj.* short
best *m.*, **bestas** animal
besydhya *v.* to baptize; **besydhys** baptized
Bethalem *m. place-name* Bethlehem
betraya *v.* to betray
beuv, beus, beu, *etc. v. preterite of* **bos** *(see*
   10A.1-2)
be va *conj. phrase.* whether *(in alternatives)*
bew *adj.* alive; **yma va yn few** he is alive
bewa *v.* to live
bian *adj.* small; **biadnha** comparative and
   superlative
bien, bies, bia, *etc. v. conditional of* **bos** *(see*
   11A.1)
biv (byma, boma), by, bo, *etc. present*
   subjunctive of **bos** *(see 19A.4)*
blas *m.* stink, stench
bledhen *f.*, **bledhydnyow** year; **nessa**
   bledhen next year; **an vledhen usy ow**
   tos next year; **bloodh** *coll.* years of age
blejen *f.*, *pl.* **blejennow** *(not attested in Middle*
   or Late Cornish) flower
blejyewen *f.*, *coll.* **blejyow** flower *(attested in*
   traditional Cornish only in **de Sul Blejyow**
   Palm Sunday)
blew *coll.* hair of the head
blou *adj.* blue
bloodh *see* **bledhen**
bò *see* **pò**
bobmen *f.*, **bomednow, bomennow**
   blow, whack
bodh *m.* wish, desire
bodhar *adj.* deaf
body *m.*, **bodys** body

bohes *pron. & adj.* little, small amount; **bohes venowgh** seldom; **bohes comfort** little comfort

bohosak *adj.* poor; *as a noun* poor man, *pl.* **bohosogyon**

boken, poken *conj.* or, otherwise

bolùnjeth *m.* wish, will

boos *m.* food

boragweyth *adv.* one morning

bord *m.*, **bordys** table

bos *v.* to be; **a wra bos** will be

bosty *m.*, **bostiow** restaurant, cafe

Bosvena *m. place-name* Bodmin

botel *f.*, **botellow** bottle

bowjy *m.*, **bowjiow** cowshed

brag *m.* malt

brâs *adj.* great, big; **brâssa** *comparative and superlative*; *as a noun* **brâsyon** *pl.* important people; **dre vrâs** for the most part

brâster *m.* greatness, majesty

brathy *v.* to bite, to wound by biting (*of snakes, dogs, etc.*)

brës, brÿs *m.* mind

bresel *f.*, **breselyow** dispute, insubordination

Bretones *f.*, **Bretonesow** Breton woman

breus *f.* judgement

brew *m.*, **brewyon** cut, wound

bro *f.* country (*this word is very rare indeed*)

broder *m.*, **breder** *brother*

brusy *v.* to judge

bry *m.* worth, account

brybour *m.*, **brybours** vagabond

bryntyn *adj.* noble; **bryntyn y gnas** of noble nature

Bryttas *n. pl.* Britons

bùs *conj. Late variant of* **mès** but

buwgh *f.*, **buhas** cow

bÿdh (bëdh) *v. future of* **bos** will be

bydner *adv.* never; *used with* **re²** *to express negative wishes*

byldya *v.* to build

bylen *adj.* villainous, ugly

bys in *prep.* to, into; **bys dhodho** to him; **bys venary** forever; **bys venytha** forever; **bys vycken** forever; **bys may⁵(th)** until

byscath *adv. Late variant of* **bythqweth**

bysy *adj.* busy; essential

bytegyns *adv.* however, nevertheless

bÿth *adj. & adv.* ever, any; *with neg.* never; **bÿth well** any better

bythqweth *adv.* ever (*in the past*)

byttele· *adv.* nonetheless

cabm *adj.* bent, wrong; *m.* step in the phrase **wàr gabm, wàr gamm** steadily

cachya *v.* to catch

cader *f.*, **caderyow** chair (*found only in place-names*)

cadnas *f.*, **canasow** messenger, delegate

cafos *v.* to get (**cavos, cawas** *and* **gawas** *are variant forms of the verbal noun.*); **kev, cav** will get *3rd singular present-future*;

Calan *m.* First day of the month; **Calan Est** Lammas' (1st August); **Cala'Me** Mayday; **De Halan Gwâv** Allsaints' day (1st November);

cales *adj.* hard, difficult

cales'he *v.* to harden, to make difficult

caletter *m.*, **caletterow** difficulty

Cambron *m. place-name* Camborne

camgemerys *adj.* mistaken

camhenseth *m.* wickedness

campolla *v.* to mention

cân *f.*, **canow** song,

cana *v.* to sing; **kenys** sung

canker *m.*, **kencras** crab

canqueyth *adv.* a hundred times

cans *num.* hundred

cansves *ord.* hundredth

cansvledhen *f.*, **cansvledhydnyow** century

cantol *f.*, **cantolyow** candle

canvos, canfos *v.* to perceive; *cf.* **convedhes**

car *m.*, **kerens** relative; (*rarely*) friend

cara *v.* to love (*for inflected tenses see 17A.1*)

caraf, keryth, car, etc. *v. present of* **cara** (*see 17A.1*)

Carasek *m. personal name* Caradog

caren, cares, cara, etc. *v. imperfect of* **cara** (*see 17A.1*)

carow *m.*, **kyrwas** stag

carr *m.* (**tan**), **kerry tan** (motor-)car

carrek *f.*, **carrygy** rock; **an Garrek Loos** St Michael's Mount

carren, carres, carra, etc. *v. subjunctive of* **cara** (*see 19A.1*)

carrjy *m.*, **carrjiow** garage

carsen, carses, carsa, etc. *v. conditional of* **cara** (*see 17A.1*)

carvyth *v.* will love; *future of* **cara**

cas *adj.* hateful; **cas yw genef** I hate

câss *m.* case, matter; **i'n câss-na** in that case; **câss lytherow** pocket-book, wallet; **câss o ganso** he was concerned

Casvelyn *m. personal name* Caswallon

cath *f.*, **cathas** cat; **Cath Ker** the Cheshire Cat

causya *v.* to cause

cav *see* **cafos**

cav *m.*, **cavyow** cave

cavos *v. variant of* **cafos**

cawas *v. variant of* **cafos**; *also* **gawas** *with permanent lenition*

Caym *m. personal name* Cain
certan *adj.* certain; **yn certan** certainly
cessya *v.* to cease, to stop
chair *m.*, **chairys** chair; **chair brehek** armchair; **chair howl** deck chair
chambour *m.*, **chambours** *chamber,* bedroom
chartour *m.*, **chartours** charter
chastia *v.* to chastise, to punish
chaunjya *v.* to change
chauns m., **chauncys** chaunce, opportunity
che (**chy**) *pron.* thou, thee (*Late variant of* **te, ty**)
cheryta *m.* charity
chy *m.*, **treven** house
chy (**che**) *pron.* thou, thee (*Late variant of* **ty, te**)
clappya *v.* to talk, to jabber
class *m.*, **classys** class
clâv *adj.* sick; *as a noun, pl.* **clevyon** sick person, patient
clâvjy *m.*, **clâvjiow** hospital
cledh *m.*, **cledhyow** ditch
cledha *m.*, **cledhydhyow** sword
cler *adj.* clear
clogh *m.*, **clegh** bell
clor *adj.* mild; **yn clor** mildly
cloud *m.*, **cloudys** cloud
clôwes *v.* to hear; to feel, to perceive, to smell; **clôwyth** will hear (*3rd singular future*)
codha *v.* to fall
coges *f.*, **cogesow** (female) cook
côk *m.*, **cûcow** fishing boat
cola *v.* to harken to (*followed by* **orth**)
coler *m.* anger
coll *m.* loss
collas *v.* lost *3rd singular pret. of* **kelly**
collenwel *v.* to fulfill; to fill up (< **cowllenwel**)
colodnek *adj.* hearty, brave
colon *f.* **colonow** heart; **gen** (**gans**) **oll ow holon vy** yours sincerely (*at the end of a letter*)
colonecter *m.* bravery
comendya *v.* to commend, to recommend
comolek *adj.* dark, overcast
comolen *f.*, *coll.* **comol** cloud (*this word is not attested in traditional Cornish*)
compes *adj.* right, faithful; straight; **yn compes** straight, directly
composa *v.* to verify
comprehendya *v.* to comprehend, to embrace, to encompass
compressa *v.* to oppress
confessya *v.* to confess
conqwerrour *m.*, **conqwerrours** conqueror

conqwerrya *v.* to conquer
conscians *m.* conscience
consecrâtya *v.* to consecrate
consydra *v.* to consider
consylya *v.* to plan, to counsel
contrary *adj.* contrary; **i'n contrary part** on the contrary; **dhe'n contrary** on the contrary
convedhes *v.* to understand
conyn *m.*, **conynas** rabbit
coodh *defective v.*; **y coodh dhybm** I must; **y codhvia dhybm** I ought to; **y cotha** ought
coos *m.*, **cosow** wood, forest
Corawys *m.* Lent
coref (LC **cor**) *m.* ['kɔrə(f)] beer; **coref clor** mild ale
cornel *f.*, **cornelly** corner
cors *m.*, **corsys** course (*all senses*)
cortes *adj.* polite, well mannered
corwyns *m.* whirlwind, cyclone
Corynthyans *pl.* Corinthians
coscar *coll.* retinue, companions
cosel *adj.* quiet
coselhe· *v.* to pacify, to quieten
costya *v.* to cost
cot *adj.* short; **cot hy anal** out of breath (*describing a female*)
côta *m.*, **côtys** coat
coth *adj.* old
cot'he· *v.* to abridge, to shorten
cothwas *m.*, **cothwesyon** old fellow
cothman *m.*, **cothmans** friend
cov *m.*, **covyon** memory; **porth in cov** remember
cowel *m.*, **cowellow** basket, cradle
cowethas *f.*, **cowethasow** society, company
cowl *m.* soup; **cowl fug-grùban** mock-turtle soup
cowl-derevel *v.* to finish building, to build completely
cowl-wil *v.* to complete
côwsel *v.* to speak; **côwsys** spoken; *3rd singular preterite* **kêwsys**, **côwsas** spoke
coynt *adj.* odd, wily
crambla *v.* to climb
cramyas *v.* to crawl
creatya *v.* to create
cregy *v.* to hang
crejyans *f.* belief, faith
cres *m.* peace
cres *f.* creed; **wàr an gres** by the creed, upon my faith
crës, crÿs *v.* *2nd singular imperative of* **cresy**
creswas *m.*, **creswesyon** policeman
cresy *v.* to believe
crefhe· *v.* to strengthen, to reinforce

creft *f.*, **creftow** art, craft
crev *adj.* strong
cria *v.* to cry, to call; **cries** called
crocer *m.* crozier-bearer
croffal *m.* complaint
crohen *f.*, **crehyn** skin
crytyca *v.* to criticize
cubmyas, **cummyas** *m.* permission, leave
cudha *v.* to hide, to cover; **cudhys** hidden
cùntell *v.* to collect, to gather
Cùntelles *f.* **Keltek** Celtic Congress
cunys *coll.* firewood, fuel
cûr *m.* cure (*of souls*)
cùsca *v.* to sleep
cùssul *f.*, **cùssulyow** advice, counsel
cùssulya *v.* to advise
cuv *m.* **colon** darling
cyta *f.*, **cytas** city
da *prep. Late variant of* **dhe** to; **da jy** *Late variant of* **dhis**, **dhyso jy** to you (*singular*); **da vy** *Late variant of* **dhybmo vy** to me
dâ *adj.* good; **dâ yw genef** I like; **yn tâ** (LC **yttâ·**) well.
dagren *f.*, **dagrow** tears
dainty *adj.* dainty, fastidious
dalhen *m.* grip, grasp; **settya dalhen in** to grasp, to seize
dall *adj.* blind
dallath *v.* to begin; **dalethys** *1st singular preterite*
dallhe· *v.* to blind, to dazzle
dalathas *v.* began; *3rd singular preterite of* **dallath**
dama *f.* mother
dampna *v.* to condemn; **dempnys** condemned, damned
danjer *m.* hesitation; danger; jurisdiction; **perthy danjer** to hesitate; **mara'n kefyth in danjer** if you get him in your thrall
dar *interj.* eh, why (*astonishment*)
daras *m.*, **darasow** (**darajow**) door; **daras ara·g** the front door; **daras delergh** the back door
darbary *v.* to prepare, to provide
darn *m.*, **darnow** piece
darwar *imperative defective verb* be careful!
dauncya *v.* to dance
dauns *m.*, **dauncyow** dance
davas *f.*, **deves** sheep
Davyth *m. personal name* David
de *adv.* yesterday
debonê·r *adj.* debonair
debry *v.* to eat; **debrys**, **debras** ate *3rd singular pret.*
declarya *v.* to declare, to announce
dëdh *m.*, **dedhyow** day
dedhewy *v.* to promise

De Fencost myttyn *adv.* (on) Whitsudnay morning
defendya *v.* to dispel; to defend
deffen, **deffes**, **deffa**, etc. *v. subjunctive of* **dos** (*see 19A.1*)
deg *v.* carries, bears *3rd singular present-future of* **don**
deg *num.* ten; **deg ha peswar ugans** ninety; **deg ha try ugans** seventy; **deg warn ugans** thirty
degens *v. see* **don**
dege·nsete *adv.* the day before yesterday
degol *m.*, **degolyow** holiday; **Degol agan Arlodhes** the Annunciation (25th March); **Degol Maria Dallath an Gwaynten** the Presentation (2nd February); **Degol Maria Hanter Est** the Dormition of the BVM, the Assumption (15th August); **Degol Maria mis Merth** the Annunciation (25th March); **Degol Myhal** Michaelmas (29th September); **Degol Peran** St Piran's Day (5th March); **Degol Stefan** Boxing Day (26th December); **Degol Stool** Epiphany (6th January)
degves *ord.* ninth; **degves ha try ugans** seventieth; **degves ha peswar ugans** ninetieth
De Gwener *m.* Friday, on Friday
degys *verbal adj.* carried (*see* **don**)
De Halan an Vledhen *adv.* (on) New Year's Day; **De Halan Gwâv myttyn** on the morning of All Saints' Day
dehen *m.* cream
dehesy *v.* to shoot, to let fly
delen *f.*, **delyow** *pl.*, **del** *coll.* leaf
dell *conj.* as *before verbs*
delyvra *v.* to deliver
De Merher *m.* Wednesday, on Wednesday; **De Merher Lusow** Ash Wednesday
De Merth *m.* Tuesday, on Tuesday; **De Merth Enes** Shrove Tuesday
den *m.*, **tus** man, person
denethy *v.* to beget, to generate
De Pask myttyn *adv.* (on) Easter morning
deppren, **deppres**, **deppra**, etc. *v. subjunctive of* **debry** (*see 19A.1*)
der *prep. variant of* **dre** through *before vowels*
derevel, **drehevel** *v.* to raise; to build; **derevys** raised
derivas *v.* to tell, to relate; to inform (*with* **dhe²**)
De Sadorn (**Zadorn**) *m.* Saturday, on Saturday
descajor *m.*, **descajoryon** teacher
descajores *f.*, **descajoresow** (female) teacher
desîrya *v.* to desire, to request

desky *v.* to learn, to teach
De Sul (Zul) *m.* Sunday, on Sunday; **wàr an Zul** on Sunday; **dhe weyth pò dhe Sul** on a weekday or on Sunday; **De Sul an Drynjys** (on) Trinity Sunday; **De Sul Blejyow** (on) Palm Sunday
delkyow *pl. Late variant of* **delyow** leaves
demedhy *v.* to marry
denaha *v.* to deny
dendyl *v.* to earn
der, dre² *prep.* through
der LC *for* **dell** *introducing indirect speech*
der *conj.* LC *for* **hadre·** until
descador *m.*, **descadoryon** teacher
desempys, dhesempys *adv.* immediately
desmygy *v.* to guess, to imagine
desmyk *m.*, **desmygow** riddle
despît *m.* ; **in despît dhe²** in spite of
determya *v.* to determine
dettor *m.*, **dettoryon** creditor
deun, deus, do, etc. *v. imperfect of* **dos** (*see 16A.3*); **deun** *also 1st person plural imperative*
deuns *v. 3rd singular & plural imperative of* **dos**
deur *defective v.*; **ny'm deur** I don't care
deus *v. 2nd singular imperative of* **dos**
deuth, deuthys, deuth, etc. *v. preterite of* **dos** (*see 16A.2*)
deuv, deuma, deus, deu, etc. *v. present-future of* **dos** (*see 16A.1*)
deuvef, deuves, deuva *v. perfect of* **dos** (*see 25A.3*)
devar *m.* duty
devedhys *verbal adj.* come (*see* **dos**)
devyn *m.*, **devydnow** portion of writing, passage
dew² *m. num.* two
dewas *m.*, **dewosow** drink
dewblek *adj.* twofold, double
dewdhegves *ord.* twelfth
dewdhek *num.* twelve
dewfrik *dual* nose
dewgans *num.* forty
dewgansves *ord.* fortieth
dewheles *v.* to return
dêwys *v.* to choose
De Yow *m.* Thursday, on Thursday; **De Yow Hablys** (on) Maundy Thursday
dha² *poss. adj.* thy, your
dhana *adv.* then
dhe *prep.* to; **dhe'm** to my; **dhe'n** to the; **dhe'th** to thy, to your
dhe'n dor *adv.* down, downwards
dhe'n leur *adv.* down, downwards
dhedhans *prep. pron.* to them, *earlier form of* **dhedhans** (*see 5A.5*)
dhe ves *adv.* away
dhia *prep.* from; **dhia bàn** *conj.* since
dhort *prep. Late form of* **dhyworth** from

dhybm (dhymm), dhis, dhodho, dhedhy, *etc. inflected forms of* **dhe²** to (*see 5A.5*); **dhe vy** *Late form of* **dhybmo vy** to me
dhyra·g *prep.* before; *conjugates like* **rag** (*see 12A.4*); **dhyrag dorn** beforehand
dhywar² *prep.* from off
dhyworta *prep. pron.* from them, *earlier form of* **dhywortans** (*see 5A.5*)
dhyworth *prep.* from
dhyworthyf, dhyworthys, dhyworto, dhyworty, *etc. prep. pron. inflected forms of* **dhyworth** from (*see 5A.5*)
dialans *m.* punishment (*Unified Cornish* **dyalans**)
diek *adj.* lazy
dien *adj.* complete
dieskyna *v. early form of* **skydnya** to descend
dis *prep. pron. variant of* **dhis** to you (*singular*)
dobyl *adj.* double
dos *v.* to come
docken, dockes, docka, etc. *v. subjunctive of* **don** (*see 19A.1*)
doctour *m.*, **doctours** learned man, doctor
dog *v. 2nd singular imperative of* **don**
dohajë·dh *m.* afternoon
don *v.* to carry, to bear; **degens** *3rd singular imperative*
dor *m.* earth, ground, **an dor** the ground, **an nor** the earth, the world; **dhe'n dor** to the ground, down
dora *v.* brings, will bring *3rd singular present-future of* **dry**; **doroy** *2nd singular imperative*
dorn *m.*, *plural* **dewla** hand, fist
dov *adj.* tame
doth *adj.* discreet, well behaved
dothyen, dothyes, dothya, etc. *v. conditional of* **dos** (*see 16A.3*)
down *adj.* deep
dowr *m.*, **dowrow** water; **dowr used for** river *before river names*
dowrgledh *m.* canal
dowt *m.* doubt, fear; **heb dowt** without doubt, doubtless; **perthy dowt** to fear
dowtya *v.* to doubt, to fear
dre² (der) *prep.* through; **dredhof, dredhos, dredho,** *etc. inflected forms* (*see 12A.4*); **dredha** *variant of* **dredhans** through them
drefen *conj.* because
dregyn *m.* harm, injury
drehedhes *v.* to reach
dres *prep.* across; **dres oll an jorna** all day long; **dres ena** over there; **drestof, drestos, dresto,** *etc. inflected forms* (*see 12A.4*)
drewgh *v. 2nd plural imperative of* **dry**

dreys *coll.* brambles
dro *v. 2nd singular imperative of* **dry**
drog, **drog-** *adj.* bad; **drog yw genef** I am sorry; I do not like; **drog-dhewas** *m.* evil drink; **drog-dhyweth** *m.* evil end; **drog-labm** *m.*, **drog-labmow** accident; **drog-ober** *m.*, **drog-oberow** evil deed, crime; **drog-oberor** *m.*, **drog-oberoryon** criminal; **drog-pobel** *f.* evil people, criminals
drog-handla *v.* to mishandle, to mistreat
drollen, **drolles**, **drolla**, etc. *v. subjunctive of* **dry** (*see 19A.1*)
dros *v.* brought *3rd singular preterite of* **dry**
drùshyan, **drùshya** *v.* to thresh
dry *v.* to bring; **drÿs** brought
du *adj.* black
Du *m.*, **mis Du** November
dùches *f.*, **dùchesow** duchess
dug *v.* carried, bore *3rd singular preterite of* **don**
dûk *m.*, **dûkys** duke
Dùrda dhe why (< **Duw roy dëdh dâ dhywgh why**) *interj.* good day
durya *v.* to continue, to persevere; to persist
dùryan *f.* east (*archaic*)
duw *m.*, **duwow** god, **Duw** God; **a Dhuw** *interj.* O God; **Duw re dalla dhywgh** may God repay you; **Duw re dhanvona** God send; **Duw re dharbarra nos dâ dhywgh** God give you a good night; **Duw re sowena dhywgh** God prosper you
duwhan *m.* sorrow, misery
duwhanhe· *v.* to sadden, to grieve
dy *adv.* thither, to that place, there
dybedna *v.* to behead, to decapitate
dyber *m.*, **dybrow** saddle
dyberth, **dybarth** *v.* to depart, to leave; *m.* separation, division; **kyns ès dybarth** before departing
dyblans *adj. & adv.* clear, clearly
dybreder *adj.* heedless, thoughtless
dydhan *adj.* entertaining, amusing
dyfedna *v.* to forbid
dyffyf, **dyffy**, **deffo**, etc. *v. present subjunctive of* **dos** (*see 19A.3*)
dyhow *m. & adj.* right(hand); (*archaic*) south
dyllas *coll.* clothes
dyllo *v.* to release, to publish
dynar *m.* penny
dynerhy *v.* to greet, to send greetings to
dynya *v.* to entice, to lure
dyowl *m.*, **an jowl**, **dewolow** devil
dyscor *m.*, **dyscoryon** teacher; learner
dyscans *m.*, **dyscansow** lesson, teaching
dyscortes *adj.* impolite, rude
dyscryjyk *adj.* unbelieving; *m.*, **dyscryjygyon** unbeliever, pagan.

dyscudha *v.* to uncover, to discover
dyscypyl *m.*, **dyscyplys** disciple, pupil
dyskybel *m.*, **dyskyblyon** disciple, pupil
dysonora *v.* to dishonour
dysqwa, **dysqweth** *v. 2nd singular imperative of* **dysqwedhes**
dysqwedhes *v.* to show; to show oneself, to appear
dystrêwy *v.* to destroy
dyswil *v.* to destroy, to ruin; **dyswrës** destroyed, ruined
dyvlas *adj.* shameful
dyvlasa *v.* to disgust
dyweth *m.* end; **wàr an dyweth** in the end, at last
dywgh *prep. pron. variant of* **dhywgh** to you
dyw² *f. num.* two
dywros *f.*, **dywrosow** bicycle
dywweyth, **dewweyth** *adv.* twice
dywysyk *adj.* industrious; assiduous
ea *interj.* yes
Ebrel *m.*, **mis Ebrel** April
ebron *f.* sky
edhen *m.*, **ëdhyn**, **ÿdhyn**, **edhnow** bird
edrek *m.* regret; **edrek yw genef** I regret
Efen *m.*, **mis Efen** *variant forms of* **Metheven** June
Efesyans *pl.* Ephesians
egery *v.* to open; **egerys** opened, open
eglos *f.*, **eglosyow** church
egoras *v. 3rd singular preterite of* **egery**
Ejyp *m. place-name* Egypt
el *m.*, **eleth** angel
ell *v. variant of* **yll** (< **gyll**) can; *see* **gallos**
ella·s *interj.* alas
ellen, **elles**, **ella**, etc. *v. subjunctive of* **mos** (*see 19A.1*)
elyn *m.*, **elydnow** elbow
emprês *f.*, **empresow** empress
emprour *m.*, **emprours** emperor
empydnyon *pl.* brains
Empyryk Angwyn *m. personal name and title of* Dick Angwyn
en, **es**, **o**, etc. *v. imperfect of* **bos** (*see 9A.1*)
en, **es**, **e**, etc. *v. imperfect of* **mos** (*see 14A.4*)
ena *adv.* there, then
encledhyas *v.* to bury
encressya *v.* to increase
enef *f.*, **enevow** soul
enep *m.*, **enebow** page, surface
Enes *m.* Shrovetide; **De Merth Enes** Shrove Tuesday
eneval *m.*, **enevales** beast (of burden)
enjoya *v.* to enjoy, get the benefit of
entra *v.* to enter (*followed by* **in**)
epscop *m.*, **epscobow** bishop
er *prep.* by; **er an leuv** by the hand
erber *m.*, **erberow** place of safety

erbynn *prep.* against (*see* **warbydn**)

erhy *v.* to command

erna²(g) *conj.* until

erof, **eroma** *v. Late form of* **esof**, **esoma** (*see 3A.1*)

ervira *v.* to decide; **ervirys yw genef** I have decided, I intend

ervys *verbal adj.* armed; **den ervys** armed man

escar *m.*, **eskerens** enemy

esedha (**sedha**) *v.* to sit

esel *m.*, **esely**, **esyly** member

esen, **eses**, **esa**, etc. *v. imperfect of long form of* **bos** (*see 5A.1*)

eskys *f.*, **eskyjyow** shoe

esof, **esoma**, **esos**, etc. *v. long form of* **bos** to be (*see 3A.1*)

Est *m.*, **mis Est** August

et *prep. Late variant of* **in** in; **et y gever** *Late Cornish variant of* **in y gever** towards him (*see* **kever**)

êtegves *ord.* eighteenth

êtek *num.* eighteen

eth *num.* eight

êthves *ord.* eighth

eur *f.*, **euryow** hour; **i'n eur-na** then

eus *v.* is (*see 4A.1-2*)

ev *pron.* he, him

Eva *f. personal name* Eve

ewgh *v. 2nd plural imperative of* **mos**

ewn *adj.* right, just, correct

ewn-gara *v.* to love rightly, to love enough

êwna *v.* to mend

exaltya *v.* to exalt

execûtya *v.* to execute, to carry out

eyl *pron.*; **an eyl...y gela** the one...the other; **an eyl...y ben** the one...the other (*with feminine nouns*)

eythyn *coll.* furze

Falmeth *m. place-name* Falmouth

fâls, **fâls-** *adj.* false; **fâls-duw** *m.*, **fâls-duwow** false god, idol; **fâls-acûsacyon** false accusation, calumny

falslych *adv.* falsely

fanja *v.* to receive

fara *v.* to fare

farwèl dhis, **farwèl dhywgh** *interj.* goodbye

fâss *m.*, **fâssow** face; *in plural* faces; pretence; minatory expression

fate·ll *adv.* how; *also* that *introducing indirect speech*

fatla *adv.* how

fa·vera *v.* to favour

fay faith *in the expression* **wàr ow fay** upon my faith

fêdh *f.* faith; **wàr ow fêdh** upon my faith; **tàn ow fêdh** upon my faith

fêkyl *adj.* false, affected (*when predicative it is prefixed*); **fêkyl-geryow** *pl.* hypocritical words

fe·nester *f.*, **fe·nestry** window

fenten *f.*, **fentydnyow** well, spring

fèst *adv.* very

fetha *v.* to conquer

fienasow *pl.* anxiety

flàm *m.*, **flabmow** flame

flattra *v.* to flatter (*followed by* **gans**)

flogh *m.*, **flehes** child; **gans flogh**, **gen flogh** with child, pregnant

floren *f.*, **florednow** lock

flour *m.* **flourys** flower; *also* **flouren** *f.*

Fôceùs *m. personal name* Photius

fol *m.*, **fôlys** fool

folya *v.* to follow

fordh *f.* **fordhow** road, way

formya *v.* to create

formyor *m.*, **formyoryon** creator

forsâkya *v.* to forsake

fos *f.*, **fosow** wall

fowt *m.*, **fowtys** fault

franchys *m.* freedom

frank *adj.* free

frankince·ns *m.* frankincense

fre *adj.* free, liberal; *adv.* freely

fresk *adj.* fresh

freth *adj.* eager, assiduous; **yn freth** eagerly, assiduously

frik *m.* nostril; **dewfrik**, **frigow** nose

frodn, **fronn** *f.*, **frodnow**, **fronnow** bridle

frût *m.*, **frûtys** fruit

Frynk *f. place-name* France

Frynkek *m.* French (*language*)

fug-grùban *m.* mock-turtle

fur *adj.* wise, sensible

furneth *m.* wisdom

fy *interj.* fie!

fyllel *v.* to fail

Fylyppyans *pl.* Philippians

fysky *v.* to rush, to hurry

gà³ *poss. adj. short form of* **aga** their

Galathyans *pl.* Galatians

gallos *v.* to be able

gallaf (**gallama**), **gyllyth** (**gylta**), **gyll**, etc. *v. present of* **gallos** (*see 18A.5*)

gallen, **galles**, **galla**, etc. *v. subjunctive of* **gallos** (*see 18A.5*)

gallos *v.*. to be able; *m.* power, might

galosek *adj.* powerful, mighty

galow *m.* call, calling

galsen (**galjen**), **galses** (**galjes**), **galsa** (**galja**), etc. *v. conditional of* **gallos** (*see 18A.5*)

galsof, **galsos**, **gallas**, etc. *v. perfect of* **mos** (*see 25A.3*)

galwaf, gelwyth, gelow, etc. *v. present-future of* **gelwel**

'gan ('n) *pron. 1st pl. infixed* us *(see 18A.1)*

gans *prep.* with

gansa *prep. pron.* with them, *earlier form of* **gansans** *(see 5A.5)*

garma *v.* to call, to shout

garow *adj.* rough, harsh

garr *f.*, **garrow** leg

gas *v. 2nd singular imperative of* **gasa**; *used in periphrastic imperatives*

'gas ('s) *pron. 2nd pl. infixed* you *(see 18A.1)*

gàs *poss. adj. Late form of* **agas** your, you

gasa *v.* to leave; **gesys** left

gavar *f.* **gever** *(also* **gyfras***)* goat

gavel *f.* grasp, hold

gell *adj.* (light) brown

gelwel *v.* to call, to name

gen *prep. Late variant of* **gans** with

genama *prep. pron.* with me *(variant of* **genef***)*

genef, genama, genes, ganso, gensy, etc. *prep. pron.* inflected forms of gans with (see 5A.5)

Genver *m.*, **mis Genver** January

genys *verbal adj.* born

ger *m.*, **geryow** word

Germogh *m. place-name* Germoe

gerva *f.*, **gervaow** vocabulary, glossary

gerys *verbal adj. Late form of* **gesys** left (< **gasa** to leave)

ges *m.* fun, mockery; **gwil ges** to jest; to make fun of *(with* **a²***)*

gesowgh *v. 2nd plural imperative of* **gasa**; *used in periphrastic imperatives*

Geverango *pl. place-name, where the four hundreds of Penwith, Kerrier, Pyder and Powder meet*

glân *adj.* clean

glanhe· *v.* to clean

glas *adj.* blue

glaw *m.* rain; **yma ow qwil glaw** it's raining

glëb *adj.* wet; **gleppa** *comparative & superlative* wetter, wettest

glow *coll.* coal

glûth *m.* dew

gobederen *f.*, **gobeder** *coll.* ankle-bone, ankle

gober *m.*, **gobrow** wage; prize

gocky *adj.* foolish

godhvedhaf, godhvedhyth, godhvëth, etc. *v. future of* **godhvos** *(see 21A.1)*

godhvëth, godhvÿth *v. 2nd singular imperative of* **godhvos**

godhvien, godhvies, godhvia, etc. *v. conditional of* **godhvos** *(see 21A.1)*

godhvos *v.* to know; **godhvedhys** known

godhyen, godhyes, godhya, etc. *v. imperfect of* **godhvos**

godra *v.* to milk *(a cow or other animal)*

godreva *adv.* in three days time

gogleth *m.* north *(archaic)*

goheles *v.* to avoid

golhy *v.* to wash

golow *m.*, **golowys** light

Golowan *m.* Midsummer's day, Feast of St John (24 June)

golowy *v.* to illuminate

goly *m.*, **goliow** wound

gonesyas *m.*, **gonesyjy** workman, worker

gonsy *prep. pron. variant of* **gensy** with her *(see* **gans***)*

gonys *v.* to work, to cultivate

gool *m.* **goliow** feast day, holy day; **gool ha gweyth** holiday and working day

gòn, goraf, godhes, gor, etc. *v. present of* **godhvos** *(see 21A.1)*

gonys *m.* cultivation; *v.* to cultivate, to sow

goos *m.* blood

gora *coll.* hay

gordhya *v.* to worship *(sometimes followed by* **dhe²***)*

gordhuwher *m.* evening, in the evening

Gorefen *m. Late form of* **Gortheren** July

gorfen *m.* end; **bys worfen bës** until the end of the world

gorfedna *v.* to finish

gorhemydna, gorhemynna *v.* to command

gorlenwel *v.* to fill up, to fill to overflowing

gormola *m.* praise

gorow *m.* male

gorowra *v.* to gild; **gorowrys** gilt

gorra *v.* to put, to send; **gorra own in** to frighten

gorsaf *m.*, **gorsavow** station

gorseth *f.* **gorsedd**, session of bards; mound, throne; **Gorseth Kernow** the Cornish Gorsedd; **Gorseth Arberth** the Mound of Arberth

Gortheren *m.*, **mis Gortheren** July

gortheby *v.* to answer

gorthyp *m.*, **gorthebow** answer

gortos *v.* to wait; **gorta** waits *3rd singular present-future*

gorvarhas *f.*, **gorvarhasow** supermarket

goslowes *v.* to listen *(followed by* **orth***)*

gosteyth *adj.* obedient

gosys *adj.* bloody, covered in blood

gothfen, gothfes, gothfa, etc. *v. subjunctive of* **godhvos** *(see 21A.1)*

gour *m.*, **gwer** man, husband; **gour ty** husband

govenek *m.* hope

govyn *v.* to ask (*followed by* **orth**); **govydnys** *verbal adj.*

gov *m.*, **govyon** smith

governans *m.*, **governansow** government

governour *m.*, **governours** governor

govys *m.*; **a'm govys vy** for my sake

gow *m.*, **gowyow** lie; **heb wow** without a lie, in truth

gowek *adj.* mendacious; *as noun* liar *m.*, *pl.* **gowygyon**

grappa *m.*, **grappys** grape; **gwedhen** *f.* **grappys** vine

grâss *m.* grace; *pl.* **grassow** thanks

grassa *v.* to give thanks; **grassaf dhe Dhuw** thank God

grauntya *v.* to grant

Grêk *m.*, **Grêkys** Greek

gromercy dhis *interj.* thank you (*informal to one person*); **gromercy dhywgh** (*to two or more people or to one person formally*)

gruthyl *v. variant verbal noun of* **gwil**

gu *m.* woe; **govy** woe is me; **gony** woe is us (*see 25A.5*)

gul *v. variant of* **gwil**

guw *m.*, **guyow** spear

gwadn *adj.* weak

gwadnhe·, **gwannhe·** *v.* to weaken; **gwadnhë·s** weakened

gwadn-rewl, **gwann-rewl** *f.* bad rule, poor arrangement

gwadn-wre'ty *f.* bad wife, adulteress

gwag *adj.* empty; hungry

gwainya *v.* to gain, to win

gwaityaf *v.* I expect, I shall expect *1st singular present-future of* **gwetyas**

gwana *v.* to pierce, to stab

gwarek *f.*, **gwaregow** bow, arch

gwarior *m.*, **gwarioryon** player, actor

gwarnya *v.* to warn

gwarnyans *m.*, **gwarnyansow** warning

gwary *v.* to play; to play music; *m.*, **gwariow** play (*in theatre*); game

gwaryva *f.*, **gwaryvaow** theatre

gwas *m.*, **gwesyon** fellow; servant

gwastas *adj.* level, smooth

gwâv *m.*, **gwavow** winter

gwaynten *m.* spring

gwedhen *f.*, **gwëdh** *coll.* tree

gwe·dhowes *f.*, **gwedhowesow** widow

gwedren *f.*, **gwedrednow** glass, tumbler

gwel *m.*, **gwelyow** field

gweles *v.* to see; **gwelys** seen; **gwel** see! *2nd singular imperative*

gwell *adj.* better *comparative of* **dâ**; **gwell yw genef** I prefer; **gwell yw dhybm** I prefer; **gwella** best *superlative of* **dâ**

gwellen, gwelles, gwella, etc. *v. subjunctive of* **gweles** (*see 19A.1*)

gwels *m.* grass

gwelta (< **gwelyth**+**ta**) *v.* thou seest *2nd singular present of* **gweles**

gwelvyth will see *3rd singular future of* **gweles**

gwely *m.*, **gweliow** bed

gwenenen *f.*, **gwenyn** *coll.* bee

gwenyn *m.* poison (*attested only in OC* **guenoinreiat** poisoner)

gwer *adj.* green

gweres *m.* help, assistance; *verbal noun* to help; *also 3rd singular present-future*

gwerhes *f.*, **gwerhesow** virgin (*used of the mother of Jesus and of virgin saints*)

gwerryor, gwerrour *m.*, **gwerrours** warrior

gwertha *v.* to sell

gwesty *m.*, **gwestiow** guest in restaurant or hotel

gweth *adj.* worse *comparative of* **drog**; **gwetha** worst *superlative of* **drog**; **in gwetha prës** unfortunately

gwethyas *m.*, **gwethysy** warden, guardian

gwetyas *v.* to expect

gwewen *f.*, **gwewednow** heel

gwil *v.* to do, to make

gwin *m.* wine

gwir *m.*, **gwiryow** right; **in gwir** truly; *adj.* true

gwiryon *adj.* innocent

gwiryoneth *m.* truth

gwith *m.* keeping, guard; **kemeres with** to take care, to mind; **in dadn with** in custody

gwitha, gwetha *v.* to keep

gwlân *coll.* wool

gwlas *f.*, **gwlasow** country

gwlascor *f.*, **gwlascorow** kingdom

gwra *v. 2nd singular imperative of* **gwil**

gwrav, gwrama *v.* I do, I will do *1st singular present-future of* **gwil**

gwreg *f.*, **gwrageth** wife; **gwreg ty, gwre'ty** wife

gwrellen, gwrelles, gwrella, etc. *v. subjunctive of* **gwil** (*see 19A.1*)

gwren, gwres, gwre, etc. *v. imperfect of* **gwil** (*see 14A.1*); *also 1st plural imperative of* **gwil**

gwrêns *v. 3rd singular & plural imperative of* **gwil**

gwres *f.* heat, ardour

gwrewgh *v. 2nd plural imperative of* **gwil**

gwrior *m.* creator

gwrug, gwrussys, etc. *v. preterite of* **gwil** (*see 13A.1*)

gwrussen, gwrusses, gwrussa, etc. *v. conditional of* **gwil** (*see 14A.3*)

gwrydnyans *m.* squeezing, extortion

409

gwryllyf, gwrylly, gwrello, etc. *v. present subjunctive of* gwil (*see 19A.3*)
gwrÿs *verbal adj.* done . (*see* gwil)
gwÿdhboll *f.* chess
gwydn, gwynn *adj.* white, pale
Gwydngala *m.*, mis Gwydngala (*also* Gwyngala) September
gwylfos *m.* wilderness
gwyls *adj.* wild
Gwyngala *see* Gwydngala
gwyns *m.*, gwynsow wind
gwynvÿs *adj.* how lucky, how fortunate (*see 25A.5*)
gwyras *f.*, gwyrosow whisky, spirits
gwysca *v.* to wear (*clothes*)
gyll *v. see* gallaf
gyllyn, gyllys, gylly, etc. *imperfect of* gallos (*see 18A.5*)
gyllvyth *3rd singular future of* gallos (*see 18A.5*)
gyllys *verbal adj.* gone; become (*see* mos to go)
gylsen, gylses, galsa, etc. *v. conditional of* mos (*see 16A.4*)
gylty *adj.* guilty
gyvvyans *m.* forgiveness, pardon
hadre·² *conj.* while; hadre vywhy as long as you (*sg.*) live
ha(g) *conj.* and; ha'm and my; ha'n and the; ha'w³ and my; hag erel et cetera
hager, hager- *adj.* ugly; hackra *comparative-superlative* uglier, ugliest; hager-awel *f.* bad weather; storm; hager-ober *m.*, hager-oberow evil deed, crime; hager-mernans *m.* nasty death
hail *interj.* hail
hanaja *v.* to sigh, to gasp
haneth *adv.* tonight
hanow *m.*, henwyn name
hanter *m.*, hanterow half
hanter-cans *num.* fifty
hanter-cansves *ord.* fiftieth
hanter-dëdh *m.* midday
hanter-our *m.*, hanter-ourys half-hour
hardlych *adv.* precisely
harow *interj.* help!, alas!
harp *m.*, harpys harp
hasen *f.*, has *coll.* seed
hâtya *v.* to hate
haunsel *m.* breakfast
hâv *m.*, havow, havyow summer
haval *adj.* like, similar (*followed by* dhe²)
heb *prep.* without; heb dowt without doubt, doubtless; heb mar of course; heb wow without a lie, in truth; hebof, hebos, heptho, *etc. inflected forms* (*see 12A.4*)
hebma *m. pron.* this, this one
hedna *m. pron.* that, that one

hedhyw *adv.* today
Hedra *m.*, mis Hedra October
hel *adj.* generous
hell *adj.* slow, tardy; yn hell slowly
Hellës *f. place-name* Helston
helma *m. pron.* this, this one (*variant of* hebma)
hèm *pron. short form of* hebma *before vowels in* bos
henwel *v.* to name, to call
herdhya *v.* to thrust, to push
hernen *f.* hern *coll.* pilchard; hern gwâv winter pilchards; hern hâv summer pilchards
Herod *m. personal name* Herod
hevel *defective v.*; yth hevel it seems; yth hevelly it seemed (*imperfect*); yth havalsa it would seem (*conditional*)
hevleny *adv.* this year
hir *adj.* long
hirwarrow *m.* cranefly, daddy-long-legs
ho *interj.* hey, ho
hobma *f. pronoun* this, this one, this female person
hockya *v.* to hesitate; in udn hockya hesitantly
hodna *f. pronoun* that, that one, that female person
hôk *m.*, hôkys hawk
holergh *adj.* late; yn holergh *adv.* late
holma *f. pronoun* that, that one, that female person (*variant of* hobma)
hòm *f. pron. short form of* hobma *before vowels in* bos
hòn *f. pron. short form of* hodna *before vowels in* bos
honen *pron.* self, *both reflexive and emphatic*; y honen oll all by himself
hordh *m.*, hordhas ram
hosket *m.*, hoskettys hogshead
hot *m.*, hottys hat
how *interj.* ho!
howl *m.* sun
howlsedhas *m.* sunset; (*archaic*) west
hunegan *m.*, huneganas dormouse
hunros *m.*, hunrosow dream
huny *pron.* one; *used only with* kettep each, lies many *and* pùb every
hùrtya *v.* to hurt
hus *m.* magic
hy *pron.* she, her
hy³ *poss. adj.* her
idn *adj.* narrow, confined
iffarn *m.* hell
ilow *m.* music. See also mûsyk
in *prep.* in; i'n in the; inof, inos, ino, *etc.* inflected forms (*see 12A.4*)

in bàn (*later* **in màn, màn**) *adv.* up, upwards

in dadn² *prep.* under

indella *adv.* thus, in that way; *also* **indelna**

indelma *adv.* thus, in this way

Inglond *m. place-name* England

in gwir *adv.* truly, really

in hans *adv.* over there; **in hans dhe²** beyond

inia *v.* to urge, to incite

iniadow *m.* urging, insistence

injynor *m.*, **injynoryon** engineer

in kerdh *adv.* away

in kerhyn *prep.* around (*often of garments*)

in ketelma *adv.* in just this way, like this

in mar veur dell *adv.* in as much as

in mes *adv.* out; **in mes a²** out of

inocent *adj.* innocent; *m.*, *pl.* **inocentys** innocent person

in rag *adv.* forward

inter, intra *prep.* between, among; **intredhof, intredhos, intredho**, *etc.* *inflected forms* (*see 12A.4*)

i'n tor'-ma at the moment, at present

in udn² *particle to make adverbial participle* (*see 25A.2*)

iredy *adv.* indeed

isel *adj.* low

i'th *prep.* & *poss. adj.* in thy, in your (*also* **in dha**)

Jafet *m. personal name* Japhet

Jene·fer *f. personal name* Jennifer

jentyl *adj.* kind

Jermany *f. place-name* Germany

Jesù Crist *m. personal name* Jesus Christ

jolyf *adj.* lively, sprightly; **yn jolyf** in lively fashion

jorna *m.* day; **an jorna-ma wàr seythen** today week

Jory *m. personal name* George

Josef *m. personal name* Joseph

joust *m.*, **joustys** joust

jouster *m.*, **jousters** jouster

Jowan *m. personal name* John

jowl *interj.* devil, heh (*see* **dyowl**)

jùj *m.*, **jùjys** judge

jùjya *v.* to judge

jùjment *m.*, **jùjmentys** judgement

jùnya *v.* to join

jùstys *m.* justice

ke *m.*, **keow** hedge

kê *v. 2nd singular imperative of* **mos**

kebmer *v. 2nd singular imperative of* **kemeres**

kebmys *pron.* as much as, as many as; **kebmys tra aral** so many other things

kefrës, kefrÿs *adv.* also, as well

kegyn *f.* kitchen

kekemmys *pron. variant of* **kebmys** as much as

kelly *v.* to lose

kelly *f.*, **keliow** grove

Kelt *m.*, **Keltyon** Celt

Kembra *f.* Wales

Kembrek *m.* Welsh language

kemeres *v.* to take

kemerren, kemerres, kemerra, *etc. v. subjunctive of* **kemeres** (*see 19A.1*)

ken *adj.* other (*precedes noun without lenition*); *pron.* something else; *adv.* otherwise; **dhe gen le** to another place

kendon *f.* debt; **bos in kendon** to owe, to be in debt

kendonor *m.*, **kendonoryon** debtor

kenedhel *m.*, **kenedhlow** generation

kensa *ord.* first; **kensa ha dewgans** forty-first; **kensa warn ugans** twenty-first

kentrevak *m.*, **kentrevogyon** neighbour

kentryna *v.* to spur

kenys *verbal adj.* (*see* **cana**)

kenyver *adj.* & *pron.* each, every, all; **kenyver den** everybody; **kenvyer onen** everyone

kepa·r ha(g) *prep.* like, as, similar to; **in kepar maner** in a similar way

ker *adj.* dear, expensive, blessed

kerdhes *v.* to walk; **kerdhes in mes gans** to go out with, to date

kerenjedhek *adj.* loving, affectionate

kerensa *f.* love; **rag kerensa** for the sake of

kerhes *v.* to fetch

Kernow *f.* Cornwall

Kernow *m.*, **Kernowyon** Cornishman

Kernowek *m.* Cornish language

Kernowes *f.*, **Kernowesow** Cornishwoman

kervya *v.* to carve; **kervys** carved

kerys, kersys, caras, *etc. v. preterite of* **cara** (*see 17A.1*)

kesen *f.*, **kesow** *pl.* (sod of) turf (*for burning*)

keskerdhes *v.* to walk together, to march

kestalkya *v.* to talk together, to converse

kessydhyans *m.* rebuke, punishment

keth *adj.* same (*precedes noun*)

kette·l² *conj.* as soon as

kyttryn *m.*, **kyttrynow** bus

keus *m.* cheese

kev *v.* (*see* **cafos**)

Kevardhu *m.*, **mis Kevardhu** December

kevelyn *m.*, **kevelydnow** cubit

kever *m.*; **in y gever** with respect to him, towards him

kewgh *2nd plural imperative of* **mos**

kêwsys *verbal adj.* (*see* **côwsel**)

kig *m.* meat, flesh; **kig bowyn** beef; **kig porhel** pork

kigor *m.*, **kigoryon** butcher

knighyas *m.* whinnying

knofen *f.*, **know** *coll.* nut

knoukya *v.* to knock, to strike

knyvyas *v.* to shear

ky *m.*, **keun** dog

kyffewy *m.*, **kyffewyow** party (*convivial*)

kyn⁵(th) *conj.* although; **kyn fe** though it be, even; **kynth usy ev obma** although he is here

kyns *adv. & prep.* before; **kyns na pell** before long; **kyns pedn** within (*of time*); **kyns ès** *conj.* before

kyny *v.* to keen, to lament

kynyaf *m.* autumn

labm, lamm *m.*, **labmow, lammow** jump, leap; **wàr udn labm** all at once

lack *m.* lack

lacka *adj. comparative & superlative of* **drog** bad; **lacka ha lacka** worse and worse

ladha *v.* to kill; **ledhys** killed

ladra *v.* to steal

lagas *m.*, **lagasow, lagajow** eye

laha *m.*, **lahys** law

lath *f.*, **lathow** yard (*measure*)

Latyn *m.* Latin (*language*)

lavar *v.* 2nd singular imperative of **leverel**

lavarren, lavarres, lavarra, etc. *v. subjunctive of* **leverel** (*see 19A.1*)

lavrak *m.*, **lavrogow** pair of trousers

lavurya *v.* to toil, to work

lavuryans *m.* labour, toil

lawa *v.* to laud, to praise (*of God*)

lawethan *m.* leviathan, monster

le *adj.* less, smaller *comparative of* **bian** small; **le ha le** less and less; **lyha** smallest, least *superlative of* **bian**

le *m.* place; **in le** instead of; **pùb le** everywhere

lebmel *v.* to jump; **labmas, lammas** *pret.* 3rd singular jumped

lebmyn *adv.* now

ledan *adj.* wide

lêder *m.*, **lêders** leader

lehe· *v.* to lessen, to diminish

lel *adj.* loyal, faithful; **yn lel dhywgh** yours faithfully (*in letter writing*)

lemen *adv.* only *following a negative*

lendya *v.* to lend (*followed by* **dhe²**)

ledn *f.*, **lednow** blanket, cloth

lent *adj.* slow

lent'he· *v.* to slow down, to decelerate

les *m.* interest, advantage

Lesard, an *m. place-name* the Lizard

lesky *v.* to burn

let *m.* hindrance, delay; **heb let** immediately

leth *m.* milk

leun, leun- *adj.* full; **leun-golon** *f. in phrase* **a leun-golon** very willingly; **leun-gresy** to believe completely

leuv *f.* hand, **dewla** *dual & plural* (*see* **dorn**)

leven *adj.* smooth, even

leverel *v.* to say; **leverys** said *verbal adj.*; **leverys, lavaras** (he) said *3rd singular preterite*

lewyas *v.* to steer, to drive

lies *adj.* many; **lies tra** many things; **lies huny** many a one, many people; **pana lies, py lies** how many

lion *m.*, **lions** lion

livya *v.* to lunch

lodn *m.*, **lodnow** bullock, animal

loor *f.* moon

loos *adj.* grey, old

losowen *f.* **losow** coll. plant, herb

Loundres *f. place-name* London

lowarn *m.*, **lewern** fox

lowarth *m.*, **lowarthow** garden

lowen *adj.* happy

lowena *f.* joy, happiness; **lowena dhis** hallo, greetings

lowender *m.* joy, happiness

lowenek *adj.* glad, merry

lowenhe· *v.* to gladden, to rejoice

lowr *m.* enough; **lowr a²** enough of, much of; **lowr gweyth** many times, frequently

lùk *pron. & adv.* enough, sufficiently

Lulyn *f. place-name* Newlyn

lùst *m.*, **lùstys** lust, desire

lybm *adj.* sharp

lycklod *m.* likelihood; **dre lycklod** in all probability

lÿs, lës *f.*, **lesyow** court (*attested only in place-names*)

Lÿs Kerwys *f. place-name* Liskeard

lyther *m.*, **lytherow** letter

lytheredna *v.* to spell

lyver *m.*, **lyvrow** book

lyverjy *m.*, **lyverjiow** library

lyvryk *m.*, **lyvrygow** little book

lyw *m.*, **lywyow** colour; **py lyw ywa?** what colour is it?

'm *pron. first person singular infixed* me (*see 18A.1*)

-ma *suffix used after definite article and noun to mean* this

mab *m.*, **mebyon** son; **mab den** mankind

mabm *f.*, **mabmow** mother

madama *f.* madam

maga⁵ *adv.* how (*before adjectives*); **magata** as well, also

maga *v.* to nurture, to rear

maghteth *f.*, **meghtythyon** maid, maiden, virgin
Mahom *m. personal name* Mahound
mal *m.* eagerness; **mal yw genef** I am eager
malbe² *prefixed adj.* devil the…; **malbe dàm** damn all; **malbe vadna** devil the drop, damn all; **malbe onen** devil the one, nobody
màn *m. and adv.* at all (*after negative verb*); zero
manaf, mydnaf, mydnys, mynta, mydn, medn, etc. *v. present-future of* **mydnas** (*see 18A.3*)
managh *m.*, **menegh** monk
maner *f.*, **manerow** manner, way
manerlych *adv.* in a fitting way, fittingly
mar(s), mara(s) *conj.* if; **mar pleg** please; **mar calsa den** if one could
marchont *m.*, **marchons** (**an varchons**) merchant, businessman
margh *m.*, **mergh** (**an vergh**) horse
marhak *m.*, **marhogyon** rider, horseman
marhas *f.*, **marhasow** market
marhogeth *verbal noun* to ride; *used only in verbal noun*
marhoges *f.*, **marhogesow** horsewoman, woman rider
Maria *f. personal name* Mary
marnas *conj.* unless; *following a negative only*
marner *m.*, **marners** mariner, sailor
marow *adj.* dead; **bos marow** to die
martesen *adv.* perhaps
marth *m.* wonder, astonishment; **marth yw genef** I am astonished
marthus *m.*, **marthùsyon** wonder, miracle
marwyl *adj.* mortal (*not attested in traditional Cornish*)
maryach *m.*, **maryajys** marriage
mâta *m.*, **mâtys** mate, fellow
mater *m.*, **maters** matter
maw *m., pl.* **mebyon** *or* **coscar** boy
may⁵(th) *adv.* where; (*with subjunctive*) so that, in order that
me (**my**) *pron.* I, me
Me *m.*, **mis Me** May
medhek *m.*, **medhygyon** doctor
medhel *adj.* soft
medhow *adj.* drunk
medhowy *v.* to become drunk, to be drunk
medn *v. variant of* **mydn** *3rd singular present-future of* **mydnas**
medra *v.* to aim, to emulate
megys *verbal adj.* nurtured, reared (*see* **maga**)
mejy *v.* to reap
mêkya *v.* to pretend, to presume
melen *adj.* yellow

mellya *v.* to bother with (*followed by* **gans**)
melo·dy *m.*, melody, tune
men *m.*, **meyn** (**an veyn**) stone
mencyon *m.*, mention; **gwil mencyon a²** to mention
menestrouthy *m.* instrumental music
meneth *m.*, **menydhyow** mountain
menjen, menjes, menja, etc. *v. variant of* **mynsen**
mentêna *v.* to support, to maintain
mênya *v.* to mean
mênyng *m.* meaning
meppyk *m.*, **meppygow** baby boy
meras, miras *v.* watch, look at (*takes* **orth**); **meras stark orth** to stare at
mercy *m.* mercy; **kemeres mercy a²** to have mercy on
merwel *v.* to die; **merwys** *3rd singular preterite* died
Meryasek *m. personal name* Meriasek, Meriadec
mernans *m.* death
mery *adj.* merry
mes a fordh *adj. phrase* out of the way, wrong; *see* **in mes**
mès *conj.* but
mêster *m.*, **mêstryjy** master; **Mêster** Mister, Mr
mêstres *f.*, **mêstresow** mistress; **Mêstres** Mrs
Mêstresyk *f.*, **Mêstresygow** Miss
mesva *f.* inch
meth *m.* shame; **meth yw genef** I am ashamed
methek *adj.* ashamed, embarrassed
Metheven *m.*, **mis Metheven, mis Efen** June
metya *v.* to meet
meur *adj.* great, grand; **meur a²** many, much, lots of; **meur-jersya** to cherish greatly
meyny *m.*, **meynys** household, family
mil *f.*, **milyow** thousand
mildir *f.*, **mildiryow** mile
milgy *m.*, **milgeun** hound, dog
milva *f.* zoo
milweyth *adv.* a thousand times
miras *v. see* **meras**
mis *m.*, **mîsyow** month
moghhe· *v.* to increase
mollath *f.*, **molothow** curse; **mollath Duw i'n gegyn** God's curse in the kitchen
mona *m.* money
molethy *v.* to curse
mor *m.*, **morow** sea
moren *f.*, **moronyon** maid, young woman
mortal *adj.* mortal

morthol *m.*, **mortholyow** hammer
mos *v.* to go; **mos warbydn** to meet
mostethus *adj.* dirty, defiled
movya *v.* to move
mowes *f.*, **mowysy** girl
moy *adj. and pron.* more *comparative of* **meur**; **moyha** most *superlative of* **meur**
munys *adj.* tiny
muskegy *v.* to go mad; **muskegys** insane, confused
muscok *adj.* insane; *m.*, *pl.* **muscogyon** madman; **tus vuscok** insane people, madmen
mûsyk *m.* music
my (**me**) *pron.* I, me
mydnas *v.* to wish; *used as auxiliary for future and conditional*; **y fynna'** (*for* **y fynnaf**) I will
mydnen (**mednen**), **mydnes** (**mednes**), **mydna** (**medna**), *etc.* *v. imperfect of* **mydnas** (*see 18A.4*)
mydnen, **mydnes**, **mydna**, *etc. v. subjunctive of* **mydnas** (*see 19A.1*)
mydnys (**mednys**), **mynsys** (**mensys**), **mydnas**(**mednas**), *etc. v. preterite of* **mydnas** (*see 18A.4*)
Myhal *m. personal name* Michael
mynna' *v. see* **mydnas**
myns *m.* size; *pron.* as much as, as many as
mynsen, **mynses**, **mynsa**, *etc. v.* would *conditional of* **mydnas** (*see 18A.4*)
mynta (< **mynnyth+ta**) *v. 2nd singular present-future of* **mydnas**
mynysen *f.*, **mynys** *coll.* minute
myrgh *f.*, **myrhas** daughter
myrr *m.* myrrh
mytern *m.*, **myterneth** king
myternes *f.* **myternesow** queen
myttyn *m.* morning; *as adv.* in the moring
-na *suffix* (*used after definite article and noun to mean* that)
na(**g**) *negative part. in subordinate question, answers and indirect speech*; *in Late Cornish often used instead of* **ny**(**ns**).
nos *f.*, **nosow** night
nâ! *interj.* no!
Nadelyk *m.* Christmas; **Nos** *f.* **Nadelyk** Christmas Eve
na fors *adv. phrase* no matter; *also* nyns eus fors
nagonen *pron.* *with negative verb* nobody
nakevys *verbal adj. Late for* **ankevys** forgotten
namnygen *adv.* a moment ago, just now
namoy *adv.* any more (*used with negative*)
naney·l *conj. & adv.* neither (*see 26A.7*)
naw *num.* nine
nawnjegves *ord.* nineteenth

nawnjek *num.* nineteen
nawves *ord.* ninth
neb *adj.* some; *pron.* somebody; whoever; *as a relative pron.* who; **neb den** somebody; **neb tra** something
nebes *pron.* a little, a few (*followed by plural noun*)
nebonen *pron.* somebody
nefra *adv.* ever (*in the future; never used for the past*)
nell *m.* power, might
nena *adv.* (< **i'n eur-na**) then
neppyth *pron.* something
nerv *m.*, **nervow** nerve
nes *adj.* nearer *comparative of* **ogas** near; **nessa** *comparative and superlative of* **ogas** nearer; nearest, next
newher *adv.* last night
neyja *v.* to fly, to swim
north *m.* north
norvŷs, **norvës** *m.* world, earth
nowodhow *pl.* news
nown *m.* hunger; **yma nown dhybm** I am hungry
nowyth *adj.* new
ny *pron.* we, us
ny *neg. part.* **nynj** (**nyns**) *before vowels in* **bos** *and* **mos**
nyns (**nynj**) *see* **ny**
ober *m.*, **oberow** deed, work
obery *v.* to work, to fashion
obma *adv.* here; **obma in ogas** near here, nearby
occasyon *m.*, **occasyons** occasion
oferen *f.* mass, eucharist; **re'n oferen** by the mass (*oath*)
offendya *v.* to offend
offens *m.*, **offencys** offence
offra *v.* to offer
offys *m.*, **offycys** office, function
ogas *adj.* near; **ogas dhe²** near, near to; **in y ogas** near him
ogasty· *adv.* almost, nearly
ogh *interj.* oh (*in sorrow or dismay*)
ola *v.* to cry, to weep
olas *m.* hearth
oll *adj.* all
ollgalosek *adj.* almighty
oma *v. emphatic form of* **ov** I am; *see* **bos**
omberthy *v.* to balance
omdho·n *v.* to carry oneself, to behave; **o·mdhon** to conceive, to breed
omdhydhana *v.* to amuse oneself
omdhysqwedhes *v.* to appear
omdowl *m.* wrestling
omdôwlel *v.* to wrestle
omdowlor *m.*, **omdowloryon** wrestler
omlath *v.* to fight'; *m.* fight

omgelly *v.* to faint
omglôwes *v.* to feel (oneself)
omsettya *v.* to resist (*followed by* **orth**)
omvetya *v.* to meet, to converge
omwheles *v.* to upset, to overturn
omwitha (**omwetha**) *v.* to keep oneself
omwolhy *v.* to wash (oneself)
ôn *m.*, **ên** lamb
onen *num.* one *in counting*; *pronoun* (impersonal) one
only *adv.* only
oos *m.*, **osow** age
opyn *adj.*, *adv.* open; **opyn-welys** seen openly, seen clearly
orta *prep. pron.* at them, *earlier form of* **ortans** (*see 5A.5*)
orth *prep.* at, against, to (*with certain verbs*)
orthyf, **orthys**, **orto**, **orty**, *etc. prep. pron. inflected forms of* **orth** (*see 5A.5*)
os jy *v.* are you, you are *variant of* **osta** (*see 6A.2*)
ost *m.*, **ôstys** host, landlord
ôstes *f.*, **ôstesow** hostess
osta *v.* are you, you are *second person singular of short form of* **bos** (*see 6A.1*); **ôta** *early variant of* **osta**
othem *m.*, **othomow** need; **yma othem dhybm a²** I need
othomak *adj.* needy; *m.*, *pl.* **othomogyon** needy person
otta *v.* behold, lo; **otta vy**, **otta jy**, **otta va**, *etc.* here I am, here you are, etc. (*see 25A6*)
our *m.*, **ourys** hour
ov, **os**, **yw**, *etc. v. short form of* **bos** (*see 6A.1*)
over-devys *verbal adj.* overgrown
overcùmya *v.* to overcome
ow³ *poss. adj.* my
own *m.* fear; **yma own dhybm** I fear; **perthy own** to be afraid; **kemeres own** to become afraid
owr *m.* gold
owt *interj.* oh, hey (*in disgust or anger*)
oy *m.*, **oyow** egg
padn *m.*, **padnow** cloth
paintya *v.* to paint
pajer ugans *num. Late for* **peswar ugans** eighty
palas *v.* to dig
paly *m.* velvet, brocade
pàn *conj.* when
pana² (< **py ehen a²**) *adj.* which?, what kind?; **pana bellder** how long; **pana dermyn** when?; **pana dhownder** how deep; **pana hager** how ugly; **pana lowr torn** how often; **pana uhelder** how high; **pana** (**pàn**, **pa**) **vaner** what kind?; **in pàn vaner** how?; **pa vaner ha sort** in which way

pandra, **pandr'** *pron.* what?; **pandr'yw an mater?** what's the matter?; **pandr'o an mater?** what was the matter?
paper *m.* **nowodhow**, **paperyow nowodhow** newspaper
pa·radîs *m.* paradise
pardona *v.* to pardon, to forgive (*followed by direct object*)
park crôkê *m.* croquet pitch
parow *pl.*; **heb parow** without equal
parys *adj.* ready
Pask *m.* Easter; Passover; **De Pask** Easter Sunday
passya *v.* to pass
pasty *m.*, **pastys** pasty
pebys *verbal adj.* baked (*see* **pobas**)
peca·r *Late Cornish form of* **kepa·r**
peder *f. num.* four
pedergweyth *adv.* four times
pedn (**penn**) *m.*, **pednow** head; **pedn bloodh** birthday; **Pedn an Wlas** *m. place-name* Land's End
pedn-scoler *m.*, **pedn-scolers** head boy
pednwyscor *m.*, **pednwyscoryon** hatter
pehas *m.*, **pehosow** sin
pejwar *num. variant of* **peswar** four; **pajer** *in later Cornish*
pel *f.* **droos** football
pell *adj.* far
pellwolok *f.* television
pellen *f.*, **pelednow** ball
Pencost *m.* Pentecost, Whitsun; **De Fencost** Whitsunday
pendhescajor *m.*, **pendhescajoryon** head teacher, principal
peneglos *f.*, **peneglosyow** cathedral
pengasen *f.* paunch end, belly
pensevyk *m.*, **pensevygyon** prince
penvêster *m.*, **penvêstrysy** headmaster
percêvya *v.* to perceive
perfeth *adj.* perfect
perhen *m.*, **perhednow** owner
perhednak *m.*, **perhenogyon** owner
perna (**prena**) *v.* to buy
person *m.*, **persons** person
personek *adj.* personal
perswâdya *v.* to persuade
perthy *v.* to bear, to tolerate; **perthy cov a²** to remember
peryllys *adj* dangerous
pes *adj.* how much, how many
pës, **pÿs** *v.* 2nd singular imperative of **pesy**
peskytter may⁵ *conj.* as soon as, whenever
pesqweyth *conj.* as often as
peswar *num.* four; **peswar ugans** eighty; **peswar ugansves** *ord.* eightieth
peswardhegves *ord.* fourteenth
peswardhek *num.* fourteen

415

peswartrosek *adj.* four-footed
pe·swora, pe·swara *ord.* fourth;
  **pe·swora warn ugans, pe·swara
  warn ugans** *ord.* twenty-fourth
pesy *v.* to pray
pëth *pron. variant of* **pÿth** what?; *m.*
  possessions, property; **pëth an bÿs** wordly
  wealth, living
peur⁵, py eur⁵ *adv.* when?
pew *defect. v.* owns, possesses
piba (peba) *v.* to play the pipes, to pipe;
  pib *3rd singular present-future*
Pilat *m. personal name* Pilate
plag *m.*, **plâgys** plague, punishment
plain *adj.* plain
plâss *m.*, **plassow** place
plegya *v.* to fold; **plegys** folded
plegya *v.* to please (*takes* **dhe²**)
plesont *adj.* pleasant
plesour *m.*, **plesours** pleasure
plêsya *v.* to please (*takes direct object*)
ple⁵(th) *adv.* where?; **ple ma va?** where is
  he?; **ple mowns y?** where are they?
plît *m.* plight, state, condition
plos *adj.* dirty
pluvak *f.*, **pluvogow** pillow
pluven *f.*, **pluvednow** pen; *also* feather
  where the plural is the coll. **pluv**
pluw *f.*, **pluyow** parish; **Pluw Paul** the
  Parish of Paul
pò *or* **bò** *conj.* or
pob *pron.* everybody
pobas *v.* to bake
pobel *f.*, **poblow** people
pocket *m.*, **pockettys** pocket
pols *m.* short time, moment
pons *m.*, **ponsow** bridge
ponya *v.* to run
poos *adj.* heavy, serious, foetid; **poos yw
  genef** I am reluctant
popet *m.*, **popettys** doll
pòr² *adj.* very
pora·n *adj.* exactly
porhel *m.*, **porhelly** pig
porposya *v.* to purpose, to intend; **yth ov
  porposys** I intend
porth *2nd singular imperative of* **perthy**
porth *m.*, **porthow** port, cove; **Porth Ia** *m.
  place-name* St Ives
pory *v.* to graze
posa *v.* to lean
posnya *v.* to poison
pôtya *v.* to kick; **pôtys** kicked
pow *m.*, **powyow** country; **Pow an
  Sowson** England
powes *m.* rest, repose *and v.* to rest, to
  repose; **powes wàr** to depend on
pows *f.*, **powsyow** garment, dress

poynt *m.*, **poyntys** point; **poynt a skians**
  good counsel, maxim; *adv. with neg. verb* not
  at all
poyson *m.* poison
practys *m.* practice, exercise
prag *adv.* why?
prais *m.* praise
praisya *v.* to praise
pras *m.*, **prasow** meadow
preder *m.*, **prederow** thought; **kemeres
  preder a²** to consider, to take thought for
predery *v.* to consider, to think; *Late variant*
  p'edery; **prederys** considered *3rd singular
  preterite*
prena (perna) *v.* to buy
prenassa *v.* to go shopping
prës, prÿs *m.*, **prejyow** time, meal
prëv *m.*, **prevas** insect
prevy *v.* to prove
prias *m.*, **priosow** spouse
pris *m.*, **prîsyow** prize; price
profet *m.*, **profettys** prophet
profus *m.*, **profusyon** prophet
promys *m.*, **promyssyow** promise
promyssya *v.* to promise
pronter *m.*, **prontyryon** priest, vicar
prow *m.* advantage; **a brow** advantageous
pry *m.* earth, clay
prydydhieth *f.* poetry
prydyth *m.*, **prydydhyon** poet
pryns *m.*, **pryncys** prince
pryson *m.*, **prysons** prison
pùb dëdh *adv.* every day
pùb den, pùb den oll *pron.* everybody
pùb huny *pron.* everybody
pùb jorna *adv.* every day
pùbonen *pron.* everybody
puns *m.*, **punsow** pound (*money*)
pùnyshment *m.*, **pùnyshmentys**
  punishment
pùnyshya *v.* to punish
pùpprÿs *adv.* always
pùptra *pron.* everything
Pwyll *m.* Pwyll (*a Welsh name; Pwyll was prince
  of Dyfed*)
py eur⁵, peur⁵ *adv.* when?
pymp *num.* five
pympes *ord.* fifth
pymthegves *ord.* fifteenth
pymthek *num.* fifteen
py *adj.* which?
py(th) *adv.* where?, whither?
pygebmys *adj.* how much, how many;
  pygebmys downder how deep;
  pygebmys hës how long; **pygebmys les**
  how wide; **pygebmys uhelder** how high
pynag oll *pron.* whoever, whatever;
  pynagoll fordh may wherever

pyneyl *pron.* which of two
pyseu·l *adj.* how much, how many
pysk *m.*, **pùscas** fish
pystyga *v.* to injure
pyteth *m.* pity, compassion; **kemeres pyteth** to have compassion
pỳth, pëth *pron.* what?
pyw *pron.* who?; **pywa** (< **pyw ywa**) what? (*in astonishment*)
qwarel *m.*, **qwarels** pane of glass
qwarellya *v.* to quarrel
qwart *m.*, **qwartys** quart
qwartron *m.* quarter
qwestyon *m.*, **qwestyonow** question
qweth *f.*, **qwethow** garment
qwît *adv.* quite, completely
radn *f.*, **radnow** part, share
rag *conj. and prep.* for; **ragof, ragos, ragtho**, *etc. inflected forms (see 12A.4)*; **rag ewn tristans** for sheer sorrow; **rag hedna** therefore
rannjy *m.*, **rannjiow** flat, apartment
ras *m.* grace; **meur ras a hedna** many thanks for that
re² *perf. part.*; **me re beu** I have been; **me re welas** I have seen
re *pron. in* **an re-ma** these; **an re-na** those
re² *adv.* too; **re a²** too much of
re²(n) *prep.* by (*in oaths*); **re Varia** by Our Lady; **re Vyhal** by St Michael; **re'm leowta** by my loyalty; **ren ow enef** upon my soul; **ren ow thas** by my father
rebûkya *v.* to rebuke
recêva *v.* to receive
recken *m.*, **recknys** bill
Redrùth *m. place-name* Redruth
redya *v.* to read
refrainya *v.* to refrain
regardya *v.* to regard, to consider
rejoycya *v.* to rejoice
reknel *f.*, **reknellow** calculator
remembra *v.* to remember
renky *v.* to grunt, to snore
repentya *v.* to repent
reqwîrya *v.* to require
res *m.* necessity; **res yw dhybm** I must; *also* **me a res** I must
resek *v.* to run (*chiefly of liquids*)
rêson *m.*, **rêsons** reason, cause; **dre rêson** because
rewardya *v.* to reward
rial *adj.* royal, majestic
robbyor *m.*, **robbyoryon** robber
rollen, rolles, rolla, *etc. v. subjunctive of* **ry** (*see 19A.1*)
rollya *v.* to roll
rom *m.*, **rômys** room; appointed place
Roman *m.*, **Romans** Roman

roncas *v. 3rd singular preterite of* **renky** snored, grunted
rônd *adj.* round
ro(y) *v. 2nd singular imperative of* **ry**
roy *v. 3rd singular present subjuctive of* **ry** (*see 19A.3*)
rudh *adj.* red
rûth *f.*, **rûthow** crowd, multitude
ruwvaneth *m.* kingdom < OCV **ruifanaid** (*not attested in Middle or Late Cornish*)
ry *v.* to give; **re** gives *3rd singular present-future*; **rÿs** given *verbal adj.*; **ros** gave *3rd singular preterite*; **rosen, roses, rosa**, *etc.* conditional
ryb *prep.* beside, near; **rybof, rybos, ryptho**, *etc. inflected forms (see 12A.4)*; **rybon** *adv.* nearby
ryban *m.*, **rybanys** ribbon
rych *adj.* rich
rygol *m.*, **rygolyow** trench, **groove**
ryver *m.*, **ryvers** river
sacryfia *v.* to sacrifice
's *pron. infixed 3rd singular feminine* her (*see 18A.1*)
's *pron. infixed 3rd plural* them (*see 18A.1*)
sa'bàn (< **sav in bàn**) *v.* arise!, get up!
saffen, saffes, saffa, *etc. v. subjunctive of* **sevel** (*see 19A.1 & C.23*)
sagh *m.*, **seghyer** bag
salow *adj.* whole, healthy
sans *adj.* holy; *m., pl.* **sens** saint
sarf *f.*, **syrf** serpent, snake
sav *m.* standing position, stance; **a'y sav** standing
savas *v.* stood, got up *3rd singular preterite of* **sevel**
savyour *m.*, **savyours** saviour
saw *adj.* safe, sound
saw *conj.* but; **saw unsel** but only
sawgh (*pronounced* [saw]) *m.* load; **worth an sawgh** by the load
sawment *m.* healing, recover'
sawour *m.*, **sawours** smell, odour
sawya *v.* to heal
Saxon *m.*, **Saxons** Saxon
scant *adj.* scarce, scanty; *with negative* hardly
scav *adj.* quick, light (*of weight*)
scodhya *v.* to support, to relie upon (*followed by* **wàr**)
scol *f.*, **scolyow** school
scoler *m.*, **scolers** scholar
scolvêster *m.*, **scolvêstrysy** schoolmaster
scobmyn *m.*, **scobmow** fragment
scon *adv.* soon; **yn scon** *adv.* soon; **sconha** sooner
scoodh *f., pl.* **scodhow**, *dual* **dywscoth** shoulder

scoos *m.*, **scojow** shield, escutcheon

Scotlond *m.* Scotland (*see also* **Alban**)

scovarn *f.*, **scovornow** ear [*****dywscovarn** *is unattested in Cornish*]

scovarnak *m.*, **scovarnogas** hare; **Scovarnak Merth** the March Hare

scrifa (**screfa**) *v.* to write; *also m.* writing; **scrif** *2nd singular imperative*

scrifor *m.*, **scriforyon** writer

scrija *v.* to scream

scryptour *m.*, **scryptours** scripture

scubya *v.* to sweep

scùmbla *v.* to defecate, to mess (*of animals*)

secùnd *ord.* second; **secùnd ha dewgans** *ord.* forty-second; **secùnd warn ugans** *ord.* twenty-second

sedha (**esedha**) *v.* to sit

sëgh *adj.* dry, thirsty

sehes *m.* thirst; **yma sehes dhybm** I am thirsty

selder *m.*, **selders** cellar

Seleven *m. personal name* (< *Solomon*) St Levan

sêlya *v.* to seal

semlant *m.*, **semlans** appearance

sêmly *adj.* seemly, beautiful

sens *m.*, **sencys** sense

sensy *v.* to keep, to hold; **sensy chy** to keep house; **sens e fast** hold him fast!

seny *v.* to sound, to play (music)'

sera *m. see* **syra**

serry *v.* to anger; to become angry; **serrys** *verbal adj.* angry; **sorras** angered; became angry *3rd singular preterite*

servont *m.*, **servysy** servant

servya *v.* to serve

servys *m.*, **servysyow** service

sêsya *v.* to seize

settya *v.* to set

seul² *adv.* the... *in incremental comparatives* (*see 24A.3*)

seul *pron.* whoever

sevel *v.* to stand; **sevys, savas** stood *3rd singular preterite*; **sevel orth** resist, abstain from

sevien *f.* **sevy** *coll.* strawberry

sewajya *v.* to assuage, to relieve

sewya *v.* to follow

seytegves *ord.* seventeeth

seytek *num.* seventeen

seyth *num.* seven

seythen *f.*, **seythednow** week; **an jornama wàr seythen** today week; **seythen alebma** a week ago

seythves *ord.* seventh

shakya *v.* to shake

shoppa *m.*, **shoppys** shop

shyndya *v.* to ruin; **shyndys** injured

sians *m.*, **siansow** whim, caprice

sin *m.*, **sînys** sign; **sin an grows** the sign of the cross

sîra *m.* father

skentyl *adj.* intelligent, clever

skeus *m.*, **skeusow** shade

skians *m.* knowledge, sense

skyber *f.*, **skyberyow** barn

smoth *adj.* smooth

sodhva *f.*, **sodhvaow** office

sogh *m.*, **soghyow** ploughshare

solabrë·s already

sols *m.* shilling

son *m.*, **sonyow** sound, noise

sorn *m.*, **sornow** corner, cranny

sorras *v.* (*see* **serry**)

soth *m.* south

soth *m.* truth

soweth *interj.* alas, unfortunately

Sows *m.*, **Sowson** Englishman

Sowsnek *m.* English language

spâss *m.* space, room

Spayn *f.* Spain

spellya *v.* to spell

spêna *v.* to spend

spessly *adv.* specially

spîtfùl *adj.* spiteful

spladn (**splann**) *adj.* bright, apparent

spladna *v.* to shine

sportya *v.* to sport, to hunt

spyrys *m.*, **spyryjyon** spirit; **Spyrys Sans** Holy Spirit

sqwerdya, sqwardya *v.* to tear; **sqwerdys** torn

sqwith *adj.* tired

sqwîthus *adj.* tiresome

sqwychel *f.*, **sqwichellow** switch

stag *adj.* fixed; **stag ena** on that very spot

stair *m.*, **stairys** stair

stankya *v.* to stamp, to trample

stap *m.*, **stappys** step

stât *m.*, **stâtys** state, condition; estate; **drog-stât** bad state, bad condition

stella *adv.* still, yet

stenor *m.*, **stenoryon** tin miner

steren *f.*, *pl.* **sterednow**, *coll.* **ster** star

stergan *m.*, starlight, stars

stoppya *v.* to stop

story *m.*, **storys** story

straft *adv.* straightway

stranj *adj.* strange

strayl *m.*, **straylyow** mat

strechya *v.* to delay

strêt *m.*, **strêtys** street

strôll *m.* mess, disorder

studh *m.* condition, state

styr *m.*, **styryow** sense, meaning

styrya *v.* to mean, to explain

sùbstans *m.* substance, nature

sùffra *v.* to suffer, to allow
Sulgweyth *adv.* one Sunday
sur *adj.* sure; yn sur surely
syght *m..* syghtys sight
sygnyfia *v.* to signify, to mean
Syr *m. in titles* Sir
syra (sera) *m.*, syrys (serys) sir
tabm *m.*, tybmyn piece, bit; dhe dybmyn
to pieces, to bits
taclow *pl. see* tra
tal *v.* (*see* tylly)
Tamsyn *f. personal name* Tamsin
tan *m.* fire
tàn! *v.* take!'; tanowgh take! *pl.*
tanow *adj.* thin, few
tansys *m.* bonfire
tarow *m.*, terewy bull
tas *m.*, tasow father; NB: an tasow the
fathers
tâstya *v.* to taste
tava *v.* to feel, to touch
tavern *m.*, tavernyow tavern, pub
te (ty) *pron.* thou, you
tê *m.* tea
tebel- *adj. & adv.* evil, wicked; tebel-
goweth *m.* bad friend; tebel-was *m.*
wicked fellow; tebel-venyn *f.* wicked
woman
tebel-dhyghtya *v.* to mistreat
tebel-wolia *v.* to wound badly
tebmyk *m.*, temygow fragment
tecka *adj. comparative and superlative of* teg
beautiful; tecka wel what a beautiful sight
exclamative adjective (see 24A.5)
tekhe· *v.* to beautify
teg *adj.* pretty, beautiful, handsome
tell *conj. aphetic form of* fate·ll how, that
tenewen *m.*, tenwednow side
tergweyth *adv.* three times
terlebmel, terlemmel *v.* to frisk, to
prance
termyn *m.*, termynyow time; an termyn
usy ow tos the future
ternos *adv.* on the next day; ternos vyttyn
the next morning
terry *v.* to break; terrys broken
tesen *f.*, tesednow cake
tety valy *interj.* pshaw, pooh
tevy *v.* to grow; teffo *3rd singular present
subjunctive;* tevens *3rd singular imperative*
tew *adj.* fat, thick
tewel *v.* to be silent
tewl *adj.* dark
tewolgow *pl.* darkness
teyr³ *f. num.* three
'th⁵ *pron. 2nd person infixed* thee, you (*see
18A.1*)
tiak *m.*, tiogow farmer

tir *m.*, tiryow land
tireth *m.*, tirethow country, district
tirnans *m.* low-lying country
tobm *adj.* hot
tobma *v.* to heat, to warm
todn *f.*, todnow wave
tolgh *m.*, tolhow hillock
toll *m.*, tell hole
toth *m.* speed
totta (< toth dâ) *adv.* very quickly
tour *m.*, tourow tower; Tour Babel the
Tower of Babel
tournay *m.* tourney, tournament
towl *m.*, towlow plan, intention
tôwlel *v.* to throw; to plan, to intend
tra *f.*, taclow, taclenow [*the plural* *traow
*is used twice by Lhuyd, probably on the basis of
Breton* traoù; *it does not occur in traditional
Cornish*]
trailya *v.* to turn, to translate
train *m.*, trainow train
traitury *m.* treachery
tramor *adj.* overseas, foreign
traweythyow *adv.* sometimes
tre *f.*, trevow town, settlement; *adv.*
homewards, home; in tre at home
tredhegves *ord.* thirteenth
tredhek *num.* thirteen
trega (triga) *v.* to dwell; yma va tregys *he
lives, he dwells*
tregereth *f.* compassion, pity; kemeres
tregereth wàr² to take pity on
trehor *m.*, trehoryon cutter, tailor
trehy *v.* to cut
tremmil *num.* three thousand
trenja *adv.* the day after tomorrow
tresour *m.* treasure
tressa, tryja *ord.* third; tressa warn
ugans twenty third
trestya *v.* to trust (*followed by* dhe²)
treth *m.* trêthow sandy beach, strand
treveglos *f.*, trevow eglos village
treven *see* chy
treveth *f.* occasion
triga (trega) *v.* to dwell; yma va trigys *he
lives (dwells), he is living (dwelling);* ev a
drig *he will live, he will remain;* trig *2nd
singular imperative*
trist *adj.* sad
tristans *m.* sadness
tro ha(g) *prep.* towards
trogh *adj.* cut, blemished, broken
tro ha(g) *prep.* towards
tron *m.*, trônys throne
tron *m.* snout
troos *m.*, treys *pl.*, dewdros *dual* foot
tros'hës *m.*, tros'hesow foot (*length*),
troyllya *v.* to wind

trueth *m.* pity, mercy

Trûrû *m. placename* Truro

try³ *m. num.* three; **try ugans** sixty; **tryugansves** *ord.* sixtieth

Trynyta *m.* Trinity

tu ha *prep. variant of* **tro ha** towards

tùchya *v.* to touch; **tùchya pib** to smoke a pipe; **ow tùchya (dhe²)** concerning, about

tus *pl. of* **den** man, person

ty (te) *pron.* thou, you

ty *v.* to swear; **me a'n te** I swear it

tyby *v.* to consider, to think; **me a dëb** I consider

tybyans *m.*, **tybyansow** opinion

tyller *m.*, **tyleryow** place; **tyller clos** secluded spot, private place

tylly *v.* to pay; **tal** is worth; **y tal dhybm** it is worth my while, I should; **y talvia dhybm** I ought; **talvyth** will have to

udn *num.* one

udnek *num.* eleven

udnlagajek *adj.* one-eyed

udnyk single, sole; **yn udnyk** only

ufern *m.*, **ufernyow** ankle

ugans *num.* twenty

ugansves *ord.* twentieth

uhel *adj.* high, tall; **an uhel-powers** *pl.* the powers that be

ùnderstondya, ùnderstandya *v.* to understand

ùnderstondyng, ùnderstandyng *m.* understanding

unegves *ord.* eleventh; **unegves warn ugans** thirty-first

Ùngarek *adj.* Hungarian

ùnpossybyl *adj.* impossible

unver *adj.* unanimous

unverhe *v.* be of one mind, agree

unweyth *adv.* once; even, at all

uskys *adv.* quick

uskys'he· *v.* to accelerate

usy *v.* is (*see 4A.1-2*)

ûsya *v.* make use of, use; be accustomed to

uthyk *adj.* dreadful, terrible; *adv.* terribly

valy *m.*, **valys** valley

vas (*lenited form of* **mas** good) *adj.* of use, worth, acceptable

venjons *m.* vengeance

venten *f. variant of* **fenten**

venym *m.* poison, venom

venymya *v.* to poison

vëth any; **den vëth** *with negative verb* nobody; **tra vëth with negative verb** nothing

vexya *v.* to annoy

voys *m.*, **voycys** voice

vyctory *m.*, **vyctorys** victory

vynyard *m.*, **vynyardys** vineyard

vyrjyn *f.*, **vyrjyns** virgin

vysytya *v.* to visit

war *adj.* wary, aware; **bëdh war!** beware!

wàr *prep.* upon; **warnaf, warnas, warnodho,** *etc. inflected forms (see 12A.4)*; **warnedha** *variant of* **warnodhans** *3rd plural inflected form*; **wàr dhelergh** back, backwards; **wàr nans** down, downwards; **wàr jy** inside; **wàr ves** outside

warbarth *adv.* together

warbydn (warbynn) *prep.* against (*see 7A.6*)

warlergh *prep.* after, behind; according to; **warlergh hedna** thereafter, afterwards; **warlergh bad maner** in a bad manner

warleny *adv.* last year

wastya *v.* to waste

west *m.* west

whans *m.*, **whansow** desire; **yma whans dhybm** I desire

whare *adv.* presently, immediately

wharvos *v.* to happen; **wharva** *3rd singular preterite*; **wharvedhys** *verbal adjective*; **wharvo** *3rd singular present subjunctive*

whath *adv.* still, yet

whedhel *m.*, **whedhlow** story

wheffes *ord.* sixth

wheg *adj.* sweet, dear

whegh *num.* six

wheghves *ord. see* **wheffes**

whel *m.* work

whelas (whilas) *v.* to seek

whensys *adj.* desirous; **yth ov whensys** I should like

wher *v. 3rd present of* **wharvos**

wherow *adj.* bitter

wherthyn *v.* to laugh

Whervel *m. variant form of* **Whevrel** February

whêtegves *ord.* sixteenth

whêtek *num.* sixteen

whetha *v.* to blow

Whevrel *m.*, **mis Whevrel** February

whilas (whelas) *v.* to seek; **whila (whela)** *2nd singular imperative*

whor *f.*, **whereth** sister

why *pron.* you *pl.*

whyrvyth *v. 3rd singular future of* **wharvos**

wolcùm, welcùm *adj.* welcome

wolcùbma *v.* to welcome

wondrys *adj.* wonderful, remarkable

Wordhen *f. place-name* Ireland

wor' tu ha(g) *prep.* towards; *see also* tro ha(g)

wosa (woja) *prep. & conj.* after; **wosa hedna** afterwards; **wosa pùptra** after all

y *pron.* they, them

y² *poss. adj.* his

y(th)⁵ *v. part. before inflected forms of verbs*

yagh *adj.* healthy

yagh'he· *v.* to heal

yêhes *m.* health
yêth *f.*, yêthow language
yeyn *adj.* cold
yeynor *f.*, yeynoryon refrigerator
yma *v.* is, are (*of position*); ymowns are
y'm beus *v.* I have (*see 23A.1*)
yn⁵ *part. used before adj. to make an adv.*; yn
   cosel quietly; yn crev strongly; yn fen
   vigorously; yn fenowgh often; yn
   heglew audibly; yn lent slowly; yn
   lowen happily; yn scav quickly; yn scon
   soon; yn sevur strictly; yn tâ well; yn
   tefry indeed; yn tien completely; yn

town in cùsk fast asleep; yn tywysyk
assiduously; yn uskys quickly; yn uthyk
horribly
yn medh *defective v.* said
yonk *adj.* young
yowynkneth *m.* youth, youthfulness
ÿst, ëst *m.* east
yth, ythys, êth, etc. *v. preterite of* mos (*see
   16A.4*)
ytho· *adv.* therefore, so
yw *v.* is (*of characteristic*)

zeg *m. variant of* seg brewer's grains, draff

GERVA SOWSNEK-KERNOWEK
English-Cornish Glossary

This is not a complete wordlist, but rather a consolidated glossary containing the words in each Vocabulary in chapters 1–39.

able *adj.* abyl; **be able** gallos (*see 18A.5*)
about *prep.* (*local and metaphorical*) adro dhe²; ow tùchya (dhe²)
above *prep.* a-ugh (*see 12A.4*); *adv.* avàn; a-uhon (*in a text*)
abridge *v.* cot'he·
abroad *adv*(= *at large, widely*) alês; (= *overseas*) dres mor
accelerate *v.* uskys'he·
acceptable *adj.* vas (*lenited form of* mas 'good'); dâ lowr
accident *n.* drog-labm *m.*, drog-labmow
according to *prep.* warlergh
account *n.* (= *value*) bry *m.*; (*in bank*) acownt *m.*, acowntys
accountant *n.* acowntyas *m.*, acowntysy
accustomed *adj*, ûsys; **be accustomed to** ûsya
acknowledge *v.* avowa; aswon
across *prep* dres
actor *n.* (*in theatre*) gwarior *m.*, gwarioryon
Adam *personal name* Adam *m.*
add *v.* addya
admit *v.* admyttya; avowa
adulteress gwadn-wre'ty *f.*, gwadn-wrageth ty
advantage *n.* les *m.*; prow *m.*
advantageous *adj.* a brow
Advent *n.* Asvens *m.*
advice *n.* cùssul *f.*, cùssulyow
advise *v.* cùssulya
affectionate *adj.* kerenjedhek
afraid *adj.* ownek; **be afraid** perthy own; **become afraid** kemeres own; **I am afraid** yma own dhybm
after (= *afterwards*) *adv.* awosa, wosa; *prep.* warlergh
after all *adv. phrase* wosa pùptra

afternoon *n.* dohajë·dh *m.*
afterwards *adv.* wosa hedna; awosa
again *adv.* arta
against *prep.* warbydn, (*earlier*) erbynn; orth (*see 5A.5*)
age *n.* oos *m.*, osow
ago *adv.* alebma; nans yw
agree *v.* acordya; assentya; agria; unverhe·; bos acordys
agreement *n.* acord *m.*, accord
ah *interj.* â
aim *v.* medra
alack *interj.* ala·ck
alas *interj.* ala·ck; ella·s; soweth
ale *n.* coref (LC cor) *m.*; **mild ale** coref clor
alive *adj.* bew; **he is alive** yma va yn few
all *adj.* oll; pùb; **all day long** dres oll an jorna
allow *v.* gasa (LC gara); sùffra
Allsaints' day *n.* (*1st November*) De Halan Gwâv
almighty *adj.* ollgalosek
aloft *adv.* avàn
alone *adj.* y honen oll
along *adv.* ahës
already *adv.* solabrë·s
also *adv.* kefrës, kefrÿs; inwe·dh; magata
although *conj* kyn⁵(th); **although he is here** kynth usy ev obma
always *adv.* pùpprÿs; pùb termyn
among *prep.* inter, intra (*see 12A.4-5*)
amuse *v.* dydhana; **amuse oneself** omdhydhana
amusing *adj.* dydhan
and *conj.* ha(g); **and my** ha'm, ha'w³; **and the** ha'n
angel *n.* el *m.*, eleth
anger *n.* sorr *m.*; coler *m.*; *v.* serry; angra

angry *adj.* serrys; engrys; **become angry** cafos anger; serry
animal *n.* best *m.*, bestas
ankle *n.*; *n.* ufern *m.*, ufernyow; gobederen *f.*, gobeder *coll.*
announce *v.* declarya
annoy *v.* ania, vexya
annoyance *m.* ancombrynsy *m.*
Annunciation *n.* (*25th March*) Degol *m.* agan Arlodhes, Degol *m.* Maria mis Merth
anoint *v.* anoyntya
answer *n.* gorthyp *m.*, gorthebow; *v.* gortheby
anxiety *n.* fienasow *pl.*
any *adj.* bÿth; **any better** bÿth well; **any more** *adv.* namo·y (*used with negative*)
anyone *pron.* den vëth, den vÿth; **does anyone know?** a wor den vëth?
apartment *n.* rannjy *m.*, rannjiow
apparent *adj.* a·pert; spladn, splann
appear *v.* apperya, dysqwedhes, omdhysqwedhes; **it appears** yth hevel
appearance *n.* semlant *m.*, semlans
apple *n.* aval *m.*, avallow
April *n.* Ebrel *m.*, mis *m.* Ebrel
arch *n.* gwarek *f.*, gwaregow
archangel *n.* arghel *m.*, argheleth
archer *n.* archer *m.*, archers
ardour *n.* gwres *f.*
argue *v.* argya
arise *v.* drehevel, derevel; sevel in bàn; **arise!** *imper. v.* sa'bàn (< sav in bàn)
arm *n.* (*weapon*) arv *f.*, arvow; *v.* arva; **armed man** den ervys; **armed men** tus *pl.* ervys
armchair *n.* chair *m.* brehek, chairys brehek
around *prep.* in kerhyn (*often of garments*)
arrears *npl.*; **in arrears** adhelergh
art *n.* creft *f.*, creftow
as *prep.* ave·ll (*see 10A.8*); **kepar dell**; *conj.* mar²; maga⁵ (*before adjectives*)
as much as *pron.* kebmys, kemmys; kekebmys, kekemmys
as often as *conj.* pesqweyth may⁵
as soon as *conj.* kette·l²
as well *adv.* kefrÿs, kefrës; inwe·dh; magata
Ash Wednesday *n.* De Merher Lusow
ashamed adj. methek; **I am ashamed** meth yw genef
ask *v.* govyn (*followed by* orth)
asleep *adj.* in cùsk; **fast asleep** yn town in cùsk;
assail *v.* assaultya
assent *v.* assentya; bos assentys
assiduous *adj.* dywysyk; freth;
assiduously yn tywysyk; yn freth (freth *in*

traditional Cornish does not mean 'fluent of speech')
assistance *n.* gweres *m.*
assuage *v.* sewajya
assure *v.* assûrya
astonishment *n.* marth *m.*; **I am astonished** marth yw genef
astronomer *n.* astronymer *m.*, astronymers
at *prep.* orth. (*see 5A.5*)
attack *v.* assaultya; settya wàr²
audible *adj.* heglew
audibly *adv.* yn heglew
August *n.* Est *m.*, mis *m.* Est
Australia *place-name* Australya *f.*
autumn *n.* kynyaf *m.*, kydnyaf *m.*
avail *v.* amowntya
avoid *v.* goheles
aware *adj.* war
away *adv.* dhe ves; in kerdh
baby *n.* baby *m.*, babiow; **baby boy** *n.* meppyk *m.*, meppygow
back *n.* keyn *m.*
back, backwards *adv.* wàr dhelergh;
bad *adj.* drog, drog-; gwadn-, gwann-; **bad organization** gwadn-rewl, gwann-rewl *f.*
bag *n.* sagh *m.*, seghyer
bake *v.* pobas; **baked** pebys
balance *v.* omberthy
ball *n.* pellen *f.*, pelednow
bank *n.* (*financial*) arhanty *m.*, arhantiow
banknote *n.* banknôta *m.*, banknôtys
baptize *v.* besydhya; **besydhys** *adj.* baptized
barn *n.* skyber *f.*, skyberyow
basket *n.* cowel *m.*, cowellow,
bat *n.* (= *mammal*) eskelly *pl.* grehen
be *v.* bos (*see 8A.3, 10A.1-2, 11A.1, 11A.3, 19A.1, 19A.4*)
beach *n.* (sandy) treth *m.*, trêthow
bear *v.* don; perthy
beast *n.* (*of burden*) eneval *m.*, enevales
beautiful *adj.* teg; *comparative & superlative* tecka; sêmly
beautify *v.* tekhe·
because *conj.* a·wos; dre rêson; drefen; **because of** a·wos, dre rêson a²
become *v.* mos; **he has become old** ev yw gyllys coth
bed *n.* gwely *m.*, gweliow
bedroom *n.* chambour *m.*, chambours
bee *n.* gwenenen *f.*, gwenyn *coll.*
beef *n.* kig *m.* bowyn
beer *see* ale
before *adv. & prep.* kyns; dhyrag; **before long** kyns na pell; *conj* kyns ès
beget *v.* denethy
begin *v.* dallath; **I began** dalethys
behave *v.* omdho·n

behead *v.* dybedna
behind *prep.* adrëv; warlergh; *adv.* adhelergh
behold *interj.* otta; **behold him** otta va (*see 25A.6*)
belief *n.* crejyans *f.*
believe *v.* cresy, crejy
bell *n.* clogh *m.*, clegh
belly *n.* pengasen *f.*
benefit *n.* prow *m.*; benefyt *m.*; **get the benefit of** enjoya
bent *adj.* cabm
beside *prep.* ryb (*see 12A.4*)
best *adj.* gwella (*superlative of* dâ)
Bethlehem *place-name* Bethalem *m.*; Bethlem *m.*
betray *v.* betraya
better *adj.* gwell (*comparative of* dâ;
between *prep.* inter, intra (*see 12A.4*)
beware! *imperative v.* bëdh war!
beyond *prep.* dres; in hans dhe[2]
bicycle *n.* dywros *f.*, dywrosow
big *adj.* brâs; *comparative & superlative* brâssa
bill *n.* recken *m.*, recknys; scot *m.*
bird *n.* edhen *m.*, ëdhyn, ÿdhyn, edhnow
birthday *n.* pedn *m.* bloodh
bishop *n.* epscop *m.*, (*Late*) ispak *m.*, epscobow
bit *n.* tabm *m.*, tybmyn; **to bits** dhe dybmyn
bite *v.* dynsel; brathy,
bitter *adj.* wherow
black *adj.* du
blanket *n.* ledn *f.*, lednow,
blemished *adj.* trogh; myshevys
blessed *adj.* benegys; **Blessed Virgin Mary** an Werhes *f.* Ker Maria
blessing *n.* bednath *f.*, benothow
blind *adj.* dall; *v.* dallhe
blood *n.* goos *m.*
blow *n.* (= *thump*) bobmen *f.*, bomednow, bomennow
blow *v.* whetha
blue *adj.* blou; glas
boar *n.* badh *m.*, badhas
Bodmin *place-name* Bosvena *m.*
body *n.* corf *m.*, corfow; body *m.*, bodys
bonfire *n.* tansys *m.*
book *n.* lyver *m.*, lyvrow
booklet *n.* lyvryk *m.*, lyvrygow
born *adj.* genys
bosom *n.* ascra *f.*
bother *n.* ancombrynsy *m.*; *v.* ancombra; ania; vexya
bottle *n.* botel *f.*, botellow
bow *n.* gwarek *f.*, gwaregow
Boxing Day *n.* Degol *m.* Stefan
boy *n.* maw *m.*, mebyon *pl. or* coscar *coll.*
brains *npl.* empydnyon *pl.*
brambles *npl.* dreys *coll.*

brave *adj.* colodnek
bravery *n.* colonecter *m.*
bread *n.* bara *m.*
break *v.* terry; **he broke it** ev a'n torras
breakfast *n.* haunsel *m.*
breath *n.* anal *f.*; **out of breath** cot y anal
breed *v.* o'mdhon
Breton *n.* Breton *m.*, Bretons
Breton (woman) *n.* Bretones *f.*, Bretonesow
brewer's grains *n.* seg *m.*, zeg *m.*
bridge *n.* pons *m.*, ponsow
bridle *n.* frodn *f.*, fronn *f.*, frodnow, fronnow
bright *adj.* spladn, splann
bring *v.* dry; **brought** drÿs *verb. adj.*
Britons *npl.* Bryttas
brocade *n.* paly *m.*
broken *adj.* terrys; trogh
brother *n.* broder *m.*, breder
brown *adj.* (*light*) gell
build *v.* byldya; derevel, drehevel
bull *n.* tarow *m.*, terewy
bullock *n.* lodn *m.*, lodnow
burn *v.* lesky
bury *v.* encledhyas
bus *n.* kyttryn *m.*, kyttrynow
businessman *n.* marchont *m.*, marchons, an varchons
busy *adj* bysy
but *conj.* saw; mès, (*Late*) bùs
butcher *n.* kigor *m.*, kigoryon
butter *n.* amanyn *m.*
buy *v.* perna, prena
by *prep.* er; **by the hand** er an leuv
cafe *n.* bosty *m.*, bostiow
Cain *personal name* Caym *m.*
cake *n.* tesen *f.*, tesednow; câken *f.*, câkys
calculator *n.* reknel *f.*, reknellow
call *n.* galow *m.*; *v.* cria; garma; gelwel; **called** cries
calling *n.* galow *m.*
Camborne *place-name* Cambron *m.*
canal *n.* dowrgledh
candle *n.* cantol *f.*, cantolyow
caprice *n.* sians *m.*, siansow
car *n.* carr *m.* (tan), kerry (tan)
Caradog *personal name* Carasek *m.*
care *v.*; **I don't care** ny'm deur
careful *adj.*; **be careful!** darwar *defective verb*
carry *v.* don; **carry out** *v.* execûtya
carve *v.* kervya; **carved** kervys
case *n.* câss *m.*, câssys; **in that case** i'n câss-na
Caswallon *personal name* Casvelyn *m.*
cat *n.* cath *f.*, cathas
catch *v.* cachya
cathedral *n.* peneglos *f.*, peneglosyow

cause *n.* rêson *m.*, rêsons; caus *m.*; skyla *m.*; *v.* causya
cave *n.* cav *m.*, cavyow
cease *v.* cessya
cellar *n.* selder *m.*, selders
Celt *n.* Kelt *m.*, Keltyon
Celtic Congress *n.* Cùntelles *f.* Keltek
century *n.* cansvledhen *f.*, cansvledhydnyow
certain *adj.* certan; **certainly** *adv.* yn certan
chair *n.* cader *f.*, caderyow (*found only in place-names*); chair *m.*, chairys
chance *n.* chauns *m.*, chauncys
change *v.* chaunjya
charity *n.* cheryta *m.*
charter *n.* chartour *m.*, chartours
chastise *v.* chastia
cheese *n.* keus *m.*
chess *n.* gwÿdhboll *f.*
child *n.* flogh *m.*, flehes; **with child** gans flogh, (*Late*) gen flogh
choose *v.* dêwys
Christmas *n.* Nadelyk *m.*; **Christmas Eve** Nos *f.* Nadelyk
church *n.* eglos *f.*, eglosyow
city *n.* cyta *f.*, cytas
claim *n.* qwarel *m.*
class *n.* class *m.*, classys
clay *n.* pry *m.*
clean *adj.* glân; *v.* glanhe·
clear *adj.* cler
clever *adj.* skentyl
cliff *n.* âls *f.*, âlsyow
climb *v.* crambla
cloth *n.* padn *m.*, padnow; qweth *f.*, qwethow
clothes *npl.* dyllas *coll.*
cloud *n.* cloud *m.*, cloudys; comolen *f.*, comol *coll.* (comolen, comol *is not attested in traditional Cornish*)
coal *n.* glow *coll.*
coat *n.* côta *m.*, côtys; mantel *f.*, mentylly
cold *adj.* yeyn
collect *v.* cùntell
colour *n.* lyw *m.*, lywyow; colour *m.*, colourys; **what colour is it?** py lyw ywa?; *v.* lywya; (= *blush*) rudhya
come *v.* dos
comfort *n.* comfort *m.*; **bohes comfort** little comfort
command *v.* erhy; gorhemydna, gorhemynna; comondya
commend *v.* comendya
company *n.* cowethas *f.*, cowethasow
compassion *n.* pyteth *m.*; mercy *m.*; tregereth *f.*; **have compassion on** kemeres tregereth wàr²
complain *v.* croffolas
complaint *n.* croffal *m.*

complete *adj.* cowl-, dien; *v.* **complete** *v.* cowl-wil; collenwel
completely *adv.* cowl-; qwît; yn tien
computer *n.* amowntyor *m.*, amowntyoryon
conceive *v.* (*reproduction*) o·mdhon; (*reproduction & thought*) concêvya
concern *n.* bern *m.*; *v.* **he was concerned** câss o ganso
concerning *prep.* adro dhe²; ow tùchya (dhe²)
condemn *v.* dampna; **condemned** dempnys
condition *n.* plît *m.*; stât *m.*, stâtys; studh *m.*; condycyon *m.*; **bad condition** drog-stât
confess *v.* avowa; confessya
confined *adj.* idn
confused *adj.* kemyskys; (*in mind*) muskegys
conquer *v.* conqwerrya; fetha
conqueror *n.* conqwerrour *m.*, conqwerrours
conscience *n.* conscians *m.*
consecrate *v.* consecrâtya; sacra
consider predery a²; consydra; regardya; tyby; **I consider** me a dëb
continue *v.* durya
contrary *adj.* contrary; *n.* **on the contrary** i'n contrary part; dhe'n contrary
converge *v.* omvetya
converse *v.* kescôwsel; kestalkya
cook *n.* (*female*) coges *f.*, cogesow
Corinthians *pl.* Corynthyans
corner *n.* cornel *f.*, cornelly; sorn *m.*, sornow
Cornish language *n.* Kernowek *m.*
Cornishman *n.* Kernow *m.*, Kernowyon
Cornishwoman *n.* Kernowes *f.*, Kernowesow
Cornwall *place-name* Kernow *f.*
correct *adj.* ewn; *v.* êwna; amendya
cost *v.* costya
counsel *n.* cùssul *f.*, cùssulyow; *v.* cùssulya
count *v.* amowntya
countenance *n.* bejeth *m.*
country *n.* bro *f.* (*this word is very rare indeed in traditional Cornish*); gwlas *f.*, gwlasow; pow *m.*, powyow; (= *region*) *n.* tireth *m.*, tirethow
course *n.* (*all senses*) cors *m.*, corsys
court *n.* cort *f.*, cortys; lÿs *f.*, lês *f.*, lesyow (*attested only in place-names*)
courteous *adj.* cortes
cove *n.* porth *m.*, porthow
cow *n.* buwgh *f.*, buhas
cowshed *n.* bowjy *m.*, bowjiow
crab *n.* canker *m.*, kencras
cradle *n.* cowel *m.*, cowellow
craft *n.* creft *f.*, creftow
cranefly *n.* hirwarrow *m.*
cranny *n.* sorn *m.*, sornow

crawl *v.* cramyas
cream *n.* dehen *m.*
create *v.* creatya; formya
creator *n.* formyor *m.*, formyoryon; gwrior *m.*
creditor *n.* dettor *m.*, dettoryon
creed *n.* cres *f.*
crime *n.* drog-ober *m.*, drog-oberow; hager-ober *m.*, hager-oberow
criminal *n.* drog-oberor *m.*, drog-oberoryon; **criminals** *pl.* drog-pobel *f.*
criticize *v.* crytyca
crowd *n.* rûth *f.*, rûthow
cry *v.* (= *call*) cria; (*tears*) ola
cubit *n.* kevelyn *m.*, kevelydnow
cultivate *v.* gonys
cupboard *n.* a·mary *m.*, a·marys
cultivation *n.* gonys m.
cure *n.* (*of souls*) cûr *m.*
curse *n.* mollath *f.*, molothow; **God's curse** mollath Duw; *v.* molethy; cùssya
custody *n.* gwith *m.*; **in custody** in dadn with
cut *n.* brew *m.*, brewyon; *v.* trehy; *adj.* trogh
cyclone *n.* corwyns *m.*
dainty *adj.* dainty
dance *n.* dauns *m.*, dauncyow; *v.* dauncya
danger *n.* danjer *m.*, peryl *m.*, peryllyow
dangerous *adj.* peryllys
dark *adj.* tewl; (*of sky*) comolek
darkness *n.* tewolgow *pl.*
date *v.* kerdhes in mes gans
daughter *n.* myrgh *f.*, myrhas
David *personal name* Davyth *m.*
day *n.* dëdh *m.*, dedhyow; jorna *m.*; **day before yesterday** *adv* dege·nsete; **day after tomorrow** *adv.* trenja; **in three days time** *adv.* godreva
dead *adj.* marow
deaf *adj.* bodhar
dear *adj.* ker; (*in letter writing*) wheg,
death *n.* mernans *m.*
debonair *adj.* debonêr
debt *n.* kendon *f.*; **to be in debt** bos in kendon
debtor *n.* kendonor *m.*, kendonoryon
decapitate *v.* dybedna
decelerate *v.* lent'he·
December *n.* Kevardhu *m.*, mis *m.* Kevardhu
decide *v.* ervira; **I have decided** ervirys yw genef
declare *v.* declarya
deed *n.* ober *m.*, oberow; dêda *m.*, dêdys
deep *adj.* down
defecate *v.* caha; (*of animals*) scùmbla
defend *v.* defendya
defiled *adj.* mostethus

delay *n.* let *m.*; *v.* dylâtya; strechya
delegate *n.* cadnas *f.*, canasow
deliver *v.* delyvra
deny *v.* denaha
depart *v.* dyberth, dybarth
deranged *adj.* muskegys
descend *v.* skydnya (*earlier* dieskyna)
desire *n.* bodh *m.*; lùst *m.*, lùstys; whans *m.*, whansow; *v.* desîrya; whansa; **I desire** yma whans dhybm; me a garsa; yth ov whensys
desirous *adj.* whansek; whensys
destroy *v.* destria; dystrêwy; dyswil
determine *v.* determya
devil *n.* dyowl *m.*, an jowl, dewolow
dew *n.* glûth *m.*
die *v.* bos marow; merwel
difficult *adj.* cales
difficulty *n.* caletter *m.*, caleterow
dig *v.* palas
diminish *v.* lehe·
direction *n.* (*of compass*) qwartron *m.*, qwartronys
dirty *adj.* mostethus; plos
disciple *n.* dyscypyl *m.*, dyscyplys; dyskybel *m.*, dyskyblyon
discreet *adj.* doth
disgust *v.* dyvlasa
dishonour *v.* dysonora
dispel *v.* defendya
dispute *n.* bresel *f.*, breselyow
distress *n.* a·wher; *v.* ankenya, vexya; **be distressed** perthy awhe·r
district *n.* tireth *m.*, tirethow; **in this district** i'n côstys-ma
ditch *n.* cledh *m.*, cledhyow
division *n.* dyberth *m.*, dybarth *m.*
do *v.* gwil (gul); **done** gwrÿs
doctor *n.* (*physician*) medhek *m.*, medhygyon; fysycyen m., fysycyens; (= *learned man*) doctour *m.*, doctours
dog *n.* ky *m.*, keun
doll *n.* baban *m.*, babanas (*this word does not mean* 'baby'); popet *m.*, popettys
door *n.* daras *m.*, darasow (darajow); **back door** daras delergh; **front door** daras ara·g
dormouse *n.* hunegan *m.*, huneganas
double *adj.* dewblek, dobyl
doubt *n.* dowt *m*; *v.* dowtya
doubtless *adv.* heb dowt
down *adv.*(*of position*) awoles; a·barth awoles; in nans; (*of motion*) dhe'n dor; dhe'n leur; wàr nans
dreadful *adj.* uthyk
dream *n.* hunros *m.*, hunrosow
dress *n.* (*woman's garment*) pows *f.*, powsyow,
drink *n.* dewas *m.*, dewosow

drive *v.* drîvya; lewyas
drop *n.* badna *m.*, banahow
drunk *adj.* medhow ; **become drunk, be drunk** medhowy
dry *adj.* sëgh
duchess *n.* dùches *f.*, dùchesow
duchy *n.* ducheth *m.*
duke *n.* dûk *m.*, dûkys
duty *n.* devar *m.*
dwell *v.* triga, trega
each *adj. & pron.* kenyver
eager *adj.* freth; whensys; **I am eager** mal yw genef ; **eagerly** yn freth
eagerness *n.* mal *m.*
ear *n.* scovarn *f.*, scovornow (*dywscovarn *is unattested in Cornish*)
early *adv.* a·brës; ava·rr
earn *v.* dendyl
earth *n.* dor *m*; (= *clay*) pry *m.*; **the earth** an nor *m.*, an norvës *m.*
east *n.* dùryan *f.* (*archaic*); ÿst *m.*, ëst *m.*
Easter *n.* Pask; (**on**) **Easter morning** De Pask myttyn
eat *v.* debry; **he ate** ev a dhebrys, ev a dhebras
egg *n.* oy *m.*, oyow
Egypt *place-name* Ejyp *m.*
eh *interj.* (*astonishment*) dar
eight *num.* eth
eighteen *num.* êtek
eighteenth *ord.* êtegves
eighth *ord.* êthves
eightieth *ord.* peswar ugansves
eighty *num.* peswar ugans; (*Late*) pajer ugans
elbow *n.* elyn *m.*, elydnow
eleven *num.* udnek
eleventh *ord.* unegves
embarrass *v.* ancombra; **embarrassed** *adj.* methek; shâmys
embarrassment *n.* ancombrynsy *m.*; meth *m.*; sham *m.*
emperor *n.* emprour *m.*, emprours
empress *n.* empres *f.*, empresow
emulate *v.* medra; gwil warlergh; omhevelly dhe²
end *n.* dyweth *m.*; gorfen *m*; **in the end** wàr an dyweth; **till the end of the world** bys worfen bës
enemy *n.* escar *m.*, eskerens
England *place-name* Inglond *m.*; Pow *n.* an Sowson
English language *n.* Sowsnek *m.*
Englishman *n.* Sows *m.*, Sowson
enjoy *v.* enjoya
enough *n.* lowr *m.*; **enough of** lowr a²; *pron. & adv.* lowr; lùk
enter *v.* entra (*followed by* in)
entertaining *adj.* dydhan

entice *v.* dynya
envy *n.* avy *m.*; *v.* perthy avy
Ephesians *npl.* Efesyans *pl.*
Epiphany *n.* (*6th January*) Degol *m.* Stool
equal *n.* par *m.*, parow; **without equal** heb parow
escutcheon *n.* scoos *m.*, scojow
estate *n.* stât *m.*, stâtys
et cetera *adv. phrase* hag erel
Eve *personal name* Eva *f.*
even *adv.* kyn fe; *adj.* leven; compes; gwastas
evening *n.* gordhuwher *m.*
ever *adv.* bythqweth (*in the past*); nefra (*in the future*)
every *adj.* kenyver
everybody, everyone *pron.* kenyver; kenyver den; kenvyer onen; pob; pùb den, pùb den oll; pùb huny; pùbonen
every day *adv.* pùb dëdh; pùb jorna; kenyver jorna
everything *pron.* pùptra; kenyver tra
everywhere *adv.* pùb le
evil *adj.* drog-, tebel-; **evil deed** drog-ober
exactly *adv.* pora·n
exalt *v.* exaltya
execute *v.* (= *carry out*) execûtya
exercise *n.* practys *m.*; *v.* omassaya
expect *v.* gwetyas; **I expect** gwaityaf
expensive *adj.* ker
explain *v.* styrya
extortion *n.* gwrydnyans *m.*
eye *n.* lagas *m.* lagasow, lagajow (*the dual* dewlagas *is confined to early Middle Cornish*)
face *n.* bejeth *m.*; fàss *m.*, fàssow
fail *v.* fyllel
faint *v.* omgelly *v.*
faith *n.* crejyans *f.*; fëdh *f.*; **upon my faith** wàr an gres; wàr ow fay; wàr ow fëdh; tàn ow fëdh
faithful *adj.* compes; lel
faithfully *adv.*; **yours faithfully** yn lel dhywgh (*in letter writing*)
fall *v.* codha
Falmouth *place-name* Arwednak *m.*; Falmeth *m.*
false *adj.* fàls, fàls-, fêkyl-; **false god** fàls-duw
falsely *adv.* falslych
far *adj.* pell
fare *v.* fara
farewell *interj.* farwèl dhis; farwèl dhywgh
farmer *n.* tiak *m.*, tiogow (*tiogyon *is unattested*)
fashion *v.* obery
fastidious *adj.* dainty
fat *adj.* tew
father *n.* tas *m.*, tasow; an tasow; sîra *m.*
fault *n.* fowt *m.*, fowtys

favour *v.* fa·vera
fear *n.* own *m.*; dowt; *v.* dowtya, perthy dowt; **I fear** yma own dhybm
feast day *n.* gool *m.*; degol *m.*
feather *n.* pluven *f.*, pluv *coll.*
February *m.* Whevrel *m.*, Whervel *m.*, mis *m.* Whevrel (*Whevrer *is unattested*)
feel *v.* tava; omglôwes (*intransitive*)
fellow *n.* gwas *m.*, gwesyon; mâta *m.*, mâtys
female *n.* benow *f.* & *coll.*
fetch *v.* kerhes
few *adj.* nebes (*followed by plural noun*); tanow
fie *interj.* agh; fy
field *n.* gwel *m.*, gwelyow
fiftieth *ord.* hanter-cansves
fifteen *num.* pymthek
fifteenth *ord.* pymthegves
fifth *ord.* pympes
fifty *num.* hanter-cans
fight *n.* omlath *m.*; *v.* omlath; strîvya
fill v.; **fill up** gorlenwel
finish *v.* gorfedna
fire *m.* tan
firewood *n.* cunys *coll.*
first *ord.* kensa; **twenty-first** kensa warn ugans; **First day of the month** *n.* Calan *m.*
fish *n.* pysk *m.*, pùscas; *v.* pyskessa
fishing boat *n.* côk *m.*, cûcow
fittingly *adv.* manerlych
five *num.* pymp
fix *v.* fastya
fixed *adj* stag.
flame *n.* flàm *m.*, flabmow
flat *adj.* plat; flat; *n.* rannjy *m.*, rannjiow
flatter *v.* flattra (*followed* by gans)
flower *n.* flour m., flouren f., flourys; blejen *f.*, *pl.* blejennow (*not attested in Middle or Late Cornish*); blejyewen *f.*, blejyow *coll.* (*attested in traditional Cornish only in* de Sul Blejyow 'Palm Sunday')
fly *v.* neyja; **let fly** dehesy
fold *n.* pleg *m.*, plegow; (*in clothing*) ascra *f.*; *v.* plegya; **folded** plegys
follow *v.* sewya; folya
food *n.* boos *m.*
fool *n.* fol *m.*, fôlys; fol *m.*, felyon
foolish *adj.* gocky
football *n.* pel *f.* droos
for *conj* rag; *prep.* rag (*see 12A.4*); **for sheer sorrow** rag ewn tristans
forbid *v.* dyfedna
forest *n.* coos *m.*, cosow; forest *m.*
forever *adv.* bys venary; bys venytha
forget *v.* ankevy; **forgotten** ankevys; (*Late*) nakevys
forgive *v.* gava (*followed by* dhe²); pardona (*followed by direct object*)

forgiveness *n.* gyvyans *m.*
forsake *v.* forsâkya
fortieth *ord.* dewgansves
fortunate; **how fortunate!** gwynnvÿs, gwydnvÿs; **how fortunate he is!** gwydn y vÿs (*see 25A.5*)
forty *num.* dewgans
forward *adv.* in rag
four *num.* peswar *m.* (*Late*) pajer; peder *f.*
four-footed *adj.* peswartrosek
fourteen *num.* peswardhek **four times** *adv.* pedergweyth
fourteenth *ord.* peswardhegves
fourth *ord.* pe·swora, pe·swara; **twenty-fourth** pe·swora warn ugans, pe·swara warn ugans
fox *n.* lowarn *m.*, lewern
fragment *n.* scobmyn *m.*, scobmow; tebmyk *m.*, temygow
France *place-name* Frynk *f.*
frankincense *n.* frankince·ns *m.*
free *adj.* frank
freedom *n.* franchys *m.*
Friday *m.* Gwener *f.*; **the first Friday** an kensa Gwener; **on Friday** De Gwener
French (*language*) Frynkek *m.*
frequently *adv.* yn fenowgh; lowr gweyth
fresh *adj.* fresk
friend *n.* cothman *m.*, cothmans; (*rarely*) car *m.*, kerens
frighten *v.* gorra own in
from, *prep.* a² (*see 5A.5*); dhyworth (*Late* dhort); dhia²; **from here** alebma; **from there** alena; **from off** dhywar²
front tâl *m.*; **in front** *adv.* ara·g; **in front of** dhyrag
fruit *n.* frût *m.*, frûtys
fulfill *v.* collenwel
full *adj.* leun, leun-
fun *n.* ges *m.*; **make fun of** gwil ges a²
function *n.* offys *m.*, offycys
furze *n.* eython *coll.*
future *n.*; **the future** an termyn usy ow tos
gain *v.* gwainya
Galatians *npl.* Galathyans *pl.*
garage *n.* carrjy *m.*, carrjiow
garden *n.* lowarth *m.*, lowarthow
garment *n.* pows *f.*, powsyow; qweth *f.*, qwethow
gasp *v.* hanaja
generate *v.* denethy
generation *n.* kenedhel *m.*, kenedhlow; denethyans *m.*, denethyansow
generous *adj.* hel; larych
George *personal name* Jory *m.*
Germany *place-name* Almayn *f.*; Jermany *m.*
Germoe *place-name* Germogh *m.*

get *v.* cafos (cavos, cawas); **get up!** *imper. v.* sa'bàn (< sav in bàn)
gild *v.* gorowra; **gilt** gorowrys
girl *n.* mowes *f.*, mowysy
give *v.* ry
glass *n.* (= *tumbler*) gwedren *f.*, gwedrednow
glad *adj.* lowenek
gladden *v.* lowenhe·
glossary *n.* gerva *f.*, gervaow
go *v.* mos (*see 16A.4*); **gone** gyllys
goat *n.* gavar *f.* gever, gyfras
God, god *n.* Duw, duw *m.*, duwow
gold *n.* owr *m.*
good *adj.* dâ
Gorsedd; the Cornish Gorsedd Gorseth *f.* Kernow;
gory *adj.* gosys
government *n.* governans *m.*, governansow
governor *n.* governour *m.*, governours
grand *adj.* meur
grant *v.* grauntya
grape *n.* grappa *m.*, grappys
grapevine *n.* gwedhen *f.* grappys
grasp *n.* dalhen *m.*; gavel *f.*; *v.* settya dalhen in
grass *n.* gwels *coll.*
graze *v.* pory
great *adj.* meur; brâs; *comparative & superlative* brâssa
Greek *n.* Grêk *m.*, Grêkys
green *adj.* gwer
greet *v.* dynerhy
greetings! *interj.* lowena dhis, lowena dhywgh
grey *adj* loos
grieve *v.* duwhanhe·
grip *n.* dalhen *m.*; *v.* settya dalhen in
groove *n.* rygol *m.*, rygolyow
ground *n.* dor *m.*; **the ground** an dor
grove *n.* kelly *f.*, keliow
grow *v.* tevy
grunt *v.* renky; **he grunted** ev a roncas
guard *n.* (= *keeping*) gwith *m.*
guardian *n.* gwethyas *m.*, gwethysy; warden *m.*, wardens
guess *v.* desmygy
guest *n.* (*in restaurant, hotel*) gwesty *m.*, gwestiow; ôstyas *m.*, ôstysy
guilty *adj.* cablus; gylty
hail *interj.* hail
hair (*of the head*) *n.* blew *coll.*
half *n.* hanter *m.*, hanterow
half-hour *n.* hanter-our *m.*, hanter-ourys
hammer *n.* morthol *m.*, mortholyow
hamper *v.* ancombra, lettya
hand *n.* leuv *f.* (*archaic*); dorn *m.*, dewla *dual & pl.*
handsome *adj.* teg; sêmly

happen *v.* wharvos
happily *adv.* yn lowen
happiness *n.* lowena *f.*; lowender *m.*; joy *m.*
happy *adj.* lowen
hard *adj.* cales
harden *v.* cales'he·
hardly *adv.* scant *with negative*; scantlowr
heal *v.* sawya; yaghhe·
harm *n.* dregyn *m.*
harp *n.* harp *m.*, harpys
harsh *adj.* asper; garow
hat *n.* hot *m.*, hottys
hate *v.* hâtya; **I hate** cas yw genef
hateful *adj.* cas
hatter *n.* pednwyscor *m.*, pednwyscoryon
have *v.* y'm beus (*see 23A.1*); **I have money** yma mona dhybm; **I have money with me** yma mona genef
hawk *n.* hôk *m.*, hôkys
hay *coll.* gora
he, him *personal pron.* ev
head *n.* pedn, penn *m.*, pednow
head boy *n.* pedn-scoler *m.*, pedn-scolers
headmaster *n.* penvêster *m.*, penvêstrysy
head teacher *n.* pendhescajor *m.*, pendhescajoryon
heal *v.* sawya; yagh'he·
healing *n.* sawment *m.*
health *n.* yêhes *m.*
healthy *adj.* salow; yagh
hear *v.* clôwes
heart *n.* colon *f.*, colonow
hearth *n.* olas *m.*
hearty *adj.* colodnek.
heat *n.* gwres *f.*; *v.* tobma
heavy *adj.* poos
hedge *n.* ke *m.*, keow
heedless *adj.* dybreder
heel *n.* gwewen *f.*, gwewednow
hell *n.* iffarn *m.*
help *interj.* harow; *n.* gweres *m.*
Helston *place-name* Hellës *f.*
hence *adv.* alebma; ahanan
henceforward *adv.* alebma rag
her *poss. adj.* hy³; *object pron.* 's (*infixed*) (*see 18A.1*)
herb *n.* losowen *f.* losow *coll.*
Herod *personal name* Herod *m.*; Erod *m.*
hesitantly *adv.* in udn hockya
hesitate *v.* hockya; perthy danjer
hesitation *n.* danjer *m.*
hey *interj.* ay; (*in disgust or anger*) owt
high *adj.* uhel
hillock *n.* tolgh *m.*, tolhow
him *object pron.* 'n (*infixed*) (*see 18A.1*)
hindrance *n.* let *m.*
his *poss. adj.* y²
ho! *interj.* how!

hogshead *n.* hosket *m.*, hoskettys
hold *n.* dalhenf; gavel *f.*; *v.* sensy; dalhedna;
  hold him fast! sens e fast!;
hole *n.* toll *m.*, tell
holiday *n.* degol *m.*, degolyow; gool *m.*
  golyow
holy *adj.* sans.
home *n.* chy *m.*, treven; trigva *f.* trigvaow;
  at home in tre; **from home** a·dre;
  home, homewards tre
hook *n.* bagh *m.*, bahow
hope *n.* govenek *m.*
horribly *adv.* yn uthyk
horse *n.* margh *m.*, mergh, an vergh
horseman *n.* marhak *m.*, marhogyon
horsewoman *n.* marhoges *f.*, marhogesow
hospital *n.* clâvjy *m.*, clâvjiow
host *n.(of tavern, etc.)* ost *m.*, ôstys
hostess *n.* ôstes *f.*, ôstesow
hot *adj.* tobm
hound *n.* milgy *m.*, milgeun
hour *n.* eur *f.*, euryow; our *m.*, ourys
house *n.* chy *m.*, treven
household *n.* meyny *m.*, meynys
how *adv* fate·ll; fatla
how deep? *interr. adj.* pygebmys downder?
  pana dhownder?
how greatly ass, assa² *v. part.*
how high? *interr adj.* pygebmys uhelder?
how long? *interr. adj.* pygebmys hës? pana
  bellder?
how many? *interr. adj.* pygebmys?; pes?
how much? *interr. adj. & pron.* pygebmys?;
  pyseu·l?; pes?
how often? *interr. adv.* pana lowr torn?
how wide? *interr. adj.* pygebmys les?
however *adv.* bytegyns
hundred *num.* cans *m.*, cansow; **hundred
  times** canqueyth
hundredth *ord.* cansves
Hungarian *adj.* Ùngarek
hunger *n.* nown *m*
hungry *adj.* gwag; **I am hungry** yma
  nown dhybm
hunt *v.* helghya; sportya
hurry *v.* fysky
hurt *v.* pystyga; hùrtya
husband *n.* gour *m.*, gwer; gour *m.* ty
I, me *personal pron.* me, my (*Late* vy)
if *conj.* a⁴; mar⁴(s), mara⁴(s)
ignite *v.* anowy
illuminate v. golowy
imagine *v.* desmygy
immediately *adv.* desempys, dhesempys;
  dystowgh; heb let
impolite *adj.* dyscortes
impossible *adj.* ùnpossybyl

in *prep.* in (*see 12A.4*); abe·rth in; **in the** i'n;
  adv. aberveth; ajy·
inch *n.* mesva *f.*
incite *v.* inia
increase *v.* moghhe·; encressya
indeed *adv.* iredy; yn certan; yn sur; yn tefry
industrious *adj.* dywysyk
inform *v.* derivas (*followed by* dhe²)
injure *v.* pystyga; shyndya
injury *n.* dregyn *m.*; pystyk *m.*, pystygow
innocent *adj.* gwiryon; inocent; **innocent
  person** *n.* inocent *m.*, inocentys
insane *adj.* muscok; muskegys
insect *n.*prëv (prÿv) *m.*, prevas
inside *adv.* (*motion into*) aberveth; ajy;
  (*position*) wàr jy
insistence *n.* iniadow *m.*
instead of *prep.* in le
insubordination *n.* bresel *f.*, breselyow
intelligent *adj.* skentyl
intend *v.* ervira; porposya; tôwlel; **I intend**
  ervirys yw genef; yth ov porposys
intention *n.* towl *m.*, towlow
interest *n.* les *m.*
Ireland *place-name* Wordhen *f.*
January *n.* Genver *m.*, mis *m.* Genver
Japhet *personal name* Jafet *m.*
Jennifer *personal name* Jene·fer *f.*
Jesus Christ *personal name* Jesù Crist *m.*
John *personal name* Jowan *m.*
join *v.* jùnya
Joseph *personal name* Josef *m.*
joust *n.* joust *m.*, joustys
jouster *n.* jouster *m.*, jousters
joy *n.* lowena *f.*; lowender *m.*
judge *n.* jùj *m.*, jùjys (*brusyas is unattested); *v.*
  jùjya; brusy
judgement *n.* breus *f.*; jùjment *m.*,
  jùjmentys
July *n.* Gortheren *m.*; (*Late*) Gorefen *m.*
jump *n.* labm, lamm *m.*, labmow, lammow;
  v. lebmel; **jumped** labmas, lammas
June *n.* Metheven *m.*; Efen *m.*, mis *m.* Efen
just *adj.* ewn; **just now** *adv.* namnygen
justice *n.* jùstys *m.*
keen *v.* kyny
keep *v.* sensy; gwitha, gwetha; **keep house**
  sensy chy
keeping *n.* gwith *m.*
key *n.* alwheth *m.*, alwhedhow; **put under
  lock and key** gorra in dadn naw alwheth
kick *v.* pôtya; **kicked** pôtys
kill *v.* ladha; **killed** ledhys
kind *adj.* jentyl
kingdom *n.* ruwvaneth *m.* (*not attested in
  Middle or Late Cornish*); gwlascor *f.*,
  gwlascorow
kiss *v.* abma (*followed by* dhe²)

kitchen *n.* kegyn *f.*
knock *v.* knoukya
know *v.* aswon; godhvos (*see 21A.1*)
knowledge *n.* skians *m.*
labour *n.* lavur *m.*; lavuryans *m.*; *v.* lavurya
lady *n.* arlodhes *f.*, arlodhesow
lamb *n.* ôn *m.*, èn
lament *v.* kyny; lamentya
Lammas (*1st Augus*) Calan *m.* Est
land *n.* tir *m.*, tiryow
landlord *n.* ost *m.*, ôstys
Land's End *place-name* Pedn *m.* an Wlas *m.*
language *n.* yêth *f.*, yêthow; tavas *m.*, tavosow
last *superlative adj.* dewetha; **at last** *adv.* wàr an dyweth
last year *adv.* warleny
late *adj.* holergh; dewedhes; *adv.* yn holergh
lately *adv.* adhewedhes; agensow
Latin *n.* (*language*) Latyn *m.*
laud *v.* lawa
laugh *n.* wharth; *v.* wherthyn
law *n.* laha *m.*, lahys
lazy *adj.* diek
leader *n.* lêder *m.*, lêders
leaf *n.* delen *f.*, delyow *pl.* (*Late variant* delkyow), del *coll.*
lean *v.* posa
leap *n.* labm *m.*, lamm *m.*, labmow, lammow; *v.* lebmel, lemmel; **leapt** labmas, lammas
least *superlative adj.* lyha; **at least** dhe'n lyha
leave *v.* gasa, (*Late*) gara; **left** gesys; (*Late*) gerys
learn *v.* desky
learner *n.* dyscor *m.*, dyscoryon
leg *n.* garr *f.*, garrow (*the dual* dywarr *is not attested in traditional Cornish*)
lend *v.* lendya (*followed by* dhe²)
Lent *n.* Corawys *m.*
less *comparative adj.* le; **less and less** le ha le
lessen *v.* lehe·
lesson *n.* dyscans *m.*, dyscansow
letter *n.* lyther *m.*, lytherow
level *adj.* gwastas
leviathan *n.* lawethan *m.*
liberal *adj.* (= *generous*) fre; larych
library *n.* lyverjy *m.*, lyverjiow
liar *n.* gowek *m.*, gowygyon
lie *v.* (= *recline*) growedha; **lying down** a'y wroweth
lie *n.* (= *falsehood*) gow *m.*, gowyow; **without a lie** heb wow
lift *v.* derevel; lyftya
light *adj.* (*of weight*) scav
light *n.* golow *m.*, golowys; *v.* anowy
like *adj.* haval (*followed by* dhe²); *prep.* ave'll (*see 10A.8*); kepar ha(g)

like *v.* cara; **I like** dâ yw genef
likelihood *n.* lycklod *m.*
lion *n.* lion *m.*, lions
Liskeard *place-name* Lÿs Kerwys *f.*
listen *v.* goslowes (*followed by* orth)
little *pron.* bohes
live *v.* bewa; (*reside*) triga, trega; **I live here** yth esoma tregys obma
lively *adj.* bewek; jolyf; **in lively fashion** yn jolyf
Lizard *place-name* Lesard *m.* an
lo *interj.* otta (*see 25A6*)
load *n.* sawgh (*pronounced* [saw]) *m.*; **by the load** worth an sawgh
lock *n.* (*locksmith's*) floren *f.*, florednow
London *place-name* Loundres *f.*
long *adj.* hir
look *v.*, miras, meras (*followed by* orth)
lord *n.* arlùth *m.*, arlydhy
lose *v.* kelly
loss *n.* coll *m.*
love *n.* kerensa *f.*; *v.* cara (*see 17A.1*)
loving *adj.* kerenjedhek
low *adj.* isel
low-lying country *n.* tirnans *m.*
loyal *adj.* lel
lunch *n.* ly; *v.* livya
lure *v.* dynya
lust *n.* lùst *m.*, lùstys,
lying *adj.* gowek
mad *adj.* muscok; **go mad** muskegy
madam *n.* madama *f.*; benyn *f.* vas
madman *n.* muscok *m.*, muscogyon
magic *n.* hus *m.*; pystry *m.*
magician *n.* pystrior *m.*, pystrioryon
Mahound *personal name* Mahom *m.*
maid *n.* maghteth *f.*, meghtythyon; mowes *f.*, mowysy; moren *f.*, moronyon
maiden maghteth *f.*, meghtythyon; mowes *f.*, mowysy; moren *f.*, moronyon
maintain *v.* mentêna; scodhya
make *v.* gwil (gul)
male *n.* gorow *m.*
malice *n.* avy *m.*; **to bear malice against** perthy avy orth
malt *n.* brag *m.*
man *n.* den *m.*, tus; gour *m.*, gwer
mankind *n.* mab *m.* den; kynda *m.* mab den
manner *n.* maner *f.*, manerow; **manners** *pl.* manerow *pl.*; cortesy *m.*
many *adj.* lies; meur a²; lowr a²; ; **many a one** lies huny; **many things** lies tra; **how many times?** pana lowr torn?
march *v.* keskerdhes
mariner *n.* marner *m.*, marners
market *n.* marhas *f.*, marhasow
marriage *n.* maryach *m.*, maryajys
marry *v.* demedhy

Mary *personal name* Maria *f.*
mass *n.* (= *eucharist*) oferen *f.*; **by the mass**
(*oath*) re'n oferen
master *n.* mêster *m.*, mêstryjy
mat *n.* strayl *m.*, straylyow
mate *n.* mâta *m.*, mâtys,
matter *n.* câss *m;* mater *m.*, maters; stoff *m.*;
   v. **it doesn't matter** na fors; nyns eus fors
Maundy Thursday *n.* De Yow Hablys
maxim *n.* poynt a skians, poyntys a skians
May *n.* Me *m.*, mis *m.* Me
Mayday *n.* Cala' *m.* Me
me *object pron.* 'm (*infixed*) (*see 18A.1*)
meadow *n.* pras *m.*, prasow
meal *n.* prës *m.*, prÿs *m.*, prejyow
mean *v.* mênya; styrya; sygnyfia
meaning *n.* mênyng *m.*; sygnyfycacyon *m.*;
   styr *m.*, styryow
meat *n.* kig *m.*
meddle *v.* mellya (*followed by* gans)
meet *v.* metya; mos warbydn
melody *n.* melo·dy *m.*, melodys
member *n.* esel *m.*, esely
memory *n.* cov *m.*, covyon
mend *v.* êwna
mendacious *adj.* gowek
mention *n.* mencyon *m.*; *v.* campolla; gwil
   mencyon a²
merchant *n.* marchont *m.*, marchons, an
   varchons
mercy *n.* mercy *m.*; pyteth *m.*; trueth *m.*;
   have mercy on kemeres mercy a²;
   kemeres pyteth a²
merry *adj.* lowenek; mery; jolyf
mess *n.* strôll *m.*
messenger *n.* cadnas *f.*, canasow,
Michael *personal name* Myhal *m.*
Michaelmas *n.* (*29th September*) Degol *m.*
   Myhal
midday *n.* hanter-dëdh *m.*
midnight *n.* hanter-nos *f.*
Midsummer *n.* Golowan *m.*
might *n.* gallos *m.*; nell *m.*; nerth *m.*; power
   m.
mighty *adj.* galosek
mild *adj.* clor
mile *n.* mildir *f.*, mildiryow
milk *n.* leth *m.* ; *v.* godra
mind *n.* brës, brÿs *m.*
minute *n.* mynysen *f.*, mynys *coll.*
minute *adj.* munys
miracle *n.* marthus *m.*, marthùsyon; merkyl
   m., merclys
misery *n.* duwhan *m.*
mishandle *v.* drog-handla
Miss *n.* Mêstresyk *f.*
mistaken *adj.* camgemerys
Mister, **Mr** *n.* Mêster

mistreat *v.* drog-handla; tebel-dhyghtya
mistress *n.* mêstres *f.*, mêstresow
mock *v.* gwil ges a²; mockya
mockery *n.* ges *m.*
moment *n.* pols *m.*; **at this moment** i'n
   tor'-ma; i'n present termyn
money *n.* mona *m.*
monk *n.* managh *m.*, menegh
month *n.* mis *m.*, mîsyow
moon *n.* loor *f.*
more *adj. & pron.* moy; **more and more**
   moy ha moy
morning *n.* myttyn *m.*, myttynow;
   morning and evening *adv.* mo ha
   myttyn; **one morning** *adv.* boragweyth
mortal *adj.* mortal
most *adj. & pron.* moyha
mother *n.* mabm *f.*, mabmow; dama *f.*
mountain *n.* meneth *m.*, menydhyow
move *v.* gwaya; movya
Mrs *n.* Mêstres *f.*
multitude *n.* rûth *f.*, rûthow
music *n.* mûsyk *m.*; ilow *m.*; (*instrumental*)
   menestrouthy *m.*
must *v.*; **I must** res yw dhybm; me a res
my *poss. adj.* ow³
myrrh *n.* myrr *m.*
name *n.* hanow *m.*, henwyn; *v.* gelwel;
   henwel
narrow *adj.* cul; idn
nature *n.* gnas *f.*; natur *m.*; sùbstans *m.*
near *adj.* ogas; *prep.* ryb; **near him** in y
   ogas; ryptho
nearby *adv.* rybon
nearer *comp. adj.* nes; **come nearer** nessa
nearest *superl. adj.* nessa
necessity *n.* res *m.*
need *n.* othem *m.*, othomow; **I need** yma
   othem dhybm a²
needy *adj* othomak.; **needy person**
   othomak *m.*, othomogyon
neighbour *n.* kentrevak *m.*, kentrevogyon;
   kentrevoges *f.*, kentrevogesow
nerve *n.* nerv *m.*, nervow
never *adv.* (*in the past*) bythqweth, (*Late*)
   byscath ; (*in the future*) nefra
nevertheless *adv.* bytegy·ns, byttele·
new *adj.* nowyth
New Year *n.* Bledhen *f.* Nowyth; **New**
   Year's Day De Halan an Vledhen
Newlyn *place-name* Lulyn *f.*
news *npl.* nowodhow *pl.*
newspaper *n.* paper *m.* nowodhow,
   paperyow nowodhow
next *adj. & adv.* nessa
next day *adv.* ternos
next morning *adv.* ternos vyttyn

night *n.* nos *f.*, nosow; ; **good night** Duw re dharbarra nos dâ dhywgh; **last night** *adv.* newher

nine *num.* naw

nineteen *num.* nawnjek

nineteenth *ord.* nawnjegves

ninth *ord.* nawves

no *interj.* nâ

no, none *adj.* vëth, vÿth *used with negative;* **I have no money** me ny'm beus mona vëth

noble *adj.* bryntyn

noise *n.* son *m.*, sonyow

north *n.* (*archaic*) gogleth *m.*; north *m.*

nobody *pron.* den vëth, nagonen (*both with negative verb*)

northwards *adv.* tro ha'n north

nose *n.* dewfrik *dual;* frigow *pl.*

nostril *n.* frik *m.* (*see* **nose**)

not *adv.* ny(ns), ny(nj); (*in subordinate clauses and in answers*) na(g); **not at all** *adv.* phrase poynt; màn

November *n.* Du *m.*, mis *m.* Du

now *adv.* lebmyn; i'n tor'-ma

nurture *v.* maga; **nurtured** megys

nut *n.* knofen *f.*, know *coll.*

obedient *adj.* gosteyth

obvious *adj.* ape·rt

occasion *n.* occasyon *m.*, occasyons; treveth *f.*

October *n.* Hedra *m.*, mis *m.* Hedra

odd *adj.* coynt

odour *n.* sawour *m.*, sawours

of *prep.* a²; **of my** a'm; **of thy, of your** a'th

offence *n.* offens *m.*, offencys

offend *v.* offendya

offer *v.* offra

office *n.* (= *function*) offys *m.*, offycys; (= *bureau*) sodhva *f.*, sodhvaow

often *adv.* yn fenowgh; lies gweyth

oh *interj.* â, agh

old *adj.* coth; loos; **old man** cothwas *m.*, cothwesyon

once *adv.* unweyth; **all at once** wàr udn labm

one *num.* onen; udn; *pron.* huny (*used only with* keuep, lies *and* pùb); **one...the other** an eyl...y gela; (*with f. nouns*) an eyl...y ben ; *pron.* (= *someone*) onen

one-eyed *adj.* udnlagajek

only *adv.* yn udnyk; only; mès, saw, marnas *after negative*

open *adj.* egerys; opyn; *v.* egery

openly *adv.* a·pert; opyn

opinion *n.* tybyans *m.*, tybyansow; opynyon *m.*, opynyons

opposite *prep.* adâ·l; *adv.* adâ·l dhyn

oppress *v.* compressa

or *conj.* pò (bò);

other *adj.* ken (*precedes noun*); aral, *pl.* erel

otherwise *adv.* poken (boken)

ought *v.*; **I ought** y codhvia dhybm

our *poss. adj.* agan

out *adv.* in mes; wàr ves; out of *prep.* avês a²

outside *adv.* wàr ves

over *prep* dres; a-ugh (*see 12A. 4*); **over there** *adv.* dres ena; in hans

overcast *adj.* comolek

overcome *v.* fetha; conqwerrya; overcùmya

overgrown *adj.* over-devys

overseas *adj.* tramor

overturn *v.* omwheles

owner *n.* perhen *m.*, perhednow; perhednak *m.*, perhenogyon

pacify *v.* coselhe·

pagan *n.* dyscryjyk *m.*, dyscryjygyon

page *n.* folen *f.*, folednow; (*archaic*) enep *m.*, enebow

paint *v.* paintya

pale *adj.* gwydn, gwynn

Palm Sunday *n.* De Sul *m.* Blejyow

pane *n.* (*of glass*) qwarel *m.*, qwarels

paper *n.* paper

paradise *n.* paradîs.

pardon *n.* gyvyans *m.*; *v.* **pardona** gava dhe²

parents *pl.* kerens

parish *n.* pluw *f.*, pluyow;

park *n.* park *m.*, parcow

part *n.* radn *f.*, radnow

party *n.* (*convivial*) kyffewy *m.*, kyffewyow

pass *v.* passya; tremena

passage *n.* (*of writing*) devyn *m.*, devydnow

Passover *n.* Pask *m.*

pasty *n.* pasty *m.*, pastys

patient *n.* clâv *m.*, clevyon

Paul *place-name* Pawl *m*; **the Parish of Paul** Pluw *f.* Pawl

pay *v.* tylly

peace *n.* cres *m.*

pen *n.* pluven *f.*, pluvednow

penny *n.* dynar *m.*

Pentecost *n.* Pencost *m.*

people *n.* pobel *f.*, poblow

perceive *v.* canvos, cantos (*cf.* convedhes); clôwes; percêvya

perfect *adj* perfeth.

persevere *v.* durya

persist *v.* durya

person *n.* den *m.*, tus; person *m.*, persons

personal *adj.* personek

persuade *v.* perswâdya

Philippians *npl.* Fylyppyans *pl.*

piece *n.* tabm *m.*, tybmyn; darn *m.*, darnow; **to pieces** dhe dybmyn

pierce *v.* gwana

pig *n.* porhel *m.*, porhelly

Pilate *personal name* Pilat *m.*
pilchard hernen *f.* hern *coll.*; **summer pilchards** hern hâv; **winter pilchards** hern gwâv
pillow *n.* pluvak *f.*, pluvogow
pipe *v.* piba
pity *n.* pyteth; tregereth *f.*; trueth *m.*; **take pity on** kemeres pyteth a²; kemeres tregereth wàr²
place *n.* plâss *m.*, plassow; tyller *m.*, tyleryow; le *is used in some contexts but has no plural*; **private place** tyller clos
plague *n.* plag *m.*, plâgys
plain *adj.* plain
plan *n.* towl *m.*, towlow; *v.* tôwlel
play *v.* gwary; *(music)* seny
player *n.* gwarior *m.*, gwarioryon
pleasant *adj.* plesont
please *v.* plegya *(followed by* dhe²); plêsya; **if you please** mar pleg; *(earlier)* dell y'm kyrry
pleasure *n.* plesour *m.*, plesours
plight *n.* plît *m.*
ploughshare *n.* sogh *m.*, soghyow
pocket *n.* pocket *m.*, pockettys
poem *n.* bardhonek *m.*, bardhonegow
poet *n.* prydyth *m.*, prydydhyon
poetry *n.* prydydhieth *f.*; bardhonieth *f.*
point *n.* poynt *m.*, poyntys; **there is no point in** ny vern *defective v.*; *v.* poyntya
poison *n.* poyson; gwenyn *m.* *(attested only in* OC guenoinreiat *'poisoner'); v.* posnya; venymya
polite *adj.* cortes
pooh *interj* tety valy
poor *adj.* bohosak; **poor man** *n.* bohosak *m.*, bohosogyon
pork *n.* kig *m.* porhel **power** *n.* gallos *m.*
pound *n.* *(money)* puns *m.*, punsow; pens *m.*, pensow
power *n.* power *m.*; nell *m.*; nerth *m.*; **the powers that be** an uhel-powers *pl.*
powerful *adj.* galosek
practice *n.* practys *m.*
practise *v.* practycya
praise prais *m.*; gormola *m.*; *v.* praisya; gormel
prance *v.* terlebmel, terlemmel
pray *v.* pesy
precisely *adv.* hardlych; pora·n
prefer *v.* preferrya; **I prefer** gwell yw genef, gwell yw dhybm
pregnant *adj.* gans flogh, *(Late)* gen flogh
prepare *v.* darbary; parusy, preparya
present *adj.* present; **at present** i'n tor'-ma; *n.* ro *m.*, royow;
present *v.* presentya
presently *adv.* whare

presume *v.* mêkya; bedha; presûmya
pretend *v.* mêkya; fâcya; gwil wis
pretty *adj.* teg; *comparative & superlative* tecka
price *n.* pris *m.*, prîsyow
priest *n* pronter *m.*, prontyryon
prince *n.* pensevyk *m.*, pensevygyon; pryns *m.*, pryncys
principal *n.* pendhescajor *m.*, pendhescajoryon
prison *n.* pryson *m.*, prysons
prize *n.* gober *m.*, gobrow; pris *m.*, prîsyow
probability *n.* lycklod *m.*; **in all probability** dre lycklod
produce *n.* ascor *m.*
promise *n.* promys *m.*, promyssyow; *v.* promyssya; dedhewy
property *n.* pŷth, pëth
prophecy *n.* profecy
prophesy *v.* profusa
prophet *n.* profus *m.*, profusyon; profet *m.*, profettys
protect *v.* gwitha, gwetha; **protect oneself** omwitha, omwetha
prove *v.* prevy
provide *v.* darbary; provia
pub *n.* tavern *m.*, tavernyow
publish *v.* dyllo
punish *v.* chastia; pùnyshya
punishment *n.* dialans *(UC* dyalans) *m.*; kessydhyans *m.*; pùnyshment *m.*, pùnyshmentys
purpose *n.* towl *m.*; *v.* porposya
push *v.* herdhya
put *v.* gorra; settya
quarrel *n.* qwarel *m.*
quarrel *v.* qwarellya
quart *n.* qwart *m.*, qwartys
quarter *n.* *(= fourth part)* qwarter *m.*, qwartrys
queen *n.* myternes *f.* myternesow
question *n.* qwestyon *m.*, qwestyonow
quick *adj.* scav; uskys
quickly *adv.* totta (< toth dâ); yn scav; yn uskys;
quiet *adj.* cosel
quietly *adv.* yn cosel
quieten *v.* coselhe·
quite *adv.* *(completely)* qwît
rabbit *n.* conyn *m.*, conynas
rain *n.* glaw *m.*; *v.* **it's raining** yma ow qwil glaw
raise *v.* derevel; lyftya; *(= rear)* maga
ram *n.* hordh *m.*, hordhas
read *v.* redya
ready *adj.* parys
really *adv.* in gwir
reap *v.* mejy
rear *v.* maga

reason *n.* rêson *m.*, rêsons; *v.* resna
rebuke *n.* kessydhyans *m.*; rebûk *m.*, rebûkys
receive *v.* recêva; fanja
recently *adv.* agensow
recognize *v.* aswon
recommend *v.* comendya
reach *v.* drehedhes
red *adj.* rudh
Redruth *place-name* Redrùth *m.*
refrain *v.* refrainya; **refrain from** sevel orth
refrigerator *n.* yeynor *f.*, yeynoryon
refuge *n.* erber *m.*, erberow
regard *v.* regardya
reinforce *v.* crefhe·
rejoice *v.* lowenhe·; rejoycya
relative *n.* car *m.*, kerens;
relieve *v.* sewajya
rely *v.* scodhya (*followed by* wàr²)
reluctant *adj.*; **poos yw genef** I am reluctant
remember *v.* perthy cov a²; remembra
repay *v.* aqwytya
repent *v.* repentya
repose *n.* powes *m.*; *v.* powes
require *v.* reqwîrya
requite *v.* aqwytya
resist *v.* omsettya (*followed by* orth); gwil resystens
rest *n.* powes *m.*; *v.* powes
restaurant *n.* bosty *m.*, bostiow
retinue *n.* coscar *coll.*
return *v.* dewheles
reward *n.* gober *m.*, gobrow; weryson *m.*; *v.* aqwytya; rewardya
ribbon *n.* ryban *m.*, rybanys
rich *adj.* rych
riddle *n.* desmyk *m.*, desmygow
ride *v.* marhogeth (*only in verbal noun*)
right *n.* gwir *m.*, gwîryow; *adj.* compes; ewn
river *n.* awan *f.*; ryver *m.*, ryvers
road *n.* fordh *f.*, fordhow
rob *v.* robbya
robber *n.* robbyor *m.*, robbyoryon; lader *m.*, ladron
rock *n.* carrek *f.*, carrygy
roll *v.* rollya
Roman *n.* Roman *m.*, Romans
room *n.* rom *m.*, rômys
rough *adj.* garow
round *adj.* rônd
round about *adv.* ader dro
royal *adj.* rial
rude *adj.* dyscortes
ruin *v.* dyswil; shyndya
ruined *adj.* dyswrës
run *v.* ponya; resek (*chiefly of liquids*)
rush *v.* fysky

sacrifice *n.* sacryfîs *m.*, sacryfîcys; *v.* sacryfia; offrynna
sad *adj.* trist
sadden *v.* duwhanhe·
saddle *n.* dyber *m.*, dybrow
sadness *n.* tristans *m.*
safe *adj.* saw
sailor *n.* marner *m.*, marners
saint *n.* sans *m.*, sens; sanses *f.*, sansesow
St Ives *place-name* Porth Ia *m.*
St Levan *personal name* Seleven *m.* (< *Solomon*)
St Michael's Mount *place-name* an Garrek *f.* Loos
sake *n.*; **for the sake of** rag kerensa; **for my sake** a'm govys vy
Saturday *n.* De Sadorn, (*Late*) Zadorn
saviour *n.* savyour *m.*, savyours
Saxon *n.* Saxon *m.*, Saxons
say *v.* leverel; **say!** lavar, leverowgh; **he said** leverys, (*Late*) lavaras; yn medh
scanty *adj.* scant
scholar *n.* scoler *m.*, scolers
school *n.* scol *f.*, scolyow
schoolmaster *n.* scolvêster *m.*, scolvêstrysy
Scotland *place-name* Alban *f.* (*found once in Lhuyd's Cornish*); Scotlond *m.* (*the traditional name*)
scream *v.* scrija
scripture *n.* scryptour *m.*, scryptours
seal *v.* sêlya
search *v.* whilas, whelas; sarchya
second *ord.* secùnd; nessa (*in a series*); **twenty-second** secùnd warn ugans
see *v.* gweles
seed *n.* hasen *f.*, has *coll.*
seek *v.* whilas, whelas
seem *v.* apperya; omdhysqwedhes; **it seems** yth hevel; **it seemed** yth hevelly
seemly *adj.* sêmly
seize *v.* sêsya; settya dalhen in
seldom *adv.* bohes venowgh
self *pron.* honen (*both reflexive and emphatic*)
sell *v.* gwertha
sense *n.* sens *m.*, sencys; skians *m.*; (= *meaning*) styr *m.*, styryow
sensible *adj.* fur
September *n.* Gwydngala, Gwyngala *m.*, mis *m.* Gwydngala, Gwyngala
serpent *n.* sarf *f.*, syrf
servant *n.* gwas *m.*, gwesyon; servont *m.*, servysy; mowes *f.*, mowysy; servyades *f.*, servyadesow
serve *v.* servya
service *n.* servys *m.*, servysyow
set *v.* settya; gorra
seven *num.* seyth
seventeen *num.* seytek
seventeeth *ord.* seytegves

seventh *ord.* seythves
shade *n.* skeus *m.*, skeusow
shake *v.* shakya
shallow *adj.* bas
shameful *adj.* dyvlas
share *n.* radn *f.*, radnow; shara *m.*, sharys
sharp *adj.* lybm; sherp
she, her *personal pron.* hy
sheep *n.* davas *f.*, deves
shield *n.* scoos *m.*, scojow
shilling *n.* sols *m.*
shine *v.* spladna; shînya
shoe *n.* eskys *f.*, eskyjyow
shop *m.* shoppa *m.*, shoppys
shopping *n.*; **go shopping** prenassa
shore *n.* âls *f.*, âlsyow
short *adj.* berr; cot
shorten *v.* cot'he·
should *v.*; **I should do it** y talvia dhybm y wil
shoulder *n.* scoodh *f.*, *pl.* scodhow, *dual* dywscoth
show *v.* dysqwedhes
Shrovetide *n.* Enes *m.*; **Shrove Tuesday** *n.* De Merth Enes
sick *adj.* clâv
side *n.* tenewen *m.*, tenwednow; tu *m.*, tuyow
sigh *v.* hanaja
sight *n.* golak *f.*; syght *m.* syghtys
sign *n.* sin *m.*, sînys; **the sign of the cross** sin an grows
signify *v.* sygnyfia
silent *adj.* tawesek; **be silent** tewel
similar *adj.* haval *(followed by* dhe[2]); **similar to** kepa·r ha(g), (Late) peca·r ha(g)
sin *n.* pehas *m.*, pehosow; pegh *m.*
since *conj.* abàn; dhia bàn
sincere *adj.* gwiryon
sincerely *adv.* yn lel ; **yours sincerely** *(in letter writing)* gans oll ow holon vy; *(Late)* gen oll ow holon vy
sing *v.* cana; **sung** kenys
single *adj.* udn-; udnyk; heb prias
sir *n.* syra *m.*, sera *m.*, syrys, serys; *(in titles)* Sir
sister *n.* whor *f.*, whereth
sit *v.* esedha, sedha; **sitting** a'y eseth
six *num.* whegh
sixteen *num.* whêtek
sixteenth *ord.* whêtegves
sixth *ord.* wheffes, wheghves **sixtieth** *ord.* tryugansves
sixty *num.* try ugans
skin *n.* crohen *f.*, crehyn
sky *n.* ebron *f.*
sleep *v.* cùsca
slow *adj.* hell; lent; *v.* **slow down** lent'he·

slowly *adv.* yn lent
small *adj.* bian; munys; **small amount** bohes
smaller *comparative adj.* le; biadnha
smallest *superl. adj.* lyha; biadnha
smell *n.* sawour *m.*, sawours; *v.* clôwes
smoke *v.* megy; **smoke a pipe** tùchya pib
smooth *adj.* gwastas; smoth
snake *n.* serpont *m.*, serpons; sarf *f.*, syrf
snore *v.* renky
snout *n.* tron *m.*
so *adv.* indella; mar[2]
society *n.* cowethas *f.*, cowethasow
soft *adj.* medhel
sole *adj.* udn-; udnyk
solve *v.* assoylya
somebody *pron.* nebonen
something *pron.* neppyth; neb tra
sometimes *adv.* traweythyow
song *cân f.*, canow
soon *adv.* yn scon
sorrow *n.* a·wher *m.*; duwhan *m.*; moreth *m.*; tristans *m.*
soul *n.* enef *f.*, enevow
sound *adj.* saw; salow
sound *n.* son *m.*, sonyow; sownd *m.*, sowndys; *v.* seny
soup *n.* cowl *m.*
south *n.* soth *m.*
space *n.* spâss *m.*
Spain *place-name* Spain *f.*
speak *v.* clappya; côwsel; **spoken** côwsys
spear *n.* guw *m.*, guyow
special *adj.* arbednek; specyal;
specially *adv.* spessly
speed *n.* toth *m.*
spell *v.* lytheredna; spellya
spend *v.* spêna; spendya
spirit *n.* pyrys *m.*, spyryjyon; **Holy Spirit** Spyrys Sans; **spirits** (= *distilled drink*) gwyras *f.*; dowr *m.* tobm
sport *n.* sport; *v.* sportya
spot *n.* spot *m.*, spottys; **on that very spot** stag ena
spouse *n.* prias *m.*, priosow
sprightly *adj.* jolyf
spring *n* (*of water*) fenten *f.*, fentydnyow
spring *n.* (= *season*) gwaynten *m.*
squeezing *n.* gwrydnyans *m.*
stab *v.* gwana
stag *n.* carow *m.*, kyrwas
stair *n.* stair *m.*, stairys
stamp *v.* stankya
stand *v.* sevel; **he was standing there** yth esa ev a'y sav ena
star *n.* steren *f.*, sterednow *pl.*, ster *coll.*
stare *v.* miras, meras stark *(followed by* orth)
starlight *n.* stergan *m.*

state *n.* stât *m.*, stâtys
steady on! *interj.* kê wàr dha gabm
steer *v.* lewyas
stench *n.* sawour *m.* poos; flerynsy *m.*
step *n.* stap *m.*, stappys
still *adv.* whath; stella
stink *n.* sawour *m.* poos; flerynsy *m.*; *v.* flerya; mousegy
stone *n.* men *m.*, meyn, an veyn
stop *v.* cessya; stoppya
story *n.* story *m.*, storys; whedhel *m.*, whedhlow; drolla *m.*, drollys
straight *adj.* compes
straightaway *adv.* straft; heb let
strand *n.* treth *m.* trêthow
strange *adj.* stranj
stranger *n.* stranjer *m.*, stranjers
strawberry *n.* sevien *f.* sevy *coll.*
street *n.* strêt *m.*, strêtys
strict *adj.* sevur
strictly *adv.* yn sevur;
strike *v.* gweskel; cronkya; knoukya
strong *adj.* crev
strongly *adv.* yn crev
substance *n.* sùbstans *m.*
sufficiently *adv.* lùk
summer *m.* hâv *m.*, havow, havyow
sun *n.* howl *m.*
Sunday *n.* De Sul; (*Late*) De Zul); **on Sunday** (*Late*) wàr an Zul; **one Sunday** *adv.* Sulgweyth
sunset *n.* howlsedhas *m.*
supermarket *n.* gorvarhas *f.*, gorvarhasow
support *n.* mêntons *m.*; scodhyans; *v.* mentêna; scodhya
sure *adj.* sur; certan ; **surely** yn sur
surface *n.* bejeth *m.*; enep *m.*, enebow; fâss *m.*
swear *v.* ty, tia; **I swear it** me a'n te
sweep *v.* scubya
sweet *adj.* wheg; *comparative & superlative* whecka
swim *v.* neyja
switch *n.* sqwychel *f.*, sqwichellow
sword *n.* cledha *m.*, cledhydhyow
table *n.* bord *m.*, bordys
tailor *n.* trehor *m.*, trehoryon
take *v.* kemeres; **take** *imperative v.* tàn!; tanowgh take! (*pl.*)
tall *adj.* uhel
tame *adj.* dov
Tamsin *personal name* Tamsyn *f.*
tardy *adj.* hell; lent
taste *v.* tâstya
tavern *n.* tavern *m.*, tavernyow
tea *n.* tê *m.*
teacher *n.* descador *m.*, descadoryon
teaching *n.* dyscans *m.*, dyscansow

tear *n.* dagren *f.*, dagrow
tear *v.* sqwerdya, sqwardya; **torn** sqwerdys
television *n.* pellwolok *f.*
terrible *adj.* uthyk
terribly *adv.* yn uthyk
than *conj.* (in comparisons) ages, ès (*see 24A.2*); ave·ll, vell *in Late Cornish*
thank *v.* grassa; **thank God** grassaf dhe Dhuw; **thank you** gromercy dhis, gromercy dhywgh
thanks *npl.* ras; **many thanks** meur ras
that, that one *pron.* hedna *m.*; hèn *before vowels in* bos; hodna *f.*, hòn *before vowels in* bos
the *def. art* an
theatre *n.* gwaryva *f.*, gwaryvaow
thee *object pron.* 'th[5] (*infixed*) (*see 18A.1*)
their *poss. adj.* aga[3], gà[3]
them *object pron.* 's (*infixed*) (*see 18A.1*)
then *adv.* (= so) dhana; (= at that time) i'n eur-na; ena; nena; i'n tor'-na
thence *adv.* alena
there *adv.* ena
thereafter *adv.* warlergh hedna
therefore *adv.* ytho·; rag hedna
these *pron. pl.* an re-ma
they, them *personal pron.* y, (*Late*) anjy·
thick *adj.* tew
thin *adj.* tanow
thing *n.* tra *f.*, taclow, taclenow (*traow is not attested in traditional Cornish*)
think *v.* predery; (*Late*) p'edery; tyby
third *ord.* tressa, tryja ; **twenty third** tressa warn ugans
thirst *n.* sehes *m.*
thirsty *adj.* sëgh; **I am thirsty** yma sehes dhybm
thirteen *num.* tredhek
thirteenth *ord.* tredhegves
thirty-first *ord.* unegves warn ugans
this, this one *pron.* hebma *m.*, helma *m.*; hèm *before vowels in* bos; hobma *f.*, holma *f.*, hòm *before vowels in* bos
this year *adv.* hevleny
thither *adv* dy
those *pron. pl.* an re-na
thou, thee *personal pron.* te, ty; (*Late*) che, chy
thought *n.* preder *m.*, prederow; **to take thought for** kemeres preder a[2]
thousand *num.* mil *f.*, milyow; **three thousand** tremmil
three *num.* try[3] *masc.*, teyr[3] *fem.*; **the three of them** aga thry; **three times** *adv.* tergweyth
thresh *v.* drùshyan, drùshya
throne *n.* tron *m.*, trônys
throw *v.* tôwlel
thrust *v.* herdhya

Thursday *n.* De Yow
thus *adv.* indella; indelma; **thus exactly**
  adv. in ketelma
time *n.* prës, prÿs *m.*, prejyow; termyn *m.*,
  termynyow; **on time** *adv.* a'brës, adermyn
tin miner *n.* stenor *m.*, stenoryon
tiny *adj.* munys
tire *v. trans.* ania; sqwitha
tired *adj.* sqwith
tiresome *adj.* sqwîthus
to *prep.* dhe²; bys; **to my** dhe'm; **to the**
  dhe'n; **to thy**, **to your** dhe'th; *with nouns*
  bys in; *with personal prons.* bys dhe²
today *adv.* hedhyw; **today week** an jorna-
  ma wàr seythen
together *adv.* warbarth
toil *n.* lavuryans *m.*; lavur *m.*; *v.* lavurya
tolerate *v.* perthy
tomorrow *adv.* avorow
tonight *adv.* haneth
too *adv* re².; **too much of** re a²
touch *v.* tava; tùchya
tournament *n.* tournay *m.*
towards *prep.* tro ha(g) ; wor' tu ha(g), tu
  ha(g)
tower *n.* tour *m.*, tourow; **the Tower of
  Babel** Tour Babel
town *n.* tre *f.*, trevow
train *n.* train *m.*, trainow
trample *v.* stankya
translate *v.* trailya
translation *n.* trailyans *m.*, trailyansow
treachery *n.* traitury *m.*
treasure *n.* tresour *m.*
tree *n.* gwedhen *f.*, gwëdh *coll.*
trench *n.* rygol *m.*, rygolyow
Trinity *n.* Trynyta *m.*; Trynjys *f.*; **Trinity
  Sunday** *n.* De Sul an Drynjys
trousers *n.* (*pair*) lavrak *m.*, lavrogow
true *adj.* gwir
truly *adv.* in gwir
Truro *place-name* Trûrû *m.*
trust *v.* trestya (*followed by* dhe²)
truth *n.* gwiryoneth (gwîrioneth) *m.*; soth *m.*;
  in truth heb wow; in gwir; in gwiryoneth
try *v.* assaya; whilas, whelas
Tuesday *n.* De Merth
tune *n.* melo·dy *m.*, melodys
turn *v.* trailya
twelfth *ord.* dewdhegves
twelve *num.* dewdhek
twentieth *ord.* ugansves
twenty *num.* ugans
twice *adv.* dywweyth
two *num.* dew² *m.*; dyw² *f.*
twofold *adj.* dewblek
ugly *adj.* hager, hager-.; *comparative &
  superlative* hackra

unanimous *adj.* unver
unbeliever *n.* dyscryjyk *m.*, dyscryjygyon
unbelieving *adj.* dyscryjyk
uncover *v.* dyscudha
understand *v.* convedhes; ùnderstondya,
  ùnderstandya
understanding *n.* ùnderstondyng *m.*,
  ùnderstandyng *m.*
unfortunate *adj.* anfusyk; **unfortunate
  person** anfusyk *m.*, anfusygyon
unfortunately *adv.* i'n gwetha prës; *interj.*
  soweth
unless *conj.* marnas
until *conj.* bys may⁵(th); erna²(g)
up *adv.* (*of position*) avàn; (*of motion*) in bàn,
  (*Late*) màn
upon *prep.* wàr (*see 12A.4*)
upper, uppermost *adv.* awartha
upset *v.* omwheles
upside down *adv.* an pëth awartha dhe
  woles
us *personal pron.* 'gan, 'n *infixed* (*see 18A.1*)
use *v.* ûsya
valley *n.* valy *m.*, valys; tnow *m.*, tenwyn
velvet *n.* paly *m.*
vengeance *n.* venjons *m.*
verify *v.* composa
very *adv.* fèst; pòr²
vicar *n.* pronter *m.*, prontyryon
victory *n.* vyctory *m.*, vyctorys
vigorously *adv.* yn fen
village *n.* treveglos *f.*, trevow eglos
villainous *adj.* bylen
vine *n.* gwedhen *f.* grappys
vineyard *n.* vynyard *m.*, vynyardys
viper *n.* nader *f.*, nadron
virgin n. gwerhes *f.*, gwerhesow (*used only of
  BVM and virgin saints*); maghteth *f.*,
  meghtythyon; vyrjyn *f.*, vyrjyns
visit *v.* vysytya
voice *n.* lev *m.*, levow; voys *m.*, voycys
wage *n.* gober *m.*, gobrow; waja *m.*, wajys
walk *v.* kerdhes; walkya; **walk together**
  keskerdhes
wallet *n.* câss *m.* lytherow
war *n.* gwerryans *m.*; **wage war** gwerrya
warden *n.* gwethyas *m.* gwethysy; warden
  m., wardens
warm *v.* tobma
warn *v.* gwarnya
warrior *n.* gwerryor, gwerrour *m.*,
  gwerrours
wary *adj.* war
wash *v.* golhy; **wash oneself** omwolhy
waste *v.* wastya
watch *v.* miras, meras (*followed by* orth)
wave *n.* todn *f.*, todnow
way *n.* fordh *f.*, fordhow; maner *f.*, manerow

weak *adj.* gwadn
weaken *v.* gwadnhe·, gwannhe·
wealth *n.* pÿth, pëth; **worldly wealth** pÿth *m.* an bÿs
weapon arv *f.*, arvow
wear *v.* (*clothes*) gwysca
weather *n.* awel *f.*
Wednesday *n.* De Merher
week *n.* seythen *f.*, seythednow; **a week ago** seythen alebma
weep *v.* ola
welcome *adj.* wolcùm, welcùm; *v.* wolcùbma
well *adv.* yn tâ
well *n.* fenten *f.* (*Late*) venten *f.*, fentydnyow, (*Late*) ventydnyow
west *n.* (*archaic*) howlsedhas *m.*; west *m.*
wet *adj.* glëb; *comparative & superlative* gleppa
whack *n.* bobmen *f.*, bomednow, bomennow
what *interr. pron.* pandra?; pëth? (pÿth?) **what's the matter?** pandr'yw an mater?
whatever *pron.* pynag oll; pynag oll dra
when *interr. adv.* peur⁵, py eur⁵; pana dermyn
when? *interr. adv.* py eur⁵?, peur⁵?; pana dermyn?; *rel. adv.* pàn
whenever *conj.* peskytter may⁵
where *interr. adv.* py(th); ple⁵(th); **where is he?** ple ma va?; **where are they?** ple mowns y?
wherever *indef. adv.* pynagoll fordh may⁵
whether *conj.* (*in alternatives*) be va
which? *interr. adj.* pana²?; py; **which of two?** pyneyl?
while *conj* hadre·²·; **while you** (*sg.*) live hadre· vywhy
whim *n.* sians *m.*, siansow
whirlwind *n.* corwyns *m.*
whisky *n.* gwyras *f.*, gwyrosow
white *adj.* gwydn, gwynn
whither? *interr. adv.* py(th)
Whitsun *n.* Pencost; **Whitsunday morning** De Fencost myttyn
whoever *pron.* pynag oll; neb
whole *adj.* salow; saw
why *interr. adv.* prag; rag fra
wicked *adj. & adv.* tebel-, **wicked fellow** tebel-was *m.*; **wicked woman** tebel-venyn *f.*
wickedness *n.* camhenseth *m.*
wide *adj.* ledan; efan
widow *n.* gwe·dhowes *f.*, gwedhowesow
wife *n.* gwreg *f.*, gwrageth; gwreg ty *f.*, gwre'ty wife
wild *adj.* gwyls
wilderness *n.* gwylfos *m.*
will *v.* (*when expressing the future*) mydnes, mednes; **he will come** ev a vydn dos

willingly *adv.* a'y vodh; **very willingly** a leun-golon;
wily *adj.* coynt
win *v.* gwainya
wind *n.* gwyns *m.*, gwynsow
wind *v.* troyllya
window *n.* fe·nester *f.*, fe·nestry; (*Late*) beister *f.*, beistry
wine *n.* gwin *m.*
wing *n.* askel *f.* eskelly
winter *n.* gwâv *m.*, gwavow
wisdom *n.* furneth *m.*
wise *adj.* fur
wish *n.* bolùnjeth *m.*
with *prep.* gans, (*Late*) gen; (*see 5A.5*)
within *prep.* ajy· dhe²; (*of time*) kyns pedn; *adv.* wàr jy
woe gu *m.*; **woe is me** govy; **woe is us** gony (*see 25A.5*)
woman *n.* benyn *f.*, benenes
wonder *n.* marth *m.*; marthus *m.*, marthùjyon; merkyl *m.*, merclys
wonderfully *adv.* wondrys
wood *n.* coos *m.*, cosow
wool *n.* gwlân *coll.*
word *n.* ger *m.*, geryow
work *n.* ober *m.*, oberow; whel *m.*; *v.* lavurya; (= *fashion*) obery
worker *n.* gonesyas *m.*, gonesyjy,
workman *n.* gonesyas *m.*, gonesyjy
world *n.* bÿs, bës; norvÿs, norvës
worse *adj.* gweth, *comparative of* drog; lacka
worship *v.* gordhya (*sometimes followed by* dhe²)
worst *adj.* gwetha, *superlative of* drog; lacka
worth *n.* bry *m.*; valew; *adj.* **it is worth seeing** y tal y weles
wound *n.* brew *m.*, brewyon; goly *m.*, goliow; *v.* golia; (*by biting*) brathy; **wound badly** tebel-wolia
wrong *adj.* cabm; mes a fordh
wrestle *v.* omdôwlel
wrestler *n.* omdowlor *m.*, omdowloryon
wrestling *n.* omdowl *m.*
write *v.* scrifa, screfa
writer *n.* scrifor *m.*, scriforyon
year *n.* bledhen *f.*, bledhydnyow; **years of age** bloodh *coll.*; **next year** nessa bledhen; an vledhen usy ow tos
yellow *adj.* melen
yes *interj.* ea
yet *adv.* whath; stella
you why; *personal pron.* gas, 's *infixed* (*see 18A.1*)
young *adj.* yonk
your *poss. adj.* agas, gàs; (*informal sing.*) dha²
youth *n.* (*period*) yowynkneth *m.*
zero *n.* màn *m.*

MENEGVA
Index

References are to sections.

'mortal' 38A.7

mos 'to go' also **mones** 16A.4; attested forms App. C.20; conditional **gylsen**, **gylses**, **galsa** 16A.4 and note; imperfect **en**, **es**, **e**, etc. 16A.4; perfect **galsof**, **galsos**, **gallas**, etc. 25A.3; present-future **av**, **êth**, **â**, etc. 16A.4; preterite **yth**, **ythys**, **êth**, etc. 16A.4; subjunctive **ellen**, **elles**, **ella**, etc. 19A.1; verbal adjective **gyllys** 25A.4

mutation, initial; anomalous mutation App. A.6; lenition (soft mutation, second state) 1A.4; 1A.5; App.A.1; mixed mutation (fifth state) 7A.3; 8A.5; App. A.4; nasalization App. A.5; omission of mutation App. A.7; provection (hard mutation, fourth state) 3A.2; App. A.3; spirantization (third state) 7A.2; App. A.2; summary of initial mutations App. A

mydnas (**mednas**) 'to wish'; as an auxiliary verb 18A.3; attested forms App. C.19; conditional 18A.4; imperfect 18A.4; present-future 18A.3; preterite 18A.4; subjunctive 19A.1

myns 'as much as, as many as' 21A.3

Nance, R. Morton; derived **brusyth* from OC **brodit** 39A.4; derived **casor* from OC **cadwur** 37A.6; devised the form **tron* 'nose' 32A.1; devised the form **Whevrer* 'February' 31A.2 note; his view of some attested forms 23A.2 note; his view on borrowings from English 29A.1; recommended the form *byghan* 'small' 31A.5; reconstructed full paradigm of **pew** 23A.3 note.

'nation' 33A.5

neb 'who'; in relative clauses 15A.4; meaning 'whoever' 21A.3

necessity 20A.4

'neither…nor' 26A.7

'never' 25A.8

'nobody' 9A.5

'nose' 32A.1

'not to' with verbs 26A.3

'nothing' 9A.5

nouns; feminine nouns with following genitive 2A.6; gender of nouns 1A.1; plural of nouns 1A.2

numerals; cardinal 1-100 10A.6; higher numerals 27A.1; miscellaneous expressions with numerals 27A.4; ordinals 1st-100th 11A.4; simplified numerical system 27A.8

obligation 20A.4

'one' (impersonal pronoun) 9A.6

'only' 9A.7; 37A.1; 37A.2

orthography 0.1- 0.4

otta 'behold' 25A.6

pàn 'when'; followed by the subjunctive 19A.6

past participle *see* verbal adjective

'people' 33A.1

perfect tense with **re²** 10A.4

'person' 32A.1

personal pronouns; disjunctive 5A.4; infixed 18A.1; suffixed emphatic 13A.4; suffixed objective 18A.2

personal suffixes (emphatic pronouns) 13A.4

pesy 'to pray, to beg' 17A.7

perthy 'to bear'; **perthy avy** 'to envy' 17A.8; **perthy awher** 'to be anxious' 17A.8; **perthy cov** 'to remember' 17A.8; **perthy danjer** 'to hesitate' 17A.8; **perthy dowt** 'to fear' 17A.8

pew 'possesses' 23A.3

'place' 35A.1

ple⁵(th) 'where?' 10A.5

pluperfect; confined to the very earliest Middle Cornish 14A.3 note; 34A.5

points of the compass; in the texts 28A.3; in Unified Cornish 28A.3 note

'poison' *n.* and *v.* 38A.8

'pound' 30A.2

prefixes with verbs 29A.4

pre-occlusion 0.3.14

prepositions and prepositional pronouns; **a²** 'from' 5A.5; **a-ugh**, **a-ught** 'above, over' 12A.4; **dhe²** 'to' 5A.5; **dhyrag** 'before' 12A.4; **dhyworth** 'from' 5A.5; **dre** 'through' 12A.4; **dres** 'across' 12A.4; **gans** 'with' 5A.5; ; **heb** 'without' 12A.4; 12A.5; **in** 'in, into' 12A.4; **inter**, **intra** 'among' 12A.4; 12A.5; **orth** 'against, at' 5A.5 ; **rag** 'for' 12A.4; **ryb** 'beside' 12A.4; **wàr** 'upon' 12A.4

present-future 17A.3

present participle; noun object of present participle 3A.3; pronominal object of present participle 7A.4

preterite 17A.5

pronunciation and spelling 0.1–0.4

proverbs, riddles and rhymes 40Y

'public house' 30A.4

quotation marks 0.4.2

reflexive verbs 22A.7

regular verb; inflection 17A.1

'rejoice' 35A.6

relative sentences 15A.1-15A.4; indirect relative sentences 15A.3; relative sentences with **bos** 'to be' 15A.2; relative sentences with **neb** 15A.4

rhymes; proverbs, riddles and rhymes 40Y

riddles; proverbs, riddles and rhymes 40Y

'river' 36A.5

'Romans' 36A.10

'room' 32A.4

ARWEDHYOW SONIETH
PHONETIC SYMBOLS

ABECEDARY KESGWLASEK SONIETH
INTERNATIONAL PHONETIC ALPHABET

[aɪ] as *igh* in English *night*.

[aʊ] as *ow* in English *cow*.

[æ] short, like *a* in southern English *cat*.

[æ:] long, the sound can vary from a drawn out version of *a* in southern English *sad* to the *ai*-sound in English *air*.

[ɑ] as *a* in southern English *half*.

[ɒ:] like the sound heard in southern English *laws*.

[b] as in English *boy*.

[ᵇm] an unexploded *b* just before the *m*, as in English *webmail*.

[d] as in English *door*.

[dʒ] as *j* in English *jam*.

[ᵈn] an unexploded *d* just before the *n*, as in English *hadn't*.

[ð] as *th* in English *this* or *that* (never as in *thing*).

[e:] long, like the pure vowel sound of *made* as heard in Wales and Northern England.

[ə] when unstressed, as *e* in English *fallen*.

[əɪ] a sequence of *a* in English *sofa* and *ee* in *see* in rapid succession, similar to the way *see* is pronounced in Cockney or Australian English.

[ɛ] short, as *e* in *bet*.

[ɛʊ] a sequence of *e* in English *may* and *oo* in *took* in rapid succession.

[f] as *f* in English *fallen*.

[g] as *g* in English *get* or *gun* (never as in *George*).

[gl] as *gl* in English *glass*.

[gɹ] as *gr* in English *ground*.

[gʷl] like [gl] but with a very short unstressed *uh*-sound between *g* and *l*; imagine saying *"guhlass"* for *glass*.

[gʷɹ]   like [gɹ] but with a very short unstressed *uh*-sound between *g* and *r*; imagine saying *"guhrround"* for *ground*.

[gz]   voiced as the *x* in English *examine*.

[h]   as *h* in English *hand* or *aha!*.

[ɦ]   a voiced variant of [h] as *h* in English *aha!* for some speakers.

[i]   when final and unstressed as *y* in English *baby*.

[i:]   long vowel as *ee* in English *seen* or *i* in English *machine*.

['i:ə]   with a stress on the *i*, as *ea* in the name *Lea* or *ia* in the name *Mia*.

[iʊ]   a sequence of *ee* in English *see* and *oo* in *took* in rapid succession. The pronunciation [ju] (as in English *you*) for this is not correct.

[ɪ]   short vowel as *i* in English *kitchen*.

[ɨ]   when unstressed, is short *i* as in English *satin*.

[j]   as *y* in English *yet*.

[k]   as *k* in English *kitten*.

[kɹ]   as *cr* in English *crate*.

[ks]   voiceless as *x* as in English *extreme*.

[kw]   as *qu* in English, *quick*.

[kʷɹ]   like [kɹ] but with a very short unstressed *uh*-sound between *k* and *r*; imagine saying *"cuhrrowd"* for *crowd*.

[l]   always a "light *l*" as in English *leave*, not a "dark *l*" as in *full*.

[lʰ]   an [l] followed quickly by [h].

[ɭ]   an unvoiced *l*, less strong than the Welsh *ll* [ɬ]; try putting the tongue in the *l*-position and say *s*.

[m]   as *m* in English *man*.

[n]   as *n* in English *now*.

[ŋ]   as the *ng* in English *young*.

[o:]   long, the pure vowel sound of *home* as heard in Wales and Northern England.

[oɪ]   as *oy* in English *boy*.

[oʊ]   as *oa* in English *boat*.

[œ]   short, as in German *Hölle* 'hell'.

[ø:]   long, as in French *peur* 'fear' or *ö* in German *schön* 'beautiful'.

[ɔ]   short as *o* in English *top*.

[p]   as in English *put*.

[ɹ]   at the beginning and at the end of a word, as well as before and after other consonants, as in Cornish English *razor*. A final *r* is never dropped as in RP and similar dialects of British English.

[ɾ]   between two vowels it is a single tongue tap, like *tt* in American English *butter* or like the *r* in Spanish *pero*.

[s]   as in English *s* in *sit* or *c* in English *city*.

446

[ʃ]   as *sh* in English in *ship*.
[t]   as in English *tall*.
[tʃ]   as *ch* in *church*.
[θ]   as *th* in English *thin*, *think* (never as in *this*, *that*).
[u:]   long *oo* sound in English *cool*.
[uɪ]   like the diphthong in English *gooey*.
[ʊ]   short *oo* sound in English *took*.
[ɵ]   when unstressed as the two *o* in English *collaborate*.
[v]   as in English *vine*.
[w]   as in English *wine*.
[ʍ]   a voiceless *w*, like the breathy *wh* in accents of English that distinguish *wear* and *where*, such as Scottish and Irish English. The sound of *wh* is not [hw] or [xw]. It is closer to the voiceless bilabial fricative [ɸ]; learners who do not have [ʍ] in their dialect may try to approximate the sound of *wheg* as [ɸʷeːɡ] (like blowing out a candle) or even [fʷeːɡ].
[x]   is pronounced strongly, as *ch* in Scottish *loch*; often pronounced more weakly: see [h] and [ɦ].
[y:]   long, as in French *lune* 'moon' or *ü* in German *grün* 'green'.
[ʏ]   short as a short *ü* sound in German *Mütter* 'mothers'.
[z]   as in English *zeal*.
[ʒ]   as *zh* in the Russian name *Zhivago*.

LYTHEREDNOW ÛSYS GANS EDWARD LHUYD
LETTERS USED BY EDWARD LHUYD

ɒ   [ɒ:]   like the sound heard in southern English *laws*.
ð   [ð]   as *th* in English *this* or *that* (never as in *thing*).
ꝺ   [ɡ]   as *g* in English *get* or *gun* (never as in *George*).
ꞵ   [ŋ]   as the *ng* in English *young*.
τ   [θ]   as *th* in English *thin*, *think* (never as in *this*, *that*).
u̜   [w, ʊ] as in English *wine*; in a diphthong, a short *oo* sound in English *took*.
ẏ   [ə]   as *a* in English *ago* or as *e* in English *fallen*.
zh   [ʒ]   as *zh* in the Russian name *Zhivago*.

Note also the letter *yogh*, **ȝ**, not used by Lhuyd but which occurs in some traditional texts:

ȝ   [ð, θ] as *th* in English *this* or *thing* in words of Cornish origin.
       [j]   as *y* in English *young* in words of English origin.

Lightning Source UK Ltd.
Milton Keynes UK
UKHW012210150221
378843UK00001B/171

9 781904 808992